Robert Crowell

History of the Town of Essex

From 1634 to 1868

Robert Crowell

History of the Town of Essex
From 1634 to 1868

ISBN/EAN: 9783337133450

Printed in Europe, USA, Canada, Australia, Japan

Cover: Foto ©ninafisch / pixelio.de

More available books at **www.hansebooks.com**

OF THE

Town of Essex.

FROM 1634 TO 1868,

BY THE LATE

Rev. ROBERT CROWELL, D. D.,

PASTOR OF THE CONGREGATIONAL CHURCH IN ESSEX.

WITH

Sketches of the Soldiers

IN THE

WAR OF THE REBELLION,

BY

Hon. DAVID CHOATE.

———•◆•———

ESSEX:
PUBLISHED BY THE TOWN.
Press of Samuel Bowles & Co., Springfield, Mass.
1868.

Most of the readers of this volume will recognize *the first chapter* as the "History of Essex (then Chebacco, a part of Ipswich) from 1634 to 1700," which was published in 1853.

In the preparation of *the rest* of the work, as well as of that first part, it was the author's plan to insert a "few *fancy sketches* of domestic, nautical and military life," in the belief, as he stated in his preface, that since these "were designed to be true to nature and in accordance with the history of the times, they would not diminish the value of the book as a history of the town. The reader," he added, "will readily distinguish, it is presumed, between the *facts* of history and the *drapery* in which some of them occasionally appear. Man is no less a reality for the dress, he may be supposed to have worn, according to the fashion of his day; nor is it difficult to distinguish between the man and his apparel."

It was also his design to introduce as many *biographical sketches* of natives and residents of the town, as could be obtained; considering that "the history of towns, is the history of townsmen, especially when acting for town or country."

And since *some mention of public affairs*—proceedings of the government, political movements, military operations and the like—by which the welfare of the people was in any way affected, or in which their leading men took part, seemed to him essential to a full exhibition of the history of the town, he aimed *to associate its successive stages* with the most important events occurring in the colony, the province and the nation, of which it was a part.

It was his intention *to close the history* with the year 1819, and yet to increase its value as a work of reference, by appending a chronological record of events from that year to the date of its publication. At the time of his death, however, the work was completed no further than the year 1814, several gaps were still unfilled, and only a few of the materials were collected and arranged for the rest of it.

The town, at a meeting held April 1, 1867, voted to purchase the manuscript for publication, and since that time efforts have been made by those, into whose possession it had fallen, to supply deficiencies and to carry out as fully as possible the plan of the author; but of necessity the book still has defects, from which it would have been free, had he himself lived to revise and finish it.

The last chapter, containing *the doings of the town with reference to the war of the rebellion and the sketches of its soldiers* in the Federal army, has been written by Hon. David Choate. Some of the biographical sketches (published originally in the newspapers), the "Walk about Town," the copious extracts from the records of marriages and deaths, and other facts have also been furnished by him. The whole work, too, has had the benefit of some revision at his hands, though he is in no way responsible for its defects.

The book is further indebted for many facts to several other citizens and particularly to Caleb Cogswell, Esq., whose researches have contributed much valuable material to the *sixth chapter*.

The author was dependent upon Rev. J. B. Felt's History of Ipswich for a number of statements, statistics and dates drawn from ancient documents; yet the most of these have been verified and all others have been taken at first hand from family papers and original records of all sorts. Some errors of dates will, perhaps, still be found, arising from unreliable sources of information, from mistakes in copying, or from oversight in the reading of the proof-sheets. Only those who have had experience in this kind of work can fully appreciate the difficulty of attaining perfect accuracy in such matters.

The *biographical sketch of the author* has been prepared at the suggestion and in accordance with the publicly expressed wish of a number of the citizens of the town.

E. P. CROWELL.

AMHERST COLLEGE, *September*, 1868.

Contents.

APPENDIX.

Biographical Sketch of the Author.

Robert Crowell was born in Salem, Mass., December 9, 1787. He was the son of a sea captain, Samuel Crowell, the commander of a privateer in the Revolutionary War, under a commission from Congress,[*] afterwards master of a ship in the East India trade, and who was supposed to have perished by shipwreck in the Indian Ocean in 1810, at the age of 55. It was not the lot of the subject of this sketch, therefore, to grow up under the watchful eye and with the guiding hand of a father. His mother, however,—Mrs. Lydia Woodbury Crowell,—to whose care alone he was thus of necessity left, was a woman of more than ordinary intelligence, of energy and discretion and of earnest piety. It was no slight testimony to the fidelity and wisdom of the early training he received from her, that when he entered a store on Kilby Street, Boston, at the age of fourteen, on learning that the clergymen of his own denomination in that city had departed from what he had been taught to believe was the truth, and were preaching error, he decided to attend public worship at a *Baptist* church. The published history of that church mentions "a remarkable revival of religion in it during the first years of the present century." And with that condition of things, it is not strange that the preaching of its pastor, Rev. Dr. Samuel Stillman, a man eminent for his piety, and "the most popular pulpit orator of his day,"—to which he thus statedly listened, should have made upon his mind, as he was wont to declare, religious impressions that were never effaced. Some three years of laborious service earned him the confidence of his employer and the promise of a partnership in trade at the age of twenty-one. But a love of books, and a desire for an education, which had been stimulated by the excellent schools of his native town, had strengthened rather than diminished by his separation from studies, and he returned to his home in 1804, to prepare for college at the Latin Grammar School in Salem, then under the instruction of Master Daniel Parker.

He had no means for defraying the cost of a liberal education and was obliged to set out on his course relying entirely upon himself. School teach-

---

[*] Captain Crowell's commission as "Commander of the schooner *Greyhound*, of forty tuns burthen, and mounting six carriage guns," is dated October, 1779, and has the signature of John Jay, President of Congress.

2

ing—the first time at Manchester when he was eighteen years old—procured him the necessary funds only in part. But he providentially found a friend in a neighbor, Mr. Joseph Hodges, who loaned him several hundred dollars, without interest or security, and who was content to wait for its repayment by installments from the professional salary of his beneficiary.

Entering Dartmouth College in the Autumn of 1807, he was fortunate in the class which he joined, not so much on account of its *numbers*, (fifty-four at graduation,) though it was the largest which graduated at that Institution during the first sixty-eight years of its history, as because of the *character* of some of its members—the real culture of a college student being more vitally affected by the intellectual ability, the degree of enthusiasm, and the scholarship of the leading men of his class, than by almost any other influences of his academic life. Of those with whom he was thus brought into the very intimate relation of class-mate, several have attained high eminence in Church and State—among them his room-mate, Rev. Dr. Daniel Poor, missionary in Ceylon for forty years, Rev. Jonathan Curtis, the first scholar of his class and afterwards a tutor in college, Joel Parker, LL. D., now Professor of Law in Harvard University, and Hon. Ether Shepley, Chief Justice of the Supreme Court of Maine. Many others have been useful and influential in the various learned professions.

While an undergraduate, his tastes inclined him especially to the study of the Greek and Latin classics, and mental and moral philosophy. But his conscientious fidelity in *all* the studies of the college course, and his eagerness to make the most of them as means of discipline and culture, have been attested not more by some who were his associates then, than by his rank as a scholar. Of this no more need be recorded than that he was a member of the Phi Beta Kappa Society, to which only a certain part of each class—the first third in scholarship—were eligible.

At his graduation in the Summer of 1811, he was at no loss in deciding upon the profession for which he should study. His Christian life, as he always afterwards believed, had begun in the Winter of his first year in college, while he was teaching a school in Reading. The consciousness of his unfitness to comply with a rule, requiring the daily sessions of the school to be opened with prayer, compelled him to an immediate and earnest consideration of the subject of personal religion, and led him, through a Divine renewal of his character, "to devote himself to God as a penitent believer in Jesus." Giving evidence of this change he had united with the Tabernacle Church, of which his mother had for many years been a member, March 10, 1810, and throughout his connection with college had been known as an active and consistent Christian. He now looked upon the work of the Christian ministry as both a duty and a privilege for himself. And impaired health and want of funds forbidding his entering the Theological Seminary at Andover, he studied divinity with his pastor, Rev. Dr. Samuel Worcester.

In 1813, he received licensure, and in June of that year preached for the first time in Chebacco. The pulpit being at that time vacant he was employed as stated supply for the remainder of the year. Several months following he spent in Home Missionary labor in Maine, and while in that work he received, in March, a call from the Church and Parish in Chebacco, to become their pastor. His acceptance of this call is dated, " Salem, June 25, 1814," and his ordination took place on Wednesday, the 10th of August following. Of the public exercises on that occasion, some account is given in this history. The relation thus constituted continued unbroken forty-one years and terminated with his death by pneumonia, November the 10th, 1855. His funeral was attended at the church on the afternoon of the 13th, on which occasion a discourse was delivered by Rev. Dr Daniel Fitz of Ipswich, from Deuteronomy 11:31, and prayer offered by Rev. Wakefield Gale of Rockport.

In his domestic life during this long period, there were some experiences of sorrow which were adapted to discipline him more perfectly for the " ministry of consolation," but of which it is fitting that only the briefest mention should here be made. Married very soon after his settlement, August 29th, to Miss Hannah H. Frost of Andover, he was deprived of her by death, December 11, 1818. His second wife, Miss Hannah Choate of Essex to whom he was united September 2, 1822, died on the 9th of February, 1837. Two children were taken from him in their infancy, and a third— Washington Choate—at the age of twenty, when a student of medicine and apparently on the threshold of a life of usefulness.

A ministry of such duration was necessarily the witness of many and great changes in the community where its offices were performed. Stretching beyond the middle of the century from a point so near its beginning, this pastorate beheld the erection of the parish into a town ; a steady and considerable increase in its population and its business ; its advance in educational privileges ; its participation in seasons of religious awakening, in the temperance reformation, and in national political excitements ; its growth in intelligence and enterprise, along with the enlargement of the nation, the wonderful progress of the age in science and the arts, and the origination of almost all the appliances of an enlightened philanthropy for the benefit of the diseased and for reclaiming the vicious, as well as for christianizing the heathen. This term of official service also spanned the life of more than an entire generation ; so that in his earliest parochial visits the pastor conversed with some who recollected the burial of Pickering, and had enjoyed the fifty years' ministry of Cleveland, with not a few who had been old enough to share in the excitements of the Revolution and had seen the beginning of the Republic; and in his latest days numbered among his congregation many whose parents had been reared under his preaching. In this long series of years he had literally followed to the grave more than eight hundred of his people.   He had officiated at the baptism of two hundred and fifty-six persons, and united in marriage three hundred and fourteen couples.

Yet even in this eventful period, and while an attentive spectator of such constant and important changes, his own ministerial work could admit of very little variety, and of nothing novel or extraordinary.   Most of his time must be spent in the seclusion of the study.   In parochial duties,—religious conversation, the visitation of the sick and the afflicted, and the burial of the dead,—there was the same unvarying routine.   Each year was a repetition of the preceding in its regularly recurring services of worship and of preaching; and his appearance in public was almost wholly limited to these occasions. His pulpit was never vacated except from sickness, and his only deviation from the round of his ordinary duties consisted in attendance upon meetings of the Association, and of the Conference and upon Councils.   His pastorate, therefore, like that of most country clergyman, could be characterized by few incidents of general or striking interest, or even such as would be fitted of themselves to reveal or illustrate the distinctive traits of his character.

His very steadfastness, however, in this undeviating and limited course of action certainly indicates that he *had* a definite plan and purpose in life to which he constantly adhered.   Of *the general features of this ideal* we may, perhaps obtain the most correct views,—though at best but glimpses—from some of his own published discourses; since the standard of clerical living which he commends to one entering the profession could hardly be other than the reflection or echo of his own sentiments, and in his delineation of a completed ministerial career would be almost unconsciously disclosed those qualities of mind and heart which seemed to himself most excellent, and which he was ever striving to attain.   At the same time in judging of *his approach to the model thus outlined* in his own words, the reader must make suitable allowance for the coloring of the picture; since near relationship, while it has the best opportunity of observation, must be incapable of impartial judgment.

Apparent on the most casual glance at the life of Dr. Crowell,* is his conscientious and exclusive *surrender to his professional calling* as he deemed it indicated to him by the finger of his Divine Master.   That such a devotion was distinctly contemplated, must be inferred from his reply to the "call" to the pastorate, which thus closes :—" To you Providence directed me in the commencement of my ministerial labors.   And to you, if I am not deceived, the same Providence is now calling me for a more permanent residence among you.   This call I would not resist, being confident in this very thing, that if God has any work for me to do, He can prepare me for it and direct me to it." His success in realizing this purpose, the language he used respecting a father in the ministry, perhaps with some abatement, describes :—" He sought to be

---

* The degree of Doctor of Divinity was conferred upon him by Dartmouth College in 1850.

a minister and nothing but a minister. He never suffered any other object to divide or distract his attention. His mind could not indeed be prevented from ranging through the works of nature that he might see and adore the wisdom of their Former and gather up truth wherever it was to be obtained, but he brought all his attainments in knowledge from whatever source derived, and laid them down at Jesus' feet. He was an attentive observer of the political prospects and changes of the world, and particularly of his own country which he ardently loved ; but all his observations he brought to bear upon that Christian ministry to which he was devoted."*

His enthusiasm in theological study was sustained, if not kindled, by this single aim to be faithful and useful in the work given him to do. It was one of his strongest convictions that "imbecility and a barren ministry must be the necessary consequence of a relaxation from studious habits and a reliance upon what has been already acquired. The itinerant preacher may travel the country with the same scanty stock with which he commenced, but the settled abiding pastor must be constantly adding to his fund of knowledge, if, like the well instructed scribe, he would bring forth out of his treasury things new and old." † With the value to the minister of a critical knowledge of the Scriptures in the original, he was deeply impressed. His everyday life testified to the sincerity and consistency with which he charged the candidate for this office to " make the searching of the Scriptures a special study. Be not content," was his injunction, " to read them in any other language than those in which they were originally written. However excellent the translations in English, yet see for yourself that they are thus faithful, that you may add your testimony to this interesting fact, and prevent if possible, evil men and seducers from wresting the Scriptures by a false appeal to the original tongues." He himself read the Hebrew and Greek Testaments systematically and carefully to the end of his life—a practice rare at his day, even among the graduates of Theological Seminaries. The meaning of every passage he was to expound and of every chapter to be interpreted at the monthly meeting of the ministerial association, was thoroughly examined in the original.

In all investigation of religious truth, it was his maxim that one should "study the scope and end of the Scriptures, and make them his only authority for what he believes and practices. He should draw his whole creed from this high and sacred source; never bringing to it any human system, however excellent in itself, or however well sustained by the authority of man, for the purpose of making the Scriptures accord with it ; but examining everything in the light of Scripture, and receiving or rejecting it according as it agrees or disagrees with this unerring standard." ‡ *Of his own religious belief*, as

---

* Sermon at the funeral of Rev. Dr. Joseph Dana, November 19, 1827.

† Charge at the ordination of Rev. J. Taylor, Wenham.

‡ Ibidem.

thus developed, his summary of Dr. Dana's would be a fair representation. "In respect to sentiment, he was a firm believer in those doctrines usually denominated Calvinistic, and which embrace as cardinal points—the Trinity—man's native and entire depravity—regeneration by the special influences of the Holy Spirit—justification by the righteousness of Christ alone—election—the perseverance of the saints—man's free agency and accountability—the resurrection of the dead—the final judgment—the eternal misery of the wicked and the everlasting happiness of the righteous." These truths he held solely because he found them in the Bible, "to which alone," like his venerated friend, "he repaired to learn what he should believe and what he should preach; and for the truth of them he was remarkable for exhibiting in all his public discourses Scripture authority."

With such a creed growing out of such a constant and reverent perusal of the inspired Word of God, as a perfect and authoritative revelation, he could not be guilty of any ambiguity *in his utterances from the pulpit*, or of any effort to win popularity by the subject matter, or the style of his sermons. "Ask not," was his admonition to the young preacher, "in the selection of your subjects for the pulpit, what will please men, but what will please the great Head of the church, and preach the preaching which he hath bidden you. Let no consideration of interest or expediency induce you to omit, in the course of your ministry, any one doctrine or duty of Holy Writ, but faithfully declare the whole counsel of God." In full accord with this precept was his own practice. His characterization of Dr. Dana's sermons was; in proportion to his ability, applicable to his own. "His statements of divine truth were full, clear and impressive. His public discourses were rich in sound instruction and persuasive exhortation, expressed in language simple and pure, and in a style grave, perspicuous and forcible. "They were noted," said Rev. Dr. Fitz in his funeral sermon, "for strength of argument, for depth of research, and for their direct and solemn appeals to the conscience and the heart."

Deriving from the same Divine source *his idea of the relative importance of the various duties* devolving on him, he always made the public presentation of religious truth from the pulpit paramount to all else. "He ever felt"—to introduce again his own words to another—"that the first and most important duty which he owed his people, besides visiting the bereaved, the sick and dying, was the preparation of thoroughly digested discourses for the Sabbath."[*] In his estimation, "no frequency of pastoral visits, no zeal in the number and continuance of religious meetings, no sacrifice of time and strength in carrying out plans for the promotion of the great public charities can atone for the neglect of this, the most appropriate and the most important of all ministerial duties, because God's chosen method of saving them that believe."[†] Yet *while making pastoral duties subordinate* to the

---

[*] Charge to Mr. Taylor.   [†] Ibidem.

preaching of the Gospel, his surviving parishoners will testify "with what affectionate solicitude he watched over their spiritual interests, and how deeply he sympathized with them in all the vicissitudes of life," rejoicing with them that rejoiced in the social circle, and at the marriage festivity, and weeping with them that wept whether in the chamber of sickness or the house of mourning.

Of his eagerness to supplement the ministrations of the pulpit in every possible way, several illustrations are worthy of record. He established a Sabbath School in less than a year after his settlement, May, 1815, when such organizations were still rare and hardly more than an experiment, and acted as its superintendent for the first season. In 1821, he taught a week-day school and "expended the avails of his labor in the purchase of books for a church library, that his church might be furnished with increased facilities for acquiring the knowledge of duty and of God."* This library was increased, until it numbered more than two hundred volumes of standard theological, and other religious works, and was for many years a source of much interest and profit to a considerable portion of the members of the church. At one period, quite early in his ministry, he was wont to call together the children of the Parish at stated intervals for catechetical instruction in the meeting-house, and this exercise was attended by a large number. At another time he gave lessons to a class in the rules of music, to prepare the way for a singing-school, and thus for the improvement of the choir. In the Summer and Fall of 1827, he taught a Bible class on the Sabbath, in which exercise questions in writing by the members of the class were handed to him for answer.

Seeking thus to do only the legitimate business of his sacred office, he had his reward in the occurrence of several seasons of special religious interest among his people, and in the addition of two hundred and fourteen persons by profession to the church, which at the time of his ordination contained but six male members, and only thirty-two in all. As the result of one of these revivals of religion which began in September, 1827, and of which more particular mention is made elsewhere in this history, eighty-three persons were admitted to the church, among them many of the members of the Bible-class above referred to. According to the recollection of some of his parishioners, his labors during that harvest season were incessant. "His style of preaching was the same as usual; his manner, earnest and impressive, manifesting a deep feeling of his dependence upon the Holy Spirit; and he often expressed the fear that he should prove an unprofitable servant. He attended most of the inquiry meetings, went from house to house holding several short meetings the same day, and conversed freely with his people wherever he met them."†

While aiming at the best possible cultivation of his own field, he could not,

---

* Dr. Fitz's funeral sermon.   † Deacon Caleb Cogswell.

however, confine his thoughts or limit his exertions to that. The same spirit of single-hearted devotion to his Master's cause, which animated him in his parochial duties, overflowed into *undertakings for the moral and spiritual welfare of others.* "The arms of his expansive benevolence embraced within them the welfare of the town, the country and the world. Whatever related to the spiritual good of man and to the glory of God deeply interested him. With grief he saw the progress of error, and lamented the wide and increasing departure of so many in this generation from the faith and practice of their pious ancestors." * One indication of his interest in the prosperity of the churches in immediate fellowship with his own, is found in the fact communicated by the present scribe of that Body, that "he took an active part in the organization of the Essex South Conference of Churches, on the 8th of May, 1827, was Moderator of the first meeting after its formation, and was rarely absent from its sessions as long as he lived." But he was especially interested in the work of laying anew the foundations of evangelical religion in several places in his own neighborhood, participating in this with the late Rev. David Jewett, of Sandy Bay, (now Rockport,) with whom he was " particularly acquainted for more than thirty years, and intimately associated in several objects of benevolence." †   " It was their earnest and united efforts," writes Rev. Charles S. Porter, the first pastor of the Congregational Church at Gloucester Harbor, " aided by a few warm-hearted laymen, that called into being the evangelical churches at the Harbor and at Lanesville, (then a part of Annisquam parish). Many were their prayerful consultations, their journeys, often on foot, to raise funds in behalf of those Christian enterprises, and frequent their visitation of those places for the purpose of preaching, at first in school-houses, and of conversing in private with the people. These churches and that in West Gloucester are so many monuments to the zeal, wisdom and fidelity of those men, erected while they still lived to perpetuate their memory on earth."   " After the incorporation of the Religious Society at Lanesville, March 6, 1828," adds Rev. Thomas Morong, its late pastor, "Dr. Crowell took a lively interest in everything pertaining to the project, both by preaching there and by uniting with a few other ministers in soliciting the funds necessary for the erection of a house of worship. Of the land, upon which that building was erected, he was made one of the Trustees. At the organization of the church, August 25, 1830, he was present, and took part in the exercises. He is remembered by that church as a constant benefactor and friend in their day of small things." Respecting similar labors in other places, Rev. Mr. Morong furnishes the following information drawn from the records of the Essex South Conference, of which he is the scribe. " On the 9th of May, 1832, the Conference, at the instance of Dr. Crowell and Mr. Jewett, resolved, 'That this Conference

---

* Sermon at the funeral of Dr. Dana.
† Sermon at the funeral of Rev. David Jewett, July 23, 1841.

views with deep interest and tender concern the moral desolations of the West Parish in Gloucester, and recommend to our churches that special efforts be immediately made to restore that waste place;' and instructed the Standing Committee on Domestic Missions, (of which Dr. C. was one,) 'to confer immediately with such persons in said parish as they may think proper, on the subject of erecting a chapel; and to secure their co-operation in such a way as may be best adapted to insure the success of the Gospel in that place.' The Committee went vigorously to work, and in a little less than two years had the satisfaction of reporting the completion of a house of worship, and the organization of an evangelical church in West Gloucester. It required, however, a great deal of perseverance and many appeals to the churches before the Committee succeeded in discharging the debt that they had contracted in their benevolent efforts. I think it safe to say that, but for Dr. Crowell and Mr. Jewett, there would have been no evangelical society, and perhaps no preached gospel at all in West Gloucester to this day. Dr. Crowell was mainly instrumental in 1835, in carrying out similar enterprises in Saugus and in Upper, now North Beverly. By his persevering efforts, houses of worship were erected in each of those places, and finally paid for. Ever afterwards he was prominent in suggesting and raising the sums which the Conference donated towards the support of those four feeble churches; and so late as the 10th of October, 1855, only a month before his death, he was made Chairman of a Committee to which was given the oversight of those churches, and the payment of money from the general fund in aid of their pastors. Besides this, he often visited them, preached in their meeting-houses on the Sabbath, and encouraged them to a hopeful perseverance. Three of these churches are now self-supporting; but of all them, it may be truly said, that Dr. Crowell was one of the main instruments, under God, of their existence."

From the same motive *he identified himself heartily with all the interests of the town* of which he was a citizen. In measures or enterprises for its greater material prosperity, such as the opening of a canal or the construction of mills, he was always ready to co-operate, because he believed that thrift and intelligence might be made tributary if not auxiliary to piety. And in his researches into the past history of the town, his chief object was to show that its political institutions and privileges were the legacy of men of the Puritan stamp, and to trace the inseparable connection between these civil blessings and that style of character, that his townsmen might be attracted into likeness to it as the true type of a model citizen. The very first, New Year's day after his ordination,—being the Sabbath,—he gave from the pulpit, in the form of an historical discourse, from Job 8 : 8, "A sketch of the history of the Second Parish in Ipswich." To the request for its publication he assented, as stated in his prefatory note, " for the benefit chiefly of the rising generation of this parish, with the hope that it may serve to in-

3

crease their knowledge of their fathers, and lead them through Divine grace
to imitate their pious and devout examples." And the chief reflection drawn
from the subject at the close of the sermon, was "the high value their ancestors attached to the institutions of the gospel."

To the cause of education in the town he contributed much time, thought
and labor. His years of service as one of the School Committee, amounted
in all to more than a quarter of a century, and he did but reiterate a sentiment which he had always felt and often expressed, when, in his last annual
school report to the town in April, 1855, he declared that "the education of
all the children in the town is confessedly the most important business in which
the town has any concern; involving its welfare for the present and coming generations, and in a measure, the good of the country at large, especially
of those parts of it in which some of our youth may establish themselves
and exert an influence for weal or woe." The estimation in which his services in this capacity were held by his fellow-townsmen, may be inferred from
a passage in the annual report of his surviving associates of the Committee at
the close of the next school year, in which they "not only deem it appropriate to pay a passing tribute to his memory because of the official relation which
he sustained toward them, but feel prompted to do so by their esteem for his
worth as a citizen, and their appreciation of his services as a friend of education and a public teacher of morals and religion." They also bear witness
that he had "evinced a most lively interest in the improvement of the schools
and a paternal solicitude for the general welfare of the rising generations,"
and declare that "his name is cherished among those of the mental and moral
benefactors of the town."*

Early convinced of the incalculable evils of all use of intoxicating liquors
as a beverage, he joined heartily in the movement which accomplished the
temperance reformation, leading the way in his own parish by his own example
and precept. "The first public meeting in town with reference to the subject was held in his church, and was opened with prayer by him. He was
one of eight to form the first Temperance Society there, July 16, 1829, and
to sign the first temperance pledge, exerted himself to have all his church-
members sign the pledge also, often afterwards preached on the subject, and
never suffered his zeal in the cause to flag to the end of his days."† Although the reform began amid bitter opposition, the influence of that society
was such that as early as 1833, no licenses were granted by the town.

And finally it is believed to be no exaggeration, in the view of those who had
personal acquaintance with him, to assert that in *his demeanor in private life*
he approximated the high and beautiful ideal thus sketched by him for another.
"In your social intercourse with your fellow-men, never forget that you are
an ambassador of Jesus. Let your conversation, therefore, be as becometh
the gospel of Christ, that a holy consistency may mark your every step, and

---

* Rev. John Prince, School Report for 1855–56.   † Mr. U. G. Spofford.

that you may be an example to the believers, in speech, in behavior, in love, in faith, in purity; not self-willed, not soon angry, not given to filthy lucre, but a lover of good men,—sober, just, holy, temperate.   As much as in you lies by kindness and forbearance, charity and condescension, live in peace with all men; yet still maintain a suitable firmness and decision of character as a servant of God, to whom you are to render your final account."*   Were any corroboration of this statement needed, it might be furnished in the testimony of Dr. Fitz, that " in the various circumstances and relations of life, decision, prudence and affection remarkably mingled in his character.   He was regardful of the feelings and the reputations of others; but he was bold in maintaining what he believed to be a right course of action, and in dispensing what he considered the eternal truth of God."   Those who knew him best could not say *less* of him in this regard, than he expressed in his tribute to the memory of his friend, Mr. Jewett : " All the relative and social duties were discharged by him with habitual tenderness and care.   His home was the bosom of hospitality and friendship, of peace and love."

But *all his traits of character*, thus imperfectly sketched, under these various aspects of theologian, preacher, pastor, citizen and friend, were but *different branches of one and the same root*,—an earnest piety shaping his entire life, " ruling every hour and act "   The Christian spirit from which they sprang was like a vital force determining the direction in which his powers should be exerted, and inspiring all his use of them, while drawing in turn its life from the revealed Word of God.   To this central quality,— the fashioning power of his character,—as thus sustained, the preacher of the sermon at his funeral, referred in the following words : " To him the truths of the gospel were ' spirit and life '   He clung to them with all the strength of a devoted faith, and with all the ardor of a quenchless love.   They were his comfort in life; they wonderfully bore him up under the pressure of repeated and sore bereavements and amid severe bodily sufferings; and they were his support when heart and flesh were failing.   He was a man of prayer. He kept up constant communion with his Savior.   He appeared to live and act with eternity in view.   With one hand he seemed to put away the objects of earth, while with the other he laid hold on those things which are above."

The ripeness of this Christian character, the maturity of this faith, found full proof at the close of his life.   " Living and feeling thus," continued Dr. Fitz, "he was calm and peaceful when the Master he served suddenly indicated to him that his work on earth was done.   As he approached eternal scenes he appeared to be supported by the everlasting arm, and to be sustained by the bread of heaven.   The precious doctrines of the gospel which he had so long and so faithfully preached, shed their radiance, and their consolations around that death-bed scene.   ' If there is one thing,' said he, ' which gives me more comfort than another at such a time as this, it is the doctrine

---

*Charge to Mr. Taylor.

that where the work of repentance and faith is begun in the soul by the Holy Spirit, it will be carried on to the day of perfection.' "

Confidence in the reality and the purity of this Christian temper had ever been the *strongest tie* between the minister and his people during his lifetime, and because of this, while they mourned him when dead, they 'sorrowed not even as others which have no hope.' On the day of his burial the church was crowded with parishioners and other people of the town,—the aged, who " had hoped that he would remain to be their comforter amid infirmities and sorrows, that he would smooth their passage to the grave, and commend their departing spirits to God," *—the young, who " had known no other pastor than the one whose sleeping dust was then before them,—to witness a scene as new as it was painful, fifty-six years having elapsed since a mourning congregation had been gathered at the interment of Rev. Mr. Cleaveland." † Around his lifeless form, were assembled as mourners, nearly all the members of the ministerial association to which he belonged. But the funeral service " though impressive was not gloomy. The hopeful and the spiritual overpowered the painful and the earthly. The craped church ; the pensive congregation ; the motionless form before the desk where it had stood for nearly half a century as the animated ambassador of Christ ; the long procession of old and young that thoughtfully followed to the grave on the open road the remains of a teacher so faithful yet so kind ; the silent weeping there ; the calm and golden sunshine ; the solemn autumn evening with its clear, immortal stars that drew on ;—all made one of those rare lulls in this stormy life when Christ's voice could be heard, speaking of eternity, saying : ' I am the resurrection and the life : He that believeth in me, though he were dead, yet shall he live.' " ‡

---

* Dr. Fitz's funeral sermon.   † Ibidem.
‡ Rev. J. M. Hoppin, in the *Congregationalist* of November 30, 1855.

History of Essex.

———•••———

CHAPTER I.

1634—1700.

FROM THE FIRST SETTLEMENT TO THE CLOSE OF THE
SEVENTEENTH CENTURY.

THE first settlement of this town commenced in 1634.
Plymouth began to be settled in 1620, Salem in 1627,
Boston in 1630, and Ipswich in 1633.

Our ancestors originally came from different parts of
England. The reasons assigned for leaving their own
country and settling in a wilderness, were, "That the
ancient faith and true worship might be found inseparable companions in their practice, and that their posterity might be undefiled in religion." *

Soon after the commencement of the Reformation in
England, 1534, the Protestants were divided into two
parties: the one adhering to Luther, the other to Calvin.
The former chose to secede from the church of Rome in
a very gradual manner, while the latter were desirous of
affecting an entire reformation at once. They contended
earnestly for the "scripture purity," in worship, as well as
in doctrine. This, together with their gravity of deportment and pious conversation, obtained for them the name
of Puritans. The Lutheran party, however, prevailed, and
their sentiments were made the basis of the Established,

---

* Morse and Parish's Hist. of N. E.

or National Church. With this church the Puritans continued in fellowship many years, although they constantly
lamented its popish forms, and sighed for a thorough reformation. At length, in 1602, a number of them formally
separated from the Established Church, and set up for
themselves a more pure form of worship. The consequence was, a violent and cruel persecution of them by
the bishops and authorities of the land. Not suffered to
live in peace where they were, nor permitted to depart,
they endured many hardships and trials. But in 1607, a
considerable number of them succeeded in leaving their
country, and removed, some to Amsterdam, and some to
Leyden, in Holland. Grieved with the corrupt examples
around them, and fearing lest their children should be
contaminated therewith, they resolved on a removal to
the desolate regions of North America. Accordingly, in
1620, August 5th, they embarked at Delft-Haven, near
Leyden, and, in November following, arrived on the bleak
and barren shores of Cape Cod. Here they anchored for
a short time only, and in the following month removed to
a place which they called Plymouth. The persecution
still continuing in England, and, in addition to the former
corruptions of the Church, a "Book of Sports on the Holy
Sabbath of God" being required to be read by the ministers of their respective assemblies, great numbers of
others, eminent for their piety, talents, and learning, embarked for this country. In 1627, Captain John Endicott,
with about one hundred persons, arrived at Naumkeag,
afterwards Salem. In June, of the following year, they
were joined by two hundred more, under the ministry of
the Rev. Messrs. Higginson, Skelton, and Bright. A part
of these soon after removed, and began the settlement of
Charlestown. In the Summer of 1630, about fifteen hundred persons, with Governor Winthrop at their head, arrived at Salem; whence they proceeded to Charlestown,
and soon settled Boston, Watertown, and Roxbury.

"In March, 1633, J. Winthrop, a son of the Governor, with twelve men, began a plantation at Agawam; which afterwards was called Ipswich. The next year, a church was gathered, being the ninth in the colony. In April, the people being destitute of a minister, *the Governor traveled on foot from Boston to Ipswich*, spent the Sabbath with them, and exercised by way of prophecy"* or exhortation. In 1634, the Rev. Nathaniel Ward came over from England, and became their first minister.

FIRST SETTLERS OF CHEBACCO.

The same year William White and Goodman Bradstreet removed toward Chebacco River, where lands were granted them by the town. Thus commenced the first settlement of this town in 1634. History gives us no account of these two families. The name of William White is first met with in 1635, in the transactions of Ipswich, as one of its inhabitants. So also are several of the name of Bradstreet: but which of them settled in this part of Ipswich, is uncertain. The land, which these first two settlers occupied, lay in what is now the north part of Essex. The next year, October, 1635, Mr. John Cogswell had three hundred acres granted him by the town, "in the farther part of Chebacco." This grant was bounded on the west by what is now the main road from Ipswich to Gloucester, and the brook which runs on the east side of the old burying-ground, and the creek running to the river; on the south by the river; on the east by the water, and on the north by the brook which runs on the north side of the farm now owned by Colonel John P. Choate.

Mr. Cogswell, before his emigration, was a prosperous merchant in London. He sailed for this country from Bristol, England, May 23, 1635, in the ship Angel Gabriel. On his passage he was wrecked in a violent storm on the

---

* Hist. of New England.

coast of Maine, in Pemaquid Bay. By this catastrophe, he lost a part of his property; but escaped safely to land with his family, where they lived for a short time in a tent. Leaving his family in the tent, he took passage for Boston, where he procured a vessel denominated a barque, commanded by Captain Gallop, and returned to Pemaquid Bay for his family and goods. He arrived at Ipswich in August, and removed to this place in the following October. His furniture and other goods were more than could be stored at one time in the vessel, from Pemaquid to Ipswich. From an inventory taken at his decease, it appears that his furniture brought from England, consisted of beds, suits of curtains, table-linen, damasks, Turkey carpets, silver plate, etc. His wife's name was Elizabeth. Their children were born in London; one was buried there, and the remaining seven,—William, John, Edward, Mary, Hannah, Abigail and Sarah,—they brought with them to this place. He had the title of Mr., and his wife, Mrs., which were given only to persons of some distinction. Their daughter Mary married Godfrey Armitage; Hannah married Charles Waldo, and removed to Chelmsford; Abigail married Thomas Clark; and Sarah married Simon Tuthill. Their first house, which was of necessity built of logs, stood, as tradition says, about thirty rods southeast of the house occupied by the late Colonel J. P. Choate.

Other settlers arrived, no doubt, soon after this. But we have no record even of their names, as residents of this part of Ipswich. Mr. Felt, in his history of Ipswich, in general, gives a valuable table of the names of the early settlers, with the year in which these names are first met with in the town records; but which, of course, does not specifiy in what part of the town they lived. Among the names which are known to have been long prevalent in this place, are the following: 1634, John Perkins; 1635, Robert Andrews, Wm. Goodhue, George Giddings; 1638, John Burnham; 1639, Andrew Story; 1648, Thomas Low,

1648, John Choate. The presumption is, that these were among the early settlers of this southern section of Ipswich, called by the Indians, Chebacco.

FIRST ROAD FROM IPSWICH TO GLOUCESTER.

Owing to the difficulty of making bridges in those early days, the roads were very circuitous, avoiding, as much as possible, the crossing of brooks and creeks. The road from Ipswich through this place to Gloucester, came by the house now occupied by Darius Cogswell, at the head of Choate's brook, entered the present Ipswich road, and proceeded as far as the lane, which leads to Colonel J. P. Choate's, which it entered, and passed on to the river by the house of Adam Boyd; crossed the river by ferry, proceeded in a southerly direction over the hills, to the head of Clark's Creek, thence by the present dwelling of Elias Andrews, thence to Gloucester, west parish, along by the site of the first meeting-house to a ferry, which crossed to the "up-in-town" parish, then the first parish in Gloucester.*

VISIT TO THE FIRST SETTLERS.

Leaving for awhile this dry, but necessary detail of facts, yet still keeping close to the lines of truth, let me invite you to go back two hundred years, and survey the place as it then was, and look in upon the settlers, and see how they managed in-doors and out. The first house which you visit, is that of Mr. Cogswell. Viewing the building, as you approach it, you perceive it is built wholly of logs, in a square form, much as children build a house of cobs; the under and upper sides of the logs being roughly hewn, that they may lie somewhat contiguous, and not admit too many of the rays of the sun, or too much of the keen air of Winter, the ends are notched to fasten them together, and the roof covered with thatch.

---

* For evidence that the first road to Gloucester went by this dwelling of Elias Andrews, see John Burnham's deed; near the close of this chapter.

4

The whole building, as it presents itself to your view, appears to be from twenty to thirty feet square. You knock at the door, and it is opened by Mrs. C., who gives you a frank and hearty reception. You are somewhat surprised to see in your maternal ancestor, not a Yankee, but an English face,—round, staid, and easy, and not like her posterity, sharp, busy, and care-worn. Her manners are English of the best stamp, for she has moved in good society at home, though not among the nobility. Her dress is neat and handsome; of the fashion of the times, though to your view exceedingly antiquated. Her whole appearance, and the appearance of the furniture, contrasts somewhat strangely with the rude appearance of the rough logs; of which the floor, as well as the walls of the house, are built. You look up and see the naked poles of the roof, and the thatch which lies upon them. At the end of the building, opposite the door, is the fire-place, constructed of rough stones, the smoothest and best that could be found in their natural state. In front of a huge back-log, eight or ten feet in length, is a bright and glowing fire, sending forth tremendous heat from sticks proportioned in size and length to the log behind. You plant your chair midway between the fire and the door, and can hardly tell by which you are most annoyed, the rushing of the winds through the crevices of the logs in your rear, or the irresistible heat in front. But by often twisting and turning, you contrive to maintain your position between such opposite and powerful foes. During the conversation with Mrs. C., and her four interesting daughters, all busy with their knitting, you glance occasionally at the objects around you. On one side of the house, you observe some handsome curtains, stretched quite across, which, with one at right angles in the middle, form two bed-rooms, one in each corner of that side of the house. The chairs in the sitting-room, or kitchen, are but few, on account of the difficulty of bringing them

across the deep. But seats are supplied by the numerous
trunks and boxes, in which they transported their beds,
bedding, clothing, table-linen, damasks, and carpets. As
the floor is too rough for their Turkey-wrought carpets,
they remain yet unpacked. But the time for supper
draws near, and Mrs. C. and her eldest daughter are busy
in preparing the repast. The old English kettle is hung
over the fire, with contents for a plentiful supper of bean
broth, to which, as you are a visitor, a nice cake of Indian
hominy is added,—which Mrs. C. contrives to bake by cau-
tiously approaching the glowing fire with her face more
than half turned away, to preserve her eyes. Presently
the father, and two of his sons, come in from their field
labor. Harvesting has commenced, and they are reaping
the first fruits of their toil in the wilderness. They have
not yet wholly lost the delicate appearance resulting from
city life and manners; though the perils of the ocean, and
the hardships of the wilderness, have done something to
give them a darker hue, and more athletic appearance.

Labor in the open air, in the cool season of Autumn,
has given them a keen appetite. The table is now set
for the social meal, covered with elegant table-linen, and
spread with basins of pewter, and spoons of silver. The
broth is poured into an elegant vase, from which each is
supplied by a silver ladle. The family gather around,
and stand with reverence while the head of the family
craves a blessing from the Author of all their mercies.

Supper being ended, and the table removed, all are
seated for the evening; the females near the light of a
pine torch, for the purpose of sewing and knitting, and
the males around the room at their pleasure.

A neighbor calls in to spend a social hour. We will
suppose it to be Goodman Bradstreet. The conversation
turns at once on the latest news from their father-land,
where they have left many dear friends, and in the government and prosperity of which, they yet feel a most

tender and lively interest. Does King Charles still continue his despotic course, despoiling his subjects of their
dearest rights, and provoking them to insurrection and
civil war? Is Archbishop Laud as full of bitterness and
persecution towards the Puritans as ever? are questions
eagerly asked, and answered affirmatively, in sad tones,
from the testimony of those who have recently arrived.
From the discussion of English politics, they turn to their
own local affairs, and touch upon the apparently peaceable
disposition of their savage neighbors, whose wigwams are
close at hand; the danger that would arise from their
getting possession of knives and fire-arms; the dangers
already existing from the ferocious beasts of the woods
near by; the difficulty of preventing cattle and sheep from
being devoured by them; the difficulty, too, of cultivating
the soil while the stumps are so thick, and there are only
two ploughs for the use of the whole town. With joy and
gratitude they advert to the goodness of God, in prosper-
ing their crops of Indian corn and English grain; preserving their lives and health, amidst so many exposures; and
allowing them the inestimable privileges of civil and religious freedom, even in the solitude and perils of the
wilderness.

When Goodman Bradstreet has retired, and the evening
is well-nigh spent, the good man of the house takes the
family Bible, and reads from it aloud those sacred truths,
which at their London fireside had been their comfort and
support; which had cheered them on the stormy ocean,
and were now their consolation and joy; and then, with
much fervency, offers the evening sacrifice of prayer and
praise, while all stand round in the silent and solemn
attitude of worship.

You are then shown to your lodging for the night,—
the bed reserved for visitors, enclosed with curtains to
exclude the night air, and the too early light of the morning. As you lie upon your pillow, curiosity prompts you

to draw aside the curtain, and take a peep through the shrunken logs. A beautiful bright star meets your eye with many others less brilliant. The woods resound with the hideous yells of beasts: among which the howling of a pack of wolves is predominant, and waxes louder and louder, till they seem at length to be close by your bed. With the bleating of the sheep, the bellowing of the cattle, and the barking of the stout mastiffs in the yard,—all is bustle, stir and alarm. The family is in motion. Mr. Cogswell and his eldest son seize their rifles, and discharge them in quick succession at the door. The flashing of the powder, and the strange report of the guns soon start off the savage pack; not, however, without their taking with them one or two poor sheep, partly devoured.

After a refreshing night's sleep, you rise with the morning sun, and breakfast and family worship being ended, you walk out to survey the woodland scenery. A dense forest of birch, oak, chestnut and maple, the growth of centuries, meets your eye in every direction. Here and there you see a cleared spot, which the Indians have burned away, and use for growing corn, or which the new settlers have cleared up for tillage. The road before you, towards the river, winds about, to avoid the larger stumps, and on the low and muddy parts of it, the straight portions of small trees are laid, covered here and there with a little earth, or with a plenty of soft brush. You look over on your right into one of the corn-fields, leaning as you look, not on substantial stone walls, but on such slender fencing of poles and brush, as the necessity of the times permits, and wonder that amidst such a multitude of burnt stumps, anything can be made to grow by ploughing or spading the earth.

INDIAN WIGWAMS AND CUSTOMS.

Following an Indian foot-path through the forest, you come out at a wide plot of ground, where are some dozen

wigwams, clustered on the sunny side of a hill, which over-
looks the marsh and Chebacco River. As you approach
their huts with the measured step and cautious eye, which
the sight of a savage always inspires, you hesitate whether
to go forward or turn back. But curiosity prevails, and
you begin to examine their premises. Their wigwams are
made of bark, fastened by strong withs to poles driven
into the earth, in a broad circle at the bottom, and brought
nearly together at the top, to save the necessity of making a roof. Leaving a hole at the top for the smoke to
escape, the fire is kindled in the center beneath; around
which, on the ground, the indolent men are lying or sitting,
while their squaws, with their papooses, are abroad, some
gathering fuel, some bringing in pumpkins and beans,
some drying the fish, and the venison taken by their lords
in their last excursion. The skin of some animal tied
about their waists, is all their clothing. In one wigwam,
into which you take a peep, you see the men busily
engaged in gambling; hazarding, and often losing every
particle of property they possessed.

In another direction, you see a company of men, women and children, gathered round a powah. He is performing, to their astonishment, some of his wonderful
feats. He can make the rocks dance, and the water
burn, and turn himself into a blazing man. He can
change a *dry snake skin* into a living snake, to be seen,
felt, and heard. All these things you see him do, and
are ready to exclaim, "There is no new thing under
the sun! That which is done is that which shall be
done." But hark! What loud and bitter cry is that,
issuing from one of the huts? It is a lamentation for
the dead, made ever and anon by the mourning family,
and the neighbors assembled with them. The man of
the hut has died, and his burial is to take place before
evening.

It is now time to satisfy the cravings of hunger, and

the women are busy preparing food. You are inquisitive
to see how it is done. At a little distance from the wigwam, the fire for cooking is kindled. One is moistening
some corn, which she has bruised in a hollow stone with
a stone pestle, by pouring water upon it from a dried
pumpkin shell, and spreading it for baking upon a thin
flat stone. Another is boiling meat in a wooden vessel,
by putting hot rocks in the water with the meat, and
changing them often. The wooden vessel is a log rudely
hollowed out by a stone gouge. As hospitality to strangers is the Indian's pride, you are, of course, invited to
partake of the repast. It is in the wigwam, where the
men are seated upon the ground in a circle, with the food
in the centre. You contrive to sit with them, though with
far less grace, and eat with them out of the common dish,
without knife or fork, or salt, or drink. The women stand
round till their lords have finished, and then in a like posture eat up what remains.

After thus dining, in Indian style, you bend your course
to the banks of the river, where are a group of Indian
children frolicking in the water, some not over three
years, swimming like ducklings. Numerous canoes of
birch bark are gliding up and down the river, for the purpose of "clamming" and fishing. The river will never
be more lively a hundred years hence.

FISH WEAR.

As you walk on the bank of the river, you see a con-
trivance for catching the river fish. It is called a wear,
and belongs to John Perkins, Jr. It consists of stone
walls, extending towards each other down the stream, till
they come in contact at an angle of forty-five degrees.
At this angle a trap is set, made of hoops and twigs, in
which great numbers of fish are taken. Mr. Perkins is
granted this privilege for seven years, beginning with
1636, and is to sell his alewives at 5s. for 1,000. Richard

Kent is also allowed to build another wear, having one already in operation.

On your return to the hill of wigwams, you see a crowd collected for the funeral. The mourners have their faces painted black. The corpse rests by the side of the grave, till they join again in their savage howl. Tears roll freely down the cheeks of old and young. The body is laid in the grave; and another dismal cry is heard. The mat on which the deceased died, is then spread over the body. His tomahawk and spear, and whatever was most precious to him, is buried with him; but his garment of skin they hang upon a tree near by, never again to be touched, but to perish with the body.

As you turn away from this solemn scene, deeply affected by their dark superstition, and their destitution of the light of Revelation, and of all the comforts and blessings of civilized life, you are more sensible than ever of your obligations to Him who made you, and who died to redeem you. Returning by the road that you came, you pass a thick swamp, and see just before you a bear with her cubs just entering it, and are glad that her eye was turned from you, till she was on her way through the swamp. A little further along, you see a wolf caught in a trap, or rather held fast by a line. He cannot pull away; for the hooks in his mouth attached to the line, cause him great agony. These hooks, four in number, had been bound together by a thread, some wool wrapped about them, and then dipped in melted tallow, till they formed a substance as large as an egg; which has proved a bait to the unsuspecting animal.

Prolonging your visit for a day or two in Mr. Cogswell's family, you call also upon their neighbors, who, though few and far between, are treasures of comfort to each other, abounding in all the sweet charities of good neighborhood. Your walk at this time lies in a north and north-west direction, on the road which leads to the centre of Ipswich.

`The first house which you come to, is William Goodhue's. He has just moved into the place, and entered his new log building, which is about a quarter of a mile north of Mr. Cogswell's. A half mile beyond William Goodhue's in the same direction, is the Bradstreet house; and nearly a mile farther, on the dark and solitary road through the woods to Ipswich, is William White's. By your brief visits to each of these families, you learn that they are thoroughly Puritan in their principles, and English in their manners and customs. Their children were born in England, and have been thus far well instructed and brought up. Their houses, though built of logs, are comfortable and well furnished. Having spent the day pleasantly in these happy and hospitable families, you return to Mr. C 's. It is Saturday evening. The pious household are making preparation for the coming Sabbath, the

> " Day of all the week the best,"

and for the proper observance of which, chiefly, they left their native land, and settled in this wilderness. Nothing is left undone which it is practicable to do, by way of preparation for holy time. On Sabbath morning, having risen at an early hour, all get ready with their best apparel to attend public worship in the body of the town. The mother is mounted upon a horse, with the youngest daughter behind her; while the other three daughters and three sons, with their father at their head, travel on foot. The mother and daughters, however, ride alternately, as fatigue requires, or choice directs. The father and eldest son go armed, to guard against the attacks of wild beasts. The road is long and rough; but love for the house of God lightens the toil. They are joined on the way by the families of their neighbors, and the excitement of social affections, and suitable conversation, makes the way seem short.

In less than two hours, you are at the door of the meet-

5

ing-house, a spacious log building, but filled with many a warm heart, and lighted up with many a heavenly countenance. The service on both parts of the day, consists of prayer, singing, and preaching. The preacher is Mr. Ward, the pastor of the church. His discourses are full of evangelical sentiment, calculated to humble the sinner, and exalt the Saviour; and you know not which most to admire, the lucid arrangement of the excellent matter, sustained at every point by Scripture quotations, or the fluency and fervor of the delivery. You mark, as a peculiarity of the times, that one of the elders or deacons, who sit in a pew adjoining the pulpit, in front, reads the psalm, one line at a time, and all in the assembly, that are able, join with him in the singing.

The services being ended at an early hour, the intermission having been short, you commence your return with the pilgrim family. Deeply interested in the preacher, you are prompted, as you walk by the side of Mr. C., to ask of him some account of the man. He cheerfully complies, and gives you the following particulars of his beloved pastor, as he has learned them from an authentic source:

"Mr. NATHANIEL WARD was born at Haverhill, England, in 1570. He was educated at one of our principal universities, and after having been for some time a student and practitioner of the law, he traveled in Holland, Germany, Prussia, and Denmark. At the university of Heidelberg, he became acquainted with the celebrated scholar and divine, David Parcus, and by conversing with him, was induced to abandon the profession of law, and to commence the study of divinity. After being occupied for some time, in theological pursuits, at Heidelberg, he returned to England, and was settled in the ministry at Standon, in Hertfordshire. He was ordered before the bishop, December 12, 1631, to answer for his non-conformity, and refusing to comply with the requisitions of the church, he was at length forbidden to continue in the exercise of his clerical office. In April, 1634, he left his native country, and arrived here in the following June; and was soon settled over us as our pastor, being sixty-four years of age."

Having reached Mr. C's. house, and supped with the family, you close the day as it was begun, with household devotions, and with conversation suited to make you more useful and happy on earth, and better prepared for the world to come. On the following day you take leave of the family, in which you have made so pleasant a visit, resolving that you will return again, if you live, and see what progress your venerated ancestors have made, in the clearing of land, in the arts of husbandry, and the comforts of life. 1138898

CHARACTER OF THE FIRST SETTLERS.

In the meantime, the settlement and improvement of the place gradually advanced. The persecution of the dissenters in England continuing, great numbers of them embarked for this country. But in 1640 the tide of emigration, in a great measure, ceased to flow. The spirit of liberty, and even of republicanism had begun then to show itself in the British Parliament, and hope was cherished by the Puritans that they should soon enjoy as much civil and religious freedom there as here. It was estimated at the time, that up to 1640, about four thousand families, consisting of twenty-one thousand souls, had arrived in two hundred and ninety-eight ships. The expense of the removal of these families was estimated at £192,000 sterling, which, including what they paid at home, and to the Indians here, was a dear purchase of their lands.*

Of these emigrants, Ipswich received a proportional share, both as to numbers, intelligence, and piety. Johnson, as quoted by Felt, remarks of Ipswich, as early as 1646, "The peopling of this town is by men of good rank and quality, many of them having the yearly revenue of large lands in England, before they came to this wilderness." Cotton Mather says of Ipswich, in 1638, "Here was a renowned church, consisting mostly of such illuminated Christians, that their pastors, in the exercise of

---

* History of New England.

their ministry, might think that they had to do not so much with disciples as judges." Of Mr. Rogers he says: " His colleague here was the celebrious Norton; and glorious was the church of Ipswich now in two such extraordinary persons, with their different gifts, but united hearts, carrying on the concerns of the Lord's kingdom in it."

FIRST MINISTERS OF IPSWICH.

As Mr. Ward had resigned his office by reason of ill health, the church elected Mr. John Norton as his successor in 1636, and two years after, chose Mr. Rogers for his colleague. They were in office together, one as pastor, and the other as teacher; a distinction chiefly nominal, as their official duties were much the same. Mr. Rogers, (Nathaniel,) was born at Haverhill, England, in 1598. He was a descendant of John Rogers, the martyr; was educated at Emanuel College, where he was eminent both as a scholar and a Christian. He came to this country at the age of forty, in company with many others, who all settled with him at Ipswich. Mr. Norton was born at Starford, England, in 1606; entered the university of Cambridge at fourteen; removed to this country in 1635; resided in Boston about a year, and then settled in Ipswich, at the age of thirty. In 1652, he removed to Boston, and was settled as successor to Mr. John Cotton.

Mr. Ward, the first minister of Ipswich, continued to preach in Ipswich occasionally after he resigned his office as pastor of that church. In 1638 he was appointed by the General Court, on a committee to prepare a code of laws. In 1639 he sends them the result of his labors. Copies of it were sent to the several towns for the consideration of the freemen. It was adopted by the General Court in 1641. It consisted of a hundred laws, called the body of liberties. Mr. Ward, it will be remembered, was an eminent lawyer before he became a minister, which was one reason, doubtless, why he was appointed on this committee. In 1640, with some men of Newbury, he commenced the settlement of Haverhill, where afterwards his son John was settled in the ministry. Having been in this country eleven years, he returned to England, at the age of seventy-five, and became minister of Shenfield, in Essex County, where he lived eight years, and died aged eighty-three. He published, after he returned to England, several tracts, and a book, entitled "The Simple Cobbler of Agawam," a satirical and witty performance.

ELECTIONS AND CITIZENSHIP.

In 1634, a law was passed, that the whole body of freemen meet in Boston, from all the towns, at the General Court of Election, and choose the magistrates, including Governor, and Lieutenant-Governor. In 1636, Ipswich, and five other towns are allowed to keep a sufficient guard of freemen at home from such a court, and to forward their proxies. This practice continued for about thirty years, when it went into disuse, and the present usage was in substance adopted. None but freemen could hold offices or vote for rulers. To become a freeman, each person was required to become a member of some Congregational church. This was doubtless owing to the peculiar situation of our ancestors at that time. They had fled from the persecution of the Episcopal church at home. Now if they had allowed men of that church, or any other church, hostile to religious freedom, to take the lead in their affairs here, in their feeble state, the result might have been the bringing in of the same persecuting power of the bishops, from which they had already suffered so much, and this would have defeated the very end for which they came here. They might as well have remained under the persecuting power of the bishops in their father-land, as to have come to this wilderness, and allowed that power to follow them, and gain the ascendancy over them. Their only security against this danger

seemed to be in a law that every voter, and every candidate for office, should be a member of some Congregational
church; i. e., a church, whose principles of government
are wholly democratic. Others might reside among them
unmolested, but not take the lead, or have any management in their civil or religious affairs. Some have taken
occasion from this to reproach them, as if they were not
willing to grant that liberty to others which they claimed
for themselves. But they stood in this matter only in
self-defence. They had bought, with a great price, their
tract of land in this part of the wide wilderness, and were
at a great expense and suffering in settling on it, for the
express purpose of enjoying their own religion in their
own way. The wilderness was wide enough for all. Others might choose their portion in it, and set up what worship they pleased, and conduct their own affairs in their
own way, on territory, the sovereignty of which they had
fully and fairly acquired. But they could not be allowed
to reside on the lands of the Puritans, at the hazard of
robbing them of their dearest rights and privileges. They
could not, therefore, become voters or rulers among them
without complying with certain specified conditions: such
conditions as our fathers deemed necessary to protect their
own liberties. The same, for substance, is true with us at
this day, though the conditions of citizenship are not the
same, because our circumstances are different. The times
of our fathers were those of infancy and weakness. The
least tendency to mutiny in the infant colony, placed
them in great jeopardy. As on board of a vessel, the
safety of the whole depends on the suppression of the
first manifestation of a mutinous spirit, and even of the
promulgation of principles tending to mutiny, by the
severest measures, if necessary; so in these infant settlements of our fathers, with savages in the midst of them,
with wild beasts around them, with scarcely any means of
defence, and themselves few and far between, the preserva-

tion of their lives, and of their dearest rights and liberties, depended on their promptly putting down all opposition to their civil government, and suppressing all insurrectionary publications.

Hence, when Roger Williams, a Welsh emigrant, appeared in 1631, and refused the oath of fidelity to the government, and taught others to follow his example; and taught that their patent obtained of King Charles, was invalid; and that it was wrong to take an oath in a court of justice, or anywhere else, unless you first knew that the person administering the oath, was a converted man; and other things equally absurd and dangerous to the civil peace, he was sent out of their colony, and proceeding to another part of the wilderness, he began the settlement of Rhode Island; which he might as well have done before attempting to overturn the government of Massachusetts as afterwards.*

And thus, too, when the Quakers appeared in 1656, with the declaration that no government was lawful unless administered by them, "That every other government but their own was a tree to be cut down,"† and carried out these insurrectionary principles, by riotous and treasonable acts,—they were sent out of the colony. On their returning with the same determination to overturn, if possible, the civil authorities, they were sent out again, with the warning that if they returned the third time, they would be subjected to capital punishment. In their infatuation, they came back, and four of them were hung on Boston Common; just as incorrigible rebels against civil govern-

---

* It is a remarkable fact, that Rhode Island, actuated by the principles of self-defence, imitated Massachusetts in that very thing, in which Roger Williams had so reproachfully condemned them; viz. excluding those religionists, whom they believed to be dangerous to civil liberty, from the privileges of freemen, or the right of choosing, or being chosen, civil officers. And this, too, in violation of the charter which they had just received from England. In March, 1663, they enacted a law, in which they say, "That all men of competent estates, and of civil conversation, *Roman Catholics only excepted*, shall be admitted freemen.—*Hist. of N. E.*

† History of New England.

ment would now be treated,—and yet this is called in all
our school histories, the persecution of the Quakers! We
have alluded to this matter because the reputation of the
first settlers of Ipswich, and of this place, then a part of
Ipswich, as well as of the colonists in general, is so deeply
concerned in it. It seems to be time that their children
should know, that the memory of their justly venerated
sires is not deserving of this foul stigma, which some have
endeavored to fasten upon it.

PEQUOT WAR.—1637.

The Pequots inhabited the borders of Connecticut River,
from its mouth to within a few miles of Hartford. They
were a fierce, cruel, and warlike tribe. They had mur-
dered several English families in that neighborhood; and
by seeking a union with other savage tribes, threatened
to destroy the whole of the English colonists. This
aroused the colonies of Plymouth, Massachusetts, and Connecticut, to unite, and make common cause against so destructive a foe. Connecticut raised 90, Plymouth 40, and
Massachusetts 200 troops. The quota of Ipswich, for this
army is 23. They are drawn out by lot. The names of
all the inhabitants, fit to bear arms, are placed in a box by
the proper authorities, and drawn out, one by one, until
the number to be drafted is completed. An order is then
sent to each of the drafted men, to appear on parade on
a certain day and hour, prepared to march in pursuit of
the enemy. The summons is doubtless received with
calmness and courage by men, who felt that the peace and
security of their wives and children, and the welfare of
the country, depended on their subduing this haughty and
cruel foe. No little agitation and solicitude, however, is
felt by the families in view of their husbands, fathers, and
brothers, being called to the battle-ground, with the uncertainty of ever seeing them again. Three of the drafted
men were from this part of the town,—Andrew Story,

Robert Cross, and John Burnham. Story probably lived
at the Falls. Burnham lived on the farm now owned by
Enoch and Caleb Haskell. His land, as appears from an
ancient deed, extended to the head of the creek, then
called Clark's Creek, and thence south-easterly, toward
Gloucester line, including the farm now owned by Ezra
Perkins, and joining upon the school farm. He was the
progenitor of the Burnhams in this place. Some of his
descendants inherited and lived on that tract of land
until within thirty years. Others settled at an early
period on land now owned by Timothy Andrews, Winthrop Burnham, Daniel Mears, William Low, and others,—
making a circuit near the woods, from the south-west
corner of the school farm, over Rocky Hill, to Chebacco
Pond.

Cross, we suppose, must have lived on a tract of land
east of John Burnham's; probably on the farm now owned
by Jonathan Lufkin; since the town records mention a
road, ordered to be laid out in 1657, from his house, to the
farther (south) side of Chebacco Ferry; the same road
probably which is now from Caleb Haskell's, by the East
school-house, to Jonathan Lufkin's.

The persons above named, went to the war, and returned
in safety; as we find them mentioned two years afterwards,
among those who were to receive from the town, a grant
of land from two to ten acres each, for their services in
the Pequot war.

We will visit Mr. Burnham's, and hear from his own
lips, the story which he may be supposed to have related
to his family and friends, on his return. It is a Summer
evening, and the family and visitors are seated in the yard
of the log house, upon logs conveniently arranged, when
Mr. B. thus begins:

"You remember the morning when neighbor Cross and I set out for the
army, with our blankets and provisions strapped to our backs, and guns in
hand. As we passed neighbor Cogswell's, he shook us heartily by the hand,

6

and said it was a righteous cause, and God would prosper us in it. They saw us coming at Goodman Bradstreet's, and the whole family came to bid us God-speed, and wish us a safe return. When we reached the corner of Belcher's lane, we found Andrew Story, from the Falls, waiting to join us. It was a painful and laborious expedition which was before us, attended with many anxieties as to whether we should ever see home again or not. But we encouraged one another in the Lord, believing that he had called us to the work of defending our lives and liberties against the attacks of a savage foe. We reached Ipswich Common, a little before the time appointed, and found there some of the drafted men of Ipswich, and those from Rowley and Newbury. Very soon Captain Dennison, and the rest of our company, came upon the ground. A number of the settlers in the neighborhood, with our beloved pastor, came also to take leave of us. We formed a line, and our captain having exercised us for awhile, requested our minister, Mr. Ward, to give us a word of exhortation, and offer a prayer, which he did. We then took up our march for the Pequot country. Having reached Salem Village, (North Danvers,) we were joined by the drafted men from Salem, and as we marched on, several others fell into our ranks. We reached Charlestown late in the evening, and encamped on the common; it was the first time that I had ever slept upon the ground, with nothing but the starry heavens for a covering. The next day, passing through Cambridge, we found there the Boston troops, with Captain Stoughton, who was to be our principal captain, having the military stores, and camp utensils. We marched nearly thirty miles that day, through thick woods, and across many small streams, halting at noon for our meals, and for rest. The Indians, with their squaws and papooses, came from their hills around, to take a peep at us. They professed to be friendly; but there was jealousy in their looks, a sort of half war, and half peace. As we went through a manual exercise, and especially when we took aim, they suddenly skulked behind their stout oaks; but soon ventured out again, when they found our guns did not speak. At evening we found an open space on the side of a hill, cleared by the Indians, and there halted for the night. Having kindled our fires, and ate a good supper of porridge, we attended, as usual, upon prayer, offered by one of our captains, and with a trusty watch, and blazing fires, we laid ourselves down, and slept safely and soundly. The next day, we found ourselves getting nearer to hostile ground, and kept a sharp lookout, lest we should feel the arrows of the Indians, suddenly flying upon us from the surrounding woods. We, however, passed along quietly that day. On the following night, the sound of the Indian warwhoop, real or imaginary, we could not tell which, together with the tremendous howling of beasts, kept me awake for awhile. But through fatigue I fell asleep, and dreamed of being in a terrible battle with the Pequots, whose arrows and tomahawks gave us no small trouble. Their awful yelling getting louder and louder, awaked me, when I

discovered one of the watch standing over me, who told me it was time for
me to get up, and take my turn in the watch. At length, after a tedious
and exhausting march of nearly a week, often through pathless woods, carrying our guns, our ammunition, and provisions, we reached the Pequot's
country, and learned that Captain Mason, with 90 Connecticut troops, and
500 friendly Indians, had attacked and captured one of the principal forts of
the Pequots, and that the remainder of them, with Sassacus, their principal
Sachem, had gone westward, and Captain Mason had returned to Saybrook.
Captain Stoughton, in consultation with his officers, concluded to march to
Saybrook. At that place, Captain Mason, being thus joined by the Massachusetts troops, 200 strong, had orders to march immediately in pursuit of
the enemy. Accordingly, on the morning of the 25th of June, we took up
our line of march in search of the remnant of this warlike and cruel tribe.
It was not long before we came in sight of some of them in small detached
parties, whom we easily captured or destroyed. But it was some time before
we could get any information of the main body of the tribe. After five days'
march, we reached Quinnipeak, (New Haven,) where we were told by a
friendly Pequot, that Sassacus and his men were in a swamp, a few miles
west of us. We pushed forward, and on the next day reached the border of
the swamp. But it was too soft and boggy for any to enter but Indians.
Our officers thought it best to surround the swamp, so as to be sure that none
of them should escape, and annoy them as we could. We found that there
was another tribe in the swamp, to the number of 300, that had never mur-
dered any of the English. Them we willingly let out. But the Pequots said
they had both shed and drank the blood of Englishmen, and were determined
to fight it out. As night came on, we cut through a part of the swamp, and
made the circle round the enemy much less, and so completely hemmed them
in, that they could not escape, even under the darkness of the night. The
enemy finding in the morning, that they were wholly shut in, made a violent
attempt to break through our lines. But we drove them back, with great
slaughter. They next tried to force the lines of the Connecticut troops; but
with no better success. The battle now was close and hot, the enemy seeming determined not to yield but at the loss of their lives. Out of about 600
of them, only 60 escaped. Our loss was 11 killed, and 20 wounded. John
Wedgwood and Thomas Sherman, of this town, were among the wounded.
We took many of them prisoners; some of whom were kept by our men as
servants, and some were sent to the West Indies, and sold to the planters.
This battle finished the Pequot tribe. The few that escaped, or were not in
the swamp, were destroyed by the friendly Indians. We took some of them
on our return. A party of them hove in sight one day, when Francis Wright,
our townsman, gave chase to them, and having no more powder and ball, he
brake his gun over them, and brought two of their heads to the camp. The
prisoners told us that more than 2,000 of their tribe had been killed in dif-

ferent battles, and more than 1,000 taken prisoners.* Our march back was less tedious, as we had less to bring; and, as we neared home, the way seemed shorter. Ipswich never seemed so pleasant before; the sight of Chebacco was still pleasanter. We owe many thanks to God for keeping us alive and unharmed in so hard and perilous a campaign, and in giving us such signal success."

Upon this, the good man offered a prayer, abounding in thanksgiving, as well as supplication; after which all retired. In 1639 eight acres of land were granted to Mr. Burnham by the town as a pension for his service in the Pequot war.

Notwithstanding the extermination of this numerous and warlike tribe, the fear and alarm excited by the Indians were not diminished, but gradually increased among the colonists. An order is issued by the Governor and Council, requiring Ipswich, Rowley, and Newbury, to send 40 men, on the Sabbath, September 2, 1642, to disarm Pasconoway, who lived at Merrimack. This was caused by the suspicion of a general conspiracy against the English. The pay of the soldiers in these wars, was 1s. per day, and of the officers, 2s. Musket balls and wampum, i. e. strings of shells, black, white, and blue, were the currency of the day.

EARTHQUAKE.

" The year 1638," history informs us, " was remarkable for a great earthquake, throughout New England. This earthquake, as did that of 1627, which was equally violent and extensive, constituted a remarkable era, that was long remembered, and referred to by the pious inhabitants of these infant colonies."

COMMONERS.

The first settlers of this town claimed all the land contained in it, having purchased it of Masconnomet, for £20 sterling. And what they did not divide among themselves, for their immediate use and improvement, or grant to

---

* Trumbull's History : Indian Wars.

others that came to settle among them, they held in common, and were therefore called commoners, and their land thus held, commonage. They appear to have been a body of proprietors, distinct from the town; for it was not till 1788, that they gave to the town all their claim to the common land, to pay the town debt. But though distinct from the town as a body, they seem also to have had some connection with it in this matter, and to have been in a measure under its jurisdiction respecting it, for we find in the records of the town, that "None but commoners shall make any use of common land," and the Selectmen are directed to petition the Court for a confirmation of this order. The Court accordingly passed a law, "That no dwelling shall have commonage, except those now built, or which may be, by consent of commoners, or towns."

OTHER EARLY SETTLERS.

In 1643, Thomas Low settled in this place, on land since owned by the late Captain Winthrop Low. His house was about thirty-five rods south of Captain Low's mansion.

In 1645, John Choate, the first of the name in this place, came from England, and took land near the head of the creek, which divides Essex from Ipswich. His house was a few rods north-east of where the late John Low's now stands. He had four sons, and a number of daughters. His son Joseph, and grandson Daniel, afterwards owned the same farm. His son John settled on the farm now owned by Darius Cogswell. Thomas settled on Hog Island. He was a great farmer, and was called Governor Choate, probably from his having the sole rule and possession of the Island. His son John, born 1697, built the stone bridge in Ipswich, called Choate's bridge. His daughter Sarah, married Rev. Amos Cheever, of Manchester.

In 1645, we are told, New England was remarkably prosperous: commerce flourished, the fishery was actively carried on, and agriculture was successful.

ANOTHER VISIT TO THE ANCIENT SETTLERS.

1649. As a marriage is to take place at Mr. Cogswell's, we will revisit the family, notice the changes that have occurred, and be present at the joyful solemnity. When there before, thirteen years since, they were living in their log house, surrounded by a dense forest, with but little land cleared, and that little full of burnt stumps, and with Indian wigwams near at hand, and the wolf, and the wild-cat, and the bear, as soon as night set in, filling the forest with their terrific notes. But though the savage man and beast remain, you see many agreeable changes wrought by the persevering hand of industry. The log house has been abandoned for a new framed house, two stories in front, the roof descending on the back side nearly to the ground, the chimney in the centre, with two spacious apartments, and their chambers, on each side of it, and a kitchen in their rear, narrow but nearly as long as the house. The chimney is built of stone, in its natural state, carefully selected, and put together with clay mortar, as high as the garret floor, where it receives a wooden chimney, daubed on the inside with clay mortar, and rising some feet above the roof. The fire-places in each of the front rooms, are spacious, but in the kitchen, of a mammoth size, so that the whole family may be seated in the corners at the ends of blazing logs, four or five feet in length. The boards were sawn by hand. Bricks being laid against the inner partition, and covered with clay, to exclude the cold, the boards on the outside, called clay-boards, are fastened in an upright posture, with narrow strips covering the interstices. The roof is finished in the same style. The house stands in from the road, and faces the south, that the sun at high noon, may look full into the windows, and by suitable marks on the window stool, may indicate the hour of the day. The windows are three feet by two, with small diamond-shaped glass, set in lead lines, and opening outwardly, on hinges. As you approach the house from the road, you pass through a beautiful garden of shrubbery, arranged after the English fashion. The whole establishment, though without the modern clap-boards and shingles, and the ornament of paint, affords a fine contrast to the rough, dark-looking log cabin, still standing just in the rear. You stand at the door, and might enter, by pulling the new nice string which hangs before you, but you choose to knock, that some one may show you in, and conduct you to the family; by whom you are cordially received, and hospitably entertained. You are as much pleased with the improvement of their dwelling internally, as externally. The fine carpets, which could not be laid upon the rough floors of the log house, are now spread upon their new rooms, comparing well with the stuffed chairs, and other furniture brought with them from England, and saved from the wreck at Pemaquid.

While the father and sons are busy in the field, the females are more than usually busy in the house, preparing for the expected wedding, and fitting the bride with a suitable wardrobe, and other articles for housekeeping. Having paid your respects to the family within, you walk abroad to see those without, and to witness the various improvements upon the premises. The black stumps in the fields are nearly all gone, and new fields added to the old ones. The woods have grown thinner, and have retired farther from the barn, and other out-buildings. The road from Mr. C's. to the ferry, is not near as dark as formerly, and is much improved for traveling. But you do not venture far; for the law of the day forbids your going beyond a mile from the house alone, or unarmed, through fear of the Indians. The Indians here have the appearance of peace; but they belong to an insidious race; and need constant watching. See there a spacious log building, with strongly fortified doors. It has been erected in conformity with a general order from the Court, to be a re-

treat for all the families around, in case of an attack from
the Indians. A watch is kept every night in all the towns,
and the discharge of a gun is the signal of alarm. In the
conversation of the evening, this matter is often referred
to, and the wish that their savage neighbors would take
up their wigwams, and leave the town, is heartily responded to by all. But there is little hope of this, and
the various ways in which they would defend themselves,
or escape from their murderous weapons, is, therefore,
freely talked of, especially by the younger members of
the family. But there is one defence surer than all others, the protecting arm of a gracious Providence; and as
the good man of the house devoutly renders thanks in
the family prayer, for their preservation thus far from so
dreadful a foe, and from other impending dangers, and sup-
plicates a continuance of the same, all unite with deeper
solicitude, and more heartfelt devotion than ever.

The morning light dawns upon the Sabbath. All prepare at an early hour for the Sabbath day's journey to the
house of God. Their home they leave under the protection of that Being, whose command they obey in not for-
saking the assembling of themselves together. As you
proceed with the men armed, you are silent, ready to catch
every sound from the deep woods, lest it should betoken
an attack from some beast, or savage foe.

The neighbors join you, as you pass their houses, armed
in like manner, and your fears are abated as your numbers
increase. On arriving at the house of God, the numerous
muskets and pikes, seen in the hands both of old men and
young, give signs of the common danger. But faith in
God, composes the mind, and prepares the heart for His
worship, Who is the source of all good, and a very present
help in trouble. But means are to be used, and, to prevent a surprise, sentinels are placed on the outside of the
church, while the congregation worship within.

PUBLIC WORSHIP.

Mr. Rogers, the pastor, begins the services with a prayer. The teacher, Mr. Norton, then reads and expounds a portion of Scripture. A psalm is then given out by one of the ruling elders or deacons, which is read and sung line by line. Mr. Rogers preaches in the morning, and Mr. Norton in the afternoon. An hour-glass is placed at one end of the elders' pew, that the sermon may not be less than an hour in the delivery. Singing, prayer, and the benediction follow the sermon on both parts of the day. Before the close of the afternoon service, the usual Sabbath collection is taken in the following manner: the whole congregation, with the magistrates and chief men at their head, pass up one aisle to the deacons' seat, where, if they give money, they drop it into a box, if anything else, they set it down before the deacon, and then pass down the other aisle to their seats. At the close, notice is given of the Thursday lecture, at eleven o'clock, A. M., which all are expected to attend, as it is a service which the parishioners have requested of their minister, for their own religious instruction and edification. As soon as the benediction is pronounced, your attention is suddenly arrested by the loud and measured tones of the town clerk, in the following announcement: "Notice is hereby given that marriage is intended between Godfrey Armitage, of Boston, and Mary Cogswell, of Ipswich." As this is the third Sabbath that the parties have been thus publicly cried, only a slight tinge of red now suffuses Mary's face. A justice of the peace must marry them; such is the law of the colony. But as religious services are proper and important on the occasion, the parents invite their pastors to be present on the following Tuesday, at eleven o'clock.

In conversation with the family, as you return, you speak of the precious privileges you have enjoyed; and of your great satisfaction that the sermons, so faithful and

7

profitable, were each of them over an hour in length.
" We could not do with less instruction from the pulpit
than this," says Mr. C.   " We therefore stipulated with our
pastors at their settlement, that in proportion as they fell
short of an hour, in their sermons, a deduction should be
made from their yearly support."

In your walk on Monday through the *North End*, you
notice with pleasure, the increased number of settlers, all
occupying framed houses, and all having some cultivated
lands nearly free from stumps, and orchards that are beginning, some of them, to yield fruit.   Nothing seems to
be in the way of their comfort and peace, except that the
bears and wolves commit depredations upon their flocks
and herds, both by night and by day, making it unsafe for
the children to be out of the sight of their parents.   The
Indians, too, frequenting the woods and the roads, and
occasionally looking into the houses, though apparently
friendly, yet occasion anxiety lest they are plotting some
hidden mischief.

MARRIAGE CEREMONY.

A beautiful bright sun dawns on the nuptial day, accompanied with a balmy refreshing air.   The company
begin to assemble at an early hour.   The best room is
thrown open, and soon filled with the invited guests, the
near neighbors, and many friends and acquaintances, from
the body of the town.   The officiating magistrate, William
Paine, Esq., with Mr. Rogers and Mr. Norton, enter together, and receive the affectionate salutations of the company.   The children are at home.   William has brought
his "intended" to partake with him the joy of the occasion.
Charles Waldo, of Chelmsford, soon to be married to Hannah, is also present.   There are two young men from the
centre of Ipswich, Clark and Tuthill, both beginning to be
troubled with some heart-beatings.   Clark has an eye
upon Abigail, and Tuthill upon Sarah, both of whom, in

some unaccountable way, have caught the same heart complaint. But whether they caught it of the young men,
or the young men of them, remains in uncertainty. One
thing is certain, they hardly dare to exchange glances, because they have not yet asked leave, and the law of the
colony is severe upon the young man that makes or mani-
fests love to a young lady without leave, formally obtained
of her parents.

The bride and bridegroom are seated by themselves opposite to the magistrate, with the brides-maid and grooms-
man in their appropriate places. The time for the ceremony having arrived, Mr. Rogers invokes the blessing of
God. The magistrate then joins the parties in marriage,
by their mutual assent to a solemn covenant, and Mr.
Norton closes with prayer. As the marriage feast is soon
to follow, the intervening time is spent in pleasant and
profitable conversation on the signs of the times, and the
news of the day, both at home and abroad. The news
from England of the execution of Charles I., particularly
engrosses their attention. They are all agreed that if
ever a murderer deserved death for one act of murder,
Charles, who, by his tyranny and cruelty, perpetually har-
assed and oppressed his subjects, robbing them of their
dearest rights and privileges, certainly deserved no less.
Cromwell, the real leader and master-spirit in this struggle
for freedom, they highly extol for his piety and courage,
his wisdom and indomitable energy, his patriotism, and
love of justice, and devoutly wish, that with the help of
God, he may be instrumental of restoring liberty to England, and establishing permanently a republican form of
government. Dinner being ended, and the company retiring, you retire with them.

THE SCHOOL FARM.

1651, Jan. 11th. The town give to the Grammar or
Latin School all the "neck beyond Chebacco River and the

rest of the ground up to Gloucester line." January 16th,
this land is leased by the trustees of the donation to John
Cogswell, Jr., of Chebacco, and his heirs and assigns forever, for £14 a year.   It includes the land on the south of
the river to Gloucester line, as far east as the creek, over
which is the lower causeway, and west, as far as the brook
near Warren Low's house.   At the date of this lease,
money by being very scarce, was of so much value, that
£14, ($67.76,) was a sufficient salary for the teacher.
But when money, by becoming more plenty, fell in value,
and would purchase comparatively but little, the salary
was altogether insufficient.   Hence, the town in 1720,
were about commencing a suit against the holders of the
school farm, to compel them to pay the original value of
the £14.   This suit they offered to relinquish, if the occupants of the farm would agree to support the school-
master; which would have cost in that day, about $200.
But this the occupants were clearly not bound to do by
the terms of the lease, as the town no doubt ascertained;
for they abandoned the prosecution, and remained satisfied
with the nominal sum.   If it had been stipulated in the
lease, that the annual rent should be more or less than
£14, according to the value of money, estimated by the
current price of certain specified articles of living, the
amount at this day would probably have been more than
$200 a year.   This, however, would not now support a
schoolmaster, as £14 did then, because, besides the difference in the price of commodities, the style of living, is
now full three times as expensive as it was then.

DEATH OF MR. ROGERS.

1655.   The funeral of Mr. Rogers, the only minister of
the town, after the removal of Mr. Norton to Boston, takes
place, and is attended by a great number of people, from
all parts of the town, and by many from neighboring
towns.   He is buried at the expense of the town, and his

grave is bedewed with the tears of many who loved him as their pastor, and whose souls had been savingly benefited by his earnest and faithful ministry. The people of Chebacco have much reason to lament his comparatively early departure from life, for often had he been with them in their houses, in scenes of joy and sorrow. He had sat with them by the side of their sick beds, directing them to Jesus, the friend and Saviour of sinners, and comforting their hearts with His promises to the penitent and believing. He had solemnized their marriages, baptized their children, and buried their dead. For sixteen or seventeen years, they had enjoyed his ministry in the sanctuary of God, on the Sabbath, and on lecture days. His sermons were of a more than ordinary character, and were listened to by large and attentive audiences. In addition to what has been already said of him on page 36, the following extract from Cotton Mather's *Magnalia Christi Americana*, published in 1702, may be added:

" In College he became a remarkable and imcomparable proficient in all *academick learning*. His usual *manner* was to be an early and *exact student*, by which means, he was quickly laid in with a good stock of *learning*, but unto all his other learning there was that glory added, *the fear of God*, for the crown of all; the principles whereof were instilled into his young soul with the counsels of his pious *mother*, while he sat on her knees, as well as his *holy* father, when he came to riper years. Having entered the ministry he was preacher to a great congregation at Bocking in *Essex* for four or five years, and for five years afterward to the parish of Assington in *Suffolk*. In both of those places his ministry was highly respected and greatly *prospered*, among persons of all qualities. He was a lively, curious, florid *preacher;* and by his *holy living*, he so farther preached, as to give much *life* to all his other *preaching*. He had usually every Lord's day. a greater number of hearers than could crowd into the church; and of those many *ignorant* ones were instructed, many *ungodly* ones were converted, and many sorrowful ones were comforted. Though he had not his father's notable *voice*, yet he had several ministerial qualifications, as was judged, beyond his father; and he was *one prepared unto every good work*, though he was also exercised with *bodily infirmities*, which his labors brought upon him. But it was the resolution of the Hierarchy, that the ministers, who would not conform to their impositions, must be *silenced* all over the kingdom.   Our Mr. Rogers, perceiving the approach of the *storm* towards himself, did, out of a particular *circumspection* in his own temper, choose rather to prevent, than to *receive* the censures of the ecclesiastical courts, and therefore he resigned his place.   Nevertheless, not being free in his conscience wholly to lay down the exercise of his ministry, he designed, a removal into New England. Setting sail at *Gravesend* he landed at Boston about the middle of November 1636 after a voyage of *twenty-four* weeks.   Soon after he accepted of an invitation to *Ipswich*, where he was ordained *pastor* of the church, on *February* 20, 1638, (1639, N. S.,) at his ordination, preaching on II. Cor. 2 : 16,— *who is sufficient for these things;* a sermon so copious, judicious, accurate, and elegant that it struck the hearers with admiration.   While he lived in *Ipswich*, he went over the five last chapters of *Ephesians*, in his ministry ; the twelfth to the *Hebrews*, the doctrine of *self-denial*, and *walking with God;* and the fifty-third chapter of *Isaiah*, to the great satisfaction of all his hearers, with many other subjects more occasionally handled.   It belongs to his character that he *feared God above many*, and *walked with God* at a great rate of *holiness*, though such was his reservedness, that none but his intimate friends knew the *particulars* of his *walk*, yet such as were indeed intimate with him, could observe, that he was much in *fasting* and *prayer*, and *meditation*, and those duties wherein the *power of godliness* is most maintained ; and as the *graces* of a Christian, so the *gifts* of a minister, in him, were beyond the ordinary *attainments* of good men, yea, I shall do a wrong unto his name, if I do not freely say that he was one of the *greatest men* that ever set foot on the *American strand.*

   " He had often been seized with fits of sickness in the course of his life ; and his *last* seemed no more threatening than the former, till the *last morning* of it.   An epidemic sort of *cough* had arrested most of the families in the country, which proved most particularly fatal to *bodies*, before laboring with *rheumatic* indispositions.   *This* he felt ; but in the whole time of his illness, he was full of *heavenly* discourse and counsel, to those who came to visit him.   It is a notable passage in the *Talmuds*, that the inhabitants of Tsippor, expressing an extreme unwillingness to have the death of R. Judah, (whom they surnamed *The Holy*,) reported unto them, he that brought the report, thus expressed himself.   *Holy men and angels took hold of the tables of the covenant, and the hand of the angels prevailed, so that they took away the tables.*   And the people then perceived the meaning of this paraboliser to be, that holy men would fain have detained *R. Judah* still in this world, but the *angels* took him away.   Reader, I am as loth to tell the death of *Rogers*, the *Holy;* and the inhabitants of Ipswich were as loth to hear it, but I must say the *hand of the angel prevailed* on July 3d, 1655, in the afternoon, when he had uttered those for his last words : '*My times are in thy hands.*'   His age was 57."

Such were the character and labors of him on whose ministry our ancestors in this place attended, and with whom some of them had come from England. If obedient to that gospel which he preached, they are now rejoicing with him among the redeemed in glory.

HAFFIELD'S BRIDGE AND ROAD.

1656. This year is memorable for the building of Haffield's bridge. On the following year, "A road is laid out," says the record, "to Goodwife Haffield's bridge, through Mr. Roger's ox pasture." This is the present road from Haffield's bridge, to the corner of the first road which came round the head of Choate's brook. A road must have been opened at the same time on this side, over the hill to the bridge. Our fathers, in beginning their homes in a wilderness, had so much to do, and so little to do with, that they found it easier to go round the creeks than to make bridges over them. Yet as soon as their means allowed, they were ready to make improvements in roads and bridges, as well as in other things, pertaining to the conveniences and comforts of life.

COURT-HOUSE AND JAIL.

As early as 1636, a court was held in Ipswich once a quarter, for the trial of such offences as were not capital. This court answered to our modern court of Common Pleas. The Supreme Court did not begin to sit in this town till 1693. A jail was built here in 1652. It was then the second in the colony. In 1656, a House of Correction was in operation. It seems to have been connected with the jail. The inmates were required to work, as the Selectmen were directed to supply them with flax and hemp.

The trials in the courts, it may be presumed, were conducted, for the most part, in the same manner as they are at this day. The jurors were then, as now, taken from the different towns of the county, and were the supreme judges in every case between man and man, and between man and his majesty's province. The justices or judges upon the bench were to decide upon all points of law, but the jury upon matters of fact, involving questions of property, or of guilt or innocence. This is the great bulwark of English liberty. All are equally free and safe, where all have the privilege of being tried by their peers. But let us go into one of the Ipswich courts, held in olden time. It is in the month of May, 1663. As we ascend the hill, the meeting-house, a handsome edifice, is on our left; a neat but smaller building on our right, is the court-house. A little north of the meeting-house, we see the jail and house of correction, a dark, comfortless looking building, with its windows guarded by iron bars. Between the church and the prison, on the same level spot, stands the whipping-post, tall and stout, with its iron hook, to fasten and draw up the culprit, while the lash is applied to the naked back. And near the post, stand the stocks. The pillory was placed there only when occasion required. We enter the court-room, while the church bell is sending forth its peculiar peals, which all understand to be an invitation to all concerned, to hasten to court. Standing in the crowd, just within, we hear the authoritative voice of the sheriff, "Make way for the Court! make way for the Court!" and begin to fear, as we can move but little, that we shall be found guilty without an indictment. An opening is made, and his Honor, the Court, passes through, and takes his seat on an elevated bench, next to the wall. The counselors-at-law sit before him in an enclosure, formed by a railing, called the bar. On the right and left of the gentlemen of the bar, are seated the jurymen. A stand or platform for the witnesses, is near the bar, and just without it, and facing the judge, is the box for criminals. As it is the first day of the court's sitting, Mr. Cobbet, one of the ministers of the town, offers an appropriate prayer. The voice of the sheriff is then heard in strong and measured accents, "Oyes, Oyes, Oyes, all persons who have anything to do before the Quarterly Court, may now draw near, and give their attendance, and they shall be heard. God save the king."

A prisoner is now brought in, and placed in the criminal's box for trial, a woman from Newbury, charged with the crime of perjury. The jury for the trial of this case are impaneled, and sworn by the clerk. With uplifted hands they assent to the oath : "You solemnly swear that you will well and truly try the issue between his majesty's province and the prisoner at the bar. So help you God."

As you listen to the closing words, and ponder upon their meaning, you are satisfied that it is a solemn appeal to God for the truth of what is said, with a consent to be saved or destroyed by Him, according as you speak truly or falsely. This is the highest obligation which man can impose upon his fellow man, to tell the truth, the whole truth, and nothing but the truth. An oath for confirmation is an end of all strife. It is as far as man can go to terminate controversies.

The criminal at the bar, in a case in which she was a witness, had, under oath, testified falsely, and thus committed the crime of perjury. The clerk reads the indictment, which sets forth with great particularity, the crime with which she is charged. This particularity, in its abundance of words, in almost every variety of form, seems to you tedious and unnecessary. But it is the result of much experience, and is, every word of it, necessary to secure both the rights of the prisoner, and of the community at large. After reading the indictment, the clerk addresses the prisoner, Leah Sapphira, (which we may suppose to be her name.) "What say you to this indictment; are you guilty thereof, or not guilty?" "Not guilty," is the reply. He then turns to the jury. "Gentlemen of the jury, the prisoner pleads not guilty, and for trial, puts herself upon her country, which country you

8

are. If she is guilty, you will say so, and if not guilty,
you will say *so*, and no more. Gentlemen of the jury,
hearken to your evidence."

The attorney for the government opens the case by
stating particularly what he intends to do, and to prove,
and then proceeds to call his witnesses. They testify,
under oath, what they know of the matter; all which
goes to prove her guilt. They are cross-examined by the
prisoner's counsel, that he may draw something from them,
if he can, which will go to refute their own testimony.
He then brings forward his rebutting testimony; calls
witnesses to prove the general goodness of her character,
and to establish the truth of the facts, to which she testified in the case in which she is said to have committed
perjury; and goes on to show, by a labored argument, that
the evidence against his client is altogether insufficient to
prove her guilt, and appeals to the good feelings of the jury,
to their love of humanity, and justice, and to their honest
perception of the failure of the government to prove the
guilt of his client, that thus he may persuade them to
bring in a verdict which shall relieve her from this state
of disgrace and distress. His majesty's counsel then addresses the jury: dwelling upon the facts in the case, and
showing, as we may suppose, that she testified falsely in
a point material to the issue of the case, by swearing to
that, which, as all the witnesses were agreed, never took
place. Her testimony, therefore, was wilfully false and
malicious.

The pleas on both sides, are able and eloquent. The
jury listen attentively, but with a conservative countenance. The judge states the case, recapitulates the evidence for and against, and charges the jury that if they
are satisfied that the evidence against her is full and conclusive, beyond all reasonable doubt, they must return a
verdict of guilty. But if they have reasonable doubts in
the case, they are bound to let the prisoner have the

benefit of them, and bring in their verdict accordingly. The prisoner hears this with a countenance marked with anxiety, and deep interest. The jury retire, but soon return to their seats. The clerk then says, " Mr. Foreman, are you agreed in a verdict?" " We are agreed," is the response. " What say you, Mr. Foreman, is the prisoner at the bar guilty, or not guilty?" " Guilty!" says the foreman. " Gentlemen of the jury, hearken to your verdict. The jury, upon their oath, do say that the prisoner at the bar is guilty. So you say Mr. Foreman, so say you all; gentlemen of the jury?" The jury bow assent.

The judge prefaces the sentence with a few pertinent remarks, on the heinousness of the crime of perjury, as striking a deadly blow at the very existence of society, by destroying all confidence in testimony, and as full of impiety and profaneness, tending to bring down upon the guilty head, the wrath and curse of the Almighty. As this, however, is her first offence, he imposes on her the lightest penalty of the law; which is, that she stand at the meeting-house door, in the town of Newbury, next lecture day, from the ringing of the first bell, till the minister be ready to begin prayer, with a paper on her head, having on it, written in large capital letters, FOR TAKING A FALSE OATHE. She is taken to prison, to be held in custody, till the sentence is executed. If you are disposed to think the penalty too light for the crime, you will remember that the culprit is a woman, perhaps of some standing and character, and the mortification must be extreme, to stand as if in a pillory, and be gazed at, for an hour, by all her neighbors and town's people, as a false, perjured woman.

MANUFACTURES.

Among the manufacturers in town, in the progress of this century, are mentioned, ropemakers, coopers, gunsmiths, wheelwrights, carpenters, glovers, tailors, soap-

makers, maltsters, ship-builders, tanners, curriers. No
shoemakers are mentioned; probably, for the reason that
the inhabitants made their own shoes, principally, if not
wholly. An aged man remembers that at a much later
period, there were traveling workmen, who cut and fitted
shoes for families, and occasionally finished them.

The first saw-mill in Ipswich, was erected on Chebacco
River, in 1656. The conditions of the grant were, that
there be liberty for cutting timber, (on commoners' wood
land,) provided none be cut within three and one half-
miles of the meeting-house, and the town have one-
fifteenth of what is sawed, and no inhabitant be charged
more than four per cent. Nine years after, Jonathan
Wade is allowed to have one on the same river. 1667:
May 23, Lieutenant Thomas Burnham is permitted to
erect one near the falls; but not so as to injure Mr.
Wade's. Four years after, another is erected by William
Story. 1682: Jonathan Wade is allowed to set up one
at the falls. 1687: John, son of Thomas Burnham, removes his mill so as to be near George Story's. No saw-
mill is mentioned during this century, in any other part
of the town: and no *grist-mill* is erected here until 1693,
when John Burnham, Jr., had leave to erect one at "the
launching place." This was, doubtless, "the launching
place" below the falls, to which the new road leads, as the
remains of the dam are still to be seen there. Why it
was that during this century all the sawing was done here,
and all the grinding on Ipswich River, we have no means
of learning. Probably, the building of vessels here, was
the reason why so many saw-mills were erected.

THE FIRST SHIP-YARD.

1668. Twelve years after the first saw-mill was erected,
the town grant "One acre of ground, near Mr. Cogswell's
farm, to the inhabitants of Ipswich, for a yard to build vessels, for the use of the inhabitants, and to employ work-

men for that end." This is pretty conclusive evidence, that our ancestors here had already begun to build vessels, as it seems altogether improbable, that a ship-yard would have been granted by the town, if it had not been asked for, and equally improbable that it would have been petitioned for, if the building of vessels was wholly unknown here. This acre for a ship-yard, was near the present bridge. Mr. Cogswell's farm came up to the main road, on the north side of Spring street; but on the south side only as far as the brook, back of the first burying-ground, and to the creek, into which this brook runs. The ship-yard, then, to be near Mr. Cogswell's farm, must have extended from some point near the mouth of this creek, south-westerly on the bank of the river, probably twenty rods, and eight rods back from the river. As it was then partly covered with timber, and bounded by marked trees, the bounds, through want of care, became obliterated.

FIRST CHEBACCO BOAT.

Tradition says, that the first Chebacco boat was built by a Burnham, in the garret of an ancient house, which stood where is now the house of Daniel Mears, south-west of the corner of the old and new road to Manchester; and that the garret window had to be cut away before they could launch her. An aged man, Parker Burnham, 1st,* says that when a child, about 1770, he distinctly remembers hearing his grandfather, then very aged, relate this fact to his father. This grand-parent was born about 1690. He had probably himself received the fact from parental or ancestral lips. Another part of the traditional account of this first boat, derived from another source, is, that the Summer after she was built, a man and a boy, Burnhams, of course, as she was built by one of that name, went in her to Damaris Cove, about one hundred and twenty miles, for a fare of fish. If we are disposed

---

*Deceased since this part of the history was first published.

to doubt whether both of these facts can be true, we must
wait till we better know the structure of the house, and
the size of its garret, and of the boat, before we can safely
set aside the tradition of the fathers.   It is certain that
there *was* a first Chebacco boat built for fishing, and a *first*
trip of this first boat.   And we may as well take the
ancient tradition concerning the matter, as any modern
suppositions.

FIRST FISHING VOYAGE.

As the season is pleasant, and the trip a novel one, we
will accompany this enterprising skipper, and his youthful
companion, down to the eastern shore, and see how they
succeed in taking a fare of fish.   It is early in June.   The
storms of Spring have passed away, and Summer's days
begin to shed their balmy influence on land and water.
As our new vessel is to sail very early in the morning, if
the wind is fair, she is taken down the river, as far as the
horse bridge, the night before.   The morning comes, and
the Summer breeze is from the west.   We must be at the
bridge at early dawn, to go on board with the captain and
his boy.   The ship is small, and will carry but two or
three tons.   But as our spirits are light, we shall not
much trouble her with our weight, so we may take our
stand upon the forecastle, unperceived by either of the
crew.   Our vessel is of a peculiar shape, sharp at both
ends, though not designed to sail either way, as a super-
ficial observer might think.   She is pink-sterned, and pos-
sesses a good rudder, the tiller of which is grasped by our
skipper, as soon as all sails are set, and all hands on board,
and she is loosed from her fastening.   We are soon under
way, with a stiff breeze, and rapidly pass the objects on
shore, among which are here and there groups of half-
naked Indians, old and young, whose curiosity is excited
at the sight of our boat, with her wide-spread canvass.
The islands appear in all their beauty, covered with verd-

ure, and bearing lofty trees, except here and there the
clearings made by the natives. We cross the bar, and as
we launch out into the bay, the sun is just lifting his broad
and ruddy face out of the ocean, shedding his glorious
beams over the vast expanse of waters, and tipping the
hill-tops, and summits of the woods, with his yellow rays.
As we come upon the swelling sea, our little bark feels
the heaving influence, and begins to roll and pitch, with
some degree of violence; yet she bears herself nobly, as
she rides over the waves. Some little fear might trouble
the minds of our skipper and his boy, as they are somewhat green in the business, did not the rolling of the boat
produce some rolling and heaving of the stomach, which
occupies their attention. But they hold on to their post
of duty, sensible that life is depending on it. Our spirits,
happily, though in sympathy with our sea-sick crew, and
partaking of the rolling and pitching of the boat, yet are
not affected with the sea malady, and have, therefore,
nothing to do, but to look abroad, and enjoy the sublime
scene before us ;—the mountain waves of the dark rolling
deep, the azure vault of heaven, in which the glorious
sun, the king of day, is pursuing his wonted course. We
adore the wisdom and power of Him who spreads out the
heavens like a curtain, and holds the waters in the hollow
of his hand. Here and there a sail is seen in the distance,
seeming to rest upon the waters like a swan, laving its
wings. The policy of our skipper is to keep near shore,
so he puts the helm for New Hampshire's port. As we
glide over the waves, we leave Plumb Island on our left,
and soon the Isle of Shoals on our right, and at mid-day
discover the village of Portsmouth, and see before us blue
Agamenticus. Our crew make but a slender repast at
noon. The sight of food is almost enough, though their
stomachs are becoming much calmer. This may be owing
to the comparative calmness of the sea. The wind has
died away. Our vessel rocks but little, and has, indeed,

but little motion of any kind. This, to sailors, is what
the giving out of a horse upon the road is to the traveler.
We lay becalmed for an hour or two, when suddenly the
sky begins to be overcast with dark and threatening
clouds, and peals of distant thunder are heard. A fresh
breeze springs up from the north : this induces our skipper
to run for Portland, to avoid the danger of a squall. The
thunder is nearer and nearer, and the lightning more and
more vivid. The wind rises; the ocean swells; our miniature vessel rocks violently; alternately she mounts and
descends, yet riding securely the foaming waves. Tremu-
lous and frail as she appears, she yet proves a safe as well
as fast sailer, and might frighten a landsman to death, before she would sink him. We are soon inside of land,
safely moored in Portland harbor. The storm is more and
more violent. The rains descend in torrents; our crew
shelter themselves in the cuddy. But we are not long
held in this uncomfortable state. The clouds begin to
break and disperse; the sky becomes clear, almost as
quickly as it gathered blackness. The sun, descending to
the horizon with his broad disc, pours forth his rays with
softer beauty, and paints upon the opposite vapor, a bow
of variegated, enchanting colors, extending in a splendid
arch across the sky, resting with either foot upon the
ocean. We leave the harbor, and turn our course easterly, for our destined cove. Night closes in with its dark
blue vault, studded with glistening stars, affording sufficient light for our pilot, especially the north star, ever
staid and steady, on which he keeps an inquisitive eye.
He is careful to keep far enough from land to avoid all
breakers, and have good sea room. Before midnight, we
are off the mouth of the Kennebeck, and soon pass the
many coves between that and the Damariscotta. Our
skipper seems well acquainted with the coast. He has
probably been here before, in some vessel from Salem, or
Boston, to fight the eastern Indians. He steers straight

for Damaris Cove Island, and entering its snug little harbor, anchors for the night. This island is owned by a *Knight* of the east, who has cleared up a little farm at the head of the harbor, and is prepared with his flakes for drying his neighbors' fish, at the rate of one-sixteenth for curing.

We anticipate the approach of morning, and are on our way out of the harbor, for fishing, by the time the first streaks of light are breaking from the east. We are soon upon the ground, and busy with our lines. The fish are very plenty, and very hungry. We have a good haul, and our little boat is soon loaded, and on her way to the beautiful little harbor. The Knight of the island and our skipper, are soon acquainted. The fish are all dressed and salted, and laid upon the flakes to be dried ; and we are on our way by noon for another load. As we come upon the ground, we find some "down-east" boys, with their lines in the water. They look with an inquisitive eye upon our Chebacco sailer,—their expressive countenances seeming to say, "that is a queer sort of water animal." But we stay not for criticisms. Handsome is, that handsome does. Again our fish are soon dancing upon the deck ; and with a second load we make for the island.

After a few such days of toil and success, we are ready for a homeward voyage, with a cargo of excellent cod. Having rested for the night, we set sail in the morning, with a long day before us. Our course is very zigzag, as the wind is against us. With a heavy load, and head wind, and home in our eye, our patience is much tried with our slow progress. But the east winds of Spring are not all expended. By afternoon we have a fresh breeze, which puts us forward with good speed. As night approaches, we are so well on our way, that we conclude to keep running till we make our own river. The day is wholly gone: but a beautiful night scene

9

supplies its place. The moon looks down upon the placid waves, and,

" With more pleasing light, shadowy sets off the face of things."

As we look up, and gaze upon the multitude of stars that fill the heavens, we are ready to exclaim with the Psalmist, "When I consider the heavens, the work of thy fingers, the moon and the stars which thou hast ordained, Lord, what is man, that thou art mindful of him, or the son of man that thou visitest him."

By the guiding hand of Providence, we safely reach our own bay, and entering the river, anchor for the night by Cross's Island. In the morning, by the help of the flowing tide, we reach the horse-bridge, and are soon greeted by friends and neighbors. Some of the same lips, that with lengthened visage, and mournful accents, prophesied that we should never see home again, now greet us with the joyful words, "Well, there! I thought so! I *knew* you would make out well."

The news of our arrival and success, spreads from house to house. Fishing boats and fish become the topics of the day. Several are determined to enter into the business; some talk of building at their doors vessels of six or seven tons, provided there is a prospect of drawing such large craft to the launching-place. Some express a wish that the town would grant them a ship-yard. Others think they shall not be able to do without one much longer, and one or two more saw-mills beside.

DEATH AND BURIAL OF MR. COGSWELL.

John Cogswell, Sen., died November 29, 1669, aged about 72. We will go to the good man's burial. Many neighbors and acquaintances are assembled within, and about the house. He lies in his coffin, upon a table in the best room of the house, which he had erected with so much care, and in which he had enjoyed so much comfort and peace. There sit his weeping widow, and mourning children and grandchildren. You raise the lid of the coffin, and gaze upon the ghastly features of him, who, but shortly before, was busy, active and useful, having a leading part in all the affairs of the town. You call to mind the sacrifices he made for his religion and his God, in coming from a home of plenty and elegance in the city of London, to this wilderness of savage beasts, and more savage men; exchanging the counting-room of the merchant for a log cabin, and a field of rough unbroken soil, to be subdued only by the labors of many a weary day. You look with admiration on the remains of such a sainted spirit, so justly venerated by his children, and all who knew him, and so heartily mourned for, by her who had shared his sufferings, and enjoyed his comforts. Both of his beloved pastors are present, Rev. Mr. Cobbet, and Rev. Mr. Hubbard, with other principal men of the church. The ministers and assembly sit in silent meditation. You may, perhaps, be expecting a sermon, or a long exhortation, from one or both of the ministers; but our pious fathers having suffered so much from their Episcopal brethren of the Church of England, were desirous of getting as far from them as they could, in all forms and ceremonies, and, therefore, would not preach at a funeral, nor have any services but a prayer. A few words only are now addressed by Mr. Hubbard to the mourning family, and then a solemn, and deeply affecting prayer is offered by Mr. Cobbet, the senior pastor. It is early in the day, for the way to the sanctuary of the dead is long and tedious, not less than five miles. The center of Ipswich was the place where our pious fathers went regularly to meeting on the Sabbath, and once a week to the Thursday lecture. In Ipswich, therefore, they must bury their dead, fast by the house of God; the way to which seemed shorter for being so often trodden.

The dead, too, must be borne all the way upon the shoulders of men; for no carriage was then to be had; and if one could have been procured, our ancestors would have thought the dead dishonored, by being drawn to the grave by a beast. But the time is come for the procession to set forth. The widow and children take a last lingering look at that dear countenance, which had so often cheered them by its smiles, now ghastly in death; and then he is borne out of his house to return no more. You look out of the window to see the procession formed. The men and the women do not walk together, according to the custom of the present day; but the men go first, two and two, after the corpse, because the deceased is a male. If it had been a woman who was to be buried, women would have gone first. The male relatives walk first, and then the female mourners behind them, some of them mounted on horses because of the weary distance. Behind them, the male part of the neighbors, and citizens, and last of all, female acquaintances, more than one often riding upon the same beast. Six neighbors, of a similar age to the deceased, take hold of the pall, while younger men bear the corpse by turns, often relieving each other of the heavy burden; and by the side of the whole, is a file of some half-dozen men, with their pikes and muskets, as a guard against their savage neighbors. In this silent and solitary manner, they bore the deceased to the old burying-ground in Ipswich, where his ashes now slumber, with that of numerous others from this place, comprising all who died here the first half century, after the settlement began.

INDIAN WARS.

In 1675, began the war with Philip, an Indian chief, in Plymouth Colony, who, for some time, had used measures to persuade the Indians in all parts of New England, to unite against the English. The eastern Indians, about the

same time, commenced hostilities, and butchered many individuals, and some whole families.

The Indians also, bordering upon the Merrimack River,
feeling themselves injured, by the increase and spread of
the English, once more resumed the bloody tomahawk.
Not only were the frontier towns in almost constant alarm,
but all others partook in a greater or less degree of the
panic. When their war parties came so near as Haverhill
and Salisbury, killing the defenceless women and children,
and burning their houses, our ancestors in this place could
not but partake of the general anxiety. Several, on different occasions, were called into the army, and went in
pursuit of the savages far from their homes. John Cogswell, son of John who had taken the lease of the School
Farm, was taken prisoner by the Indians, some time in
October, 1676, during an expedition to the eastward.
Some years after, a man by the name of Dicks, of this
place, was killed near Casco.

MODE OF LIVING.

We will spend a day at Wiliam Goodhue's, whose house
stood near the present dwelling of William Marshall, in
the north district. Without ceremony, we will call at an
early hour. As welcome guests, we are invited to sit down
with the family to a breakfast consisting of a dish of bean-
porridge. Each has a pewter basin and spoon before him,
which is filled to the brim, from the large iron kettle standing upon the hearth. Some Indian hoe-cake is added to
the repast. Having breakfasted, thanks are given, and
mercies supplicated, in prayer to Him, who is the source
of all good. While the hired men repair to the field for
making hay, the father tarries awhile, and gathers the
children around him for reading and spelling. A portion
of an hour, spent in this way, after each repast, is all the
schooling the times will allow. The women, having set
the house in order, proceed to their daily employment.

One repairs to the loom in the chamber, and begins the wholesome task of throwing the shuttle, which vies with time in its swiftness. Another arranges the spinning-wheel, and commences that music, which, if it does not delight the ear, will clothe and warm the body. The younger ones are busily employed in knitting. By and by, the men and boys come in from the field for their luncheon of bread and cheese. The large pewter mug is set on, full of malt beer, out of which, they all drink in turn. "I wish," says one of the hired men, "we could have a little strong water. I was up at Goodman White's the other day, and he gave all hands a little, which put us in fine spirits, and spurred us on mightily in our work, while it lasted: and if we could have had a little now and then, it seems to me, we should have done double the work." "But an order," says Mr. Goodhue, "has come from our Great, and General Court, forbidding us to give wine or liquors to our work-men, because it gets them into an evil practice, and trains up the young, by degrees, to habits of excess. You feel better on strong water for awhile, and so much worse after that to make up for it. And then you want more and more, the longer you take it, till you get to be a drunkard; or, at least, you are always in danger of this. The only safe way, is never to drink any." "But the law," replies the workman, "forbids it, except when it is neces-sary. Now, I think, if it is ever necessary, it is in the Winter, on very cold days, and in the Summer, when mow-ing, on very hot mornings." "But the law," replies Mr. G., "means that it is necessary when people are not very well." "Then I ought to have some," says another, "for my stomach is mighty weak." "And I, too," says another, "for at times I feel weak all over." "At this rate," says Mr. G., "you will make it out that it is necessary all the time, and then what is the law good for?" But they must hasten to the field, and make hay while the sun shines.

At length, the hour for dinner has come ; for the sun lies in square at the window. Anna has been watching the mark for noon, and hastened her dinner, so as to be in season. She blows the horn at the door, and all in the field, and in the house, hear the welcome sound, and hasten to the social board. The dinner is of soup, or the liquor in which salt meat or pork has been boiled, thickened with meal, together with some vegetables. The dish and the plates are of pewter. The drink, of malt beer. This is their daily fare. After dining, the children again read and spell. The labors of the day are then resumed. " Come, girls," says the mother, " you know the law requires that we spin three pounds of flax, three of wool, and three of cotton every month, or pay our fine. But the worst fine would be, the shame of not doing so well as our neighbors. Our class-leader, Goodwife Bradstreet, will be here this afternoon, to do her duty, and see how we get along. Let us make the wheels go with a good loud hum, and reel off all we can."

The day now begins to decline, and as night draws on, the cows are brought up for milking. A good supper of hasty pudding and milk follows. In the evening, as the workmen rest themselves a little before bed-time, the conversation turns on the use of tobacco. " It seems to me," says a young man, who was getting on the wrong side of thirty, without any signs of establishing himself in a family state, " that a few whiffs from a good pipe, do much to rest one after a hard day's work. I learned to smoke in England, and could never see any harm in it. I don't understand why your law is so severe against it, that I must wholly leave smoking, or be liable to a fine of 10s. every time I buy any tobacco. Some, I find, do get round the law by raising it in their gardens. But this does not help a stranger. It seems to me that some of you are as much afraid of tobacco as of rum." " We are so, indeed," says Mr. G., " for we have marked, that, too commonly, those

who like the one, like the other.   And here let me remind
you of the law among us, that requires every single man
to put himself under the supervision and control of some
head of a family, as it seems to me you are in great danger of its pains and penalties."

But it is time for us, reader, to retire.   And in leaving
this worthy family, we must not think that we have been
treated impolitely, because they kept the wheels, and the
loom, the scythe and the rake, going so fast, that we had
but little time to talk with them; or because they did not
give us coffee or tea, or nice cake, for these things were
never heard of till more than a hundred years after.

FORMATION OF THE SECOND PARISH IN IPSWICH.

In the year 1676, the people of this place began to talk
in earnest of seceding from the parish in the center of
the town, and of becoming a parish by themselves.   They
had now, for more than forty years, traveled over difficult
roads, four or five, and some of them six or seven miles,
to their place of worship.   The fathers and mothers who
had fled from persecution in England, and knew by contrast the value of freedom of conscience, thought but little
of the tediousness of the way to the house of God; especially as they were sensible that they could not sustain
the institutions of the gospel any nearer to their homes.
But their children, less sensible of the value of religious
privileges, were less inclined to make so great a sacrifice
to enjoy them.   The consequence was, a growing disposition to tarry at home on the Sabbath.   It was this, perhaps, chiefly, which stirred up the more considerate and
religious among them, to take measures for the establishment of the gospel ministry in this place; which they
were now sufficiently numerous and able to sustain.   Accordingly, in February, 1677, they held a meeting for
consultation on this subject, at the house of William
Cogswell, which stood a little north of the dwelling now

occupied by Albert and Jonathan Cogswell, on the same side of the way. The record of this meeting, is the beginning of our first parish record, which contains several interesting documents and entries, of the proceedings of our fathers, in relation to their separation from the first church and parish in town. Their mode of writing and spelling, and their use of capitals, differed from ours. For our own convenience, the extracts we may make from this record, will be chiefly in the modern style. One or two of the shorter ones, will be given in the ancient style as a specimen.

The date of the first meeting is in the record, February, 1676. But the year at that time, did not begin till the 25th of March, and so continued, till altered by an act of Parliament, in 1752, when the year was ordered to begin January 1st, and eleven days were added to it, so as to make February 3d, (for example,) February 14th. The date, then, of February, 1676, was, in our style, February, 1677. To prevent confusion in regard to the years, we shall place the new style under the old, where a difference occurs; thus, February 167$\frac{6}{7}$.

PETITION FOR LEAVE TO HAVE PREACHING.

" At this meeting," says the record, " the inhabitants of Chebacco, considering the great straits they were in, for want of the means of grace among themselves, unanemously agreeing, and drawing up a petetion and presented it to the towne of Ipswich, at a publick towne meeting, which was to desire of the towne that they might have liberty to call a minester to preach among themselves : but the towne would not grant it, neither did they seeme to refuse it, but would not vote concerning it."

In conversation with some of the leading men of the town, the people here were given to understand, that the former had no objection to their having preaching among them, especially if they continued to support the ministry

10

in Ipswich. But still as a town, they would not vote for,
or against the prayer of the petitioners. This made it
necessary for them to carry their petition to the General
Court. The Court refused to grant the petition, but recommended them to make further application to the town,
and the town to give their answer at the next session of
the Court. This the town did, and the result was that the
Court judged it not meet to grant the petition then, but
recommended to the town "as soon as may be, to contrive
the accommodation of the petitioners in the matter petitioned for." This was October, 1677.

The next town meeting was held, as the Record says,
February 19, 1677, (new style, March 2, 1678,) at which
the town voted that the Selectmen confer with the Chebacco neighbors, about what they petitioned, and report
at the next town meeting. The inhabitants here chose
William Cogswell, John Andrews, Thomas Low, and William Goodhue, a committee to confer with the Selectmen.
Several conferences were held, but without any decisive
result.

FIRST PREACHER IN CHEBACCO.

At length, when they requested of the Selectmen leave
to call Mr. Jeremiah Shepard to preach among them, a
part of the Selectmen assented, and the rest made no objection. The call was extended to Mr. Shepard, January
19, 167⅞, who came, and preached in a private house.
Finding that no private house was sufficiently large to
accommodate the people, "They agreed to build a plain
house, and, if they could obtain leave of the town or
Court, to put it to the use of a meeting-house: if not, to
some other use." But before this was done, Mr. Shepard
gave notice after the religious services of the Sabbath,
that he had received a letter from an honorable brother
in Ipswich, saying that the church there was dissatisfied
with the proceedings of the brethren here, and therefore
he should desist from preaching.

SECOND PETITION AND ACTION OF THE TOWN.

Upon this the people here again petitioned the town, but without effect. This petition is dated February 4, 167⅜.

On the 15th of the next March, the Selectmen, in behalf of the town, sent to the General Court a petition and address, in which they made many heavy charges against the people of Chebacco. The charges are contained in the following reply, which, as it was addressed to the Honored Court, who had the Ipswich document before them, and in the issue were favorably inclined toward the people here, we may believe contained a true statement of the charges, and a proper and sufficient reply to them.

"A declaration and vindication of the transactions of the inhabitants of Chebacco, in the precincts of Ipswich, in reference to their late proceedings in obtaining the ministry of the gospel among them: May 28, 1679.

"This Honored Court may please to remind that the inhabitants of Chebacco have once and again applied ourselves to your Honors, that we might be eased of our long and tiresome Sabbath days' journeys to the place of public worship in our town, humbly hoping that your Honors would so far sympathize with us, and favor our shattered condition as to grant us relief, and we cannot but gratefully acknowledge your fatherly care, especially in our last application of ourselves to this Honored Court, in seriously recommending our case to the town of Ipswich: that our friends and neighbors there might relieve your humble supplicants in the matter petitioned for, that so we might obtain the ministry of the word amongst ourselves, which is our hearts desire ; but contrary to the direction of this Honored Court, and cross to our expectations, our friends and neighbors in the town were regardless of our suffering condition : whereupon, after due waiting, and due deliberation, we did apply ourselves to the town, February 19, 1677, to be informed whether or no, they would accommodate us according to the direction of this Honored Court ; our necessity, also, calling for relief, the town did take so far cognizance of our demand, as to refer our case to the Selectmen, to consider with us what might be best for our accommodation ; whereupon, we had a treaty with the Selectmen : but the Selectmen turned us going, with dilatory answers, which were :

" 1. They alleged that those farmers towards Wenham, were they that were meant by the General Court that they should be accommodated with us : we replied, that could not be, because the return from the General Court was that we should be accommodated amongst ourselves in the matter petitioned for, which was a meeting-house amongst ourselves, and we did not care how many neighbors joined with us, provided that we might have the means of grace amongst ourselves.   •

" 2. They alleged that the war was not yet past, and God's judgments were yet hanging over us, and the town was at great charge ;—to which we replied, that when we sought to have the means amongst ourselves, we looked at it as our duty, and therefore, when the judgments of God were amongst us, that it was rather an argument to stir us up to our duty than to lie under the omission of it : neither would we put the town to charge, either to erect our meeting-house, or maintain our minister.

" 3. They alleged we belonged to the town, and, therefore, were obliged to help the town to bear the charges, and they could not spare our money ; to which we replied, that they alleged at the General Court, that we paid but 17 or 18 pounds to the ministers of Ipswich, and there were three ministers to whom the town paid 200 pounds per annum, and if the town would supply us with one of them, we would pay one of them 50 pounds towards his maintenance yearly. Then they replied, that could not be, and that our want was only in the winter, and if we could get a minister to preach to us in the winter, they would free us from paying to the ministers in the town, in the winter season, and we should come to the public worship in the town in the summer, and pay there.

" This last proposition was the most rational and candid that we have yet obtained : which hath been a grand encouragement in calling a minister to accommodate us this last winter season ; though we are now considered heinous transgressors in so doing.

" 4. They alleged, that the Rev. Mr. Hubbard, their teacher, was gone to England, and they desired us to wait till he came home again : we answered, the direction from the General Court came a considerable time before the Rev. Mr. Hubbard took his voyage to England ; yet if they would engage to supply us as soon as the Rev. Mr. Hubbard came from England, we were willing patiently to wait : which we have done ; but as yet feel no relief. Thus having applied ourselves to the Honored General Court, who seriously recommended our case to the town of Ipswich, and they referring the agitation of our case to the Selectmen, and they making a proposition to us to provide a minister for the winter, and the extremity of the winter season putting us upon great inconveniences, in regard of our attending public worship in the town, whereupon, we were put upon a kind of necessity to seek for relief, if possibly we could obtain the means amongst ourselves ; and, accordingly we applied ourselves to Mr. Shepard to help us in our present exigency, till the winter season was over, engaging to pay our wonted dues to the town as formerly, as also to recompense Mr. Shepard for his labors. We applied ourselves to him January 1, 1678. Mr. Shepard taking our motion into consideration, and after some space of time we desiring his answer, he told us he was willing to see his way clear, and therefore desired us to consult with those that were betrusted with the affairs of the town, that he might understand how they approved of our proceedings : whereupon, some of the principal of our inhabitants, who had the betrustment of this affair, obtained a meeting of the Selectmen, January 9, 1678 : they desired liberty to call a minister to preach with us at Chebacco, and having permission from the Selectmen, none of them contradicting our motion, they again applied themselves to Mr. Shepard, importuning him to help us, according to our former request : we obtained his labors, and were willing to encourage ourselves that we should still enjoy him ; comforting ourselves in this, that we hoped we should obtain both the pity and favor of this Honored General Court, and accordingly we put ourselves in a posture for the entertaining the gospel, and were willing to lay aside our self-interests, that we might build a house for the worship of God, which we were the more vigorous in, by reason that we had experienced much, in a little time, of the sweetness and good of that privilege in enjoying the means amongst ourselves, whereby the generality of our inhabitants could comfortably attend the public worship of God ; of which some hundreds do not, nor, with convenience, can attend the public worship at town ; and, of so considerable a number of the inhabitants as are amongst us, scarce fifty persons the year throughout, do attend the public worship of God on the Sabbath days.   The house that we have been busied about, for the place of public worship, was ever intended for such an end, always with this provisal, that this Honored Court do authorize the same, or countenance our proceedings therein : if not, we shall ever own ourselves loyal subjects to authority ; and therefore the same is erected upon a propriety, that if this Honored Court see not meet to favor our proceedings, we may turn our labors to our best advantage.   This Honored Court may further be informed that after we had enjoyed the benefit of Mr. Shepard's labors for some considerable time, a man of principal worth in the town, sent a letter to him, which signified that offence was taken at our proceedings, which letter has date, February 19, 1678, which Mr. Shepard gave us information of, the Sabbath day following, and ever since hath desisted preaching amongst us,—and information was given thereof to our Reverend Elders at town ; yet, notwithstanding, a complaint was exhibited against us at the Honored Court of Assistants, March 4, 1678, which signified that Mr. Shepard still continued preaching, and we prosecuting our desires, resolving to enforce our demands : whereas Mr. Shepard had for a considerable time before desisted preaching, and we resolving to quiet ourselves with the determination of this Honored Court in reference to our proceedings : and whereas we are complained of to the Honored Court of Assistants, as persons of more unpeaceable spirits than those that reside in the other Hamlet, wherein, as is asserted, are persons of worth, &c., which yet are so ingenuous as to be quiet hitherto, and not to seek a rending of themselves from the body :—to which we might reply, that the worthiness of our neighbors in the other hamlet, should not cause us to derogate from the worth of our poor souls, nor prevent us from laboring after the ordinary means of salvation : and whereas their ingenuousness is applauded for not seeking a rending of themselves from the body, we hope our ingenuousness may merit a recommendation of the like nature, who do abhor a rending away either from the church or town of Ipswich, as the town will be sensible of by our rational and fair propositions : and whereas it is asserted in the complaint that we have acted contrary to our agreement with, and engagement to the town, April 11, 1678, we reply that we are utterly ignorant of any engagement, and therefore admire that our neighbors should render us so scandalous in the face of the country : but we hope we may with all good conscience plead our innocency in this and all other reflections that are cast upon us. These things we desire to leave with this Honored Court, as a declaration of our cause, and a vindication of our innocency, and are ready farther to inform this Honored Court in what they may please to demand, or in what may be alleged against our proceedings.''

The Court, or rather the Council, notwithstanding this able and unanswerable vindication, decided that Chebacco should desist from all further proceedings in this matter, and sent to our fathers an order to this effect. But before they received this order, "The sills of the meeting-house were laid in Mr. William Cogswell's land, and the timber in place ready to raise."

RAISING THE FIRST MEETING-HOUSE.

"While we were in this great conflict, that all things seemed to act against us, some women, without the knowledge of their husbands, and with the advice of some men, went to other towns, and got help, and raised the house, that we intended for a meeting-house, if we could get liberty."* This was in the Spring of 1679.

This bold and decisive act of the good women, though without the knowledge of their husbands, we may be sure was not done without much previous whispering and privacy among themselves. We may suppose they had a social visit at Mrs. Varney's, just opposite the corner,—the

---

* Records, p. 18.

site of the intended meeting-house,—on the afternoon of the day before the raising, to talk over matters, and see what they could do to help their husbands out of this trouble. It was only a neighborly visit, though some of them were from distant parts of the town.

If you had stood that afternoon at what is now the corner of Colonel J. P. Choate's lane, you would have seen them coming upon their saddles and blankets from over the river, across the horse bridge, and from the Falls, and from the North End, wrapped in their riding hoods, to protect them from the chilling blasts of Spring, and with countenances betokening important business in hand. As they reach the corner, they cast an inquisitive eye upon the timber, lying in exact order upon the ground in Mr. Cogswell's field, and seeming to invite some skillful, if not fair hands, to raise them up and give them union, beauty, and strength. They are soon dismounted at Mrs. Varney's door, and housed in her best room. It is an important meeting, and well attended, though got up without any public notice. Let not the men any longer say that women cannot keep a secret, for the whole is planned, and will be executed without the knowledge of their husbands. Let not the men any longer think that they can build a church, or fit it up, without the knowledge and concurrence of the women. As men are not invited to this social gathering, we cannot, of course, be present, and have no means of knowing what discussions were had, or what votes were passed. But we *guess* that all the various difficulties and objections in the way of their arduous enterprise, were freely talked over, and that, when one spoke of the danger of offending the Great and General Court, another bright mind and sparkling eye, suggested that the Court had not said a word about the *women*, and only forbidden the *men* doing any thing further in this matter. Another eloquent tongue remarked, that the order sent by the Court, mentioned only *Chebacco* men. They had good friends in Gloucester and Manchester, who could come and raise the house without any danger. We *guess* that Mrs. Martin, and Mrs. Goodhue, and Mrs. Varney, were appointed, or mentioned, or volunteered, to be a board of managers to go,— one to Gloucester precinct, the other two to Manchester, to *raise* men, and bring them on to the ground the next day. For, early the next morning, Mrs. Varney, mounted on the old family horse, with Mrs. Goodhue behind, and their hired man Chub, on another horse, to protect them, and Abraham Martin and his wife on another, were seen riding together, over the horse bridge, and returning before noon, with parties of men from Manchester, and the "precinct," and conducting them to the timber in the corner of Mr. Cogswell's field. Nothing is said by the Chebacco folks: but with great alacrity and cheer, their neighbors go to work, and join timber to timber, and fasten joint to joint, and soon a whole broadside is seen going up; and by and by another; and no stop, no stay, till the ridge-pole is in its place, and then three hearty cheers indicate that the work is done. Many women upon horses had already arrived, with well filled sacks pending from their saddles, the contents of which they deposit at Mrs. Varney's. Their kind neighbors from abroad are invited to the supper, without any other entrance fee than *the good frame* they have been in. The tables are spread with a suitable variety of edibles; among which there is a plenty of good *tongue*. Chebacco *men* are scarce that day, so the good neighbors have to be thanked for their labor of love by the ladies alone.

On the next Tuesday, the constable came down from Ipswich, with the following warrant from "our Honored Major General:"

"*To the Constable of Ipswich:*—You are hereby required to attach the body of Abraham Martin, and John Chub, and bring them before me on Tuesday next, about one of the clock, to answer for their contempt of authority in helping to raise a meeting-house at Chebacco. You are also, at the same time to bring with you the wife of William Goodhue, the wife of Thomas Varney, and the wife of Abraham Martin, for procuring, or abetting and encouraging the raising the said house : and so make return hereof under your hand."

They were accordingly tried in Ipswich, and found guilty, and bound over to the next court in Salem.

ACTION OF THE GENERAL COURT AND ITS COMMITTEE.

But the General Court, having cognizance of the case, at their session, May 28, 1679, ordered that they appear at Salem Court, and make their acknowledgment in these words, viz :

" That they are convinced that they have ofended in soe doeing, for which they are sorry, and pray it may be forgiven them, and soe to be dismissed without any farther trouble, charge, or attendance, in that respect, or farther attendance on the councell for that theire offence. Attests, Edward Rawson, Secretary."

This Court also chose a committee, consisting of Joseph Dudley, Richard Waldron, Anthony Stoddard, William Jonson, and Henry Bartholomew, for the settlement of the business of Chebacco, touching the place of public worship amongst them, and the settlement of a minister. This committee sat here the 23d of July, 1679, and heard the statement of a delegation from Ipswich, that the town and the church were satisfied with the acknowledgment made by those active in raising the meeting-house, and heard also the reasons presented by them for removing Chebacco meeting-house nearer the centre of Ipswich, to accommodate the people at the farms. But the committee, in their decision, say, that "though a removal of the house farther toward Ipswich, might accommodate some more of the inhabitants, and farmers of said town, yet as the people here are competent to support a minister by themselves, and the proposed removal of the house would greatly discommode those living at the head, and over the

11

river of Chebacco; therefore, the place where the house
now standeth, be, and is, hereby allowed by us; and they
have liberty to proceed to the finishing of said meeting-
house." The committee further say:

"Respecting the settlement of an able, pious, and orthodox minister
among them, for the due management of the worship of God, we find, by a
paper presented to us, that they greatly desire the settlement of Mr. Shepard,
as their minister, but as he hath not professed his subjection to the order of
the gospel amongst us, in joining to any particular Congregational Church,
we see not reason at present to advise Mr. Shepard's preaching or settlement
amongst them."

We see here a continuance of the same fear which
manifested itself in the first settlement of the colony, that
Episcopacy, or some other church power, should gain the
ascendency, and triumph over civil freedom.   As Congre-
gationalism was purely democratic, it excited no fears, and
was ardently cherished.   The committee farther advised
the people here, seriously to consider, with invocation of
God's name, of some meet person, learned, able and pious,
to manage the public worship of God amongst them, and
to report to them between that and the day before the
meeting of General Court, in October following.   At that
time, a delegation from this place, appeared before the
committee, and stated, that for want of time, or some other
considerations, Mr. Shepard had not complied with their
advice ; but that their desires were still towards him.
Upon which, the committee appointed the 2d Tuesday in
April, 1680, for a further hearing of this matter.   At that
meeting, the delegation of this place presented to the
above committee, Mr. John Wise, as one in whom they
were unanimously agreed to be their pastor, and who was
approved and accepted by the committee.

Mr. Shepard doubtless left Chebacco, July, 1679, according to the advice of the committee ; otherwise the
people here would have become offenders by employing
him, and would have been summoned to Court as such.
Mr. Shepard was the son of Rev. Thomas Shepard, of

Cambridge. He was graduated at Harvard College, 1669. After leaving this place, he was settled in Lynn, and continued in the ministry there 41 years, being eminent in his profession.

SITE AND DESCRIPTION OF THE MEETING-HOUSE.

After leave obtained of the Court, our ancestors doubtless proceeded to finish the meeting-house, in part, at least, that same Summer and Autumn. As the site of this first house of worship is a matter of doubt with some, we give the following facts, which show that it must have been the lot of land now covered by the house and barn of Captain Joseph Choate.

The people here petitioned the town, February, 1679, for leave to set this house on the common land, by Thomas Varney's which was opposite to where Captain Choate's house now is. This being refused, "The sills were laid," says the record, "on said William Cogswell's land, and the timber in place ready to raise." *

At a parish meeting, August, 1693, it was voted that the two short seats in the meeting-house be given to William Cogswell and his heirs, on condition that he, or they, give to the parish a legal assurance of land under said house and adjoining. Mr. Cogswell's land extended from the head of the lane, which is now Spring street, to the head of the lane leading by Colonel Choate's house, then the road to Gloucester.

The north-western corner of his field, (now Captain Joseph Choate's house-lot,) was near to that lot on the common, or parsonage, which our fathers selected, but which the town would not grant. It was the most central, as the corner where three roads met. The deed of Captain Choate's house lot, recognizes the fact of its having been owned by Adam Cogswell, a son of William, and gives the dimensions thirteen rods by three, which were suitable for a meeting-house lot.

---

* Records, p. 12.

The record says that the site of that first meeting-house was four and a half miles from Ipswich meeting-house, which is precisely the distance of Captain Choate's house, to Ipswich north church.

When the author came here, forty years ago, there were several aged people living, whose fathers and mothers had worshiped in the first house, (as late as 1719,) and whose testimony was, that it stood on the site of Captain Choate's house, which in their younger days was called Meeting-House Hill.

The second house, built in 1719, was fifty-two feet by forty-two. From which we may conclude, that the first house was somewhere about forty-two by thirty-six. It faced the west, as we learn from the record; had two doors in front, with wooden latches, and "good and sufficient strings" for lifting the latches. There were galleries on three sides of the house: the pulpit stood on the eastern side, opposite to the doors, with a solid and elevated sounding-board, over the head of the preacher, and a handsome cushion for the Bible. Only two or three pews were built at first; the rest of the floor of the house was covered by long and short seats: the same in the galleries. A turret was built on the centre of the house, "after the fashion, and in the proportions of the turret in Andover." In this turret a bell was hung. The salary of the sexton, for ringing the bell, and sweeping the house, and setting the bason with water for baptizing, was 20s., and freedom from parish taxes.

SELECTMEN—MODE OF SEATING THE CONGREGATION.

The committee of the parish were styled, the Selectmen of Chebacco. Their stated business was to assess the tax for the support of the minister, and for defraying other parish expenses. Occasionally, they were instructed to see that the pulpit cushion was repaired, that the broken glass in the windows was mended, and the strings of the doors kept in order, that they might be easily shut and opened.

After the house was so far finished as to be convenient for public worship, a committee was chosen " to dignify the seats;" with instructions to begin at the centre seats, as first in dignity, and account the others more or less honorable, as they approached to, or receded from, the centre. Annually, a committee was chosen to seat the people in the more or less honorable seats, according to the amount of taxes which they paid, or the offices which they filled. If the reader is surprised at these aristocratic notions in our ancestors, they may find some apology for them in the fact that they came from a land of aristocracy; or perhaps a better apology in the fact that something of the same custom prevails at this day; with this difference only, that people now choose for themselves more or less costly seats, as best suits their own notions, and thus dignify their own seats. In our fathers' days, the assignment to a lower seat by the committee, because one did not pay so much as his neighbors, never gave satisfaction and there were not unfrequent rebellions against the lawful authorities on this account, though the practice continued for many years.

The parish vote that the Selectmen cause posts to be set round the house, that Mr. Cogswell's fence may not be damnified by the tying of horses. Several flat rocks with steps, were, according to the custom of the day, placed in convenient position for mounting the horses.

DEDICATION OF THE HOUSE.

Everything in and about the house being thus arranged, and Mr. Wise, whom they had chosen to settle with them, having arrived, April, 1680, measures are taken for the dedication of the house to the service of God. It is on Wednesday, the day usually selected for ordinations and dedications. The occasion, as a matter of course, excites much interest among the people here, who begin early in

the day to prepare for attendance. Their neighbors in
Manchester and Gloucester West Parish, who raised the
house, we may well suppose, were there, and many of
their friends with them.

We will go to the North End, and attend the dedication.
As you approach the house, you see many collected, and
many others coming, some on foot, and some on horseback.
The posts are all occupied with horses, and Mr. Cogswell
is so exhilarated with the day, that he will not complain
if his fence suffers a little by the many that are fastened
thereto. Standing opposite to the house, you look up and
see a plain two story building, with a double row of diamond glass windows, and a turret on the middle of the
ridge-pole. The sharp sound of the bell tells you that the
hour of service is near at hand; you walk up to one of
the doors, and enter by pulling the string which hangs
gracefully down. A side aisle is before you, and you are
shown to the strangers' seats. Before the service begins,
you notice the appearance of the inside of the church;
above, all is open to the roof; the beams and rafters are of
solid white oak. The boarding of the roof is new, and
not yet occupied with the spiders' webs and swallows'
nests. The walls above the galleries are not yet plastered.
You look for the singers' seats, but such a thing is not
even imagined. All that can sing in the house, are "the
singers." The pulpit is plain, but lofty, with a spacious
window behind, and a massive sounding-board above, to
prevent the voice of the speaker from ascending to the
ridge-pole. In front of the pulpit is a high seat, or pew,
for the deacons, and a pew by the side of the pulpit for
the minister's family. The deacon's seat is empty, as the
church is not yet organized. One suitable to fill the office
of deacon, is chosen by the parish, to read the psalm or
hymn, and pitch the tune. As you glance at the audience,
you see the women by themselves on the short seats, on
both sides of the house. They are covered with thin hoods
and short cloaks. The gentlemen on the long seats in the

middle of the house are clad in homespun coats and deer-
skin small clothes, blue or gray stockings, with shoes and
broad buckles. The whole presents to you a very ancient
appearance, as yours will to posterity, two hundred years
hence. But soon the minister enters and ascends the pulpit. Mr. Wise is a tall, stout man, majestic in appearance,
of great muscular strength; his voice is deep and strong;
his sermon is adapted to the occasion; and by appropriate,
fervent prayer, he consecrates the house to God. The
singing is apparently by the whole assembly, and though
not of the most refined kind, it is hearty and strong.
Books are scarce in that day, so the psalm is read for singing, one line at a time. After the benediction the numerous audience, interested, and, perhaps, edified by the services, retire from the sanctuary; when all the friends from
abroad are cordially invited by the people here, to go with
them to their homes to partake of the rich repast, which
had been previously made ready.

The people of this parish while they supported their
own minister, continued to pay their accustomed rates for
the support of the two ministers in Ipswich, till February,
1681. In October, 1680, they petitioned the Court to be
set free from paying ministerial taxes in Ipswich. In answer to this the Court say:

"We judge it meet that all the people, inhabitants of Ipswich, shall continue their several proportions to the maintenance of the ministry there,
unless those of Chebacco be discharged from payment to the ministry of
Ipswich, and left to maintain their own minister.

"A true copy,—Attest,   EDWARD RAWSON, *Secretary.*"

At a town meeting held the 15th of the following February, the town accepted this latter part of the Court's
order, and discharged Chebacco from any farther taxes to
support their ministers.

BOUNDARY LINE OF CHEBACCO.

At this meeting they also defined the boundary line
between Ipswich, and Chebacco, or between the first and

second parishes of Ipswich, viz: from the head of Choate's brook to run down to Castle Neck River, as the creek runs into the river and so to the sea; also from the head of said brook to Marbles', thence including Knight's farm, and to run on a straight line from the southerly corner of said Knight's farm, to the double U. tree on Wenham line, and so on the south-east upon the neighboring towns to the sea. This the Court afterwards so far altered, as to have Knight's farm belong to the Hamlet. The present bounds do not touch Wenham.

GRAVE-YARD.

At this same meeting, February 15, 1680, they granted one acre of ground to Chebacco for a grave-yard.

SETTLEMENT OF MR. WISE.

Mr. Wise continued to supply the pulpit stately, for more than three years, before he was ordained their pastor. The reason for this delay is not stated. Probably the church in Ipswich was slow in being reconciled to the thought of parting with so many of its members. The members of that church residing here, sent in a request, dated September 6, 1681, to be dismissed, for the purpose of being organized into a church in this place. How soon this request was granted, does not appear; but the church was not organized here till about two years after; and of course those making the request still remained members of Ipswich church during that time.

In February, 1682, the parish extended a formal call to Mr. Wise to settle with them as their pastor. Again in May following they chose a committee to treat with him about a settlement. They offer him for his support, ten acres of land, which they had bought for this purpose of Richard Lee, to be his own and his heirs and assigns forever. This was called his settlement. His annual salary was to be £60, or about $290,—one-third in money, and two-thirds in grain, at the current price,—forty cords of oak wood by the year yearly, and eight loads of salt hay. In addition to this they agree to build, and keep in repair, for his use, a parsonage—house and barn; the house to be equal in every respect to Samuel Giddings' house; which seems to have been a model house in that day. He was also to have the use of the parsonage lands and the strangers' contributions. This was a generous support. Comparing the value of money and grain, and the common style of living in that day, with the present, we may safely say that it would require at least $800 per annum to support a minister as well at this day.* The parsonage-house stood on the parsonage-land, now owned by Josiah Low, at the north end of that enclosure. The remains of the cellar are still to be seen. The ten acres given him for his settlement were in the rear of the house owned by the late John Mears, senior.

ORGANIZATION OF THE CHURCH AND ORDINA- TION OF MR. WISE.

Mr. Wise, the pastor elect, was born at Roxbury, and educated at Harvard College. He was twenty-one years old when he left college. As he did not commence preaching here till he was twenty-eight, he doubtless spent much, if not all, of the intervening time, in preparing for the ministry, and in supplying vacant pulpits. On the day of his ordination, August 12, 1683, he was a little more than thirty-one years of age, having been born July, 1652. The church was organized on the day of his ordination, and by the same council which set him over it as pastor.

As William Cogswell had been a leading man in establishing the parish and church, and in building the meeting-house on his own land, we may naturally suppose that the council met at his house, which was not far from the meeting-house, on the afternoon of August 11th.

The first church record kept by Mr. Wise, was lost. We have therefore no copy of the letter-missive sent to

---

* 1853.

the churches for their attendance in council, and no means of knowing what churches were sent to, except in the case of the Wenham church; whose record notices the letter to that church from Chebacco, inviting them to be present by their pastor and delegates, to aid in organizing a church, and ordaining Mr. Wise as their pastor. This is the only record extant of the origin of this church, August 12, 1683. The Wenham record proceeds to say that the church voted to comply with the request, and chose Captain Fiske, George Gott, Deacon Fiske, with their pastor, Rev. Joseph Gerrish, to attend in the proposed council.

William Cogswell married Martha, the daughter of Rev. John Emerson of Gloucester; so that he was doubtless present with his delegates. Rev. Messrs. Cobbet, and Hubbard, respectively the pastor, and teacher of those who were to be gathered into a church, could not of course be absent. Rev. Edward Payson of Rowley was also a native of Roxbury, a graduate of the same college with Mr. Wise, and of nearly the same age, and was of course invited to be on the council, with his delegates. Rev. Jeremiah Shepard of Lynn, who had been with this people in their first separation from Ipswich church, and to whom they were ardently attached, as a minister of the gospel, would also receive an invitation to attend the council. The church in Manchester as a near neighbor, and whose good men had kindly helped our women in raising the meeting-house, would not of course be passed by. Their preacher, Rev. Mr. Winborn, was not settled over them as pastor, yet he was doubtless present with the delegates from that church. The church in Roxbury, in which Mr. Wise had been brought up under the ministry of the venerated Elliot,—styled the apostle to the Indians, from his benevolent labors among them,—we might suppose would be invited to be present with their pastor and delegates, were it not for the great age of Mr. Elliot, then in his eightieth year, and the difficulty of traveling so great a distance, in that day.

Aside from the Roxbury church, we have six others, which were doubtless here by their pastors and delegates, making a council of twenty or more. Their first business, after organizing at the house of Mr. Cogswell, was to examine the documents respecting the proposed organization of the church; such as the request of church members here to be dismissed, for this purpose, from the church in Ipswich, and the vote of the Ipswich church to grant this request, with the accompanying letter of dismission and recommendation. These being found regular by the council, they proceed to examine, and pass judgment upon those relating to the ordination of Mr. Wise; the call of the parish extended to him, and his answer, his church standing, and letter of dismission and recommendation, that he may be a church member here; together with his licensure to preach, usually given in that day by some church that had examined the candidate. Being satisfied with these papers, the next business of the council is to examine Mr. Wise, as to his theological attainments and soundness in the faith, and religious experience. This examination takes up the rest of the day, and the council adjourn to an early hour in the morning. Assembled in the morning, they express by vote their satisfaction with the pastor elect, and proceed to designate the ministers who are to perform the several parts in his ordination, and also those who are to lead in the services at the organization of the church. They then proceed in procession from Mr. Cogswell's to the meeting-house. Great numbers are in attendance from this and the neighboring towns.

The day is warm and every door and window of the house is thrown open; the bell from the turret sends forth its peals with more than usual animation; every eye sparkles, every countenance brightens; the crowd at the door open to the right and left for the council to pass in; then all enter that can; every seat is filled, every aisle crowded; the many without are not far from the pulpit, and can readily hear through the open doors and windows.

The services are all of an interesting character to puritan hearts, and are listened to with devout attention, especially by those who are thus to receive a spiritual watchman and guide. The council are seated in front of the pulpit, the persons to be organized into a church are on each side of them, the men on the right, the women on the left. Mr. Cobbett, the oldest minister on the council, and of course its moderator, commences the services by prayer; he then calls upon those who are to be formed into a church to rise, that they may in that public and solemn manner give their assent to the confession of faith, and covenant, previously prepared. The confession of faith is doubtless a brief summary of that which had just been adopted by all the puritan churches in a general Synod in Boston, and which contains the doctrine of the Triune God, Father, Son, and Holy Ghost; of the native and entire depravity of man; regeneration by the Holy Spirit; justification by faith in the atoning blood of Christ; the perseverance of the saints; the everlasting happiness of the righteous; the eternal misery of the wicked; with other kindred doctrines, involved in them, and growing out of them. The covenant administered to them, is in these words:

You do in the name and fear of God (as in the presence of God, men and angels,) take God, Jehovah, Father, Son, and Holy Ghost, to be your only portion, and chiefest good ; giving up yourself and yours unto His use, and service, in the sincerity and uprightness of your hearts ; you do promise by the assistance of Divine Grace, to walk in His fear, according to the rule of worship and manners towards God and men, all your days, as He shall reveal His mind to you out of His holy word and truth ; farther you do by your own choice and act, (highly esteeming the privileges of God's household,) yield yourselves, as members of the Church of Christ, before which you now stand. Expecting its faithful watch over you ; and you promise subjection to the discipline of Christ in it, both corrective and directive, while God shall continue you members of it ; also promising all love and watchfulness over your fellow members, you do resolve to discharge all your duties both to God and men, Christ by His grace assisting you.*

---

* Mr. Pickering, successor to Mr. Wise, says in his Record, that Mr. Wise's son, Rev. Jeremiah Wise of Berwick, Me., handed him this covenant, as the original covenant of this church.

Having given their assent to this covenant, and confession of faith, Mr. Cobbet, in the name of the council, declares them to be a regular church of Christ, in fellowship with all sister churches.

The ordination services immediately follow. Judging from the usage, which has come down to us from our fathers, we may naturally suppose that these services were performed by the following persons. Introductory prayer, Mr. Winborn; prayer before the sermon, Mr. Shepard; sermon, Mr. Hubbard; ordaining prayer, Mr. Emerson; charge to the pastor, Mr. Cobbet; right hand of fellowship, Mr. Payson; concluding prayer, Mr. Gerrish; benediction by the pastor. The services close sufficiently early to allow all to partake of the hospitalities of dinner, and to ride to their several homes before sunset. Thus was organized the first church and parish in this place, which took the name of "the second church and parish in Ipswich." Soon after its organization, the church chose John Burnham, and Thomas Low, deacons.

TRAINING-DAY.

The jealousy, and hostility of the Indians made it necessary for our ancestors to be in constant preparation to defend themselves. As early as 1634, it was ordered that every trained soldier, pikeman and others, be equipped for service. Training was to be eight times in the year. Lads from ten to sixteen formed platoons by themselves, armed with small guns, half pikes, or bows and arrows; and boys under ten, who on training days came to look on, were formed into a platoon and drilled by some officer appointed for the purpose by the captain. This gave to them a courage and hardihood which accounts for some remarkable feats performed by children. One in particular has come down to us from olden time by tradition. The scene is in the edge of the woods where the late Asa Burnham resided. A lad by the name of Burnham, about ten years old, was walking in the woods, and came sud-

denly upon two cubs. He amused himself with them for
a few moments; when to his terror he saw the old bear
coming fiercely upon him with a wide yawning mouth.
He instantly seized a pine knot, which lay near him, and
as she came up, thrust it with all his might down her
throat, and then ran for the house; but it was enough,
she could not follow him. When his father came out with
his gun, he found her in the struggles of death. The
jagged edges of the knot caused it to stick fast, till she
was completely choked.

But we will go upon the common, and see the soldiers
upon parade. It is the first training day ever witnessed
in Chebacco, (1683.) Previous to this all able to bear
arms, were obliged to travel to the center of the town,
with all their accoutrements, eight times in a year, for a
military muster. But Chebacco has now become the second parish in Ipswich, with a minister settled among them,
and they must have a military company for their honor,
and defence. Lieutenant John Andrews is commander of
the company, William Goodhue, ensign, Samuel Ingalls,
corporal, and Thomas Varney, sergeant. Early in the
morning Sergeant Varney, with the drummer and fifer,
are seen traversing the place, reminding all by beat of
drum to assemble on the ground according to previous
notice. "The spirit-stirring drum, and the ear-piercing
fife," raise up the buoyant spirits of the young, who anticipate a large share of pleasure on this day of parade.
But the older men, aware of the dangers of war, especially
of the insidious, and bloody assaults of the Indian, cannot
but look grave, though it be training day. The hour of
muster is come. They are formed into a line sixty-four
in number. At the end of the line on the left is the platoon of boys from ten to sixteen years, and still farther
on, those under ten. The roll is called with loud and
measured tones, and answered by the no less solemn and
significant, " here."

You are particularly struck with the appearance of the

officers, as they stand out in front of the line. Lieutenant
Andrews, in the military style of the day, is dressed in
red small-clothes, and red stockings, with a profusion of
gold lace upon his three-cornered hat.

You look upon the long line of men, and see countenances of steady courage, and manly sense, with bodies of
great muscular strength: their dress is not perfectly uniform, yet they·have all deerskin small-clothes, and blue
stockings, with coats of good homespun cloth, spun and
woven by their wives, and daughters. The platoon of boys,
with wigs encircling their rosy cheeks, and small-clothes
buckled at their knees, with long stockings, and broad
buckles upon their shoes, appear like men in miniature.

As fire-arms are scarce, only about two-thirds of the company have muskets; the rest have pikes, and the pikemen
are by law dressed with head-pieces and corselets. Bullets too are scarce, and smooth stones fitted to the bore of
the gun, are substituted for them. On the left, beyond the
boys, is a group of Indians with their squaws and pappooses,
looking on with much curiosity and earnestness. They eye
the scene with a keen and jealous look; often curling the
lip with contempt at seeing the English boy handling the
cross-bow; which, however, is suddenly changed to fear
when the white men's guns all speak together.

It was, with the blessing of God, the Englishman's gun
of which the Indians had not learned the use, nor obtained
possession, which saved him from the deadly massacre of
the tomahawk. But, see, while we are moralizing, the
whole company is in motion; they are marching and coun-
termarching, with a quick step in accordance with the
music. All the spectators are in motion following them
round, back and forth, with exhilarated feelings, inspired
by martial sounds. Even the half-naked Indian children
feel the inspiration, and set their little feet in motion to
keep time with the drum. Presently the soldiery are on
their way to the North End, closely followed by all the
lookers on; they halt in front of the meeting-house, and

perform various evolutions; they proceed to the house of
the pastor and offer the customary tokens of military respect. By the time they reach the common again, it is
high noon. They ground their arms, and have a recess
for two hours, to visit their homes for dinner. In the
afternoon all are together again, each in his place, ready
to take arms at the word of command. Most of the aged
men, and nearly all the women, old and young, have come
out to witness the first training.

Mr. Wise is present, full of patriotic emotions, and ap-
preciating fully the importance of the day, as one of preparation to defend their country, and their firesides from the
deadly foe. Wars, and rumors of wars, are all around.
This saddens the hearts of fathers and mothers, as they
look upon their sons, and think of their liability to be
called to the battle-ground. But the regimentals and the
music, and the waving banner, and the variety of involu-
tions and evolutions banish all sadness from the hearts of
the young, and they think of nothing but the holiday
scene before them, and associate with training day only
bright ideas and joyous emotions. The afternoon is diligently spent by the trainers in their various military exercises, and laboriously enjoyed by all the spectators. Before night they are dismissed and retire.

The constable with his long black staff tipped with
brass, is on the alert in accordance with his oath of office,
to see that none loiter behind for any evil practice, but
that all may find an early home, and an early bed.

FRENCH AND INDIAN HOSTILITIES.

The latter part of this century, the inhabitants of New
England generally experienced much alarm, and suffering,
from the bloody assaults of the Indians, who were insti-
gated to these murderous attacks by the Canadian French.
It was therefore deemed desirable to carry the war into
the French dominions; and an expedition was fitted out
for that purpose under the command of Sir William Phips.

He sailed in August, 1690, with a fleet of thirty-two sail, and arrived before Quebec in the following October. But owing to several unpropitious circumstances, the expedition failed, and in November, the troops arrived in Boston. "The expedition involved the government in a heavy debt; a thousand men perished, and a general gloom spread through the country."

The Indians continued their depredations, and butcheries for several years, exhausting the resources of the Colonists, and depressing their spirits. The inhabitants of this town were often called on to defend their neighbors at the eastward, and nearer home, during this destructive Indian war. It is pleasing to reflect that our forefathers made no aggressive wars. They treated the Indians kindly, buying their lands of them at a reasonable, and fair price, and using every effort to civilize and christianize them. It was not till, without provocation, the savages sought to destroy them with their wives and little ones, that they took arms in their own defence, and were compelled to use them, till their foes were nearly all destroyed, or driven back into the interior of the country.

INDEPENDENCE DECLARED, 1687.

On the death of Charles II., James II. ascended the throne. Under his reign, Sir Edmund Andros was appointed Governor of all the New England Colonies. In 1687, he caused a tax to be levied upon the people of this colony of 1d. on £1, which was a violation of their charter rights, and their rights as Englishmen, not to be taxed without their consent in a Legislative Assembly.

The minister of this place, feeling that the liberties of the country were in danger, went with two of his parishioners, John Andrews, Sen., and William Goodhue, to the centre of the town, to confer with friends there on the subject. A meeting for consultation was held at the house of John Appleton, who lived, it is said, not far from where the Railroad Depot now is. At that meeting, after much

13

patriotic discourse flowing from hearts glowing with the flame of liberty, it was determined that it was not the duty of the town to aid in assessing, and collecting this illegal and unconstitutional tax.

In a general town meeting the next day, August 23, which had been called for this purpose, remarks were freely made to this effect by several; and Mr. Wise, in particular, made a bold and impressive speech, in which he urged his townsmen to stand to their privileges, for they had a good God and a good King to protect them. We have no record of this speech; but with his sentiments and language before us *in his printed work on the liberty of the churches,* we may well suppose that he spoke in substance as follows:

Mr. Moderator :—The question before us is one of the deepest concern to us all, involving our dearest rights and privileges; it is not a mere question of property, whether we will pay the amount of tax levied upon us by his Majesty's servant, the Governor of this Province, but whether we will surrender the right so dear to every Englishman's heart, and so essential to his civil freedom, that of levying our own taxes, and controlling our own means of subsistence. This right is inherent in the British Constitution, and is guaranteed to us by our Provincial Charter. It is essential to our civil and religious freedom, to our personal safety and welfare, and to the security, and tranquillity of our firesides.

For it is plain that if any portion of our property, however small, may be taken from us without our consent, then by the same principle, the whole of it may be taken, and our persons and families be rendered penniless, and houseless, and subjected to the most abject and cruel servitude. Thus reduced to a state of vassalage, we subsist wholly by the clemency of the despot, and may be destroyed at any moment of arbitrary caprice or displeasure. Need I say, Sir, that such an assumption of power would not be tolerated for a day, no, not for a moment, in our father-land? Is not the principle that taxation and representation go together, as familiar there as household words? Has it not been argued, and demonstrated in letters of blood, that not the house of Lords, nor the Monarch upon the throne, but the Commoners only, the real agents of the people, can impose taxes? Have we lost this inestimable privilege by being at a greater distance from Parliament than some of our brethren? Are we not Englishmen still, living under the royal government, and entitled to all the privileges and immunities of British subjects? And can we then tamely surrender these rights, by the payment of this illegal and unconstitutional tax, thus admitting a precedent and a principle so destructive of all our liberties?

We go sir, for law, and order, and authority; but we insist that by the law of nature, which is the law of God, and of right reason, all power and all authority in civil matters, have their origin wholly with the people. In their natural state every man is his own master, and protector ; and if he could secure his own welfare, and safety with equal efficiency single-handed, it would be folly for him to sacrifice any portion of his natural liberty, in which he is his own king and councilor. But this not being possible, he enters a civil community, the chief end of which is that those thus associated, may be secured against the injuries, to which they are liable from their fellow men. This end is best answered by a government substantially democratic ; in which the people have a voice in all that concerns their safety, liberty, and property.

Such a government, it is said, is the British empire ; a limited monarchy based upon a noble and efficient democracy ; where the concurrence of the Lords, and Commons, in making and repealing all statutes or acts of Parliament, is necessary ; and thereby hath the main advantages of an aristocracy, and of a democracy both, and yet is free from the disadvantages of either. It is such a monarchy, as by most admirable temperament, affords very much to the industry, liberty and happiness of the subjects, and reserves enough for the majesty and prerogative of any King, who will own his people as subjects, not as slaves. All this we would fain believe true of the British Constitution ; and yet we look back upon the republics of Greece, and see some very desirable principles of liberty, which though they failed under paganism, we are confident may be sustained, and carried out under the conservative influence of Christianity. Of the Athenian Commonwealth, Plato writes, " The original of our government was taken from the equality of our race. Other states there are, composed of different blood and unequal lines ; the consequence of this is tyrannical or oligarchical sway, under which men live in such a manner, as to esteem themselves partly lords and partly slaves. But we, being all born brethren of the same mother, do not look upon ourselves as standing in so hard a relation, as that of lords and slaves. The purity of our descent inclines us to keep up the purity of our laws, and to yield the precedency only to superior virtue."

It seems manifest that most civil communities arose at first from the union of families, nearly allied in race and blood. And though ancient story makes frequent mention of Kings, yet it appears that most of them were such as had an influence in persuading rather than a power of commanding. So Justin describes the kind of government as the most ancient, which Aristotle styles, heroic ; which is no ways inconsistent with a democratic state. I am aware, Sir, that it will be said that in such reasoning, and remarks, we are holding forth the language of sedition, and rebellion against the powers that be. But we disclaim all such intention ; we hold ourselves loyal subjects of a government, which is itself regulated by the constitution and laws of the land. And it has been well said, that where the laws of the land are the measure, both of the sovereign's commands, and the people's obedience, the one cannot invade what by concessions and stipulations is granted to the other ; nor the other deprive them of their lawful and determined rights.

The prince therefore, or magistrate who strives to subvert the fundamental laws of the country, is in reality the traitor, and not the people, who endeavor to defend and preserve their own laws and liberties.

It is most apparent, through the whole ministry of the world, that it is the duty of all public officers to administer according to the plain rules of the public state, and not by their own fancy, or wills. And so in this case, the chief ruling officer is obliged to lead the government according to its plain and settled principles, and not to hesitate or vary to suit his own convenience or wishes. It is the saying of those who are skilled in the law, *Rex in regno duo superiores habet, Deum et Legem.* The king has in his realm two superiors, God, and the Law. All the nobles and great ministers of the kingdom must look upon the law as the watchful eye of some dire divinity, restraining them from all deviations and violations. All Englishmen live and die by the law,—the law of their own making

The English government is a charter party, settled by mutual compact between persons of all degrees in the nation, and no man must start from it but at his peril. Englishmen hate an arbitrary power, politically considered, as they hate the wicked one. Through immemorial ages they have been the owners of very fair enfranchisements, and liberties; and the sense, favor, and high esteem of them, have been, as it were, *extra ducem* transmitted with the elemental materials of their essence, from generation to generation, and so ingenite and mixed with their frame, that no artifice, craft, or force, can root it out. *Naturam expellas furca, tamen usque recurret.**

And though many of their incautelous princes have endeavored to null all their charter rights and immunities, and aggrandize themselves in the serene state of the subjects, by setting up their own will for the great standard of government over the nation; yet they have all along paid dear for their attempts, both in the injury of the nation, and in interrupting the increase of their own grandeur, and their foreign settlements and conquests. On the first appearance of this monster, Tyranny,—upon the holding up of a finger, or upon the least signal given,—on goes the whole nation upon the Hydra. The very name of an arbitrary government, is ready to put Englishmen's blood into a fermentation. But when it actually comes in person, and shakes its whip over their ears, and tells them it is their master, it makes them stark mad; and being of a mimical genius, and inclined to follow the court mode they turn arbitrary too. Some writers who have observed the governments, and humors of nations, thus distinguish the English. The king of Spain is the king of men. The king of France the king of asses; and the king of England the king of devils; for the English can never be bridled and rid by an arbritrary prince.

We trust, sir, that in this province we shall prove true to the blood that flows in our veins; true to our country, and to our God. We may have to suffer by refusing to pay this unconstitutional tax; but we have a good God

---

*You may drive out nature with violence, but she is sure to return.

and a good king, and shall do well to stand to our privileges at all hazards. We shall suffer more by a servile compliance with so unjust a demand, than we can by a manly refusal. We shall in that case inflict a blow upon our rights and liberties, which may prove mortal. In the alternative of slavery or death, freemen cannot hesitate. If we must fall, let it be by the hand of tyranny, and not by any act of our own. Let us die as martyrs in a glorious cause and not as guilty self-murderers. I doubt not, Sir, that when the vote is tried, we shall all be of one heart, and one mind, not to surrender our rights. In this way we shall obey God, and honor the king.

As the above is *chiefly in Mr. Wise's own words*, the reader may consider it as a specimen of his mode of reasoning, and style of writing on the great subject of civil and religious freedom. He was then thirty-six years of age, combining the fire of youth with the firmness and wisdom of manhood.

TRIAL AND PUNISHMENT OF MR. WISE AND HIS FELLOW-CITIZENS.

A report of Mr. Wise's doings, and of the action of the town was made to the Governor, and the consequence was that he, and five others, John Andrews, William Goodhue, Robert Kinsman, John Appleton, and Thomas French, were arrested and committed to jail in Boston; being denied the privilege of giving bonds for their appearance in court. They were all found guilty of contempt and high misdemeanor, and kept in prison twenty-one days longer, before sentence was passed. But we will let Mr. Wise tell the story in his own words:

" We, John Wise, John Andrews, Sen., Robert Kinsman, William Goodhue, Jr., all of Ipswich, about the 22nd of August, 1687, were, with several principal inhabitants of Ipswich, met at Mr. John Appleton's and there discoursed and concluded, that it was not the town's duty in any way to assist that ill method of raising money without a general assembly, which was generally intended by above said Sir Edmund, and his Council, as witness a late act issued out by them for such a purpose. The next day in a general town meeting of the inhabitants of Ipswich, we the above named J. Wise, J. Andrews, R. Kinsman, W. Goodhue with the rest of the town, there met, (none contradicting) and gave our assent to the vote then made. The ground of our trouble, our crime, was the copy transmitted to the Council, viz: 'At a legal town-meeting, August 23, assembled by virtue of an order from John Usher,

Esq., for choosing a commissioner to join with the Selectmen to assess the inhabitants according to an act of His Excellency the Governor, and Council, for laying of rates. The town then considering that this act doth infringe their liberty, as free English subjects of His Majesty, by interfering with the Statute Laws of the land, by which it was enacted, that no taxes should be levied upon the subjects without the consent of an Assembly, chosen by the freeholders for assessing of the same, they do therefore vote that they are not willing to choose a commissioner for such an end, without said privilege, and, moreover, consent not, that the Selectmen do proceed to lay any such rate, until it be appointed by a General Assembly, concurring with Governor and Council.'

"We, the complainants, with Mr. John Appleton and Thomas French, all of Ipswich, were brought to answer for the said vote out of our own county thirty or forty miles into Suffolk and in Boston, kept in jail for contempt and high misdemeanor, as our mittimus specifies, and upon demand, denied the privilege of *habeas corpus*, and from prison overruled to answer at a Court of Oyer and Terminer in Boston. Our Judges were Joseph Dudley of Roxbury, Stoughton of Dorchester, John Usher of Boston, and Edward Randolph. He that officiates as Clerk and Attorney in the case, is George Farwell. The Jurors only twelve, and most of them (as is said) non-freeholders of any land in the colony, some of them strangers and foreigners, gathered up (as we suppose) to serve the present turn. In our defence was pleaded the repeal of the Law of assessment upon the place; also the Magna Charta of England, and the Statute Laws, that secure the subject's properties and estates, &c. To which was replied by one of the judges, the rest by silence assenting, that we must not think the Laws of England follow us to the ends of the earth, or whither we went. And the same person (J. Wise abovesaid testifies) declared in open council, upon examination of said Wise, 'Mr. Wise, you have no more privileges left you, than not to be sold as slaves,' and no man in Council contradicted. By such Laws our trial and trouble began and ended. Mr. Dudley, aforesaid Chief Judge, to close up a debate and trial, trims up a speech that pleased himself (as we suppose) more than the people. Among many other remarkable passages to this purpose, he bespeaks the jury's obedience, who (we suppose) were very well preinclined, viz: 'I am glad,' says he, 'there be so many worthy gentlemen of the jury so capable to do the king's service, and we expect a good verdict from you, seeing the matter hath been so sufficiently proved against the criminals.'

"NOTE.—The evidence in the case, as to the substance of it, was, that we too boldly endeavored to persuade ourselves we were Englishmen and under privileges, and that we were, all six of us aforesaid, at the town-meeting of Ipswich aforesaid, and, as the witness supposed, we assented to the aforesaid vote, and, also, that John Wise made a speech at the same time, and said that we had a good God and a good King, and should do well to stand to our privileges.

"The jury return us all six guilty, being all involved in the same information. We were remanded from verdict to prison, and there kept one and twenty days for judgment. There, with Mr. Dudley's approbation, as Judge Stoughton said, this sentence was passed, viz: John Wise suspended from the ministerial function, fine £50, pay cost, £1,000 bond; John Appleton, not to bear office, fine £50, pay cost, £1,000 bond; John Andrews, not to bear office, fine £30, pay cost, £500 bond; Robert Kinsman, not to bear office, fine £20. pay cost, £500 bond; William Goodhue, the same; Thomas French, not to bear office, fine £15, pay cost, £500 bond. These bonds were for good behavior one year. We judge the total charges for one case and trial under one single information, involving us six men, above said, in expense of time and moneys of us and our relations for our necessary succor and support, to amount to more, but no less, than £400, money. Too tedious to illustrate more at this time, and so we conclude.'' *

The town afterwards made up the loss which these persons had sustained. After the expulsion of James from England and the introduction of William and Mary to the throne, Andros was put down by the people of Boston, and sent over to England. Before a new governor arrived, Mr. Wise and Nehemiah Jewett were chosen by Ipswich to meet in Boston with the representatives of the other towns to consult with the council about the public affairs of the Colony. Sometime after, Mr. Wise brought an action against Chief Justice Dudley for denying him the privileges of the *habeas corpus* act, and recovered damages.

EDUCATION—THE FIRST SCHOOL.

Our forefathers, it is well known to all acquainted with their history, were intelligent, and well educated men. They knew therefore how to appreciate the importance of a good education for their children. But while in a wilderness, few and far between, and with scanty means of living, they could not build school-houses, and hire teachers, and if they could have done it, the dangers from wild beasts would have rendered it hazardous for their children to go, and come from school. As late as 1723, wolves were so abundant and so near the meeting-house that parents would not suffer their children to go and come from worship, without some grown person. The education of their children, however, was not neglected.

* The Revolution in New England, justified: as quoted by Felt.

They were taught at home to read, write, and cipher, and were instructed in the great principles of religion, and the principal laws of their country. And when in 1642, it was found that some parents were not faithful in these and other duties to their children, the Selectmen of the town were directed, "To see that children neglected by their parents are learned to read, and understand the principles of religion, and the capital laws of this country,. and are engaged in some proper employment." The same year the town voted that there should be a free school. Cambridge College was established in 1638. A few years after this, aid was solicited from all the families to support charity scholars at this institution, that educated men might be raised up for rulers, physicians, and ministers. The representatives from the towns, and ministers in their several parishes, were desired by the General Court to use their influence, that each family give to the College at least one peck of corn, or a shilling in money.

In 1651, a Latin school was begun in this town to prepare youth for entering College. And in about half a century, thirty-eight young men from Ipswich were graduated at Cambridge. Eleven of them became ministers of the gospel, three of them physicians, and the rest served in civil, or judicial capacities.

Toward the latter part of this century, the inhabitants of this part of Ipswich began to think of establishing a free school among themselves. But such a thing could not be done without consultation, and general consent. A general meeting must therefore be held in the meeting-house, of all the voters in the parish to advise respecting it. The minister of the parish is present and a goodly number of the parishioners. Mr. Wise is, of course, expected to address them on this subject, and we may suppose that in substance he spake as follows:

"*Brethren and Friends:* We are met this afternoon to advise on a subject, which I trust we all feel to be of vast importance to our children, to our country, and to the church of God.

"What are children, what are men and women, without education? Just like the savages that we see around us? Of this we have been more or less convinced, and have long struggled under many difficulties, to give our children what schooling we could at home. But you know full well the temptation to grow remiss in this duty under the pressure of very many domestic labors in the house and in the field. Besides your children, you well know, cannot make much progress in learning their lessons, amidst the many interruptions of home. I see before me a few, a very few of our aged friends, who had their education in England. They will bear me witness, that with all their care, and toil in teaching their children, they have not been able to do for them, what their fathers in England did for them. And is it not equally true that *their* sons, and *their* daughters have not done as much for their children, as was done for them. And will not this downward progress inevitably continue, if we keep on in this way. The less schooling our children have, the less will they appreciate learning, and, of course, the less will they be likely to bestow upon their children. I know it is the opinion of some that you had better continue, in what they call the good old way; that if you set up a school here, you will have to build a school-house, and pay the salary of a school-master, which will make your taxes a heavy burden; that you have already taxes to pay, and some of you an annual rent for your farms, to support the Latin school in the body of the town; that some of your children will have a long way to travel to school, and that yourselves, or your older sons will have to accompany them to keep off the wild beasts. But are these difficulties of any importance, compared with the proper education of your children?

"You have, some of you, the same difficulties to encounter in coming here to worship God on the Sabbath, and on lecture day. But still you come, and those of you that are farthest off, are usually first at meeting. Where there is an object of sufficient importance, difficulties vanish. Rest assured, if you keep on in the old way, things will go from bad to worse. Already the number among us that neglect the instruction of their children has begun alarmingly to increase.

"There is no prospect, in my judgment, of effecting any reformation, and securing the proper instruction of your children, but to have a school under the charge of a faithful master. Even if all parents were faithful in teaching their children at home, still their education would not be so complete, as if assembled together in school, and passing the whole day in school exercises. The presence of one, animates another, and the striving of some to excel in well doing, stimulates others to the like effort; so that a collection of children, well managed in a school, will, I venture to say, make double the progress they would separately in their houses, with the best care and attention.

"I must, therefore, very earnestly exhort you to go forward in this good work, and spare no pains, nor expense, in giving your children a good education. You, and your fathers before you, have done what you could to establish a grammar school, and a college, that you may have well educated

14

ministers, and rulers. But of what use is it to have intelligent rulers, if
the mass of the people are uneducated ? Ignorance is no friend to virtue, or
to liberty. It is no friend to religion. The most inattentive hearers of the
word, are usually those of the least education. If you would secure virtue,
piety, liberty, and prosperity to your descendants, you must liberally patronize
the cause of education."

In this earnest manner, and with many other words, did
he testify and exhort, saying, "Save your children from
ignorance, infidelity and vice."

Others present, expressed, their minds on the subject :
a few doubtingly, and discouragingly ; but the most part
with resolution and zeal, in favor of an onward course.
The result was, the choice of a committee to hire a teacher,
and provide suitable accommodations for a school.

This committee made choice of Nathaniel Rust, Jr., who
opened his school in June, 1695, and taught through the
Summer with such acceptance, that the next Summer they
invited him to settle with them, as their school teacher.
This invitation he accepted, and taught here several years.
The town gave six acres of pasture for the benefit of the
school, and one quarter of an acre to Mr. Rust, to set his
house on. The house which he then built, is the same, as
to most of the timbers, with that now owned by William
H. Mears. It was remodeled and enlarged about seventy-
five years since. The school pasture was on the north and
west, of Mr. Mears' land, and became merged in the old
parsonage pasture. The school was probably taught in a
room in Mr. Rust's house, as no school-house was built till
the beginning of the next century.

ROADS AND BRIDGES.

As at the beginning, there was first a ferry for crossing the
river near the dwelling of the late Adam Boyd, which continued till 1666, and was then superseded by a horse-bridge,*

---

* At a town meeting held February 6, 1671, " John Burnham makes request to the
town for some help from them toward making up the bridge over Chebacco River,
which was broken down by the storm. The town granted £10, of the £20, then due
from Mr. William Cogswell."—*Ipswich Town Records.*

so toward the close of this century, there was first a ferry for crossing where the mills now are, and then in 1700, a bridge was built. There was, doubtless, when the ferry was in operation, some kind of a road over the marsh to Thompson's Island. But when the bridge was built, or soon after, the old causeway was probably built. The ferriage at the lower ferry, was 2d. a passenger; at the upper the same for a person, and 4d. for a horse. The road from Col. Choate's lane to the present bridge, was no doubt opened at an early period, and that gradually, as the convenience of settlers required. It must have been completed as early as 1668, when the ship-yard was laid out. In 1697, a road is ordered through John Cogswell, senior's, farm, (the school farm.) This is doubtless the present road from Thompson's Island to the lower causeway.

1699. A road is to be made from Gloucester line to John Cogswell's upland. This was to meet the preceding road.

1700. A bridge is to be built over Burnham's Creek, the same that was called Clark's Creek, to connect the two roads above mentioned.

BOUNDARIES OF DEACON BURNHAM'S FARM.

In 1694 a committee empowered by the town to settle disputes as to the boundaries of lands, met in this place. A report was spread, that Deacon Burnham had encroached on the commoner's land. But the committee, so far from finding this to be true, found that the bounds had never been determined, on that side of Deacon Burnham's farm; which was the south-west side, near to the house of the late Elias Andrews, Sen. They, therefore, after due consideration, and consultation with the neighbors, and with Deacon Burnham's son John, to whom he referred the whole matter, determined, and settled the boundaries as in the following document:

John Burnham's Deed, to be entered into Record, August 13, 1694.

We the Committee Impowered to look after Incroachments, and to Settle the bounds where they prove not Settled, being informed that Deacon John

Burnham, Senr., had Incroached of the Town's Common Land, on the South-westerly thereof; between his Land and the New Pasture Land, so called. We having been upon the place formerly, and examined the matter, and finding the bounds uncertainly Settled, Discoursed with the said Deacon Burnham, he having committed all into the hands of his son, John Burnham, Consenting to what agreement should be made between him and us; he the said John Burnham paying the charge of the Committee.

We have thus settled his Bounds, beginning at the head of the Creek, called Clark's Creek, near Joseph Andrews, his house, and run by the Instrument on the Course of 58 degrees eastwardly from the South, by the Circumferentor without variation, and marked by a white oke tree within the fence near the said Creek, and so, on that Course, Cross the field, to a small pine tree, on the brow of a hill within the Inclosed Land; then further to a white oke tree on the hill without the fence, then a Small Walnut tree, then further on the same Course to a hollow oke Just by the Rode that Leads to Gloster, then further to a white oke tree within two rods of Gloster Line, and further to Gloster Line to a white oke, being a bound tree, marked with the marking Iron. All which said trees are marked for his bounds, he bordering all the way upon the New Pasture Land, from the said Creek onwards, about one hundred and twenty-five Rods to a white oke tree, marked for the corner of said Pasture Land, now belonging to Mr. John Cogswell, and the other two rods onward, bordering upon the land reserved by Ipswich men, Lying between the land of the New Pasture and Gloster line, which said Bounds, as by the marked trees, we settle for his Bounds, and by Consent of the parties concerned, viz. Mr. John Cogswell for himself, and we in behalf of, and with the power of the inhabitants of Ipswich. To have and to hold the said Bounds, for his Bounds.

DEATHS OF PROMINENT MEN.

1694. November 5, died, Deacon John Burnham, the ancestor of the Burnhams in this place, and one of the first deacons of the church here.

On the last month of this century, December, 1700, William Cogswell, son of John Cogswell died, Æ. 81. He had been a very active, and highly useful citizen in this place, and his death was much lamented.

We have now reviewed the principal events and transactions relating to our ancestors in this place, from their settlement here, to the close of the 17th century. We have seen something of their trials, and sufferings, their energy and enterprise, their mode of living, and daily pursuits; their regard for the Bible and the Sabbath; their love for the worship of God; their obedience to his commands; and their regard for the best welfare of all among them.

If, in glancing at their civil regulations, we have been disposed to smile at some of them, as too particular, and interfering too much with the personal concerns, tastes and habits of private life, we must remember that they are not to be judged of, in these respects, by our modern views of civil, or national affairs. In the infancy of their settlements, they more resembled one large family, with several branches on the same plantation, than a state or a nation. And in their family state, their laws and regulations would, of course, resemble those, which are adopted in every well regulated family, rather than those, which are enacted by the government of a nation. Judged in this light, we see the wisdom as well as the benevolence, and watchful care, which marked all their social, civil, and ecclesiastical regulations. One thing is certain that whatever fault we may find, as to the shape, and appearance of the tree, which they planted, or their manner of setting it in the ground, it has proved a healthy, long-lived tree, and borne the best of fruit. And is not the tree to be judged by its fruit? Shall we then be wise in cutting down this tree, and planting one of an opposite nature? Shall we not do well to cherish the same principles of piety and virtue, which our fathers so warmly cherished, and follow in the same steps of sobriety, holiness and truth, in which they walked, if we would like them, hand down the blessings of a well regulated community to children's children? Happy is that people, that is in such a case; yea, happy is that people, whose God is the Lord.

CHAPTER II.

TO THE DIVISION OF CHEBACCO INTO TWO PARISHES.

At the close of the seventeenth century, *Chebacco Parish, in Ipswich,* contained a population of about three hundred souls, a church with a settled pastor, a school, and a military company.* A house of worship had been erected. Five saw-mills were in operation. A ship-yard had been laid out. Three bridges and two causeways had been built on the road from Ipswich Centre to Gloucester. The business of the place consisted chiefly of farming, fishing and boat-building.

In the mother country, King William was still upon the throne. He lived, however, but a short period in the eighteenth century, expiring on the 8th of March, 1702; and was succeeded, on the same day, by Queen Anne.

Dudley was the first Governor of Massachusetts appointed after the opening of this century, Gov. Bellamont having died March 5th, and Lt. Gov. Stoughton, July 7th, 1701. On Stoughton's death the executive office devolved for the first time upon the Council, a body consisting of twenty-nine members elected annually by the House of Representatives, and which corresponded to our Senate. Gov. Dudley arrived in 1702, and continued in office fourteen years. His administration during all this period was odious to our fathers; for though a native of Massachusetts, he was an enemy to popular liberty; and was, therefore, opposed, in most of the acts of his government, by the representatives of the people. When he was Chief

---

* "In 1683 Chebacco has 64 infantry besides troopers."

Justice, under Gov. Andros, he kept the minister of this place and some others from Ipswich in prison, in violation of the rights of Englishmen. We allude to these State affairs because they were matters in which our fathers in this town took a deep interest, and in which their representatives acted an important part, so that they were of course, exciting topics of conversation by their firesides. There were then but two parties in the colony: the royalists, and the friends of liberty. The great body of the people were on the latter side; on the former, only the officers of the crown, and a few others, who sought their patronage. As a prerogative of the crown and its officers, Dudley insisted on a fixed and permanent salary. But neither the House of Representatives nor the Council would allow it, but granted him such a sum only from year to year as they thought best. Dudley, after a long contest, was compelled to submit. The people triumphed as they did also in similar contests with other royal Governors.

1702. It appears from the following entry in the Parish Records that the *first school-house* was erected this year:

"Whereas it was left to the Selectmen (of Chebacco) to appoint a place for the erecting a school-house in Chebacco, we, the subscribers, having duly considered the same, have appointed that the said house be built on the right hand of the way as you go from the Meeting-house to Dea. Thomas Low's, upon a handsome, rising, dry piece of ground, right opposite to Mr. Adam Cogswell's barn, which is accounted to be pretty near the centre of the place. Near by said place stands a shrubbed white oak.

NATH. RUST, JR.,
BENJ. MARSHALL,
JOHN CHOATE,   } *Selectmen.*"
NATH. GOODHUE,

This school-house, therefore, stood on "the common," in front of the house now owned by William H. Mears, and continued to be used for school purposes till 1757, when it was sold, and a new one built. What its dimensions were, we are not informed. It was doubtless small, designed to accommodate all the children in the place—about fifty in number. The school, which had been originally commenced in this parish in June, 1695, had been hitherto kept in the private house of the teacher, Nathaniel Rust, Jr. (now Mr. Mears' dwelling-house.) The erection of this first school-house was, in that day, a great affair in the little community of our fathers, and excited, no doubt, great interest among them. In generations to come, it will be interesting to their posterity, as education advances, to trace it back to this small beginning. May they never have occasion to say that they are doing less in proportion to their numbers, and ability for the education of their children, than did their fathers in 1702. The privilege of six months' schooling was then given annually to every child and youth in the place, even at a time when, in addition to other hardships, they were obliged to do their part in maintaining expensive and harassing wars with the French and Indians. Generally at that day the only books used in the schools were reading and spelling books. Arithmetic was taught by the master's writing the rules and examples in the scholars' manuscripts, to be wrought by them on the slate. As the parents had been required by law to instruct their children in the principal laws of the country, and in moral and religious truth, so the same was expected of their school-teacher. The school-masters at that time were chosen by the parish. Among the earliest whose names are known, were Samuel Phillips in 1709, a graduate of Harvard College in 1708, and afterwards pastor of the South Church in Andover; and William Giddings, in 1713.

1703. It is a fact that may serve to show the comparative importance of Ipswich in the early settlement of the country, both in civil and military affairs, that it paid a higher County and State tax in 1703, than any other town in the County, Salem not excepted.

Before the close of this year a French and Indian war broke out, which lasted through ten long years at the expense of much blood and treasure. Every fifth man, it was stated in a public document, was called into the military service. This war commenced with the attack of the

Indians on Deerfield in the Connecticut valley. Three years before, ninety men, of which this town furnished its quota, had been drawn from the Essex regiments to be stationed at Haverhill, Amesbury, Wells, and Kittery, to prevent surprise from the enemy. In 1704, Col. Church, known for his exploits in former wars, was sent to the province of Maine to operate against the enemy, with five hundred and sixty men. He proceeded to the Penobscot River, and there killed and took captive many Indians. He then went up the river St. Croix, and took the town of Menis. There were doubtless several from this place in this, as in other expeditions. One-fifth of the men called out to war, would require ten or twelve from Chebacco to be more or less constantly absent from home. On the 18th of May, this year, a public Fast was observed " to pray," as the proclamation stated, " for her majesty, that her forces, and those of her allies, and of this Province may prevail, that the sea-coast, and inland frontiers be protected and that there be a plentiful effusion of the Holy Spirit of God for a thorough reformation of all evils."

About this time, as we learn from the parish record, Mr. Wise built for himself a house on the ten-acre lot, which the parish had bought and given him, at his ordination for a settlement. The old parsonage-house, it will be remembered, stood in the parsonage-lot, nearly opposite the residence of Capt. Joseph Choate, at the north end of said lot. There Mr. Wise had lived for about twenty years, when he built this house on his own land, on the spot where the house of the late John Mears, Sen., now stands, fronting the same way, and, as tradition says, with the same yard before it. On enlarging his cellar in 1844, Mr. Mears found a shoe-buckle brush, with the initials of Mr. Wise's name on the handle. It appears that before Mr. Wise built his house, the parish had engaged to build for him a new parsonage ; and also to give Mrs. Wise £100, in case she should be left a widow in the parsonage-house ; as she would then be obliged to remove from it. But at a sub-

15

sequent meeting, they offered their minister £50 if he would release them from these obligations, and give bond to pay the parish £80, if he left them to settle over any other people. It stands on the record in these words with some abridgments:

"May the 21, 1701. It was then voted, that, provided the Rev. Mr. John Wise forgive us all the behindments relating to his salary until the beginning of this present year; and also that he forgive us all the stone wall that the place is yet obliged to do about the pasture, and also doth acquit and discharge us from all repairs of the parsonage-house, except shingling and groundselling and clapboarding; and also from a house this place was formerly obliged to build for him; and from the £100 it was formerly voted to Mrs. Wise, provided she was left a widow,—it is voted that we will give to our minister, Mr. John Wise, the full sum of £50. He, the said Mr. John Wise shall give bonds," etc.

This offer of the parish Mr. and Mrs. Wise accepted; and in a few years after, he removed to his own house; receiving during his life the rents of the old parsonage-house; which, at his decease reverted to the parish.

Let us visit the first minister in his new dwelling. The way is familiar but the scenery of olden time is new to us. Extensive forests confine our view chiefly to the road and adjacent fields. As we go from the Centre to the North End, we leave the new school-house on the common upon our left, Capt. Adam Cogswell's house and barn upon our right, and soon the meeting-house, also upon our right, and the old parsonage upon our left, and after a short distance farther, we come to the new parsonage, as it is called. Mrs. Wise receives us at the door, and entertains us with much hospitality. Mr. Wise is in his study. The younger children are at school, while her daughters in the kitchen are preparing the repast for noon. On inquiring for the welfare of her children, the good lady gives us the following particulars: Jeremiah, the eldest, was graduated at Harvard College about four years since. Having studied theology and been licensed to preach, he is settled in the ministry at Berwick in the Province of Maine. Lucy was married about a year since, to the Rev. John White of

Gloucester. Joseph is living in Boston. Ammi Ruhami, Henry and John are at school. The hour of dinner having come, Mr. Wise is called from his study, and we take our seat with him at the social board. Presently the boys come in from school, and are seated with us.

" Well my boys," said the father, " what has Master Rust said to you to-day ?"

" After repeating our Catechism, he asked us who was the governor of the Province, and who was queen of England, and the name of her sister, that was queen before her."

" And could you tell ?" inquired their father.

" Yes," says one ; " I knew that Governor Dudley is our governor."

" And I knew," said another " that Anne is our queen ; for I heard you speaking of her, the other day, and of her sister Mary as the wife of King William, and daughter of King James. But Master Rust is going to ask us more questions about it, and wants us to find out how James came to be a Catholic, and his daughters Protestants, and what the story is about Anne's running away from home, when Mary and her husband came to take away their father's throne."

" Well, boys, I will tell you the story after dinner," added the father.

Dinner being ended, we are invited into the study—the south-west corner chamber—that its occupant may have the most light and heat. The library before us is not extensive, though sufficient to acquaint and enlarge the mind with a knowledge of history, philosophy, the ancient classics, and especially theology. The Hebrew and Greek Scriptures, with their respective Lexicons, are upon the table for daily use. We notice Gurnel's "Armor of Light" by the side of Dalton's " County Justice," upon the shelf, showing that the pastor must have the law for civil action, as well as the gospel for spiritual direction.

" Now for the story about King James and his daughters," says the father to the sons. " I will make it short, that you may remember and tell it to your teacher. The two brothers, Charles and James, after their father Charles the First was beheaded, were in exile with their mother in Papal countries, and were brought up Catholics. Charles, when he came to the throne of England after Cromwell's death, was secretly a Catholic. But he knew that he could not be king of England without declaring himself a Protestant. He had no children to succeed him. His brother James, then Duke of York, would be his successor, if living at his death. But he seems to have thought that he should live as long as his brother, that the daughters of James would be his successors, and that it was as necessary that they should be educated Protestants as that he should declare himself one.   So with his kingly power, he took his brother's daughters, Mary and Anne, and placed them in Protestant families, under Protestant teachers.   But James outlived Charles; and came to the throne a bigoted papist.   This of course, could not be endured by Englishmen.   Secretly a conspiracy was formed against him.   William, Prince of Orange, who had married his daughter Mary, then at the head of the Dutch nation, was invited by the conspirators to come over to England, and take the throne with his wife, who was the next heir to the crown.   William and Mary came, and after fighting several battles, James was obliged to flee from the country.   Anne, who had married George, Prince of Denmark, was at home, when William and Mary landed on the western shores of England. Wishing to join her sister, she improved the opportunity of her father's absence, who was at Salisbury eighty miles distant, to escape privately.   Lady Churchill, her particular friend, communicated to some of the leading conspirators her wish to do so, and in a few hours everything was arranged.   Accompanied by a friend and two female attendants, she stole down the back-stairs in a dressing-gown and slippers, at dead of night, and gained the street unchallenged.   A hackney-coach was in waiting.   Two men guarded the humble vehicle.   One of them was the bishop of London, her old tutor.   The carriage drove to his house, where she was secreted for the night.   The next day she joined the army of the insurgents.   When James reached home and found that Anne had gone, he exclaimed in agony " God help me ! my own children have forsaken me.''

To this story our school-boys listened with the greatest eagerness, and will, no doubt, be able to give their teacher the principal facts, if not all the particulars.   As the children are retiring, the father expresses his satisfaction at the progress of education among us,—that we have now a school of six months for all the children in the place, taught by a faithful, industrious and well-qualified teacher. He alludes also, with much pleasure, to the fact that five young men, have participated in the privileges of the Latin school in the town, have enjoyed the advantages and honors of Harvard University, and are pleasantly and usefully laboring in the ministry.   We inquire of him his opinion of the late act of Queen Anne in declaring war against France.   At this he expresses his deep regret, as involving us in all the horrors of another French and Indian war.   But we must trust in God, he says, and buckle

on the armor for self-defence. It is a day that calls for
courage and bodily strength, as well as for faith and prayer.
But hark! Some one is knocking at the door below. Mr.
Wise is called down to see a stranger. We look from the
window into the yard, and see that the stranger has tied
his horse to a post within, and hear him say to our pastor,
" Sir, my name is Chandler, of the town of Andover; hearing that you were a famous wrestler, and having myself
some success that way, having thrown all in our region, I
have come all the way from Andover to take hold with
you." " No objection to that," is the pleasant reply. They
take hold in earnest, and after a few struggles, Mr. Chandler is laid upon his back. On rising, he is not satisfied,
and wishes for another trial. The result is that Mr. Wise
not only lays him a second time upon his back, but gently
puts him over the fence into the street. " And now," says
Chandler, " if you will just throw my horse over after me,
I will go along." With this amusing incident, we take
leave for the present of the pastor's house.

1705. The snow was so deep during the Winter that
there was no moving about without snow-shoes, and what
was very remarkable, horses had to wear them as well as
men.

1707. September 15th, Rev. Francis Goodhue, a native
of this place, died at Rehoboth in Bristol County.

" He was the successor in the ministry at Jamaica, L. I., of the Rev. John
Hubbard, a native of Ipswich who graduated at Harvard College, 1695, settled over the Presbyterian Church in Jamaica, February, 1702, and died
October 5, 1705, aged 28. Mr. Goodhue was settled the same year that Mr.
Hubbard died. He was a native of the same place and probably had been a
companion of Hubbard in childhood, as he was but one year younger, and
both pursued their studies preparatory to college in the Ipswich Grammar
School. He was a son of Dea. William and Hannah Goodhue, and was born
in Chebacco Parish, Ipswich, Mass., October 4, 1678. His grandfather,
William, was one of the most influential, and respectable men in the colony
of Massachusetts, whose " many virtues " are said to have " conferred honor
upon his name and family." Francis Goodhue graduated at Harvard in
1699, and was settled at Jamaica in 1705. At the close of the summer of
1707, he went from that place on a journey to New England to visit his rel-

atives, but died of fever on his way, at Rehoboth, Mass., where he was buried. The ministry of Goodhue was short, but it was eminently useful in keeping the congregation together under its adverse circumstances. It is deeply affecting to contemplate the situation of the congregation called thus to mourn over the early graves of two ministers, who, having been pleasant and lovely in their lives, in death were not far divided. A literary friend has kindly furnished me with the following elegant lines on Mr. Goodhue, taken from the Boston News Letter of February 28, 1723:

"'Libertas nomen; bonitas conjuncta colori Cognomen præbent; Insula Longa gregem. Nascitur Ipsvici; dissolvitur inter eundum; Seconchæ lecto molliter ossa cubant. Doctrina, officium, pietas, adamata juventus, nil contra jussam convaluere necem. Pars potior sedes procedit adire beatas, gaudens placato semper adesse Deo.'

" Which may be thus translated:

" Liberty gives him a name (Francis;) good joined to hue, a surname; Long Island, a flock. Born at Ipswich, he dies whilst traveling. His bones softly repose in their bed at Seekonk. Learning, sacred office, piety, amiable youth could avail nothing against death decreed. The immortal part enters into Paradise, rejoicing to be forever in the presence of God reconciled."*

His library was brought home to his father. Two volumes of it—"Calvin's Institutes" and "Elton on Colossians,"—printed in London in 1634, and containing his autograph, are now in the author's possession.

1710. It was during this year that Mr. Wise wrote and published his treatise on the liberty and independence of the churches, under the quaint title, "The Churches' Quarrel Espoused." The occasion of his putting forth the treatise was as follows: At the meeting of ministers in Boston on Election week, May, 1705, several questions were proposed and discussed relating to councils, and the best method of conducting the government and discipline of the Congregational churches; and the consideration of them recommended to the several associated ministers in the different parts of the colonies. They adjourned, and met again in Boston on the same subject, in September following, and again in November, and finally agreed on several "Proposals" to be printed and circulated among the churches. These proposals were sixteen in number,

* " History of the Presbyterian Church in Jamaica, L. I., by J. M. MacDonald, pastor. 1847."

under two general divisions; the first eight respecting the action of associated ministers in licensing candidates for the ministry, determining when it was expedient for councils to be called, and the propriety of each pastor submitting such cases of discipline as would be likely to produce any embroilments to the consideration and advice of his associated brethren, before proceeding to any action on them in his church. The second division of the proposals related to standing councils, to consist of associated ministers, and lay delegates from their respective churches, to meet at least once a year, and as much oftener as the association of ministers might determine. These proposals, however honestly intended for the good of the churches, obviously contain principles, which, if carried out, must tend to subvert their liberties. So it was considered by some in that day, and the danger thus threatening the churches drew from the pen of our first minister here a sharp and able reply; which is still numbered among our standard works in ecclesiastical affairs.

This year, news arrives that William Cogswell of this place is killed by the Indians; probably in some one of the frequent skirmishes that occurred in Maine.

1712. April 12th, died, Dea. Thomas Low, aged 80. He left a widow, Martha, and seven children, Samuel, Jonathan, David, Martha Dodge, Joanna Dodge, Sarah and Abigail Goodhue. He was one of the deacons of the church here from its commencement to his decease. Besides the management of an extensive farm, he entered largely into the business of making malt. He was a prominent man in the church, and for several years parish clerk. His will, made four years before his death, thus begins:

"In the name of God, Amen. I Thomas Low, of Ipswich, in the county of Essex, in the Massachusetts Bay, Maltster, not knowing how soon it may please God Almighty to call me to my long home, and to the grave, the place appointed for all the living; therefore I make this to be my last Will and Testament. First of all I commit my immortal soul into the gracious hands of God, that gave it, and my body to the grave, and a decent burial, in hope of a glorious resurrection through the merits of the Lord Jesus Christ, my only Redeemer. And for what of worldly goods or estates it hath pleased God to bless me with in this life, I do hereby give and bequeath to my beloved wife and children, as hereafter followeth."

The will is dated, "17th of June, 1708, in the seventh year of the reign of Queen Anne."

Let us visit the house so recently deprived of its possessor and head. Following the road to the bridge, we turn to the right through a gate, near the present dwelling of Abel Story, and traveling about sixty rods westerly, come to the mansion, so well known a hundred and fifty years ago, as Dea. Low's. There are some pleasant enclosures near the house; but the trees are so thick we cannot see the river, and the cattle have their pasture in woods, but little thinned as yet by the axe. On entering the dwelling, we find the afflicted widow occupying "*the new end*" of the house, which the Deacon had built but a few years before his death. Samuel, the oldest son, occupies the other part of the house, where he has lived since his marriage. His (Samuel's) family, especially the prattling babes, are a source of much comfort to the bereaved grandmother. We find her meekly submissive to the will of God, though heavily afflicted in the departure of one with whom she had lived in the conjugal state more than fifty years. She speaks of her loss in accents of sorrow, yet relieved and consoled with the hope of soon being with him in a brighter and better world. She dwells with fond recollection on his many virtues as a Christian husband and father, and particularly of his love to her expressed in the ample provision which he had made for her in her widowed state. As she perceives by our looks that we desire her to go on, she enters into particulars, and states that he had left her the use of the new end, in which they had lived together the last few years of his life, with all their ancient furniture, and provisions more than enough for her use, consisting of two hundred weight of pork yearly, with ten barrels of Winter apples, and all the Summer fruit she needed, two barrels of cider, six bushels of malt, three of Indian corn, and one of wheat, besides ten shillings in money, fourteen pounds of wool and twelve of flax, wood for one fire, the milk of two cows, and a horse to ride at her pleasure and convenience, together with the garden at the end of the house.

As her husband was a maltster, she invites us out to see the establishment in a building near by, where the business is still carried on by her son Samuel. On entering, we notice many bags of barley lying on one side, ready to be made into malt. The kiln or oven is upon the ground before us. In a sort of chamber, seven feet above the oven, bars of wood are laid stretching from beam to beam, crossed by others laid on them, so as to form a lattice, over which is spread a hair cloth, eight or ten feet square. The barley is first washed, then spread upon this hair cloth to be dried. Small openings in the kiln beneath are constantly sending up heat and smoke for the drying process. It is then cleansed by a sieve prepared for the purpose, and carried to a mill in the other end of the building, where it is ground, and comes out malt. The barley, when wet, increases in size sufficiently to pay the maltster, by returning measure for measure. The whole presents a busy scene. Boys as well as men are employed. Some are washing the barley, and carrying it aloft for spreading. Others are removing what is dried, for the purpose of sifting and carrying it to the mill. Another is tending the fire beneath, and keeping the horse in motion in his never-ending circle; and all to furnish a drink, which shall be both palatable and harmless. We learn, however, from the maltster, that the business is declining, since it is found that apples, even of the meanest kind, make a more exhilarating as well as cheaper drink, and that this branch of his business is increasing yearly, while the other is decreasing. From the malt-house we go to the cider-mill, and look in upon its operations. Here is no trouble of washing the materials. Heaps of apples lie upon the ground just as they were

11

taken from under the trees, crabbed, wormy and rotten. We retire from these manufactories of liquors, fully convinced by the teachings of experience, that the more "strong drink," the more thirst, and that health and morals can be secured only by entire abstinence from all that intoxicates.

This same year died Dea. William Goodhue, (or Capt. William Goodhue, as he was more generally called,) aged about seventy years. As captain of the militia in this place, he was no doubt often called upon to engage in excursions against the French and Indians. He filled, at several different periods, the office of selectman of the town, and of representative to the General Court. He was a leading man in the parish and church, and was highly respected, eminently useful and greatly beloved. It was stated in Chapter I. of this History, that he accompanied Mr. Wise to the caucus held in the center of the town, to devise measures for resisting illegal taxation, and was imprisoned for so doing by Gov. Andros. This honor is given in Felt's History to William, his father, who resided in the center of the town. But the father was then more than seventy years of age, and had retired from public life; while William, the son, was about forty-five years old, an intimate friend and near neighbor to Mr. Wise, and therefore most likely to accompany his minister on such an expedition, (especially as it was unsafe in that day to travel alone.) Dea. Goodhue left a widow and six children, viz: Hannah Cogswell, Margery Giddings, Bethiah Marshall, Nathaniel, Joseph and John.

1714, August 1. Queen Anne departed this life at noon, having reigned a little more than twelve years. Mr. Wise in his preface to "The Churches' Quarrel Espoused" thus eulogizes her while living:

" My conclusion is with the devoutest application to the supreme throne, that the Almighty God will bless the great Anne, our wise and Protestant princess, New England's royal nurse, and the great benefactress, that she may live to see all her Protestant churches, through her vast empire, more virtuous, and more united, and as they all meet and center, with their differing persuasions, by their love and loyal actions, in her person and government, let her most excellent majesty, next to Christ, continue absolute in her empire over their hearts, and as she has made such a complete conquest of all differing parties within her dominions, by her wise and virtuous measures, and thereby won all the fame of rule and sovereignty from her royal progenitors, who could never so charm such mighty nations, let her reign continue the exactest model for all courts in Europe ! And when she is full, repleat and satisfied with length of days, and the most glorious effects of a prosperous reign, let God favor her lasting, and flourishing name with an unperishing monument, on which justice shall become obliged to inscribe this memento : ' Here lies in funeral pomp the princess of the earth, the store-house of all ennobling, and princely perfections.' ''

On the same day that Queen Anne died, George, elector of Brunswick, is proclaimed king of Great Britain. After the news arrived here, Gov. Dudley issued his proclamation, September 17th, declaring George the First to be king of the Province; and soon after retired. He was succeeded by Gov. Shute, the son of an eminent citizen in London, whose family were generally dissenters, or puritans. In early life he went into the army under King William, was made a captain and afterwards a colonel. He was esteemed at Court, had the character of a friend to liberty, and was of an open, generous and humane disposition. He arrived in Boston, October 14, 1716; was received with the usual parade.

1716. COMMONERS' LAND.

" At a legal meeting of the proprietors of the common and undivided lands in the town of Ipswich, the 27th of January, 1716," a committee was chosen to divide the common lands " into eight parts, lying each part as near as may be for the accommodation of such as lie nearest to it, and to have respect to quantity and quality." The committee in their report say, " In order hereunto we have measured the said commons, and find it to amount to 7,335 acres, and we have divided it accordingly. " We laid out *one-eighth* convenient for the proprietors of Chebacco ; with a line beginning twenty polls and an half to the Eastward of the Widow Choate's corner ; and running Southwardly to a stake and heap of stones standing to the Northward of Chebacco pond ; and so from said stake on the same line to the pond. (The stake stands twenty perch and an half more Eastwardly than it did at first.) And to the *East* of this there are 1,084 acres, which we account 873 acres."

1717. We find this year, for the first time, mention made of the existence of Slavery among us. From a bill of sale still extant, dated July 30, 1717, it appears that Joshua Norwood of Gloucester sold to Jonathan Burnham of Chebacco, for £64 in bills of credit, a negro boy whom he had bought of Thomas Choate of Hogg Island.* During most of the last century, slaves were held by our fathers in this and the neighboring towns, and in the colonies generally. How shall we justify them in that which we now condemn? While we have such exalted views of the integrity and piety of our puritan ancestors, can we say that being slave-holders, they could not have been Christians? But while compelled to admit, that it is possible for a slave-holder, who treats his slaves well, to be a Christian, we have in the case of our fathers some things to say in their behalf, *as to the way* in which they became slave-holders, and their conduct in reference to it. They did not send vessels to Africa to bring slaves to this country. They did not enter at all into the slave-trade, nor willingly give it any encouragement. On the contrary, they remonstrated most loudly against it. All the slaves here were originally brought from Africa to this country in English ships, and forced upon the colonies. "England," says Bancroft "stole from Africa, from 1700 to 1750, probably a million and a half of souls, of whom one-eighth were buried in the Atlantic, victims of the passage, and yet in England no general indignation rebuked the enormity. Massachusetts unremittingly opposed the introduction of slaves. In 1701 the town of Boston instructed its representatives to put a period to negroes being slaves. In 1705, the General Court imposed a tax upon those who brought slaves into the market, of so much for every slave sold." All the colonies at the South, as well as the North, were always opposed to the African slave-trade. But England per-

---

* This must have been *Gov. Tho. Choate*, so called ; as his son, Lieut. Thomas, would have been but 24 years old in 1717, and the sale to Norwood might have been a considerable time before, thus making Lieut. Thomas, perhaps, a minor.

sisted in bringing them and landing them upon our shores. But why did our fathers buy them? The only apparent reason is that of humanity or necessity. If they had not taken them into their families by purchase, they might have been left to perish in our streets, or subjected to all the horrors of another passage over the Atlantic to be sold to some other country. If they had been left unprovided for, upon our shores, they must have perished; for they were as incapable of providing for themselves, as the most neglected and ignorant child. "The concurrent testimony of tradition," says Bancroft, "represents the negroes at their arrival to have been gross and stupid, having memory and physical strength, but undisciplined in the exercise of reason, and imagination." Their condition, therefore, was at once improved as soon as they came into the possession of our fathers. They dwelt under the same roof; their wants were all cared for; they worked shoulder to shoulder with their masters in the field; sat by the same fire with the children, were taken to church with them on the Sabbath, and instructed in the great truths of Christianity, and when our fathers were made free, they were made free with them. There is nothing in these facts to diminish aught of England's guilt in the enormities of the slave-trade; but they certainly furnish some apology for our fathers in giving a home to those who were already bondmen.

During this year Mr. Wise publishes another treatise, entitled "A Vindication of the Government of the New England Churches, Drawn from Antiquity, the Light of Nature, the Holy Scriptures, its Noble Nature, and from the Dignity which Divine Providence has put upon it." Two years before this, he received a written request from the ministers in Gloucester to print a new edition of his former treatise, couched in the following language:

"Reverend Sir: We have had the favor and satisfaction of reading, and according to our measure considering the transcendent logic, as well as grammar and rhetoric of your Reply to the Proposals; by which our eyes are

opened to see much more than ever before we saw of the value and glory of
our invaded privileges, and are of opinion that if your consent may be obtained to a new edition it may be of wonderful service to our churches, if God
shall please to go forth with it. However it will be a testimony that all our
watchmen were not asleep, nor the camp of Christ surprised and taken before they had warning   We are, &c.,   SAMUEL MOODEY.
                                              JOHN WHITE.

"*Gloucester, March* 25, 1715."

Mr. Wise probably delayed complying with this request,
till he had completed his second treatise, and then published them both together in one volume.   Another edition of them was published some years after, together
with the Platform adopted by the churches in 1648, and
the Confession of Faith in 1680.

In the month of April, this year, much anxiety and
alarm were felt by the people in this place, as on all the
sea-board, on account of pirates cruising on our coast.

1718.   ERECTION OF THE SECOND HOUSE OF WORSHIP.

This year a new house of worship was erected.   Two
years before, it had been voted at a Parish meeting—

" That when there shall be a vote for building a new meeting-house in
Chebacco, said house shall be erected upon the land lying on the easterly side
of a white oak tree, on the right hand of the highway, beyond the school-house ;
said tree being about thirty rods westerly of said school-house."

A committee was chosen by the Parish—

" To wait on Mr. Wise to see if he be willing that the new meeting-house
shall be removed from the site of the old one so far as the plain by Moses
Rust's, and he expose himself to come so far from the new parsonage to carry
on the service of God's holy worship there."

In October of the year preceding this, viz., 1717, it was
voted to build a meeting-house fifty-two feet by forty-two,
and twenty-one in height, and that it be erected the ensuing winter.   The site first chosen was near where the
pound now is.   But afterward another spot was selected,
and by much labor prepared for the new house.   This was
in the rear of the house now owned by Henry Mears.

The road in that day, in passing the corner from the North End to the Falls, was over the high land, westerly of its present course. Gravel was dug for the highway near the lower house now owned by Adam Boyd, in the rear of which, and near Mr. Boyd's upper house stood Mrs. Johannah Rust's house. The Record styles it, "The first knowle of land southerly from the gravel pit, which is on the front side of Mrs. Johannah Rust's dwelling-house."

Forty-seven voters entered their names on the Parish Record in favor of this new location for the meeting-house. But in May, 1718, it was voted—

"That, whereas, there was a place of late that has been in nomination, and also a considerable quantity of labor has been done by said inhabitants upon said place in order to level the same for the raising said house ; yet upon the urgent request of Mr. Wise, our Reverend Minister, that they would alter their designs concerning the same, and would be pleased to gratify his desire concerning said house, and raise it upon the plain spot of land by Moses Rust's, which formerly was voted by said inhabitants, for said service, and also, in viewing said plain and considering thereof, it is the opinion of most of said inhabitants, that the latter is far more commodious than the former to accommodate the erecting said house ; wherefore it was voted that our new meeting house shall be raised upon the plane spot, agreeable to the former vote for setting the house there. The vote was further tried in the negative and no hand was held up."

When it is considered that the question of locating a meeting-house has generally proved a very difficult one, and has often done more to divide and alienate from each other the members of a parish, than almost anything else, we must give credit to our fathers for a spirit of mutual forbearance and conciliation, in coming to a unanimous vote on such a vexed question. It was also voted at this meeting—

"That the building committee, with the parish Clerk, shall take account of what people offer to do in raising the house, and also take care of such things as shall be given in, for the benefit of said work, and shall order and direct the workmen, upon the day of raising, to the several places of entertainment whereat people have promised to make provision for them."

The house was accordingly raised and nearly completed that Summer. Liberty is granted to certain individuals that desire it, to build pews around the house, next to the walls. These pews had lattice-work on the sides of them near the top, as is recollected by some aged persons now living. The rest of the house is filled with seats on each side of the broad aisle. Galleries are erected on three sides of the house. The pulpit, with an hour-glass upon it, is on the west side, opposite to the front door. A door is at each end north and south. A turret is on the center of the roof, for the new bell, which has been recently purchased, the rope of which hangs down in the middle of the house below. The roof on the inside remains unfinished, the beams and rafters and ridge-pole being all in sight. A short ladder is kept standing on a platform resting on the cross-beams, and reaching to the bell.

After the dedication of the house, a committee is chosen " to dignify the seats and seat the people." This is a delicate and difficult task. There are certain rules, however, which, according to the customs of the day, govern and direct in this matter. The highest seat in dignity is in the middle of the house. The rest grow less and less in dignity as they recede from this, whether toward the pulpit or toward the door. The men occupy the seats on the right of the broad aisle, as you enter the house, the women those on the left. The women are seated according to the dignity of their husbands, or, if widows, according as the dignity of their husbands had been. Magistrates have the pre-eminence. Next to them come military officers in their various grades, from the major-general down to the corporal. Respect is also shown to the aged, and to those who have done special service for the benefit of the parish, or who pay the largest sum for the support of the ministry. In all these cases, however, a suitable abatement is made if a man is known to be in debt; he must take a lower seat in proportion to what he is owing. If we are disposed to object to this ancient custom, we must consider that it is in agreement with the public sentiment of the day. We must consider, too, that when the seats

are free, some system for assigning them to individuals
and families, as their places of sitting from Sabbath to
Sabbath, must be adopted by the parish, to preserve order
and prevent confusion.   Having removed to their new
house, the old one (on Meeting-House Hill) in which our
fathers had worshiped for nearly forty years, and in which
they had held all their parish meetings, is left desolate,
and soon after sold, pursuant to a vote of the parish.

The site of the second house was near the Town Pound.
Thus " the common " more than a hundred years ago, was
occupied with a parish-church and school-house, leaving
room besides for the regular military musters, and all the
accompaniments of a training day.

If we seem to make too much of these matters, it should
be considered that they were the germ of the liberty and
independence of our whole land.   Our towns, and schools
and churches were the birth-places and the nurseries of
that liberty and equality, order and prosperity, which
grew into manhood, and, in due time, threw off the
shackles which our mother country imposed upon us.

" In the settlements which grew up on the margin of the greenwood," says
the historian Bancroft, " the plain meeting-house of the congregation for public worship was everywhere the central point. Near it stood the public school
by the side of the very broad road, over which wheels did not pass, to do more
than mark the path by ribbons in the sward. The snug farm houses, owned
as freeholds, without quit-rents, were dotted along the way, and the village
pastor among his people, enjoying the calm raptures of devotion, ' appeared
like such a little white flower as we see in the spring of the year, low and
humble on the ground, standing peacefully and lovingly in the midst of the
flowers round about ; all in like manner opening their bosoms to drink in the
light of the sun.' In every hand was the Bible ; every home was a house
of prayer ; in every village all had been taught ; many had comprehended
a methodical theory of the divine purpose in creation, and of the destiny of
man."   Again he says : "*All New England* was an aggregate of organized
democracies.   But the complete development of the institution was to be
found in Connecticut and the Massachusetts Bay.   There each township was
also substantially a territorial parish ; the town was the religious congregation ; the independent church was established by law ; the minister was
elected by the people, who annually made grants for his support.   There,
too, the system of free schools was carried to great perfection, so that there

17

could not be found a person born in New England, unable to read and write. He that will understand the political character of New England in the eighteenth century, must study the constitution of its towns, its congregations, its schools, and its militia."

1720. This year the Ipswich Grammar school was placed under charge of a native of Chebacco—Henry Wise. Being a classical as well as English school, it had already afforded him the requisite preparatory training for college, when it was under the instruction of Mr. Daniel Rogers, a son of President Rogers of Harvard College. Of the fifteen students who were fitted for college by Mr. Rogers during the period in which the school was under his charge (1687–1715,) eight were from Chebacco, whose names were as follows: William Burnham, Benjamin Choate, Francis Cogswell, John Eveleth, Francis Goodhue, John Perkins, Henry Wise, and Jeremiah Wise. Mr. Perkins was a son Abraham Perkins, and a descendant of William Perkins, who emigrated to Ipswich about 1632. He was graduated in 1695, studied medicine, and first settled as a physician in Ipswich, but afterwards removed to Boston. He died in 1740. Mr. Cogswell was a son of Jonathan Cogswell, and a grandson of Dea. William Goodhue, from whom he received by bequest, the library of his uncle, Rev. Francis Goodhue. He was graduated at Harvard in 1718. Henry Wise was a son of the minister. His connection with the Grammar school as a pupil closed in 1713, when he entered Harvard College. He was graduated in 1717. For nearly three years he resided in Boston, and was engaged in mercantile business. He then removed to the center of Ipswich, and on June 20, "at a meeting of the Selectmen, Mr. Henry Wise accepted the offer the Selectmen made him for keeping the school for the year ensuing. Accordingly the Selectmen delivered the key of the school-house, and he began to instruct the Grammar school." His salary was £55 in bills of credit. He continued to be the Preceptor of the school for eight years. It is not certainly known when his death occurred, but it was on or before the year 1732. It was some time during this year, also, that the tenants of the school-farm refused to pay their rents, on the ground that "no power had been given by the town to their Trustees, to appoint successors in that trust, for receiving and applying the rents, or of ordaining and directing the affairs of the school." The town, by their Selectmen, assumed the control of the school and its property. And the next year, (1721,) an action at law was brought against the tenants of the school-farm, which lingered until 1729, when the town "received £100 of Gifford Cogswell on account of charges at law about the school-farm." This sum the town very properly ordered to be distributed to the several parishes "to be used towards the support of reading and writing schools." Under this order, £20 were paid to the Chebacco Committee.

1721. This year is memorable for the extensive spread, and great mortality of the small pox in Boston, and other towns; and also for the introduction of inoculation to modify the disease, and render it less fatal. Dr. Cotton Mather, one of the principal ministers of Boston, becoming acquainted with the good effects of inoculation in some parts of the old world, earnestly recommended to the physicians of Boston, to make trial of it. They all refused, except Dr. Boylston, who, to show the confidence he had of success, began with his own children. This brought upon him great obloquy. The minds of most people were struck with horror at the thought of taking active measures to bring the disease upon any. The pastor of the church here, Mr. Wise, was among the very few who stood boldly forward, amidst strong prejudice and violent opposition, to advocate, and urge on, the remedy of inoculation. In this he showed his wonted independence of mind, and benevolence of heart.

1722. Great difficulty and distress were experienced about this time, and onward, from the great quantity of Province Bills issued by our General Court. This reduced

the value of currency, and consequently raised the price
of labor and of all articles of consumption. The depreciation of the Province bills, however, arose, not only from
their quantity. but from the want of confidence on the
part of the people that they would ever be redeemed, except at a very great discount. The reasons for issuing
these bills to so great an extent, were the great depres-
sion of trade, and the heavy debts incurred by the French
and Indian war. But instead of being a remedy, or any
relief, they only increased the difficulties already existing,
and a flood of evils was brought by them upon the whole
community. It fell with more weight upon those who
were living upon a stipulated sum for their services. The
parish here had from time to time increased Mr. Wise's
salary, but had not come up to the original value even
when they had added forty pounds. On the motion to
make up the full value, the vote was in the negative.
Mr. Wise, therefore, entered a complaint against them,
September 25, 1722, at the Court of the General Sessions
of the peace, held in Newbury. The result was that the
parish added fifty-five pounds to the original sum, thus
increasing the salary to one hundred and fifteen pounds.
This civil suit does not seem to have interrupted the goodwill and harmony existing between pastor and people.

WORSHIP IN THE NEW MEETING-HOUSE.

Let us attend church on Sabbath morning with our ancestors in their new house. As we stand in front of it,
we see it to be a very plain edifice, without the ornament
of paint or blinds, though having the advantage of being
new and comparing well with the public buildings of that
day in other places. The common has but few trees on
it. A shrub oak is near the school-house. A tall and
flourishing one spreads its lofty arms behind the church.
The hills in the rear are covered with forest trees of an
ancient growth. Only two or three houses are in sight,
with small cultivated fields around them bordering upon

thick woods. On our right, in the rear of the school-
house, is the dwelling of the teacher, Moses Rust. On
the opposite side of the road, is the barn of Capt. Adam
Cogswell, and a little north of that, his house—the ancient
dwelling of his father, William Cogswell, one of the primitive settlers. On our left, in an elevated position, stands
the house of the widow Rust, and just south of that we
see the cleared spot, which had been leveled and prepared
for the meeting-house, but which our fathers abandoned
for the more convenient location before us. Before entering the church, sad news is spread from neighbor to neighbor which occasions many a sorrowful countenance. On
the evening before, a fishing boat arrived, which had a
narrow escape from pirates in the Bay; and which saw
them capture a Chebacco boat, and put several of their
piratical crew on board to convey her with our captured
men to a distant port. This is especially distressing to
those who have fathers or husbands, sons or brothers at
sea. The bell which calls us into the church, though new
and larger than the one upon the old house, is yet small
and shrill in its tones. As we enter the front door, the
pulpit is opposite to us, and a body of long seats before
us on each side of the broad aisle, while a tier of pews
line the walls on each side. The galleries are spacious
and well-filled. The view of so many aged men sitting
together, whose heads are covered with red caps, some of
worsted and some of velvet, attracts our attention. We
know the *Squire* of the place from his sitting at the head
of the most dignified seat. In the same seat with him
are those who bear the various military titles. In the
seats next to the pulpit are the children, that they may
be the more easily watched and cared for. While the
men with their sons are thus seated on the right of the
broad aisle, according to their various dignities, their wives
and daughters sit on the left side. The pulpit is lofty,
with a high sounding-board. In front of it and joined to
it is the elders' pew, and before that the deacons' seat.

In looking up, our eye meets the ridge-pole, and naked beams and rafters. Swallows have already begun to make their nests there. A basin of water is in its accustomed place before the pulpit. Nearly all the children born in the place,—five and twenty or thirty annually—are brought in their infancy for baptism. Mr. Wise enters and takes his seat in the pulpit, and the bell stops tolling. His appearance is quite changed since we first saw him in the pulpit forty years since. His white locks indicate advancing years. But though three-score and ten, his voice is yet firm and distinct. He commences the services of divine worship by reading a psalm from the old collection of Tate and Brady. This, one of the deacons repeats line by line, and pitches the tune, that it may be sung by the whole congregation. Mr. Wise in his prayer is solemn and fervent. In words of adoration, thanksgiving, confession and supplication he expresses the devotion and the desires of the worshiping assembly. He intercedes also for others, not forgetting the rulers of the land, the governor and council, and the representatives of the people, the king in the father-land, with the Parliament and all in authority. He remembers all that are in danger, in perils by land, in perils by sea, and prays especially for the deliverance of those neighbors and friends, that had fallen into the hands of pirates. "Great God," he fervently cries, "if there is no other way, may they rise and butcher their enemies;"—an expression long remembered, because the event showed that on that morning they rose upon the pirates and slew them, and thereby safely reached home. After another singing the sermon is delivered. Though not written, it has been well studied, for it is connected, instructive and impressive. As he occasionally holds up his notes, we see that they are written on a mere scrap of paper, a few inches square, containing in brief only the heads of the discourse, and a few leading thoughts. After sermon, an infant is brought forward for baptism. Its name is Aaron Foster. We look with deep interest upon

this infant face, for as we are spirits from a later age, we
can tell, without the gift of prophecy, what manner of
child this shall be. We can follow him through his childhood and youth, and see him rise into manhood. We see
him a young soldier in the combined army at the taking
of Louisburg. We behold him traversing the ocean, as the
captain of a vessel. We follow him into the Revolutionary army, fighting the battles of his country for liberty.
We see him after the war at the head of a numerous family, and find him still living in the nineteenth century.
And after his departure from life, we see at his funeral, not
only children, but a retinue of grandchildren, growing up
to respectability and usefulness, among whom we recognize Moses Foster of Wenham, Thomas Foster, and David
Choate of this place, and Rufus Choate of Boston. But
our thoughts have suddenly run down to a late day. We
recall them to witness the baptismal service; after which
a prayer is offered, and the assembly dismissed by the
apostolic benediction. As we retire we almost unconsciously reflect on the vanishing nature of earthly scenes.
How changed the congregation to-day, from that which
we saw in the old house forty years before, almost a whole
generation having passed away. The pastor remains, but
the deacons have gone, and with them all that were then
aged; and the young then that have escaped the stroke
of death, are now in the seats of the old.

1725, March 29. The parish assemble in the meeting-
house at nine o'clock, A. M., to see what measures they will
take to procure a preacher; as Mr. Wise, by reason of sickness, is unable to preach. They make choice of Theophilus Pickering, a young man recently licensed to preach, to
supply the pulpit for four Sabbaths, and choose Capt. Jonathan Cogswell to go to Salem and invite him to come. They
also vote that if he come he shall board at Capt. Cogswell's
which is near the church. At this meeting, also, they direct the trustees of the Parish to build a Pound. This is
doubtless the same that is now in use. In compliance with

their request. Mr. Pickering came and supplied the pulpit.
Mr. Wise lived only ten days after this, expiring on the
8th day of April. At the decease of Mr. Wise, the old parsonage, and the parish land reverted to the use of the parish, and they chose a committee to let the same for such
rents as they should judge proper. . They also voted £30
to defray the expenses of Mr. Wise's funeral. It was the
custom at that time, at the funeral of one who had been in
public life, or otherwise distinguished, to present gold rings
and gloves to the bearers, and other distinguished persons
present, besides making a general entertainment, in which
alcoholic drinks were freely dispensed according to the custom of the day. This accounts for the fact that a hundred
dollars should be expended at the funeral of a minister, including also, however, the monument for his grave. Mr.
Wise was buried from the new meeting-house, where for
the last seven years of his life he had preached on the Sabbath, and on Thursdays, the weekly lecture. How solemn
the scene, to behold the venerable form which a Sabbath
or two before had appeared in the pulpit in all the vigor
and activity of life, now lying in his coffin below, a pale,
breathless corpse. The house is filled, and every countenance is solemn and sad. The funeral sermon is preached
by Rev. John White, pastor of the first church in Gloucester, from II. Cor. iv. 7, first clause. Under the "*Improvement*" of the discourse, the preacher remarks:

"Fourth and lastly: Let us be duly affected and humbled when these
earthen vessels are broken to pieces, and can hold this treasure no more.
'Tis not to be so much wondered at, as lamented when earthen vessels are
dissolved. They are frail and infirm, and liable to many disasters. And
the more capacious and serviceable any such vessel was, the more reason we
have, to lay their dissolution to heart. On this sad occasion, God is calling
you in this Precinct to bitter mourning; and to lament with the church of
old, (Lam. v. 16.,) 'The crown is fallen from our head : Woe unto us that we
have sinned.' And I would heartily mourn with you. The very late decease of your reverend, aged, and faithful pastor has made a deep wound,
and wide breach. Your loss is great. Infinite Wisdom furnished, and suited
him for you ; and Infinite Love gave him to you, and continued him even to
old age among you ; and the Sovereign God has taken him from you. I

dare not presume (nor will the time allow me) to attempt to give you the *character* of the venerable Mr. Wise. He that would do it to the life must have his eloquence. Such as knew him best had the most honorable opinion of him and reverend respect for him. His kind, condescending, and most generous, and obliging carriage has often brought to remembrance, what is said of Titus Vespasianus, the Roman Emperor, viz., that no man ever went out of his presence sorrowful. And some who had viewed him at a distance through a false glass, when they have visited him, and familiarly conversed with him, have been charmed, and even ravished. They have beheld majesty mixed with affability, gravity with facetiousness, charity with severity; charity to the persons, and severity to the opinions of his antagonists. However he might be thought of, or represented by some, he had a high value and veneration for men of his *character* and *order:* and this was his language, living and dying, which he uttered to those about him on his death-bed, viz., I would have you pay a special veneration to your ministers. They are your great interest. Magistrates indeed preserve your lives and estates; but your ministers' business is to save your souls. Wherefore esteem them highly for their work's sake; and cultivate this spirit and principle into your children. He was zealously affected towards his country and the civil and sacred liberties and privileges of his country; and was willing to sacrifice anything but a good conscience to secure and defend them. And the thing he had most at heart was the wellbeing of the churches; and no risks were too great to run, no pains too great to take, to defend and confirm the *order* and established Constitution, or promote the purity and peace of the same. And when by reason of bodily infirmities the nearest and dearest relation would not draw him from home, the service of the churches would. And this was his *finishing work.* The success of these, his travels and labors, was to admiration. And some cases were attended with difficulties to an ordinary conduct and courage insuperable. I need not say to you, who were witnesses of these things, how prayer and patience carried him through all. He told me in the beginning of his sickness that he had been a man of contention, but the state of the churches making it necessary, upon the most serious review, he could say he had fought a good fight, and had comfort in reflecting upon the same. He was conscious to himself of his acting therein sincerely. At the same time he expressed his nothingness, and unworthiness: and as he needed the divine compassion and mercy, so he entirely depended upon, and earnestly prayed for the free grace of God in Christ. Can I do less than say (on this mournful occasion) as the surprised and inspired prophet Elisha, when he beheld the prophet Elijah ascend in a chariot of fire: "My Father, my Father, the Chariot of Israel and the Horsemen thereof."*

---

* "The Gospel Treasure in Earthen Vessels. A Funeral Sermon on the mournful occasion of the Death of that Faithful Servant of God, the Reverend Mr. John Wise, Pastor of the Second Church in Ipswich. Preached to his Flock on the 11th day of April, 1725. By John White, A. M., Pastor of the First Church in Gloucester. Zech. i. 5. Boston. Printed for N. Boone, Cornhill, 1725." A copy of this sermon is now in the library of the Salem Athenæum.

18

We see in the procession, as it moves in slow and solemn pace from the church to the grave-yard, the bereaved widow and children and grandchildren, with other relatives, and the officers and members of the church, and of the parish, with many strangers. The bearers or pall-holders were all ministers, who wore white leather gloves —the badge of mourning common in that day, and presented to them on this occasion by the parish. Mr. Wise's remains were interred near the centre of the *grave-yard*, and soon afterwards the mound was covered with a slab containing the following inscription:

UNDERNEATH LIES THE BODY OF THE
REV. JOHN WISE, A. M.
FIRST PASTOR OF THE 2D CHURCH IN IPSWICH.

Graduated at Harvard College, 1673.
Ordained Pastor of said Church, 1681.
And died April 8, 1725,
Aged 73.

FOR TALENTS, PIETY AND LEARNING,
HE SHONE AS A STAR OF THE
FIRST MAGNITUDE.

In 1815 the slab was elevated upon four granite pillars, and a copy of this inscription cut in slate, inserted in place of the original which had been broken.

By his will it appears that Mr. Wise left a widow and seven children. To three of his sons, Jeremiah, Henry, and Joseph, he had given a collegiate education. To John the youngest, he bequeathed his real estate—a house, barn, and ten acres of land—out of which Mrs. Wise was to have her maintenance. She, however, deceased October 18th of the same year. To the other children he left a thousand dollars to be divided equally among them. His library was to be divided between Jeremiah and Henry, with the exception of the following books bequeathed to John: *Gurnel's Armor of Light, Dalton's County Justice*, and *Speed's Chronicles of England.*

Three deacons of his church had deceased during Mr. Wise's ministry: John Burnham, November 5th, 1694,

Thomas Low, April 12th, 1712, aged 80, William Good-hue, 1712. The number of church members at the time of his decease was 91. One of the vessels of the communion service purchased during his ministry, is still in the possession and use of the church. It is a cup, marked "*C. C.*" (Chebacco Church,) "1712."

The principal events in the life of Mr. Wise have been already noticed. In addition to these, it is of some interest to know that his labors as a minister were not limited wholly to this parish. Before coming to Chebacco, he had preached a year at Northampton, and had a call to settle there. On the 5th of July, 1690, he was appointed by the General Court, chaplain in an expedition which had just been planned against Canada. The occasion of this expedition was the fact that on the breaking out of a war between England and France the previous year, the offer of colonial neutrality had been rejected by England; that parties of French and Indians had attacked and destroyed Schenectady, Salmon Falls, Casco, and other frontier settlements, and that French privateers from Nova Scotia were infesting the coasts of New England. The provinces therefore formed the bold and hazardous design of reducing Canada to subjection to the crown of England, as the only means of securing their own permanent peace and safety. Accordingly, on the 9th of August, a force of thirty vessels, and about two thousand troops sailed from Boston, under command of Sir William Phips, and arrived at the Isle of Orleans, four miles below Quebec, on the 5th of October, having been retarded by unavoidable accidents. But the troops from Connecticut and New York, who were to march from Albany on Montreal, and prevent Count Frontenac from re-enforcing Quebec, did not succeed in reaching their destination. The garrison at Quebec was, therefore, so much increased in numbers, its fortifications so much strengthened, before the arrival of Phips and his little army, that the expedition was entirely unsuccessful. After two attacks upon the town the assailants withdrew, and re-embarking, reached Boston November 19th.   It is recorded of Mr. Wise that he distinguished himself in this expedition by his *heroic spirit* and *martial skill*, as well as by the faithful discharge of the sacred duties that more immediately devolved upon him.   His services to his country in the army, as well as his sufferings in prison at an earlier period, show that his zeal for her cause was pure, intense, and unceasing.   And from all his public career, we are assured that he was a great and good man.   Every good work of every kind, he favored and encouraged.*

His writings furnish abundant proof that he was an original thinker, a close reasoner, a profound scholar, an energetic writer, aiming not to display himself, but to unfold and inculcate his subject.†   As a preacher, he was instructive, impressive, and persuasive.   His ministry was eminently successful.   Not less than two hundred hopeful converts, as is inferred from a comparison of facts, were added to the church during his pastorate.   Testimony to the excellence of his character is found in the standard works on the lives of our Puritan fathers.   The printed copy of the sermon at his funeral, which has been already quoted, also contains what is entitled, "A character of the Reverend Mr. John Wise, by another hand :"

"On the 8th of April, died at Ipswich the Rev. Mr. J. Wise, the worthy Pastor of the church of Chebacco, and on the 11th, was decently buried amidst the honors, and lamentations of his distressed friends, and of his loving and generous flock, and at their expense.   Nor would they be satisfied without his Interment with them.   Who being their Glory while among the living, even his lifeless body might be an ornament in the Dormitory of the Dead.   He was a gentleman of such uncommon merit, that it is no easy task to do justice to his character, and pay a suitable deference to the honor of his mem-

* 1720, Thomas Symmes, having issued his dialogue to promote the revival of singing by note more extensively, remarks in it, "I received a letter from Mr. Wise of Ipswich, wherein he gave it as his judgment that when there were a sufficient number in a congregation to carry away a tune roundly, it was then proper to introduce that tune."

† From the numerous allusions and quotations in his works, it is plain that his library must have contained the best of the Greek and Roman classics, and works upon Greek, Roman, Ecclesiastical, and English History; and that he must have been as thoroughly conversant with ancient literature and philosophy, as with Christian theology and Biblical science.

ory. He was richly adorned with the beauties of Nature and Grace, and brightly polished with the Ornaments of the best Erudition. The graceful structure of his manly body, majestic aspect, and sweet deportment, were but an emblem of the mighty Genius, and brighter excellencies of his superior soul. He had a strong and elevated Fancy, solid Wisdom, steady Fortitude, great Generosity, Courtesie, and Integrity; and above all a zealous Piety, and liberal Charity, which nobly furnished him for the great services that Providence designed him for, and employed him in, and were so many gems in the crown of honor, that shone upon his hoary head to the close of his life, and ever commanded the love, and veneration of all about him. He was a great Divine, and an able Minister of the New Testament, and had a peculiar Talent for composing Church controversies, and Ecclesiastical difficulties, and was happy in a constant success in it. He was a learned scholar, and an eloquent Orator, as his excellent writings and discourses testify. He was of a generous and publick spirit, a great lover of his country, and our happy Constitution; a studious assertor, and faithful defender of its liberties and interests. He gave singular proof of this at a time when our Liberties, and all things were in danger. And with undaunted courage he withstood the bold invasions that were made upon us. He was next called (in his own order) to accompany our forces in an unhappy expedition, where not only the pious discharge of his sacred office, but his heroic spirit, and martial skill, and wisdom, did greatly distinguish him. A third remarkable was his appearing in defense of our Church Constitution both by his valuable writings, and observable actions, and when great dissensions arose in some churches, and difficulties thereupon, (though to others insuperable,) yet his wise counsels, forcible arguments, irresistible eloquence, inimitable zeal, courage, candor, and diligence did so happily succeed, as to accommodate all things, and procure and establish the Peace, and Order of the Churches wherever he was called. And upon the whole, justice and gratitude both oblige us to give him the Title of a Patron of his Country and a Father in Israel, and to join with an eminent minister in his publick mention of him, that he was our Elijah, the Chariot of Israel, and the Horsemen thereof, our Glory and Defense."

The precise time when the church and parish gave a call to Mr. Pickering to become their pastor, cannot now be ascertained. He accepted their invitation, however, on condition that the salary they had proposed to give him should be increased, giving his reasons for this in the following language:

" Whereas our Lord Jesus has required of his people a suitable support for his ministers, as yourselves know and believe, and whereas it nearly concerns every minister upon settlement to see to it that he has a convenient maintenance, and as far as may be to prevent any after difficulties that might be prejudicial to the peace of the place and success of the ministry, I have, therefore, after due deliberation, thought it best that I should freely offer my thoughts unto you referring to this head of maintenance. We all know that a minister cannot live creditably without considerable expenses, and we also know that what was wont to be a middling salary formerly, in a moderate value, is equivalent to £150 or £160 in our paper money. Indeed such a sum makes a great sound in a man's ears; but ordinarily men don't seriously consider (unless it be in case of their own interest,) how our Province bills are depreciated, nor how the price of goods and provisions rises, and for this reason salary men in many towns almost suffer for want. For my own part I cannot (and I think I ought not) be contented unless I have wherewithal conveniently to answer my duties and necessities, and to furnish me with such helps and advantages as whereby I might be enabled in my best manner to serve your true interests and maintain the character of a minister as it should be; which to be sure will not be displeasing to any of you, for I am confident it would not offend you to have your minister a credit to you."

With these views the parish harmoniously concurred, and the result was that they agreed to give him the use of all the parsonage lands, they keeping the fences in repair, and £120 annually in semi-annual payments, to be increased or diminished in proportion to the value of money (silver) at 8s. per ounce troy-weight; and the avails of the customary contribution taken on the Sabbath. For a settlement, they agreed to give him the buildings on the old parsonage, and £100 toward building a house for himself. The house which he built and lived in during his ministry, was the one subsequently owned by the late Mrs. Mary Choate. The commoners also gave him the common land north of the meeting-house, being about three-fourths of an acre. The terms of settlement were agreed on in July, but the ordination was deferred to a season less busy for farmers. Accordingly on the 23d of October following, with the usual solemnities and interesting services, he was ordained in the new meeting-house to the work of the gospel ministry in this place.

1726. While occupied with the affairs of the parish, we would not forget that our fathers are still citizens of Ipswich. To the body of the town they go for the trans-

action of all town affairs. Once a year, in the month of
March, the legal voters are expected to assemble in the first
parish meeting-house for the choice of town officers and
other business, and in April, annually for the election of
Province officers. All intending marriage go to the centre
for certificates of publishment. Families needing a physician must send five miles for him. The poor are provided for in the body of the town, where is the alms-house
upon the common, built of logs, forty feet long, sixteen
wide, and six high. The tenants of the school farm on
the south side of the river still carry to the centre their
annual rent of £14 for the support of the Grammar school.
The Indians have nearly all disappeared; but the wild
beasts still inhabit the woods and set up their nightly howl.
With the closing of this year ends the first Record book,
which contains the transactions of the parish for the first
fifty years, including those connected with its origin.

1727. This year there was experienced in this place,
in common with others, a great earthquake. It occurred
on the 29th of October. About forty minutes after ten
at night, when there was a serene sky, and calm but sharp
air, a most amazing noise was heard, like to the roaring
of a chimney when on fire, as some said, only beyond all
comparison greater. Others compared it to the noise of
coaches upon pavements, and thought that the noise of
ten thousand together would not have exceeded it. The
noise was judged by some to continue about half a minute
before the shock began, which increased gradually, and
was thought to have continued for the space of a minute,
before it was at the height, and in about half a minute
more, to have been at an end, by a gradual decrease. The
noise and shock of this, and of all earthquakes which preceded it in New England, were observed to come from the
West and go off to the East. At Newbury and other
towns on the Merrimack, the shock was greater than in
any other part of the State. No buildings were thrown
down, but parts of the walls of several cellars fell in and

the tops of many chimneys were shaken off. The earth burst open in several places, and more than a hundred cart loads of earth were thrown out. The seamen upon the coast supposed their vessels to have struck on a shoal of loose ballast. More gentle shocks were frequently felt for some months after. " There have seldom passed above fifteen or twenty years without an earthquake, but there had been none very violent within the memory of any then living. There was a general apprehension of danger, of destruction, and death ; and many who had very little sense of religion before, appeared to be very serious and devout penitents. But too generally as the fears of another earthquake went off, the religious impressions went off with them." * In this place the earthquake was followed by a powerful revival of religion, in which many gave evidence of having become new creatures in Christ. The number of church members at Mr. Pickering's ordination was ninety-one. It was soon increased to one hundred and seventy-seven, seventy-six of whom were added to the church as the fruits of this revival.

Upon the death of George I., this year, his son, George II., ascended the throne of England. To our fathers the death of one sovereign and the accession of another were events of the deepest interest, since the appointment of their governor depended on the pleasure of the crown, and the whole aspect of their political affairs took its hue from the royal countenance. On the accession of George II., Burnet, a son of the bishop of Salisbury, who was at this time governor of New Jersey and New York, was appointed governor of Massachusetts and New Hampshire. Gov. Shute had returned to England three years before this, with many and bitter complaints against Massachusetts, as not sufficiently loyal, and too much inclined to independence. The consequence was that Massachusetts was obliged to accept an explanatory charter, which confirmed the right of the governor to negative the speaker

---

* Hutchinson's History of Massachusetts.

of the House, and forbade the House to adjourn for more
than two days without his consent.   During Gov. Shute's
absence, Lt. Gov. Dummer, a native of Newbury, managed
the affairs of the Province.   He continued to act as governor till Burnet arrived, and again at his death till Belcher
took the gubernatorial chair.   Gov. Dummer, at his decease,
bequeathed a valuable estate in Byfield toward supporting
a grammar school there.   This is now Dummer Academy.

1728.   As Capt. Thomas Choate has been the representative of the town to the Great and General Court for
several years, we will make an excursion to Hogg Island,
and learn of him something of the political affairs of the
Province, and of the doings of the Court.   Mr. Choate is
a man of strong mind, extensive information, and well
qualified to express what he knows with clearness, precis-
ion and force.   Though living upon an island, his influence
is felt in all public matters.   Ipswich, which stands next
to Salem, and near to Boston in political importance, would
not be represented in the government of the Province by
a man of inferior abilities.   Our visit is on a bright summer's morning, when the sun gladdens all the salt meadows,
and the birds carol from the neighboring bushes and trees,
reminding us of the poetic words of the Ettrick shepherd:*

> " O never before looked a morning so fair
> Or the sunbeam so sweet on the lea !
> The song of the merl from her old hawthorn tree
>   And the blackbird's melodious lay,
> All sounded to him like an anthem of love,
> A song that the spirit of nature did move,
> A kind little hymn to their Maker above
>   Who gave them the beauties of day."

As we approach the island we see that like most other
portions of the town it is in a great part covered with a
thick forest.   Mr. C. has cleared for himself an excellent
farm, and has vigorous sons to cultivate it.   Eleven children with himself and wife constitute the family.   After

---

*James Hogg.

an introduction and remarks on the weather, &c., we express to him our desire that he would give us some little account of affairs in Boston, and of our prospects for civil and religious liberty.

"I can relate to you a few things," he says, "which have come under my own observation during the few years I have been at Court. Aside from our trouble with the Indians, which I hope is nearly at an end, our chief labor and difficulty have been to preserve our rights and liberties from royal encroachments. Our kingly governors set their mark too high for the prerogatives of the crown, and for their own independence above the will of the people. They require not only a large salary, but also that we should place it beyond our own control, by making it permanent, or during their continuance in office. This, we think, is contrary to our liberties and privileges, as Englishmen, given us by Magna Charta. It is true his majesty has a salary fixed for life. But he is the father of his subjects, while our governors have no other interest with us, than to fill their purses and carry away what they can. There is no other way, we think, to ensure their good behavior, and make their administration for the public good, than to make them dependent for their living on those whom they serve. If the people furnish the money for all public uses, it belongs to them to say how it shall be disposed of. The keys of their own treasury they have a right to keep in their own hands. For this most essential principle of liberty, we have been obliged to contend with all our royal governors. Dummer has been more pacific and yielding, in some respects, than the rest of them ; yet he has contended for a portion of the people's money, in a yearly stipend, without the people's yearly consent. So wearisome have been our contests with his majesty's servants on this point, and so unbecoming their language often to us, that when, on a certain occasion, a motion was made for a grant to a governor to bear the expense of his lady's funeral, an old representative dryly remarked that he objected to a grant for the governor's *lady ;* had the motion been for a grant to bury the *governor* himself, he should have thought the money well laid out.

"Another dark spot in our political horizon is the increased issue of Province bills. This is owing to the mistaken notion that an increase of currency in bills of credit, will not only revive trade, but be a remedy for all the evils felt from the depreciation of bills already in circulation. This is much the same as if a man, whose blood is in a corrupt state, should seek to restore it by high living. We look for the time when both of these dark clouds, which so strongly threaten our peace and prosperity, shall with the blessing of heaven, break and disappear."

In full concurrence with these sentiments of Mr. Choate, we take leave, and return from the island.

1729. This year a native of Chebacco, a son of our

first minister, has the honor of preaching the Election Sermon in Boston. It was delivered, as the title-page says, "Before his Excellency, William Burnet, esq., the Honourable, the Lieutenant-Governor, the Council and representatives of the Province of the Massachusetts Bay, May 28, being the day for the election of his Majesty's Council. By Jeremiah Wise, M. A., Pastor to a Church of Christ in Berwick. Sold at the Bible and Three Crowns near the Town Dock, Boston." The text is Rom. xiii. 4 : "For he is the minister of God to thee for good." The subject of the discourse is, "Civil Rulers should improve all their power and influence for the best good of a people." Among the various ways mentioned of doing this, is, taking care of the education of youth, and making suitable provision for the support of it. We give the following extracts as a specimen of the sermon :

"The education of youth is a great benefit and service to the publick. This is that which civilizes them, takes down their temper, tames the fierce-ness of their natures, forms their minds to virtue, learns them to carry it with a just deference to superiors, makes them tractable or manageable, and by learning and knowing what it is to be under government, they will know bet-ter how to govern others when it comes to their turn. And thus it tends to good order in the State. Yea, good education tends to promote religion and reformation as well as peace and order; as it gives check to idleness and ignorance, and the evil consequences thereof. Further by this means men are fitted for service for publick stations in Church and State, and to be pub-lick blessings. The publick would greatly suffer by the neglect thereof, and religion could not subsist long, but would decay and even die without it. The public weal depends upon it, and therefore it ought to be the publick care, and so it has been in the best formed Commonwealths who have erected and endowed publick schools and colleges for the education of youth.

"This was our fathers' early care, even in the infancy of the country, and their pious zeal for the glory of God and the good of their posterity, has been remarkably blessed. Learning has flourished greatly under the care of the government, new colleges have been erected, and God has raised up gen-erous friends to become benefactors to them."

In his address to the rulers, he says:

"It is worthy of your serious inquiry, whether there has been enough done to guard the sanctity of the Sabbath, and to prevent the disorders, which too many in country towns are guilty of, in the intervals of divine service and on the evenings after it. Whether there may not be something further done to prevent the growth of intemperance, which has increased so much by yearly accessions, and threatens to deluge the country."

The sermon consists of fifty-four printed pages, and does honor to the talents, learning, and fidelity of the author. Gov. Burnet's administration was short,—a little more than a year, and almost wholly spent in warm altercation with the Honorable House, in regard to a fixed salary. His want of success affected his spirits. He fell sick of a fever and died on the 7th of September, 1729. He was succeeded by Jonathan Belcher, a native of Massachusetts, but at that time a merchant in London. He arrived in the following August. Like his predecessors, he proposed a fixed salary. · Like them he saw the proposal repelled with decision and firmness. Seeing the cause to be desperate, he obtained leave from the crown to receive such grants as should be made to him. Thus ended the controversy which had been carried on for more than forty years. Our fathers triumphed and maintained their liberty in the face of all the opposition of the British court, and the strenuous efforts of the royal governors.

1732. The fishery was successfully carried on here, and in the centre of the town. The town by a vote passed the year before, require the names of all the crews of the fishing vessels in the town to be entered with the town clerk, on penalty of £20 for every omission.

Leonard Cotton, the school-master, is allowed by this parish the use of the school land. He had taught one year before this, and continued one year after.

1733. Died July 9th, Dea. John Choate, eldest son of the first settler of that name, and brother of Capt. Thomas Choate. He was born in 1660, married Miss Elizabeth Giddings, and settled on the farm now owned by Darius Cogswell. He had six sons, four of whom died young. In 1712, he was chosen deacon of Mr. Wise's church. His age was 73.

Jonathan Cogswell, commissioned a justice of the peace, October 26, 1733, was a great-grandson of the first settler of that name and was the father of the late Col. Jonathan Cogswell. He was married July 1, 1731 to Miss Elizabeth Wade of Ipswich, and resided on the Cogswell farm which he inherited. He died May 2d, 1752. There is good traditional authority for believing that the frame, chimneys, and a large part of the wood-work within, of the house, which was the residence of the late Adam Boyd, were built by Mr. Cogswell. One of the volumes, which, as a magistrate, he must have had frequent occasion to consult, has been preserved to the present time. It is a large, heavily bound book, entitled " Acts and Laws of his Majesty's Province of the Massachusetts Bay in New England, passed by the Great and General Court or Assembly of the Massachusetts Bay, published in 1726." The oldest enactments in it are dated, 1692. His commission, with the signature of the Province officers, is also extant. The following is an exact copy of it:

" George the Second, by the Grace of God, of Great Britain, France and Ireland King, Defender of the Faith, &c. To all unto whom these Presents shall come, Greeting : Know ye that We have assigned and constituted, and do by these Presents assign, constitute and appoint our trusty and well-beloved Jonathan Cogswell, to be one of our Justices to keep our Peace in the County of Essex, within our Province of the Massachusetts Bay, in New England, and to keep and cause to be kept the laws and ordinances made for the good of the Peace and for the Conservation of the same and for the quiet Rule and Government of our People, in the said County, in all and every the articles thereof, according to the force, Form and effect of the same, and to chastise and Punish all Persons offending against the Form of those Laws and ordinances, or any of them, in the county aforesaid, as according to the form of those Laws and ordinances shall be fit to be done, and to cause to come before him the' Said Jonathan Cogswell those that shall break the peace, or attempt anything against the same, or that shall threaten any of our People in their persons, or in *burning* their houses, to find sufficient security for the peace and for the good behaviour towards us and our people, and if they shall refuse to find such security, then to cause to be kept safe in Prison until they shall find the same, and to do and perform in the county aforesaid all and whatsoever according to the laws and ordinances of our province afores[d] or any of them, a Justice of the Peace may and ought to do and perform, and with other our Justices of the Peace in our said county (according to the Tenour of the commission to them Granted,) to enquire by the oaths of good and lawful men of our said County, by whom the truth may be the better known of all and all manner of thefts, Trespasses, Riots, Routs and unlawful assemblies whatsoever, and all singular other misdeeds and offences of which Justices of the Peace in their general Sessions may and ought to inquire, by whomsoever or howsoever done or perpetrated, or which shall here-after happen howsoever to be done or attempted in the county aforesaid con-trary to the form of the Laws and ordinances aforesaid made for the common good of our Province afores[d] and the People thereof, and with other Justices in our s[d] County (according to the Tenour of the commission to them Granted as afores[d]) to hear and determine all and singular the said Thefts, Trespasses, Riots, Routs, unlawful assemblies, and all and singular other the Premises, and to do therein as to Justice appertaineth according to the Laws, Statutes and ordinances aforse[d]; In Testimony whereof We have caused the Publick Seal of our Province of the Massachusetts Bay aforesaid to be hereunto affixed.

"Witness Jonathan Belcher, our captain-General and Governour-in-Chief of our Province, at Boston, the twenty-sixth Day of October, 1733, In the seventh year of our reign.

"By order of the Governour, with the advice and consent of the Council.
"J. WILLARD, *Sec'y.*   J. BELCHER."

THE FIRST COLLEGE GRADUATE FROM CHEBACCO.

1734. Rev. John Eveleth, whose death occurred August 1, of this year, was the first Chebacco boy who received a liberal education. He was the son of Joseph and Mary Eveleth, and was born in Gloucester on the 18th of De-cember, 1669, of which town his grandfather, Sylvester Eveleth, (or Eveleigh as it was then written,) became a resident about the year 1648. When John was about five years of age, in the year 1674, his father removed with his family to Chebacco where he spent the remainder of his life and where he died December 1, 1745, at the extraordinary age of 105 years. "It is said that he was remarkable for his piety, and that a few years before his death (probably in 1740), he was visited by the celebrated preacher, Rev. George Whitefield, on one of his journeys through this town from Boston to Newburyport, who, in accordance with an ancient custom kneeled down before this venerable patriarch and received his blessing." John was fitted for college at the Ipswich grammar school, and was graduated at Harvard College in 1689. As soon as he had studied divinity sufficiently, he commenced preaching at Manchester, and continued to supply the pulpit there until 1695. On the 13th of May, 1700, he was invited to preach in the town of Stowe. He accepted this· invitation and remained there seventeen years, although the organization of a church, and his ordination as its pastor, did not take place until three or four years after his call. Dismissed. in December, 1717, he was settled again in 1719, at Arundel (now Kennebunkport, Me.,) and his pastorate there extended to the year 1729. During three years of this ministry, he divided his services equally between the towns of Arundel and Biddeford. He also acted as chaplain to some provincial forces stationed in the vicinity, from January 11, 1724, till the middle of 1726, or later. He resigned his ministerial charge much against the wishes of the inhabitants, " as he was not only their minister and school-master, but a good blacksmith and farmer, and the best fisherman in town." His remaining years, at least till 1732, were spent in the same town. He was buried "in the town of Kittery, near Eliot." Mr. Eveleth's brother James was the father of Aaron Eveleth, and the grandfather of the late Jonathan Eveleth.

John Burnham, 3d, has the improvement of the school pasture, as school-master of the place. In addition to what is raised here, a committee is appointed to receive from the town their proportion of £100, raised for the support of schools in the several parishes.

At a meeting in May, a committee is chosen to wait on Mr. Pickering, and inquire on what terms he will sell to them the lot of land given him by the commoners, lying on the north of the meeting-house, joining upon Joseph and Robert Rust's land, Thomas Varney's, and the Gloucester road, measuring one hundred and twenty-three square rods. Mr. Pickering afterward conveyed this lot to the parish by deed. At a meeting in August they

voted, that in consideration of their love and affection to
the Rev. Theophilus Pickering, they do freely, fully and
absolutely give, grant and convey to him, and his heirs and
assigns forever, all their right, title and interest in the land
on which the fence in front of his house stands, and the
land enclosed by the same, and also in the well dug by
him on the south-easterly side of the road. This year they
add fifty pounds to his salary, on account of the depreciation of currency. They had been gradually increasing
it years before, and continued so to do till his salary
amounted to two hundred and thirty-two pounds.

1735. The most extensive and fatal epidemic which had
been known in New England since its settlement by our
fathers, prevailed in this and other towns. It was called
the *throat distemper*. The throat swelled with white or
ash colored specks, an effloresence appeared on the skin,
there was a great debility of the whole system, and a
strong tendency to putridity. The distress and anguish
were often indescribable. The writhings and contortions
of the patient seemed as great as if he were on a bed of
burning coals. It spent its force chiefly in the northern
part of this county, and in some of the adjacent towns
in New Hampshire. It was confined to no season of the
year but prevailed and continued with more or less severity through every month. Some families lost all their
children. In some towns one-seventh part of the population were cut down by it.

The parish, relying upon the constable, who had unexpectedly gone to sea, to collect their taxes, and the time
for legally choosing a collector having gone by, are compelled to petition the State authorities for leave to choose
one out of season. The form then used may give us some
idea of the olden time in such matters:

" To his Excellency Jonathan Belcher, esq., Captain-General and Governour-
in-Chief in and over his Majesty's precincts of the Massachusetts Bay in New
England, and the Hon. his Majesty's Council, and the Hon. the House of
Representatives in General Court assembled in June, 1735, the petition," &c.

This year the vegetable potato was brought into the place for the first time. Mr. Cavies, whose house stood near the dwelling of Mrs. Griggs, being in Salem and seeing potatoes on board of a coasting vessel, bought a small quantity and sold them to his neighbors for seed. They were first planted in beds, and for some years after, a bushel was considered a great crop. The mode of cooking was to cut them in slices and boil with soup.

1738. The parish direct the trustees to take down the turret, lest it should fall and damnify the meeting-house. They afterwards erected a new one.

As this is a leisure season, and somewhat dry (historically), we will accompany our fathers to the woods on a deer hunt. As deerskin is a staple article for small clothes, and mittens, and can be had only by hunting, and the flesh is fine venison, such excursions are not infrequent. We assemble with our hunting party on the common by the school-house, on a fine moonlight evening in November. A moderate fall of snow makes the woods more light and pleasant, and will help us in our hunting match. We enter the woods just north of the common, between Joseph Rust's and Thomas Varney's, taking a west-north-west direction. Our huntsmen have their horns and their dogs, and the scene is greatly enlivened by the blowing of the one and the barking and frisking of the other. Plenty of hand-sleds are taken with us to draw back the fruit of our game. Our cheering and shouting and barking are responded to by the howling of the wolves, which are on the alert. They are disposed to approach us, but the flash and report of a gun now and then starts them off again. We now come to Belcher's lane, and as we cross it we see the light from his dwelling. On entering the thick woods again, we incline towards the hills on the left. Occasionally a fox is seen darting swiftly before us. They are out of their holes in the stillness of the night to gather up their wonted food. Some of our huntsmen let fly at them, and the dogs bound off in pur-

20

suit, but they are too swift and wary to be taken, so the dogs are called back. Our most experienced huntsmen caution us to take care of ourselves when we come upon the deer. Though timid animals, they are full of craft, and when hard pushed, without any way of escape, are apt to rush upon their assailants, and do injury with their furious horns. There are signs of a herd not far off, and we are directed to restrain all noise and proceed softly. The dogs take the hint, and are as mute and cautious as any of us. Approaching the foot of a hill we come in sight of them. The whole herd are upon their feet listening to our approach, and in a moment they bound off, but not till our guns have brought some of them to the ground. Our huntsmen follow and the dogs are in full chase. Some that were wounded are held at bay by the hounds, the huntsman's spear finishes the work of death upon them, and all gather round blowing the horns in triumph for such a victory. We load up our victims and set out for our return. As we traverse the thick forest our spirits anticipate the day, a hundred years later when all these trees will disappear, and through this lone valley, the steam engine may be flying with greater rapidity than the deer, drawing scores of busy travelers after it. Such a suggestion to our fathers, however, would appear like the wildest of all dreams.

1740. John Varney, a fugitive British man-of-war's man, stopped at Esquire Choate's door, and asked for food, which was given him. He was also allowed to spend the night. By way of payment for the favor, he began to chop wood at the door, and remained with the family until he had cut all the wood, and helped about the farm. The "commoners" or land-holders, at some meeting, voted that Varney might have a certain poor rocky piece of land, situated about two miles south-west from the meeting-house. Varney was very industrious, built walls, planted fruit-trees, and brought the land into a good state of cultivation. Varney was a conscientious church-goer. At

Christmas the old people far and near would visit him, carrying provisions for him in wallets upon their shoulders. Poor Varney would talk of "Old England," and weep like a child because he would never see it again. "Skipper" Wesley Burnham, when a very small boy, ate of the fruit which Varney raised; the trees were standing but a few years ago. The land is now the property of the heirs of the late Zaccheus Burnham, and the site of the house and barn is still pointed out; although it is at present a heavily timbered woodland. The smallness of the inclosures, for the stone walls are still standing, is a curiosity, not to say a mystery, as very little use could apparently have been made of them.

1742. The house of Joseph Belcher was consumed by fire. The Parish vote that the money which they had taken by contribution on the Sabbath for sufferers by fire in Carolina, but which had not been sent on there, should be given to their neighbor, Mr. Belcher. They also request their minister to have another contribution taken for the benefit of some others that were found to be needy among them.

This year they vote for the first time that their school shall be taught two months of the year on the south side of the river, and two months at the Falls. They had been in the habit, for a series of years, of uniting with the Hamlet parish in hiring a teacher for the year, who was to divide his time between the two parishes as their respective school committees might agree. When the Hamlet did not join with them, they usually voted to employ a teacher for the year in this place. It was at such times probably that they allowed it to be taught four months in other parts of the town, in rooms provided by the inhabitants in those neighborhoods, while the other eight months were spent in the school-house. This tells nobly for the zeal of our fathers in the cause of education. In addition to their portion of the town's money for schooling, they taxed themselves as a parish for the same purpose, to the amount of £20 or more. At one time they petitioned the town for a portion of the grammar school rents; at another, that the grammar school might be taught a portion of the year in Chebacco, both of which were unsuccessful.. They vote, this year, that the parents shall pay three pence per week for each child sent to school. The administration of the new governor was a subject of much conversation at this time with our fathers. Gov. Shirley was born in England and bred a lawyer. Having a numerous family, he removed to this country, and opened an office in Boston. When the news came of his being appointed governor, July, 1741, he was in Rhode Island, as counsel for Massachusetts before a court of commissioners appointed to settle the bounds between the two Provinces. It was matter of much speculation with the politicians of the day, what course he would pursue in regard to the great points of controversy between the people and the crown. Events, however, soon showed that he was disposed to favor the people by following the royal instructions according to their spirit as he apprehended them, and not strictly according to their letter. His favorite measure for the taking of Louisbourg, caused him to yield still more to the people, that they might be disposed to yield to him.

1744–5. News of war with France and Spain being received, preparations began to be made for the invasion of Nova Scotia. These were not completed till March of the following year, when the troops sailed from Boston— the land forces thirty-eight hundred in number, under the command of Col. William Pepperell, the naval force under Commodore Warren. The grand design was the capture of Louisburg, styled the Dunkirk of America. Its fortifications had employed French troops twenty-five years, and cost thirty millions of livres. Among the three thousand troops called out from the several towns for this expedition Ipswich, as usual, furnished its full proportion, which included several from this part of the town. Tradition mentions Aaron Foster among them, then a young man of twenty-three. We will call at his father's at the old Foster house, at the Falls, near the south-westerly junction of the old and new roads to the Center, and hear from the young soldier the account which he may be supposed to have given on his return. Several of the neighbors are in, and the youthful adventurer thus proceeds:

"After we were drafted, we put our fire-arms in order, and equipped ourselves for a campaign of several months. On receiving notice we repaired to Boston, and were put on board one of the transports; all of which, convoyed by the Shirley, sailed from Nantasket roads the next morning, 24th of March. We had pretty good weather for the season; but owing to some head winds we did not pass Cape Sable under several days, and it was not till the 2d of April that we began to steer more northerly for the Gulf of St. Lawrence, and on the 4th we put in at Canso. Here we were joined by the troops of New Hampshire and Connecticut, making our whole land force above four thousand strong. Learning that there was so much ice about the island of Cape Breton, that it would be of no use for us to proceed, we waited three weeks in the harbor of Canso. Soon after we had orders from the General to get under way, and our whole fleet made for Cape Breton, and on the 30th of April anchored in Chapeau Rouge Bay. We were discovered early in the morning, and a detachment of one hundred and fifty men was sent to prevent our landing. But our General was crafty, and making a pretence of landing at one place drew the enemy there, while a hundred of our men landed at another. These were soon attacked by the enemy, but we killed six of them and took as many more prisoners. We should soon have taken the whole, if they had not fled to the town, for our men were fast landing, one upon the back of another. About a mile beyond us on the same point of land was the grand battery to guard the entrance to the town from the harbor. A quantity of pitch, tar, and other combustibles in the storehouses that we burnt, caused a thick smoke, and the wind driving it directly into the battery the enemy were terrified, fearing that our whole force was upon them. They deserted the fort at once, having spiked their cannon and thrown their powder into a well. A small party of our men went up to the fort first, but discovering no signs of life suspected a plot and were afraid to enter, but a Cape Cod Indian crept slyly in, and finding it empty, soon made the fact known and our men rushed in just as the French were returning to take possession of it. Thus was a stronghold gained by us without any expense of blood or treasure. Maj. Pomeroy of Northampton in our Province, was placed at the head of twenty of our soldiers, that were smiths, for the purpose of drilling the cannon which had been spiked. They soon had them in readiness for use again, and the enemy's fire from the town and from another battery on an island in the harbor was briskly returned by us, with great damage to the houses in the town. Several attempts were made to take the island, but in vain. At the last attempt we had sixty killed and one hundred and sixteen taken prisoners. There was no hope left but to scale the walls, which could not be done without planting our cannon and mortars near, to cover our men in the attack. This was a difficult problem to work out, for there was a boggy morass to be crossed over, which wheels could not pass, and men would sink to their middle in the mud. In despair of getting over the bogs it occurred to one of our officers, Capt. Noyes of Newburyport, that there were several hundred pairs of snow-shoes in camp, in expectation of a winter's campaign. He put on a pair, and found he could walk upon the morass perfectly well. This removed the difficulty. Drags were constructed by our carpenters, twenty feet by sixteen, smooth and flat at the bottom. Noyes had the cannon placed upon them, and selecting fifty men accustomed to snow-shoes, and fixing a long rope to the drag, we walked the morass at the dead of night without difficulty, and placed the cannon where Col. Vaughan directed, covering them well with sea-weed, so that where there appeared only a mass of sea-weed at night, a formidable battery rose in the morning. The approaches were then begun in the mode which seemed most proper to our plain, common sense men. Some more learned in military tactics began to talk of zigzags and epaulements, but we made ourselves very merry over this, and went on in our own way. By the 20th of May we had erected five batteries, one of which mounted five forty-two pounders and did great execution. We also erected a new battery upon the light-house point which silenced many of the guns of the island battery. English ships of war were continually arriving, which added such strength to our fleet, that a combined attack upon the town was resolved upon. But before this was effected, Duchambon, the French commander, becoming disheartened, offered to capitulate. On the 17th of June, the town, the city, fort and batteries were surrendered to us, and we marched in in triumph. As we entered the fortress and looked upon the strength of the place, our hearts for the first time sunk within us. All seemed to be deeply affected with the wonderful providence of God in making everything favorable for us, and in filling the heart of the enemy with fear, so that they gave up to us, an army of un-disciplined mechanics, farmers and fishermen, a fortress impregnable by any force that we could bring against it. Many of our men during the siege had taken colds, and many were seized with the dysentery, so that fifteen hundred men were taken off from duty at one time ; but the weather proving remark-ably fine, during the forty-nine days' siege, they generally recovered. The day after, the rains began and continued ten days without cessation. If this had occurred before, it must have been fatal to many of us, as we should have had nothing better than the wet ground to lie upon, and our tents were not sufficient to shelter us against a single shower.''

In addition to this account of the returned soldier, we may say, on the best authority, that this expedition was one of the most remarkable events in the history of North America. When the news reached Boston, the bells of the town were rung merrily, and all the people were in transports of joy. The intelligence spread rapidly through all the towns, carrying with it equal gladness, and affecting the hearts of all Christians with a sense of the wonderful interposition of God in behalf of the colonies. And well they might rejoice and give thanks. Their commerce and fisheries were now secure, and their maritime cities relieved from the dread of an attack from a formidable foe. The next year the French made extraordinary exertions to retrieve their loss, sending a powerful fleet to the American coast, the news of whose approach spread terror through every town. But a succession of disasters prevented it from inflicting any injury and compelled its speedy withdrawal.

March 3, (1745,) died Capt. Thomas Choate. He was a son of John Choate, the first settler of that name in Chebacco, and was the first resident of Hogg Island. In both parish and town affairs he was a leading man, and was a representative to the General Court in 1723–27.

CHAPTER III.

THE TWO PARISHES AND THEIR REUNION.

1746. THIS year was made especially memorable in the annals of Chebacco by the division of Mr. Pickering's church and the organization of a new church and society. Two years before, twenty-six of his church members had presented to Mr. Pickering a statement in writing of certain "grievances or occasions of disquietude" toward him, and notified him of their intention to withdraw from his preaching, unless the causes of their disquietude should be removed. These grievances were, in reality, accusations of the gravest character—charging him with not preaching plainly the distinctive doctrines of the Bible, with a want of interest in his ministerial work, with worldliness of spirit and conduct, and with opposition to the great revival of religion of the preceding years. The general attention to religion to which they referred, was effected, so far as human means were concerned, largely by the preaching of Rev. Mr. Whitefield, who, in 1740, visited New England for the first time, and preached in many places. During his tour to the eastward, on which he started from Boston, September 29th, he "preached at Ipswich to some thousands." Respecting this occasion he wrote, "the Lord gave me freedom, and there was a great melting in the congregation." * He also visited Chebacco at the same time. Of this revival these disaffected brethren afterwards gave the following account:

"In the year 1741 and onwards, it pleased God, out of his rich, free and sovereign grace, to bring upon the minds of many in this parish a deep concern

* This scene was on the hill in front of the First Congregational meeting-house in Ipswich Center.

about their future state, and what they should do to be saved ; and although something of this concern then spread itself over the land, and in some places was very remarkable, we believe it was in none more so than in this place, where before, we were as careless, worldly and secure as any, if not more so. But now the face of things was changed ; and engagedness to hear the word preached, Christian conferences, private meetings for religious worship, and assistance to each other in the way of life, were what the minds of many appeared to be deeply concerned in, and engrossed much of our time. And we have undoubted grounds to conclude that at this time the free grace of God was richly displayed in the saving conversion of many among us."

Mr. Pickering had declared himself not unfriendly to revivals of religion, but had objected to some of the measures adopted by Mr. Whitefield to promote them. His treatment of the aggrieved, however, having only served to increase their alienation of feeling toward him, they laid their grievances before the church. Their accusations were decided to be unsupported by evidence, but in the hope of bringing about a reconciliation, final action in the case was postponed. Soon after this, their application for a mutual council to decide the question at issue, was refused, on the ground that by their withdrawal they had forfeited their claim to it; but the church reconsidered this action in the year 1745, and unsolicited, twice proposed to the aggrieved to unite in calling such a council, which proposal they in turn both times refused. A little later, an agreement was made that the controversy should be terminated by Mr. Pickering's resignation of his charge, provided that a majority of the church should consent to his going, that a purchaser should be found for his estate, and that mutual forgiveness should be exercised. These conditions, however, were not complied with. On the 13th of January, 1746, sixteen members of the church "assembled at the house of Daniel Giddinge, and resolved to separate from him and his church, and set up for a distinct society, unless he would consent to resign his pastorate." Of this meeting, Capt. Robert Choate was moderator, and William Giddinge, clerk, and a committee was appointed to confer with Mr. Pickering. At an ad-

21

journed meeting two days later, this committee made a report of their interview, and "there being now a church-meeting held at the meeting-house, our society in general," says the record, "went up to said meeting, and declared to Mr. Pickering and to the church publicly, that they had separated themselves from them." On the 20th of the same month the formation of a "Separate Society" was completed, thirty-eight men entering into and signing "a solemn covenant and league to set up the worship of God agreeable to his word revealed in the Scriptures." At another meeting held the 2d of May, William Giddinge, Lieut. Thomas Choate, Ensign James Eveleth, 'Squire Francis Choate and Daniel Giddinge were chosen a committee to invite the churches in Mansfield, Canterbury and Plainfield, Conn., and the "Separate Church" in Boston, to assemble in council and organize a new church. At about the same time, the Separatists also declined the proposal of a council, which had been called by the Second Church, to make that council a mutual one by inviting such other churches as they might select, to form a part of it. When this council, which had been in the meantime enlarged, so that nine churches were represented on it, again met on the 20th of May, 1746, it again invited the aggrieved to refer their matters of difference with the church to it. This offer was refused, though they "at length consented that the members of the council should as private Christians have an hearing of their case, and presented all their articles of complaint and their evidence to sustain it."

This council consisted of the first and second churches in Gloucester, the first and third churches in Ipswich, two churches in Beverly, two churches in Rowley, and the church in Wenham. Rev. John White was moderator. They appear to have made a thorough and impartial investigation of the whole matter. The accusations made by the aggrieved were considered one by one, and the evidence for and against each, including several of Mr.

Pickering's sermons, was heard and weighed. The judgment of a majority of the council upon each charge, as
well as their advice to the parties concerned, was given
apparently with great candor, impartiality and discrimina-
tion, in their "result," which was adopted at an adjourned
meeting held June 10th. In Mr. Pickering's sermons
"they could not discern any of the alleged defects, but,
on the contrary, no small number of the doctrines of
grace, handled in a judicious manner." In their judgment, there was no ground whatever for the charge of a
want of interest in his ministerial work, or of a neglect of
pastoral visits; no reason for doubting his piety, nor for
believing that he had been worldly in spirit, or had conducted improperly in business affairs. They were of the
opinion, however, that he had been "negligent about examining candidates for admission to the church respecting
their religious experiences," that he had been "wanting
in ministerial duty in not early and thoroughly examining
into the nature of the religious appearances among his
flock," and that his treatment of the aggrieved at first
"had given them just ground of offence, but that he had
offered them such satisfaction, that they ought to forgive
him." The conclusion of their *result* is as follows:

"We can by no means approve of said aggrieved members withdrawment
from the Communion of the Church, to which they belong, and from the
public ministration of the word by the Pastor: yea, we look upon this their
conduct as very unjustifiable and reproachful to Religion, and more especially
since they have also, contrary to the known order of these churches, set up
a separate Assembly for solemn Worship, and invited and encouraged Persons of doubtful character, and coming to them in a disorderly manner, to
teach them from time to time; which last thing in particular may be of most
pernicious influence, to introduce among themselves and neighbors, dangerous
corruptions in Doctrine, as well as set an evil example. We advise the
church that at present great tenderness and even long suffering be extended
towards the separating members, that if possible they may be won thereby.
In cordial love to the pastor we advise him to ask pardon of his great Master,
for any such false steps of his, whereby his brethren may have been made to
stumble: Also that he be ready, with Humility to acknowledge them, on
proper occasions: and that he use all wise, endearing and condescending

methods, which God in his Providence may at any time give him opportunity of taking to gain his offended Brethren."

From this decision a minority of six—including three ministers—expressed their dissent as follows:

"As to many main articles of charge exhibited, the aggrieved have real grounds of grievance with their pastor, and it appears to us that these grounds of grievance do still remain. We cannot concur with the council, that the withdraw of the aggrieved is unjustifiable and reproachful to religion: neither that they have exposed themselves to the censure of the church thereby. And it highly concerns the pastor and the church to remove the stumbling blocks out of the way of the said withdrawing brethren, by that confession and reformation which is their duty, and which may draw them into a re-union with themselves."

Even *they*, however, add:

"We cannot justify their withdraw in *all* the circumstances of it; and we think the aggrieved brethren should greatly desire and carefully endeavor a re-union, by acknowledging and putting away what has been unchristianlike in their spirit or behavior, either towards Pastor or Church."

The seceders, however, did not wait for the decision of this body, nor even for its deliberations. The council which they had voted to call, on which, however, only the churches in Boston and Canterbury were represented, met by their invitation on the same day (May 20th), at the house of Mr. Francis Choate. The reasons for the with-drawal which have been already stated were also laid be-fore it. *This* council justified the separation, assisted in the preparation of "articles of faith and discipline and a covenant," and in its presence these were signed by nine men and thirty-two women, on the 22d of May. Thus was constituted the "Fourth Church in Ipswich." On the 30th, Francis Choate was elected moderator, and Rev. Ebenezer Cleaveland ("our preacher") acting scribe.

Rev. Ebenezer Cleaveland, the first preacher to this new Society, was born in Canterbury, Conn., January 5th, 1725. He entered Yale College in 1744, but a few months after, November 19th, for the offence of "attending the ministra-tions of a lay exhorter of the Whitefield stamp," though it was in vacation and in company with his parents and was

not known to be in violation of any rule, and for his refusal
to acknowledge that he deserved censure for the act, was
expelled from College, on the ground that it was a sanction
of "measures deemed subversive of the established order
of the churches." The government of the College afterward rescinded the vote of expulsion, and enrolled him as
a graduate of the class of 1748 to which he had belonged.
He preached in Chebacco from the Spring of 1746 until
nearly the close of that year. The "Fourth Church," after
he left them, gave him a "letter of recommendation to
the work of the Gospel ministry," in which it is mentioned
that he "did dwell with and preach the Gospel unto us
for several months." In 1751 he commenced preaching
at Sandy Bay—now Rockport, and in February 13, 1755, a
church was organized, of which he was ordained pastor in
December of that year. He continued to be its minister
until May, 1784. In the French war of 1758, and the Canada expedition in 1759, he was a chaplain in the army.
He also entered the continental army in the same capacity,
in June, 1775, and served about three years. After his dismission he preached several years in Landaff, N. H., and
then returning to Rockport, resided there the remainder
of his life, occasionally preaching in destitute places. His
death occurred July 4, 1805. On his tombstone it is recorded that he was "a faithful pastor and a godly man."

On the 17th of December, 1746, the "Fourth Church"
proceeded to the election of permanent officers. Francis
Choate and Daniel Giddinge were chosen *Ruling Elders*,
and Eleazer Craft and Solomon Giddinge, *Deacons*. Several years later (in 1751), these office-bearers were formally set apart to their work by ordination at the hands
of the pastor. Still later in its history (November 20,
1765,) Dea. Craft was made a Ruling Elder, and Stephen
Choate and Thomas Burnham, Deacons. At the same
meeting Mr. John Cleaveland, present by invitation, was
"desired to declare his principles," which he did, and was
then unanimously elected pastor of the church. In this

action the Society concurred, and the invitation thus extended, Mr. Cleaveland accepted, December 26th.

1747. His ordination took place on the 25th of February following. The council called for this purpose consisted of Rev. John Rogers and delegates from the church in Kittery, Me., delegates from the New Church in Exeter, N. H., and Rev. Nathaniel Rogers and delegates from the first church in this town. Other churches were invited but the inclemency of the weather prevented their attendance. The council assembled the day before at the North End, at the house of Mr. Francis Choate, (the same as to its frame as that now owned by Mr. John Burnham,) for the purpose of examining the candidate and assigning the parts for the ordination. Rev. John Rogers was chosen moderator, and Rev. John Phillips scribe. An elevated platform was erected in front of the house to accommodate the council during the public exercises, while the congregation stood in front of that. The services commenced at ten o'clock. The ordaining prayer was offered and the charge given by the Rev. John Rogers, and the fellowship of the churches expressed by Rev. Nathaniel Rogers. Notwithstanding the severity of the season, tradition says that a large audience were in attendance.

This opening year of Mr. Cleaveland's ministry also witnessed the death of Rev. Theophilus Pickering, after a short illness, on the 7th of October,* at the age of 47. He was the second son of John and Sarah Pickering, and was born in Salem, September 28, 1700. The family had been one of much prominence in olden time in that city, and afterwards some of its members were distinguished in the affairs of State. His grandfather, John Pickering, was born in England in 1615, and emigrated to Salem in 1637. His nephew Timothy was a Colonel in the Revolutionary War, and Secretary of War and afterwards of State, under

---

* It has been found impossible to account for the discrepancy between this date of Mr. Pickering's death taken from the records, and that carved on his tomb-stone. Both have been correctly copied.

the second administration of Washington. John Pickering, another relative, was an eminent lawyer of the present century, distinguished also for his classical learning. Theophilus graduated at Harvard University in 1719, and though he soon after came into possession of considerable property at the death of his father, June 19, 1722, he determined to devote himself to the work of the ministry. He was laborious and successful in his pastoral office, and during his ministry about two hundred persons were admitted to the church. As a Christian man and teacher, he had the confidence of most of his brethren in the ministry, and there is no reason to doubt the conscientiousness of his opposition to the course of the Separatists. The estimation in which he was held by his own church is plainly seen in the language used respecting him in the "Answer of the Second Church to the Chebacco Brethren's Plain Narrative:"

"We at Chebacco have (as we verily believe,) had among us a man of God, a learned, orthodox, prudent, faithful minister of Jesus Christ, though not without failings even as others; one whom we heard teaching and preaching the truths of the Gospel, with pleasure, and we hope, with profit; and whose memory will, we trust, be ever dear to us notwithstanding the reproaches that have been plentifully cast upon him."

He was a diligent student, was well versed in theology, and, in the judgment of his contemporaries, was a man of vigorous intellect and of superior ability as a logician and a writer. From a list of his books which is preserved in a collateral branch of the family, it appears that he was possessed of a very valuable library. His genius for mechanism was great. Many specimens of his mechanical labors still remain. As a testimony to his learning and abilities, it has been said to the author by some aged people who remembered him, that Whitefield, after considerable debate with him on the cardinal points of Christianity, acknowledged that he was a man of great ingenuity, though he regretted the erroneousness of his views. Mr. Pickering was never married. His will, which was dated October

4. 1747. begins as follows: "I, Theophilus Pickering, being of sound mind and memory, but laboring under sickness, and realizing my mortality." In it he distributed seven thousand pounds, *old tenor*, to his sisters and their children, and gave the residue of his estate to his brother Timothy. His tomb-stone in the old grave-yard contains the following inscription:

HERE LIES BURIED THE
Body of ye Revd Mr
THEOPHILUS PICKERING,
WHO DEPARTED THIS LIFE
Sept ye 19th, 1747,
AGED 47 YEARS.

Three deacons of the church had died during his ministry. John Choate in 1730, Seth Story in 1732, aged 73, and John Burnham (chosen deacon in 1732,) in 1746. The number of church-members at his death was forty. Four vessels used at the communion service, marked "Ipswich Second Church"—two of them having the date, "1728," and the other two, "1732"—are still in the possession and use of the church, venerable for their antiquity, and prized for the associations connected with them.

1748. Shortly after Mr. Cleaveland's ordination, Mr. Pickering had published a pamphlet, entitled "A Bad Omen to the Churches in the instance of Mr. John Cleaveland's Ordination over a Separation in Chebacco Parish." This was immediately answered by Mr. Cleaveland, in another pamphlet, entitled "A Plain Narrative of the Proceedings which caused a Separation of a Number of Aggrieved Brethren from the Second Church in Ipswich: or, a Relation of the Cause which produced the Effects that are exhibited in the Rev. Mr. Pickering's late Print, entitled 'A Bad Omen to the Churches.'" Mr. Pickering's preparation of a rejoinder he did not live to complete, but his church after his death carried out his purpose in the publication early the next year of "An Answer to the Chebacco Brethren's Plain Narrative—the

Pretended Narrative convicted of Fraud and Partiality; or a Letter from the Second Church in Ipswich to their Separated Brethren, in Defence of their deceased Pastor and Themselves against the Injurious Charges of the said Separated Brethren in a late Print of theirs, by giving a more Just and True account of the things that preceded the Separation." In answer to this, another pamphlet appeared, supposed to have been written by Mr. Cleaveland, entitled "Chebacco Narrative Rescued from the Charge of Falsehood and Partiality." "These pamphlets are all written with great spirit, and show that the minds of the several writers were stirred to their inmost depths."

The Second Church, however, instead of carrying the controversy further, determined to submit the proceedings of the Separatists, subsequent to their withdrawal, to the judgment of others. Accordingly by their desire a council of delegates from the South, the old and new North churches of Boston, the third church of Salem, the first church of Reading, and the first church of Cambridge, met at Chebacco on the 19th of July, 1748, relative to the settlement of Mr. Cleaveland there. On the 30th they met by adjournment in Boston. They concluded "that Mr. Cleaveland's church was not a Congregational Church, and that the first church in Ipswich and the church in Kittery were not justifiable in assisting at his ordination." They advised Mr. Cleaveland's church to be reconciled with the Second Church. The ministers of the council present were Rev. Joseph Sewall, moderator, Benjamin Prescott, Nathaniel Appleton, William Holby and Andrew Elliot.

A drouth of unusual severity is thus alluded to in the records of the "Newly Gathered Congregational Church in Chebacco," and the action of the church with reference to it thus expressed :

"August 7. Whereas the frowns of God are manifestly upon us, not only in his withdrawal of spiritual showers, but also in his withholding the rain of heaven from the dry and thirsty ground, causing a melancholy drought : we do, therefore, look upon it as a very loud call to us to call a solemn assembly

22

for fasting and prayer, to confess our sins and the sins of the land and nation and of the whole earth, and beg mercy for the same, and we do appoint Tuesday next, the 9th instant, to be kept by us as a day of Fasting and Prayer."

1749. January 3d. The second Parish voted to concur with the Second Church in the choice of Nehemiah Porter of the Hamlet Parish in this town to be their minister. Mr. Porter had previously supplied the pulpit for some time. His salary is £500 in Province Bills, to vary according to the price of certain specified articles, together with the use and income of the parsonage rights. In the list of articles, butter is put down at 7s. per pound, pork at 2s. 6d. and molasses at 20s. per gallon. Mr. Porter was ordained January 3d, of the next year but there is no record of the ordination services.

It was during the session of our General Court this year, that an act was passed to redeem the Province Bills, by paying a Spanish milled dollar for every 45s. of the old tenor, or for every 11s. 3d. of the new emission. As the bills had depreciated, and were no longer in the hands of the first holders, it was insisted that to redeem them at their original value would impose a new tax on the first holders themselves. The money by which they redeemed the bills was the specie remitted to them from the royal exchequer as a re-imbursement for their expenses in the capture of Louisburg.

July 6th. Major Ammi Ruhami Wise, son of Rev. John Wise, died of fever, in Boston, in the sixty-first year of his age. He resided in Ipswich, and was a noted merchant, Justice of the Court of Sessions, and representative to the General Court in 1739 and 1740. In 1740 he also commanded a company of troops, in the expedition to the Spanish West Indies.

1750. The Court of Sessions met here about this time for the purpose of opening a road to Manchester, from the corner near Thompson's Island, by the houses of William Low and Amos Andrews. Previous to this there had been a private way from Joshua Burnham's to William now

Warren Low's, with a gate at each end. This was now made a public road, and carried through the woods to Manchester.

FORMATION OF THE SIXTH PARISH.

1752. As parishes were territorial organizations, all persons residing within their limits were subject to taxation by them for the current expenses of the parish. The members of Mr. Cleaveland's society were, therefore, obliged at first to carry a double burden, from which for a time they had sought release in vain. As late as January 19, 1750, the Second Parish, in answer to their memorial "that they may not pay a tax levied on them by that body," said "We know no minister of their own regularly called and settled, either with respect to the laws of the Province, or the order of these churches." And although their petition to the General Court for an act of incorporation had been sent in the very next year after the formation of the society, it was not granted until the 8th of December, 1752. Opposition to their request had now ceased, and having presented evidence that they had "come to an agreement with the standing part of the Second Parish," it was ordered that "the petitioners, being fifty-seven in number, with their families and estates be made a distinct and separate precinct." This organization took the name of the *Sixth Parish* in Ipswich, though connected with the *Fourth Church*, because soon after the formation of the latter, Line Brook and the South Parishes had been incorporated.

Joseph Perkins, grandfather of the late John Perkins, was its clerk from its formation until its union with the Second Parish, and for most of that time its treasurer also. Its house of worship was erected this same year on the site of the present edifice of the North Congregational Church. It had the same shape as the second meeting-house, on the common, but had no turret or bell. It was built and owned at first by proprietors, but in April, 1761, was purchased of them by the parish. There is no record of its dedication. The congregation had worshiped in private houses, and a part of the time in William Cogswell's barn, until its completion. While our fathers and mothers, too, were thus divided in their opinions as to the best mode of conducting the affairs of the church, and had different places of worship, yet, as tradition testified to the author through the lips of the aged more than forty years ago, they were charitable and kind in their intercourse with each other, and such was their respect for the rights of conscience, that often the husband would convey his wife upon the same horse to one meeting, and then ride himself to the other, and when worship was ended, return to take up his conscientious spouse, that they might be one again in the domestic circle.

1753. November 26th, died at Kingston, N. H., Rev. Benjamin Choate, M. A., aged 73. Mr. Choate was a native of this place, a son of John Choate, the first settler of that name, and a brother of Thomas Choate, the first resident of Hogg Island. He was born in 1680, fitted for college in the Ipswich Grammar School, and was graduated at Harvard College in 1703. He then spent some time in the study of theology, and was chaplain of the garrison at Deerfield for about two years from November, 1704. Soon after, he emigrated to Kingston, N. H., with the first settlers of that place, in the capacity of a preacher, and resided in garrison with them. There is a record on the town books, as early as 1707, of an agreement to pay Mr. Choate a salary, but the town was so much disturbed by Indian hostilities that he probably did not go there to reside permanently till 1713. He was ordained as an Evangelist before going to Kingston, and acted as minister till 1720, when according to the records of that town, other preachers began to be employed. The church there was not organized till 1725. Rev. Ward Clark was the first pastor. From the year 1720 Mr. Choate was employed as school-master by the town for many years, and his name appears on the town books as moderator of town meetings, and as holding various other offices.

1755. On the 18th of November, between the hours of four and five in the morning, there was a great earthquake, which threw down stone walls and the tops of many chimneys, and bent the vanes on some of the steeples. It did much damage to many houses in this town. Its moral influence was felt in this place, as Mr. Cleaveland states in a pamphlet published soon after, awakening some to reflect on their ways, and from a conviction of sin and guilt, to seek reconciliation with their God and Saviour.

1756. January 21st, died Rev. Jeremiah Wise, eldest son of Rev. John Wise, aged 76. He was born in Chebacco in 1680, graduated at Harvard College in 1700, studied theology with his father, and on the 26th of November, 1707, was ordained pastor of the Congregational Church in South Berwick, Me. His ministry there continued until his death. In a "sketch of eminent ministers of New England," published about the year 1765, he is spoken of as a man of learning, discretion, and of eminent piety—a prudent, faithful and useful minister in his day." Several of his sermons were published.

March 9th, died Francis Cogswell, A. M., aged 58. He fitted for college at the Ipswich Grammar School, and graduated at Harvard College in 1718. March 14, 1728, he was married to Miss Elizabeth, daughter of Rev. John Rogers of Kittery, Me. Mr. Cogswell resided in Ipswich, and became a wealthy merchant. He represented the town in the General Court in 1750, 1751, and 1752. He was also a Justice of the Peace.

A specimen of the newspaper reports of local intelligence is found in "The Boston News Letter" of October 23d, of this year:

"Last Tuesday, se'n night, a barn at Chebacco, in Ipswich, was struck by lightning, and consumed, with all that was therein. A young man being at work in the field, observing the squall coming on, ran to the barn for shelter ;

but he had hardly got in before it was set on fire. 'Tis tho't he was instantly struck dead by the lightning; and was burnt to a great degree before he could be got out."

1757. An increase of interest in the cause of education is indicated by the erection of a new and more commodious school-house in Chebacco. It was built "upon the site of the old one" (near Mr. W. H. Mears' house), was twenty-one feet in length, and eighteen in width, eight feet stud, and contained five windows. Its cost, £250, old tenor, or about $25 in gold, was defrayed by "a subscription founding a school-house in Chebacco," made at a meeting held April 5th, at Mr. Joseph Perkins' house (which is still standing near Mr. John C. Choate's), and signed by seventy-four of the inhabitants. The care of the school-house was entrusted to a committee chosen annually by the subscribers or "proprietors." From the very full records of their meetings from this year until 1801, it is ascertained that the teachers of this school were sometimes nominated by the proprietors and appointed by the selectmen of the town, and sometimes chosen by the proprietors' committee, and that the average length of the schools per year during the remainder of the century, was four months. It further appears that Chebacco's proportion of the money raised by the town for schools, and of the income of the school-lands, was expended for the support of this school, and that the session was often "lengthened out" by money raised by subscription. The wages of the teachers per month, so far as recorded, varied from $5.50 to $9.33. The latter sum was paid only when a "Latin teacher" was employed.

That the "proprietors" early appreciated the importance of furnishing to all the children of the place the opportunity of entering upon a course of liberal education, is indicated by their vote, in 1764, that *Latin* should be taught in their school; and by their instructing their committee "to employ as teacher some person capable of teaching it." Pelatiah Tingley was the first Latin teacher, during the

Winter of 1764–5, and his successor, for the next two years, was Jonathan Searle, Jr. The use of the school-room, for a weekly singing-school through the Winter, was given by the proprietors in 1764, and for many years following. An evening school was also held first in 1765. Of eleven teachers of this school mentiond in the records, only three or four were natives of the place. One of these, Dea. Thomas Burnham, taught it eight years. Among the others were David Burnham, Jr., and Dr. Russ. After the erection of the first school-house at the Falls in 1761, and the first one on the south side of the river in 1779, the owners of what had been " the school-house in Chebacco" styled themselves "the Proprietors of the North School Division," or " the North School Society. in Chebacco."

In 1791 this North school-building was moved to a site near the location of the present engine-house, and continued in use until 1801—forty-four years in all.

1758. Rev. Mr. Cleaveland enters the army this year as chaplain of the "Third Provincial regiment of foot." His commission under the signature of Gov. Pownal and Secretary Oliver, bears date 13th March, 1758. His orders were to join his regiment at Flat Bush, five miles above Albany. The whole army under Gen. Abercrombie, nine thousand Provincials and about seven thousand British Regulars, were to rendezvous at Albany, on the west bank of the Hudson. The field officers of his regiment, were Col. Bagley, Lieut. Col. Whitcomb, Maj. Ingersoll. The staff officers, John Cleaveland, chaplain,[*] Richard Sikes, adjutant, Caleb Rea, surgeon, William Taylor, quartermaster. The fourth company in the regiment was commanded by Capt. Stephen Whipple of the Hamlet, First Lieut. Nathan Burnham, Second Lieut. Stephen Low, and Ensign Samuel Knowlton, all of Chebacco. In a let-

---

[*] Bancroft makes mention of him in connection with this expedition of Abercrombie as one of those " chaplains who preached to the regiments of citizen-soldiers a renewal of the days when Moses with the rod of God in his hand sent Joshua against Amalek."—*History of United States*, vol. 4, chap. 13.

ter to his wife dated at Capt. Van Buren's, Flat Bush, New York. June 10, 1758, he says:

' " I arrived here last night; had a very tedious route through unknown ways. We left Boston on Thursday, stopped at Spencer (Worcester Co.) and spent the Sabbath with Mr. Eaton, an eminent servant of Christ. Brother Ebenezer Cleaveland preached in the forenoon and I in the afternoon. Col. Bagley came up and attended service and then rode on to overtake his regiment. Our Surgeon Dr. Rea, Ebenezer, and I went through Springfield to Sheffield where we came across the Connecticut forces in which was our brother Aaron. My health has been very good, though greatly fatigued with my ride upon my very dull horse. Uncommon health prevails throughout the army, and all are in good spirits, anxious to be doing something. Gen. Abercrombie and Lord How have gone before us to the Lake. We expect to be marching in a day or two. If God is for us we shall have success. The regiments during their march have all been very civil except the Marblehead company, whose conduct has been extremely bad. I am now performing the duty of Chaplain for Col. Ruggles' regiment, our own not having yet arrived. We have found the locusts in the wood through which we have come very noisy and annoying. Brother Ebenezer not having received his commission as chaplain was about to return; but Col. Preble, whose chaplain, Mr. Little, had failed to come on, engaged brother to take his place."

Some extracts from a journal, which Mr. Cleaveland kept during this campaign, may give us some idea of the privations and hardships of a camp life, as well as of the events that then occurred:

"June 15th. Col Bagley has arrived at Greenbush. He expresses a wish to be moving forward—says, two or three men in Col. Ruggles' and Col. Nichols' regiment are sick, and that he apprehends danger of small-pox from the constant visits made to the city (Albany). Col. Bagley's regiment is coming in; and Capt. Whipple's company have all come—except Jacob Lufkin left behind disabled. Prayed with three or four companies of our regiment this evening. I am much pleased to meet our friends of Chebacco.

"June 16th, Friday. This morning attended prayers with several companies of my regiment.

"A sad affair has occurred in our regiment. Several persons in Capt. Morrow's company put under guard for killing some of our landlord's cattle.

"17th, Saturday. Attended prayers. Lieut. Col. Whitcomb was present for the first time. The Court-martial condemned three of the men who killed the cattle. Two of them were moderately whipped.

"Sabbath, 18th. This day preached to a large and attentive auditory. Visited a sick man and prayed with him.

"Tuesday 20th, at Schenectady. Think it well situated; about as large as Charlestown.   A stone Church—Dutch minister and Dutch residents. The regiment called to prayers at evening.   Col. Bagley present for the first time.   Col. B. has ordered the Captains to attend every day while they tarry here at 6 A. M. and 7 P. M.

"22d, Thursday.   Last night orders arrived from Gen. Stanwix for the two companies of Col. Whiting that are in town, and for one company and half of another, in our regiment to march directly to Half-Moon.   We attended prayers and then supped at our new lodgings, having dined with Dominie Vroom, the Dutch minister of the town.

"23d, Friday.   Prayers delayed by reason that Col. Bagley gets orders to march towards Fort Edward.   Officers and soldiers are pleased with the idea of joining the army.   The Lord God be with us in all our marches and engagements.

"24th, Saturday.   Gave a short word of exhortation to the soldiers.   Mr. Johnson of Carisbrook was present and prayed.   Soon after a soldier, while exercising in the Prussian way, unwittingly discharged his piece loaded with two balls.   One man was killed, another wounded and another hit.   At evening made a speech of some length as they were to march next day.

"25th, Sabbath.   After prayers, set out for Half-Moon, and arrived about sunsetting : a march of the best part of 20 miles.   I cautioned the regiment in the morning to remember the Sabbath day to keep it holy ; and they did behave quite civil in general.   But I never saw just such a Sabbath before. We took a long Sabbath day's journey for our march.   At Half-Moon we found two Connecticut regiments, Col. Lyman's and Col. Wooster's.   This night we encamped on the hard floor, with a blanket under us, and another upon us.

"26th, Monday.   Very rainy.   Tarried at Half-Moon all day.   Wrote a letter to my wife and another to Francis Choate, Esq.   Colonels Lyman and Wooster marched off towards Fort Edward.

"27th, Tuesday.   We set out and reached Stillwater about noon.   There overtook Col. Wooster's regiment ; dined with Col. Wooster in the Fort.

"28th, Wednesday.   From Stillwater to Saratoga Fort ; where we put up and tarried all night.   Fourteen miles from Stillwater to Saratoga.

"29th, Thursday.   Marched from Saratoga to Fort Miller, five miles ; and from there to Fort Edward, seven miles.   Lodged in Commissary Tucker's tent, and fared well.

"July 1st, Saturday.   Having sent back my horse with sundry articles of clothing to Capt. Van Buren's, I set out on foot for Lake George.   Dined at Half-Way Brook with Col. Nichols.   Col. Cummings and Mr. Morril, the Chaplain reached the lake before sunset ; somewhat fatigued, and lodged with Mr. Furbush, Col. Ruggles' chaplain.

"2d, Sabbath.   Our regiment joined with the regiment of Col. Ruggles in the services of the day.   Mr. Furbush preached in the forenoon from Exodus xvii., on Moses sending Joshua to fight against Amalek, while he with the rod of God in his hand went upon the hill with Aaron and Hur.   An

23

excellent sermon and well adapted.   In the afternoon I preached to a large concourse from Ephesians vi. 18.   There was remarkable attention in the assembly both parts of the day.

"3d.   Prayers quite early this morning, because the regiment was to be viewed by the General at seven o'clock.   Took my brother E. C. with me and visited John Brainerd, chaplain to Col. Johnston, of New Jersey regiment, Mr. Ogilvie, chaplain to the Regulars, Mr. Spencer of the New York regiments; and in the afternoon went with the above chaplains except Ogilvie, to the Connecticut forces, where we had an agreeable interview with their four chaplains, Messrs. Beckwith, Eels, Pomroy and Ingersol, and agreed with them to go in a body the next morning and pay our compliments to his excellency, Gen. Abercrombie.   Also agreed to spend some time in prayer.

"4th, Tuesday.   This morning after breakfast, Messrs. Beckwith, Eels, Pomroy, Ingersol, Brainerd, Spencer, Furbush, my brother and myself went to the General's tent and paid our compliments to him.   Mr. Beckwith made a short speech or address to him in the name of the whole.   He treated us very kindly, told us he hoped we would teach the people their duty and be courageous.

"This day we had orders to be in readiness to strike our tents at day-break, and be on board the bateaux at five in the morning."

Mr. Cleaveland gives in his journal a pen-drawing of the northern extremity of Lake George, and of South Bay, showing the position of Ticonderoga, a fort, and the line of the French entrenchments.   But as we cannot copy this, we ask our young reader to look on the map, and he will see that Ticonderoga is on the west side of Lake Champlain, not far from the northern end of Lake George. Our army is now on the eastern side of Lake George. To reach Ticonderoga it must embark upon this Lake, sail down towards its northern extremity, and land on its west side.   Let us take a view of the army just ready to embark; a larger army of European descent than ever before in America; having for its object not a war of ambition and oppression, but merely of self-defence; at least so far as the colonies were concerned in it, whose sole design was to subdue a foe that had for more than half a century stirred up the savage tribes, and brought them by stealth upon the homes of our fathers to butcher indiscriminately men, women and children.   Assembled for this righteous cause, we see on the shore of the Lake nine thousand provincial troops, and about seven thousand British Regulars. With the provincials, we see Maj. Rogers with his six hundred rangers, taken from the boldest and hardiest of the yeomanry of the land, armed with firelock and hatchet and carrying packs of twice the ordinary weight. This whole armament is about to embark upon the beautiful lake, in nine hundred small boats, one hundred and thirty-five whale-boats, and the formidable train of artillery mounted upon rafts. But to return to Mr. Cleaveland's journal:

" July 5th, Wednesday. At day-break the drums beat ' The General,' when the tents were immediately struck, and everything packed up and carried on board; and by five we were rowing our bateaux. The whole army was upon the water; the Regulars in the middle column; Colonels Treble, Ruggles, Bayley, and Williams on the right wing; Gen. Lyman, Colonels Whiting, Fitch, and others, on the left; the artillery in the rear of the main body; and Col. Partridge, with the Royal Hunters, brought up the rear. The rangers were in the front. We rowed above twenty miles, and had orders to draw up with our bateaux to the western shore (to rest). We pitched our tents on the shore, and lay till about eleven o'clock, when orders came to go all on board, and row immediately to the narrows.

" 6th, Thursday. By day-light arrived at the entrance of the narrows, where we halted till the whole army came up, and every regiment took his own place, according to the General's orders, and then orders came to row immediately up to the landing and land; where we expected a very warm reception from the enemy's advanced guard. My heart was much inclined to pour out desires to the God of heaven that he would appear for us, and intimidate the enemy. And it is wonderful how God did appear for us; for though the enemy had four battalions in the advanced guard, and several cannon, yet by nine o'clock, in the morning we were all safely landed; the French only fired a few small arms, which did no harm, and then ran off. But as they burned the bridges on the river, (the river which connects Lake George with Lake Champlain,) the army marched through the thick wood, to go round the bend of the river; and when we had marched about two miles, we were attacked in front, by about 3000 French and Indians. At hearing the first fire, Col. Bayley's regiment in which I was, was ordered to form to the right and run up to the enemy. There was a very smart engagement for about one hour. My Lord How was killed; and about 24 of our men were missing when we came into the camp, where we landed, and several were brought in wounded. We captured of the enemy 159, and it was judged, that we killed as many more of them.

" 7th, Friday. This day they marched out again to build the bridges, so as to march down the wagon-road and take possession of the saw-mills there, where the enemy have some small strength; and about the same hour, the army began their march to take possession of the ground near the fort; and a little after sunset Gen. Johnson arrived with his regiment. What number of Indians he has brought, I cannot get intelligence. This night I lodged in a bateau and laid my head on the barrels.

" 8th, Saturday. This morning Gen. Johnson with his Indians marched after the army, before sunrise, to Ticonderoga. This has been a most bloody fight. Our troops attempted to force the French entrenchments, with small arms, and met with great loss. Our men acted with the greatest intrepidity; and one or two companies of the Highlanders and Regulars were almost entirely cut off. Many were slain, and many came in wounded. The number of both is not known; but it is conjectured that a thousand are among the killed and wounded. Capt. Whipple received a ball in his thigh, which lodged there; Lieut. Nathan Burnham received a mortal wound in his bowels, and Lieut. Stephen Low (both of Chebacco) was slain, as we suppose; the last that was seen of him, he was sitting down, with a heavy wound. The conduct is thought to be marvellous strange, to order the entrenchment to be forced with small arms, when they had cannon not far off, and numbers sufficient to keep the enemy off till we had entrenched and placed our cannon and mortars so as to play upon the enemy. Most of our forces retreated towards the landing where the bateaux lay.

" 9th, Sabbath. This morning, to the general surprise of the whole army, we were ordered to embark in the bateaux, to leave the ground we had possessed, and return to Fort William Henry. We left the ground, at about nine o'clock in the morning, and arrived at Fort William Henry before sunset. All dejected, partly on account of our returning, and partly on account of our being without much food for three days. This evening Lieut. Burnham (Nathan) was buried, having died upon the water, of his wound. I understood he inquired much for me, and desired to see me before he died; but I was in another bateau, and could not be found, the lake being full of them.

" 10th, Monday. Orders are given out to make a return of the killed, wounded and missing; which, according to the information I have had, amounts to eighteen or twenty hundred in the whole army, principally among the Regulars and Highlanders. In Col. Bayley's regiment six were killed, two officers and four privates; eleven are wounded, including Capt. Whipple. I find people, officers and soldiers, astonished that we left the French ground, and commenting on the strange conduct in coming off.

" 11th, Tuesday. Wrote a letter this day to my spouse, to be sent by Mr. Thompson. Whale-boats and bateaux, by order, unloaded. People begin to sicken, partly, perhaps, because they were scant of provisions, while down the Lake, and nothing to drink, but lake-water, and partly through dejection and discouragement, arising from disappointment.

" 12th, Wednesday. This day wrote a letter to Col. Choate. Spent considerable time with Mr. Furbush, in reading and conversation. Towards evening, the General, with his Rehoboam Counsellors, came on, to line out a fort on the Rocky Hill, where our breast-work was the last year. Now we begin to think strongly, that the Grand Expedition against Canada is laid aside, and a foundation is going to be laid, totally to impoverish our country."

This apprehension of the journalist as to Abercrombie's design was well founded. Having in his fright after his repulse by the French, hurried back over Lake George to his former quarters on the south end of the Lake, he entirely abandoned his project of capturing Ticonderoga. He remained, however, in his quarters with his whole army through the rest of the Summer. Mr. C. continued his instructive and interesting journal, till his return in the Autumn, embracing sixty-nine pages. It would be desirable, if we had room, to give the whole of it. But a few more brief extracts must suffice:

" 15th, Saturday. Much indisposed in body. This afternoon came in three deserters from Ticonderoga, who say there were but 3500 there, when we attacked their entrenchment. Had we forced them thence, their design was to betake themselves to their whale-boats, which lay ready, run down to Crown Point, lay it in ashes, and then repair to Chamblee, and there make their stand, where they could have relief from Canada. But our return saved them a deal of trouble.

" 22d, Saturday. This morning Jonathan Marshall of Chebacco broke out with small-pox, and was sent to the Hospital at Fort Edward. The Lord prepare us for all his will. At 10 o'clock A. M., all the provincial chaplains that were at the Lake, met at Mr. Emerson's tent for prayer, and agreed to meet every Tuesday and Friday at 10 A. M., for prayer. This evening Col. Schuyler, and Mr. Clark taken at Oswego, and who came home last Fall on a furlough, set off from here with a flag of truce, consisting of twenty-one, with one French prisoner taken in 1755, to go to Ticonderoga, where the Col. and Mr. Clark design to resign themselves up to the French, the parole being out. Also received this evening a letter from my wife, which informs me of the near approach of her and my dear brother Nehemiah Dodge to the gates of death. The Lord appear for him, and give him to triumph over death and hell. Also at the same time received a letter from my good and cordial friend William Story of Boston.

" 23d, Sabbath. This forenoon preached with some freedom from Malachi 1 : 6. The people gave good attention, and many Regulars were present. Oh that God would set the truths of the gospel home upon the hearts of all, that my heart may be encouraged, and my hands strengthened in the work of God ! Preached again in the afternoon, from the same words, to a more unmerous auditory, consisting not only of my own regiment, but of Regulars and Highlanders.

" 25th, Tuesday. This forenoon one of the Regulars was hanged for theft. He confessed on the ladder that gaming, robbery, theft and other sins had brought him to this shameful and untimely death, and warned his fellow-soldiers against such vices. He desired the prayers of the people standing by, for his poor soul, and praying for himself, was hove off the ladder. The Lord make this sad spectacle the means of effectually warning all from the bad vices that the soldiers are much addicted to."

1760. Our fathers have this year a new king set over them. George II. died suddenly in the seventy-seventh year of his age and thirty-third of his reign; and was succeeded by his grandson, George III., who was the son of Frederick, Prince of Wales, and Augusta, Princess of Saxe-Gotha. His father died when he was young. George III. was our last sovereign. Sir Francis Bernard was our royal governor at this time. He commenced his administration, August 2, 1760, and retired August 1768. History says of him, that he was haughty, morose and tyranical. He left the administration of government in the hands of Lieut. Gov. Hutchinson. Our representative this year was Col. John Choate.

March 13th. The town vote that such private soldiers, as are in the war, exclusive of tradesmen and carpenters, shall be excused from their poll-tax. " A way is opened from North-gate by John Baker's through P. Kinsman's land, to Chebacco road." This is the road which, after passing Hatfield's bridge, leads us to the way conducting to the beach.

The *Quarterly Fast* of the churches in Ipswich has its origin, this year, in this parish. Mr. Cleaveland's church " agreed to spend one day every quarter of the year, in a congregational fasting and praying for the outpouring of God's Spirit upon them, and upon all nations, agreeable to the concert of prayer first entered into in Scotland some years before." The First and South Churches and the church at the Hamlet, in the year 1780, began to unite in the observance of this Fast which from that time was held

alternately in each of the four churches.   It is indicative
of stability that a religious observance which commenced
ninety-four years ago, (1854,) should still be maintained by
these churches, all of them originally of the same town.

1761.   The town grant a lot of land for a school-house
in Chebacco, near the limekiln.   Tradition places this
at the Falls, on the north-west side of the lane leading to
Jacob Burnham's, near the entrance of this lane.   A school
had been taught there two months a year, after 1741, in
a private house.   The limekiln was beyond the school-
house, and near the woods, for the convenience of procuring fuel.   Lime was then made from clam-shells.   Lay-
ers of wood and shells were alternately placed in the
kiln.   After the burning, the powder from the shells was
run through a sieve.   The location of the school-house in
this lane was then convenient to accommodate the families in the South End and near the woods, as well as at the
Falls.   This was the first school-house erected in that part
of the town.   Capt. William Story is said to have been the
first teacher at the Falls.   He was succeeded by Master
David Burnham, who had taught in the North school.

1762.   Previous to this year there had been no public
conveyance from Ipswich to Boston.   The mail had been
carried through Ipswich in passing from Boston to Portsmouth, on horseback, for several years before this, and continued to be for several years after.   It occupied six days
in going and returning.   But this year a curricle or stage-
chair, as it was called, drawn by two horses, commenced
running from Portsmouth to Boston through this town,
for the accommodation of passengers here and elsewhere,
occupying five days in going and returning.   The fare
through, each way, was three dollars and ten cents.

The drought this year was so excessive, that it cut off
most of the hay and corn, an event very afflictive and distressing at that time, because these articles could not then
be procured from any other source.   Their cattle, which
they could but poorly spare, were many of them butchered

for want of fodder, while they themselves were put to great inconvenience, if not to suffering, for want of bread.

1763. A very remarkable revival of religion commenced this year in Mr. Cleaveland's society, which resulted in the hopeful conversion of very many. About one hundred persons were added to the church. From a narrative of the revival, published by Mr. Cleaveland, we give the following brief extracts. After noticing the Quarterly Fast, the conference and prayer-meetings of the church, as preceding this revival and probably the means in the Divine hand of producing it, he proceeds to say:

"Some time in the month of October, this year, the Rev. Francis Worcester came to preach to my people one Sabbath, and I supplied his place. He came early in the week, and preached several lectures before the Sabbath, and several after, and took his leave of us with a lecture to young people; and as their attention had been aroused by his other discourses, several things in this took such a fast hold of their consciences that they could not shake them off. A little while after, I exchanged with the Rev. Samuel Chandler of Gloucester, and as he understood there were a number of persons under awakenings in my congregation, he adapted his discourses to their case, and his preaching that day was owned of God, for the begetting convictions in some and for increasing them in others. Their concern evidently increased, especially on the Monday evening before the anniversary Thanksgiving, which was on the 8th day of December.

"The next day after Thanksgiving, we had a conference meeting, and a considerable number of the youth attended. On the succeeding Sabbath there was a very solemn assembly. I desired the distressed to come to my house the next evening. But on Monday, early in the day, many came, bowed down under a sense of their lost and perishing condition, and my house was filled all that day. Some found comfort before the evening, and by sunset or a little after, so many resorted to my house that it could not hold them; and we repaired to the meeting house which was soon filled. On Tuesday my house was filled with persons wounded in spirit, and some in the greatest agony of distress in every room. This day and evening several persons received relief to their distressed souls. While my house this evening was thus filled, the Rev. Jonathan Parsons of Newburyport came in, having heard of the religious concern here; and a lecture was appointed to be the next day in the afternoon. On this occasion, Mr. Parsons preached a very suitable sermon. The meeting-house was full of people. People came from the parishes all around us. There was a solemn silence through the whole assembly, during the time of divine service, and a sacred awe on every countenance. As the people were now inclined to assemble for religious exercises, and their attention was roused, I appointed another lecture to be on Friday, this week ; and from this time till the Spring business came on, we had two lectures in the meeting-house every week, on Tuesdays and Thursdays.   Our meeting-house was crowded both on the Lord's day and on week days.

"Divers persons from other towns and parishes were brought under concern, and several hopefully converted.   Towards the last of February, twenty-two persons were added to the church.   About a month after this we took into the church thirty-two more, and the whole number of those we admitted in the space of seven or eight months was upwards of ninety.   In the ensuing Fall there was not only a considerable revival of those who had received comfort, but several new instances of hopeful conversion.   As to the nature of this· work, so far as it appeared, it consisted in the conviction of sin and righteousness, as the leading things ; conviction of sin brought them into distress, as by it they saw they were undone and perishing ; conviction of righteousness opened the door of hope and comfort to their souls, as by it they saw an all-fulness of supply in Christ the Mediator."

1764.   News arrived from England that the British Parliament on the 10th of March passed an act for granting certain duties in America, which, after declaring that it was just and expedient to raise a revenue there, imposed duties on silks, sugar, wines, coffee and some other articles.   This was justly considered by our fathers, as a blow aimed at their dearest rights.   If our trade may be taxed, said the people of Boston, in the instructions which they gave their representatives, why not our lands ?—why not the products of our lands and everything we possess or use ? "Taxation without representation is tyranny," was the universal watchword.   The unrighteous and oppressive act, was the topic of conversation at every fireside, and the subject of universal reprobation.   Meetings were held in different towns to express their disapprobation and to instruct their representatives to remonstrate against, and petition for its repeal.   Our fathers in this town had, on former occasions, when their liberties were threatened, given similar instructions to their representative.   Nearly all the colonies in the. country took the same ground against England, affirming that the imposition of duties and taxes, by the Parliament of Great Britain upon a people not represented in the House of Commons, was absolutely irreconcilable with their rights. This was the same ground that was taken by Ipswich seventy-seven years before, for which Mr. Wise and some others were imprisoned and fined.

As another connecting link between the present (1854) and nearly a hundred years ago, we may say that Parker, son of David, Jr., and Elizabeth Burnham, was baptized by Mr. Cleaveland, July 1st of this year. [Mr. Burnham died in 1856 aged 92.]

1765. The British Parliament instead of rescinding any of their oppressive acts, add another still more odious. On the 22d of March the famous Stamp Act received the royal sanction. By this act most of the written instruments in legal affairs and in ordinary business, such as deeds, indentures, pamphlets, newspapers, advertisements and almanacs, were subject to tax. The news of this produced a strong sensation in almost every mind throughout the country. It evinced to our fathers a settled determination on the part of England to invade our rights and reduce us to a state of bondage. It was time therefore for them both to speak and to act in such a manner as to show an equally determined resolution, never to submit to such oppression. Our House of Representatives passed a resolution that it was expedient for the colonies, so agreeing, to meet by their respective delegates in a general Congress, to consult together on the present circumstances of the colonies; and to consider a humble address to his Majesty and the Parliament for relief. This measure originating in our town, as well as others, through their representatives, on being communicated to the colonies was received by most of them with cordial approbation; and on the 7th of October this Congress, the first ever held in America, met at New York, and agreed upon a memorial to the House of Lords, and a petition to the King and Commons. In these documents, they acknowledged their allegiance to his Majesty, and their readiness to obey the constitutional acts of Parliament; but the stamp act and other acts of Parlia-

ment, they declared to be subversive of the rights and
liberties of the colonies, and in violation of the fundamental principles of the British Constitution. The proceedings of this Congress, though agreed to only by the
deputies of six colonies, yet were warmly approved in
every part of the country, and soon received the sanction
of the other colonies.

In the meantime the people everywhere were determined that none of the stamps should be sold or used.
The day on which the stamp act was to go into operation—the first of November 1765—was ushered in, in
many places, by funeral processions, the tolling of bells, and
hoisting colors of vessels at half mast. Business was suspended, and shops and stores closed. But by this time
not a single sheet of all the bales of stamps sent from
England, could be found in any of the colonies except
Delaware, Virginia and Georgia. They had either been
burnt, reshipped to England, or concealed and safely
guarded by the royalists, through fear of the popular fury.
The consequence was, that no business requiring stamp-
paper could be legally transacted. To this, our fathers
and mothers submitted as a less evil than slavery. Even
their sons and daughters upon the eve of marriage chose
to postpone it indefinitely rather than be married by
stamped certificates of publishment. Courts of justice
were shut, and an absolute stagnation in all the social relations of life prevailed. Printers of newspapers alone
went in the face of the royal edict, because they knew a
worse thing than the penalty of the law would happen
to them if they did not. When intelligence reached
England of the state of things here, it produced a great
sensation. Business there received a heavy blow from the
suspension of business here.

1766. March 10th, Col. John Choate departed this life
at the age of 68. He was a son of Capt. Thomas Choate,
the first settler of Hog Island and was born there in the
year 1697. His parents were his early teachers, as they

were of all their children, faithfully and diligently instructing them in the rudiments of learning, and the principles of morality and piety.   John rose to much eminence in civil society.   In addition to strong native talent, he possessed extensive information on civil, military and judicial affairs. He resided, after his marriage, in the center of the town, and represented the town at the General Court in 1731–2–3–5, 1741–2–3–5–6–7–8–9, 1754–7 and 1760.   He was a member of the Governor's Council from 1761, to 1765 inclusive, Justice of the Court of Sessions and Court of Common Pleas, and Judge of the Probate Court.   When in 1764, the town and county bridge was rebuilt, he was chairman of the committee for that business.   Under his direction chiefly, and upon a plan drafted by him, although he had never seen a bridge of that sort, it was built with two stone arches, resting on one solid pier in the middle of the river.   On exhibiting the plan and during the progress of the work, the whole of which he superintended, many expressed strong doubts of its capability of sustaining any considerable weight, and some confidently predicted that on the passing of the first loaded carriage, the arches would give way and fall into the river.   Though confident himself of success, yet as the experiment was new, and there was a possibility of failure from some unpropitious circumstances, he deemed it wise to be prepared for the worst.   Hence when the bridge was completed, and many were gathered to witness the passage of the first loaded team, he stood, it is said, with his horse saddled and bridled, ready to mount, if the arches began to give way, and turn his back upon the prophets all ready to shout, " We told you so!—we knew it could not stand!" But victory was completely on his side.   To the disappointment of some, and the admiration of many, the arches never yielded to any pressure ; and the bridge, by order of the Court of Sessions, was labelled in durable letters which the traveler reads, " *Choate bridge, built in* 1764."

Col. Choate was eminent as a Christian, as well as a

civilian and Jurist. To purity of morals, he added the worship of God, and the honoring of his Redeemer in obedience to every gospel requirement. Morning and evening
his house was the house of prayer. He was an active and
useful member of the South Church under the ministry
of the Rev. John Walley. By his talents, learning and
usefulness, he did honor to the place of his birth ; of which
we may say, that few islands of the same extent of territory, with land enough for only three farms, have given
birth to so many active, useful *and distinguished men.*
Besides the many Christian fathers and mothers who live
to bless the communities to which they emigrated, it numbers among its children living or dead, an elder of the
church, two pastors' wives, the wife of an eminent physician, several justices of the peace, four representatives
to the General Court, a judge of several courts, a justice
of the Court of Sessions, a senator of the Commonwealth,
and a senator of the United States.

This year the pastoral relation between the Rev. Nehemiah Porter and the Second Church and Parish was dissolved. Mr. Porter was born in Ipswich, March 20, 1720,
at the Hamlet (now Hamilton.) He was prepared for
college by his pastor, Rev. Mr. Wigglesworth, and graduated at Harvard in 1745. In the possession of the author
is a Hebrew Lexicon, *published in 1607,* which was the
property of Mr. Porter and contains his autograph with
the date 1744. It doubtless formed a part of his apparatus for study during the Senior year and it gives ample
evidence of having been well thumbed. His first wife—
Rebecca Chipman of Beverly—died in this place October
28, 1763, aged 36. She left nine children. Rev. Charles
S. Porter of South Boston is the son of one of them.
Mr. Porter's pastorate in Chebacco lasted sixteen years.
During the greater part of this time he lived very happily
with his people. But for a few years before his dismission, difficulties existed between them which rendered his
situation more and more unpleasant, and occasioned sev-

eral councils. In April of this year, referees mutually
chosen by the parties, met here and decided that it was
expedient for his connection with them to be dissolved if
his parish pay him £340 L. M. which included arrearages
of salary for a few of the past years. The parish complied, and in June he took his dismission. The same summer he took passage in a vessel for Yarmouth, Nova Scotia,
where some emigrants from this town resided. There he
founded a Congregational Church which still lives and
prospers. Having preached to that church several years,
he returned to Massachusetts and was installed pastor of
the church in Ashfield, December 21, 1774.

" Being then about 54 years of age, some at the parish meeting for giving
him an invitation to settle, urged as an objection that on account of his age
they could not expect to enjoy him long, as their minister. But he sustained
the pastoral relation with them forty-five years, and for the most part of that
long period was very active, and highly useful. He visited the people here
when nearly eighty, and conducted the services of worship both parts of the
Sabbath. Even after a colleague pastor was settled in 1808, Mr. Porter
did not entirely suspend his active labors though he was then in the eighty-
eighth year of his age. He continued to preach occasionally for many years
afterwards, and sometimes exhorted and prayed in public with edification to
his hearers, until he reached his hundredth year. In June 1819 a second
colleague was ordained. Memorable indeed were the novel and interesting
scenes of that ordination day—the venerable appearance of the Senior Pastor, bending under the weight of almost one hundred years, as he passed
along the broad aisle leaning on his two staffs, the firm and steady step with
which he ascended the pulpit stairs without aid, the fervency with which he
engaged in the consecrating prayer, and the distinct, audible, and appropriate
manner in which he addressed a few dying words to his beloved flock in the
form of a charge.

" As a preacher Mr. Porter sustained a very respectable character. If not
a star of the first magnitude, yet he shone with a clearness and degree of
lustre, which rendered him an ornament to the church. That divine light
and truth which irradiated and sanctified his own soul, he diffused to the utmost of his ability into the souls of others. The doctrines he had imbibed and
firmly believed as the only foundation of his hope and comfort for time and
eternity, were such as are emphatically called the doctrines of grace. These
he labored to inculcate in all his preaching and exhortations. His sermons
were always plain and simple, well calculated to instruct and impress the
mind, and delivered with remarkable animation and pungency, and holy fervor. For several years before his death, religion was the constant theme of

his conversation. It may be truly said that he preached daily to those who visited him in his own house. He spoke in a distinct voice, and with wonderful propriety of language. He expressed great confidence in God ; and spoke of death with much composure. At nine o'clock p. m., February 29th, 1820, he calmly fell asleep in Jesus, having completed his hundredth year into one month. His funeral was attended on the following Friday, by the neighboring clergymen, and a numerous concourse of citizens. Rev. John Emerson of Conway preached an appropriate sermon from Psalms cxvi. 15."*

The surviving descendants of Mr. Porter at the time of his decease were supposed to be upwards of two hundred and thirty in number.

On the 19th of March, this year, the bill was passed in the British Parliament for repealing the American stamp act. This caused great joy in England. The vessels in the Thames displayed their colors, and the city of London was illuminated. But the joy here was greater still. The intelligence was received with acclamations of the most sincere and heartfelt gratitude by all classes of people. The bells were rung, and public thanksgivings were offered up in the churches. In the midst of their joy, however, they overlooked the declaratory act passed at the same time, that the British Parliament had the right to tax the colonies ; but their attention was soon turned to this by other oppressive acts of Parliament in relation to our trade.

1767. The British Parliament in maintenance of their declared right to tax the colonies, levied duties upon glass, paper, pasteboard, white and red lead, painters' colors, and tea ; and passed an act establishing a new board of custom-house officers in America. These acts, when they reached the colonies, again excited universal alarm. It was seen at once, that new duties were only a new mode of drawing money from the colonies ; and the same determined opposition to the measure was exhibited, which had been shown to the stamp act. Their fears were still further increased by the arrival soon after, of a body of British troops in Boston, which was hypocritically said to have been driven in, by stress of weather. The governor undertook to provide for their support out of the public treasury. The conduct of the troops was such as to confirm the suspicions, that they were brought in by design. Our Legislature remonstrated with their usual firmness against the oppressive exactions of public money by the governor, and against the imposition of duties for the support of crown officers and the maintenance of troops among them. It was during this session that they passed a resolution, to address a circular letter to the other colonies, inviting them to a union, not of resistance to the mother country, but of remonstrance and petition for redress of grievances.

1768. This circular letter which was sent February 11th, created no little alarm in the British Cabinet, union and concert of action among the colonies being a peculiar object of dread to the ministers. The Earl of Hillsborough, therefore, wrote a letter expressive of his Majesty's displeasure, and requiring the House of this year to rescind the obnoxious resolution; and directing the governor, in case of their refusal, to dissolve the General Court. This letter, dated April 22d, the governor laid before the House, on the 21st of June. On the 30th of June the House voted not to rescind, 92 to 17. Our representative this year, Dr. John Calef, was unfortunately in the minority. Our fathers wide awake on the subject of liberty, kept a watchful eye on the representatives to see if they did their duty, and claimed the right in town meeting of approving or condemning, as the case might require. Accordingly they assembled on the 11th of August, and voted, that the town of Ipswich highly approve the conduct of those gentlemen of the late House of Representatives, who were for maintaining the rights and liberties of their constituents, and were against rescinding the resolves of a former House. Voted, that the thanks of the town be given to the worthy and much esteemed ninety-two gentlemen of the House of Representatives,

for their firmness and steadiness in standing up for, and
adhering to the just rights and liberties of the subject
when it was required of them at the peril of their political existence, to rescind the resolves of the then former
House of Representatives. The conduct of these ninety-
two was highly applauded throughout the colonies. Dr.
Calef recanted and made public confession, and was thus
restored to the confidence of his townsmen, September
19th. The town in compliance with a proposal of the
selectmen of Boston, elect Michael Earley to represent
them in a convention, to deliberate on constitutional
measures to obtain redress of their grievances. This
convention met in Boston, September 23d, and disclaim-
ing legislative authority, petitioned the governor, expressed its aversion to standing armies, to tumults and
disorders, its readiness to assist in suppressing riots and
preserving the peace: and after a short session dissolved.

1769. June 27th, a visit is made to Mr. Cleaveland's
house by 77 ladies. Such parties assembled at the parsonage soon after breakfast. They brought flax and wheels
with them and spun the whole day industriously, except
the time for dinner and supper. At 11 o'clock A. M., such
men of the Society as pleased came and paid their respects to the spinners. Among the presents made to the
minister's family was all the yarn made at the meeting;
then very needful to supply them with homespun linen.

1770. March 19th, the town voted that

" We are determined to retrench all extravagances; and that we will, to
the utmost of our power, encourage our own manufactures; and that we will
not, by ourselves, or any for or under us, directly or indirectly, purchase any
goods of the persons who have imported or continue to import, or of any
trader who shall purchase any goods of said importers, contrary to the agreement of merchants in Boston and the other trading towns in this government
and the neighboring colonies, until they make a public retraction, or a general
importation takes place. And further, taking under consideration the excessive use of tea, which has been such a bane to this country, voted, that we
will abstain therefrom ourselves, and recommend the disuse of it in our families,
until all the revenue acts are repealed."

25

Our fathers were wise in barely recommending the disuse of tea in their families, for if our mothers had not
been as patriotic as their husbands, they could hardly have
kept tea from their tables. But the women of that day,
our fathers have told us, were not less patriotic than the
men, and were ready to sacrifice all for the good of their
country. Said a lady of ninety, not long before her recent
death, " The oppression of the British, I well remember
was an exciting topic of conversation at all our firesides,
and in all companies: a subject into which the women
entered as zealously as the men, and all were ready to resist, even unto death."

The importance of manufacturing their own clothing
and other articles, was deeply, universally felt. In this
way alone could they be free from a servile dependence
on the mother-country. The growth of sheep was to be
encouraged for the sake of their wool. No lambs were to
be butchered. "We will eat no lamb, we will drink no
tea, we will wear no mourning at funerals, we will dress
wholly in home-spun," was the universal cry, the total-
abstinence pledge of the day. Deer-skin furnished an important article of clothing. But deer were becoming
scarce in our woods at a time when they were much
needed. Hence our fathers in town-meeting this year,
voted that the deer-reeves of Ipswich join with those of
other towns, to prevent these animals in Chebacco woods
from being extirpated. Fishing was also much encouraged among us. From twenty-five to thirty Chebacco
boats with two men and a boy in each, went to Damaris
Cove and brought their fish ashore here to be cured.
Fish flakes were to be found on Hog Island, on Ware-
house Island at the north end, on Thompson's Island, and
at Clay Point.

This year for the first time the people of Chebacco were
favored with the residence of a physician among them.
Dr. Ebenezer Davis, a young man, now commenced practice here. After his marriage he lived in the " Pickering

house." A few years later he removed to Squam Parish, Gloucester, and was succeeded here by Dr. Russ.

1771, October 25th. Daniel Giddinge died, aged 67. He was an elder in the Fourth Church, and a representative of the town in 1758. He left eight children.

1772. A fever of the nervous putrid type commenced here, which continued for some time, and in its progress proved very fatal. It prevailed chiefly among the young. The most vigorous were the first to yield to it. It carried off in the whole, fifty persons.

December 28th. A town-meeting is called to hear the report of a committee appointed at a previous meeting, in pursuance of a circular from Boston, urging upon the towns the importance of a unanimous expression of their feelings with regard to the conduct of the British ministry, and the appointment of committees of correspondence. The report of the committee was unanimously adopted. It contained for substance a statement of their grievances,—that the governor and judges and board of commissioners of the customs were paid by the crown, and thus made independent of the Legislature, that regular troops were posted in the Province, and taxes levied without the voice of the people. It declared their right to dispose of their property as they pleased, to petition the king and Parliament for a redress of grievances, and to continue so to do until redress should be granted.

It affirmed that Parliament in assuming the right to tax the colonies, acted contrary to the opinions of eminent men in Parliament, as well as of the whole community here; made a full declaration of their firm attachment to his Majesty and his royal family, and of their desire to the utmost of their ability to support government, and promote quietness and good order, and at the same time not to submit to oppression, but to stand firmly for their rights. It instructed the representative of the town to use his influence that the governor and judges be paid by the Legislature and not by the crown; and that an agent of the House be appointed to represent the condition of the Province to the king or his ministers; and if the governor refuse to allow grants of the House for such an agent, that the House recommend to the several towns to pay the agent. A committee of correspondence was also chosen at this meeting. By these committees, the doings of the several towns were reported to the Boston committee, and by them sent abroad to similar committees in other colonies, and thus a confidential interchange of opinion was kept up between the colonies. Great unity of sentiment was the consequence, and the value of the measure was fully developed in the struggle which afterwards ensued between the colonies and the parent country. When by royal power our Legislatures were dissolved or prorogued, our democratic town-meetings became, under God, the salvation of the country. Through them the people could both speak and act.

1773. Parliament enact that the East India Company may export their teas to America, with a drawback of all the duties paid in England. By this regulation tea would be cheaper here than in England, and it was supposed that the colonists would be willing on this account, to pay the small duty levied upon it. Large quantities of tea, were, therefore, shipped to this country. Before its arrival, the inhabitants of the principal sea-ports determined that, if possible, it should not be even landed.

When news was received in Ipswich, that the cargoes of tea which had arrived in Boston had been thrown overboard in the night-time by men disguised as Mohawk Indians, our fathers met in town-meeting, and voted:

" 1. That the inhabitants of this town have received real pleasure and satisfaction from the noble and spirited exertions of their brethren of Boston and other towns to prevent the landing of the detested tea, lately arrived there from the East India Company, subject to duty which goes to support persons not friendly to the interests of this Province.

" 2. That they highly disapprove of the consignees of the East India Company, because of their equivocal answers to a respectable committee of Boston, and their refusal to comply with the wish of their countrymen.

" 3. That every person who shall import tea, while the act for duty on it continues, shall be held as an enemy.

" 4. That no tea be sold in town, while this act is in force ; that if any one sell it here, he shall be deemed an enemy.

" Voted that these resolves be sent to the committee of correspondence of Boston."

1774. The two religious societies, after a separate existence of more than twenty-eight years, are at length united and become one again under the name of the Second Church and Parish with the Rev. Mr. Cleaveland for their pastor. The choice of a committee by the Second Parish within three months after Mr. Porter's dismission " to treat with the Sixth Parish concerning a union of the two," and similar action on the part of the latter, soon after, the arrangement entered into less than two years later, March 12th 1768, to worship together,—half of the year in each meeting-house, a renewal of overtures by the Sixth Parish in 1769, and again in 1773, a further agreement in 1770, that the Second Parish should pay four-sevenths and the Sixth Parish three-sevenths of Mr. Cleaveland's salary, afford conclusive proof that there had been little if any personal alienation of feeling between the individual members of the two bodies. These measures also served to prepare the way for the formal and perfect union which was now to be effected, first, however, as was becoming, between the two *churches.* By invitation of the Fourth Church, in response to a proposal for union made by the Second Church on the 30th of March, 1774, a joint meeting of the two bodies " for conference relative to a union " was held at the " Centre school-house " on the 8th of April, at which each church passed a unanimous vote " to bury forever as a church all former differences between them and the other church, and to acknowledge the other a sister church in charity and fellowship." At an adjourned meeting at the same place, on the first Monday in June, each church " voted to unite in calling an ecclesiastical council to assist and advise the two churches in uniting in one ;" and in this action the two

parishes concurred on the 1st of July. Five churches
were represented on this council—the first, third (Hamlét),
South and Line-brook churches in Ipswich, and the church
in Byfield. It convened on the 4th of October at "the
new meeting-house." Rev. Mr. Leslie of Byfield was its
moderator, and Rev. Joseph Dana, scribe. On consideration of the question "whether the way was clear to proceed to the act of uniting the two churches agreeably to
their desire," it was found that the Fourth Church had
given offence to the church in Manchester by admitting
to communion some members of that church resident in
Chebacco who were under censure, and it was therefore
deemed advisable "for the peace and harmony of the
churches" to request the Manchester church, if they think
proper, to state whether they had any objection to this
union. At the adjourned session of the council on the
25th of the same month, the Manchester church, through a
committee, signified their approval of the proposed union,
on certain conditions which were referred to the Fourth
Church and accepted by them. This reconciliation having been effected, the council next appointed a committee
to draw up a plan of union, articles of faith and a covenant. On the afternoon of the next day, the plan reported
by the committee, having been unanimously accepted and
recommended "as a proper plan of union all things considered," was distinctly read to both churches, unanimously
accepted by them, and subscribed in the presence of the
council by Dea. Seth Story, moderator, and five other
brethren of the Second Church, and the pastor and twenty-
two brethren of the Fourth Church. This compact was
as follows:

" *Heads of Agreement for uniting the Second and Fourth Churches
of Ipswich into one Congregational Church, come into, in the presence of a Council of Churches.*"

" 1. We, the Second and Fourth Churches of Ipswich, covenant and agree
to become one Congregational Church, under the name or style of the Second
Church of Ipswich.

" 2. We covenant and agree that, by the act of union, this united church
shall be entitled to all the rights, powers and privileges which belonged to
each church before the union, that is to say : The officers of each church,
whether pastor, ruling-elders, or deacons, shall, by the act of union, become
the officers of the united church ; And the church vessels and furniture for
the Holy Communion, and every other peculiar privilege and grant whatsoever, made or belonging to either, said Second Church or the said Fourth
Church, shall be the property of this united church, under the name or style
of the Second Church in Ipswich as aforesaid.

" 3. We covenant and agree to receive the word of God contained in the
Scriptures of the Old and New Testament to be our absolute and only rule
relative to the doctrines of faith, the worship of God, church-government and
discipline, all relative duties, and a virtuous life and conversation.

" 4. As we aim to be a true *Protestant* Church in our united state, we covenant and agree to profess unity of faith with the Protestant church in general,
by adopting that system of Christian doctrine held forth in the Westminster
shorter catechism and the New England Confession of Faith ; it being a sound
orthodox system or summary of Scripture doctrine, according to our understanding of the word of God.

" 5. And, as we aim to be a strictly *Congregational* Church in point of
church-government and discipline in our united state, we covenant and agree
to adhere to the platform of church-government and discipline drawn up by a
synod at Cambridge in New England. A. D. 1648, as containing our sentiments in the general, relative to a church-state, its power, its officers, their
ordination, the qualifications for church-membership, admission of members,
the communion of churches, &c., &c.,—in a word relative to church-government in general.

" And now, as a visible political union among a number of visible saints
is necessary to constitute them a particular Congregational Church, and this
political union or essential form is a visible covenant, agreement or consent,
whereby they give up themselves to the Lord to the observing of the ordinances of Christ together in the same society ; so a visible political union between us *as churches* is necessary to constitute us one particular Congregational Church :

" Wherefore, we, the Second and Fourth Churches of Ipswich, having
agreed to become one united Church of Jesus Christ for the worship of God
and the observing of his ordinances together in the same society, and having
before as distinct Churches covenanted with God and one another in a distinct covenant respectively, do now as churches, consistent with sacred regard thereto, covenant together to be one church of Jesus Christ, and solemnly renew covenant with God in Christ to walk and worship together as
one body, by signing together the following form or covenant which is in
substance the same as is understood to be the original covenant of the Second
Church of Ipswich, in which it (that is the Second Church) was founded.

" In testimony of our holy resolution in the strength of Christ to stand and walk together in the fellowship of the Gospel, in a careful observance of this covenant and the foregoing heads of agreement, we not only call Heaven and Earth to witness, but set our names hereunto, in the presence of an Ecclesiastical Council, this 20th day of October, 1774."

" It was then desired that if any of the congregation had aught to object to the articles, they would signify it. There was no objection. Thereupon the moderator, in the name and by the unanimous vote of the council, saluted the Brethren as a united church by the name of the Second Church in Ipswich, and gave the right hand of fellowship to them as a sister Church ; also gave the right hand of fellowship to the Rev. Mr. Cleaveland as Pastor of the united church, and the other Elders of the council, did the same. The united church voted their thanks to the council, and the business of the day was concluded with singing the one hundred and thirty-third and a part of the one hundred and twenty-second Psalms, and with prayer by the moderator."*

Before the union of the two churches, the following officers had died : of the Second Church, Dea. John Andrews, March 25, 1753 ; Dea. Zechariah Story, February 16, 1774, aged 90 ;—of the Fourth Church : Elder Daniel Giddinge, October, 1771. The officers of the *united church* (all of both churches continuing in office), were : elders, Francis Choate, Eleazer Craft ; deacons, Seth Story, Solomon Giddinge, Stephen Choate, Thomas Burnham. The additions to the Second Church during this period of separation numbered 23, to the Fourth Church, 155.

The two *parishes* did not become legally united until the next year. On the 23d of January, 1775, a committee was chosen by each, to prepare " conditions of union." The terms proposed by this joint committee were adopted by both parishes, March 2d, and a " petition to the General Court for a confirmation of said union," was prepared, accepted March 29th, and sent to Boston by a joint committee. On the 10th of April, " the General Court passed an act uniting the Second and Sixth Parishes into one, to be called the Second Parish." The united congregation continued to worship half the year in each meeting-house, until the present one was built.

---

* Church Records.

CHAPTER IV.

TO THE CLOSE OF THE EIGHTEENTH CENTURY.

1774. WHILE thus engaged in the work of perfecting union among themselves in religious matters, the people of Chebacco were by no means indifferent to the further encroachments made upon their political rights during this same most eventful year, nor did they fail to do their part in the preparations made for resistance. They fully shared in the universal indignation, excited by the news, received in the Spring, of acts of Parliament, closing the port of Boston against all trade; altering the charter of their Province, so as to make the appointment of the Council, justices, judges, sheriffs and even jurors, dependent upon the king, or his agent; forbidding all town-meetings except the annual meeting, without leave of the Governor in writing, and a statement of the special business proposed to be done; authorizing the Governor, with advice of the Council, to send any person for trial to any other colony, or to Great Britain, for any act in violation of the laws of the revenue; and of the appointment of Gen. Gage, with almost unlimited powers, not only as Governor, but also Commander of his Majesty's forces in America. With the rest of the Province, they regarded the election by their House of Representatives of five of its members, as delegates to a Continental Congress to meet in Philadelphia in September, as by far the most important business transacted by that body, at its first session under the new governor, on the 25th of May.

The *town meetings*, which were held from month to month on account of the dark and threatening aspect of

26

the times, our fathers in this parish were not at all backward to attend, especially as they were led on in the way of duty by their pastor, who was full of patriotic zeal, and ready to make any sacrifice for the cause of liberty. On the 29th of August, delegates were elected by the town to a county convention to meet at Ipswich September 6th, " to concert measures in these distressed times." This convention passed several resolutions, recommending peaceable measures as long as they would answer, but a resort to arms as preferable to slavery; and such measures of defense as might make resistance, if it must come, more successful.

On the 26th of September the town met to give instructions to their representatives to the General Court, which had been ordered by the Governor to convene again at Salem, October 5th. The patriotic language in which they addressed their representatives on that occasion is as follows:

" As it is a day of much darkness, this Province in particular suffering under ministerial vengeance, it requires wisdom and firmness so to act, as by the blessing of God, to convince our enemies, that we shall stand for our rights. We instruct you not to countenance that unconstitutional council appointed by the king, in submitting to act with them in one particular, and that, if the governor will not allow the council chosen by the people to sit as the second branch of the Legislature, that you do not proceed to do one single act, unless it be to pass such resolves as may be judged necessary to attest your abhorrence of slavery, and all attempts that but serve to have a tendency that way. We agree with the advice given by a Congress of this country, that a provincial Congress be formed and meet together to consult on what is to be done by this people as a body; and we would have you unite with such a Congress. We think it would be better to have each town send more persons to this Congress, than the law allows representatives to the General Court, and we would have you exert yourselves for this."

The House of Representatives, though the governor had changed his mind and by proclamation forbidden it to assemble, met at Salem, resolved itself into a Provincial Congress, and adjourned to Concord. There, October 26th, they took a step decisive of war. This was the organization of the militia, consisting of all the able-bodied men of the colony, and the election of general officers. They also constituted one-fourth of the militia minute-men to be frequently drilled and held in readiness for service at a minute's warning. Before the close of the year, the busy note of preparation resounded throughout the whole Province. The committee of safety were indefatigable, in providing for the most vigorous defense in the Spring— procuring all sorts of military supplies for the service of twelve thousand men, and every town was active in carrying out their plans.

In Chebacco a military company of foot, consisting of 68 men, was formed. The meeting for organization was held on the 20th of December. Lieut. Jacob Story was chosen chairman and Rev. John Cleaveland clerk. Before proceeding to the election of officers the following preamble and resolutions were passed unanimously:

" We, the training Company of Chebacco, in Ipswich, being assembled to choose Military Officers for the said Company agreeable to the advice of the late Provincial Congress, this 20th Day of December, A. D. 1774, previous to our proceeding to the choice of said Officers, think it proper to enter into the following Resolutions, viz :

" 1. Resolved, That the persons who shall be chosen by the majority of the training Band now assembled, shall be military Officers of the company in this place, in case they accept of the choice, till others shall be chosen or appointed in their Room.

" 2. Resolved, That the officers, who shall be chosen and shall accept of the choice, shall hold themselves obliged to inform themselves well into the military Art and Discipline, and to use their best Endeavors to teach the company in this place the military Art and Discipline, by frequently calling them together to exercise them in the way ordered by his Majesty in 1674 ; also, in obedience to their superior Officers appointed agreeable to the advice of the Provincial Congress, to send us forth to action in the Field of Battle in Defence of our constitutional privileges, whensoever there shall be a manifest call for it against our common Enemies.

" 3. Resolved, That, in case of manifest Failure of performing the Duties of their office as hinted at in the above Resolutions in any or either of the officers that shall be chosen, we reserve the power in our hands of dropping such delinquent officer or officers, and of choosing others in their room.

" 4. Resolved, That we will yield such Obedience to the commands of the Officers that shall be chosen, and shall accept of the choice, as the provincial Laws respecting the Militia require; and submit to such punishments, in case of Delinquency in us, as the said Laws also require.

"These resolutions being read once and again, the chairman put them to vote one by one to the Training Band, and all four of the above Resolutions unanimously passed in the affirmative.

"Attest,   JOHN CLEAVELAND, *Clerk of said meeting.*"

The officers elected were as follows: Jonathan Cogswell, Jr., Captain; David Low, Lieutenant; Francis Perkins, Ensign. The record of the transactions of this meeting in the hand-writing of Mr. Cleaveland, was preserved by Capt. (afterwards Col.) Cogswell, and is still extant.

1775. January 3d, the inhabitants of the town met and chose Michael Farley to represent them in the Provincial Congress to be held at Cambridge on the 1st of February. January 19th, they met again to instruct their representative:

"1. To use his influence so that Congress may appoint an early Fast because of degeneracy from the good ways of our fathers, and of increasing wickedness and infidelity in Great Britain.

"2. To inquire if any towns have neglected the resolves of the Provincial Congress, and if so to publish them: and if any persons have not complied with association agreement, to have their names advertised.

"3. While enemies among ourselves say, that we are seeking after independence, when we are not, endeavor that the Congress alter the Government, so as to agree with our last charter.

"4. We approve of the wise recommendations of the late Provincial Congress, as to our manufactures We should like some particular method pointed out for promoting them."

As our fathers say at this town meeting, revolution and independence were not what they were seeking, but redress of grievances. Amelioration of treatment for the present, and assurance of kindness in future, were all that the colonies asked of Great Britain. But what they sought was not granted. Instead of any redress, coercive measures were threatened. After the first blood in the opening of this great drama had been shed by the British, in the battle of Lexington, on the 19th of April, our fathers had no longer any doubt what course to pursue. About thirty thousand militia were soon assembled in the neighborhood of Boston, ready to do justice to themselves and their country.

On the 21st of April, two days after the battle of Lexington, a scene of terror and confusion was witnessed in this town, which extended itself to several of the neighboring towns and has since been called, "The Great Ipswich Fright." The news of the Lexington fight in all its exaggerated details, had just been received. Terrible stories of the atrocities committed by the dreaded "Regulars" had been related, and it was believed that nothing short of a general extermination of the patriots,—men, women, and children,—was contemplated by the British commander. Under this excitement, a rumor which no one attempted to trace or authenticate, was spread from house to house, that the British had landed, and were marching upon the town. The terror was indescribable. What should they do? Defence was out of the question, as all the young and able-bodied men of the town and of the entire region had marched to Cambridge. No relief was left them but in flight. All that could, left their houses and fled from the town. Almost simultaneously the people of Beverly were smitten with the same terror. How the rumor was communicated no one could tell. It was there believed that the enemy had fallen upon Ipswich, and massacred the inhabitants without regard to age or sex. As our people ran northerly for safety, they found that the rumor had gone before them, and that the people of Rowley had run to Newbury, and the people of Newbury to Salisbury; and the fright extended up the river as far as Haverhill, whose inhabitants fled across the river in boats to Bradford. It was not till the next morning that the fugitives were undeceived. Such of our town's people as could not, or would not, leave their homes, became convinced that the terrible rumor was wholly unfounded. A young man from Exeter, who happened to be in town, mounted his horse, and followed after the flying multitude, undeceiving all whom he overtook, and thus before the next night, they were all quietly lodged again in their homes.

Soon after the battle of Lexington, the Continental Congress again assembled at Philadelphia. By a unanimous vote of this body, George Washington, then a member of Congress, was appointed, June 15th, Commander-in-Chief of the army then raised, or to be raised, for the defence of American liberty. Before his arrival at the camp in Cambridge, General Ward had the command of the army. The troops had been together now nearly two months, and were impatient for some action against the British. Col. Prescott was sent on the 16th of June, with a detachment of about a thousand men, to occupy a station on Bunker's Hill. On viewing the eminence he saw at once that it was an unsuitable spot, and looking along to the right, he found that a spur of that hill now called Breed's Hill was the most proper situation in every respect for a battle-ground. There he threw up a temporary fortification; and having, on the morning of the 17th, been reinforced by several hundred men, making the whole force about seventeen hundred, he was attacked and driven from the hill by three or four thousand of the British. Of the men from this parish who were in that battle, the names of six are known: James Andrews, (father of the late Israel Andrews,) Benjamin Burnham (father of the late Abner Burnham), Nehemiah Choate, Aaron Perkins, Jesse Story Jr., a minor,* (brother of the late Ephraim Story,) who was killed, and Francis Burnham (a brother of the late Capt. Nathaniel Burnham), who was wounded. Two Chebacco boys, Aaron Low and Samuel Procter, belonged to a Gloucester company which reached Cambridge on the

---

* In the House of Representatives—"Resolved that there be paid out of the public Treasury of this State to Jesse Story of Chebacco in Ipswich (father of Jesse Story Jr., under 21 years of age) the sum of £5. 15s. in full for the loss he sustained in arms, ammunition and wearing apparel by the death of his said son who was killed at the battle of Bunker's Hill, as will appear in the account and certificate."—*Records of General Court.*

afternoon of the 16th, and were at work all that night making cartridges.

Francis Burnham's father lived in the old mansion near the ancient grist-mill at the Falls. We will call and hear from him the particulars of the battle :

" We began our march," he says, " from the camp about nine o'clock in the evening, and on reaching Bunker's Hill we lay upon our arms, till our Colonel, with his engineers, had fixed upon the spot for a fort. We were then set at work to gather up what materials we could, suitable for a fortification, and first built a redoubt, as it was called, about one hundred and forty or fifty feet square, with two open passages. On the left of the redoubt running north-easterly, we made a solid wall of sods, four feet high, for a breastwork. From this breastwork we built a line of rail-fence, and parallel to it a post-fence with four feet of space between them. This space we filled up with new mown grass ; treading it down so that it made quite as good a screen for us, as the redoubt or the breastwork of sods. Early the next morning a British ship of war began a cannonade upon us, but without any damage. Very soon the battery on Copp's Hill was opened against us, and the first shot killed one of our men ; but what is very remarkable, though the roar of cannon from this battery was incessant, yet no further damage was done by it. The next motion of the enemy that we discovered, was the landing at Morton's Point of ten companies of grenadiers and ten of light infantry with some artillery. They spent some little time in reconnoitering our position, and then sent some of their officers back to Boston. In an hour or two they came back with more troops. Though at first much superior to us in force, yet it seems they were afraid to advance. This gave us more confidence in our fortifications. About three in the afternoon they began to advance up the hill, halting occasionally to let us see what their artillery could do, but the angle of elevation was such that it did us but little harm. We had no ammunition to waste, for we had a scanty supply at best. We were ordered to put four buckshots to a bullet, and not to fire till they were within point-blank shot distance. They continued to approach us with a steady column and firm step, till we could see the whites of their eyes and then we poured in upon them a most destructive fire. The effect was tremendous. Their whole line was broken in confusion. We had ample time after we had loaded again, to see the blood flowing down the hill from the great number killed and wounded. At length they formed and advanced towards us again, but not with the same resolute step. We kept cool and waited as before, till every shot should tell, and then mowed them down like grass. Their line was broken into greater confusion than before, and it was some time.before the officers could get them to rally. By this time the whole of Charlestown, about four hundred houses, was all in a blaze. This we supposed the British did from revenge, and to terrify us. We expected to have to retreat soon, for most of our ammunition was gone, and but few of us had bayonets. They did not, however, dare to come up as before. A portion of them took a circuitous route to the south side of our hill, and soon scaled our works. We were now attacked on both sides, and the contest became very hot. Story and I were side by side, when a ball struck his head, his brains flew into my face and he fell back into the ditch, which ran along behind the fence. Another shot gave me a slight wound upon the shoulder, which made me stop for a few moments to get breath. A boy was standing not far from me, by the side of his father. When his father was just ready to apply the lighted torch to a cannon, a shot struck him and he instantly fell. The boy at once seized the torch from his father's hand and touched off the cannon, which did great execution upon the enemy. But after fighting awhile under the greatest disadvantage, we had to retreat, and more of our men fell while retreating, than when standing at the breastworks. Providentially for us, a fine, large company of Connecticut troops that had not been in the hottest of the action, moved up in good order near Mystic River and covered our retreat. One thing I forgot to mention, which was greatly in our favor. The wind blowing strong from the west, drove all the smoke directly into the face of our enemy, but as it rose a little above them we could see under the cloud, and point our guns breast-high."

The minister of this parish is chaplain of Col. Little's regiment—"the 17th Foot, Continental army—enlisted July 1, 1775," at Cambridge. He practiced as he preached. It was remarked to the author by aged people, forty years ago, that Mr. Cleaveland preached all the men of his parish into the army, and then went himself. Three of his four sons were in the service for a longer or shorter time. One of them, Nehemiah, enlisted in his sixteenth year, and served in the army investing Boston, and, at a later period, in New Jersey and at West Point. "Not only by his professional services as Chaplain, but by various contributions to newspapers, he did much to encourage and further the great enterprise which had its issue in our national independence."

From printed documents it appears that Ipswich furnished more men for the army this year than any other town in the county except Salem.

On the 9th of August, the Falcon sloop-of-war, having chased an American vessel into Gloucester harbor, dispatched three boats with about forty men, to bring her off, when the party were so warmly received by the militia, who had collected on the shore, that the captain thought it necessary to send a reinforcement, and to commence can-· nonading the town. A very smart action ensued, which was kept up for several hours, but resulted in the complete defeat of the assailants, leaving upwards of thirty prisoners in the hands of the Americans. Many people there were so alarmed at the approach of the enemy that they fled with their valuables into the interior. Some only came as far as this place, bringing silver plate and other valuables with them, and tarried awhile until the danger seemed to be over. For the defence and protection of the coast of Cape Ann, a force of militia from the more inland towns was drafted, to be stationed there. On their march thither they passed through Chebacco, halted and were paraded on the common (near the present North meeting-house), where they received their Chebacco fellow-soldiers. On this occasion, a prayer was offered by the ardent and patriotic Cleaveland. While he was praying in his stentorian voice "that the enemy might be blown "—"to hell and damnation," loudly interrupted an excited soldier—"to the land of tyranny from whence they came," continued the undisturbed chaplain, without altering his tone or apparently noticing the interruption.

The Continental Congress this year established a line of posts, from Falmouth (now Portland) in New England to Savannah in Georgia, and unanimously appointed Benjamin Franklin postmaster-general. The Provincial Congress had before this, in the month of May, appointed a post-office for Ipswich, and James Foster postmaster. This was the first post-office ever opened in Ipswich. The year before, a stage with four horses commenced running twice a week, from Newburyport through Ipswich to Boston: which was a great improvement upon the open stage-chair running once a week only from Portsmouth to Boston.

1776. The Massachusetts militia in Washington's army

27

near Boston, in which Chebacco was well represented, had increased on the first of March to about six thousand, and in the work of fortifying Dorchester heights, on the night of March 4th, which compelled the evacuation of Boston by the British, our men bore their full share.

At this stage of the war it began to be seen that something must be done upon the water, as well as upon the land, to guard the sea-coast and make reprisals upon the enemy's property upon the ocean. Our Provincial Congress encouraged the fitting out of private armed vessels, which were very successful in capturing British vessels, containing merchandise, provisions and ammunition. Some of our best merchants and sea-captains were engaged in the business, under authority of government. It was with some reference to nautical affairs, probably, as well as to other measures of safety and defence, that the inhabitants of this town on the 24th of April met and chose a committee, " to meet with other sea-port committees, of the county at the tavern near Beverly meeting-house this day, and consult on measures to be taken for our safety in this difficult time." The Continental Congress during this year fitted out thirteen vessels of war, five of thirty-two guns, five of twenty-eight and three of twenty-four guns. At a meeting in April the town chose delegates " to attend a county convention to meet here this month relative to an equal representation, by every man's having a like voice in the election of the legislative body of this colony." This convention met, and drew up a memorial in favor of this, to be presented to the Provincial Congress.

At a town meeting, June 10th, it was voted " that the representatives be instructed, if the Continental Congress should for the safety of the colonies, declare them independent of Great Britain, that the inhabitants here will solemnly pledge their lives and fortunes to support them in the measure." Similar resolutions were passed in most of the towns. After the Declaration of Independence was passed in Congress July 4th, printed copies were circulated and read in all the churches on Sabbath afternoons, at the close of public worship, and the Declaration recorded in the Town books, according to the order of the State Council.

From January to August, four of our men died of disease in the army. Thomas Emerson Cole, aged 25; Jonathan Cogswell, 3d., aged 22; William Jones, aged 50; and David Goodhue, aged 22. · In the Fall, Joseph Marshall Jr., was killed by a cannon ball at Lake Champlain.

In accordance with orders of the 15th of September, every fifth able-bodied man under fifty years of age was drafted into the army. The militia were also called upon for further active service. Jonathan Cogswell, Esq., of Chebacco, had been elected by the House of Representatives, on the 15th of February, Colonel of the third regiment in this county, embracing Ipswich, a part of Rowley, Topsfield and Wenham. As appears from the testimony of the aged, he rendered important aid to his country as a military officer, during the whole of the Revolutionary struggle. If the particulars of his military course, could all be ascertained, they would doubtless afford abundant confirmation of this testimony. His regiment had been already reduced in numbers by the frequent drafts made upon it, for sea-coast men and various expeditions, before he took the field. From documents which he left in his family, we gather that he was at Fairfield, Ct., with his regiment, on the 19th of October, at Rye, November 3d, and at North Castle, on the 20th of the same month. While at Fairfield, as appears from his "return," his regiment, which was then a part of Gen. Parsons' Brigade, consisted of six companies—19 commissioned officers, 5 staff officers, 22 non-commissioned officers, and 309 rank and file. Nineteen of the latter were sick or absent on duty elsewhere, leaving 290 privates fit for duty; making his whole effective force 336. The Chebacco company in the regiment, under command of Capt. Perkins, contained 2 Lieutenants, 4 Sergeants and 55 rank and file, " present, fit for duty." An order received by Col. Cogswell there, in the handwriting of Washington, was preserved among his papers, and is now extant. The following is a copy of it:

" Whatever Troops are on the road from Connecticut towards Marroneck (in New York), are hereby ordered and directed to advance towards Marroneck, and there put themselves under the command of the Senior Officer, until further Orders; who is, with the whole of his Troops, to use every possible means to protect the Stores of Provisions at the Saw Pitts, and give their best assistance in sending them off to places of safety. Given under my hand this twenty-first day of October, 1776. GEORGE WASHINGTON."

Fairfield being a sea-port on Long Island Sound, he was doubtless there, to protect the coast and prevent the landing of the British. How long he had been there his papers do not say. From other sources, we know that he was at the battle of White Plains, thirty miles north-east of New York. His minister, the Rev. Mr. Cleaveland, was also there at the same time as chaplain of his regiment, as was also Mr. Cleaveland's son, Nehemiah, a private. This battle was fought on the 28th of October. The attack was made by the British, with a view to get possession of the eastern roads, and thus cut off the supplies which Washington was receiving for his army. But, though there were many killed on both sides, the British failed of their object. Washington maintained his ground, till the night of the 30th, when he removed his army to North Castle, a town three miles north-east of White Plains. Leaving here most of the New England troops under General Lee, Washington crossed the Hudson, and pressed by the British, soon after retreated across New Jersey. Some of our Chebacco men were with him in this retreat, as we have often heard them say. We must follow them, for the history of towns, is the history of townsmen, especially when acting for town and country. The British army under Lord Cornwallis follow hard after Washington through New Brunswick, Princeton and Trenton. At the Delaware they expect the river will delay him, and they with their superior force shall crush him at once. But he has just crossed over as they come up. Having no boats to pass with, they encamp and wait for the river to freeze. Washington, having called in some detachments of his army and being strengthened by 1500 militia under General Mifflin, determines to recross the Delaware, and surprise the British posts at Trenton. With the greatest difficulty, this bold undertaking is accomplished on the night of the 25th of December, by a part of the army, led by Washington himself. After much toil and suffering and loss of time, the force reaches Trenton at eight o'clock in the morning. Col. Rahl, the commanding officer of that post; attempts a defence, but he is mortally wounded at the first fire, and his troops in dismay seek to escape by the Princeton road, but Washington intercepts them, and defeats their design, and they are compelled to surrender. Of our troops, two are killed and two are frozen to death. Not wishing to hazard what he has gained, he recrosses the river with his prisoners, and six pieces of artillery, a thousand stand of arms and some military stores. Two days after, he crosses the Delaware again, and takes possession of Princeton. Lord Cornwallis, leaving a part of his troops at Princeton, marches with the rest of his army to give battle to Washington at Trenton. But our wise and skillful General, aware that his force is much too inferior to hazard a battle, resorts to stratagem. Leaving his fires burning briskly, and some small parties to throw up entrenchments within sound of the British sentinels, that his army might not be missed, he silently decamps in the night, and by a circuitous route, gains the rear of the enemy between Princeton and Trenton. Two British regiments are coming from Princeton to join Cornwallis. A conflict ensues. Our troops give way. But Washington rallies and leads on the main body, and victory is ours. We press on toward Princeton, where one regiment is left. A part save themselves by flight. The rest fall into our hands. Cornwallis hearing the firing towards Princeton, suspects the whole

at once, and immediately turns his troops towards Princeton. that he may save his stores at New Brunswick.
Washington, on his approach retires to Morristown, January 6, 1777, where he entrenches.   Cornwallis goes into
winter quarters at New Brunswick.   All the rest of New
Jersey, except Amboy, falls into the hands of our people.
These remarkable exploits, so signally blessed of heaven,
kindle new life in the breast of every soldier, and send a
thrill of joy throughout the country.   In our little community here, from which most of the men are gone, the
news flies from house to house, and female lips exclaim,
" Glorious news from the Jerseys."

1777.   February 27th, the town offer a bounty and extra
pay to every soldier enlisting in the continental army for
three years; first year, £6; second year, £8; third, £10.
If they die while in service, the same shall go to their
heirs; or such soldiers shall have £18 at the end of three
years.

June 9th.   The town instruct their representatives " to
oppose the repeal of the Price Act; to act against the
General Court's forming a new plan of government; to
try for the removal of this Court to some country town ;
for having all the State's money redeemed with continental
currency, so that there be but one kind of currency in the
United States, and for giving encouragement to the raising
of flax and wool."

August 18th.   Voted, " that the committee hire men,
who shall be called to serve during the war."   Thirteen
men of Chebacco are reported this month by the Colonel
as already in service in the northern army.   Six more
are now drafted from the military company here to serve
in that army, which number (six), according to Capt. David
Low's " return " of August 15th, was one-sixth part of the
able-bodied men at home.   In September, Lieut. John
Choate makes return of eight others, " who marched out
of Capt. David Low's company in Chebacco, with said Capt.
Low, to re-enforce the northern army."   September 17th,

voted, " that the selectmen supply the families of soldiers
who are in the continental army."

As we have twenty-eight men in the northern army
under Gen. Gates, we will go there and witness some of
the operations.   The British General Burgoyne, has come
from Canada with an army of eight thousand regular
troops, to effect a junction with the British at New York.
He has taken Ticonderoga with its numerous artillery, and
the important post of Skenesborough (now Whitehall);
has the full command of Lake Champlain and Lake George;
after much labor and fatigue, and the loss of about two
hundred men in skirmishes by the way, has now reached
the Hudson River, and by a bridge of boats has crossed
over from the east side to Saratoga on the west.

As the British advance, our army leaving Saratoga, fall
down the river and finally encamp near the confluence of
the Mohawk and the Hudson on Bemis Heights.   The
camp is the segment of a circle, with the convex towards
the enemy, and is connected with the river by a deep in-
trenchment covered by strong batteries.   The right is also
covered by a deep hollow descending to the river and
·thickly wooded.   On the 19th of September, an alarm
being given about noon that the enemy is approaching,
Col. Morgan with his riflemen is sent forward to meet
them, and soon the regiments from New Hampshire, Connecticut and New York follow, and by the middle of the
afternoon, the action becomes general; and our Massachusetts troops act their part with great bravery.   The British have four field-pieces in operation.   But the ground
occupied by our troops, a thick wood on the border of the
open field, does not admit of the use of artillery.   On the
opposite side of this field, on a rising ground, in a thin
pine wood, the British troops are drawn up.   As soon as
they come forward in the open field, the fire of our marks-
men, drives them back in disorder; and whenever our
troops push forward into the open ground, the British
rally, charge, and drive them back.   This alternate ad-

vancing and retreating is continued and repeated perhaps not less than a dozen times. Every time our troops drive them back, their artillery falls into the hands of our men; but the ground is such, that they cannot bring off the guns, nor keep them long enough to use them against the British. The contest is furious, and the fire of musketry and the shout of battle continue till the darkness of the evening shuts in upon us. The British remain upon the ground, and claim the victory. Our troops return to their camp, and feel that in maintaining their ground, they have gained a decided triumph. The field is covered with the dead and the wounded. The British have lost more than five hundred; our loss is less than three hundred. Among the badly wounded, is one of our Chebacco neighbors, Joseph Burnham, who continues in much pain and distress about two weeks, and then closes his eyes in death.

In our camp all is preparation for another trial with the British. In the meantime, news is brought that a detachment of militia, under Col. Brown, has taken the posts at the outlet of Lake George, with three hundred prisoners, and also several armed vessels upon the lake. This cut off Burgoyne's communications with Canada, so that his situation became more and more critical. Provisions for his army were daily diminishing, without any hope of renewing the supply, except by the conquest of our army. But this was becoming every day less and less probable, for our success in the recent battle was noised abroad as a great victory, and the militia were coming in to join us in great numbers. Burgoyne must, however, retreat or risk another battle, for his troops are already suffering severely from a scanty supply of provisions. On the 7th of October, therefore, he makes an advance upon our army. As soon as this is discovered, our whole force is in motion. The British are so furiously assailed that amidst a shower of grape and musketry they begin to give way, and with difficulty reach their camp. Col.

Brooks, afterwards our governor, attacks a German brigade in their intrenchments, forces them from their ground at the point of the bayonet, and captures their camp equipage and artillery, and a supply of ammunition, which was a great relief to our poorly supplied troops. Night coming on, the battle is interrupted. But our troops sleep upon their arms, ready to renew it as soon as light returns. Burgoyne, having lost four hundred men, with artillery, ammunition, and tents, thinks it best to steal away in the night while our troops are asleep. In the morning, we see him at a distance, drawn up in order of battle, on some high grounds in the rear. The day is spent in skirmishing. The next day he retreats to Saratoga, in the midst of a rain that falls in torrents, and which prevents our army from giving him any annoyance. But his situation is desperate. A council of war advises him to open a treaty of capitulation. He surrenders October 16th. It is a triumphant day for the colonies, when the proud Burgoyne, under the gaze of more than twenty thousand eyes, walks up to our General—Gates, and, as a conquered foe, delivers to him his sword. We see our Chebacco soldiers intently looking on. Among them is a youth in his seventeenth year, who lives to repeat the story in his ninety-fifth year, recalling the scene with all the enthusiasm of youth. This ceremony of delivering the sword being ended, the British troops, to the number of nearly six thousand, march out of their camp with the honors of war, lay down their arms under an engagement never more to serve against the United States, and are conducted to Boston to embark for England. Five Chebacco men were drafted to form a part of the force which guarded these prisoners of war while they were encamped in Charlestown awaiting transportation. With the fall of Burgoyne, all the posts north of us to Canada line soon fell into our hands.

Some of our Chebacco men are stationed at Albany, the rest join the body of the army under Washington, at Val-

28

ley Forge, in Pennsylvania. Though sent in November, in a body of five thousand northern troops, by Gen. Gates at the request of Washington, yet, being detained by Gen. Putnam in the neighborhood of New York, they did not reach the Southern camp till December, when they were joined by two thousand more from Gen. Gates. Washington's troops, consisting of about eleven thousand, were now in Winter quarters at Valley Forge, a piece of ground on the south side of the Schuylkill, about twenty miles from Philadelphia. The soldiers are quartered in log huts, nearly eight hundred in number, arranged in rows, each hut containing fourteen men. But they are in destitute condition—almost without clothing, and poorly supplied with provisions. Many, for want of blankets to lie on, are obliged to sit and sleep by the fire at night. Destitute of shoes, their late marches had been tracked in blood over the frozen ground !

Leaving the army at Valley Forge, we turn our attention to the efforts made by our people to resist the enemy upon the sea. Something was done by our public armed ships, but more by swift-sailing privateers, which scoured every sea—even those about the British Islands. They were very successful in capturing merchantmen and ships laden with provisions and military supplies, and thus not only weakened the enemy, but supplied our distressed countrymen with bread and military stores, of which they were destitute. There were some from this parish engaged in privateering—though but few, compared with the number that entered the army. With their vessels of war, the English were at this time masters of all our coasts, on some parts of which the most wanton and cruel depredations were inflicted. On the 1st of August Col. Cogswell is informed by Brigadier Farley that "a fleet of a hundred sail of large vessels were seen from the highlands in Gloucester standing to the northward," and is ordered "to have his regiment in readiness for what may happen." During this year a British frigate was off our bay. Boats were sent from her into the harbor of Annisquam.　Mrs. Marshall, a resident on Hog Island, said to the author that she distinctly saw the flashes of the guns in their boats, and of the guns of our people on shore.　A guard of twelve men, she said, was quartered upon the Island to prevent their landing.　At one time their boats were seen approaching to effect a landing, when all upon the Island fled, except one resolute woman, the wife of William Choate, grandmother of the late Hon. Rufus Choate, who declared she would stay and keep house if all the rest ran.　She staid with two of her children, and received no harm.

October 15th, Francis Choate died aged seventy-six. He was a brother of Hon. John Choate of Ipswich Centre, and was born on Hog Island in 1701.　He was a ruling elder in Mr. Cleaveland's church, and one of his prominent supporters.　In 1754, he was made Justice of the Peace, and in town affairs, and as a town officer, he was prominent for many years.　His second son, William, was the father of the late Mr. David Choate, and of George Choate, Esq.

1778.　January 12th, the town voted to take under consideration, "The Articles of the Confederation and Perpetual Union between the United States of America, as proposed to the Legislature of this State"

January 19th.　"Voted, to instruct the representatives to vote that the delegates from Massachusetts favor the Articles of Confederation."

April 6th.　"Voted, that a committee meet with others here at Treadwell's, on the 15th instant, to consider the Constitution and form of government proposed."

June 4th.　The vote respecting the proposed Constitution stood, one for, and one hundred and ninety-one against.　The whole sum voted by the town this year for the families of soldiers is £800 in Continental bills, equal to $533.33 cents.

January 30th.　The King of France enters into a treaty with our government, recognizing the independence of these United States.　In this treaty it was stipulated, that France and the United States should make common cause, that neither should make peace with England, without the consent of the other, and neither should lay down arms till

the independence of the United States was secured.   This
treaty when received, May 6th, spread joy through all the
towns in the country.   The hereditary hatred of France,
which had pervaded the country, was suddenly changed
into gratitude, respect and love.   Thanks were returned
in all our churches for the special interposition of Providence, and prayers offered for blessings upon our allies,
the French.   This was rarely omitted on the Sabbath, the
aged tell us, by the patriotic Cleaveland.   When the news
of the French treaty arrived, Washington was still encamped at Valley Forge, with a force insufficient to meet
the British in the open field.   But the news of expected
aid from abroad, inspired all with courage, and tended to
depress and discourage the enemy.   As the Delaware was
liable to be blocked up by a French fleet, the British were
obliged to evacuate Philadelphia, and to return to the
Highlands of Navesink, where, by entrenchments, they
secured themselves from further attack.   In the Summer,
an attempt was made by our forces under Gen. Sullivan
to drive the British from Newport.   Count D' Estaing
with a French fleet was to co-operate with him, and appeared off Newport on the 29th of July, but was soon
after defeated in an engagement with Admiral House, and
left Sullivan to contend alone.   A battle was fought at
Quaker Hill, and Sullivan narrowly escaped falling with
his whole army into the hands of the British.   By good
generalship he effected a retreat.   The operations of the
enemy for more than a year, in Rhode Island, were the
occasion of the frequent call upon our men to march to
that quarter.   Our town records more than once speak
of our men having marched to Providence to strengthen
our forces there.   August 2d, Captain David Low makes
return to Col. Cogswell of "ten men in my company that
have engaged to go to Providence, in the service of these
States."   All the militia from Massachusetts Bay, while in
Sullivan's army, were enrolled in Col. Wade's regiment.
Frequent requisitions were also made for men " to join the

guards at Cambridge under Maj. Gen. Heath." On the 26th of September, Col. Cogswell was ordered by Brigadier Titcomb "to repair to Boston and take command of the men ordered to be raised the 7th inst., out of my Brigade." Among Col. Cogswell's papers is an autograph order of Gen. Gates received while he was holding this command. It is as follows:

"BOSTON, December 3, 1778.

"To Col. Cogswell, Third Regiment, Essex Militia—Sir: You will please immediately to supply the bearer with Two Officers, two Sergeants and thirty Rank and File, to assist in removing some cables of the Somersett man-of-war, now on board a vessel at Gray's wharf. I am y^r hble serv^t,

"HORATIO GATES."

Toward the close of the year, the enemy seemed disposed to remove the seat of war to the Southern States. From our church records we learn, that this year the following soldiers died abroad: James Rust, a prisoner at Halifax, aged 20; Stephen Kent, aged 50; Jonathan Andrews, aged 40 or more, at Albany; Abraham and Isaac Jones, Israel Andrews, Nathaniel Emerson, and Abijah Story (negro), in the army; Nehemiah son of Nehemiah Choate, soldier at sea, of the small pox, at Bilboa.

1779. Some definite idea of the militia organizations of this time may be obtained from the following extracts from a "Return of the Third Regiment of Militia in the county of Essex, commanded by Jonathan Cogswell, Esq., made on the 12th of January." Nine companies belonged to the regiment at this time. The first company belonged in Ipswich Centre; the second at the Hamlet; the third at Chebacco; three others also in Ipswich, two in Topsfield, and one in Wenham. The list of officers is as follows:

"Jonathan Cogswell, Colonel, commissioned February 14, 1776; Isaac Dodge, Ipswich, Lieutenant Colonel, commissioned February 14, 1776; Charles Smith, Ipswich, First Major, commissioned February 14, 1776; Joseph Gould, Topsfield, Second Major, commissioned February 14, 1776; John Heard, Ipswich, Adjutant, commissioned May 7, 1776. Whole Number of the Training Band present, including officers, 514. Ditto Alarm List, 257. Whole Number of Training Band absent, viz., in the Continental army, 119; in the State's service, 37. Absent, of the Alarm List, 6."

The return of the Chebacco company of the same date is as follows:

"A return of the Third Company of the Third Regiment of Militia in the County of Essex: David Low, Captain, commissioned May 16, 1776; John Choate, First Lieutenant; Ephraim Davis, Second Lieutenant. Training Band, present, viz: Clerk, 1, Sergeants, 4, Drummer, 1, Rank and File, 71. Ditto absent, viz., in Continental Service, 1 Subaltern, 22 Privates; in State Service, 1 Colonel, 6 Privates; 9 in private armed vessels, 4 in captivity, 4 seamen at sea. Alarm List present, viz., under 50 years of age, 14; between 50 and 60, 23; between 60 and 65, 7; total, 44. Alarm List absent in State service, 3 Privates; in private vessels, 2; seamen at sea, 2. Whole number of males above 16 years of age, not included either in the Training Band or Alarm List, viz., Whites, 5, Blacks, 4."

The "alarm list" was composed of those who were more than forty-eight years of age. The persons exempted at this time by law were, all under sixteen years of age, the officers and students of Harvard College, ministers of the gospel, grammar-schoolmasters, Indians, negroes and mulattoes. The equipments required were as follows:

"Fire-arm; steel or iron ramrod; Spring to retain; Worm; Priming wire; Brush; Bayonet; Cutting sword or Hathor; Pouch; 100 buckshot; Jack or sack knife; Tow; 5 flints; one pound of powder; 40 balls; Knapsack; Blanket; Canteen or wood bottle."

One of Col. Cogswell's "orders" of this year is also preserved, and is of considerable interest for the information it furnishes respecting the military customs of the Revolution:

"IPSWICH, June 13, 1779.

"To Capt. David Low—Sir: You are hereby directed to detach from your Company, two men to serve in the State of Rhode Island until the first day of January next, unless sooner discharged, said detachment to be made indiscriminately from the Training Band and the Alarm List. Said men are to be mustered before the County muster-master, and to be armed and equipped according to law. Their pay is to be sixteen pounds per month, in addition to the Continental pay. One hundred dollars for a further encouragement is to be advanced to each man by the selectmen of the Town where said men are detached, as a Bounty. Also two shillings a mile as mileage money from the Town where they are detached to the place of their destination. Any person detached for the service aforesaid, and shall not within twenty-four hours after he is detached pay a fine of thirty pounds, or procure some able-bodied man in his room, properly armed and equipped, he shall be held as a soldier in said detachment, and treated as such. The fines you are to procure other men with, until your quota is completed. Hereof you will not fail, and make return of the men without loss of time.

" JON^a Cogswell, Col."

June 28th. The town votes £12,000, O. T., equal to $1,000 or $1,500, to hire recruits now called out. The currency in old tenor, was at this time, not only very much depreciated, but very fluctuating. The English ministry were so lost to all principles of honor and honesty, as to counterfeit our bills, and send over whole chests of them, which they continued to distribute among us, and which were so well executed, as to be with difficulty distinguished from the genuine bills.

This year the first school-house on the south side of our river was built. It stood near a well, now belonging to the dwelling-house owned by Daniel Poland and William H. Burnham. There were at this time, only thirty-two houses on the south side of the river, ten of which were on the Gloucester and Manchester roads, and twenty-two on Thompson's Island. Now* there are on that side of the river, one hundred and twenty-five dwelling-houses, a church, and three school-houses. The frame of the first school-house was removed in 1814 to the site of the present school-house, in the South District, and improved for a school-house there for a number of years. It is now the frame of a dwelling-house in Manchester. Among the natives of Chebacco, who taught in this "good frame," may be mentioned Elias Andrews, William Cogswell, Jr., David Choate, his three sons, David, Rufus and Washington, and Samuel Gorton, Jr.

August 9th. The town elect five delegates to the convention to be held at Cambridge, for framing a new State Constitution. Among these are Stephen Choate, Esq., and Col. Jonathan Cogswell.

August 16th. Two are chosen to meet in convention at Concord, to regulate the prices of goods. The town

---

* 1855.

sanction the doings of this convention fixing the prices of various articles of merchandise.

But little was done this year in the field either by our people or the British. The campaign at the South was a failure. Washington from his camp in New Jersey, was more successful against the British on the Hudson. The fortress of Stony Point, which had been taken by the British, was retaken by a detachment of troops mostly from New England, under Gen. Wayne, who stormed the fort, on the night of the 15th of July. This was considered one of the most gallant exploits of the war.

1780. Unusually severe and stormy weather prevailed at the close of the last year and the opening of this. The snow fell in frequent storms from the middle of December, to almost the middle of January, when it lay upon the ground more than three feet in thickness on a level. Loaded teams passed over the walls, in every direction. The cold was intense and without interruption, for many days. It was long remembered as the hard winter. The spring also was cold and remarkably backward.

Friday the 19th of May was long remembered by the inhabitants of the Commonwealth and of some portions of the neighboring States, but especially by the residents of this county as "The Dark Day." Mrs. Marshall, whose maiden name was Hannah Choate, gave the author the following account of this strange phenomenon, as it was witnessed on Hog Island. She was then 17 years of age.

"The sun rose clear, but it soon began to be lowery, with some showers. Toward nine o'clock, it seemed to be breaking away; but everything had a yellow appearance. Soon after nine, a dark, heavy cloud was seen rising from the north-west, which gradually spread itself till it covered the whole heavens, except a narrow space near the horizon. About ten, this was also covered, and the darkness increased so that we had to light a candle. All the folks out of doors left their work, and came in. Fear and anxiety were manifest on every countenance. It was quite dark when we set our dinner-table. Early in the afternoon, the darkness began to abate, and before sundown it was light, but cloudy, with a yellow, brassy appearance. After sundown, it grew dark very fast, and the evening was more remarkable than the day.

It seemed like darkness that might be felt. Some of our family who tried to go to the neighbors, had to come back. We sat up quite late, knowing that the moon rose at nine, and expecting it would make some difference as to the darkness, but it did not till after eleven o'clock, when some glimmer of light began to appear from it."

Other accounts tell us, that those who were traveling in the evening had to dismount from their horses, as they wholly refused to go on, and that horses could not be compelled to leave their stables, when wanted for service. It is remarkable that, according to the testimony of our fishermen, some of whom were then at sea, there was no unusual darkness upon the water. The general opinion of scientific men of that time was, that this phenomenon was caused by the unusual thickness of the clouds, and the vast quantity of smoke arising from burning woods. It is said that there were at that time about thirty miles square of woods on fire in the vicinity of Ticonderoga and nearer.

March 30th, Ebenezer Cleaveland, son of our pastor, died of jail fever, on board of the Continental ship-of-war Eustis, aged 26. He had sailed from Salem in October, 1779, for the West Indies for his health, had been taken by the British, and retaken by the French; had been in jail, as a prisoner, at Gaudaloupe, and was now, by some means, in a ship-of-war of his own country.

The town furnishes this year, as its required proportion, 106 shirts, 106 pairs of stockings and shoes, and 33 blankets; raises 60 men for six months, and 12 horses for the public service; votes £1,200, to hire soldiers for the continental army; furnishes as its proportion 31,800 pounds of beef; accepts a report to pay its soldiers in hard money, as resolved by the General Court; votes £1,850 of new emission, or £74,200 of old emission, to pay for its army beef; votes not to accept the new constitution for the State, unless the proposed amendments are allowed. The same was voted by Danvers and some other towns. The constitution, however, was adopted by the people.

The quota of Ipswich for the continental service, this year, was fifty-two, equal to that of Salem, and larger than that of any other town in the county. Besides furnishing its proportion of these, Chebacco was called upon in June, for eleven six months' men, and the same number of three months' men, who were accordingly drafted from Capt. David Low's company.

Our men were in various parts of the army, some at the South and some at the North. Whether any of them were in the force under the immediate command of Washington, when the treason of Arnold was detected, is not known. But one of the line officers in that part of the army, at that time, was Maj. Caleb Low of Danvers, who was a native of Chebacco, and was brought up here. He was present at the execution of Andre. The following letter addressed to him by Washington, the original of which is in the hands of Maj. Low's grandson, Col. Caleb Low of Danvers, is taken from Hanson's History of Danvers:

"Sir: You will be pleased to march early to-morrow morning, with all the militia under your command, and proceed to the landing at West Point. You will send an officer to this place, by whom you will receive further orders. Col. Gouvior, the bearer of this, will apply to you for an officer and a small party of men. These you will furnish. I am, sir, with esteem, yr. mo. obe't ser't,   GEO. WASHINGTON."

"Head-quarters Robinson's House, 25th September, 1780, ½ after 7 o'clock P. M. "Major Low, at Fishkill."

Maj. Low was the son of Caleb and Abigail Low, and was baptized by Mr. Pickering, July 8, 1739. He had been a soldier in the French and Indian war, had served as captain at Ticonderoga, and was promoted to the rank of major at the beginning of the Revolutionary struggle. He had two brothers, who were also in the army and stood firmly in defence of their country. Their birthplace was in the ancient mansion which stood where the dwelling of Josiah Low now stands.

1781. In the meetings of the town it is voted:

"March 20th, that £500 be raised for soldiers and remainder of beef; June 22d, that we supply the army with 25,204 pounds of beef, 106 pairs of stockings and shoes, 106 shirts and 42 men ; August 13th, that £400 be raised to pay men hired for three months, and £200 for army clothing ; August 20th, that £220 be given for soldiers at Rhode Island who have been there five months."

Besides bearing its part of these burdens, Chebacco of its penury also contributes £5. 13s. for inhabitants of South Carolina and Georgia who are left in extreme destitution by the ravages of the enemy, the seat of war this year being chiefly at the South.

The British had overrun Georgia and the Carolinas and were attempting to subdue Virginia. But the success of our arms was such that most of the lost ground was recovered, and Cornwallis was compelled to entrench himself at Yorktown. Washington marched from New York, and arrived at the head of the Elk about the time that Count de' Grasse with twenty-five sail of the line entered the Chesapeake. By the help of the French fleet, he removed his army from the head of the Elk to the vicinity of Yorktown ; and on the 6th of October, the allied forces began the siege, which they pressed so vigorously that on the 19th Cornwallis was obliged to surrender. This was the last contest in our struggle for liberty, and under the good Providence of God, the long protracted war terminated at length wholly in our favor. The success of the siege of Yorktown excited universal joy throughout the country. The day after the capitulation, Washington ordered, that those who were under arrest should be pardoned, and announced—

" That Divine service shall be performed to-morrow, in the different brigades and divisions. The commander-in-chief recommends that all the troops that are not upon duty, do assist at it, with a serious deportment, and that sensibility of heart, which the recollection of the surprising and particular interposition of Providence in our favor, claims."

Congress also resolved to go in procession to the Dutch Lutheran Church, and return thanks to Almighty God, for the signal success of the American arms: and they issued a proclamation, recommending to the citizens of the

United States, to observe the 13th of December as a day of public thanksgiving and prayer.

1782. There is a suspension of hostilities this year. England is disposed to make peace with us, if it can be done without inflicting too deep a wrong upon the nation's pride. Much time, however, is required to adjust the whole matter, and until the treaty is made and ratified, our army must be kept in the field and sustained. Our fathers in town-meeting, vote £440 to pay men lately engaged to serve in the army, and other soldiers; and to raise nineteen men for the continental army.

Notwithstanding all their privations, hardships and sufferings during this long and bloody contest, which had almost drained Chebacco of men, especially young men, our citizens here still sustain the cause of education, even with increased zeal. Three schools are now in active operation. One at the Falls, one on the south side of the river, and the ancient North, now removed from the common to the gravel-pit, a little north of where the hay-scales now are. We will visit the school and learn something of its prosperity. Its teacher is Northern Cogswell, son of Dr. Cogswell of Rowley, who was a native of Chebacco. The school-house is considered one of good size; and yet forty scholars fill nearly all the seats. From the register on the master's desk, we see that the whole number belonging to the school is forty-five, thirty-one boys and fourteen girls. Twenty-one boys and eight girls are marked as perfect in their attendance. This register now in our possession, is written in the teacher's large and fair hand, and contains the names of all the scholars and the punctuality of their attendance. The number of girls in the school is comparatively small, for it is not the custom of the day for girls in general to attend. Only those most ambitious to be something, are seen at school, or as a man of years now expresses it, "only those who thought a good deal of themselves." The government of the school is mild and paternal, with but little use of the rod.

Yet the order is excellent, and the industry commendable. The master has the reputation of being one of the best of teachers, though yet a young man. The exercises of the school are confined to reading, writing, spelling and ciphering. We hear them read in the psalter, and spell from Dilworth's spelling-book. The "cipherers" have their sums, as they are called, written by the master, in their manuscripts, to be wrought out by them on the slate. The more indolent occasionally, copy the process by stealth from their more studious neighbors. The penmanship of the master is very fine, and the proficiency of the pupils consequently remarkably good. The amount of knowledge acquired in such a school, though very limited, is yet of incalculable importance; and besides this, the mental discipline, the habits of punctuality, of order, of subjection and attention thus early gained, and the imbibing of moral and religious truth, are of inestimable value. If we were strangers, we should say with the poet, as we look around upon this group of bright-eyed children:

> "Boys are at best but pretty buds unblown,
> Whose scent and hues are rather guessed than known."

But as we know their future career, it is pleasant to look upon them in childhood, and to see in their habits of punctuality and attendance, as marked by their teacher, their future industry, intelligence and usefulness. Two of them are still living with us, at the age of more than eighty. Two of the children of Dr. Davis, then the physician of the place, are living in Gloucester. The remainder, for the most part, we ourselves have followed to the grave, as parishioners, neighbors, and friends. One studious boy we see there, eleven years old, whose literary career is remarkably brilliant, as he passes from the district school to the academy, and to the university, and to the study and practice of law in a neighboring city. But his career is as short as it is brilliant. At the age of thirty, death lays him in the grave. Two brothers are sitting together, John and Francis Choate. John, as he advances upon the stage of life, becomes master of a vessel, and perishes at sea, being wrecked on the coast of France. Francis dies in early life, of a fever, at the age of seventeen.

1783. This was a memorable year in the annals of the town as well as of the country. A treaty of peace was made with England, in which the Independence of the United States was acknowledged, a right to the fisheries granted, and as much territory yielded as was expected or asked for. On the 19th of April, just eight years from the day when at Lexington the first blood was spilled, peace was proclaimed in the American army by Gen. Washington. In the Autumn, the army was disbanded, and our fellow-citizens returned to their homes. Forty years ago, as the author visited from house to house, he heard from the lips of these Revolutionary soldiers, descriptions of many scenes, which they had witnessed in the camp and on the battle-field, of the most thrilling interest. The impression made by the accounts they gave of their experiences of army life, of their battles, and of their sufferings from fatigue, hunger, cold and sickness, is still deep and vivid. Some of them had crossed the Jerseys with bare feet, on frozen ground, tracking the way with blood. Others at times had had nothing to keep them from starvation but melted suet. And after their service was ended, they lost most of their pay, because their exhausted country was almost literally bankrupt. Of the value of their services, of their hardships and their condition at the close of the war, we may form some adequate conception from a part of a speech of Hon. Rufus Choate, in Congress, in 1832, on the Pension Bill. It is as follows:

" From my own observation, from the testimony of other gentlemen given in this discussion, from the uniform concurrence of opinion expressed by all, who, at any time heretofore, have advocated in Congress the adoption or extension of the pension system, I am satisfied that, as a general fact, the survivors of the War of the Revolution, are in reduced pecuniary circumstances, although often considerably above want; the precise condition of life which this charity pre-eminently blesses. Sir, we know why they are in such circumstances. They left the army at the average age of thirty-two or thirty-three.

The prime of life was already nearly past. Before that age, the foundations of most men's fortunes are laid, and their destinies fixed. Many of them had families immediately dependent and expensive. The business which they followed before they went to the war, it was not perfectly easy at once to resume. Their health, and let us admit, sometimes their habits, were a little shaken by the life they had been leading. War never leaves the individual who actively mingles in it, any more than it leaves the nation, exactly where it finds him. The idleness of camp, and the excitements of camp, are alike unfavorable to morality and to industry. The chances were that when they went back to their places in society, and the land rested from the agitation with which it had so long been heaving, they would all, if the expression may be pardoned, have sunk at once to the bottom. The chances were, that they would become the 'cankers of a calm world and a long peace.' Many of them did so. Others struggled and rose to something like competence and comfort, but not above the necessity of partaking of this relief. I cannot refrain from reminding you, in this connection, that the ten years which immediately followed the war of independence, that period in which these men were called to put off the garments of the camp, and, breaking their swords into ploughshares, to resume as well as they could, the habits and pursuits of civil life, were a time the most unfavorable to morality, to industry, to the acquisition of property, and the formation of stable and elevated character, which this country ever saw. There was no opening to enterprise for anybody, and, least of all, for the penniless, disheartened and war-worn soldier. Manufactures we had none, and under such a government as the old Confederation, admitting the unrestrained importation of the foreign article, we should have never had any. Commerce and the fisheries were annihilated; agriculture was languishing to death. A great pressure of debt was bearing upon the confederacy, the States and the citizen. There was no circulating medium in existence, except a depreciated, worthless paper, wholly unfit to develop and vivify the industry of a community, but very fit, and very likely to make us a nation of gamesters and jockeys. Undoubtedly this was as severe a crisis as the sharpest agony of the war. Such was the world which the disbanded soldiers began life in ; and stronger and more affecting proof of the truth of this description, and of the disastrous influences which that hard season shed on all their after fortunes, you need not seek, than is afforded by the fact, that far the larger number of those, who received their settlement certificates from the government at the close of the war, were obliged to sell them in the course of the ten years following, at an average of two shillings and six pence in the pound.''

THE IMPORTANCE AND WORTH OF THE MILITIA.

" There was not a campaign or battle from the beginning of the war to the end, in which the militia did not bear an important part along with the continentals. I do not say that they generally mustered in equal numbers, nor that they ever learned to stand fire quite as well in the open field. We know they did not.   But I do say they served everywhere, and fought everywhere, under regular contracts of enlistment from which they could not break—or under compulsory levy for a prescribed term, and that they contributed an important and as yet, an unappreciated and uncompensated share to whatever of success crowned the American arms.   I promised to avoid details, but I will remind you that the army which shut the British up in Boston, and finally drove them from it, consisted when the siege was raised, of twenty thousand men of whom six thousand were militia.   That siege began, you may say, in April or May, 1775, and down to August 1775, the entire besieging force was a mere militia.   The Continental line did not exist in name or in fact until August 1775.   That other army which captured Burgoyne, consisted of ten thousand men, of whom thirty-eight hundred were militia ; and at Yorktown the American forces amounted to nine thousand, of whom four thousand were militia.   Besides this they shared in every triumph and every defeat, which successively illumined or darkened the long and changing scenes of that awful drama.   The brilliant victory at Cowpens, which, in its consequences, rescued two States from the enemy, was won by an army two thirds of whom were militia.   It is interesting too, to call to mind, how many of what may be termed the turning incidents of the war—how many of the more showy and startling achievements, which produced a permanent and extended influence upon the temper and feelings of the people and the enemy, and upon the course and issue of the struggle—how many of these you owe to the single handed daring of the militia.   Gentlemen have reminded you of Lexington and Bunker's Hill.   Yes, sir, the children in the infant schools can tell that the men who fought there never heard the beat of an enemy's drum before in their lives.   But how few of all the battles of history have produced such results or drawn after them such consequences, and how little of all the blood shed in war has been shed to such good purpose as this   The capture of Burgoyne was an eventful incident of the war.   The most popular of our historians, in his peculiar expression, remarks that ' this event was the *hinge* on which the Revolution turned '   It secured to us the alliance of France and put the ultimate independence of the country beyond hazard.   He says, with much more accuracy I think, that ' the battle of Bennington was the first link in the grand chain of causes which finally drew on the ruin of the royal army.'   All that glory, too, was gathered by the militia—by ' Stark's own.'   That high-spirited soldier sent the official account of the battle, not to the Continental Congress, but to the Legislature of Massachusetts, and the trophies of the victory are hanging up to-day in her Senate-house.

    " I do not wonder that some students of this portion of our history have exclaimed that we owe our independence to the militia   Remember, too, that it happened more than once during the war that a seasonable recruit of these soldiers saved, when nothing else perhaps could have saved, the army of Washington itself from disappearing and dissolving away.   Every week almost, requisitions were made on them for direct co-operation with the continental troops to meet the various emergencies of the war.   But in two or three memorable instances they saved the army.   One happened when Washington lay before Boston early in 1776, and another some time subsequently in the Jerseys.   It was in the gloomy period of the short enlistments—the old were expiring, the new were not yet nearly filled, and a prompt and strong levy of yeomen and mechanics, alone enabled him to present to the enemy the show of a considerable armed organization.   But it is needless to pursue this topic.   There can be no doubt that this force, whenever exerted, powerfully aided the cause of the Revolution.   It prevented the enemy, to some extent, from undertaking those predatory incursions upon the coast and frontier, which were so distressing when undertaken.   It protected to some extent the agricultural labor of the country, without which the war could not have been maintained two years.   It kept down disaffected persons.   It sustained the spirit of the people and of the leaders of the people, by lightening in some degree the burthen, and breaking off the horrors of civil war.   And, is there any reason to doubt that *the sufferings, priva-tions,* and *perils* of the *militia-man,* who served his nine months in the field, were as severe as those of the continental soldier who served his?   Gentlemen say that nine months' service, in a seven years' war, is below the regard of this prosperous and grateful country.   Why, nine months is a long campaign ; and a very short campaign has many times, in modern war, changed the face of the world.   All the peculiar hazards of that civil war the soldiers of both classes *(continental and militia troops)* incurred together.   They ran the same risk of falling in the field, of the prison-ship, and the scaffold.   Nay, I take it that those who served in the earlier scenes of the war before it assumed the form of recognized and national hostility, came much nearer to the pains and penalties of rebellion than those who entered later.   In other respects, I have thought the lot of the militia-men the harder of the two.   Generally they were older ; oftener they had families, and a business which required their attention.   They could not have left home to attend Court, as jurors for a fortnight, without inconvenience, and yet they were often summoned without the preparation of a moment, to a campaign of twelve months.   They were called up at midnight to leave comfortable dwellings, happy but helpless families, and fields ripening to the harvest ; and they knew that if they survived to return, it might be to find those fields trampled down by an enemy's cavalry, and those families without a house over their heads."

SOLDIERS OF THE REVOLUTION FROM CHEBACCO.

The following is a list of the soldiers of the Revolution from Chebacco, as far as has been ascertained, including all who enlisted for a longer or shorter time.   It is not to be supposed that the roll is a complete one :

KILLED.—Jesse Story, Jr., Joseph Marshall, Jr.

DIED IN THE ARMY.—Israel Andrews, Jonathan Andrews, Joseph Burnham, Lieut. Samuel Burnham, Nehemiah Choate Jr., William Choate Jr.,

30

Jonathan Cogswell, 3d, Thomas E. Cole, Nathaniel Emerson, David Goodhue, Abraham Jones, Isaac Jones, William Jones, Stephen Kent, Enoch
Marshall, James Rust, Abijah Story, Seth Story, Jr., Jeremiah White, Solomon White, John White.

IN THE ARMY DURING THE WHOLE WAR.—Benjamin Burnham, Sergt.
Isaac Burnham, Joseph Burnham, Thomas Burnham, Lieut. John Cleaveland Jr., Aaron Eveleth, Joseph Story, Capt. William Story.

OTHERS IN ACTIVE SERVICE.—Amos Andrews, James Andrews, Joseph
Andrews, Jr., William Andrews, Ammi Burnham, Jr., Amos Burnham,
Charles Burnham, David Burnham, 3d, Ebenezer Burnham, Enoch Burn-
ham, 1st, Enoch Burnham, Jr., Francis Burnham, Maj. John Burnham, Jr.,
Jonathan Burnham, Mark Burnham, Jr., Nathan Burnham, Thomas Burn-
ham, 3d, Wesley Burnham, William Burnham. Jr., William Burnham, 3d,
John Butler, William Butler, John Cavies, Abraham Channel, Aaron Choate,
David Choate, Ebenezer Choate, James Choate, Jeremiah Choate, Jr., Nehe-
miah Choate, Solomon Choate, Rev. John Cleaveland, Nehemiah Cleaveland,
Dr. Parker Cleaveland, (Assistant Surgeon), John Cogswell, 3d, Col. Jona-
than Cogswell, Rufus Cogswell, Jr., William Cogswell, Jr., Aaron Crafts,
Joseph Eveleth, John Fips, Aaron Foster, Moses Foster, Thomas Foster,
John Goodhue, William Holmes, Aaron Low, Asa Low, Capt. David Low,
Peter Low, Robert Low, Nathaniel Lufkin, Thomas Lufkin, Jr., Antipas
Marshall, Moses Marshall, Aaron Perkins, Francis Perkins, Abner Poland,
Asa Poland, Jonathan Procter, Joseph Procter, Samuel Procter, Samuel
Pulsifer, Timothy Ross, Philemon Smith, Andrew Story, Elisha Story, Jacob
Story, Sergt. Nathan Story, Primas Story, Seth Story, John Wise, Joseph
Wise, Isaac Woodbury.

WHOLE NUMBER—105.

1785. The singers begin to sit in the gallery facing
the minister. Until 1768 "congregational singing" was
the usage—one of the deacons "lining the hymn." From
that date the singers sat together in pews assigned them
on the floor of the house, the congregation still uniting
with them in the service, and the deacons continuing to
line the hymn. In 1774 the church voted "to choose
some of the brethren skilled in singing, to lead the church
and congregation in the service of singing praise to God."
The first choristers chosen were Joseph Perkins, John
Choate and Abraham Perkins. When the singers took
their seats in the gallery this year, Watts' Psalms and
Hymns were introduced as a substitute for Prince's Bay
Psalm-Book which had been in use before. Not long after

this, Daniel Sanford taught a singing-school, and at the close of it, introduced his pupils to the singers' seats. They were so numerous that they filled all the seats of the front gallery.

October 19th.   Mr. John Cleaveland, Jr., the eldest son of the Chebacco minister, is ordained pastor of the church in Stoneham, Mass.   He was born in Chebacco and was baptized in infancy, January 7, 1750 :

" His father had originally designed to give him a public education, and fitted him for admission into Yale College ; but his low state of health prevented him from pursuing his studies there.   Sometime after he had recovered his health, the Revolutionary War commenced, and his patriotism inclined him to join the continental army.   He soon obtained a lieutenant's commission, and continued in the service until peace was obtained and the army was disbanded.   As a soldier and a subaltern officer, he sustained a fair and amiable character through the whole period of his military services.   When he left the service of his country, he turned his attention to the work of the ministry, for which his piety, his early acquaintance with the learned languages, and his general knowledge of men and things, concurred in various respects to qualify him.   He was at no loss where to apply for theological instruction, and having read divinity a suitable time with his reverend father, he was examined and approved as a candidate for the ministry, by the association of ministers in his native county.   While a candidate, he preached in various places to general acceptance, and at length he received a call from the church in Stoneham, May 19, 1785, to become their pastor, which he accepted, September 17, 1785."

As he was a native and a resident of this place, this church of which he was a member was one of those which were invited to sit in council at his ordination.   Isaac Procter, Grover Dodge and Joseph Perkins were chosen delegates.   His father preached the sermon from Acts xx. 26 : "Gospel ministers must be wise, faithful and exemplary, in order to be pure from the blood of all men." His pastorate at Stoneham terminated October 23, 1794, and he was installed pastor of the North Church in Wrentham, June 6, 1798.   His ministry there ended with his death by consumption, February 1, 1815, at the age of sixty-five.   The Rev. Dr. Emmons, the celebrated theologian, who was his neighbor and intimate friend, preached

his funeral sermon, and paid the following tribute to his
worth :

" The one great object which lay the nearest to his heart, was the good of
souls; and this dictated the subjects of his public discourses, and the manner
of his public speaking. He had a good understanding of the gospel scheme
of salvation, and knew how to set the most important doctrines in a clear and
profitable light. His discourses were more solid than brilliant; more senti-
mental than declamatory; and better adapted to assist the memory, enlighten
the understanding, awaken the conscience and penetrate the heart, than to
excite the admiration or gratify the vain curiosity of his hearers. His age
had not impaired his mental powers, nor unfitted him for the service of the
sanctuary. His sun did not set in a cloud, but in its full brightness. He
retained the free and full exercise of all his rational powers, and his faith
and hope in his Divine Redeemer, disarmed death of its sting and the grave
of its terror."

The "Panoplist" for February, 1816, also contained a
sketch of his character, some of the most prominent traits
in which are thus delineated :

" Mr. Cleaveland was a man of a clear and discriminating mind, who, from
the Bible as his unerring guide, formed his own theoretical and practical sentiments, and who steadily and uniformly acted agreeably to them. He
exhibited great propriety and consistency of character in every situation and
circumstance of life. He appeared manifestly to act from principle, in all his
public and private conduct, and to carry religion with him wherever he went.
He devoted himself wholly to his work, and never suffered his secular concerns to interfere with his pastoral duties. These he diligently and laboriously performed. He composed his sermons with care, expressed his thoughts
with perspicuity, and delivered his discourses with tenderness, deliberation
and solemnity, and without the least affectation in language, in tone or in
gesture."

Mr. Cleveland was twice married, but had no children.
1786–7. August 11th, Elder Seth Story died. He was
the son of Dea. Seth Story, who succeeded Dea. John
Burnham in Mr. Wise's day. Dea. Seth Story, was the
son of William, who was the son of Andrew, who came
from England, and settled in this place as early as 1636.
He took up a large tract of land, extending from the
southern part of Belcher's lane to the river, bounded on
the east by White's Hill, and land of Dea. Thomas Low,
on the south-west and west by land of Reynold Foster,

on the west and north-west by common land belonging
to Ipswich. William's son, Seth, was married and lived
with him, and on condition of his maintaining him the
rest of his days, he conveyed to him by deed of gift the
farm, which he inherited from his father. This deed is
dated, April 13th, 1693. This same year his grandson,
Seth, was born, who lived nearly a hundred years on a
part of the same farm, filled the office of elder in the
same church in which his father had been deacon, and in
which his brother Zechariah was deacon during the time
that he was an elder. From these families have sprung
a very numerous offspring, who have become related by
marriages, to most of the families in the place.

Owing to the exhausted state in which the country was
left at the close of the war, business was interrupted and
almost suspended; many found it difficult to collect or pay
their debts; great numbers of suits were pending in the
courts, the termination of which, threatened to involve
many in embarrassment if not in imprisonment for debt.
In the western counties of the state, the discontent was
so great, that it broke out in open rebellion. About fifteen hundred insurgents under Daniel Shays, who had
been a Captain in the Continental army, entered Worcester
on the 5th of December, 1786, and prevented the sitting of
the Supreme Court there. On the 25th of December, having marched to Springfield he took possession of the court-
house in that town, and closed it against the entrance of
the Court.

The insurgents demanded that the collection of debts
should be suspended, and that the General Court should
authorize the emission of paper currency for general circulation. To suppress this insurrection Gov. Bowdoin
called out four thousand of the militia from the counties
not disaffected. The quota of Ipswich was twenty-five,
seven of whom went from this parish. They were Lieut.
Aaron Perkins, Sergt. Aaron Low, Daniel Burnham, Samuel Eveleth, Abraham Knowlton, Joseph Knowlton, and

Edward Perkins.   They were enrolled in "Capt. John
Baker's company detached from Col. Nathaniel Wade's
Regiment."   We have often heard them tell the story of
their short campaign, which is in substance as follows :

" We were enlisted for forty days, and ordered to meet in Boston, the 19th
day of January, 1787.   The cold was severe, and the winter was an unusually hard one.   But we were pretty well prepared to endure it, being
young and well-clad.   Soon after our muster on the common, we began our
march, under Gen. Lincoln, for the valley of the Connecticut, where we expected to have some warm work.   News reached us on our way, that Gen.
Shepherd, with a small body of western militia, was at Springfield, to guard
the United States arsenal there, and that Shays, with two thousand insurgents,
had entered the town, to take possession of the arsenal.   He was repulsed, however, and, as we approached Springfield, retreated before us, first up the river
and then in a north-easterly direction to Pelham, where he encamped on the
high hills, which were almost inaccessible by reason of the deep snow.   We
were marched back to Hadley, and kept in comfortable quarters a few days,
the weather being very severe.   When news came on the 3d of February,
that the insurgents had started towards Petersham, we set out in pursuit at six
o'clock in the evening, and marched during the night forty miles, facing a
north-east snow-storm all the way.   Early in the morning we entered Petersham, and taking them by surprise, captured one hundred and fifty of the
number.   We then marched into Berkshire County, and the rebels there
dispersed without making any stand against us.   After being under arms
twenty days longer than the period of our enlistment, we were discharged
and came home."

The population of Chebacco, as taken by young Joseph
Perkins this year, is 1200.

James Perkins is chosen deer-reeve of Chebacco woods
—the last election to this office, as few or none of the deer
were found in our woods after this.

1788.   January 9th, a convention met in Boston, consisting of delegates from the respective towns of the Commonwealth, to consider the Constitution of the United
States as adopted in the National Convention and offered
for acceptance to the several States.   The delegates from
Ipswich were Gen. Michael Farley, Daniel Noyes, Hon.
John Choate and Col. Jonathan Cogswell.   Mr. Choate,
according to the record of the proceedings, addressed the
Convention twice—first, in favor of the section giving to

Congress power to levy duties, excises, imposts, etc., and second, on the ninth section, concerning the power of regulating trade, etc. On the 6th of February the Convention "assented to and ratified the Constitution for the United States of America" by a vote of 187 to 168, all the Ipswich delegates voting in the affirmative. Before the close of the year the Constitution was adopted by all the States except Rhode Island and North Carolina, both of which ratified it not long after.

March 18. Solomon Giddings, a deacon of the church in this parish, died in his seventy-fourth year, at the South Parish, where he had resided the last seven years of his life.

Maj. Andrew Story leaves this place with his wife and children, in a long wagon, painted red, covered with canvas and drawn by two yoke of oxen, for a settlement in Ohio. They go in company with other families from Hamilton, Beverly and Salem. Maj. John Burnham, of this place, a descendant of the first settler of that name, and living on the same ancient homestead, a Revolutionary officer, is employed by the party to raise a company of sixty men, and march to Ohio to protect the new settlers from the Indians. He commences his tour, months in advance of this party of emigrants. Some of the wagons bear upon the outside, in large letters: "For Marietta on the Ohio." They were eight weeks in performing the journey. So rough and steep were some of the hills in Pennsylvania, that the men had to carry a part of the load from the wagons to the top of the hill, before the oxen could draw the wagons up. The men slept in their wagons, while the women and children, or a part of them, often found a lodging in some house by the way. They carried with them their utensils for cooking, and experienced much hospitality, in being allowed to cook by the fires of the houses which they passed. Mr. Story and his family had special cause for joy and sorrow during the journey. They buried a child and had a child born. During one of the warm days of June, when the canvas was rolled up at the side, a lovely young son, leaning too far from the wagon, was precipitated under the wheel and instantly killed. This so disheartened the father, that he proposed to his wife to turn back. But her resolution exceeded his, and she would hearken to nothing but pressing onward. The same resolute woman, when a widow of more than eighty years of age, made us a visit a few years since, performing the journey each way alone. Such was the beginning of Ohio from New England emigration. A State now containing more than two millions of inhabitants, had its origin, in these few covered wagons, that were seen winding their slow way, through many a town and village, a distance of more than seven hundred miles.

1789. There is to be an exhibition of dramatic and single pieces, by the North School, in the meeting-house on the hill, in the evening. The house is brilliantly lighted, and many are hastening to witness the scene. As we enter we see before us a large and convenient rostrum, erected on the top of the pews, in front of the pulpit, with a carpet, and hung round with handsome curtains. Dr. Russ, the teacher of the school, is present, busy in superintending the whole affair. The scholars have been thoroughly trained by him, and drilled in their several parts. To avoid any interruption of their school duties, as well as to be more thoroughly prepared for the occasion, they have met for rehearsal at each other's houses. The design is to exhibit their proficiency in the art of speaking, and to furnish an intellectual entertainment which shall be gratifying to parents and all lovers of education. Among the numerous spectators, we see the pastor of the church, ever interested in the training of the young, the School Committee to whom is intrusted the cause of education, and the smiling countenances of many parents, whose beloved offspring are for the first time " to speak in public on the stage." Various dialogues, military, humorous and grave, are exhibited by the speakers, with appropriate dresses and implements of action. Several heroic and didactic

pieces, in prose and verse, are also pronounced, with a clear
and full· voice and suitable gestures. Portions of the
speeches of Pitt and Burke in the British Parliament,
in defence of our Revolutionary movements, are heard
with great interest. "Romans, countrymen, and lovers!
Hear me for my cause," etc., is uttered with great spirit.
Brutus and Cassius, are set forth in the military style, with
much show of courage, and frequent reference to the broad
sword. The speaking is considered by all as remarkably
good. Parents are especially gratified, who see, in the
juvenile performers, the military officers, or legislators, or
judges of future days. We who have gone back for the
occasion, in the car of time, can distinctly see future men
and women in some of these boys and girls. There is
Col. Andrews in miniature, and his wife, Elizabeth Goodhue. They are engaged in a dialogue together. Capt.
James Perkins is before us, in the character of Washington
or La Fayette, with a sword much longer in proportion to
his coat, than when subsequently at the head of the Light
Infantry. Elizabeth Cogswell appears upon the stage,
under the eye of the *teacher*, and becomes the wife of the
physician. We might mention others still living, and
acting an honorable part on the stage of life, but we for-
bear. We come back from the occasion, fully convinced
that our fathers were not in the least behind the times
in the matter of schooling, and that if we would surpass
or even equal them, in proportion to our far more abundant means, we must do far more than we are now
doing.

October 30th. The President of the United States,
George Washington, on his tour to the North. visits this
town. If we go with our fathers and mothers to the
centre of the town, we shall have many to accompany us,
some on foot, and some on horseback, every horse almost
carrying double. The gathering in town is great. The
continentals are all present to see their old General once
more. A numerous cavalcade is formed to go to the Ham-
31

let, and escort him to the body of the town. We see in
that numerous body of horse, our minister, Mr. Cleaveland,
now approaching three-score years and ten, yet with his
large and muscular frame, sitting as erect upon the saddle
as any young man. We wait patiently for their return.
But we have not to wait long ; for the General is always
up to the mark. The whole cavalcade is in sight, and, as
they near us, every eye is fixed to discern the father of his
country. An address is made to him expressive of gratitude for his services, and bidding welcome to the hospitalities of the town ; to which he respectfully and briefly replies. A regiment is on the ground to do him honor,
which, after dining at the inn, he reviews in military style.
Having received many visits, and spent three hours in
town, he takes his departure for Newbury. The vast multitude assembled cannot let him go without a special token
of regard. They form a line on each side of the way,
comprising men, women and children, and reaching through
the village ; through the midst of these long lines of animated countenances and grateful hearts, the General
slowly rides, ever and anon making his grateful respects.

1790. May 28th, Eleazer Craft, died, aged 78. He was
the last of the ruling elders in Mr. Cleaveland's church ;
and lived near the site of the late Richard Burnham's
house, not far from the corner of the old and new road to
Manchester. He was highly esteemed for his ardent piety
and uniform Christian deportment.

1791. July 7th, John Choate Esq., died of consumption, aged 54. He was born on Hog Island, 1737, a son
of elder Francis Choate. His residence was at the North
End, in the same house where his father died, now owned
and occupied by John Burnham. He was much in public
life, for five years a representative to the General Court,
feoffee of the Grammar school, and Justice of the Sessions
Court. "A man highly respected in public and private
life, for his abilities and integrity."

THE FOURTH MEETING-HOUSE.

1792–3. In July of 1790 the parish had voted to erect
a new meeting-house, and at their meetings on the 2d,
6th, 9th and 12th days of that month, they matured the
whole measure and sold every pew. There was considerable difference of opinion, however, as to the proper location for it, some of the parish thinking that it ought to be
placed on the corner near the gravel-pit. After many
long and protracted discussions, it was finally agreed to
build it on " meeting-house hill," where the *South* meeting-
house stood. That building was accordingly taken down ;
and the new house was raised on the 3d and 4th of July,
1792. According to the testimony of the ·late Mr. John
Choate, who remembered to have seen the house raised,
although then only three years old, Capt. Jonathan Story
was the master-builder of the frame and the outside, and
gave orders at the raising. The tower up to the bell-deck
was framed together on the common, and was raised to its
place by ropes. The dimensions of the building were
forty-four feet by sixty-two, and twenty-six feet post ;
height of bell-deck, sixty feet ; height of " ball," ninety
feet ; tower, twelve feet square. A new bell was purchased,
in part by subscription and in part by the sale of the old
one. At the west end there was also a porch, admitting
both to the floor of the house and to the galleries. On
the floor of the house were fifty-three pews, and in the
galleries twenty pews and a number of free seats. The
pulpit was on the side opposite the street or main entrance, and was reached by a flight of stairs. Behind it
was a large, curtained window. Over it was a bell-shaped
sounding-board, suspended by an iron rod from the ceil-
ing. In front of the pulpit was the " elders' seat," reached
from a landing on the stairs, and directly before that, but
lower down, an enclosure containing the communion-table.
There were no stoves in the building until the year 1819.
The meeting-house was not completed until the Autumn of

1793; and on the 8th of October, was dedicated to the service of God. the Father, Son, and Holy Ghost. The pastor preached on the occasion from, Acts x. 33: "Now therefore are we all here present before God, to hear all things that are commanded thee of God." The house was full of people. The sermon was appropriate and impressive ; the singing was conducted with great animation and power, the choir being led by Isaac Long of Hopkinton, N. H., one of the builders of the house. The text was inscribed on a tablet and placed over the canopy of the pulpit. This tablet is now to be seen in the basement-room of the church. Forty-seven pews on the floor of the house and twenty in the gallery were sold for the sum total of £667.15 ($2,225.83). A list of the purchasers is before us, fifty-three in all, not one of whom is now among the living.

The old North meeting-house, which had been built in 1718, was standing as late as the 7th of November 1791, as is proved by an allusion to it in the " Chebacco School Records" of that date, yet, according to the testimony of several aged people, the Sabbath service, while the new house was building, was held in the barn of Dea. Jonathan Cogswell (the grandfather of Albert and Jonathan Cogswell). The pulpit was taken from the meeting-house and placed in the middle of the " bay " between the two "floors," on the back side of the barn, and the scaffold opposite to it on the front side, between the two barn-doors, was occupied by the choir of singers.

1797. " April 3 th. A letter-missive from the Second Church of Rowley to this church, requesting the assistance of this church with such a number of delegates as we shall choose, to join with a large number of churches in the ordination of Mr. Isaac Braman over them as pastor, being communicated, voted to comply with the request, but postponed the choosing a delegate till they should hear Mr. Braman preach a sermon or two.

" May 28th, the church being stayed after divine service, P. M., having heard Mr. Braman preach to good acceptance three sermons, proceeded to choose our brother Thomas Choate as our delegate to go with our pastor to New Rowley to sit in Council the 7th of June next, to assist in the ordination of said Mr. Braman."

At the ordination of Rev. Mr. Braman, Mr. Cleaveland made the consecrating prayer.

1798. "November 18th. A letter-missive from the Third Church in Newbury to the Second Church in Ipswich, requesting the assistance of our pastor with delegates, in the ordination of Mr. Leonard Woods to the pastoral office in that church, being communicated to the church by the pastor this day, the church voted to comply with the request, provided the weather at this late season of the year and our aged pastor's health will admit of attending the council. And our brother Abraham Perkins, being nominated as delegate of this church to go with our pastor, was chosen."

This is the last record in Mr. Cleaveland's handwriting.

1799. April 22d, the Rev. John Cleaveland departs this life, after a long, faithful and successful ministry. He was 77 years old, the day on which he died. He was born in Canterbury, Connecticut, April 22, 1722. In early life, he exhibited a taste for books, and a contemplative mind. Having passed through the preparatory course of study, he entered Yale College at the age of 19. While a member of this Institution, he exhibited on a trying occasion, that independence and moral courage for which he was distinguished in after life. Although the cause of Mr. Whitefield, doctrinally considered, was only Puritanism revived, it was conducted by measures deemed subversive of the established order of the churches, and was on this account obnoxious to the government of Yale. Ignorant, however, that he was violating any rule of the College in so doing, young Cleaveland, when at home in vacation in company with his parents and friends and a majority of the members of the church to which he belonged, attended a meeting of Separatists and listened to the preaching of a lay-exhorter or "new-light preacher" as the followers of Whitefield were called. On his return to college at the beginning of his Senior year, he was arraigned for this offence, and required to confess that he had done wrong. On refusing he was expelled from College. As some atonement for the injury thus inflicted, the government of the college unsolicited conferred on him his degree in

1764, and recorded his name among the graduates of his class—the class of 1745. Soon after his dismission from college, he was licensed to preach; and it was in consequence of that zeal for the *old doctrines* and the *new measures*, which the treatment he had received had awakened in him, that he was invited to preach to the Separatist Society in Boston, meeting in the Huguenot Church in School street "where the expatriated Bowdoin's and Amory's had before worshiped." The call however, which that Society gave him, after he had been their acting pastor for two years, he declined. But very soon after he accepted the invitation of the "Newly-gathered Congregational Church" in Chebacco, and was ordained their pastor when at the age of twenty-five. About the same time he received the honorary degree of Master of Arts from Dartmouth College. In this parish he continued in the faithful discharge of the duties of the ministry for more than fifty-two years. His last sickness, as we were informed by a member of the family, was vehement and of short duration. He was aware that the time of his departure was at hand; spake of it with calmness and Christian resignation: yea, more, he desired to depart and be with Christ. His conversation with those who visited him at this time, and with his family, was instructive and impressive. He often joined with them in social prayer, and expressed his full confidence in the God of his salvation. With this lively confidence and peaceful serenity, he descended into the vale of death, and, as we doubt not, was received up into glory. His funeral was attended by a large collection of people. The Rev. Dr. Dana of the South Parish, preached on the occasion from II. Kings ii. 12. The parish voted eighty dollars for the expenses of his burial.

Mr. Cleaveland's first wife and the mother of his children, was Mary, the only daughter of Parker Dodge, of the Hamlet. Her mother was Mary Choate, born on Hog Island. Of *her* grandchildren, one was a minister of the

Gospel, and two were physicians. Of her great grand-children, one was a professor in Bowdoin College, two are ministers, one a pastor's widow, and one a lawyer at New York. We mention these among the products of the Island. Mrs. Cleaveland died of a cancer, April 11, 1768, in her forty-sixth year. Mr. Cleaveland married for his second wife, Mary, widow of Capt. John Foster of Manchester. She died at Topsfield, April 19, 1810. An address was delivered at her funeral, in our parish church, by Rev. Asahel Huntington of Topsfield. The names of Mr. Cleaveland's children were Mary, John, Parker, Ebenezer, Elizabeth, Nehemiah, and Abigail.

Mr. Cleaveland resided from the year 1749 to the close of his life on what is now called Spring Street, in an ancient mansion, which stood on the spot now occupied by the house of Hon. David Choate. His farm included all the land now belonging to this homestead. It was bought for his use and benefit, by a number of his parishioners, and became his, as from time to time he paid the original value, without rent or interest.

In his personal appearance, Mr. Cleaveland was tall, yet of fine proportions and very erect, of a florid countenance, blue eyes, firm in his gait even to old age, moderate in his motions, but of great muscular strength and activity. He had a most amiable and benevolent eye, and was a man into whose face everybody loved to look. He usually conversed in a low tone of voice, was social and pleasant, abounding in facts which he related at times with great animation, was grave, instructive and impressive, when occasion so required. He could sometimes, however, forego the dignity of the ministerial character and amuse himself and others. He had a lady in his church who was strongly suspected of neglecting to read her Bible. In order to satisfy himself of the fact, when one day on a visit at her house, he watched his opportunity, while she was out of the room, and put her spectacles, (not having bows upon them,) into her Bible, and closed the book. The very

great length of time that elapsed before the finding of
the spectacles, but too plainly proved the suspicion well
founded.

In his public performances, Mr. Cleaveland usually began in a low tone, but would soon raise his voice, to a stentorian pitch. So powerful and distinct was his utterance
that persons sitting at an open window on the opposite
side of the street, when the windows and doors of the
church were open, have distinctly heard the greater part
of his sermon. Before the close of his sermon, which
commonly occupied an hour or more in the delivery, most
of the men in the Winter season, impelled by the cold,
would be upon their feet, still listening however, with close
attention to the end. His discourses were chiefly extem-
pore, from brief notes containing the heads and some of
the leading thoughts. We have in our hands some of
these briefs, written almost one hundred years ago, consisting of four pages : each four inches long, three wide,
and containing the date when the sermon was preached,
the text, some ten or twelve heads and many leading
thoughts, in a hand so small as scarcely to be legible. His
delivery was accompanied with appropriate gestures, frequent and energetic, his hand descending upon the cush-
ions, with such power as to drive sleep from the most
drowsy hearer. We have been told by clergymen, his
contemporaries, that he was esteemed one of the most
popular and instructive preachers of the day. He was a
diligent student and an able writer, as his published pamphlets fully testify. The light in his study was usually
burning at a late hour. The subjects on which he was to
preach, were carefully and thoroughly digested. He
never offered that, for a sacrifice to the Lord, which had
cost him nothing. As his memory was not so prompt in
his last years, he began then to write out his sermons in
full, instead of trusting to brief notes, yet his manner in
the pulpit, was still lively and vigorous. On the last Sabbath but one before his death, he preached with his usual

animation and energy.   His familiarity with the Scriptures
was proverbial.

" His prayers were congenial with his sermons. Without a careful and
orderly arrangement of topics, they were the effusions of a heart in close communion with God, and carried with them the affections of his hearers.   Mr.
Cleaveland's character was uniformity.   While he constantly held intercourse
with heaven, he consecrated particular days to private fasting and prayer.
With him, love to the Savior and to the souls for which he died, was the ab-
sorbing sentiment.   This was habitually manifest in methods altogether unos-
tentatious yet impossible to be misunderstood.   He thus secured the conscientious approbation of the community generally and the warm love of the
pious.   Though his life was spent for the most part in comparative seclusion,
his good influence was felt much beyond the immediate sphere of his labors." *

Through life he tenaciously maintained that freer system of ecclesiastical order, and that stricter system of evangelical doctrine, which characterized the advocates of Mr.
Whitefield in New England.   From convictions of duty
he contended zealously for what he believed to be the truth
and right, whenever occasion required.   During no small
part of his ministry, therefore, he was obliged to maintain
somewhat of a controversial attitude.   Besides his printed
pamphlets in his controversy with Mr. Pickering, he afterwards published :

" An Essay on important Principles of Christianity, with Animadversions
on Dr. Jonathan Mayhew's Thanksgiving Sermon ;" A Rejoinder to Dr.
Mayhew's Reply ; "A Justification of the Fourth Church in Ipswich, from
the Strictures of the Rev. S. Wigglesworth of the Hamlet, and the Rev.
Richard Jaques of Gloucester ;" "An attempt to nip in the bud the un-
scriptural Doctrine of Universal Salvation ;" "A Dissertation in support of
Infant Baptism ;" and "Defence of the result of a late Council at Salem
against Dr. Whittaker's Remarks."

Yet all his intercourse with his fellow-men was marked
by affability, candor and kindness.   Such was the benevolence of his heart, the mildness of his manners, the consistency of his deportment, that under his ministry, two
churches which had been long at variance were brought
to a permanent union.   No higher encomium could be

---

* Rev. Dr. Dana in Sprague's Annals of the American Pulpit.

passed upon his conciliatory manners and uniform propriety of conduct.

Mr. Cleaveland's authorship was not confined to his controversial tracts. Among his other published productions were "A Narrative of a Revival of Religion in the Fourth Church, Ipswich," and "A Sermon at the Ordination of Rev. John Cleaveland, Jr., at Stoneham." In 1774 he wrote several political articles for the Salem Gazette. Others upon the state of the country and its interests appeared in the same paper from time to time down to 1798 from his pen, over the signature of *"Johannes in Eremo."*

On the 2d of June following, Rev. Dr. Parish of Byfield, by request, preached a sermon to the bereaved church and congregation, on the occasion of his death. The text was Psalms cxvi. 15. The concluding portion of the discourse was as follows:

" The confines of time do not bound the hopes or joys of man. Beyond the veil of death the regions of immortality invite his attention. From the deserts of life, the City of God presents Edens of delight, palaces of glory, thrones of honor. To the piercing eye of faith, the prospect is real, the objects are distinguishable, the view is ravishing. As from Pisgah's summit the Hebrew Lawgiver beheld the promised land, Gilead, and the snowy tops of Lebanon, the vale of Jericho and the city of Zoar; so the Christian surveys the New Jerusalem, her walls of jasper, and her gates of pearl. He no longer trembles at the approach of the king of terrors. Often he desires to depart. Serene and pleasant are his last hours. The choirs of heaven participate in the blissful scene. Cheerfully they leave their thrones to hover round the dying saint, to soothe his last moment, to convoy his holy spirit to his final home, to the bosom of his God. God himself delights in the departure of his people from the dreary wilderness of mortality. Is not this subject calculated to afford comfort to mourners contemplating the departure of a Christian friend? And does not the subject address itself with particular emphasis to this assembly. The faithful husband, the tender parent, the kind neighbor, the laborious minister, the man of universal benevolence, is no more. But is it not great consolation that he believed and obeyed the Gospel of Jesus Christ? May not a transient recollection of his character revive in your minds the delightful impression, that his death was precious in the sight of God?

" In that period which is apt to be dazzled with the charms of popular applause, he voluntarily bore the cross, and suffered reproach for *what he conceived* the cause of truth and vital religion. Scrupulous in his ideas of right and wrong; ardent in his feelings; daring in his temper; he followed the convictions of his own mind, little regarding what might be the impression upon others. Though of a mild spirit, he was decided in his opinions; though gentle in his manner he was independent in his conduct, never was he snared by the fear of man.

"That he was a person of consummate prudence, of irreproachable conduct, we have ample evidence in the union which has taken place under his ministry, between the two churches and congregations, which now compose this Society. At first he was minister of only one of those, when very probably both possessing the spirit of the times might not unjustly be compared to two clouds, which at every moment disgorge the thunder, and dart terrific flames; but by the attractive influence of him whose death we all deplore, the clouds, dissolving lost their awful form, the storm was hushed, the darkness fled. The gentle shower, the peaceful bow succeeds. This union under him seems not unnatural, when we recollect his pleasing address, his meekness of temper, the suavity of his manners, and the uniform propriety of his deportment. His life was such as carried conviction to every acquaintance that he was a man of unaffected *goodness.*

"He was a careful observer of Providence, being in the habit of seeing God in every event. Every circumstance he viewed as a providence of God, constituting a necessary part of a great, a glorious whole. This belief soothed his mind in the darkest hour. The Bible was his constant companion. He was a scribe well instructed in the sacred oracles. They seemed to be treasured in his memory, and with great pertinency he applied texts to different characters and tastes. His industry was uniform. His knowledge of men and things general and extensive. A particular and tender affection he had for his brethren in the ministry. With the most cordial hospitality he welcomed them to his dwelling. Most punctual in *all* his engagements, nothing but necessity could prevent his being with them at their stated meetings. And rarely did he retire from their society without giving a word of timely instruction, of pious advice, of paternal admonition. Active and enterprising, he repeatedly, left the silence of his study for the din of war; the joys of domestic peace, for the dangers of the bloody field. Four years of his life as chaplain of her forces were devoted to his country. The waters of Champlain, the rocks of Cape Breton, the fields of Cambridge, and the banks of the Hudson, listened to the fervor of his addresses. Though he *rigidly* reproved profanity and vice of every kind, such was the mildness of his *manner*, that he seldom or never gave offence. To him another species of warfare was still more familiar. For a great part of his life, he was frequently engaged in polemic disputes. He was wont to contend for what he believed 'the faith once delivered to the saints.' But this did not in the least sour his temper, ruffle his spirit, or excite that asperity which is too frequently the effect of religious controversy. Charity and good nature were prominent features of his character. As a minister, he was laborious and successful, never sparing himself when duty called to action. Zealous

in his religious performances, he was apparently the means of awakening and
comforting many. A son of thunder to the wicked, an angel of consolation to the pious, he saw much fruit of his instruction. One period of solemnity was remarkable. The word of the Lord was powerful. In a short
time a goodly number, a cloud of witnesses, was added to the church, who
were their pastor's comfort while living, and we trust will be his crown of
rejoicing at the great day. An impassioned lover of his country, he viewed
with horror the disorganizers of the world, with sacred indignation he contemplated those who defend, or apologize for their conduct. In his opinion
to make an excuse for a nation of atheists was irreligious and anti-Christian.

"As a father, tender and indulgent, he carefully instructed his offspring in
the great doctrines and duties of Christianity. By his example and precept
he taught them to be useful, to be happy and respectable here, and blessed
hereafter. He commanded their affection and perfect esteem. He reigned
in their hearts.

"With the companion of his youth, and the worthy consort who closed
his eyes, he lived in the most endearing harmony. To lose such a friend,
husband and minister is distressing. It would be more than insensibility not
to mourn. For a friend like him Jesus wept. But is it no cause of thank-
fulness that such a blessing has been enjoyed so long? Has not such a person been highly favored of the Lord? The tears of grief are wiped away
by the spirit of gratitude. Those circumstances which enhance the loss, heal
or soothe the bleeding heart."

On Mr. Cleaveland's tombstone, in the old graveyard, is
the following inscription:

THIS MONUMENT
PERPETUATES THE MEMORY AND SINGULAR VIRTUES OF THE
REV. JOHN CLEAVELAND, A. M.,
Who died April 22d, 1799, which day completed
HIS 77TH YEAR.

"He was ordained to the pastoral office in this place, February 25, (O. S.,) A. D.
1747, and for more than fifty-two years was eminently a faithful Watchman, being
ever ready and apt to teach. His zeal and attention to the duties of his office,
evinced the purity of his motives. His mind was richly stored with useful science,
and in the Holy Scriptures he was eminently learned. His undeviating virtue commanded respect, and confirmed the hope of his blissful immortality.

"His soul, released from cumbrous clay,
Expatiates in eternal day;
And with the great Jehovah dwells,
Who, wonders new and vast, reveals."

Of the officers of Mr. Cleaveland's Church, Dea. Choate
and Dea. Giddings removed to Ipswich before the close of
his ministry, and only two of the others survived him—

Dea. Thomas Burnham, who died the next month (May 18th), aged seventy-two, and Dea. Jonathan Cogswell, (elected April 7, 1780), who died February 12, 1813, aged eighty-six. The youngest of these officers died at the age of seventy-two; the eldest (Dea. Story), at the age of ninety-three. Dea. Burnham was the last of the deacons who "lined" the psalm or hymn and "set the tune." In addition to his services as school-teacher, he was much employed in writing wills and deeds and in settling estates. His house was not far from the dwelling of the late Capt. Moses Andrews.

The number of members who withdrew from Mr. Pickering's church and formed Mr. Cleaveland's in 1746, was 82; received from the Second Church at the time of union in 1774, 15; other admissions during his ministry, 187; total, 234; remaining at Mr. Cleaveland's death, 47.

Nov. 13th. Rev. Josiah Webster was ordained pastor of the church as successor to Mr. Cleaveland. Rev. Stephen Peabody of Atkinson, N. H., preached the ordination sermon.

CHAPTER V.

BEING THE YEAR OF THE INCORPORATION OF CHEBACCO AS THE TOWN OF ESSEX.

1800. At the close of the *eighteenth* century the population of Chebacco had increased from three hundred to more than eleven hundred, and instead of one school district there were three. Progress in *educational* matters was now further indicated by the erection of new schoolhouses. At the Falls one was built in 1800, in accordance with a vote passed "at a meeting of the school proprietors held at the house of Mr. Isaac Allen," February 24th, at which meeting Capt. Jonathan Story was moderator, and Capt. Nathaniel Burnham and Messrs. Jacob and Elisha Story were appointed a building committee. In accordance with another vote passed at that meeting, this building was erected on the spot where the old one stood, (the first school-house at the Falls and built in 1761.) This location was near the dwelling of the late Nimrod Burnham. The second school-house on the south side of the river was also built by proprietors, the next year (1801), and was located on land bought of Joshua Burnham, and situated "on the easterly side of the Gloucester road at the parting of the way to Gloucester and Manchester." On the 15th of April of the same year, "the subscribers to a new school-house" in the North district, at a meeting of which Mr. Ebenezer Low was moderator, voted to erect a building suitable for a "reading and writing school, of the following dimensions: twenty feet square and nine feet post, with a chimney and six· windows, with a hyp'd Rough" (i. e., a hip roof,) and to place it "on or near the spot where Mr. Goodhue's ale-house formerly stood." i. e., a few rods north-east of Jonathan Low's. The cost of the building was divided into thirty shares. The building committee were George Choate, Esq., and Messrs. Samuel Giddings and Samuel Hardy.

1802. A social library is established here. The company at its formation, consists of thirty-four men, comprising the physician, the minister and many of the leading men of the parish. But they have all since gone to their graves, save one. The library contained an excellent selection of books, and was of great utility in disseminating knowledge and promoting a taste for reading. It continued in active operation for more than forty years, and contained at one period, four hundred volumes. When books became cheaper and found their way into families, as a part of the household furniture, and more especially, when newspapers and periodicals began to multiply, and to constitute the principal part of family reading, the "Social Library" was more and more neglected, until at length its existence became merely nominal.

1803. February 28th, Joseph Perkins, Esq., died at Salem. He was born July 8, 1772. His parents, at the time of his birth, resided in the ancient house now owned by the heirs of John Choate. His father, Joseph Perkins, built the large house directly opposite the North Church. His ancestors, both on his father's and mother's side, were among the early settlers of this place.* When about four-

---

*PARTIAL GENEALOGY OF THE PERKINS FAMILY.

1. William Perkins emigrated to Ipswich about 1633.

2. John Perkins, born in England and emigrated with his father.

3. Isaac Perkins.

4. Abraham Perkins, born about 1668; John Perkins, graduated at college in 1695, died in 1740.

5. Joseph Perkins (son of Abraham), born March 12, 1720 (O. S.); married Elizabeth Choate (born August 2, 1723, and a daughter of Lieut. Thomas Choate); died April 4, 1805, aged 85. He was one of the founders of the Sixth Parish (Rev. Mr. Cleaveland's), was its clerk from its organization until its union with the Second Parish, and its treasurer for the most of that time. In the school records he is styled an innholder.

6. Joseph Perkins, born September 3, 1752; married his cousin Mary Foster (born

teen years of age, he began the study of Latin in the district school, no objection being made by the district, and
the teacher kindly favoring it, by devoting to him extra
time. We may say, therefore, with propriety, that this
eminent lawyer and scholar was indebted to the district
school for his literary career, just as the majestic river
must be traced back to its bubbling fountain. Before he
was seventeen years of age, he entered Phillips Academy
at Andover, where he was soon known for his studious
habits, and proficiency in the learned languages. He remained there a little more than a year, and then in 1790
entered Harvard College, at the age of eighteen. His
college life was one of uncommon brilliancy, as a correct
scholar, close thinker, and popular writer and speaker.
Several of the productions of his pen, written in the early
part of his college life, were published in the Massachusetts Magazine, the only literary periodical then printed
in Boston. At the early age of twenty, he seems to have
become a regular contributor to this work, in addition to
all his college duties. His essays and orations at the private exhibitions of his class, which he has left in manuscript, show great maturity of thought and strength of
mind. It had long been the custom at Harvard for the
Sophomore class to challenge the Freshmen to a wrestling
match, a challenge which the Freshmen must accept, or
endure worse evils. This custom was the source of much
difficulty, and was deeply deplored by the friends of the

March 13, 1752, and a daughter of John Foster, born August 7, 1724, and Mary
Choate Foster, born June 24, 1731); died February 1, 1806, aged 53. He had
twelve children, four of whom died in infancy or early youth. The names of the
others were as follows :

7. Joseph, Esq., the subject of this sketch, "born at the mansion-house of my
grandfather, July 8, 1772," died February 28, 1803 ; John, born June 7, 1774, "married February 19, 1801, Lydia, daughter of the late Capt. William Choate," died
May, 1856 ; Elizabeth, born November 28, 1777, died May 19, 1806 ; James, born
January 2, 1780 ; Mary, born October 22, 1781, died August 7, 1801 ; Jeremiah, born
April 15, 1785 ; Sarah, born July 17, 1787, died May 25, 1804 ; Aaron, born August
26, 1789.

8. Children of John : Thomas, Mary (married U. G. Spofford), Sarah (married
John Burnham), Lydia (married John Cressy), Clara (married R. W. Burnham),
Harriet (married Oliver Burnham).

college. But who shall break up a time-honored custom, to which so many impulsive young men are strongly and passionately attached? *It remained for a lad from one of our district schools to effect this, simply by the power of his pen.* He wrote and delivered before the college, a satirical piece, entitled an apology for wrestling, and the custom was never heard of afterwards. At the close of his college course, in selecting the performers for "Commencement Day," the government of the college placed him at the head of his class. Among so many scholars, who afterwards distinguished themselves in the various walks of life, this was no small honor for our Chebacco student. On that occasion, he pronounced an oration on Eloquence, which was universally admired. It was afterwards published in the monthly magazine, and of it the editors say:

"The following oration delivered on the day of public commencement at Harvard University, we are happy to insert in our magazine. The applause with which the delivery was received, the intrinsic excellence of the performance, and a wish to make our monthly museum a repository of knowledge and useful entertainment, unite in an inducement to present it entire to the patrons of our publication."

After leaving College at the age of twenty-two, Mr. Perkins became an assistant in Phillip's Academy at Exeter, over which the late Dr. Abbot presided with so much celebrity for a long succession of years. He remained as teacher in this Academy only one year, during which time, he gave some attention to the law, under the direction of Hon. Oliver Peabody of that place. From Exeter he went to Gloucester, Mass., and took charge of a Proprietors' School in that place for one year. At Gloucester, also, he read law, under the direction of John Rowe, Esq. In the Autumn of the year 1796 he began to read law at Salem, in the office of William Prescott, Esq., a distinguished attorney. In July of the following year, he pronounced an oration on Genius at the public commencement at Cambridge, and took his honorary degree of Master of Arts. On the following October, having read law for three years,

33

he was admitted to the bar, and opened an office in Salem.
His first case in the practice of law, was before the Court
of Common Pleas, when he addressed a jury for the first
time in behalf of Marcus Feely, a young Irishman, in-
dicted for theft. He was successful in the case, and Feely
was acquitted. June 2, 1798, he married Miss Margaret
Orne, daughter of Timothy Orne of Salem. By her, he
had one son. His wife lived only about two years after
their marriage. Of her death, he speaks in his journal in
an affecting manner, bearing testimony to the excellence
of her character. In 1801, he was appointed attorney for
the country. In 1802, July 4th, his only son died in this
place. In his journal, the father makes the following entry:

"My son, Timothy Orne, died at my father's, in Chebacco, where he was
on a visit, aged three years, four months and six days, after an illness of five
or six days. I was with him during his last painful night; and he expired
before my eyes. Thus I am stripped of all. But the Lord gave, the Lord
hath taken away; blessed be the name of the Lord. His body was carried
to Salem in the evening, and deposited in the Orne family tomb with the remains of my dear, departed wife."

The next entry in his journal relates to the death of his
mother here.

"I was prevented," he says, "by indisposition from visiting her for ten
days before her death, and was unable to attend her funeral. Thus within
two years and a half I have been deprived of a *beloved wife*, a kind grandmother, an affectionate sister, an only child, and a dear mother. Have pity
upon me, O ye my friends, for the hand of the Lord hath touched me."

This bears date August 5, 1802, and on the next February he himself departed from this world to another, at
the age of thirty years. He died of consumption, which
was doubtless aggravated, if not brought on, by his domestic sorrows and trials. He was a communicant at the
Episcopal Church in Salem, and an officer in that church.
His pastor, the Rev. Mr. Fisher, preached a sermon on the
occasion of his death from I. Cor. xv. 53: "This mortal must
put on immortality." He thus speaks of the deceased:

"Endued by nature with a clear and solid judgment, with a disposition
formed to please, and with an heart to do good, great, and justly so, were

the expectations of his friends concerning his progress and usefulness in life. Possessed of an enlightened mind and a pure heart, his abilities were equally applicable either to elegant literature or professional studies. With an understanding which felt its own strength, he decided whatever came before it with promptitude and propriety. He was peculiarly happy in communicating his ideas and in illustrating his conceptions. On whatever subject he conversed, he discovered modesty, taste and correctness. His humanity and benevolence were so active and conspicuous as to interest him sincerely in the welfare of all about him, and to engage their respect and esteem in return.

Though sober and temperate in all the habits of his life, and given to severe application in the duties of his profession, he delighted in the convivial society of his friends. In all the domestic relations of life, such as that of a son, brother, father, husband, lover and friend, he felt and was governed by the tenderest of charities. His rectitude and integrity will remain forever unimpeached and revered, even by hypocrisy and dissimulation themselves. Although emulous and coveting the best gifts, the improvements and graces of others could excite in him no envy. He felt a strong sense of religious truths, and gave the most unequivocal proofs of his possessing the faith of a Christian by living in obedience to the doctrines and precepts of the Gospel."

In one of the Salem newspapers, soon after his death appeared a sketch of his character, of which the following is an extract:

"With an undeviating rectitude of heart, and stability of understanding, in his practice he was indulgent without weakness, and firm without severity. He was clear and cool in debate, and the tones of his voice sweet and musical. He always examined his propositions and opinions with great care and industry, and if he retained them with firmness, he had adopted them with caution. Patient and laborious in study, ardent and accurate in investigation, with a penetration of mind that permitted nothing valuable to escape it, and a tenacity of memory that suffered nothing useful to be lost; he had added the solidity of science to the natural beauties of his native genius, and would have ripened ' *in his season* ' to be an ornament to the bar, as he was of society. In private life he was amiable and exemplary. To the attainments of the scholar were united the accomplishments of a gentleman. His manners were retired without moroseness, and polished without the false refinements of fashion. His conversation was interesting and instructive, as he mingled in it the fruits of the study, unmixed with its pedantry. With a countenance and features of a manly and pleasing conformation, he possessed a well-formed person, and was calculated to embellish polite society. Attentive to the duties of religion as well as to the domestic and social duties, ' modern degeneracy had not reached him;' he exhibited constant evidences of his belief in the holy scriptures, and a uniform practice of the sacred doctrines enjoined in them."

1804. About this time forty sail of boats were engaged in the fishery on the Eastern shore; a few were employed in the Bank fishery. The fishing business diminished as ship-building increased and was found more profitable. The former was mostly discontinued about 1821.

1805. December 19th, the physician of this parish, Dr. Parker Russ, died in the thirty-seventh year of his age. Dr. Russ was born in this place; a descendant of "Master" Rust the first school teacher. He was the son of Joseph and Mary Rust. His father died when he was quite young. His widowed mother married Rev. Paul Park of Preston, Ct., and removed there with her son, then three years old. Parker received his education in Connecticut, and remained there until prepared to practice medicine, when he came to this place, about the year 1788, and succeeded Dr. Davis, as the physician of the parish. The first Winter of his residence here, he taught the North school with great success. He resided in the ancient Rust house, where he was born, now owned by William H. Mears. In 1800, December 14th, he married Elizabeth, daughter of Jonathan Cogswell, Esq., who died June 5th, 1803. Dr. Russ was well-skilled in his profession, and successful in his practice. Integrity, decision and energy were prominent traits in his character.

Dr. Reuben D. Mussey succeeded him as physician of the place. He came while Dr. Russ was sick, a short time before his death. His first lodging was in a tavern, kept by Amos Burnham, on Thompson's Island. Dr. Mussey was born in Pelham, N. H., June 23, 1780; graduated at Dartmouth College in 1803, studied medicine with Dr. Nathan Smith of Hanover, N. H. He continued here in successful practice for a few years only; became a member of the church here, and officiated as its clerk. In September, 1808, he went to Philadelphia to attend a course of medical lectures. On his return, he settled in Salem, and continued in full practice there till 1814, when he was appointed professor at Dartmouth College. In 1838 he removed to

Cincinnati, where he was appointed professor in the medical college. Dr. Mussey left many warm friends here, some of whom still live. He made them several visits, after removing his residence from town, and on one occasion lectured in the North Church, on the deleterious effects of chewing and smoking tobacco or using it as snuff, as tending to destroy health and shorten life.* Dr. Mussey was succeeded here by Dr. Thomas Sewall.

1806, February 15. From a document still extant, it appears that an effort was made to build a school-house and establish a school somewhere in the center of the parish, for the study of Latin a part of the year, and English studies another part. This was to be a sort of high school, into which all the older scholars of the place were to be admitted, while the district school-houses were to be used for primary schools, to be taught by females. The project received the approbation and patronage of several in remote parts of the parish, as well as of some in the center. If it had been carried into execution, it is our opinion that education among us would have been advanced by it more than half a century. We insert the document, with the subscribers' names:

"Whereas the inhabitants of Chebacco are deprived of the advantages of the Grammar (Latin) school in the town of Ipswich, the distance being so great that we cannot send our youth to it; and thinking it necessary, that they should be instructed in grammar; and as there is no school-house in this parish, in a suitable place, for such a purpose, it is thought advisable to build a school-house in some central place to accommodate a (Latin) Grammar school a part of the year, and a school with the common English studies another part, leaving the district school-houses to school dames in the summer, and likewise to accommodate singing schools.

"Therefore, we, the subscribers, do engage to pay for the several shares set to our respective names for the purpose of erecting and completing a school-house on that piece of land granted by the Commoners in 1729, for that purpose; said house to consist of forty shares; and as soon as thirty shares are engaged, the subscribers to meet in some suitable place, to agree upon the

---

* Dr. Mussey was a member of the Faculty of Dartmouth College from 1814 to 1838,—the first six years of that time Professor of the Theory and Practice of Medicine and of Materia Medica, and afterwards Professor of Anatomy and Surgery. He died at Roxbury, Mass., June 21, 1866, aged 86.

plan of the house, the method of building it, and to act upon any other business relative to the same, that may then be thought necessary.

"*Chebacco, February 15th*, 1806.

"Subscribers' Names: one share to each name, viz., William Holmes, Jonathan Cogswell, George Choate, Jonathan Story, Jacob Story, Abraham Perkins, Moses Marshall, Thomas Burnham 3d, Moses Marshall, Jun., Thomas Choate, Thomas M. Burnham, David Choate, Jonathan Cogswell 3d, John Perkins, Daniel Low, Abner Burnham."

On the 6th of March, a military company was organized, called the "Ipswich Light Infantry." A petition to the General Court for leave to form such a company having been presented and granted in January, the following order was issued from head-quarters:

"February 26th. The Commander-in-Chief being authorized by a resolve of the General Court on the petition of John Perkins and others, and having the advice of Council thereupon, orders that there be raised by voluntary enlistment, a Light Infantry Company in the town of Ipswich in the Second Regiment, Second Brigade, Second Division of the Militia, to be annexed to said Regiment, and subject to the rules and regulations established by law for governing and regulating the Militia. By order of the Commander-in-Chief,   WILLIAM DONNISAW, *Adj. Gen.*"

April 4th, a constitution prepared by Jonathan Cogswell, Jr., as committee was adopted and signed. The preamble is as follows:

"We, the subscribers, do enlist and agree to form ourselves into an association or company to be called the Ipswich Light Infantry; and as it is indispensably necessary for the promotion of good order and discipline that we should meet frequently in private, and as the existence of the company depends on the most implicit subordination,—in order to enforce it and to strengthen the bond of our union, do hereby establish, in addition to the general provisions of the law, the following articles."

The number of members at the formation of the company was thirty-two. The uniform was "a short blue coat, trimmed out with red, with a collar and facing; dimity pantaloons, waistcoat with red seams and binding, black half-gaiters, and Grecian caps." Knapsacks and canteens were afterwards obtained. Its first officers were as follows: Jonathan Cogswell, 3d, Captain; John P. Choate, Lieutenant; Jeremiah Choate, Ensign; Sergeants, Solomon Choate,

John Perkins, Thomas Burnham 3d, Caleb Marshall. October 20th, the company made their first appearance at "general muster" with a band of music from Salem. Captain Cogswell continued to command the company until 1810, when he was elected Colonel of the regiment. His successors down to the year 1826, so far as appears from the company records, were John P. Choate, William Andrews, Joseph Choate, James Perkins, William Choate, Joshua Low.

Rev. Josiah Webster having requested a dismission, a mutual council is called, and by their advice his pastoral relation is dissolved, July 23. Mr. Webster was much beloved by his church and people, who deeply regretted his leaving them. At his settlement, the parish gave him $500 as a donation, or settlement, as it was called. His annual salary was $334, and the parsonage. As the currency diminished in value, his salary became insufficient. The parish voted to add $100 from year to year as should be found necessary. The pastor was satisfied with the addition, and only insisted that it should be made a part of the original contract. The parish thought their pastor should have confidence in their good will, to vote the addition yearly, along with the rest of the salary. This, however, did not satisfy, and the parish will, as is usually the case, becoming stouter and stronger, the result was as stated above. Mr. Webster was afterwards settled in Hampton, N. H., June 8, 1808, where after a quiet and successful ministry, he died March, 27, 1837, aged sixty-five. In the twelfth volume of the American Quarterly Register was published a biographical sketch of him, from which the following extracts are taken:

"Rev. Josiah Webster, the son of Nathan and Elizabeth Webster, was born in Chester, N. H., January 16, 1772. His father was a farmer, barely in circumstances of comfort, with patient, laborious industry, providing for the wants of a large family, and therefore unable to furnish more than a common school education for his children. Josiah, the eldest, in his sixteenth year went to reside with an uncle, whose affairs he managed in his many and long absences. But for a long time he had felt a strong desire to become a minister of the gospel, and though he had acquired only sufficient property to defray the expense of preparation for college, and was distressed and discouraged by the opposition of his friends, in his nineteenth year he repaired to the Rev. Mr. Remmington, of Candia, under whose hospitable roof he began his studies. Afterwards he spent a year under the tuition of that eminent Christian, Rev. Dr. Thayer of Kingston, and completed his preparation at the academy in Atkinson. It was at Kingston that he indulged the hope of reconciliation to God, and of the commencement of the Christian life, A deeper consciousness of sin than he had ever felt before, pressed upon his heart, so full of distress and alarm, that for several days he was unable to pursue his studies. After a season of deep conviction, light broke out upon his mind, ' like a morning of Summer just as the sun rises, when the winds are hushed, and a solemn but delightful stillness prevails everywhere and the face of nature smiles with verdure and flowers.' From Atkinson he took a journey of more than eighty miles to Dartmouth College, for the mere purpose of examination and admission to college. His poverty prevented his remaining a single week to enjoy its advantages. Returning to Atkinson, he pursued his studies under the instruction of the preceptor, Stephen P. Webster, till the Spring of 1795, when with little improvement in the state of his funds, he rejoined his class in college, and completed his first year. At the close of the vacation, though disappointed in every effort to raise money among his friends, he once more set his face towards college. By a mysterious providence of God he fell in company with a stranger, who, learning his condition, without solicitation offered to relieve his necessities by a loan of money to be repaid whenever his circumstances should permit. The traveler was afterwards ascertained to be a merchant of Newburyport. After graduating in the year 1798, he studied theology with the Rev. Stephen Peabody, the minister of Atkinson, about a year, and was then licensed to preach the gospel by the Haverhill Association. Soon after, he was invited to preach as a candidate in Chebacco parish, Ipswich, where, November 1799, he was ordained. After his dismission from that pastorate on account of the inadequacy of his support, he was invited to preach to the church at Hampton, N. H., and was installed there, June 8, 1808. During his ministry at Hampton there were several revivals of religion, as the fruit of which one hundred and seventy persons were gathered into the church. It deserves to be recorded to the lasting honor of Mr. Webster, that he perceived the evil effects of the use of ardent spirits, at a period when even the eyes of good men, were generally closed to the subject. Almost from the first of his ministry he preached against intemperance, and for years before the temperance reformation, observed entire abstinence from all that intoxicates. He was also deeply interested in the cause of education. To his influence and agency, the academy in Hampton, one of the most respectable and flourishing institutions in the State, is indebted for much of its character and usefulness. Attached to the faith and institutions of our fathers, the doctrines of grace he understood and loved, and preached to the very close of his life. His last public act was the preaching of the sermon at the ordination of his son, Rev.

John C. Webster, at Newburyport, as seaman's preacher at Cronstadt, Russia, March 15, 1837. Anxious to perform the service assigned him on that occasion, he made an effort his impaired health was unable to sustain. The day following he returned home, and taking his bed, remarked, that he thought his work on earth was done. 'Well,' said he, 'if it be so, I know not with what act I could close life with more satisfaction.' He died of inflammation of the lungs. During his sickness, his mind was often alienated, but in lucid intervals he uniformly expressed confidence in the mercy of God, and cast himself upon the blood of atonement. His funeral sermon, preached by the Rev. Dr. Dana, is highly commendatory of his ministerial qualifications, devotion to his proper work, and his extensive usefulness. Mr. Webster published five discourses delivered on different occasions."

Mr. Webster's wife was Elizabeth Knight of Hopkinton, N. H. Of their seven children, two were natives of Chebacco. Eliphalet Knight was born May 3, 1802, studied medicine at Dartmouth College, and has been for many years a physician in Boscawen, N. H. Josiah, Jr., was born October 25, 1803, spent his life as a farmer, and died of cholera in Princeton, Ill., September 3, 1852. His other sons graduated at Dartmouth College. John C. became pastor of a church in Hopkinton, Mass.; Col. Joseph D. was chief of Gen. Grant's staff at the battle of Pittsburg Landing, in the late war, and was a most efficient officer in turning the tide of battle there; and Dr. Claudius B. became the Principal of a Seminary in Norwich, Ct.

A private way over land of Samuel Hardy, running partly to Hog Island, is laid out this year.

1807. The Fourth of July is celebrated by the Light Infantry and citizens of Chebacco generally, by a parade and public exercises in the meeting-house. By their invitation an oration is delivered by Dr. R. D. Mussey, to a large audience. A part of the closing address of this oration (which was published at the request of the hearers) is as follows:

"Gentlemen of the Light Infantry: I am happy to address you on the present occasion. The patriotic zeal, the generous ambition, the noble ardor, which prompted you to unite, and devote to the acquisition of military skill, more time and expense than usual, have met the applause and best wishes of all your friends. They view with pleasure the spirit of harmony which has

prevailed among you, and the handsome improvements and respectable appearance you have made.   They have the fullest confidence that you will
always maintain the honorable ground you now hold, and that your deportment will always draw admiration and respect from your military brethren.
Much of the safety of a free people depends on such men as you ; I mean
on a well disciplined militia.   It is undoubtedly a true maxim, that 'the
way to keep peace is to be ready for war.'   You will not suffer idleness and
amusements to unstring all your powers, and prepare you for base servitude.
Study the 'hardihood of antiquity,' and cherish those masculine habits, which
give firmness and strength to the body, resolution and ardor to the soul.
Cincinnatus could drive the Volsci and Æqui from his country, after harden-
ing his muscles at the plough.   May you never be called into action, and
may the din of battle never again be heard on the fields of Columbia.   But
you have enemies who watch your freedom as a panther watches a roe ; and
the voice of your country may cry 'to arms, to arms.'   You will not then
hesitate.   Your Eagle and Indian will be the place of rendezvous.   You
will rally round that standard, and pour out your blood before it shall be
touched by the polluted hand of despotism.   Let yours be the cause of religion and genuine liberty, you need not fear.   Remember the trophied glories
of Marathon.   There a handful of gallant Athenians put to flight the vast
legions of Persia.   Remember Leonidas and his three hundred intrepid
Spartans, who, at the narrow pass between Thessaly and Phocis, cut their
way into the midst of the millions of Xerxes, spread terror, like a cloud, over
his whole host, and saved their country from fire and sword.

   " Think of the dear-bought liberties you now possess.   Think of Lexington, Bunker-hill and Monmouth, and the many patriots who fell in the heat
of battle, or sunk away amid the ten-fold horrors of a lingering dissolution in
loathsome prison-ships.   Look round on this assembly.   Behold your venerable fathers, whose locks, now white with years, once 'whistled to the wind
of British bullets' to purchase the independence you now celebrate, the
festive joys of this day.   You cannot, you will not part with a gem for which
such a price has been paid."

   1808.   March 26th, David, the son of William and
Mary Choate, departed this life in the fifty-first year of
his age.   He was born upon Hog Island, November 29,
1757.   He inherited his father's farm on the island, and
lived there till 1800, when, still retaining his farm, he pur-
chased the parsonage, so many years occupied by Mr.
Cleaveland, and built a new house on the same spot.
His first wife was Mary, daughter of Dea. Jonathan
Cogswell, who died about two months after her marriage.
In 1785, February 22, he married Miriam, daughter of

Capt. Aaron Foster, by whom he had two daughters and four sons, and who survived him more than forty years. Mr. Choate was highly esteemed for his talents and acquirements, his integrity and public spirit. He was deeply interested in the cause of education; and at different times, taught the school both on the north and south side of the river. He was also active and influential in promoting the political welfare of the country, as appears from the following extract from a letter addressed to the author by Hon. Asa W. Wilder, of Newburyport:

"From the late Dr. Cleaveland of Topsfield, I understood that Mr. Choate (David) was member of a convention (whether in relation to the adoption of the Constitution of Massachusetts or that of the United States, I am unable to say); that he was a prominent debater, and wrote much in the papers over the signature of 'Farmer;' that Mr. Choate became known as the writer over that signature, and that being attacked by some leading debater, he (Mr. Choate) defended and sustained the 'Farmer;' that, in one instance, the late Chief Justice Parsons himself was thought to be the writer. Mr. Parsons was aware that some of the insinuations and innuendoes of the speaker were intended for him; and immediately after the debate had closed, Mr. Parsons (letting it pass so far as the authorship was charged to him,) went to Mr. C., saying, 'If I were the author, as some would seem to think, you have defended and sustained the position of the "Farmer" better than I myself could have done.' I think there can be no doubt, that what I have above related must have taken place in one of the many public conventions, —which one, I have no means of knowing. I recollect distinctly the Doctor stating the fact of what Mr. Parsons said to Mr. Choate. The occasion of his mentioning it, was in reference to the distinguished talents of Rufus Choate, about the time he came to the bar."

The following obituary notice, from the pen of Dr. Reuben D. Mussey, appeared in the Salem Gazette:

"Mr. Choate was a man of uncommon intellectual endowments. To a quick and accurate perception, a ready and full recollection, he added a *judgment ever* ready to decide, and was never under the necessity of making more than one decision on the same subject. From childhood, books were among his dearest companions, and though denied the advantages of a regular education, he arrived at a degree of improvement often unattained by men of the first opportunities, and possessed talents which would have been an honor to a statesman. In the social circle, none were his superiors. Without any efforts to draw attention, he had the admiration of all around him; and if envy herself ever raised a sigh at his power of pleasing, she immediately lost it in a less ungenerous emotion—the love of *being pleased.* The learned found instruction and amusement in his company, and the ignorant went away satisfied that they were persons of information, because they had been conversing easily on subjects before unknown to them. His friendship was firm and unabating. The man who possessed his confidence had a safe deposit for the most important facts, and such facts gained much in value, by being thrown into such a deposit. His attachment to his family was ardent and tender. As a husband, he was all that the best of wives could desire; as a father, all that a fine family of children need. He lived, the friend and supporter of virtue, order, and steady habits, and died in hope of a happier state, through the mercy of a Redeemer. A widow, five children, and the whole town lament his death."

April 5th. A new religious society is formed, called the Christian Society. From its first records, we learn that it had its origin in the preaching of some Methodist ministers,* which seems to have had considerable effect upon the minds of a few persons, and they united together for private religious meetings. Afterwards, " Elder H. Pottle preached several times. The people were attentive to hear and appeared serious while hearing. He baptized two. Early in 1806 Mr. John Rand visited this place and spent some time in preaching and in holding religious meetings. His preaching appeared to be attended with considerable effect." On the 28th of March, twenty-two persons, who had been previously baptized, "were embodied as a Church of Christ by Elder Elias Smith, Elder Abner Jones and Brother John Rand." They adopted the name of " Christians, in accordance with Acts xi. 26; and in general the system of belief held by that denomination, agreeing to lay aside all the party names now in fashion among professors, with all the creeds, articles of faith, platforms, church covenants and everything contrary to the New Testament." A house of worship was built in 1809, and owned by proprietors. This was taken down in

* Dea. Aaron Burnham once said the first preaching of the kind he heard was at Manning's factory building in Ipswich. He told his wife, on coming home, he had heard something like one of the old prophets. It was upon his personal invitation, that Messrs. Rand, Elias Smith, Elders Jones, Stinchfield, and others left Ipswich and commenced holding meetings at Chebacco.

1843. Mr. Rand preached to this society about seven years. During the first eight years the church continued to receive some accessions. "It ceased to exist as an active organization near the close of the year 1827."

Sometime in this year a second road to the Falls was built. It extends from the old road near Foster's brook over the hill south-westerly, joining the "old road" again near the houses of Abraham Perkins and Andrew Burnham.

1809. The Second Parish having been without a settled minister two and a half years, gave a call, together with the church, to the Rev. Thomas Holt, to be their minister. This call he accepted, and was installed pastor of the church, January 25th. Rev. Dr. Samuel Austin of Worcester preached on the occasion; Rev. Daniel Tomlinson of Oakham offered the consecrating prayer; Rev. Dr. Dana of the South Parish gave the charge, and Rev. Mr. Kimball of the North Parish, the right hand of fellowship. Mr. Holt was esteemed a sound, scriptural preacher. But after hearing him two or three years, his parishioners began to complain of a want of sufficient variety in his discourses, which they first imputed to his not writing them. They therefore chose a committee to wait on him and request him to write his sermons. With this he complied, but as the evil in their judgment was not removed, they respectfully requested him to resign. With this also he complied, and on the 20th of April, 1813, he was honorably dismissed by a Council. The parish gave him $100 to defray the expense of his removal, and he returned to his farm in Hardwick where he was formerly settled, and where he died. Mr. Holt was born in Meriden, Ct., November 9, 1762: graduated at Yale College, 1784: continued there most of the year ensuing, in the study of theology, and then removed to North Haven, where he finished his preparatory studies for the ministry, with Rev. Dr. Trumbull, and was ordained at Hardwick, June 25, 1789. He resigned his pastorate there, March 27, 1805. He died in 1836, aged 74.

1811. The bridge over our river, and the causeway connected with it, were much out of repair. At full tide it was very difficult, and at times impracticable for travelers to pass. This was a great inconvenience and detriment, not only to the people of this place, but also to people passing to Gloucester from other towns. Several attempts having been made by partial repairs to remove the evil, but without effect, the town voted $1,500 for thorough and effectual repairs. The county appropriated the same amount. But $3,000 not being sufficient, the town added $1,000 more, and it is believed that the county added nearly as much more, making the whole cost of bridge and causeway, as it now stands, not much less than $5,000. A new bridge was built some two or three rods south-westerly of the old one, a new piece of road opened to it from the top of the hill, about one half of the causeway built anew, and the old part joined to it and leading to Thompson's Island, thoroughly repaired. One of the abutments of the old bridge is still seen east of the mill.

1812.   February 12th, died Dea. Jonathan Cogswell. His father, William Cogswell, was the eldest son of Lieut. John, and Mrs. Hannah Cogswell, was born September 24, 1694, and was married, September 24, 1719, to Mary, daughter of Capt. Jonathan Cogswell. This Lieut. John was born in 1650 and died in 1710; was the son of William, (born in 1619, and died in 1701,) and the grandson of John Cogswell, the first settler of that name, (emigrated in 1635, and died 1669.) Dea. Cogswell was born May 9, 1725, and was married, December 28, 1752, to Mary, daughter of Benjamin Appleton. He was seven years old when his father built the present mansion now occupied by Albert and Jonathan Cogswell. Dea. Cogswell had thirteen children, several of whom died young. His farm descended to his sons, the late Benjamin and Aaron Cogswell. Benjamin was born August 15, 1766, and died January 17, 1841. His children were Polly, (Mrs. Winthrop Low,) Sally, (Mrs. Daniel Cogswell,) Jonathan and

Humphrey C., also Abigail, who died young, and Abel, who died very young of croup. Aaron was born December 28, 1771, and died July 20, 1847. His children are Aaron, Albert, Lucy, (Mrs. Aaron L. Burnham), and Jonathan. On the "Cogswell Coat of Arms," in the possession of Mrs. Aaron Cogswell, is the following inscription :

" These Arms appertaineth to the name of Cogswell, being first granted to Lord Humphrey Cogswell in the year 1447 from whom it descends to the ancient family of Cogswell."

From Dea. Cogswell's uncle Nathaniel (born 1707, died 1783) have descended Dr. William, died 1831, aged 70, (and his son—Rev. Dr. William, died 1850, aged 62.) Dr. Joseph Cogswell, born 1764, died 1851, (and his son Rev. Eliot Colby, graduated at Dartmouth College in 1838.)

In the company of militia drafted from the Second Regiment for three months' service, and stationed at Gloucester during the Autumn of this year, were eight men from this place : Sergeant, Abel Andrews ; Privates, Benjamin Andrews, Charles Andrews, Samuel Andrews, Ezra Burnham, Joshua Burnham, John Butman, William Lufkin.*

The number of pupils in the three schools in the parish had increased, in 1811, to 296.—83 in the North District. 107 at the Falls, and 106 in the South-east District. Partly on account of this large number in the last mentioned district, and partly because of the great distance of many families from the school-house, the people on the south side of the river take measures this year for a division of their district. Accordingly a petition, signed by Moses Burnham and others, was presented at town meeting on the 17th of March, and referred to a committee, consisting of Maj. Joseph Swasey, Jabez Farley and George Choate, Esquires. The report of this committee in favor of a di-

---

* The following named soldiers belonging to Chebacco, also served in the same company at Gloucester for the same time, viz : Moses Andrews, Ebenezer Andrews, Elisha Burnham, Isaac Burnham, John Durang, Edward Lee, John Lull, Matthew Vincent ; also Nathaniel Burnham. Jr., Moody Cogswell, and John Harlow, Jr., served as soldiers in Marblehead, in the company of Lieut. Pritchard, for three months.

vision into three districts, was adopted, May 13th; and the "division," subsequently made by the same committee in obedience to the direction of the town, was adopted, November 12th. It was as follows:

"No. 1. The Island, and extending along the Manchester road as far as Levi Andrews' house, and on the Gloucester road as far as John Cogswell's house, both included; also, Nathan Burnham's and Elias Andrews' houses; all the inhabitants within said limits, with their estates, shall make one district by the name of Thompson's Island * District.

"No. 2. Beginning at Seth Burnham's house, and extending on the Gloucester and Squam roads to the Gloucester line, including the house belonging to the heirs of Francis Burnham, Jr., deceased; and all the inhabitants within the described limits, with their estates, shall make one school district by the name of the Chebacco Eastern School District.

"No. 3. Beginning at William Cogswell, Jr's., on the Manchester road, extending to the Manchester line, including the house of Daniel Andrews on the north side of the road, and Samuel Groton on the south side of the road; and all the inhabitants not included in the districts No. 1 and 2, with their estates, shall form one district by the name of the Chebacco South School District."

At this time the Thompson's Island District contained thirty-six ratable polls, the South District twenty-eight, and the East District, sixteen. The first meeting of the Thompson's Island District was held November 30th. Elias Andrews was moderator, and Thomas M. Burnham, clerk. In accordance with a vote passed at this meeting, the school-house of the old South-east District, with the land under and adjoining, which had been built in 1801, and owned by proprietors, was now purchased of them for $304, and became the district school-house.

1813. The first meeting " of the legal voters of the East School District was holden by lawful authority, at the house of Mr. Ebenezer Burnham," March 2d. William Lufkin was moderator, and Capt. John Butler, clerk. Voted to build a school-house sixteen feet by twenty, and to

---

* Thompson's Island was so called from one Joseph Thompson, who purchased the whole of it of John Cogswell, Jr., son of the first settler, and lived near the spot where is now the house of William Burnham, 4th. He subsequently sold it to Thomas Burnham, Joseph Burnham, Aaron Low, and Benjamin Marshall, and removed to the State of Maine.

raise the sum of $200 for that purpose. Ebenezer Haskell, John Procter and Ebenezer Burnham were chosen building committee. At a meeting held March 30th, the site of the present school-house was selected as the proper location, and the house was erected this year.

December 21st. A meeting of the South School District, called by the selectmen at the request of several voters, was held, of which William Cogswell, Jr., was clerk. It was voted to raise $150 for the purpose of procuring a district school-house.

October 13th. Deceased, Col. Jonathan Cogswell, Jr. He was born July 14, 1783,—

"The only son of Jonathan Cogswell, Esq., who has been long known to us from his usefulness in public life. Early in life Col. Cogswell prepared himself for a university education, but for want of health was under the necessity of relinquishing his design. Endowed, however, with good native genius, by industry and application to private study, he became well-versed in modern literature We believe but few of his age better understood our political relations. Had Providence designed him for longer life, we might have expected important services to his country. To the military he was a promising acquisition. In 1806, he was active in instituting, and was chosen commander of a company of Infantry in his town, whose harmony and discipline have ever been an ornament to the regiment to which it belonged. In 1810, he was promoted to the rank of Colonel of the regiment. This office he sustained with honor to himself, and had the approbation of all under his command. Naturally modest, unassuming, none but his intimates knew his real worth. In private, he was respected and loved by all who knew him. In life, he was exemplary. In his illness, which was short but distressing, he was patient, and in death yielded up his spirit, trusting in the merits of an all-sufficient Saviour. Perhaps but few instances of mortality are marked with circumstances so afflictive to the surviving relatives. With them we drop the tear of sympathy. His remains were interred with military honors, attended by the officers of his regiment, a band of music, and the company of infantry he formerly commanded. A numerous concourse of citizens from this and the neighboring towns, followed in the procession of the mourners, with great solemnity and decorum."

1814. The amount of school money expended by the town for Chebacco this year was as follows: North district, $158.52; Falls, $124.13; Thompson's Island, $48.73; South $41; East, $40,17; Hog Island, $27,77; Total, $440,32.

August 10th. The Second Church and Parish, having

35

extended a call to settle with them in the ministry to Mr. Robert Crowell of Salem, who had supplied their pulpit, the great part of the year after Mr. Holt left them, he is this day ordained as their pastor. The council for ordination assembled in the house of George Choate, Esq., the same in which the council for the settlement of Mr. Cleaveland had convened sixty-seven years before. The services of the occasion, were as follows: Introductory prayer by Rev. Mr. Thurston of Manchester; sermon by Rev. Mr. Abbot of Beverly, ordaining prayer by Rev. Mr. Holt of Epping, N. H.; charge by Rev. Dr. Dana of this town; right-hand of fellowship by Rev. Mr. Kimball of this town, and concluding prayer, by Rev. Mr. Emerson of Beverly. Dr. Hopkins of Salem was moderator, and Rev. Mr. Kimball, scribe. The council was composed of eleven churches—eleven ministers and ten delegates. Dr. Worcester of Salem, the pastor of the candidate, was present, and would have preached the sermon, but for a mistake that had been made, then too late to be corrected. The council objected to a condition in the call of the parish, viz., that the contract between the parish and the minister might be dissolved at the option of either party, after having given six months' notice of such an intention. The objection was, that such a condition would naturally tend to invite a separation, and make the ministerial relation of short continuance. But the relation has continued more than forty years, and no inconvenience has resulted from the condition. The officers of the church since this ordination have been as follows: Deacons, Nathan Burnham, Samuel Burnham, (1821), David Choate (1828), Francis Burnham (1834); Treasurer, Samuel Burnham (1821); Clerks, David Choate (1823), Caleb Cogswell (1863).

September 14th. The town vote that the Committee of Safety superintend military affairs, and purchase what is needed. They also vote this year, that the drafted men, who by themselves or substitutes have been in actual service, shall have wages made up by the town, with government pay, to fifteen dollars a month, as long as they continue in service.

British frigates are seen from our hills in the bay, and not far from our islands. But there is no report of their landing, and consequently no "Ipswich fright."

1815. February 17th, peace is proclaimed, and our little community take measures for the due celebration of the occasion. An address on peace is to be delivered in the afternoon, and a supper provided in the evening. The pastor of the Congregational Church is invited to give the address. The Light Infantry Company is under arms, commanded by Capt. Joseph Choate, and in due form, they escort the speaker from his house to the church, and back again, after the services. The entertainment in the evening is provided by John and James Perkins, whose house opposite the church, is brilliantly illuminated. A numerous company sit down at their tables, and peace and goodwill crown the social board.

May. The first Sabbath-school is commenced among us in the Congregational Church.* The only teacher, for the first few months, is the pastor. The school is opened at the ringing of the first bell in the morning, and the hour spent in a general exercise, consisting of the rehearsal of passages of Scripture, and remarks by the teacher. In the Autumn, the school is arranged in classes, with a teacher for each class, the pastor acting as superintendent.

October 19. Dea. Stephen Choate, died of a cancer. He was a son of Thomas and Elizabeth Choate, was born on Hog Island, 1727, and baptized November 5th, of the same year. In 1757, he married Mary, daughter of David Low, who died in 1768. In 1765, he was chosen Deacon of the Fourth Church. In 1770 he married Elizabeth Potter (a widow), who died in 1814. He had nine children by his first wife, and four by his second. He was frequently employed in town business; was feoffee of the

---

* A less formal beginning of a Sabbath-school had been made in the Autumn of 1814 by the pastor, as is well recollected by aged persons, some of whom attended.

Grammar School; on the Committee of Correspondence and Inspection in the Revolution; Justice of the Sessions Court; Representative from 1776 to 1779 inclusive; a Member of the Senate from 1781 to 1803, inclusive. He removed his relation from the church here, to the South Church, in 1783. "He so improved the honors of this world, as to render himself more influential in adorning the religion of his Savior."

1816, June 12th. About this time the weather was more remarkable for the degree of cold prevailing, than was probably ever before experienced at this season of the year. The snow fell more than once, and ice was seen one-fourth of an inch thick. In Williamstown, Vt., the snow on the 8th inst. was twelve inches deep. It was seen on the neighboring mountains for several days. "Great coats and mittens," says a letter from that quarter, "are almost as generally worn as in January, and fire is indispensable." There was frost every month of the year, and the corn crop here was wholly cut off. Corn was sold at two dollars per bushel.

In the Autumn of this year, a debating society was formed, which met weekly and continued till all the customary questions before such bodies were fully discussed and decided. The physician and minister of the parish, John and James Perkins, Capt. Joseph and Col. J. P. Choate, Dr. Asa Story, afterwards of Manchester, the late Jonathan Story, Esq., and several others were members of the club.

1817. Graduated at the Dartmouth College Medical School, Asa Story. He was the son of Capt. Jonathan Story, and was born July 20, 1794. He was fitted for college at Atkinson Academy, N. H., and entered Dartmouth College in 1813, but at the close of his Sophomore year was compelled to leave on account of disease of the eyes. Not long after, he began the study of medicine in his native place with Dr. Thomas Sewall. He also studied for a time with Dr. Shattuck of Boston, and attended the usual courses of medical lectures at Hanover, N. H., in

1816 and 1817. Entering upon the practice of his profession in Wenham, he removed after a short time to Frederic City, Md. After a residence of a year or two there, he returned to this State, and commenced practice at Manchester, in 1820. There he spent his life, continuing in the active duties of his profession until a week before his death. He died February 11, 1860, of consumption of the blood. He was a faithful, kind, and skillful physician. A man of extreme diffidence which was never fully overcome, his worth was not immediately appreciated by strangers. But as a neighbor and citizen, he was very highly esteemed by his fellow-townsmen. To the welfare of the town where his professional life was spent, he contributed his full share of time, influence, and means. For a long time, he served on the school committee, with great credit. He was also, during the larger part of his residence in Manchester, a member of the Orthodox Congregational Church and Society. To all benevolent causes he gave liberally. He was married April 22, 1823, to Miss Eliza B. Farnham, of Newbury, who, with several children, survived him.

The new road to Manchester is opened this year. The Court of Sessions meet at Manchester to consider and decide on the necessity and expediency of such a road. Much opposition is made to it by Ipswich town. One of the Court, Dr. Parker Cleaveland of Byfield, passing through this place to Manchester, invites the pastor to accompany him. On entering the woods by the old road, the naked rocks and ledges are so prominent that there is no other way of safety for man or carriage, but for the Doctor to hold up the chaise with both hands, while the minister leads the horse, and this for the space of about a mile. This argument in favor of a new road is so sensibly felt by the Doctor, that he gives his decision before reaching the court; the woods re-echo and confirm it, and Ipswich has no argument, in the hearing, of sufficient power to overturn it.

1818.   Graduated at Harvard College, George Choate.
He was the son of George Choate, Esq., and was born
November 7, 1796.   In the winter of 1810, he began the
study of Latin under the tuition of the late Rev. Dr. William Cogswell, then master of the North District School.
There was much opposition made to the teaching of "the
dead languages," at that time, but such was the popularity
and influence of Dr. Cogswell that all objection was overruled.   He subsequently spent one year at Byfield, and
one at Atkinson Academy, and entered College in 1814.
After graduation, Mr. Choate was for two years master of
the "Feoffees' Latin School" in Ipswich, and during the
same time was engaged in the study of medicine with the
late Dr. Thomas Manning.   Two years more were spent
in the office of the late Dr. George C. Shattuck of Boston.
In 1822 he received the degree of M. D. at the Massachusetts Medical College, and the same year entered upon
the practice of his profession in Salem.   For several years
Dr. Choate has been president of the Essex South District
Medical Society, and president of the Salem Athenæum.
He has also represented the city of Salem on its board of
aldermen, and in the Legislature of the State.   In 1825,
Dr. Choate was married to Miss Margaret M., daughter of
Capt. Samuel Hodges.   His four sons are graduates of
Harvard College.   The eldest is a physician and superin-
tendent of the State Lunatic Hospital at Taunton.   The
other three are in the practice of law.

CHEBACCO PARISH BECOMES THE TOWN OF ESSEX.

1819.   The movement for the separation of this parish
from the town of Ipswich appears to have *begun* towards
the close of the year 1817.   At a meeting of the Second
Parish, held December 23d of that year, a committee consisting of George Choate, Esq., William Cogswell, Jr., Col.
John P. Choate, John Dexter, Capt. Jonathan Story, 4th,
Joseph Story, William Lufkin, Capt. Winthrop Low, and

Nathan Choate, were appointed " to petition the Legislature of the Commonwealth, as early as may be, to be incorporated into a town, bounded by the limits of Chebacco, and to draw our proportion of property belonging to the town, and whatever else they may think proper to ask for in said petition : provided that the other religious society in Chebacco shall unite with us in the petition, and obligate themselves to pay their proportion of the expenses."

On the 5th of January, 1818, a " meeting of the inhabitants of Chebacco ward, in the town of Ipswich, was held at the North meeting-house in said ward,"—George Choate, Esq., chairman, and Joseph Story, clerk — at which the following votes were passed :

" 1. That the freeholders and other inhabitants of this ward unite in petitioning the Legislature to be incorporated into a town, bounded by the limits of Chebacco. 2. That the petition presented to this meeting be accepted with such alterations as their committee and attorneys see fit to make. 3. That the following persons serve as a committee to give the petition a general circulation and to carry the same into effect, viz: George Choate, Esq., Nathan Choate, Capt. Nathaniel Burnham, Capt. Jonathan Story, 4th, Jacob Story, Elias Andrews, William Cogswell, Jr., Joseph Story, John Dexter, Capt. Winthrop Low, Col. John P. Choate, Capt. Francis Burnham, William Lufkin, Capt. John Butler, Capt. James Perkins, Dr. Thomas Sewall, and Jacob Burnham. 4. That this committee be authorized to employ one or more attorneys, as they shall think necessary, and to fix on a name for the town, provided an act of incorporation is obtained."

This committee met at the house of Capt. James Perkins, on the 8th of the same month, organized by the choice of George Choate, Esq., chairman, and Joseph Story, clerk, and selected a sub-committee, consisting of George Choate, Esq., Mr. William Cogswell, Jr., Capt. Winthrop Low, Mr. Nathan Choate, Capt. Jonathan Story, 4th, Mr. Elias Andrews and Mr. John Dexter, to carry the petition to the Legislature and attend, all or a part, as they shall think necessary, to effect the object of said petition. The petition which was presented to the Senate, January 21st, was as follows :

" To the honorable Senate and the honorable House of Representatives of the Commonwealth of Massachusetts, in General Court assembled :

" The petition of the subscribers hereof, inhabitants of the Second Parish of Ipswich in the county of Essex, humbly shews, that whereas the town of

Ipswich in said county of Essex, in said Commonwealth, is very extensive, being upwards of fifteen miles in length on the travelling road ; and that the Second Parish thereof, is a compact parish in the south part of said town, the southern part of which is upwards of seven miles from the court house in said town, which is the usual place of doing town business, the roads being very bad, especially in the spring of the year, at the usual time of doing town business, which makes it extremely inconvenient and almost impracticable to attend town meetings ; and that there reside within the limits of said parish upwards of two hundred and fifty ratable polls, upwards of two hundred of which are voters, and that their average travel is about five and a half miles to said court house, which makes upwards of twenty-two hundred miles travel to attend each of the several town meetings, which must necessarily be held in the course of every year :

" Therefore your petitioners pray that they may be set off from said town of Ipswich, and be incorporated into a separate town by the limits of said parish, with all the inhabitants within said limits, and their estates, with all the privileges of a town ; and that they may hold their proportion of all the town's property which is now held in common, and their proportion of the money arising from their Grammar school lands, a part of which lies within said limits ; and that they may not be held to pay any part of the money voted to be hired or voted to be raised and assessed in said town of Ipswich on the first day of January current for the purpose of purchasing a new and expensive establishment, to consist of a farm and new buildings, for the convenience and support of their paupers ; and that the remaining burdens of the town may be equalized between the two incorporations in such manner as shall be just and reasonable ; and that said Second Parish may be authorized to tax all the lands within said limits to help defray parish charges. And as in duty bound will ever pray.   Daniel Low, and 205 others.

January, A. D. 1818.

" The town of Ipswich having been officially notified of this action of the parish, on the 6th of April, appointed a committee, consisting of Hon. John Heard, John Choate Esq., Capt. Joseph Farley, Asa Andrews Esq., and Nathaniel Lord, Esq., to take the petition into consideration and report. In accordance with the report of this committee, which was accepted on the 20th of April, the town voted, That John Choate, Esq., Asa Andrews Esq., and Capt Joseph Farley be a committee to examine the records and evidence and all facts, and draft a remonstrance to lay before the town for their approbation at the adjournment of this meeting, and that they be agents of the town to present said remonstrance, and use all reasonable means to prevent the granting the prayer of the petition of Daniel Low and others before the Legislature of this Commonwealth, and to hear proposals from the petitioners, and treat with them on the subject of their petition. Voted, That one-third part of the town meetings be holden in future in the parish of Chebacco, or the Second Parish, whenever a majority of the said parish request it."

On the 14th of May the remonstrance drafted by this committee was accepted by the town. It was as follows:

" To the honorable the Senate and House of Representatives of the Commonwealth of Massachusetts in the General Court to be assembled at Boston on the last Wednesday of May, A. D. 1818.   The remonstrance of the inhabitants of the town of Ipswich in the county of Essex against the petition of Daniel Low and others, inhabitants of the Second Parish in said town, praying to be set off as a separate town, respectfully represents :

" That your remonstrants notice one grievance only in said petition as the cause of the petitioners' desire to be set off as a separate town, to wit : the traveling to attend town meetings, to which we must observe, that there always has been, and now is, a disposition on our part to accommodate them, as will appear by several votes of the town, offering them their share and proportion of town meetings to be held in that parish, but we have good reason to believe that the real reasons are not named in their petition, to wit : to avoid the burthens, which they are under obligations to bear, in common with the rest of the town.   And as a proof of this assertion, there appears to have been a fixed determination on their part to obtain from the town large expenditures on their roads and bridges, far beyond their due proportion, in that part of the town, to pave the way for an advantageous separation on their part, and the town of Ipswich have indulged them far beyond any other part of the town, in this respect.   And now with these large sums secured to them in roads and bridges, they ask to be set off and to have their full proportion of the property held in common, and to be exempted from moneys voted by the town and for their benefit.   We therefore beg leave to state, that in the early settlement of Ipswich its nearness to the sea induced the inhabitants to attempt commerce and the fisheries, which condensed to the centre of the town a considerable population and buildings, but on settlement of other places commerce and the fisheries declined, and the buildings become of small value about the body of the town, and a greater proportion of poor than in the other parts, whereas in the Second Parish the buildings are of greater value, and much more productive property, less poor in proportion to the whole number, nearer a good market, fuel within their own limits, and if a separation takes place, burthens, now legally belonging to the petitioners, placed on the residue of the town.   Your remonstrants therefore most solemnly protest against a separation, unless an indemnity or equivalent is given by them for the large sums of money expended and drawn from us by artifice, and expended in that section of the town ; and they pay a sum of money for the support of the large number of paupers, which will be left as a great burthen on us.   We protest against their drawing or holding any of the property held in common, against their having any of the moneys arising from the donations to the Grammar school, as the conditions under which the gifts and grants were made are such as are out of the powers of the Legislature to alter, and such as might become void if turned from the source for which it was

36

granted and given. We also must insist on their paying their proportion of all monies voted to be assessed by said inhabitants before their incorporation, as well as all debts due from the town; and we with confidence believe the Legislature will never interfere with the solemn contract and engagement made by said inhabitants of said parish, when they were made a parish, ' not to tax for ministerial or parochial charges any lands or buildings belonging to the inhabitants of the other parishes.' All which is with great respect submitted.''

The opposition of Ipswich proved unavailing, however, and the town of Essex was incorporated in accordance with the following act of the Legislature, approved by the Governor, February 5th, of this year.

" *Commonwealth of Massachusetts.   In the year of our Lord one thousand eight hundred and nineteen.   An Act to incorporate the Second Parish in Ipswich into a Town by the name of Essex.*

"SECTION 1. Be it enacted by the Senate and House of Representatives in General Court assembled, and by the authority of the same, that all the part of the town of Ipswich in the county of Essex called the Second Parish in Ipswich within the boundaries herein after mentioned, together with the inhabitants thereof, be and the same is incorporated into a town by the name of Essex, and invested with all the powers, privileges and immunities, and subject to all the duties and requisitions to which towns in this Commonwealth are by law entitled or subjected, the said town of Essex being bounded and described as follows, viz.: Beginning at the north-westerly corner of William Cogswell's land, at a small stone bridge at the head of Choate's Brook, so called, thence running south-westerly on the boundary of said Second Parish to Hamilton line, thence running on a different corner easterly and southerly by said Hamilton line till it comes to Manchester line, thence running easterly by said Manchester line to a heap of stones to Gloucester line, thence by said Gloucester line to the sea.   Then beginning again at the bounds first mentioned, and running down said brook to the creek, so called, thence continuing down said creek to the river, thence down the channel of said river on the north side of Hog Island to the sea.

"SECT. 2. Be it further enacted, that the said town of Ipswich shall have, hold and enjoy to their own use and benefit forever, the court-house situated in said town, the powder-house with the military stores therein, the Grammar school-house with the lands, hereditaments, rent and profits heretofore received and belonging to said Grammar school, and also the farm with the buildings, stock and utensils and all their other personal property thereon and thereto belonging, lately purchased by said town of Ipswich for a public poor-house.

"SECT. 3. Be it further enacted, that the said town of Essex shall pay to the treasurer of the said town of Ipswich, within the term of six months, their proportion of the debt due by and from said town of Ipswich and outstanding at the passing of this act, in the proportion of thirty-one cents per dollar on the whole amount thereof, which amount shall be ascertained by a committee of three persons from each of the said towns; and in case of their disagreement, then to be ascertained by three referees to be appointed by the Circuit Court of Common Pleas for said county of Essex. And said town of Ipswich shall pay to, or set off with, said town of Essex the sum of twenty-two hundred and seventy dollars.

"SECT. 4. Be it further enacted, that the said towns of Ipswich and Essex shall respectively support and maintain all such as now are, or hereafter may be, inhabit; ants of the said towns respectively, or who were born in or have a derivative settlement through any person born in or deriving settlement from any ancestor, and are or m iy become chargeable as paupers according to the laws of this Commonwealth, and who have not gained settlement elsewhere.

"SECT. 5. Be it further enacted, that all taxes assessed and not collected at the time of passing of this act, shall be collected in the same manner and paid to the treasurer of the town of Ipswich as if the separation of said town had not taken place.

"SECT. 6. Be it further enacted, that the agreement between the said town of Ipswich and the said Second Parish, made on the twenty-first day of December, in the year of our Lord one thousand and seven hundred and fifteen, be and remain as before the separation, and unaffected hereby in any respect whatever.

"SECT. 7. Be it further enacted, that any justice of the peace for the said county of Essex, is hereby authorized to issue his warrant directed to any freeholder in the said town of Essex, requiring him to warn the inhabitants thereof to meet at such time and place as may be appointed in said warrant, for the choice of all such town officers as towns are by law required to choose at their annual meetings.

"The foregoing is a true copy of an attested copy of the act of incorporation of the town of Essex. Attest,   JOSEPH STORY, *Town Clerk.*"

The agreement referred to in section six, has reference to the boundary line between Chebacco and the rest of Ipswich. Some dispute had arisen respecting this in 1715, and on the 6th of December of that year the inhabitants of Chebacco appointed Lieut. Nathaniel Goodhue and Mr. Thomas Choate a committee " to petition the General Court for a confirmation of the limits of the district of Chebacco, according to our . . . . * ever since our first being set off from the town of Ipswich and to make a settlement of bounds with such committee as may be appointed by said town of Ipswich." The town having been served with a copy of this petition " in compliance therewith and to prevent any further charge or trouble to said precinct of Chebacco " appointed a committee to confer with the Chebacco committee. This joint committee reported in favor of the same boundaries which had been established by the town in 1681,† and having made report to the town, at a meeting held March 10, 1716, it was " voted that the foregoing settlement of the lines of Chebacco Precinct be confirmed." The matter was again laid before the General Court however, by some of the inhabitants of the Hamlet who were still dissatisfied; and that body on the 29th of November 1716, confirmed the settlement of the boundary which the town had made, " except-

---

* Word illegible in the Records.   † See Chap. 1, p. 87.

ing Knight's farm which is hereby directed and ordered to lie to the Hamlet."

May 4, 1820, Essex appointed George Choate, Esq., Jacob Story and John Procter a committee to meet a committee from Ipswich to settle and establish the line between said towns from the head of Choate's Brook to Hamilton line. As these committees were unable to agree, the selectmen were authorized and empowered by the town, October 16th, to join the committee from the town of Ipswich in leaving the settlement of the line between Ipswich and Essex to a reference. The referees—David Dodge, Temple Cutler and Azor Brown—July 20, 1821, made the following award:

" Beginning at a small stone bridge in the road at the north-westerly cor-ner of Mr. William Cogswell's* land, thence running easterly in the road 31 rods to a stake and stones on the southerly side of the road, thence South 28½ degrees West to a stake and stone on Hamilton line."

FIRST TOWN MEETING.

The first town-meeting was held at the North meeting-house, on the 1st of March, a warrant having been issued by George Choate, Esq., in accordance with the act of in-corporation. Esq. Choate was chosen moderator; and it was then voted " that this and every annual town-meeting be opened with prayer." The following town officers were chosen: Joseph Story, town clerk; George Choate, Esq., Capt. Jonathan Story, 4th, Elias Andrews, William Cogs-well, Jr., and William Andrews, selectmen, assessors and overseers of the poor; Nathan Choate, town treasurer; the selectmen, with Rev. Robert Crowell, a committee to visit, oversee and regulate the schools. At a meeting held March 9th, voted $1,000 for the support of the poor, and other town charges (which was increased, April 5th, to $1,200;) voted $400 for the support of the schools; voted that $555.83—the expense incurred in obtaining an act of incorporation—be assumed and paid by the town; voted $460 for highways. In accordance with the third section

---

* The father of Mr. Zaccheus Cogswell and grandfather of Mr. Darius Cogswell, both of whom lived on the same farm.

of the act of incorporation, George Choate, Esq., William Cogswell, Jr., and Elias Andrews, were appointed a committee, on the 9th of March, "to meet with a committee of the town of Ipswich to ascertain the amount of the debt of said town previous to the incorporation of Essex, and, if possible, to make a final settlement with them." The report of this committee was accepted, December 21, 1819, and the town treasurer authorized to settle with the town of Ipswich agreeably to it. The debt of Ipswich at this time was $17,000—31 per cent. of which was $5,270. The share of Essex in the public property of Ipswich was $2,270, leaving, as a balance to be paid by Essex to Ipswich, $3,000. For the payment of this sum, together with the expense incurred in obtaining the act of incorporation, (which amounted to $555.83), Essex raised, in 1819, $1,000, in 1820, $1,000, and in 1822, $1,500.   .

LOCATION AND CHARACTER OF THE LAND.

As thus constituted, the latitude of Essex is 42° 38', its longitude 70° 47' 10". It is bounded by Ipswich, Hamilton, Manchester, and Gloucester. Its greatest length from north to south is 5¼ miles, and its mean length 4½ miles. Its greatest breadth from east to west is 4 miles, · and its mean breadth 3¼ miles. The soil is chiefly argillaceous, loamy, gravelly, and marshy. In 1855 there were 262½ acres of tillage, 937 of English and upland mowing, 78 of fresh meadow, 1949 of salt marsh, 2460 of pasture, inclusive of orchard pasturage, 1301 of woodland, exclusive of pasture land enclosed, 49 unimproved, and 120 incapable of improvement. There were also 100 acres of roads, and 2000 acres covered with water. Its real and personal estate at the time of incorporation was valued at $248,813. Its population was 1107. The number of paupers was 21, and the expense of maintaining the same per annum, $756.

Col. JONATHAN COGSWELL, Sen.

April 19th, died Jonathan Cogswell, Esq., aged 79. Col. Cogswell was a great-great-grandson of the first settler of that name, and a cousin of Dea. Jonathan Cogswell, their mothers having been sisters.   He was born July 11, 1740, at the "Cogswell farm."   February 4, 1768, he was married to Miss Elizabeth Wise, grand-daughter of Rev. John Wise.   She was born September 19, 1744, and died October 31, 1838.   By great industry and economy after coming of age, he soon cleared off a heavy debt, with which the estate inherited from his father had become encumbered, through the mismanagement of his guardian who had charge of the property after his father's death, and made the farm a profitable one.   In 1791, he purchased and removed to the "Pickering Place"—a house built by Rev. Mr. Pickering, and occupied by him during the most of his life.   Mr. Cleaveland rented it a few years, and it was afterwards purchased by Rev. Mr. Porter.   His family resided in it during his absence in Nova Scotia.   Dr. Davis, the first resident physician in Chebacco, purchased it of him, and Esq. Cogswell was the next owner.   Esq. Cogswell "was on the Committee of Correspondence and Inspection in the Revolutionary War; Captain of the military company raised in Chebacco in 1774; Major in 1775; Colonel of the Second Regiment from 1776 to the close of the war; Delegate to the United States Constitutional Convention of Massachusetts; Representative* in 1776, 1792, 1793, 1800—1813; Justice of the Sessions Court; and feoffee of the Grammar School."   His character was briefly delineated in two obituary notices published in the newspapers soon after his death, one of which is as follows:

" Died, Jonathan Cogswell, Esq., aged 79, an officer in the Revolution, one of the delegates in the Convention of this State who voted for the adoption of the Constitution of the United States, for many years a member of the House of Representatives of Massachusetts, a useful citizen and magistrate, a sincere Federalist, a devout Christian and an excellent man.   But what authorizes us thus to eulogize him ?   Ask of his fellow-townsmen how he acquired the reputation of a good citizen, and they will answer ' by performing every duty incumbent upon him.'   Though he never sought, yet when through solicitation he accepted an office, he executed the trust with scrupulous fidelity.   Ask of his political companions what were his princeples, they will say he was never found the advocate of party spirit, but he supported every measure which he in conscience approved, and exhibited a model of generous candor and undeviating consistency. Ask of his associates in the Legislature what was his character there, and they will tell you that though the persuasive appeal of eloquence never burst from his lips, wisdom and sound sense were closeted in his heart and always at his command. The poor man's gratitude acknowledges his benevolence, and the uniform uprightness of his deportment declares his fervent piety.

" More than half a century, passed in the enjoyment of connubial felicity, proved him an attentive, affectionate husband, a kind, indulgent father. And though in the close of life he was severely afflicted by the loss of an only son, who had reached the period of life when hope elevates and joy is lively, and who was just about to form a connection the dearest of all on earth, though she to whom he looked as a staff on which in the infirmity of old age he might lean and find support, was suddenly torn from him, this virtuous man bowed his head in pious resignation, for he knew God could not err. It was in the retirement of domestic life and its peculiar pleasures, that Col. Cogswell chiefly delighted. Surrounded by his family, and in the circle of his friends, his countenance wore the smiles of benevolent sociability and hearty good nature. He was polite and affable, given to hospitality, fully blessed with that most excellent gift of charity. Free from all appearance of selfishness, the happiness of others seemed the study of his life. His religion, as it had been the guide of his youth, became the comfort of his age, and virtues, like the rays of the setting sun, beamed softly and beautifully, as he descended to the tomb. We mingle our tears with those of his widow and surviving daughter, and would with them chant the solemn requiem of peace to his ashes. May the mantle of his excellence fall on us who remain, and when called to leave this region of sorrow, may we meet him in Heaven."

" In public life," adds the other sketch, " he manifested a sound judgment and unshaken integrity. In private, he exhibited all the amiable and useful qualities of a good citizen, a peaceful neighbor, a judicious adviser and friend, a benefactor to the poor, a kind husband and affectionate father. It was a remarkable trait in his character that he carefully avoided speaking of the faults of others, and, as if like measure were meted to him again, it was rarely if ever that any were found to speak against him. He retained in an unusual degree his bodily and mental vigor to the last; though family bereavements together with a love of retirement, for several years had led him to decline all public service. In his death his bereaved family and this now incorporated town have sustained an irreparable loss."

A daughter, Mrs. Mary Choate widow of the late John Choate, Esq., of Ipswich, survived him forty-one years, and died, in the same house, June 28, 1860, in her 83d year.

" Mrs. Choate was the seventh in descent from the noble old martyr, John Rogers. Margaret Rogers, daughter of Dr. John Rogers, a President in Harvard College and great-grandson of the martyr, having married the Hon.

John Leverett, F. R. S., another President of Harvard; by this marriage there were two daughters; the younger, Mary, married Col. John Denison, of Ipswich, by whom he had a daughter; this daughter married John Wise, son of Rev. John Wise, the first ordained minister of Essex (then Chebacco Parish), and who was distinguished for his courage, great strength, intellectual attainments, and elevated piety, and who, was tried, deposed from the ministry, and heavily fined and imprisoned in Boston for advising the town not to comply with the order of Sir Edmund Andros for raising a Province tax, it being, as he affirmed ' contrary to charter rights.' Of this marriage was born Elizabeth Wise, mother of the deceased."

RUFUS CHOATE.

Graduated at Dartmouth College, Rufus Choate. He was born upon Hog Island, October 1, 1799, the son of David and Miriam Foster Choate. When at the age of six months, his father removed with his family from the Island to the centre of the town. Of this parent he was deprived by death when less than nine years old. He commenced the study of the Latin Grammar, either near the close of 1809, or in the Spring of 1810, with Dr. Thomas Sewall, who about that time became a boarder in the family of Mr. Choate's mother, and who subsequently married her eldest daughter. Dr. Sewall's educational influence upon many of the young men of Chebacco, will long be remembered. In the Summer of 1810, Rev. Thomas Holt, then recently installed in the ministry at Chebacco, opened a private school and gave instruction to Mr. Choate in the Latin language. Mr. Choate's next teacher in the languages, was Mr. William Cogswell, who taught the district school in the Winter of 1810 and 1811, also during the school term of the next year. Mr. Cogswell was afterwards the Rev. Dr. Cogswell of Gilmanton, N. H. The subsequent teachers of Mr. Choate, during his preparation for college, were Center Merrill, then teaching a private summer school at the Falls, Samuel Sewall, who for some months had a private class in the languages, John Rogers of Londonderry, N. H., then teaching the North School, and the Rev. Robert Crowell, D. D. He finally entered at Hampton Academy, N. H., in January, 1815, James Adams, Esq., preceptor, where he remained seven months reviewing his studies, and entered Dartmouth College in August of that year. His public career as a statesman and orator, has been briefly sketched by Edwin P. Whipple, the essayist. The principal facts in his life, he gives as follows :

" He entered College in 1815 and was distinguished there for that stern devotion to study and that love of classical literature which have accompanied him through all the distractions of political and professional life. Shortly after graduating he was chosen a tutor in college ; but selecting the law for his profession he entered the Law School at Cambridge, and afterwards completed his studies in the office of Judge Cummins of Salem. He also studied a year in the office of Mr. Wirt, Attorney General of the United States. He commenced the practice of his profession in the town of Danvers in 1824. But a considerable portion of the period between his first entry into his profession and his final removal to Boston in 1834 was passed in Salem. He early distinguished himself as an advocate. His legal arguments replete with knowledge, conducted with admirable skill, evincing uncommon felicity and power in the analysis and application of evidence, blazing with the blended fires of imagination and sensibility, and delivered with a rapidity and animation of manner which swept along the minds of his hearers on the torrent of his eloquence, made him one of the most successful advocates at the Essex bar. In 1825 he was elected a representative to the Massachusetts Legislature from Danvers ; and in 1827 he was in the State Senate. He took a prominent part in the debates, and the energy and sagacity which he displayed, gave him a wide reputation. In 1832, he was elected member of Congress from the Essex district. He declined a re-election and in 1834 removed to Boston, to devote himself to his profession. He soon took a position among the most eminent lawyers at the Suffolk bar, and for seven years his legal services were in continual request. In 1841, on the retirement of Mr. Webster from the Senate, he was elected to fill his place by a large majority of the Massachusetts Legislature,—an honor which Massachusetts bestows on none but men of signal ability and integrity. Since Mr. Choate resigned his seat in the Senate he has been more exclusively devoted to his profession than at any previous period of his life. The only public office he now holds (1847) is that of Regent of the Smithsonian Institute. The country is principally indebted to his efforts for the promising form which that institution has now assumed."

Mr. Choate was appointed attorney-general of Massachusetts in 1853, which office he filled one year. On the 29th of June, 1859, he set sail for England, on a tour for the restoration of his health ; but prostrated by disease,

37

landed at Halifax, N. S., where he died, the 13th of July
following.

Mr. Choate's "Works, with a Memoir of his Life, by
Rev. Samuel G. Brown, D. D.," then Professor in Dartmouth College and now President of Hamilton College,
were published, in two volumes, in 1862.

Notwithstanding an extensive examination of many of
the recent town histories proves that biographical sketches
of the inhabitants both earlier and later, who have distinguished themselves among their fellow-men, make an interesting part of such town history, yet a *fear oppresses
those of us who have anything to do with completing the
history of Essex,* that the balances will betray the fact that
they were sometimes held by an unsteady hand, and that
more is said of some and less of others than strict impartiality demands.   Had the original design of the author
been carried out, all fear of this kind would have been
taken away by a close of the history with the incorporation of the parish of Chebacco as the town of Essex.   The
unmistakable demand of the town however, as expressed
at the annual town meeting, *that the history should be
brought down to the present time,* imposes new duties as
well as much additional labor.   And in relation to the
sketch above begun by Mr. Whipple, while it might with
great propriety have been left where it is by him, yet
some extracts from remarks by members of the Suffolk
bar, with a few others, will, it is hoped, be excused by all,
while they may perhaps be said to be *demanded* by some
who still regard old Chebacco as their cherishing mother:

*Extract from the Address of Hon. Charles G. Loring, at a Meet-
ing of the Suffolk bar, on the occasion of Mr. Choate's decease.*

"Having been for more than twenty years after Mr. Choate came to this
bar, his antagonist in forensic struggles, at the least, I believe, as frequently
as any other member of it, I may well be competent to bear witness to his
peculiar abilities, resources and manners in professional service. And having in the varied experiences of nearly forty years, not infrequently encountered some of the giants of the law, whose lives and memories have contributed
to render this bar illustrious throughout the land,—among whom I may include

the honored names of Prescott, Mason, Hubbard, Webster, Dexter, and others among the dead, and those of others yet with us, to share in the sorrows of this hour,—I do no injustice to the living or the dead in saying, that for the peculiar powers desirable for a lawyer and advocate, for combination of accurate memory, logical acumen, vivid imagination, profound learning in the law, exuberance of literary knowledge and command of language, united with strategic skill, I should place him at the head of all whom I have ever seen in the management of a cause at the bar.   *   *   *   *   *

"His remembrance of every fact, suggestion, or implication involved in the testimony, of even the remotest admission by his adversary,—his ready knowledge and application of every principle of law called for at the moment,—his long forecast and ever watchful attention to every new phase of the case, however slight,—his incredible power of clear and brilliant illustration,—his unexampled exuberance of rich and glowing language,—his wonderfully methodic arrangement, where method would best serve him, and no less wonderful power of dislocation and confusion of forces, when method would not serve him,—his incredible ingenuity in retreating when seemingly annihilated, and the suddenness and impetuosity with which, changing front, he returned to the charge, or rallied in another and unexpected direction,— and the brilliant fancy, the peerless beauty and fascinating glow of language and sentiment, with which, when law and facts and argument were all against him, he could raise his audience above them all as things of earth, while insensibly persuading it that the decision should rest upon considerations to be found in higher regions, and that a verdict in his favor was demanded by some transcendent equity independent of them all, at times surpassed all previous conceptions of human ability."

Richard H. Dana, near the close of his remarks on the same or a similar occasion, said:

"One word more, sir. It is not so generally known, I suppose, of Mr. Choate. that certainly during the last ten years of his life, he gave much of his thoughts to those noble and elevating problems which relate to the nature and destiny of man, to the nature of God, to the great hereafter; recognizing, sir, that great truth—so beautifully expressed in his favorite tongue—in sacred writ, [expressed in Greek,] *things not seen are eternal.* He studied not merely psychology; he knew well the great schools of philosophy; he knew well their characteristics. and read their leading men. I suspect he was the first man in this community who read Sir William Hamilton, and Mansell's work on the Limits of Religious Thought; and I doubt if the Chairs of Harvard or Yale were more familiar with the English and German mind, and their views on these great problems, than Mr. Choate. He carried his study even into technical theology. He knew its genius and spirit better than many divines. He knew in detail the great dogmas of St. Augustine; and he studied and knew John Calvin and Luther. He knew the great principles which lie at the foundation of Catholic theology and institutions, and the theology of the evangelical school; and he knew and studied the rationalistic writings of the Germans, and was familiar with their theories and characteristics.

*   *   *   *   *

"I meant to have spoken of his studies of the English prose writers, among whom Bacon and Burke had his preference. But he read them all and loved to read them all; from the scholastic stateliness of Milton, warring for the right of expressing thoughts for all ages, to the simplicity of Cowper's letters.

"But all this is gone for us! We are never to see him again in the places that knew him. To think that he, of all men, who loved his home so, should have died among strangers! That he, of all men, should have died under a foreign flag! I can go no further."

The Hon. B. R. Curtis, in presenting to the Supreme Court the resolutions of the Suffolk bar, on the 20th day of September, 1859, followed them in a speech of great power and eloquence, but we are precluded from inserting it by want of space, and can only make room for a portion of Judge Sprague's reply, as follows:

"It is not to be understood by any means," said Judge S., "that Mr. Choate's highest merit consisted in his rhetoric. That, indeed, was the most striking. But those who had most profoundly considered and mastered the subject, saw that the matter of his discourse, the thought, was worthy of the drapery with which it was clothed. His mind was at once comprehensive and acute. No judicial question was too enlarged for its vision, and none too minute for its analysis. To the court he could present arguments learned, logical and profound, or exquisitely refined and subtle, as the occasion seemed to require. But it was in trials before a jury that he was pre-eminent. Nothing escaped his vigilance, and nothing was omitted that could contribute to a verdict for his client. His skill in the examination of witnesses was consummate. I have never seen it equaled."

Upon another point the court remarked, "No man was more exempt from vanity. He seemed to have no thought for himself, but only for his client and his cause. The verdict was kept steadily in view. His most brilliant efforts had no indication of self-exhibition or display. Magnificent as they were, they seemed to be almost involuntary outpourings from a fulness of thought and language that could not be repressed. From feeling, reflection and habit, he was a supporter of law, and of that order which is the result of its regular administration. We cannot but sympathize with the bar, in a bereavement which has taken from us such an associate and friend, by whom the court has been so often enlightened and aided in their labors, and whose rare gifts contributed to make the 'light of jurisprudence gladsome.'"

CHAPTER VI

1820. TOWN STATISTICS: population, 1.107; number of polls, 258; real and personal estate, $248.813.

The *Essex Canal Company* was incorporated this year. A canal was opened by them from Chebacco River to Fox Creek (a branch of Ipswich River,) of about half a mile in length, for the transportation of ship-timber and lumber from the shores of the Merrimac, through Plumb Island Sound and across Ipswich River, to this place. The stock was divided into twenty-seven shares of $40 each; and the cost of the canal was nearly $1,100. For about thirteen years, the dividends of the company were from five to six per cent.

A chapel was built by proprietors near the meeting-house, for the accommodation of the Congregational Church in social religious meetings, and for the promotion of sacred music. Its dimensions were twenty-four feet by thirty-six, and its cost $640, including the land under it. Besides the audience-room there were two smaller rooms, one of which became the library-room of the " Essex Social Library," and the other, the selectmen's office. The building committee were Joseph Choate, John Dexter and William Andrews, Jr. On the 11th of December, it was dedicated by appropriate religious services. The text of the discourse preached by the pastor on the occasion, was the first verse of the 127th Psalm. The two-hundreth anniversary of the landing of the Pilgrims. was also observed in it, December 22d, by religious exercises and the preaching of a sermon from Exodus xv. 2. "Many will recollect with pleasure the numerous interesting and profitable meetings they attended in that building, during the thirty years in which it was used for religious purposes." A more convenient room for a chapel or vestry having been prepared in the basement of the church in 1842, this building was disposed of by the proprietors, and is now occupied as a store.

COMMISSION GRANTED FOR A POST-OFFICE.

1821. There was no regular post-office before the one established by government. But letters and papers were brought by individuals from Ipswich, and left at the house of the late John Choate. In the Autumn of 1819, a petition for a post-office in Essex, and a post route from Ipswich to Gloucester, was prepared and signed. It was presented to Congress by Hon. Jeremiah Nelson in 1820, and, "through his application and perseverance," was granted this year. Dudley Choate having been "proposed as a suitable person for post-master, and conveniently situated near the meeting-house," by "George Choate and a number of other citizens," and his name having been recommended by Mr. Nelson, was appointed the first postmaster. He kept the office in a small building attached to the house now occupied by George Norton. In 1826 he was succeeded by Amos Burnham, who removed the office to the house now occupied by his grandson, Charles A. Burnham, then used as a tavern, and who continued in office six years. In 1832, Enoch Low was appointed postmaster, and from that year the office was kept near the bridge until 1864. Albert F. Low succeeded his father in 1854, and was succeeded in 1864 by Charles W. Proctor. Since his appointment, the office has been kept in a store upon the causeway.

At the annual town meeting in March, it was voted that it be the duty of the school committee to prepare a written system of discipline for the government of the respective district schools of the town. The school committee chosen this year were Rev. Robert Crowell, William

Cogswell, Jr., Col. William Andrews, Capt. Noah Burnham, Capt. Winthrop Low, Capt. Jonathan Procter, Capt. Jonathan Eveleth.

1822. Washington Choate, son of David and Miriam Foster Choate, deceased, was born January 17, 1803, and died February 27, 1822. He was, at the time of his decease, a member of the Junior class in Dartmouth College. The following extracts from a eulogy by a college classmate, Charles Walker, (now the Rev. Dr. Walker of Pittsford, Vt.,) never before published, and delivered in a few weeks after the subject of the eulogy died, are so truthful and graphic as to supersede the necessity of any other remarks. It was delivered in the college chapel, and commences as follows:

" Where is our beloved Choate! Alas! the eye of ardent expectation searches for him in vain. He who was so lately one of us, is not here, but gone forever. The sphere of human action was too circumscribed for the operations of a mind like his. The celestial spirit has taken its flight to engage in more exalted and more congenial employments. Well may we weep. The pride and glory of our institution lies low in the tomb. The finest flower in our academic grove has withered, even while opening its fragrant blossoms to the morning sun. He was a rising luminary which our eyes beheld with admiration, as a planet whose dawn was auspicious; but ere the full brilliance of the rays was emitted, a dark and portentous cloud has forever concealed the glowing lustre from mortal view. In ordinary cases, panegyric casts some borrowed rays around its object; but here it can serve little else except to conceal an original and resplendent blaze. Seldom indeed, have the annals of any literary institution furnished an instance where the grave has so early closed over a more beloved and affectionate youth, a fairer candidate for fame, or a brighter example of ardent and exalted piety. But I shrink from the attempt to portray the varied excellencies of his character. With mingled emotions of reverence and affection, I can only delineate some of the more prominent features, and leave it for you who knew him, to fill up the outline and complete the picture.

" Washington Choate was born at Ipswich,* Mass., January 17, 1803. He very early gave indications of uncommon merit, and the discerning mind cast forward a prophetic glance, and indulged the pleasing anticipations of future greatness. The common amusements of children could not satisfy *him*. His judgment was so mature, and his moral sense so delicate, even when a boy, that his school associates always fixed upon him as an umpire in

---

* The present town of Essex, then Chebacco Parish in Ipswich.

their disputes. He had a strong sense of right and wrong, and was remarkably scrupulous in all his acts. His natural temper was unusually amiable.
' I never,' says a gentleman who once resided in the family, ' I never met
with a child whom I loved like Washington Choate.' An ardent thirst for
knowledge early appeared, as one of the most distinguishing traits in his character. His opportunities for acquiring knowledge in the early part of his life
were little superior to those enjoyed by most boys ; but they were well employed. Almost entirely by his personal exertions he became familiar with
the Latin, and made considerable proficiency in the Greek. Here probably
he laid the foundation for future eminence by the habits of vigorous application which he acquired.

    " He entered the academy at Andover in the Autumn of 1818. His su-
perior talents and amiable disposition soon secured him the admiration and the
love of all who knew him. The unremitted and vigorous exercise of his extraordinary powers, in a short time raised him entirely beyond the reach of those
with whom he was associated. Gentlemen best qualified to judge, pronounced
him the best and most lovely scholar that ever belonged to that institution.

    " The senior class well recollect what high expectations were raised, when
he commenced his collegiate course ; with what enthusiasm the members of
college singled out the individual of whom they had heard so much. These
expectations were more than realized. His views were so enlarged and so
elevated, that even the wonderfully successful efforts of his mind could not
satisfy him. Hence the smile of self-complacency was never seen playing
upon his countenance. There was a restless panting after perfection in whatever he engaged, which appeared to arise from his native greatness ; and the
struggles of his manly spirit seemed sometimes to threaten the entire demoli-
tion of its earthly tenement. The motives of ordinary ambition had little
influence on *his* mind. He sought indeed the approbation of the wise and
good ; but an unconquerable, ever growing attachment to the pursuits of
literature and science was the strong motive which impelled him forward.
After he became pious, love to his Redeemer supplied a far nobler and more
efficient incentive. With such views and under the influence of such motives,
we saw him incessant in his exertions. No one in college, I presume, knows
how much he accomplished. His retired and modest habits were such that it
could not be easily ascertained. It is well known, however, that he had
familiarized himself with the most important parts of ancient literature. His
compositions partook largely of classic elegance and taste, vigor and manli-
ness. Words, however harmoniously arranged, afforded him no gratification,
unless they embodied some valuable thought. He had made very considerable proficiency in some of the modern languages, and had selected, and eagerly
perused a large number of the best English authors. What this extraordinary
young man effected in so short a time, and a view of him in different situa-
tions of life, afford conclusive evidence that his native talents were of the first
order. The whole current of his thoughts and affections and his successful
exertions, evinced a mind elevated above the generality of scholars ; and even

the most distinguished were ready most cheerfully to allow a superiority which he by no means claimed. He thought with unusual clearness. His mind darted forward like lightning. He was delighted with the investigation and discovery of mathematical truth,—and satisfied every one who noticed the efficiency of his mind, that his reasoning powers were of no ordinary grade. The flashings of his fancy were uncommonly brilliant, and he possessed an inexhaustible fund of invention and keen native wit. But no trait of excellence was more conspicuous than the purity and correctness of his taste. Indeed, his mind seemed to have been cast in the finest and most delicate mould. He had a strong relish for the elegances of polite literature, and readily detected whatever did not deserve the name. Rarely can there be found so discriminating a mind at so early an age.

"We all know the unaffected modesty and simplicity of his manners. The sweetness of his disposition and the generous ardor of his affections seemed to entwine themselves with every ligament of his soul. His delicate spirit recoiled at the voice of adulation. His uncommon diffidence and reserve, however, could not conceal the excellences of his character. The veil was too transparent to hide such glowing lustre. When the ardor of social feeling thrilled through his heart, what an expressive smile was lighted up in his countenance. Yet with all this softness and delicacy, there was nothing of effeminacy. The native dignity of his mind was conspicuous in his whole demeanor."

ESSEX MILL CORPORATION.

By an act of the Legislature approved June 15th, John Dexter, Winthrop Low, William Andrews, Jr., George Choate, Dudley Choate, Enoch Low, Ezra Perkins, John Choate, Joshua Low and James Perkins, were incorporated as the Essex Mill Company with a capital of $10,000; with power to build a dam across Chebacco River at or near the great bridge with gates twenty feet wide for the passage of boats free of toll, and to erect saw-mills and other mills; "provided said Corporation shall make in or at the end of said dam a good and sufficient lock or locks fifteen feet wide and fifty feet in length, for the passage of flat-bottomed boats, gondolas and other water-craft, and shall attend and admit the same free of toll through said locks for the ordinary purposes of business." The stock was divided into one hundred shares. Of these, sixty-nine only were taken up. The whole cost of the locks and mills was about $10,000, and for the balance of the expense

38

money was hired, for the payment of which the stock of
the company was pledged. At the first meeting of the
corporators, held July 1st, George Choate was chosen
chairman, William Andrews, Jr., clerk, and a committee
of three appointed to obtain subscriptions to the stock.
The same month James Perkins was chosen treasurer, and
George Choate, John Dexter and John Choate a committee
to purchase a spot, and superintend the building of a dam
and a saw-mill, and to make the necessary assessments.
The next year the same committee were empowered to
erect a grist-mill, and to purchase and set up in it a card-
ing-machine and lathe.   In 1825, Charles Dexter was
elected clerk, and George Choate, William Andrews, Jr.,
and John Choate, directors.   The directors chose George
Choate, president, and John Dexter, agent. . The same
year an adjoining piece of marsh was purchased of Elliott
Woodbury for $375.   In 1826, a canal was dug through
this marsh, and a wharf three hundred and twenty-five
feet long built near the grist-mill.

1823.   The Selectmen were authorized to build a new
road at the Falls to the "landing."   This cost $320.

A draw was built to the "great bridge."   The cost of
this, together with the rebuilding of one of the abutments
and other repairs, was about $1,400.

Graduated at Yale College John Dennison Russ, the
son of Dr. Parker and Mrs. Elizabeth Cogswell Russ.   He
was born in Chebacco, September 1, 1801.

" Having finished his studies preparatory for college, under the venerable
Dr. Abbott of Exeter, N. H., he entered Yale College, and graduated from
that institution in 1823.   He began the study of medicine in the office of
John D. Wells, M. D., Professor of Anatomy and Physiology in Bowdoin
College, continued it in the Baltimore and Massachusetts Medical Colleges,
and received his Doctorate from Yale in 1825.   After spending a year abroad
in the hospitals of Paris, London and Edinburgh, he commenced the practice
of medicine in New York city.   The next year his attention was directed to
the famishing condition of the Greeks, then engaged in a desperate struggle
with the Turks for liberty.   Full of zeal for their cause, he availed himself
of the wide-spread feeling which laid almost every city and village under
contribution, and took charge of the brig 'Statesman,' which sailed from

Boston in June, 1827, laden with supplies. Other vessels followed in rapid succession, the majority of whose cargoes it fell to his lot to distribute. In the accomplishment of this work, he visited almost every village in Greece. He also established a hospital at Poras, of which he had the charge for fifteen months. Having determined then to erect a hospital more commensurate with the wants of the country, and having been furnished with a site at Hexamelia on the Isthmus of Corinth, he commenced and nearly completed a building two hundred feet in length and two stories high, when sickness compelled him to leave the work to others. In the Spring of 1830, Dr. Russ left Greece, and on his return visited Malta, Sicily, Italy and France. He reached Paris a few days before the breaking out of the Revolution, and brought the first intelligence of it to this country. He recommenced the practice of his profession in New York city, and during the prevalence of the cholera soon after, he was assistant physician at the cholera hospital at Corlears Hook in that city. At a little later period, he became interested in the condition of the children in the city nurseries, who were very generally suffering from ophthalmia, and many of whom had lost their sight by this disease. At his own cost, he began the instruction of seven blind children—which was the first attempt of the kind in America. Finding the apparatus for their instruction, used in other countries, exceedingly rude and ill adapted to their use, he made many improvements in that used for the study of Arithmetic and Geography, and substituted for the old maps used with chords and pins, paper maps. These maps, first introduced by him, are now in use wherever civilization has caused the blind to be regarded.

"Having retired from the direction of the New York Institution for the Blind, he next devoted his energies to the amelioration of prison discipline. In this cause he expended much gratuitous service, and distinguished himself as the author of several voluminous and highly important reports on that subject. He was for many years Corresponding Secretary of the New York Prison Association. The over-crowded state of the City Penitentiary also excited his sympathies, and he commenced an agitation of political sentiment respecting this matter. The first meeting for the consideration of the subject was called by him, and it was a report written by him which led to the erection of the present noble edifice known as the New York Work-house. He was also instrumental in the establishment of the Board of 'Ten Governors,' for the better regulation and oversight of the Penitentiary and Work house. In 1837, Dr. Russ wrote a letter to Henry Clay, then President of the Colonization Society, in which he appealed to that statesman to aid in carrying out his views in relation to the gradual emancipation of the slaves. The plan proposed in it was the purchase of every female slave as she arrived at maturity, with the understanding that her master should retain her services until she was twenty-one years of age, and should cause her to be instructed in reading, writing and arithmetic. By this slow and gradual process, he thought slavery might be abolished in about twenty-five years, at an estimated cost of three hundred millions of dollars, without any violent organic change in society, and with the education of the slaves for the responsibilities of freedom. In 1848, Dr. Russ was chosen a member of the Board of Education of the city of New York. During the last two years of his connection with it, through his influence and efforts, the laws regulating public instruction in the city were so altered as to unite the different organizations then existing, in one, and to build up that splendid system of school instruction which places New York city in the van of common school education. The suggestions and plans of Dr. Russ also led to the establishment of the New York Juvenile Asylum, in which the neglected children of the city, taken from the guardianship of their parents, are protected and educated by the State. He drew the act of incorporation, urged it through the Legislature, became Secretary of the Board, and since 1853, has been the Superintendent of the Asylum. To him, also, the Board are indebted for the plan of the edifice they now occupy. In the year 1830, Dr. Russ was married to Miss Eliza P. Jenkins, daughter of a captain in the English navy."

1824. March 24th, the town voted $125 to repair the long causeway.

October. The town voted $600 for the purchase of a fire engine of four and one-half inch chamber, twenty-four buckets, two fire hooks and four long ladders, and the erection of an engine-house on a piece of land near the meeting-house. In 1838, by vote of the town, this engine-house was moved to the spot which it now occupies near the "Centre gravel-pit."

POOR-HOUSE AND FARM.

1825. Though a committee had been appointed in March, 1821, "to consider the expediency of providing a permanent place for the poor," it was not until March of this year that the town voted "to purchase an establishment for the poor for their permanent residence." Up to this time the poor, as in other places, were let out to the lowest bidder. A committee, consisting of George Choate, Esq., Jonathan Story, Esq., John Dexter, Col. William Andrews, Capt. Francis Burnham, Capt. James Perkins, Capt. Winthrop Low, were chosen to purchase a poor-house and farm, and were authorized to draw on the treasury for the cost. In December, the committee reported that they had purchased the house and farm of Capt. John Procter for

$4,600. The house measured thirty feet by fifty, and had seven lodging-rooms for the poor. It had been built about a century. The farm contained about one hundred acres of upland, fifty of marsh and twenty acres of woodland. A committee of three was then chosen "to stock, furnish and prepare said farm for the reception and accommodation of the poor," and the sum of $800 was voted to defray the expense of the same. In March, 1826, $600 more were voted for the same purpose. Mr. William Lufkin, Jr., was the first superintendent, with a salary of $200. The number of paupers, when the house was opened, was twenty-one. In 1833, there were twenty paupers, "almost all of whom were impoverished either directly or indirectly by intemperance."

April 4th. The town voted "that the selectmen allow no bills for liquor on the highway." At the same meeting, it was also voted "that the constables present to the grand jury, or otherwise prosecute, all persons that may be guilty of a violation of the law providing for the due observance of the Lord's day."

1826. February 8th, died George Choate, Esq., aged 64. At the time of his death he was treasurer of the town and of the parish. The following obituary notice appeared in the Salem Gazette :—"Few men have so well discharged the duties of husband, parent and citizen as Mr. Choate. He was for many years a member of the Legislature from Ipswich, and the first representative from Essex, and was much employed by his townsmen in the management of their concerns, deservedly enjoying their highest confidence, respect and esteem. By them his usefulness will be long remembered. To a strength and purity of mind there was united a quiet, peaceful and amiable disposition, which greatly endeared him to his friends and acquaintances. So mindful was he of the rights of others that, as he never made an enemy, so certainly he has not left one ; and we cannot but admire and wish to imitate that discipline of mind and feeling, which he so

eminently manifested, and which enabled him to perform
the duties and sustain the fatigues and ills of life without
a murmur or complaint. The virtues of honest fidelity
and benevolence will not perish with the body. For the
upright and faithful there remaineth a rest. He was always deeply interested in the cause of education, and
gave his hearty and constant support to the institutions
of religion."

February 10th. Died, at Byfield, Dr. Parker Cleave-
land, aged seventy-four years. He was a son of Rev.
Mr. Cleaveland, and was born in Chebacco, October 14,
(O. S.,) 1751.

"He was not favored with the advantages of a collegiate course; but having received as good a medical education as the country then afforded, he began the practice in the parish of Byfield, at the early age of nineteen. At
the breaking out of the Revolutionary war, he sought employment in the service of his country, was appointed chief surgeon of a continental regiment,
and discharged the duties of that office during the first year of the war. Dr.
Cleaveland repeatedly represented the town of Rowley in the General Court;
and was one of three, including the venerable Ex-President Adams, who
were members of the *two* State conventions, of which, one formed and the
other revised and amended the Constitution. For forty years he was an
acting magistrate. In these and other public trusts, he displayed equal ability
and faithfulness. At once active and patient, ardent and discriminating, had
he been early trained to public speaking, he might have made himself felt and
valued in any deliberative assembly. He was an intelligent and skillful physician. Throughout his life, he read every medical work of importance that
came in his way; and though he adopted no opinions upon trust, or without
the most considerate examination, yet far was he from shutting his mind upon
the advancing light and improvements of the age. He was carefully observ-
ant of every symptom and rarely erred in his judgment or prognostic.

"He was a firm believer in the doctrines of revealed truth. It was indeed
to the grand and beautiful system of the Gospel that he directed the chief
force of his acute and vigorous understanding. The ablest and most abstruse
discussions of the great masters in theology, were the subjects of his close and
successful investigation. Notwithstanding his professional and public duties
and many distracting cares, he found time to read much, very much, both in
practical and polemic divinity. He called no man master. His religious
opinions were adopted only after the most patient and scrutinizing examination
and comparison, and they were held with that meek firmness which is the
natural result of convictions thus grounded. In his sentiments he was strictly
orthodox. But let it not be supposed that his religion was a system of cold

speculation. It were difficult to do him greater injustice. He possessed not merely a well-furnished and argumentative head, but a heart replete with the best affections and graces of the Christian character. He was faithful, and affectionate, benevolent, humble and devout. Emphatically might he be called a *man of prayer*. Often at the bed of sickness has he administered to the sinking body, and cheered with holy hopes the desponding spirit. At different periods of peculiar religious attention, his pious and useful influence has been eminently conspicuous. Firmly confiding in the justice and the mercy of every providential dispensation, he endured with Christian resignation the trials of life. Called repeatedly to part with those who were dear to him, doomed in the decline of life to struggle with adverse circumstances, his firmness, his cheerfulness never forsook him. In the love of his Redeemer, he could find relief from every earthly solicitude; this was the theme of his delightful contemplation. Although for many months before his death his health had been evidently failing, he was confined to the house but for a few weeks previously to that event. He seemed fully apprehensive that his dissolution was approaching, yet did not his principles, his faith or his hope desert him. He knew in whom he had trusted, and could therefore look back with satisfaction, and forward with unfaltering trust. In the death of such a man, it is superfluous to say that his family, his friends, his neighbors and the church have sustained an irreparable loss."[*]

His children were the late Prof. Parker Cleaveland, LL. D., of Bowdoin College and the Rev. John P. Cleaveland, D. D., of Billerica, Mass.

March. The town voted "to choose a School Committee of five, to be sworn and paid for their services: that David Choate, Winthrop Low and Charles Dexter be a committee to inquire into the condition of the several schools: that the selectmen subscribe for the American Journal of Education."

July 4th. The fiftieth anniversary of the Declaration of Independence was celebrated by the Essex Light Infantry—the town uniting with them. An oration was delivered in the meeting-house by Rufus Choate, Esq., then of Danvers, but a native of Essex. The dinner following the public exercises, was served up in the inclosure belonging to Col. William Andrews, west of his house. The officers of the Light Infantry on this occasion, were Joshua Low, captain; Moses Andrews, Jr., lieutenant; John F. Burnham,

[*] Boston Recorder, March 3, 1826.

ensign; committee of arrangements, David Choate, U. G. Spofford, Charles Dexter and Winthrop Low. The preceding year the name of the company had been changed to "Essex Light Infantry." The uniform had also been changed at the same time to "a blue coat with gilt trimmings and bell buttons, black varnished leather cap with gilt trimmings and a white plume, white trowsers and black half-boots."

1827. A revival of religion in the Congregational Church commenced in September, as the result of which more than eighty persons united with the church during the years 1828 and 1829. The following account of the beginning of this revival is taken from the minutes of the clerk in the records of the church:

"September. First Sabbath evening. A special meeting of the church to pray for the effusion of the Holy Spirit. A meeting also was held by appointment at the house of the pastor, for any who might be anxiously inquiring what they must do to be saved. *Two* persons attended this inquiry meeting.

"Second Sabbath evening. Church meeting by adjournment at brother D. Choate's. Much engagedness manifest. The second inquiry meeting at the pastor's. Number of inquirers increased to ten.

"Third Sabbath evening. At the meeting for the anxious, about thirty persons came in distress of mind to 'ask the law at the priest's lips.'

"The usual Thursday evening lecture at the chapel was attended fully and with uncommon solemnity. Such an attention to the things of eternity has become apparent, as has not been witnessed *within the memory of any but the aged.*

"A prayer meeting appointed to be holden at the chapel on Sabbath morning between the first and second bell ringing; well attended and solemn; is to be continued, if it should be attended in such numbers as to justify such continuance.

"October. Inquiry meeting continued weekly, on Tuesday evening, at the pastor's; also on Friday evening, at a private house in the Falls district; number of inquirers exceeding thirty.

"December. The hopeful appearances of a revival of religion continue deeply interesting, though without much perceptible increase. Inquiry meeting and lectures continued as usual."

1829, March. The town appropriated $150 for the repair of the great bridge and causeway.

THE TEMPERANCE REFORMATION.*

Some interest in the temperance movement had been previously awakened, but the first public address upon the subject was delivered on the 16th of July, in the Congregational meeting-house, by William C. Goodell of Boston, the editor of a paper devoted to good morals and particularly to temperance. To most of the audience in attendance, the theme was a new one, and they were startled by the form in which it was announced by the speaker: "Ardent spirits ought to be banished from the land. What ought to be done can be done." The effect of the lecture, however, was seen in the formation of *the first temperance society*, at the same meeting. Its constitution bears the following title: "Essex Temperance Society, on the principle of total abstinence; formed July 16, 1829. Prov. vi. 27, 28; Col. ii. 1." It was drawn up by Mr. Goodell and Rev. Mr. Crowell, and its third article reads as follows:

"The members of this society, believing that the use of intoxicating liquors is, for persons in health, not only unnecessary but hurtful; and that the practice is the cause of forming intemperate habits; and that while it is continued, the evils of intemperance can never be prevented, do, therefore, agree that we will abstain from the use of *distilled spirits*, except as a medicine in case of bodily infirmity; that we will not allow the use of them in our families, nor provide them for the entertainment of our friends, or for persons in our employment; and that in all suitable ways we will discountenance the use of them in the community."

Seven persons only responded to the call to organize that society, and to sign the pledge that evening. Their names are as follows: Winthrop Low, Samuel Burnham, John Choate, John Perkins, Jonathan Eveleth, Francis Burnham, David Choate. Capt. Winthrop Low was elected the first president of the society. Rev. Mr. Crowell's name for some reason, was not added until a few days after, though he was decided and earnest from the first in favor of the whole movement, and, in fact, had been the first to

---

* Furnished by Mr. Uriah G. Spofford.

introduce the subject to the notice of the people. Within
a year following, forty others enrolled their names to the
pledge, twenty-nine of whom were ladies. The names of
the men were as follows: Robert W. Burnham, John S.
Burnham, Philemon S. Eveleth, Zaccheus Burnham, Elias
Savage, Thomas Perkins, U. G. Spofford, J. C. Perkins,
James Perkins, Aaron Cogswell, Caleb Cogswell.

Within a short time after the formation of the society,
Mr. Goodell, Capt. Low and Mr. Crowell canvassed nearly
all the town in behalf of the cause, presenting the subject
to the people at their homes, and urging all to adopt the
pledge. The public discourse and the conversations in
private caused a good deal of excitement and commotion
in the community. Many who were themselves well-dis-
posed, kept aloof from the movement from the fear that
they could not obtain workmen, unless they furnished
liquor to their employes. But there was also great and
bitter opposition in all parts of the town. Some ridiculed.
Others declared that the temperance men were aiming to
bring about a union of Church and State. The strongest
opponents were those who were engaged in the traffic in
liquor, and those whose views were determined by their
appetite for it. Such contended against the movement
with all their might. The members of the society however were full of zeal in the cause. Weekly meetings
were held in the chapel, and lectures were delivered in the
meeting-house. From time to time, there were additional
signatures to the pledge, and the reform went steadily onward, although from the opposition it encountered, its
progress was slow for a number of years. So deep-rooted
had become the custom of the social use of intoxicating
drinks on all occasions, that, when Mr. Spofford succeeded
in moving a building by the aid of the neighbors, without
" treating " them, it was considered a remarkable feat, and
was always remembered as the first instance of the kind.
Opposition to the cause was most strongly manifested, of
course, when the town began to take action with reference

to it; but such was the influence of the society, that as early as 1833 no licenses were granted by the town.

It was not long before an advance was made by the advocates of temperance to the position of total abstinence from all *fermented* as well as from all *distilled* liquors. Rev. Mr. Frost was the first lecturer in town, who urged this application of the principles of temperance. He was followed by Mr. Moses B. Parish, who illustrated his argument to prove that cider contained alcohol, by the use of a distilling apparatus in his lecture. It required considerable time and discussion, in those days, to convince many people of this fact.

That public sentiment was essentially revolutionized and the foundation of the reform firmly laid in those opening years of the temperance movement, the efficiency of the subsequent temperance organizations, the sobriety of the inhabitants and the prevailing condition of public opinion have clearly shown. A sufficient illustration of the state of public sentiment on this subject is found in the result of the State election of 1867, in which there was a majority of sixty votes in town in favor of the prohibitory law.

1830. Town statistics: Population, 1,333; three persons over ninety years of age, and eleven between eighty and ninety years of age; number of polls, 319; valuation, $322,298; number of dwelling-houses, 157.

THE ESSEX UNIVERSALIST SOCIETY,

Which had been formed April 20, 1829, was legally organized on the 20th of April of this year, at a meeting held by virtue of a warrant issued by Jonathan Story, Esq., at the request of ten members. The officers chosen at this meeting were Parker Burnham, Jr., moderator; Oliver Low, clerk; Enoch Low, treasurer; William Andrews, Jr., Benjamin Burnham, Jr., Parker Burnham, Jr., committee. The number of members at the formation of the society was forty-six. The next year, by vote of the society passed April 25, 1831, preaching was supported by subscription.

1832. A school-house was built at the Falls this year. It was thirty-three feet by thirty, and eleven feet post. The building and the land on which it stood cost $800. The changes made in it in 1845, together with its repairs, cost $300.

Graduated at Amherst College, Jonathan Cogswell Perkins. Mr. Perkins was born November 21, 1809, and was fitted for college at Phillip's Academy, Andover, of which school he was a member in 1827 and 1828. Commencing the study of law in the October following his graduation at college, he was a student in the office of Hon. Rufus Choate until January, 1834, and then a member of the Cambridge Law School until May, 1835. Having finished his legal studies in the office of Hon. Leverett Saltonstall, of Salem, he was admitted to the bar at the September term of the Court of Common Pleas, the same year, and immediately commenced the practice of law in Salem. In the years 1845 and 1846, he was one of the representatives of Salem in the Legislature, and the next two years was a member of the State Senate. In June following his second term of service in the Senate, he was appointed one of the Judges of the Court of Common Pleas, which office he filled until 1859. In 1850, Judge Perkins, was elected one of the trustees of Amherst College. He had already rendered valuable service to his Alma Mater, when a member of the Legislature. In 1846, a donation of $25,000 was received from the State, by that college, with reference to which Dr. Hitchcock, at that time president, remarked on a public occasion: "The report and efforts of the Hon. Jonathan C. Perkins as chairman of the committee of the Legislature, exerted a strong influence in giving the college success in its application for aid from that body." Judge Perkins was in 1853 a member of the convention for revising the Constitution of the State. For many years he has also been distinguished among the members of his profession, for his editions of various foreign legal works, with additions and copious annotations of his own. With reference to one of these, Hon. Simon Greenleaf, one of the highest legal authorities in the country, remarked in 1844:

" From my knowledge of Mr. Perkins as a well-read and exact lawyer eminently fitted for the work, I anticipated, from the first announcement of his design to furnish notes for an edition of Brown's Chancery Reports, a rich contribution to the stock of our equity jurisprudence. I have examined his notes with some care, and find my expectations more than realized. His notes are practical, and in neatness, comprehensiveness and accuracy, are not surpassed by any editorial notes which I have seen."

In 1867, Mr. Perkins received from Amherst College the degree of LL. D.

1833. March 14th, died Joseph Story, familiarly known as " Master Story." He was born December 12, 1760, was a soldier of the Revolution, and served through the whole of that war. He was in the Northern army when Gen. Burgoyne and his army surrendered. Mr. Story taught school thirty years, twenty-seven of them in the Falls District. He was town clerk, from the incorporation, and held that office much longer than any successor has done, and was clerk of the First Parish for a long series of years; the exact number is not known, as there is a break in the record from 1775 to 1818. Mr. Story was clerk at that time (1818), and continued to be until 1825.

NEW POOR-HOUSE.

1834, March. The town voted to accept the report of a committee appointed in March, 1833, to consider the expediency of erecting a new poor-house, and to report respecting the material, size and expense of the same; also voted to build a poor-house, and to expend $2,000 for the same. Jacob Story, Charles Dexter and Samuel Hardy were chosen building committee. In 1835, $914 more were voted to defray the balance of the cost of the house, and the thanks of the town were voted to the building committee.

MILLS AT THE FALLS.

This year a bark-mill was erected at the Falls, by Capt. Francis Burnham, in connection with his tanning estab-

lishment. Three mill privileges at the Falls seem to have
been improved from a very early period, although from
the level of Chebacco pond to high water mark at the
head of the creek at the "Falls Landing," there is a fall
of only forty feet (according to a careful measurement
made some years since.) The first mill-site was granted
by the town in 1665, to a Mr. Wade, for a saw-mill. This
was, according to authentic tradition, where Mr. Perkins
Story's saw-mill now is, and this spot is believed to have
been occupied for that purpose ever since. Mr. Story's
present mill was erected in 1837. In 1667, the town
granted leave to Mr. Thomas Burnham "to set up a saw-
mill upon Chebacco River, not prejudicing Mr. Wade's."
This was upon the same dam upon which the *bark-mill*
now is, but on the other side of the stream. In 1687,
John Burnham, a son of Thomas, having raised the dam
two feet higher, which was "likely to damage the town
very much by flowing the town common (commoners'
land), and killing the wood if the dam be not removed,
and the said John Burnham now moving the town to have
a place below where the dam now stands to set up the
said mill, which place will be little or no damage to the
town, only the flowing one acre or two of the town's common, voted and granted unto the said John Burnham, in
consideration of the grant to his father and the charge he
will be at in moving his mill, liberty to set up his saw-mill
upon the place now propounded for upon said river near
to G. Story's mill; and he is not to damnifie any former
grant." In 1698 or 1700, the saw-mill was removed, and
a grist-mill took its place, as appears from an old account-
book now in the possession of Mrs. Job Burnham; and this
spot has ever since been occupied by a grist-mill until quite
recently. The last one was built about the year 1800, and
was disused in 1847. It was torn down in 1862.

    1835, April 20th. The town voted "that the inhabit-
ants, with their estates, north of the North school-house
(which stood a few rods north-east of the house of Jona-

than Low) be called the Essex North School District, and
the residue of the late North School District be called the
Central School District." On account of some supposed
illegality connected with this division of the North District, or some defect in the statement of the boundary line
between the two districts into which it was divided, the
subject was brought again before the town, at a meeting
held December 10, 1837; and it was then

" Voted, that the section of territory which, previous to the year 1835, was
called the North School District, be divided into two school districts by a
direct line running due east and west, and drawn through the center of the
spot of land upon which the North School-house, so called, stood, and from
which it was removed in 1835.

" Voted, that the two districts, so constituted, be known and called by the
name of the North and Central School Districts."

The Central District purchased a lot of land of John
Perkins, and erected upon it a school-house twenty-eight
feet in width by thirty-eight feet in length, and two stories
in height. The building and land cost $1,925. It was
opened for school purposes in December 1835. The first
teacher in it, and the only one until December, 1842, with
the exception of three winter terms, was Hon. David
Choate, who, in addition to the town school in the winter
months (except as above), taught a private school in it the
remainder of the year. During this period, the average
number of pupils per term was sixty. Many of them
were from other towns.

Among the features of this school of especial interest to the pupils, as recollected by some of them, were the use of apparatus to illustrate the principles
of natural philosophy and astronomy, and of instruments in the study of surveying; courses of lectures on natural philosophy, and on other subjects;
instruction in music and in Latin; the constant use of outline and other
maps, with which the school-room was abundantly supplied; a school-library;
prizes for excellence in various branches, and a record of scholarship and of
demerit; and every morning a unique " general exercise " of half an hour
for the whole school This usually consisted of a familiar lecture by the
teacher, on various subjects outside of the regular course of study, in which
were communicated truths, aphorisms, instructive historical and biographical
anecdotes, and a mass of information of all kinds, adapted both to stimulate
and to enrich the minds of the pupils. In their estimation, it was the most

interesting as well as profitable exercise of the day. Besides the regular studies, which were pursued with great thoroughness, and towards which a remarkable degree of enthusiasm was excited in the minds of the scholars, there were frequent exercises in singing, accompanied by the piano; and at intervals, dialogues, moot-courts, readings from entertaining books, and excursions to places and objects of interest.

On the 29th of October, 1837, the district voted that the school be divided; that the younger scholars be taught in the chamber of the school-house, by a female teacher; and that the division be made by the teacher, the Prudential Committee, and the clerk, at their discretion.

On the 30th of April, the first meeting of the new North District was held. Nehemiah Dodge was chosen moderator; John Burnham, clerk; Josiah Low, prudential committee. By vote of the district, a school-house lot, of six square rods of land was purchased of John Burnham for $12, the school-house of the old North District aforesaid was purchased for $48.78, removed to its present position, and the sum of $315 expended in repairs upon it. In 1846, further repairs were made upon it, for which the sum of $100 was raised.

By vote of the Thompson's Island School District, at a meeting held March 21st, a new school-house was built in that district, on "a lot of land in front of the house of William Burnham, 4th, and on the corner of the Manchester and Ipswich roads," and the sum of $1,000 appropriated for the payment of the house and land. Benjamin Courtney was chairman of the building committee. The old school-house, which stood between the present dwelling-houses of Moses Knowlton, Jr., and Aaron Burnham, Jr., and the land under it, were sold. In 1845, the school-house was divided into two rooms and painted, and the sum of $200 raised to defray the cost of the same. In 1850, the building was raised from the underpinning, another story built beneath it, and the whole was painted. To defray the cost of these improvements, the sum of $650 was raised.

September 1. Died, Mr. Westley Burnham, aged eighty-

eight years.   He was the grandson of David Burnham who
lived in the house since occupied by his great-grandson,
the late Abner Burnham, at the south-eastern end of Chebacco pond ; and who was a vessel-builder.   The following
sketch has been furnished by Mr. Robert W. Burnham.

"This David Burnham is known to have built a brig, at the foot of what is
now Addison Cogswell's hill, near the creek.   It would seem that the family of
Burnhams had been shipwrights from time immemorial.   Their system was, for
a considerable period, thought to be peculiar to themselves, as it was different
from any now in vogue here, but it has recently been found in a book on
naval architecture, which was brought from England about thirty years ago.

"Mr. Burnham's father was also named Westley.   He died June 28,
1797, aged seventy-eight.   The mother of the subject of this sketch was
Deborah, the daughter of Dea. Zechariah Story.   She was born in 1723, in
the old house now belonging to Aaron Story, 2d, and died November 24,
1821, *aged ninety-eight*.

"Mr. Burnham was born August 27, 1747.   In his early life, he was a
sailor.   At the age of seventeen, he made a voyage to Lisbon, and rowed in
a boat over the site of *Old Lisbon*, which had been destroyed and sunk by an
earthquake in 1755.   He became a successful navigator, although his education had been only such as Chebacco afforded.   No vessel commanded by
him was ever wrecked or dismasted ; and his judgment in maritime matters
was very highly esteemed.   He was always styled 'Skipper Westley.'   For
several years in succession, he made voyages to Virginia.   The cargoes in
those days, usually consisted of fish, lumber, and New England rum.   In
exchange for these, corn, raccoon-skins, snake-root and rice were obtained,
and brought into Chebacco, or disposed of at other harbors in the country.
Mr. Burnham was also a fisherman, and made many trips to the 'Grand
Banks.'   He afterwards followed the hereditary occupation of vessel-building.
He was a man of extraordinary strength.

"For a short time, Mr. Burnham served as a soldier in the war of the
Revolution.   Afterwards he entered the privateering service.   In an engagement with the enemy, the vessel in which he sailed was captured, and with
the rest of the crew he was carried to England.   An order of the admiralty
gave permission to any American prisoners to go on board his majesty's ships
and do sailor's duty, except fighting, if they should choose to do so, in preference to lying in prison.   After remaining some time in the 'Mill Prison,' he
took advantage of this order, and entered the seventy-four gunship Preston.
While on a cruise on the West India station, he was taken sick with the small-
pox, and was left in hospital in Jamaica.   He was so near to dying there,
that one man who returned to this country from that island reported to his
family that he was dead.   On his recovery he immediately took ship for Boston, and on arriving there, walked to Chebacco.   His arrival was noised
40

abroad, and as he expressed it, 'that night all Chebacco was at the house to
see one who had risen from the dead.' Though not a member of the church,
he was a constant church-goer, and a strict observer of the Sabbath, which in
his belief and practice commenced on Saturday evening. For a considerable
length of time, he was totally blind. And it is a very significant fact with
reference to his intelligence and mental training, that he was then accustomed
to spend his evenings in listening to the reading of a grandson (who was for
several years a member of his family), partly for his own entertainment, but
also for the sake of knowing what the boy was in the habit of reading, and
of training him to a correct pronunciation. Mistakes in accent and in emphasis were carefully criticised, and passages were required to be read over
and over again, until their meaning was properly and fully expressed.

"In 1771, he was married to Molly, daughter of Robert Woodbury of
Beverly Farms. Mrs. Burnham was born July 29, 1749, and died April
27, 1830, at the age of eighty years and nine months. To these parents,
each of a robust and long-lived race, were born ten children, and the lon-
gevity of these children has been as remarkable as that of their parents.
Molly (Mrs. Caleb Andrews.) was born October 13, 1772, and died February 18, 1847. Westley was born September 14, 1774, and died June 21,
1811. Nathan was born May 26, 1776, and died September 23, 1860.
Asa was born September 9, 1778, and died May 23, 1850. Michael was
born April 3, 1781, and died October 28, 1862. Henry was born June 23,
1783, and died 1867. Anne (Mrs. Abner Burnham,) was born July 14,
1785, and died March 3, 1862. Samuel was born October 28, 1787.
Richard was born December 9, 1790, and died January 1, 1855. Ruth
(Mrs. Jacob Burnham,) was born March 16, 1793. The eldest son only,
of all these children, has died before reaching old age.

"Even he, however, left seven children—Zaccheus (born November 13,
1797, died July 28, 1856); John Story; Hannah (born October 8, 1801,
died February 2, 1858); Mary (Mrs. Luke Burnham); Robert Woodbury;
Edith (Mrs. Eli Burnham), and Elizabeth (Mrs. Caleb Cogswell). Deprived of
their father at such an early age, these children, the eldest being less than fourteen at the time of his death, were fortunate in their mother, who trained them,
and who lived to see the results of her tuition and solicitude. She was Hannah
Story, the daughter of John and Hannah Perkins Story; was born October 10,
1775, and died May 18, 1847. Her father was a son of Elder Seth Story.

"The grandchildren of *Skipper Westley* have numbered *eighty-one*. His
favorite employments have, to a great extent, been adopted by his descendants, though few of them have had as much experience of a sea-faring life
and so many nautical adventures to relate as his son Samuel. One of *his*
most memorable voyages was made when he was about twenty-two years of
age. In January of the year 1809 or 1810, he sailed in a top-sail schooner,
Capt. Jacob Woodbury commanding, from Beverly to Baltimore, Md., thence
to Oporto, Portugal, and from that port to Archangel, Russia. There the
vessel lay frozen in the harbor from September 21st until the following May.

On the passage home, they kept "off shore" in order to avoid the French cruisers, and sailing across in from 73° to 75° north latitude, they saw the sun for six days and nights in succession. Their return cargo was invoiced at $80,000. It consisted of iron, hemp, linen diaper and mats.

"The life at sea of one of the grandsons—the late Mr. Zaccheus Burnham—was also marked by incidents of interest, and escapes from the dangers common to those who 'do business in great waters.' Sailing from Salem, in November, 1821, he made a voyage to the port of Batavia, in the Island of Java, thence to Samarang on the Malay coast, back again to Batavia, and thence to Boston, arriving September 4, 1822. Off the Cape of Good Hope—as appears from his log book—the ship encountered a gale of wind which lasted six days. She was also struck by lightning, and several of the crew were stunned, but no one was killed. On the homeward passage, 'September 9, 1822, in latitude 12° north, longitude 40° west, saw a sail ahead, judged to be a pirate. Bore away for her, and made preparations to engage her; knocked open our ports, (the Delphos was a heavy ship, and showed ports like a sloop-of-war); showed our teeth—quaker guns and all—and gave her a gun, when she immediately clapped on all sail and steered to the westward.'"

1836. This year the town appropriated $800 for school purposes. From the incorporation of the town to 1823, the sum of $400 per annum had been raised for schools; from 1823 to 1834 inclusive, the sum of $600 annually, and in 1835 the sum of $750.

April 23. Died, William Andrews, Jr., aged sixty-two. after a very short illness. "His death has occasioned not only a severe and irreparable loss to his relatives and friends, but is also a public calamity to the town in which he lived, and of which he was a most worthy and valuable citizen. He was an industrious and thriving member of one of the most universally industrious and thriving communities. He was a good husband, an obliging and estimable neighbor, a courteous and social companion. Many offices of trust and honor have been bestowed upon him by his fellow-citizens, all of which he has executed with singular zeal and fidelity. His friends and fellow-townsmen will long deeply feel that in the death of Col. Andrews[*] they sustain the loss of one of the most respectable, intelligent and useful citizens, cut off in the midst of his

---

[*] Col. Andrews was a son of Jacob Andrews. His brothers were Jacob, Ebenezer, Tyler, Daniel, Samuel and Moses; and his sisters, Mary and Sally.

days, in the midst of his hopes. What shadows we are,
what shadows we pursue."*

A UNIVERSALIST CHURCH,

Was erected this year, by proprietors, on shares of $50
each. Its dimensions are as follows: length fifty-six feet,
width forty-two feet, height to the bell-deck forty-five feet,
height to the vane seventy-five feet. The building committee were Jacob Story, Oliver Low, John Dexter, Parker
Burnham, 2d, and Samuel Hardy. The cost of the house
and land was $4,500. More than this amount was received
from the sale of the pews—fifty-six in number—at auction.
The church was dedicated " to the worship of God and the
purposes of religion " on Wednesday, December 14.

"After a night of severe storm, the day was not inauspicious. Many
from neighboring towns gathered together. The dedicatory services were as
follows: 1, Anthem ; 2, Reading of the Scriptures by Rev. J. M. Austin
of Danvers ; 3, Introductory prayer by Rev. J. H. Willis of Stafford, Ct. ;
4, Anthem ; 5, Dedicatory prayer by Rev. S. Brimblecom of Danvers;
6, Hymn ; 7, Sermon by Rev. Thomas Whittemore, from Acts xvii. 19, 20 ;
8, Anthem ; 9, Benediction. In the afternoon a sermon was preached by
Rev. Thomas Starr King of Charlestown, from I. John iv. 16. In the evening
a conference was held, to which Christians of all denominations were most
cordially invited. The services even to the last were attended by overflowing
congregations, more being present than could be seated. The house is a very
neat edifice. It is the handsomest in Essex and has a very fine location in
the center of the population."†

In 1866–67 the interior of the church was thoroughly
repaired, and furnished with a new pulpit and new pews,
and upholstered, at a cost of $3,500. An organ was also
purchased, the cost of which was $1,000.

The pastors or preachers to the Universalist Society,
have been the following:

April, 1838, to 1840, Rev. Augustus C. L. Arnold ; May, 1840, to
November, 1844, Rev. John Prince ; June, 1845, to April, 1849, Rev. H.
H. Baker ; July, 1849, to 1850, Rev. Willard Spaulding ; March, 1851, to
1853, Rev. C. H. Dutton ; May, 1852, to July, 1856, Rev. John Prince ;
October, 1856, Rev. Emmons Partridge ; March, 1858, Rev S. Goff ; April,
1859, to May, 1861, Rev. J. H. Tullee.

---

* Salem Gazette.   † Universalist Trumpet, Boston.

In 1844, the society received a legacy of eighteen acres of land, valued at $3,000, from Mrs. Betsey, wife of Jacob Story. Her will was dated December 18, 1844. This property has since been sold.

1837. February 26, died at Topsfield, Nehemiah Cleaveland, M. D., aged 76, the youngest son of Rev. John Cleaveland, late of this place. •

" He was born in Chebacco, August 26, 1760. After his service in the army of the Revolution, he spent some time at home, taking upon himself during that critical and distressing period, almost the entire support of the family. The importance of his services there, and the want of means, prevented him from obtaining a collegiate education.

" Having studied physic with his brother and with Dr. Manning of Ipswich, he entered on the practice at Topsfield, in 1783. Together with his employment as a physician, his services were often required in various public offices. A zealous Federalist in politics, he was for five years a useful member of the Senate, and his weight of character, knowledge, judgment and good sense were felt and acknowledged by his associates at that board,—among them some of the first men in the State. In 1814, he was appointed a Session Justice of the circuit court of common pleas. From 1820 to 1822, he was Associate Justice of the Court of Sessions, and from 1823 to 1828, he was Chief-Justice. For this station, he was well-fitted by his knowledge of business, his sound discretion, and his unyielding firmness in all questions of principle and duty. In 1824, he received from Harvard College the honorary degree of Doctor in Medicine.

" Dr. Cleaveland was nursed in the Puritan strictness of earlier times. His character, early formed and invigorated under the pressure of hardship and stern necessity, and amid the thrilling scenes of the Revolution, exhibited in his maturer years the strength and firmness which might be expected from such training. There was no effeminacy about him. He regulated his life with the closest regard to principle. If his strictness sometimes bordered on severity, his severity was of the wholesome kind. With all this, his natural sensibilities were quick and tender.

" In public affairs and political questions, he took, from his first entry into active life, a lively interest. Of his political opinions, his children will never feel ashamed, for they can say they were those of Hamilton, Jay and Washington. As a physician, he was much esteemed by those who had opportunity to learn his worth. He made, indeed, no pretensions to extensive medical lore—he attempted no difficult surgical operations. But he had—what all the schools of medicine of themselves cannot supply—an observing mind, a retentive memory, a good judgment, and a high sense of responsibility. Nor did he, like too many country physicians, neglect the reading of medical books and journals. His practice was always prudent and cautious—qualities which young and ardent physicians are not apt sufficiently to admire. He was punctual in attending calls, and kind and cheerful in the sick-room. He possessed, in a high degree, the qualities which ensure to a physician the confidence and attachment of his patients. But the country doctor finds many opportunities and calls to do good, for which the faculty, as such, give no prescriptions. Happy he, who has the power and disposition to meet such calls. During the fifty years of his practice in Topsfield, few days probably passed, when his opinion or assistance was not sought in some matter aside from his profession. There were few occurrences or questions, incident to common life, in regard to which he had not formed an opinion, or could not give judicious advice. Indeed, the mere fact that through so long a series of years, confidence continued undiminished—the oracle being consulted to the very last—proves that the responses had not been found unsafe or fallacious. The happy influences of so long a course of beneficent action are not to be estimated. How many quarrels have been arrested—how many lawsuits prevented —how much needless expense and trouble saved, in a thousand instances, by the timely, the un-feed advice of a judicious and peace-making neighbor.

"Trained in the orthodoxy of primitive times, his early opinions were confirmed by the personal and careful investigation of his maturer years, and he was abundantly able to give a reason for his faith, as well as his hope. Opinions so decided—so cherished—could not be without their influence; they moulded his character and shaped his conduct. The diffusion of truth—the suppression of vice in every form—the spread of religion, pure and undefiled—were objects for which he loved to pray—for which he labored, and to which he contributed liberally of his substance. Yet after a long life employed in doing good, his hopes, his dependence, were in Christ alone. Thus soothed, 'faded his late declining years away.' Thus sustained, from the midst of the affectionate circle, which had learned of him to venerate true worth, with undisturbed serenity and undiminished hope, he sunk gently to the tomb.

"His form was well-proportioned and he was of large stature, erect and of commanding aspect. His constitution was vigorous and his health unbroken until his fiftieth year; from that period he suffered much from one of the most painful of maladies."*

His first wife, who died childless in 1791, was Lucy, the daughter of Dr. Manning. His second wife, the mother of nine children, was Experience, the daughter of Dr. Elisha Lord, of Pomfret, Ct. She died in 1845, at the age of eighty-one. Five of her children were living in 1856—William N. Cleaveland, Esq., now of Boxford; Nehemiah Cleaveland, Esq., of Brooklyn, N. Y., (now of Topsfield,) a distinguished teacher and scholar, a graduate of Bowdoin College; John Cleaveland, Esq., a lawyer in New York city, a graduate of Bowdoin (since deceased); Rev. Elisha L. Cleaveland, D. D., pastor of a church in New Haven, also a graduate of Bowdoin (now also deceased); and Mary, the widow of the late Rev. O. A. Taylor of Manchester.

* Boston Medical and Surgical Journal.

April. The town voted that its proportion of the "surplus revenue" of the United States should be applied to the payment of the town's debt. The first three installments amounted to $2,835.26.

This year, in accordance with a provision of law, the Light Infantry company was disbanded. Its last officers were John S. Burnham, Captain, Asa R. Andrews, Lieutenant, Uriah G. Spofford, Ensign. The militia company, which included all males between the ages of eighteen and forty-five, except the " uniform company " and persons especially exempted by law, had its last "May training " and was also disbanded. It numbered, at this time, about sixty members. Its last officers were Isaac Farnham, Captain, Nathan Burnham, Third (afterwards First), Lieutenant, Seth Story, Acting Ensign and Clerk. After this time the militia were merely enrolled.

The powder-house, still standing, was built in 1820 by the town for the use of the Light Infantry and the militia, at a cost of $95.

August 23. Graduated at the Wesleyan University, Middletown, Ct., Thomas Sewall, Jr.:

He was born in this place, April 28, 1818, and received his academic education at the Wesleyan Academy, Wilbraham, Phillips Academy, Andover, and the Wesleyan Seminary, Readfield, Me. His orations at the " Senior exhibition," November 29, 1836, and on " Commencement day," when he closed his connection with the university, are still remembered for their remarkable excellence and power, by some who were his teachers then. In the year 1838, having completed his theological studies, Mr. Sewall entered the ministry of the Methodist Episcopal church ; and has been engaged in duties of his profession since that time, with the exception of five years. One of these was spent in a tour to Europe and the East. During the other four, he was compelled by symptoms of pulmonary disease to retire from the pulpit, and visit the South. By President Taylor he was appointed United States Consul to Santiago de Cuba, and remained there ten months, but was not permitted to exercise the functions of his office because he was a Protestant clergyman. Returning home, he was appointed to a desk in the Department of the Interior at Washington, and was afterwards transferred to the Department of State under Daniel Webster. Resigning this position in 1853, he resumed the active work of the ministry. Most of his professional life has been spent in Maryland and Virginia. He is now (June, 1868,) pastor of a church in Brooklyn, N. Y. In 1864, Mr. Sewall received the degree of Doctor of Divinity from Dickinson College, Carlisle, Pa.

1838.   The town appropriated the sum of $1,000 for school purposes. A committee of three was also chosen "to make improvements in the grave-yard, and to enlarge it."

1840.   Town statistics: Population, 1432; number of polls, 465; town valuation, $439,906.

1841.   By vote of the South School District, a lot of land south-east of the old school-house lot, consisting of five rods, was purchased, and a new school-house erected on it, at an expense of $589.82.   The building-committee were Jeremiah Cogswell, Warren Low, and Winthrop Burnham, Jr.   They were authorized by the district to sell the old school-house.

REMODELING OF THE CONGREGATIONAL MEETING-HOUSE.

1842.   The Congregational meeting-house was changed and improved in structure and appearance:

At a meeting of the First Parish, held February 7th, "John Choate, Samuel Procter, Capt. Francis Burnham, Caleb Cogswell, Col. II. C. Cogswell, William H. Mears and Issacher Burnham were chosen a committee to consider the subject of making any repairs or alterations in the meeting-house, to sketch a plan of such alteration and the probable expense of it, and report at the adjournment."   On the 18th of the same month this committee reported a plan for remodeling the meeting-house, which, with some changes made at a subsequent meeting, was adopted.   Soon after, Caleb Cogswell, William H. Mears, Adam Boyd, Capt. Francis Burnham and Nathan Burnham, 3d, were appointed a committee to carry the contemplated alteration into effect, and were instructed to complete the work on or before the first of October following.   The pews in the old meeting-house were appraised by a committee consisting of John Punchard, Esq., of Salem, Dea. John Safford of Beverly and Dea. Jabez R. Gott of Rockport, chosen by the parish for this purpose.

The contract for remodeling the church was taken by Mr. Uriah G. Spofford. The master-mason was Mr. Whipple of Hamilton, and the master-painter Mr. William Moseley of Ipswich.   The floor of the audience-chamber was laid sixteen inches below the old "gallery girth," giving a hight of seventeen feet for the audience-chamber, and of eight feet for the lower story.   The pulpit was designed by the contractor, and was built by Mr. David C. Foster, formerly of Essex.   During the alteration of the house, the church and congregation worshiped in the "basement," the old pulpit standing on the floor directly under the place where it had previously been.

October 31st, the parish voted that the pews in the new meeting-house be rented for the purpose of raising money to support their minister, and to defray the other parish charges, and that the rent of the pews be paid quarterly in advance; that Winthrop Low, John Burnham and Dr. Josiah Lamson be a committee to apportion the rent on the several pews according to their location in the house, and to let the pews at auction on Friday, November 4th; and that the money which may be received for the choice of said pews shall go towards paying for the old pews.

The church was dedicated on Thursday, November 3d. The sermon on this occasion was preached by the pastor, from the text, "Make not my Father's house a house of merchandise;" John ii. 16. Other clergymen present, most of whom took part in the exercises, were Rev. Messrs. Kimball and Fitz of Ipswich, Gale of Rockport, Nickels of Gloucester, O. A. Taylor of Manchester, and Kelley of Hamilton.

The improvements which have been made since in the meeting-house have been as follows: In 1846–7 the north porch was removed, and the north end repaired, which, with painting a part of the outside, cost $200. In 1849–50, the sum of $450, the net proceeds of "Fairs," conducted by ladies of the parish, was expended in fitting up and furnishing the "basement" and providing blinds for its windows. In 1852, the upper part of the tower was thoroughly repaired, a new spire erected, the corners each side of the tower filled out, the gallery moved back, and four flights of stairs built in the space thus gained, two chimneys built, and three sides of the exterior painted, at an expense of $1,425. The frescoing and graining of the interior, in 1853, cost $335, which sum was raised by the "Female Benevolent Society," chiefly by means of a "Fair." An organ was purchased by subscription in 1854, the cost of which was $700.

The cost of remodeling and furnishing the house, and of all these improvements, exclusive of the organ, was $4,550. Of this sum, $1,700 were obtained by the sale of the parish lands, the parish having voted, July 4, 1842, to sell them for this purpose, and having appointed "Winthrop Low, David Choate, Francis Burnham, Caleb Cogswell and Samuel Procter a committee to sell and convey all of the parsonage pasture, tillage-land, wood-land and marsh, and in the name of the parish to give deeds thereof, and also to signify by said deeds the assent of the parish to the conveyance of said lands by their minister, which assent is hereby given." These parish lands were originally "commoners' land," and amounted to about fifty acres in all. Benevolent associations and individuals, at different times, contributed $1,392, and the parish raised $1,458 by tax. The old pews were appraised at $367, while the "choice-money" for the new pews amounted to $210. "The Ladies' Sewing Society" contributed the carpets and pulpit-furniture, and the Sabbath-school gave the clock.

41

This year also was organized the "Essex Washington Total Abstinence Society." The objects of the society, as stated in its constitution, were "to reclaim those who are unfortunately addicted to habits of intemperance, and to banish from the community the sale and use of intoxicating liquors as a beverage, by the use of moral suasion, and by exerting an individual as well as associated influence in all laudable ways." The condition of membership was "the signing the pledge of total abstinence from everything that can intoxicate, except for medicinal purposes." The pledge also contained the following clause. "And above all, the members of this society, agree that they will use their utmost endeavors to reclaim and restore to temperance those that are unfortunately addicted to drunkenness." "It shall be the duty," adds another article of the constitution, "of every member of this society to cheer and encourage those who have reformed, and to endeavor by a well directed and proper personal influence to induce others to "go and do likewise." The pledge has the names of 385 persons affixed to it. The first officers were Uriah G. Spofford, president; Humphrey C. Cogswell, secretary and treasurer; Thomas H. Griggs, Sylvanus Hardy and Capt. Winthrop Low, managers. The last entry in the records of this society is dated, February 21, 1849.

1845. Died, April 10th, in Washington City, D. C., in the fifty-ninth year of his age, Thomas Sewall, M. D.

"Dr. Sewall was born April 16th, 1786, in Augusta, Me. He received his academic education, and began the study of medicine, in his native place. His professional studies were continued with Dr. Jeffries of Boston, and in the medical college there. After practicing medicine a few years in Chebacco, he attended the lectures of Rush, Barton and others in Philadelphia, in 1811, received the degree of M. D. at Harvard College, August 26, 1812, and immediately resumed his professional work. In 1819, he removed to this city. His practice soon became extensive and lucrative ; and it is believed has not been exceeded, in either respect, by that of any other of the local faculty, several members of which rank among the most eminent physicians in the Union. In 1821, he was appointed Professor of Anatomy in the National Medical College, connected with Columbia College, in Washington, and retained a chair in it as he did also his membership, during the residue of his life. From the year 1825, when the school went into operation, till the close of the season next preceding his death, he was punctual in delivering the periodical lectures, and in discharging the other duties appropriate to his professorship. His professorship at the time of his death was that of the "Theory and Practice of Medicine in the Columbia College." Amid the pressure of official engagements, and an onerous professional business, he was enabled by a methodical arrangement of his time to gain leisure for composition. Several of his works, especially the Essays on Phrenology and the Tract on Temperance, the latter of which was translated into the German language, obtained a wide circulation, as well in Europe as in this country, and fixed the reputation of the author as a profound and exact inquirer, and as an accomplished writer. The professional merits of Dr. Sewall are too deeply felt in this community, and too diffusively known abroad, to need illustration. Though endowed by nature with a bold and penetrating genius, and though rich in all the learning of his science and vigilant in marking its progress, he never allowed his judgment to yield to the fascination of theories, or to the authority of systems ; but founded his practice on the solid basis of experience. Ever mindful of the maxim of the great master of medical philosophy, that the physician is only the minister of nature, he rested on this safe monitor with a confidence which was fully vindicated by his long and successful practice. As a conscientious and faithful servant of the public, it is believed that he could not have been surpassed. His constitution was feeble ; several of his organs were chronically disordered ; and for the last twenty years of his life he was fighting off the fatal *consumption*. But these considerations could never persuade him to turn a deaf ear to the call of sickness, though made often in the most inclement weather and often in the dead of night. Such a call, at all times, and under all circumstances, he promptly obeyed ; and with the skill of a physician, carried to the bed of the sick or the dying, the tenderness of a friend. It was in a course of long and self-sacrificing attentions to a patient that he contracted the disease which was the proximate cause of his own death.

" The subject of this notice was scarcely more distinguished in the profession of his choice, than he was exemplary in all the relations of life—religious, domestic and social. In 1828, he became a professor of religion, and joined the Methodist Episcopal Church. In the discharge of his duties as an officer of that church he was scrupulously regular. It was his rule to attend public worship twice on every Sunday, however numerous and exacting might be his professional engagements ; and, though sometimes they constrained him to go late or to come away suddenly, his adherence to the rule was invariable. The faith which he professed, was his guide through life and his consolation in death. From an early period of his malady he despaired of recovery ; but that despair of life *here* was brightened by the hope of life *hereafter*, and by his lively but humble trust in the promises of the Gospel—a trust which gave him power to bear with resignation the most excruciating bodily pain. Intent to the last on doing good to his fellow-men, he employed the intervals of ease in admonitions, as fervent as they were gentle, to the friends who, from time to time, were permitted to draw near his bedside. His mind continued un-clouded throughout his long and agonizing sickness; and only an hour before his death he gave thanks, in brief and affecting terms, to God for his mercies. This hasty notice would be even more imperfect than it must be, without some allusion to Dr. Sewall, as a kind and affectionate kinsman and faithful friend. But to do more than allude to these prominent features of his character might touch harshly on grief too deep, and as yet too fresh, to be approached." *

His widow, Mrs. Mary Choate Sewall, died at Rockville, Md., March 29, 1855.

Early Tuesday morning, the 22d of July, a destructive hail-storm passed over the center of the town from west to east, breaking about three thousand panes of glass, chiefly in the houses of the central village. It accompanied a terrific thunder-storm, and occurred after several days of intensely hot weather:

"About three o'clock, a severe thunder-storm occurred, accompanied by a high wind, copious showers, and a considerable quantity of hail. The evening previous was delightfully clear and pleasant, and the change in the aspect of affairs appeared remarkably sudden to those who were aroused from their slumbers by the storm. The flashes of lightning were incessant, and the hail and the thunder, although not very alarming here, indicated a severe conflict of the elements among our neighbors at no great distance. In Essex, we understand the hail-stones were of immense size, and destroyed a great quantity of glass. One gentleman stated that the arm, which he put out of his window in shutting the blinds, was so pelted with the lumps of ice as to be seriously hurt and lamed. It is said that some of the hail-stones measured seven inches in circumference an hour after they fell, and that they would average about the size of pullets' eggs. One man states that he counted a thousand panes broken, within half a mile, as he came along the road. The hail fell in a very narrow vein, and with such force as to break through the blinds on the meeting-house." †

The present school-house of the East District was built this year.

1848, March. The town appropriated $1,300 for school purposes. It also voted "that the selectmen set up bounds to, and open and fix for use, the landing near the shop of Samuel Hardy, near the eastern end of the causeway, and that the sum of $100 be raised for this purpose."

---

* Washington Daily Globe, April 11th, 1845.   † Salem Register, and Gazette.

This year the Christian Baptist Society was reorganized, at a meeting assembled by virtue of a warrant issued by Ezra Perkins, Jr., Esq. William E. Burnham was chosen moderator, Nathaniel Macintire, clerk and treasurer, W. H. Burnham, John C. Burnham, William G. Burnham, society committee. By vote of the society, a new house of worship was erected in 1849, called the "Century Chapel." It is forty by forty-six feet, and contains forty-six pews. It was designed that this should be a *free church*, and the original plan was to have it built on shares of $5 each. But a sufficient amount not having been secured by this method, it was concluded to sell the pews. From this sale a larger sum was received than the entire cost of the building, which was $1,500.

1849. The "Chebacco Division No. 19 of the Sons of Temperance of Massachusetts," was organized on the 27th of June, at which time fifteen persons were initiated:

" Eighty-one persons united with the Order afterward. The number of members at the time of its dissolution, October 13, 1855, was forty-two. The whole amount of money paid into the treasury was $1,160. Of this sum $478 were paid out in benefits to sick members and to defray funeral charges. The sum of $75 was paid to lecturers and in the circulation of documents on the subject of temperance. Eleven lectures were given by gentlemen from abroad under the direction of the " Division," and eighteen public meetings were held in the different school districts of the town, in all of which free debate was allowed.

" Under the auspices of the Sons of Temperance, a section of the Cadets of Temperance was formed, which numbered in all fifty-seven members. This was an association of boys, pledged against the use of intoxicating drinks, tobacco in all its forms, and the use of profane language. Besides the regular business of the " Order," the Cadets engaged in declamations, readings, debates and mock-courts, with a great deal of interest and profit to themselves, and satisfaction to the audience. This organization was abandoned in May, 1851. The Sons of Temperance had a library formed by contributions from the members. On the 13th of August, 1855, a vote to surrender the charter of the Division was passed. The property was divided, the books returned to those who had contributed them, and the funds divided among the members."

1850. April 4th, died, in Boston, Mr. Thomas Marshall Burnham, aged 64. He was the son of Thomas Marshall

Burnham, and was born and brought up in Chebacco. His brothers were Benjamin, Obed Zeno, Azor, and George W., a trader on Thompson's Island and whose son succeeds him in the same business. About the year 1808, Mr. Burnham married Abigail (born March 25, 1787,) daughter of Daniel Low, and sister of Enoch and the late Capt. Winthrop Low. In early life he was a trader, at first in his native parish, and afterwards at Ipswich Centre; but at the close of the war with England, he removed, with his family, to the eastern part of Maine. About the year 1825, he went to Boston, and was for a time a dealer in furniture. Not long after, he established a store for the purchase and sale of second-hand books. The business was at first on a small scale, his capital being very limited; but it prospered and grew from time to time until his stock in trade filled two stores of four or five stories each, and "Burnham's antiquarian bookstore," in Cornhill, became generally known as the first and largest establishment of the kind in the country. For many years, it has been famous everywhere for its extensive and valuable collection of old and rare books, in almost all branches of literature and science, and in a great variety of languages, ancient and modern; and has, therefore, been a favorite place of resort for antiquarians, authors and scholars generally. The idea of this unique kind of trade seems to have been original with this native of Chebacco, and by it he amassed a fortune.

September 30, died, Jonathan Story, Esq., aged 75:

"He was a man of uncommon powers of mind, and in attempting to delineate them, we feel that there is danger of seeming to be extravagant. While he was living, it might have been said with much truth, however, that 'none knew him but to love him;' and now he is gone, it may be also said with equal truth, 'none name him but to praise.' But mere expressions of regret for the loss of such a man do not seem to be all that such a case requires. Nothing, indeed, of ours can now reach *him*, or in any way affect the dull, cold ear of death. It may be of use, however, to the living and certainly affords a serious gratification to our own minds to attempt some sketch of Mr. Story's character and life. He was born in Chebacco, in Ipswich (now Essex), in 1775, and spent his early life in laborious occupations upon his father's farm and in the mill. Although he inherited a good constitution and had uninterrupted health, in consequence of which he accomplished a great amount of manual labor, both as a mechanic and a farmer, yet he did not overlook the cultivation of his mind. Books, indeed, were not abundant nor always accessible at that day, but all that he read he understood and remembered. There seemed to be a natural foundation for knowledge in his mind. New ideas delighted him always, to the end of his life, and yet he appeared like one who had thought of the same thing before—a proof of having a mind of high order. He required less labor to understand a subject than men generally do. His ear was always open to receive instruction, and every important fact or principle, that came under his observation, found a place of deposit in his mind. Four months' residence at Dummer Academy under that prince of teachers, Mr. Moody, in addition to the common schools, afforded the only advantages of which he was able to avail himself. But a love of knowledge was kindled up in his mind, which traveled on through life without weariness or decay. He studied geometry and surveying with Father Moody, and soon became one of the most eminent surveyors in the State. While the saw was running through the log in his father's mill, young Story would draw his diagrams with a piece of chalk on a board or piece of bark, and thus continue the studies that made him afterward so distinguished. As a surveyor, Mr. Story was accurate, but it was his superior judgment and long experience that made his services so valuable. He was far more than a mere *artist*. Others might perhaps take angles as accurately and ascertain quantities as well, but he was an *arbitrator* always, remembering that another party was interested in settling the boundaries of land, and that other party often, or generally absent. It was *natural* for him to do justice between man and man, and he had the pleasure of satisfying both the parties, whether in settling disputed lines as a surveyor, or litigated questions as a magistrate, in more cases than is common among men. He had the geography (so to speak) of that great tract of wood-land extending from Beverly to Gloucester and from Essex to Manchester, fully in his mind and could have mapped out all the great and small divisions upon paper with as much ease as a school-boy would make the multiplication table. Unfortunately all this knowledge has died with him. After the experience of fifty years which he had, it is not too much to say that no man living can begin to make his place in these respects in society, good. *As a magistrate*, Mr. Story may be said to have dealt out justice with an impartial hand. Never hasty in deciding, he rarely felt himself under the necessity of revising his own decisions or found them reversed by the higher tribunals. His knowledge of law was extensive. When present in the higher courts, he was awake to everything, and heard the arguments of counsel with the deepest interest, perceiving their fallacy or admiring their truth as the case might be, but listening always with the profoundest veneration to everything that fell from the court. But he was *a peace-maker*. Many, many causes have been settled or left to referees by his advice, and thus expensive litigation has been prevented, so often ruinous to the parties and which has so often separated so many chief friends. He was a man of uncommon discernment, being quick to discover and read out the character of others and to take their intellectual guage and dimensions. And as he was rarely under the necessity of making more than one decision upon the same subject, so he was generally correct in his first estimate of persons. *The social qualities* of our deceased friend must not be overlooked, for they will not soon be forgotten, having formed so amiable a part of his character. His wit was keen, and while it was innocent and harmless, he could make a thousand smile whenever he was so disposed ; though generally, his pleasantry had some useful bearing, and would often operate to settle a doubtful question far better than the language of gravity and wisdom itself. He had a faculty of adapting himself to the different classes of men whom he met. With gentlemen of the bar, when business brought him in contact with them, he was at home, receiving instruction and imparting delight. So with the other professions ; and yet he would turn himself with perfect ease to old acquaintances in their working dress ; and while he would seem on a level with the humblest of men, none ever forgot for a moment to respect and honor him, thus showing that true worth will after all be appreciated and understood everywhere. He was *benevolent* in a very important sense of the term. Nobody, it is believed, ever sought his advice and counsel, without finding him ready to impart it, even though it had cost him much study and reflection to enable him to give it. And when he did give his opinion and advice, it came as free as the mountain breeze, and was none the less valuable for being gratuitous. The poor and the fatherless and he that had none to help him, always found a friend in him. He would not indeed squander his sympathies upon unworthy objects, but wherever there was an oppressor, he took the part of the oppressed, and in many such ways as these he has caused the widow's heart to sing for joy. He enjoyed the confidence of his townsmen in an unusual degree, having represented the town many years successively in General Court, and having long filled various town offices. It is not pretended that Mr. Story was a perfect man. That he had failings we are not disposed to deny. But these failings belonged to the infirmities and not to the vices of humanity. As a *husband*, a *father* and a citizen, he certainly lived and acted usefully and well. And it is exceedingly to be desired that our young men, especially, who are to be the architects of their own characters and fortunes should carefully study and well consider the steps by which our departed father and friend rose to a position so respectable and so useful. Mr. Story's views of religion were those generally denominated orthodox. For the support of this faith, he contributed regularly through life, and declared a short time before his death, that his only hope of future happiness was in a crucified Redeemer. He said he felt himself to be a great sinner, and desired the prayers of all Christians that he might be prepared for the retributions of eternity. He expressed to his minister his most ardent desire that all his relatives and friends would immediately seek an interest in that religion which alone can prepare the soul for death and heaven. Mr. Story leaves a widow and one son only, but the whole community unite with them in lamenting his death." *

1851. By vote of the town, a new fire-engine was obtained, and an engine-house built for it on "Thompson's Island" near the causeway, at an expense of $800. For the management of it, the "Essex Fire Association attached to the Essex Engine No. 2" was formed November 19th, consisting of thirty-five members. The first officers were John J. Clark, foreman; Andrew Howes, assistant foreman; William B. Cary, clerk.

In the Autumn of this year was established the "Essex Lyceum." The "Lyceum" successfully conducted an extended course of entertaining, instructive and valuable lectures during each Winter of its existence. In addition to occasional lectures from the resident clergymen of the town, the managers from time to time obtained the services of eminent lecturers from abroad, whose lectures were attended by large audiences. Meetings were also held for the mutual improvement of the members, the exercises consisting of declamations, select readings, oral discussions and occasionally the reading of a paper entitled the "Essex Lyceum Talent," its contents being composed mostly of original articles written by members of the Lyceum, with occasional contributions from some of the ladies of the village. The officers of this lyceum have been as follows: presidents, Aaron L. Burnham. O. H. P. Sargent, John Prince; vice presidents, Norman Story, Sylvester Eveleth, Ira Otis Burnham, J. Perkins Spofford; corresponding secretaries, John Prince, O. H. P. Sargent; recording secretaries, Aaron Low, J. M. Richardson. W. B. Cary, Samuel P. Haskell, W. W. Pendergast. Andrew Howes; treasurers, Josephus Burnham, Aaron Low; managers, Timothy Andrews, Jr., Norman Story. S. P. Haskell, John H. Burnham. In the year 1856. the lyceum was merged in the "Chebacco Library Association," which was organized on the 5th of June of that year, in accordance

* "D. C.," in the Salem Gazette.

42

with an act of incorporation passed by the Legislature
and approved by the Governor, May 1, 1856. Section 1 of
this act is as follows:

"John Prince, O. H. P. Sargent, Samuel P. Haskell, Andrew Howes,
Charles Howes, Nathan Burnham, 4th, &c., their associates and successors,
are hereby made a corporation by the name of the Chebacco Library Association, to be established in the town of Essex, for the purpose of instituting and
sustaining a library and reading-room, and promoting public instruction by lectures or otherwise, with all the powers and privileges, and subject to all the duties, liabilities and restrictions set forth in Chapter 44 of the Revised Statutes."

Section 2 provides that the said corporation may hold real and personal
estate for the purposes aforesaid, to an amount not exceeding $10,000.

At the first meeting of the petitioners, the charter was
accepted and a constitution adopted. Article 2 of this
instrument is as follows:

"No person shall be an active member of this association, or enabled to
vote in its regular business meetings, or be eligible to any office therein, unless he be a *working man*—the term *working man* being understood as sig-
nifying a person who follows any respectable calling or pursuit, whereby he
obtains his livelihood, and who does not derive his support without industry,
from wealth already inherited or accumulated. Any person *not* thus disqualified, may become a member by signing the constitution and paying one dollar." The officers are to be chosen semi-annually except the Trustees who
are to be chosen for a term of years; and no presiding officer shall be chosen
a second time until every other member who is willing to officiate shall have
been elected and shall have served one term."

The first officers were: John Prince, president; Andrew Howes and Charles Howes, vice-presidents; John
H. Burnham, Andrew Howes and John Prince, trustees;
Samuel P. Haskell, secretary and librarian. "The inau-
guration of the Chebacco Library Association took place
December 24, 1856. The meeting was called to order by
the president, who briefly stated the object of the association. By invitation, prayer was offered by Rev. J. M.
Bacon; after which speeches were made by Messrs. Partridge, Choate, Spofford, Bacon and others." In September, 1857, the association numbered seventy-four members
and had a library of four hundred and forty-two volumes.
In 1867, the number of volumes was six hundred.

THE SPRING STREET CEMETERY.

1852. In accordance with a vote of the town, a lot of land consisting of two acres and twenty rods was purchased and prepared for use as a cemetery, and called from its location, the "Spring Street Cemetery." The cost of the land was $856; of the fence, $635; of the trees and posts, and grading in front of the yard, $200; of grading the yard itself, $275; total, $1,966. It contains one hundred and eighty-nine whole lots, fifteen feet by twenty in size, and appraised at $7 each; and seventy-seven half lots, nine feet by fifteen in size, and appraised at $3 each.

" This new burial-ground was publicly set apart by appropriate consecrating ceremonies, on the afternoon of Wednesday, October 27, 1852. A large concourse of people assembled on the ground at two o'clock, when the following *original Ode*, written for the occasion by Rev. John Prince, after having been read by him, was sung by a large choir, composed of the principal singers of the town, under the direction of Mr. Robert W. Burnham, many others of the assembly also joining :

" Borne hither to this chosen spot,
    Henceforth, as years shall onward glide,
Will forms now animate with thought,
    Repose, enshrouded, side by side.

" Withdrawn by Death's mysterious power,
    Life's scenes they'll leave, at every stage,
From blithesome childhood's sunny hour
    To manhood's prime, and trembling age.

" With folded hands across the breast,
    With lips that move no more at will,
And features calm,—they here shall rest,
    With upward look, serene and still.

" And when, from earth's enthrallment free,
    The soul ascends, in joyful trust,
Still sacred shall the relics be,
    Though motionless, insensate dust.

" Here oft shall names be fondly read,
    While flowers above the mounds shall spring,
Of souls from mortal vision fled
    On stainless and ethereal wing.

" As to the Patriarch, in his dream,
    So unto us such faith be given,
That hence this hallowed ground may seem
    ' The house of God, the gate of heaven.' "

"A brief consecratory prayer was then offered by Rev. Dr. Crowell; at the close of which, under the direction of Hon. David Choate, as Chief Marshal, the people walked in procession, preceded by the officers of the town, to the basement story of the North Church, where an address was delivered by Rev. Dr. Crowell. It had originally been designed that all the services should take place upon the ground, within the enclosure; but, at the time appointed, the coolness of the weather, (although the day was pleasant, for a period so late in the season), rendered it expedient, both on account of the speaker and the audience, that the address should be delivered within doors. The occasion was one of solemn interest, which the inhabitants of the place will long remember."*

The following is an extract from the address delivered at the consecration of the cemetery:

"For the space of nearly half a century our venerated fathers the first settlers of this town carried their dead to the centre of Ipswich. They would not bury them on their own lands, for to this they had not been accustomed in their native country; and because, too, their private property might change hands, and the graves found on it might not be treated in a manner sufficiently sacred. Hence there is no tradition of any burials on private lands, and no such graves or remains of our fathers have ever been found among us. According to the views and habits in which they had been trained, they buried their dead near the sanctuary where they assembled from Sabbath to Sabbath to worship Him, who is the God both of the living and of the dead. Though no carriages were used in that day, and but very few horses, and the corpse was borne the long distance of five miles on the shoulders of men, yet by frequent changes on the part of under-bearers, as they were termed, and by the habit of walking, which prevailed in that day among all classes of society, the service was by no means so burdensome as it might now seem to us.

"If, indeed, there had been carriages and horses, yet such was the custom of the day, such their veneration for the dead, that anything other than the bier upon the shoulders of men would have been considered an unsuitable vehicle for conveying the corpse to the grave. That custom and those feelings continued among us until somewhat less than forty years since; and when in that late day the change to the use of a hearse was talked of, some of the older people strongly objected to it, as too near an approach to the desecration of the dead.

"It was not till twelve years after the burial of Mr. John Cogswell (the first settler) in the centre of Ipswich, during which time more of the original settlers were there laid in their graves, that a burying-ground was opened here. This is our ancient grave-yard, judged to be now so filled with the dead as to admit of but few more; thus creating the necessity for procuring and opening this our new and spacious cemetery.

---

* Appendix to the Address delivered at the Consecration of the Cemetery.

" If Mr. Cogswell, who was the original owner of this spot of ground, were with us, to-day, in his venerable form, with what pious benignity would he look upon the scene before us: a portion of ground once his own, enclosed, arranged and prepared, with a simplicity, neatness, convenience and ornament, so well becoming the sacred use for which it is designed. With what satisfaction and delight, too, would he lift up his eyes, and survey the whole prospect around,—the beautifully cultivated fields, instead of the dark and dense forests, which, in his day, covered hill and dale; the cheering hum of business, instead of the howl of wild beasts and savage men; the comfortable and ornamented dwellings, the beautiful churches and school-houses, and the many fruits of industry, frugality and temperance, marking the temporal prosperity of the place. Would that he could witness an equal degree of moral prosperity among us; the fear of God, the observance of his Sabbaths, the reverence of his name, and obedience to his word. Would not the good man's joy in these respects be much abated? But our hope and our prayer is that better days will come, when this whole people shall be as distinguished for righteousness, godliness and truth, as they are now for intelligence, industry, economy and thrift.

" It is a fact of much interest that one or more *families of the Aborigines* once dwelt on this now consecrated ground and *buried their dead under this soil.* In preparing the ground, the remnants of the bones of two adults and a child, as is supposed, were discovered, all lying in the same direction, with a sea-shell by their side. Not far from this, the remnants of wood-ashes and clam-shells gave indubitable proof that an Indian wigwam had been there located. The inference that these bones are the remains of those Indian families seems unavoidable. In all probability they have lain there not far from two hundred years. We look upon them with interest and veneration, not only as the bones of human beings, but as mementos of a race once living and active on this soil, but now wholly passed away. 'Tread lightly on the ashes of the dead,' is a venerated maxim. They were owners of the ground under which they laid their dead. Shall we not acknowledge their title, and give these sacred remains a resting-place, near where they were found, with some simple monument that shall tell the interesting fact?

" During the hundred and seventy-one years that our *ancient cemetery* has been in use, *not less than two thousand persons have been buried there,* according to the nearest estimate that can be made from the Parish Records.*

" Truly we may say, in view of this fact,—' How populous is the grave.'

*Among these were the first three ministers, whose pastorates together cover a period of one hundred and eighteen years. The oldest grave-stone in this burial-ground, whose inscription is legible, bears the date, 1710. The inscription is as follows:

ADAM COGSWELL,
SON OF
LIEUT. ADAM COGSWELL AND MRS. ABIGAIL COGSWELL,
Died February ye 4th, 1709-10,
AGED 19 YEARS.

More lie buried on that one acre of ground than are now living and active in their daily concerns, in the whole town. How striking the fact, that all this busy population may be gathered under the sod of a single acre. In that silent house lie our fathers and mothers, our brothers and sisters, our children and grandchildren. Once they were full of life and activity. Their voices were heard in these dwellings, in accents of friendship and love. They walked these streets ; they trod these fields, and their hands were diligently employed in their several pursuits. They were subject, also, as we are, to the sorrows and afflictions of life. Nearly all of them, we may suppose, fol- lowed their dead to that ancient yard, and with tears of anguish looked for the last time into that narrow house, the grave, soon to be their dwelling and resting-place for the body. In view of the more than two thousand burials there, each spreading sorrow and grief through many hearts, we see that our ancient cemetery has been truly a place of weeping. *There* have been buried, not only the dead, but along with them many cherished hopes, many fond ex- pectations, many comforts and joys, leaving the heart desolate and sad, to be relieved, sustained and cheered only by the sweet promises and animating hopes of holy writ. *That cemetery will still be dear to us.* It will not be forsaken. It will be visited by the living, though it can contain but few more of the dead. Tears of grief will still be shed there in the recollection of those who have been taken from our affectionate embraces, and whose faces we shall see no more on earth.

" What that ancient field has been, *so will be this, which we now consecrate to the same mournful and hallowed purpose.* Here provision is made for more than four thousand graves, which in process of time will all be filled. In the interval of less than two centuries, judging of the future from the past, there will enter this field of the dead more than four thousand funeral pro- cessions. What a picture of grief is here for the imagination to contemplate ! Each single procession, as it approaches with slow and mournful step, indi- cating the heart full of sadness and sorrow, is an affecting and impressive rep- resentation of human woe. What, then, must the whole be, when you have brought to your view one hundred such mournful scenes, yea, a thousand, and even four thousand ?

" But this is not a theme for the imagination only. It will soon be matter of bitter experience to many of us, as one loved friend after another is taken from us, and we bear his remains to this hallowed ground. Let us bless the God of providence and of grace, that in the midst of such scenes of sorrow which await us all, we have so many sources of consolation and support set before us ; that when called to bury our dead, we have so safe, commodious and desirable a resting-place for their remains. *Here we may come* and indulge in many tender recollections and profitable medi- tations. Here, as in the ancient ground, we may learn the frailty of man, the uncertainty of life, the vanity and emptiness of earthly things, and the value of the Bible, in the light which it sheds on the darkness of the grave. Here, from the Christian epitaphs that will be inscribed on the monuments of

the dead, we may gather wholesome instruction, and find the cemetery a
school of morals, and piety, as well as a resting-place for our departed friends.
Here, as in the ancient yard, we will cherish the Christian hope of a general
resurrection, and direct our thoughts to that final scene. How solemn and
eventful that great day, when all that are in their graves shall come forth,
and all that are alive upon the earth shall have their bodies made immortal,
and the innumerable throng be caught up together with the Lord in the air, to
receive from the lips of their Judge their final destination. 'Seeing then that
all these things shall be dissolved, what manner of persons ought ye to be in
all holy conversation and godliness ; looking for and hasting unto the coming
of the day of God.'"

1855.   A new road was laid out by the county commissioners from the Falls to the Central Village.   Its cost
was $1,961.88.

The town statistics were as follows :

Number of inhabitants, 1,668 ; paupers, 7 ; persons over ninety years of
age, 5 ; persons of foreign birth, 128 ; negroes, 12 ; number of polls, 430.
Of the legal voters, 96 were of the name of *Burnham ;* 46 of the name of
Story ; and 45 of the name of *Andrews.*   Number of families, 383 ; dwellings, 294.   Pupils in the Winter schools, 351 ; in the Summer schools, 294.
Value of real estate, $548,685 ; of personal estate, $297,358 ; total, $846,043.
Value of the town's property, $6,494.   Town debt, $1,039.14.   Cost of maintaining paupers per annum, $262.   Expended upon highways, $1,456.   Ap-
propriated for schools, $1,500.

1856.   Rev. James M. Bacon was installed pastor of
the Congregational Church and Society, July 9th.   The
public exercises were as follows : invocation by Rev. Jeremiah Taylor of Wenham ; reading of the Scriptures by
Rev. Mr. Mordough of Hamilton ; sermon by Rev. Edward
N. Kirk, D. D., of Boston ; installing prayer by Rev. R.
Campbell of Newburyport ; charge to the pastor by Rev.
Daniel Fitz, D. D., of Ipswich ; right-hand of fellowship
by Rev. J. E. Dwinell of Salem ; address to the people
by Rev. L. Withington, D. D., of Newbury ; concluding
prayer by Rev. D. T. Kimball of Ipswich.

There were frequent and destructive thunder-storms
this year.   Mrs. D. W. Bartlett was killed by lightning,
June 30th ; also, Mr. William Burnham, July 4th.   The
lightning struck in twenty or more places in town.

Several cattle, also, were killed by it during the Summer. Such was the frequency with which the lightning struck in Essex, while nothing unusual of the kind occurred in neighboring towns, that it became an object of interesting and scientific inquiry in the Essex Institute, a society of literary gentlemen in the county, whose central place of meeting is Salem.

1860. The town statistics were as follows:

Population, 1,701. Value of real estate, $597,508; of personal estate, $357,598; total, $955,106. Town debt, $1.536. Amount of money raised by taxation, $5,920.93, viz: State tax, $280; county tax, $1,047.05; for schools, $1.500; for highways and overlaying, $1,122.15; other town charges, $1,800; overlaying, $171.73.

ROPE-WALKS.

This year a rope-walk—the fourth in town—was built by Mr. John Mears, Jr.

Prior to 1820 the rope-making business had been carried on at the Falls by Capt. Nathaniel Burnham and Mr. Jonathan Burnham in company, and at the North End, by Mr. Samuel Hardy. A son of the last mentioned, the late Mr. Daniel Hardy, was the first manufacturer of fishing-lines on any considerable scale. In 1836, he removed his factory from the Hardy farm to its present location in the Central District. The late Mr. John Mears, Sen., entered upon the same business about the year 1825, also at the North End. In 1840, his sons, Messrs. David and William H. Mears, formed a partnership for the manufacture of lines, leasing for this purpose a part of their father's "walk." After the dissolution of this partnership, Mr. William H. Mears' rope-walk, on the hill, was built in 1845, and Mr. David Mears, a few years later, purchased his father's "walk" and moved it to a spot near his house. For several years he employed steam-power for spinning cotton and laying lines, but the work is now wholly done by hand. The number of workmen employed in the factories averages from ten to fifteen.

Some hemp has been worked since 1820. But the stock used at the present time, and for many years past, is cotton warp or yarn—to the amount of about twenty-five tons a year on the average. Mackerel-lines were made to a considerable extent during the first part of this period (1820–1868), but since then, cod lines principally. The length of a cod line is twenty-six fathoms or one hundred and fifty-six feet. About three thousand five hundred dozen of these are now made yearly—chiefly in the Winter and Spring—and are sold in the market for $15,000, on the average. They are marketed chiefly in Gloucester, Boston, Beverly and Marblehead.

MUSICAL PRECOCITY.

A rare instance of the early development of musical talent is exhibited, this year, in a child three years old— Martha S. P. Story, a daughter of Mr. Andrew Story, 2d. The following account is chiefly condensed from a "Biographical Sketch by Miss Hannah C. Marshall," published this year:

In 1859, Martha, then only two years and nine months old, startled her parents by playing a part of a familiar psalm-tune on the melodeon. Miss M taught her the air and bass of a few simple tunes; and soon after, she began to imitate what she heard others play. Before the close of the year she could play eight tunes. In May of this year, she could play more than fifty different pieces, with both hands, in perfect harmony of two, three or four parts, in good time, with ease and with great expression at the first attempt. In February, she played for the first time on the piano. She also played the organ at one of the churches in town one Sabbath. The little musician was not merely an imitator, however, but *composed several tunes* which were written down in musical characters, while she was playing them, and two of which were published. April 6th, she gave a concert in town, playing fourteen pieces. Not long after, she gave several concerts in Gloucester, Salem and Boston, which were attended by large audiences. "Her·performance," wrote B. P. Shillaber, Esq., in the Boston Saturday Evening Gazette, "is not the mere child's play of picking out a tune by the single finger, but she gives the expression of the whole harmony, and all without the least apparent effort. She is an artless and simple child, and plays with as much natural ease and unconsciousness as a bird sings." In the judgment of Mr. Paine, a musical critic, "for a child of her age, her performance upon the melodeon and piano-forte were absolutely marvellous, for no indications of *rote playing* or automaton execution were observable." According to the reporter of the Daily Bee "she played the *Prairie Flower,* arranged as a schottische, in an admirable manner; also *Sweet Home, Hamburg, Old Cabin Home, Lightly Row, The Troubadour,* and several other tunes, which were heartily applauded, especially *Hail Columbia.*"

December 31st, occurred the centennial observance of the "Quarterly Fast," by the Congregational Church:

"In the forenoon a sermon was preached by Rev. Dr. Fitz of Ipswich, on the subject of unused talent, from Matthew, 25 : 25. The afternoon was occupied by the pastors present—Rev. Messrs Bacon, Fitz and Mordough—and Deacons Francis Burnham and David Choate, in giving reminiscences of former ministers of this ancient church, particularly of Rev. Mr. Cleaveland, as the existence of the *Quarterly Fast* depended so much upon that veteran

43

preacher and patriot. A large delegation from the South church in Ipswich was present, strongly reminding many of the former years, when the fullest meetings of the year were on the Quarterly Fast day."

1861. In March, Dr. Josiah Lamson closed his practice as the physician of the town. A native of Topsfield, he was fitted for college at Bradford and Dummer Academies—his preceptor at the latter school being Benjamin Allen, LL. D. In 1814, he graduated at Harvard College. The three years following he spent in the study of medicine with Thomas Kittredge, M. D., of Andover. He also attended the medical lectures of the Harvard College Medical School in 1816 and 1817, and in the Autumn of 1817 received the degree of M. D., from the Censors of the Massachusetts Medical Society. Soon after, he was invited to Chebacco by a committee of the parish, and began the practice of medicine here in 1818.

Dr. John D. Lovering began the practice of medicine here immediately after Dr. Lamson's retirement from the active duties of his profession.

Dr. William H. Hull began his practice in town, January 29, 1859.

1862. Hon. John Prince, after a residence in Essex of more than twenty years, removes to Washington, D. C. Mr. Prince was born in Beverly, April 18, 1820. His great-grandfather, Dr. Jonathan Prince, was the first resident physician in Danvers, and of extensive practice throughout a wide circuit. His grandfather, Capt. Asa Prince, was an officer in Col. Mansfield's regiment in the War of the Revolution. His mother was a daughter of Abner Day,* for more than thirty years a deacon of the South Church in Ipswich, and a man very highly esteemed. In his boyhood, Mr. Prince learned the printer's trade, and worked as a journeyman for several years. At the age of nineteen, having availed himself of such opportunities

---

* The maiden name of Mrs. Day's grandmother was Choate. She married a Mr. Martin. After the death of Mrs. Day's father (Potter), her mother was married a second time to Dea. Stephen Choate, her first cousin. The late Amos Choate, Esq., register of deeds, was their son.

as were afforded for cultivating his powers as a writer and
speaker, he commenced preaching. In May, 1840, he became the stated minister of the Universalist Society in
Essex, and continued in that relation until November,
1844. While in this position, he was a member of a convention of anti-slavery Universalists in Lynn, in the Autumn of 1841, and as chairman of a committee appointed
for that purpose, wrote an address to the denomination on
the subject of slavery; which was adopted by the convention. This was published the same year in the Christian
Freeman, Boston, and in the National Anti-Slavery Standard, New York, and was the first anti-slavery document
issued by any assemblage of the Universalist denomination. For four years from the close of his pastorate in
Essex, Mr. Prince had charge of a society in South Danvers. The next four years he spent in lecturing before
lyceums, upon temperance and upon political subjects;
while preaching, also, in various places—at Meredith
Bridge, N. H., in 1850 and 1851. In May, 1852, he again
became pastor of the society in Essex, which office he
finally resigned, July, 1856, after a pastoral service of
nearly nine years in all. While in this relation, he officiated at more than a hundred and fifty marriages. During
his residence in Essex, Mr. Prince was an active supporter
of the temperance cause, and devoted much time to educational and literary matters. Of the town school committee he was a member fourteen years—nine of them in
continuous succession, and during several of them officiated as chairman. In 1843, he established a printing
office—the first in town. Besides "job work" of various kinds, he published for a few months, "The Essex
Cabinet," a weekly newspaper of medium size, neu-
tral in politics and theology. Subsequently for some
months, he printed a smaller paper, entitled "The Universalist Cabinet." Besides the entire labor of editing,
the larger part of the work of setting the type and of
the press-work was done by his own hands. In the field

of authorship, Mr. Prince's productions have been as follows:

Rural Lays and Sketches, a small sized volume of versification, printed by the author for circulation among personal friends and acquaintances only; *Lectures on the Bible*, originally delivered in South Danvers, an 18 mo. volume of 464 pages, published in 1846; *A wreath for St. Crispin, being Sketches of eminent Shoemakers*; also, in pamphlet form, *An Address delivered at a Temperance Celebration* of the anniversary of Washington's birthday, February 22, 1844, in Annisquam Parish, Gloucester; and a *Valedictory Discourse*, delivered in the Universalist Church in South Danvers, in 1848.

Mr. Prince entered political life in 1843, when at the age of twenty-two, he was elected to represent the town in the State Legislature. He was also a member of the House of Representatives in 1853, 1855 and 1860, and a member of the State Senate in 1858. In the course of these official terms, he served on the standing committees on towns, public buildings, parishes and religious societies, and fisheries. In 1860, he was commissioned justice of the peace by Gov. Banks. An article in the Hingham Journal of March 2, 1860, written by a man of another political party (from which source, indeed, many of the facts already mentioned have been derived), contains a sketch of him, of which the following is an extract:

"Mr. Prince is generally and favorably known as a preacher and a politician, having been several times in the Legislature, and during political campaigns one of the most zealous and efficient speakers that has taken the stump. He was originally a Democrat, though always a decided and zealous anti-slavery man. He joined the Liberty Party soon after its organization, at the time when it cast less than a dozen votes in his town in a poll of about 400, and continued a member of it until, in 1848, it was merged into the Free Soil Party, and he was merged with it. In 1854, he was active in the "Know Nothing" movement, which prepared the way for the ascendancy of the Republican party. At the session of the Legislature in 1855, he was assiduous by voice, personal effort and tactics, in securing the elevation of Gen. Wilson, to the United States Senatorship. Mr. Prince is a man of quick, keen perception, takes a broad view of men and questions, and is ever indomitable and unwearied in defending what he regards as the right. He takes an active part in debate, speaks with energy and point, and is often impassioned in his manner. Among his colleagues he is noted for his wit and humor as well as for his oratory. Of the specimens of both, which might be mentioned, the following are conspicuous."   *   *   *   *

" In 1855, Mr. Prince, being a member of the House. spoke thus on the question of adopting an amendment to the Constitution, prohibiting any person to vote, or hold office, unless he was born within the jurisdiction of the United States.

"*None but Americans should rule America* is the motto of the party now in power in this State ; and this has been many times and emphatically reiterated here during this discussion. I accept it as expressive of sound doctrine. But what is it to be an ' American,' in the sense of a qualification or fitness to rule ? Is it merely to be born on the soil, designated by the geographical name of *America*, and so narrowed down in interpretation as to signify just what is now included, neither more nor less, within the *United States* of America ? I know some persons born in Massachusetts, who are far from being *American* in feeling and in character, if by *American* you mean anything akin to sympathy for freedom, justice, republicanism, or faith in human improvement. Some natives of our own State, are ingrained aristocrats, downright monarchists, to all intents and purposes,—having little sympathy for mankind, and little trust in the capacity of the people for self-government. I would not vote for *such Americans* to legislate or administer, either in our Commonwealth or anywhere else. By an *American I* mean one who is such in character—one who is *American* or republican in *principle*, feeling, sympathy, and impulse. A man's birthplace cannot determine anything in this respect.   *   *   *   *   *

"*Mr. Speaker :* Does the gentleman intend to intimate, that I am not an original, genuine native American ? I am half disposed Sir, to branch forth in a regular, spread-eagle, Bunker Hill, Fourth-of-July speech, full of star-spangled-banner allusions ! *I* not a true *native !* Why, sir, I was born on American soil, (at least so they tell me,) and so were my father, grandfather, and great-grandfather before me. Moreover, I sprang from Revolutionary stock. I am the grandson, nothing shorter, of a man who served as a captain all through the eight years of the Revolutionary war—who was at Bunker Hill in the thickest of the fight—who ran across Charlestown Neck, following the lead of General Putnam, while a British frigate in the river was sweeping the Neck with cannon balls, and who while running, accidentally dislocated his ankle, and sitting down immediately slipped the bone back into the socket, and then resumed his flight, hearing distinctly all the while the whizzing of the balls through the air ! He shared the deprivations and sufferings of the army during the hard winter of 1777. The muster roll of his company, the paper yellow with age, may be seen in this very building, in the Secretary's office. *I* not a genuine, true-blue, original, thorough-going, out-and-out *native* American ! The idea is preposterous, Mr. Speaker ! "

After leaving the Legislature, Mr. Prince was employed a year in the office of the Secretary of the Commonwealth, and then a year in the Custom House at Salem. In May, 1862, he was appointed to a clerkship in the Treasury Department at Washington, D. C., and he has since resided in that city. November 7, 1841, he was married to Miss Mary Parker, daughter of Capt. Parker Burnham. Of three children now living, two daughters are married and reside in town, and a son is with his parents in Washington.

1863. Died, on Sabbath evening the 18th of October, John Choate, Esq., aged seventy-four years and six months. The Essex Statesman of November 18th contained the following obituary:

"Mr. Choate was so widely known in our community for his integrity and sterling value as a public man, as well as by the virtues which adorned his private life, that it would be unpardonable to allow him to pass away without some tribute to his memory. His entire life was spent in this, his native village; and his departure, in the midst of his usefulness, after a sickness, rapid and violent, has produced a deep sensation upon every mind. A newspaper sketch must of necessity be short, but a word may be said upon a few of the leading traits of his character, though, after all, it is life as a whole that we look at in making up our estimate of men.

"In the *private circle*, Mr. Choate had the admiration of his family and friends for his social qualities. He was, of course, more open and accessible to immediate friends and associates, than to others, and who is not? But who ever had occasion for even a business interview with him, without feeling, at the close of it, that he had formed a valuable acquaintance? You always knew where to find him. What he said, *he said;* and notwithstanding his premises were often laid down and his conclusions drawn, with almost lightning quickness, yet he was rarely under the necessity of making a second decision upon the same subject. There, is, perhaps, no man who does not have occasion to change his opinion sometimes, but our departed friend saw truth *so intuitively,* that it may be said, as before, he rarely had occasion to alter an opinion once formed. The Hon. Leverett Saltonstall, late of Salem, after such an acquaintance as often springs up between counsel and client, is remembered to have often spoken with admiration of Mr. John Choate, of Essex.

"Mr. Choate was *benevolent* above many. This trait of character, however, did not expend itself by throwing down a shilling and then forgetting it; but it led him *to give employment* to people in humble circumstances. Even here, however, he would not squander his sympathies upon unworthy objects, but they were always judiciously bestowed. His most agreeable *manner* on such occasions was always such that no one ever felt himself *degraded* by receiving anything from him. Even when he was laying you under the deepest obligations, the *manner* was so alleviating, that the objects of his favors would go away with a smile, feeling that the *giver* was almost as much indebted to them for *receiving,* as they were to him for giving.

"Mr. Choate, in his more *public capacity*, will long be remembered for his devotion to the interests of the town.   He was for many years Chairman of the Board of Overseers of the Poor, and as such, contributed largely to the public interest.   In a day when paupers are so easily and so often sent from town to town for trifling causes, there is frequently need of such an officer as a standing Solicitor to examine cases legally, and few laws are more difficult to be administered than pauper laws.   Mr. Choate consulted the decisions of the Supreme Court upon these matters with all the assiduity of a student of law, and frequently with quite as much success.   While he held the office of over-seer, the number of paupers was somewhat, and most justly, reduced, and it is believed to have been largely owing to the almost gratuitous labors of himself.

"And as Mr. Choate sought and promoted the interests of the town, so he was equally devoted to that of the Parish and Society where he worshiped. His views of religion were those usually denominated orthodox, and he is believed to have derived the strongest consolation from the faith he professed for more than thirty years.   He once remarked to the writer of this sketch, that, as he sometimes stood and looked upon the broad sheet of water adjoin-ing the islands which constituted his farm, in some calm morning when the whole surface was like a mirror, it gave him, as he thought, a good idea of the full ocean of God's love, in which the soul of the Christian would lave itself after the winds and storms of life were over.   We believe he is now enjoying the full fruition of that vision which then presented itself to his mind.

"Mr. Choate was a man of great *originality* of character.   No justice can be done to this element in this brief space.   Indeed originality did not seem to be an *element* of his mind, but was rather the *mind itself*.   While his views on ordinary subjects, would to some extent, be modified of necessity, by those of other men, yet they were often strikingly *peculiar*.   He seemed many times to take a kind of *poet's view* of men and things, and then ex-press himself in corresponding language—language which, though highly fig-urative, was, nevertheless, perfectly natural as well as striking.   His peculiar style of expression upon many subjects will long be remembered, as it made him to be greatly admired.   If his early inclinations had led him to prepare for professional life, it is believed he would have stood without a rival; for, although not much given to public speaking, even in town affairs, yet the usual *training* he would have had, with the strong mind and affluent and metaphorical language which was so natural to him, would have qualified him to shine at the Bar.   The lines of Gray are applicable in his case :

> "'Full many a gem of purest ray serene,
>   The dark, unfathomed caves of ocean bear.'

"Let no one, however, suppose that these elements of greatness led him to exercise any feeling of superiority over others; for whoever else might be led to view him in the light we have attempted to describe, no suspicion of such a thing ever seemed to have entered his mind.   He was the firm and consist-ent friend of the Temperance cause in the day when its friends were few, and remained so through life. In short, he lived the supporter of good order, and died in hopes of a happy immortality, through the merits of a Redeemer. Four daughters and two sons remain to mourn his loss—a loss for which they have the sympathies of all who knew him."

1864. June 21st. Hardy's Hall and the engine-house opposite, at the easterly end of the causeway, were destroyed by fire. The next year a new engine-house was built, at a cost of $1,130.

December 26th. The Sabbath-school of the Congregational Church celebrated the fiftieth anniversary of its establishment, by public exercises in the afternoon and evening. The pastor presided, and an historical address was delivered by the superintendent.

1865. The town statistics were as follows:

Population, 1601. Number of persons of foreign birth, 82; of colored persons, 21; of persons over eighty years of age, 21; of deaf, dumb, blind or insane, 15; of paupers, 5 (three of them over eighty years of age); of legal voters, 442; of families, 434; of dwellings, 319; of schools, 9; of pupils between the ages of five and fifteen, 342.

Value of real estate, $568,378; of personal estate, $318,168; total $886,546. Value of the town property, $8,000. Town debt $20,760.51, of which all but $1,535.91, was incurred during the War of the Rebellion Number of acres of land taxed, 7,917. Number of horses, 137; of oxen, 118; of cows, 315. Amount of money raised by taxation, $13,688.31, viz: State tax, $4,700; county tax, 1,049.90; towards the payment of the town debt, 2,000; for schools, $2,000; for other town charges, $3,500; overlaying $396.50; highway tax of non-residents, $40.25; delinquent highway tax, $1.66.

VESSEL BUILDING.*

Mention was made on pages sixty and sixty-one of the location of the first public yard granted by the town in 1668, for vessel-building and of the origin of this business. But it was not until the early part of the present century that it began to be one of any considerable importance. Even then it was confined almost entirely to the construction of "standing-room," "pink-stern" boats of ten or twelve tons burthen. These had two masts, but no bowsprit. They were decked over with the exception of a

---

* Furnished by Caleb Cogswell, Esq.

space in the middle, where were two rooms across the boat nearly to the sides, for the crew to stand in while fishing. In rough weather these rooms were covered with hatches. The deck had no railing. The stern was sharp like the bow. *The building yards* then were for the most part near the dwellings of the builders, in some instances not more than twenty feet from the front door. Some of the yards were more than a mile from the river. The vessels when completed were loaded on two pairs of wheels with string pieces, one on each side, to keep them steady and upright. When hauled to the launching place the wheels were run into the river until the vessel was " water-borne." and then she unloaded herself. The largest vessel hauled and launched in this way was one of fifty-five tons, built by Charles Choate on the premises now owned and occupied by Jonathan Low. These yards were gradually given up as the demand for larger vessels increased ; and " boat-haulings" went out of vogue about the year 1835. The *last pink-stern* vessel was one of thirty-five tons, built in 1844 by Ebenezer Burnham.

The *first square-stern* vessel was built by the late Parker Burnham, 1st.* The largest square-stern vessel before the last war with England was the brig Silkworm of two hundred and twenty tons, built in 1811 at Hardy's Point in the North District, by *Capt.* Parker Burnham.† As the fishing business in which the people had been largely engaged, decreased and was gradually given up—cod-fishing about the year 1825, and mackerel-fishing about ten years later—vessel-building was entered into more extensively. The road to the Falls landing was opened in 1823 to furnish additional

---

* Parker Burnham, 1st, was born in a house near Chebacco Pond, and lived there the most of his life, but was a member of the family of his son, David Burnham, in the Central District, at the time of his death, which occurred in 1856, when he had reached the age of ninety-two. It is said that he was never under the care of a physician for a single day in his life. Mr. Burnham was considered one of the best constructors and master carpenters of his day, and in later years was frequently consulted by builders who needed the benefit of his experience and skill.

† Parker Burnham, 2d, (son of Enoch and nephew of Parker, 1st,) He made several voyages, as master, in this brig, the first one to Lisbon.

44

facilities for the growing business, and for many years the work was carried on there. Vessels of a larger class also began to be more commonly built—barks, brigs and three-masted schooners—some of them of upwards of three hundred tons measurement. In 1828, forty vessels were built and for four years up to 1834, the average amount of tonnage annually built was two thousand five hundred tons. The average price per ton then was $25.

The prosperity of the business has greatly varied, but not a single year has passed in which at least *one* vessel has not been built. From November, 1851, to November, 1852, sixty vessels, of seventy-five tons burthen on the average, were built—the largest number in one year. The average price per ton was $35; the number of workmen employed, about one hundred and fifty. *The greatest number* built in one year, *by one man*, was *thirteen*, viz., by Andrew Story. In 1856-7, Aaron Burnham, 2d, built twenty-two vessels in twenty-two months. The *shortest time* in which a vessel has been *entirely* built, was *one month*. It was the schooner "July," of fifty tons, built by Capt. Parker Burnham, in the month of July, 1837. *The largest vessel* ever built in town was the ship "Ann Maria" of five hundred and ten tons. It was constructed in 1842, at Clay Point, by a company of workmen, of which Ebenezer Burnham was the agent, and Jacob Burnham, 2d, the master-carpenter. The next in size, was a three-masted schooner of four hundred and seven tons, built by James & McKenzie on the "corporation" wharf, in 1855. For ten or twelve years past, the vessels have generally been of a larger class than formerly. In March, 1864, there were twelve on the stocks, the average measurement of which was one hundred and ten tons.

The yards now used are ten in number, and are on or near the main road through the town from the Central to the East District. It is estimated that the *amount of capital* employed in the business, for the last twenty years, has been from $150,000 to $200,000.

In the construction of these vessels, all kinds of oak timber are used. The stem and stern posts are usually of white oak. Rock maple is used for keels. Birch, maple and elm are also used in the frame. The top-timbers and the " out-board " plank are of white oak. The " in-board " plank is of the same material, of a cheaper quality. The deck-plank, masts and bowsprits are of white pine and the small spars of spruce. For the most part, the timber used has been obtained in this State. Some of it has come from Maine and New Hampshire. For several years before the late war, much of the white oak planking was brought from the Southern States. The masts and small spars are obtained chiefly in New Hampshire. Sticks for bowsprits, and trees suitable for deck-plank, are still found to some extent in our own woodlands. Half a century ago, *rigging* for vessels was made in town by Capt. Nathaniel Burnham and Mr. Samuel Hardy. Anchors also were made here by our blacksmiths. But for many years past, rigging, sails and anchors have been procured and brought here by the purchasers of the vessels.

The two most active and prominent builders for forty years from the close of the war with England in 1815 have been Mr. Abel Story and the late Mr. Adam Boyd. Mr. Boyd built, in all, about two hundred vessels—a larger number than any other man. *Other builders* from 1816–20 to 1840 have been as follows:

John Boyd, Benjamin Burnham, 2d, Eli F. Burnham, Gilman M. Burnham, Issacher Burnham, John S. Burnham, Michael Burnham, Moses Burnham, 3d, Nathan Burnham, Nathan Burnham, 3d, Noah Burnham, Parker Burnham, 2d, Samuel Burnham, Zaccheus Burnham, Charles Choate, Dudley Choate, John Choate, Joseph Choate, John Dexter, John Hardy, Thomas Hardy, Enoch Low, Joshua Low, Charles Roberts, David Story, Epes Story, Ephraim Story, 2d, Jacob Story, Jonathan Story, 3d, Michael Story, 2d, Perkins Story.

Builders from 1838–40 to the present time and still engaged in the business (with the exception of Parkhurst & Courtney) are as follows:

Aaron Burnham, 2d, Ebenezer Burnham, Jeremiah Burnham, Luke Burnham, Oliver Burnham, Willard R. and Daniel Burnham, James & McKenzie, Job Story, Joseph Story and Brothers, Benjamin Courtney, Charles B. Parkhurst.

EMIGRANTS FROM ESSEX.

The many and valuable contributions which this town has made to the population of other places from time to time, particularly during the last century, should not be forgotten or overlooked in its published annals. The sons and daughters of old Chebacco and their descendants are scattered throughout New England and in many of the Middle and Western States. Several towns have been in part, settled by them. Among these is *Dunbarton, N. H.,* the centennial celebration of whose settlement occurred *September 13th of this year.* On that occasion, Rev. A. W. Burnham, D. D., of Rindge, N. H., delivered an address commemorative of the early inhabitants, some extracts from which, with other facts furnished by him, are as follows:

"The *Storys and Burnhams* came from Ipswich, Mass., Chebacco parish, the hive of these names, and were trained under the ministry of Rev. John Cleaveland, one of the "new lights" and able preachers of his day, a disciple of Whitefield. They emigrated from Chebacco about 1765–70, and settled in a cluster in one neighborhood in the beautiful southern section of this town. They were all respectable and useful citizens, and have left good families.

"The *Burnhams* were Asa, Nathan and Thomas, who were brothers, and Abraham, John, and Samuel cousin to John. *Samuel* Burnham was the son of Samuel, and was born in Chebacco, October 5, 1744. He married Mary Perkins. They had fifteen children, all but two of whom lived to mature years. At first, after their settlement in Dunbarton, they with two children were wont to ride one horse seven miles to meeting on the Sabbath; and were obliged to send their children two miles on foot through the woods to school. Of their seven sons, four were educated at Dartmouth College. These were Samuel, *fitted for college on the plow-beam,* graduated in 1795, the first college graduate from the town, a teacher, and the first principal of Pinkerton Academy, Derry, N. H., who died in 1834, aged 67; Rev. Abraham, D. D., graduated in 1804, pastor of the Congregational Church, Pembroke, N. H., forty-two years, died in 1852, aged 77; John, graduated in 1807, a lawyer, a man of uncommon energy and an accomplished scholar, died in 1826, aged 45; and Rev. Amos Wood Burnham, D. D., born August 1, 1791, graduated in 1815 and at Andover Theological Seminary in 1818, the first principal of Pembroke Academy, N. H., pastor of the Congregational Church in Rindge, N. H., from November 14, 1821, to November

14, 1867, forty-six years, and then dismissed at his own request. Of the *forty* college graduates from this town of less than a thousand inhabitants, *one-half are descendants of Samuel Burnham.*

"The wives of the brothers *David and Daniel Story* who emigrated to Dunbarton at the same time, were also Burnhams, sisters of Abraham. *David Story, Esq.*, was a son of Stephen and grandson of Jacob Story. He was first cousin to Jacob (father of Mr. Abel Story), and to Jonathan (father of Esq. Jonathan Story). Of a sound and well-balanced mind, looking well to the interests of the town and acting always according to his convictions of duty, he was a leader in all public affairs through life. He was seventeen times moderator in town-meeting, town clerk eleven years, selectman six years, representative to the Legislature six years, and one of the two justices of the peace for a long period. Rev. Dr. Harris of this town (Dunbarton), pronounced him among the best citizens, and the best magistrate within his knowledge. Like Samuel Burnham, he was a staunch old-fashioned Federalist. He was a man of rather impressive presence. As the custom then was, we boys made our bows to every passer by, whether in the road or around the school-house. In this matter we were very exact when Esq. Story passed, on his stately horse, with whip in hand in perpendicular position; and we felt honored by his invariable response, 'brave boys—brave scholars.' He had three sons, David, Warren and Abraham Burnham Story, Esq., (who graduated at Brown University in 1799,) and five daughters."

Somewhat later, several Chebacco people migrated to *Londonderry*, in the same State, of whom the following statement is made in the history of that town, published in 1851:

"About 1785–90 the town received a valuable accession of settlers from Ipswich, Mass. They were of the true Puritan race and retained all those excellences of character, that distinguished the pilgrim band which settled that ancient town. They had been trained up under the ministry of Rev. Messrs. Rogers, Cleaveland, Frisbie and Dana, men distinguished for learning and piety. Many of them became distinguished not only as intelligent and useful citizens, but as efficient members of the church, and their descendants are among the most valuable inhabitants of the town."

Of the twelve emigrants mentioned by name in that history, seven were natives of Chebacco: John Burnham, Aaron Choate, James Choate, William Choate, Joseph Cogswell, Benjamin Procter and Joseph Procter.

John Burnham was a brother of the Samuel who settled in Dunbarton, and was born in Chebacco, December

10, 1749. The following account of his services in the Revolutionary war is derived from his own statement:*

Soon after the battle of Lexington, he was appointed first lieutenant in a company raised in Gloucester, marched to Cambridge the last of May and was in the battle of Bunker's Hill. His company reached *the fort* just as the action began, and fought bravely to the last. In 1776, he was in the battles of Long Island and of Trenton. January 1, 1777, Lieut. Col. Brooks appointed him captain, and gave him recruiting orders. "Next morning, having traveled about eight miles, heard firing and supposing the armies had come together, *returned and went out to the advance party.* Fought on a retreat till we came into Trenton. The next night we marched to Princeton, and *took the enemy there.* Then I went to Gloucester, and raised a company. In the Spring, was ordered to the Northern army, where Col. Brooks appointed me captain of the Light Infantry company in his regiment, the Eighth Massachusetts. Was in all the actions until the surrender of Burgoyne, including the storming of the works at Saratoga."

The next winter we find Capt. Burnham, in Washington's army at Valley Forge ; and in the following campaign in the engagement at Monmouth, and in the storming of Stony Point, in which daring and successful assault, he was the second in command in his regiment. In the campaign of 1780, he served first under Lafayette, and then under Gen. Greene. In the siege of Yorktown, "I had the honor to be in a party under Col. Alexander Hamilton, which stormed one of the two batteries, which were first taken from the British." Early in 1782, his regiment was quartered near the Hudson River. On one occasion while there, it was paraded for inspection by Baron Steuben, the Inspector General. After the other formalities of the inspection, "he told me to order my company to 'search arms.' At the word, the men opened pans, drew ramrods, and letting them down with a little force, they rebounded very well. The Baron lifted up both hands, and exclaimed, 'Mine Gott! It is all silver.' He then said to the officers with him, ' Come here and help me admire this companie.' Next, turning to me, he said, ' You need not show me your books. I will not inspect your companie. I will admire it.'" The general orders, of the day following a general review of the army, soon after, contained this high compliment. " *The commander-in-chief,* (Washington) *did not think he ever saw a company under arms, make a more soldier-like and military appearance than did the Light Infantry company of the Eighth Massachusetts Regiment.*" His Colonel (Brooks, afterwards Governor of Massachusetts) subsequently said, "I know Capt. Burnham well. He was one of the best disciplinarians and most gal-

---

*The year before his death, being then totally blind but with mental faculties unimpaired, he dictated a narrative of his experiences in the war, the whole of which is of thrilling interest, and which was published in the Farmers' Monthly Visitor, Manchester, N. H., in 1852.

lant officers of the Revolution." Gen. and Gov. Pierce, (father of ex-President Pierce,) also said, " Capt. John Burnham was a most excellent disciplinarian. He was not second to any man in the army of his rank. Duty, with him, superseded every other consideration. I was in the Eighth Regiment with him about six years, and a witness to his indefatigable services." On the 9th of January, 1783, "after having commanded this *beautiful companie* six years, and been with them in every action, I was commissioned Major." January 1, 1784, he was discharged, when the last regiments were disbanded ; leaving behind him a record of service for his country, of which his family and his native Chebacco may well be proud.

After the close of the war, Maj. Burnham married Abby Collins of Gloucester, and for a time lived on the same homestead as his ancestor, Dea. John Burnham, the first settler. Towards the close of the last century he removed to Derry. In 1798, he was dismissed from the Chebacco church to the church then about to be formed in that place, and in 1810 was chosen deacon of it. He died June 8, 1843, aged 94. His children were six in number, Samuel, John, George, and three daughters, one of whom, Mrs. Abigail, wife of Jonathan Ireland, Esq., of Dunbarton, is still living. Maj. Burnham is remembered in Derry, as a robust, soldierly-looking man ; and by those most competent to judge, was very highly esteemed as a man of well-balanced and vigorous mind, unflinching integrity and decision, of unblemished moral character and a stern patriot. He has left a precious memory in the town of his adoption.

Of the other emigrants to Derry, the following facts have been collected : .

James Choate, who served under Maj. Burnham, was a son of Humphrey Choate. After the battle of Long Island, August 27, 1776, when Washington's army was to effect a retreat by water, under cover of night, from close proximity to a victorious enemy, he was one of those who were "detailed for boat service, being so much of a *sea-boy,*" and aided in rowing the troops across from Brooklyn to New York. Of the scenes of that night, (August 29,) he was wont to give his children vivid descriptions in after years, as he would also of the execution of Andre, which he witnessed. Mr. Choate married a Miss Perkins of Chebacco, and removed to Derry in February, 1786. He was selectman seven years, and filled other important offices. Two of his sons, Nehemiah and Humphrey, are still living. *William Choate* was a second cousin of James, and married his sister. He was several times representative to the Legislature, and was often moderator of town meetings and selectman. His son William, still living, was for nearly a quarter of a century moderator of town meetings, treasurer of Pinkerton Academy, and in all town affairs a very active citizen. *Aaron Choate* was a first cousin of James, and they married sisters. He was also a soldier of the Revolution. He went to Derry a little later than James, and like him was prominent in civil affairs.

Among the emigrants from Chebacco to various other parts of the country, who have not been already mentioned in this history, was *Jonathan Burnham*, a son of Jonathan Jr., and Elizabeth Procter Burnham, and a first cousin of the late Capt. Nathaniel Burnham. He was born in 1738. He removed to Rye, N. H., and entered the Revolutionary army from that town. During the war he rose to the rank of Colonel; and through life was "a man much respected and of much influence." He died in Salisbury, Mass., March 17, 1823.

THE CLAM BUSINESS.

For the last twenty years about fifty men and boys have been employed chiefly in the Spring and Fall, in digging clams for fishing-bait. For this purpose the clam-flats in each town, are, by law, free to all its residents, and to no others. Five bushels of clams in the shell, it is usually reckoned, make one bushel of "meats;" about two and a half bushels of the latter are put into each barrel, and this quantity an able-bodied man can dig in three tides. One bushel of dry salt is used for each barrel. During this period of twenty years, about two thousand barrels of clams have been dug yearly, on the average and sold at an average price of six dollars per barrel. Deducting for the cost of the barrel $1.00, and of the salt for it $0.75, the sum of $4.25 per barrel or $8,500 per year has been earned in this business. The bait is marketed chiefly in Gloucester.

1866. August 31st, died Capt. Winthrop Low. The following sketch of his life and character appeared not long after in the Salem Register:

"Notwithstanding the lapse of time since the decease of Capt. Low, the writer of this sketch is unwilling that his memory should pass quite away, without one small effort to prevent it. Nearly the whole of his fourscore years having been passed in his native village, and his habits having been so eminently social, he was a man whom everybody knew, and with more truthfulness than perhaps is common, it may be said, his loss is one which many will regret.

"In early life Mr. Low was for a time a student at Atkinson Academy, and subsequently, an instructor in the common school. The retirement and occupations of his father's farm, however, were more congenial with his feelings, ever taking time, however, to inform himself fully on matters of public interest. He was a constant reader even in his youth, of the ablest Boston papers, selecting them with the greatest care. His reading subsequently, however, was by no means confined to the issues of the newspaper press; this, the monthlies upon his table and the substantial volumes in his library, abundantly show. In a knowledge of the public finances, both of the State and the nation, it is believed that few were his superiors, and in relation to the theory of government, few it is believed had studied it more assiduously than he.

"The social character of our friend, before referred to, led him to enjoy the discussion of such subjects as from time to time agitated the public mind, whether relating to political, moral or educational interests. He was among the firmest friends of Common Schools, acting at times upon the town school committee, and at other times visiting them unofficially. It was about the year 1837, when visiting at Claxton and Wightman's, makers of philosophical instruments, in company with the writer, that Capt. Low purchased from his own ample funds, a fine case of valuable instruments, which he presented to the Central School in Essex, thus supplying a great necessity and affording facilities for advanced scholars, altogether unknown in the town before.

"One of the noblest chapters in the life of our friend, is that which relates to the stand taken by him in the early days of the temperance reform. It was near the commencement of Mr. Goodell's labors, that he presented the subject in Essex, and it may be said too, it was a time when it cost something to raise the temperance flag. When volunteers were called for by Mr. Goodell, at the close of his address, the first man to rise was Capt. Winthrop Low, followed by six more only, at that time. He never receded from the ground then taken, either in theory or practice, to the last hour of his life, except to make the rule more stringent and comprehensive.

"Capt. Low was a consistent, liberal supporter of the institutions of religion, according to what is usually called the orthodox faith. Ministers of the gospel were welcome at his house; indeed for several years last past, his doors were opened to the weekly prayer meeting in its turn.

"His mind was well stored with Bible truth, having always been as wakeful a hearer, as he was careful a reader. His power of attention was so great, even in his childhood, that he could recollect particular expressions in the prayers of Rev. Mr. Cleaveland, uttered sixty years before, and repeat them as he did to a grandson of Mr. C., but a short time before he died. In cul-

45

tivating this power of attention, our departed friend was certainly an example worthy of imitation by all young people.

"I have spoken of Capt. L.'s fondness for discussion ; but it should not be forgotten or misunderstood, that although he was often earnest and even ardent, it by no means follows that he was passionate. A tendency in this direction is somewhat natural to man, perhaps, and it is not improbable that even he may have found it needful to guard against it. As bearing upon this point, and at the same time expressing a desire paramount in importance to all others, I present the following slip found amongst his papers, and believe it will be regarded by all his friends, now that he is gone, as of inexpressible value :

"'1818, June 21. I hereby promise through God's assistance, to live in peace with all men. May He be pleased to give me that peace of mind and that hope of a glorious immortality, which is rather to be chosen above all the riches and honors that can be conferred upon me by my fellow-men.   WINTHROP LOW.'

"Mention has already been made of Mr. Low's knowledge of the Bible. He usually read without a commentary, not that he undervalued such aids, having had Scott at least always at hand ; but he appeared to prefer the language of the Bible itself. And it was remarked by his watchers and others, in his last illness, that his quotations of scripture were given with verbal accuracy.

"As Capt. Low strongly felt for, and sympathized with the sick and sorrowful, so he in turn received the sympathies and kind offices of his family and friends in his last sickness with deep gratitude. But he is gone ; and though the places that once knew him will know him no more, yet there are few who knew him that will soon forget the kind and benevolent heart of Capt. Winthrop Low. He died at the good old age of 81 years, much respected and lamented."

FAMILY RELICS.

In the possession of Capt. Low's family is a cane with a head of bone, encircled by a broad band of silver where it is joined to the cane, which was brought from England. On it is this inscription, "Owned in ye Family, Eng^d about 1573 ; D. L., U. America, March 14, 1803." But the most highly prized memorial of antiquity owned by Capt. Low was a copy of the Scriptures printed in 1579, pp. 554, quarto, brought to this country by Capt. John Low and handed down in the family from father to son as an heir-loom. It is, therefore, nearly three hundred years of age, and is undoubtedly the oldest bible in town. "It is what is called the Geneva edition, and was translated by Miles Coverdale, one of the earliest of the English reformers, William Whittingham, and other eminent Hebrew scholars. They were more than two years in completing the version, and they very closely adhere to the original tongues. The 23d Psalm commences thus :

"'1. The Lord is my Shepcheard, I shal not want. 2. He maketh me to rest in greene pasture, & leadeth me by the stil waters.'

" The title-page and several leaves at the beginning are missing, but at the close of the Gospels the printer has given his name and the date of publication, of which the following is a fac simile :

Imprinted at Lon-
don by Chriſtopher Barker,

Printer to the Queenes moſt
excellent Maieſtie dwelling
in Paternoſter Rowe,
at the ſigne of the
Tygres head

Anno 1579.

" Besides the Scriptures, the book contains the celebrated version of the Psalms in meter, by Sternhold & Hopkins—a rare curiosity—under the following title : The whole Booke of Psalmes collected into English metre by Thom. Stern, John Hopkins and others, conferred with the Ebrue, with apt notes to sing them withal. At London, Printed by John Daye, dwelling over Aldersgate. An. 1578. *Cum Privilegio Regiae Majestatis.*

" This in part, was the music our forefathers sung. Among the tunes, which are in diamond notes, and consist of the air only, is the ' Qld Hundredth,' written nearly as we now sing it. The version of the 18th Psalm which has greatly puzzled the wits of the critics and which one of them avowed that he would rather have made, than to have been Emperor of Brazil, has the two following stanzas which are still retained in some of our hymnals :

'The Lord descended from above,
and bowed the heavens hye,
And underneath his feete he cast
the darkness of the sky ;
On cherubes & on cherubins
full royally he rode,
And on the winges of all the windes
came flying all abroade.'

" The volume is also enriched with various comments, tables, indices, etc., which attest the skill and laudable painstaking of the learned translators. It has, also, a valuable chronological record under the following quaint title :

" ' A perfite supputation of the yeeres and times from the creation of the world vnto this present yeere of our Lord God 1578.' "

On the blank leaves of the book are written the following names : " Susana Low her Book 1677, May 19 ;" " Thomas Low his Book " (apparently written about the same time) ; " Samuel Low," and " John Low."

THE GREAT BRIDGE.

The third " great bridge " on the present site was built by Mr. Uriah G. Spofford. The first one, which had no draw, was built in 1811 by order of the Court of Sessions

by Moody Spofford, Esq., of Georgetown.   Up to that time
the bridge and the course of the highway had been north-
east of the space now occupied by the mills.   In 1823 a
second bridge with a draw twenty-four feet wide, was built
by Jonathan Story, Esq.   In 1842, all above the piers of
this bridge was built anew by Mr. John Choate.

In re-building this year (1866), the abutments remained the same.   On the
old mud-sills which were two feet four inches below low water-mark, a *new
foundation* consisting of ten sticks of timber, six of them twenty-two feet
long, fourteen inches wide and ten inches thick, was laid across the river, and
bolted to the old timbers.   Four sills each thirty-five feet in length, twelve
inches thick and sixteen inches wide, were placed on this new foundation and
secured by bolts, the vacancies between the timbers filled with stone and
gravel, and the whole ballasted with stone.

The *frame* of the bridge consists of four piers, each having three posts,
two of which are ten inches by twelve, and the third ten inches by ten, a cap
twelve inches by fourteen, and one tier of girts ten inches by ten.   The gird-
ers from pier to pier are also ten inches by ten, and there are seventy-two
braces in all, each four inches by six.   Every part of the frame is of oak,
and the timbers are pinned together by seasoned locust pins one and one-
eighth inches in diameter.   The covering timbers are of the best pine, seven
inches by sixteen, except the draw-timbers which are nine inches by fourteen.

The roadway is covered with four-inch spruce plank, and on the sides has
a tight board fence.   The draw is hoisted in the same manner as before.
The length of the bridge between the abutments is seventy-two feet; the
roadway is fifteen feet above the foundation, and twenty-four feet in width,
except the draw, which is twenty feet eight inches in width.   The cost of the
structure was $3,800.

The *chief improvement* over the old bridge consists in
a nearly level roadway, the rise being only four inches.
The idea of this was first suggested by D. W. Bartlett,
Esq., and the application of it made by the builder.   The
draw hangings were also invented as well as constructed
by Mr. Spofford, the peculiar features being a truss timber
attached to each draw-timber underneath, and another on
the top of each outside draw-timber at the end where
they meet.

1867.   October 12th, Richardson's Hall was dedicated.
It is situated in the Central Village near the junction of
the three roads to Ipswich, Gloucester and Hamilton, its

dimensions are thirty-five by fifty feet, and the cost of the building was $5,000.

December 5th occurred the dedication of a new school-house in the Falls District. This building is located upon the northerly side of the highway leading from Essex to Hamilton, and opposite the entrance to the road leading to the "landing." It is thirty-one feet in width by forty-one feet in length, and two stories in hight; was commenced May 9, 1867, and finished November 25th. The builder was Mr. Procter P. Perkins. The cost of the land on which it was erected was $402.50; of the foundation, $360; of the building itself, $3,750; of the fencing and grading, the stoves and other furniture, the blinds and bell, such as to make the whole expenditure nearly $6,000. The two school-rooms contained in it are each thirty feet square, and together can conveniently accommodate one hundred and twenty scholars. The number of pupils in attendance in both departments on the opening of the building for school purposes, was one hundred and twelve. Capt. Francis Burnham presided at the meeting convened for the dedication of the house, assisted by Mr. Perkins Story and Capt. David Low as vice-presidents. The exercises were as follows:

Introductory address by the President; singing by a choir consisting of Nehemiah Burnham Esq., Mr. Coeleb Burnham, Mrs. Lucy M. Burnham, Mrs. Mary F. Morris and Miss Susan E. Story; Historical sketch by Mr. Nathaniel Burnham; Singing; Poem by Mr. Coeleb Burnham; Singing; Dedicatory address by Mr. Michael Burnham; Reading of letters from William W. Pendergast, Esq., of Hutchinson, Minn., Capt. Samuel Burnham and Hon. David Choate; Dedicatory prayer by Rev. J. M. Bacon; Singing of "America" by the audience.

1868.   Daniel W. Bartlett, Esq., was appointed post-master, July 1st, and the post office removed to Richardson's building on Martin street.

CHAPTER VII.

THE DOINGS OF THE TOWN WITH REFERENCE TO THE WAR OF THE REBELLION,

WITH SKETCHES OF THE SOLDIERS,

COLLECTED FROM THEM, EITHER VERBALLY OR IN WRITING.

BY HON. DAVID CHOATE.

[SOME account of the doings of the Town, and of the soldiers it has furnished, during the late Rebellion, will form an appropriate close to the foregoing History. And it may properly be premised, that in speaking or writing of *passing or recent events,* DIFFICULTIES must obviously be encountered, entirely unknown and unfelt when dealing with the *dead past.* And in speaking of PERSONS, reading, thinking *persons,* the difficulties referred to, are *immeasurably augmented,* for reasons too obvious to require explanation. The simple fact that one soldier may have but a small space assigned to him, while another, no more meritorious perhaps, may have pages assigned to him, may sometimes call forth *criticisms* and perhaps *denunciations.* A little reflection, however, will show that, for nearly every sketch of those now living, the compiler, from the nature of the case, must be beholden to the soldier himself or his personal friends; and further, that while many of our brave men kept no journal of events, others did keep them, and more or less full and copious according to their opportunities and fancies. Nothing, therefore, is to be inferred on the score of *comparative merit,* from the amount of space allotted to different men. Of some, even the briefest descriptions have been drawn out only after *repeated solicitations,* while others have furnished statements cheerfully and more fully than could be inserted.

But the difficulties of *arrangement* have also been quite as insuperable. Like the author of the "Great Rebellion," we must say that "being compelled to write the sketches of the soldiers, just as the materials presented themselves, or could be found, all regard to arrangement was abandoned of necessity." Some substitute for this may be found in the Summary or Recapitulation forming an Index to this chapter; but such have been the difficulties in this case, that the compiler can only hope that a generous indulgence will be conceded by every reader, and especially by the soldiers themselves, or their surviving friends.]

THE PRESIDENT'S FIRST CALL FOR VOLUNTEERS.

It was not until the 3d of May, 1861, that the President issued his call for volunteers for three years or during the war. Massachusetts was requested to furnish three regiments of this number; and such was the patriotic ardor in the State, that Gov. Andrew urgently requested that he might be allowed to double that number. The

number of regiments was accordingly increased to *seven*.
And on the 17th of June, 1861, ten more regiments having
been offered by the State, were accepted by the general
government, and they were all put into the field by the
8th of October in the same year.   Under the above mentioned call, the following named persons, forty-eight in
number, enlisted from Essex, viz.:

Andrews, Charles E.	Butman, John C.	Lee, John F.
Andrews, Cyrus	Claiborne, George C.	Low, William B.
Andrews, Mon. Misson	Clifford, David E.	Low, William E.
Andrews, Prince A.	Coose, William D.	Lufkin, Charles P.
Andrews, Reuben	Crafts, John, Jr.	Lufkin, William
Andrews, Stephen P.	Dodge, George	Martyn, John L.
Andrews, William A.	Duggan, Daniel	McIntire, Edward E.
Burnham, Harlan P.	Hardy, George C.	Mears, Henry C.
Burnham, John B.	Haskell, James Frederic	Morse, Charles F.
Burnham, Mark F.	Haskell, William P.	Morse, Thomas A.
Burnham, R. W., Jr.	Hatch, Jason	Ross, George
Burnham, Rufus	Hayden, William	Sargent, George H.
Burnham, William H.	Howard, William S.	Sargent, O. H. P.
Burnham, William H. H.	Howes, Edwin A.	Story, Aaron Herbert
Burnham, Zenas	Howes, Erastus	Swett, Simeon
Butman, Ancill K.	Jones, Samuel Q.	Wentworth, George S.

TOWN ACTION.

At a legal town meeting on the 17th of June, 1861, it
was voted to pay the sum of $1.50 per week to the wife
and each of the children, under sixteen years of age, of
any inhabitant of the town who has been, or may hereafter be, mustered into the military or naval service of
the United States, and a like sum to any child, parent,
brother or sister of such inhabitant, who, at the time of
his enlistment, were dependent on him for support.   Also
voted to appropriate $1,000 to carry this vote into effect.

Another meeting of the town to aid the families of
volunteers was held July 27, 1861, at which it was voted,
—agreeably to a report made by O. H. P. Sargent, U. G.
Spofford, Oliver Burnham, D. W. Bartlett and Moses
Knowlton, Jr., being a committee previously appointed
for that purpose,—to pay to any single person dependent

on the volunteer for support, *two dollars per week; for two persons*, three dollars per week; for three persons, four dollars per week; for four persons, four dollars and fifty cents per week; for five persons, five dollars per week, and provided that in no case shall any family receive more than five dollars per week.   And the votes passed at the meeting on the 17th of June, (above recorded) were reconsidered.

On the 1st of June, 1862, a company of cadets from Boston, and a company from Salem, were ordered to Fort Warren to do garrison duty for six months.   Capt. Staten of the Salem company received orders to recruit his company with volunteers, and the following named persons volunteered into his company from Essex, viz:

Allen, Joseph G.	Bartlett, Jacob	Gilbert, John F.
Andrews, Alburn	Burnham, Alfred M.	Howes, Webster
Andrews, Ira, Jr.	Burnham, Jesse	Low, Edward
Andrews, William H.	Burnham, Otis	McIntire, William H.

They were ordered to Fort Warren in Boston Harbor on the 30th of June, 1862, for six months.

THE PRESIDENT'S NEXT CALL FOR THREE HUNDRED THOUSAND MEN.

On the 1st day of July, 1862, President Lincoln issued his next call for volunteers to form new regiments and to fill old ones.

TOWN ACTION.

A town meeting was held on the 21st of July, 1862, " to see what action the town would take to encourage enlistments;" whereupon, it was voted that a bounty of $150 be paid to each man who should enlist under the President's call.   The following persons enlisted and received the bounty of $150, viz.:

Andrews, Horatio N.	Burnham, David B.	Burnham, Wilbur
Andrews, Timothy, Jr.	Burnham, George S.	Channel, John C.
Burnham, Albert F.	Burnham, George W.	Coy, Michael
Burnham, Charles A.	Burnham, James Horace	Dodge, William G.
Burnham, Daniel	Burnham, Osgood E.	Guppy, George F.

Hart, John F.

Haskell, Albert A.

Hull, William H.

Jones, John S.

Lander, Edward L.

Mears, Rufus E.

Mears, Samuel, Jr.

Parsons, John J.

Poland, Jeremiah, Jr.

Story, Asa

Story, David L.

Tucker, Joseph W.

Varnum, John

Wentworth, George S.

THE PRESIDENT'S FIRST ORDER TO DRAFT THREE HUNDRED THOUSAND MEN.

On the 4th of August, 1862, the President, by proclamation, ordered a draft of three hundred thousand militia to be immediately called into service.

TOWN ACTION.

A meeting was held agreeably to legal notice, " to see what action the town would take to fill its quota." It was voted to pay a bounty of $200 to each man, the town's quota being thirty-two, and the following named persons enlisted, pursuant to the President's said call, and to the action of the town, viz.:

Andrews, Israel F.

Andrews, Lyman B.

Burnham, Albert F.

Burnham, George F., 2d

Burnham, Horace

Burnham, Ira F.

Burnham, Lamont G.

Burnham, Leonard

Burnham, Lewis

Callehan, Daniel

Callehan, Maurice

Chase, Lyman B.

Crafts, Franklin

Crafts, John, Jr.

Crockett, Charles P.

Duggan, Morty

Hardy, Alphonso M.

Hayden, Luther

Howes, Charles

Jackson, Andrew

James, Washington W.

Kelleher, John

Kimball, James B.

Low, Aaron

Mahoney, Thomas

Marston, Charles, Jr.

McEachen, John

Mears, Francis Gilbert

Prest, Robert

Procter, Charles W.

Procter, Joseph, Jr.

Riggs, Solomon A.

In order to a continuous history of the town in its connection with the Rebellion, it may be stated that in the case of this draft, the quota of the State was nineteen thousand, instead of fifteen thousand as before. Gov. Andrew consequently issued an additional order for twenty-six more men from this town. Upon ascertaining, however, that the State quota was filled, the Governor released the town from responding further. Previously to the filling of the State quota, the town had *taken action* at a legal meeting for that purpose, and promptly voted $200 each for the twenty-six men additional, making $5,200, and placed the same in the Governor's hands for the purpose of securing the extra enlistments above. On discovering the State quota to be full, as before stated, the money was refunded to the town.

SECOND DRAFT OF THREE HUNDRED THOUSAND.

This draft took place July 8, 1863, and the Essex quota was forty-seven; being one hundred per cent. in addition to the town's true number of twenty-three. The following persons were drafted, to wit:

Adams, Moses - - - - Hired substitute.
Andrews, Albert - - - Accepted, and sent to the war.
Andrews, Edward N. - - Exempted.
Andrews, Elias C. - - - Exempted.
Andrews, Ezra - - - Exempted.
Andrews, Frederic Sanborn - Hired substitute.
Andrews, Rufus - - - Joined heavy artillery, unattached.
Annable, Elisha B. - - Exempted.
Annable, John J. - - - Exempted.
Burnham, Daniel - - - Accepted, and sent to the war.
Burnham, Franklin - - - Paid commutation.
Burnham, Francis C. - - Exempted for physical disability.
Burnham, James Howe - - Accepted, and sent to the war.
Burnham, Leander - - - Exempted.
Burnham, Luke Roswell - - Exempted for disability and hemoptysis.
Burnham, Nathaniel - - Exempted.
Burnham, Nehemiah - - Hired substitute.
Burnham, William A. - - Hired substitute.
Burnham, Zenas - - - Exempted.
Channel, John O. - - - Exempted.
Choate, Francis, - - - Hired substitute.
Choate, William C. - - Hired substitute.
Cogswell, Charles Berry - - Exempted.
Cogswell, Daniel Webster - - Hired substitute.   [physical disability.
Guppy, George F. - - - Accepted, but afterwards discharged for
Haskell, David L. - - - Exempted for physical disability.
Haskell, Francis P. - - Exempted for physical disability.
Haskell, Oliver S. - - - Exempted for physical disability.
Haskell, Stephen - - - Exempted.
James, John F. - - - Exempted.
Lufkin, Albert E. - - - Joined heavy artillery.

Lufkin, Alfred	· · ·	Joined heavy artillery.
Lufkin, Sewall	· · ·	Exempted.
McKenzie, Jacob	· · ·	Exempted.
Mears, Solomon P.	· · ·	Exempted.
Perkins, Gustavus S.	· · ·	Was in the navy at the time of the draft.
Perkins, Leverett	· · ·	Exempted.
Procter, John N.	· · ·	Exempted.
Reardon, Michael	· · ·	Hired substitute.
Story, Charles A.	· · ·	Exempted.
Story, Emri	· · ·	Exempted for diseased eye.
Story, Epes S.	· · ·	Exempted.
Story. Hervey	· · ·	Hired substitute.
Story, John C.	· · ·	Exempted.
Story, Newton, 2d	· · ·	Hired substitute.
Story, Pierpont	· · ·	Exempted.

THIRD DRAFT OF THREE HUNDRED THOUSAND.

The President, by his order of October 17, 1863, called for three hundred thousand men, and unless raised as volunteers by the 5th day of January, 1864, a draft was to take place. The quota of Essex was *twenty-three.* The sum of $2,600 was raised by subscription. The following named persons enlisted, but received none of the town's bounty:

Andrews, Rufus	Chase, Lyman H.	Lufkin, Alfred
Andrews, Stephen P.	Duggan, Daniel	Poland, Jeremiah, Jr.
Burnham, Abner	Howes, Edwin A.	Prest, Robert
Burnham, Robert .W., Jr.	Lufkin, Albert E.	Swett, Simeon

The following named persons enlisted from Essex, under the President's call, and received the citizen's bounty of $125 each:

Burnham, Constantine	Burnham, Mark F.	Haskell, William
	Fields, Charles H.	

The following named men were hired by the citizens' committee raised for that purpose:

Berry, John	Constantine, William	Murray, John
Brabbury, Jacob	Crawley, John	Peasley, Joseph
Butler, Thomas	Hubbard, William R.	Sunbeig, John
Cohre, Henry	McDonnell, John	Travers, Charles

And the following is a list of strangers hired by the town, twenty-seven in all, viz.:

Anderson, Charles	Cummings, Philip	Power, James
Ayres, James	Dowley, Thomas	Reed, Francis
Bannan, Thomas A.	Duffy, George	Robinson, John
Beers, William	Goss, James P.	Smith, James
Bennet, James	Huntley, Loring	Sullivan, John
Brown, John	Mackay, William	Thomson, George
Callchan, George H.	Morris, Elisha C.	Thomson, James
Collins, Richard T.	Morton, William F.	Wenborne, Arthur J.
Creighton, Samuel	Murphy, Michael	Williams, Thomas

Under an order of the President for a draft issued May 4, 1864, to fill the quotas of different States that had failed to furnish their full number of men under previous calls, the number drafted from Essex was five, as follows, viz.:

Andrews, Zeno P. - - - - -	Hired substitute.
Boyd, Charles - - - - -	Hired substitute.
Story, Charles O. - - - - -	Paid commutation, $300.
Story, William H. - - - -	Exempted.
Smith, Willard - - - - -	Hired substitute.

SKETCHES OF ESSEX SOLDIERS.

We now proceed to give a sketch of the Essex soldiers, officers and men. The apology for the length of the first article, if any such is needed, is, that the sketch may be said to apply to *large numbers* of the Forty-eighth, and although repeated attempts have been made to *use the scissors*, it has been found increasingly difficult to perceive where the work of retrenchment could most properly be made. And for the extreme brevity of a portion of the sketches, as before intimated, our apology is the scantiness of the materials, which we deeply regret.

CAPTAIN CHARLES HOWES.

Capt. Charles Howes, was born at Chatham; came to reside in Essex as a ship builder, in 1850; resides in a beautiful cottage built for himself in front of the Orthodox Church. The company (E), of which he was at first Lieutenant, and afterwards Captain, was raised in Salem and Essex, with a few exceptions. The first encampment was at the barracks in Wenham, and lasted from the 15th of September until the 4th of December, 1862, when the regiment left for Readville. On the 27th of the same month the troops were ordered to New York, where they arrived on the 28th. From New York the regiment again embarked on the 2d of January, 1863, for Baton Rouge, where they arrived on the 4th of February, and encamped about one mile from the river, at Camp Banks. The regiment was brigaded with the One Hundred and Sixteenth New York, Forty-ninth Massachusetts, and the Twenty-first Maine, under command of Col. Chapin of the One Hundred and Sixteenth New York. The muskets were received soon after the arrival at the camp, and from that time the drilling became incessant. On Monday, March 9th, orders were received to be ready to march at a moment's notice. The large tents were struck, and the shelter tents pitched. These consist of two pieces of cotton cloth, each five feet square. Two of these are buttoned together, and form a tent under which two men can sleep. Each man carries one of these pieces, when on the march. On the night of Thursday, the 12th, at eight o'clock, orders were received to report next morning at the steamboat landing, at three o'clock, in light marching order, and with one day's rations and sixty rounds of ammunition. Although these orders betokened a busy and perhaps a bloody day, yet the activity and desire of the troops to be there and to meet whatever might betide, is manifest from the fact that they were at the landing before the hour appointed, and immediately embarked on board the "Sallie Robinson." Two other steamers took the Second Louisiana and two companies of cavalry, viz: McGee's and Godfrey's, both Union troops.

Essex may well be proud of this specimen of her soldiers, for when it was first understood by the heading of the boat up the river, that their destination was Port Hudson, a long, loud shout, almost enough to shake the Sallie Robinson, rang from stem to stern. After steaming up eight miles, they arrived where the convoy were waiting, consisting of the famous gunboat Essex, as Capt. H. well designates her; the gunboat Albatross, the steam sloop-of-war, Hartford, also three mortar boats and one small armed steamer. When within five miles of Port Hudson, at a place called Springfield Landing, the troops disembarked. They took up their march at right angles with the river, and were obliged to cross a swamp half a mile in extent, appropriately called the Devil's Swamp, the water being to their waists in several places. The march was continued some seven miles into the interior, where they struck the great road from Baton Rouge to Port Hudson, and proceeded on to Baton Rouge. This seems to have transpired on Friday, the 13th of March, and the object, Captain Howes states, was to reconnoitre the road to Port Hudson, "to ascertain if any preparations had been made by the rebels to check the advance of our troops in that direction. During the excursion, several shots were fired by the rebel cavalry, damaging nothing, however, except a few of the horses." This enterprise was considered one of the most daring exploits made in that department. With a force numbering but little over one thousand men, cut off, as they were, from all support the moment they left the river, it was surprising, as the Captain well observed, that they met with no more resistance. The result was sufficient to establish the character and military prowess of the Forty-eighth. It was a march of twenty-four miles, and the first raid they had then undertaken.

And no sooner were they arrived in camp, than they received orders to march again the next morning at four o'clock. So great, however, was the exhaustion that they were permitted to rest until eight o'clock, when they were detailed to guard the rear baggage train. They were ready on time, with full ranks, and took up their march over the same road as on the day before. Their first halt was at Montecino Bayou, a stream of water eight rods wide, crossing the Port Hudson road. Captain Howes was now in command of four companies viz: Company E (his own), Company I, one company of the Massachusetts Forty-second, and one of the native Louisiana (colored). The two first named were detailed to guard the bridges, and the two latter to repair them.

With these companies, Capt. H. established a line of pickets a mile in extent around the bridges to guard against surprise, and the two companies above mentioned employed to repair the bridges, received orders from Capt. Howes where to form in case of an attack. At eight o'clock, Col. Clark, chief of Gen. Banks' staff, arrived in an ambulance, having been shot in the leg on the very road over which Capt. H. and his one thousand men had passed the day before. At the same time also, a message was received by Capt. H. from head-quarters, stating that there were from eight hundred to fifteen hundred rebel cavalry on his flank, and that they would probably attempt to destroy the bridges before morning; the orders were imperative that the bridges must be defended at all hazards. Capt. Howes then caused ropes to be stretched across the road from tree to tree, and had the covering plank taken up from the centre of one of the bridges, so that it was impossible to cross it; he also barricaded the other bridge (a pontoon) with carts, timber and other obstructions, so that the bridges might have been easily defended against almost any force. Our men, (says Capt. H.) "slept upon their arms until ten o'clock, when they were alarmed by the sound of approaching cavalry. They were at their posts in a moment," thus showing themselves ready for any emergency. The alarm proved groundless, as the approaching troops were found to be a body of Rhode Island cavalry, which had been ordered back to Baton Rouge.

Just about this time, the bombardment of Port Hudson was commenced by our fleet. Notwithstanding the intervening fifteen miles, the flashes of the guns could be seen and the reports heard. And as if to add to the sublimity of the scene, the light of the ill-fated Mississippi steamer (Union), could be seen as she went down the river on fire. Her magazine exploded when nearly opposite our camp, with a crash which seemed to shake the earth to its center. Our troops returned from before Port Hudson on the next day. Eight companies of the Forty-eighth, before quite reaching their old camping ground, received orders to return and encamp near the bridges at Montecino

Bayou, the stream before referred to, as crossing the Port Hudson road. Capt. Howes' company was detailed for picket duty on the Clinton road, running parallel, as it does, to Port Hudson road and a half mile distant, a company of the Twenty-first Maine being already there. These two companies relieved each other every four hours, thus giving a brief opportunity for sleep, which was taken under the piazza of a house near by. The company on duty, whichever it might be, was stationed in the forest. The night was one of the most rainy and disagreeable kind, and when it is recollected that the men were nearly exhausted, having been broken of their rest for the two previous nights, we begin to have some faint idea of the hardships of a soldier's life. After twenty-four hours of duty here, the company was relieved and returned to camp, where they learned that orders had been received requiring them to be ready to march at four o'clock next morning. "We were up at two A. M." says the gallant captain, and struck and packed our tents, and after waiting for marching orders until noon in vain, the tents were once more pitched and remained until Friday morning, when the whole army was ordered back to Baton Rouge, where they arrived at three P. M. In these perils, a few of the Essex men were unable to participate on account of sickness. Solomon A. Riggs and Horace Burnham, had been removed to the Hospital at New Orleans, some days before, while Ira F. Burnham and Charles P. Crockett were in the hospital at Baton Rouge. Two others, viz., Luther Hayden and John Kelleher, had been detailed for guard duty, and consequently did not go up the river on the occasion above described, but joined us the next day."

The testimony of Capt. Howes to the courage and soldier-like qualities of our Essex men is of the most honorable kind. "I CAN SAY," he writes, "IN FAVOR OF THE ESSEX MEN, THAT NONE WERE MORE PROMPT AT THE CALL OF DUTY, NONE MORE OBEDIENT TO COMMANDS, NONE WHO MADE LESS COMPLAINT DURING THE FATIGUING MARCH."

To this it may be added, that Gen. Banks issued an order in which he stated that the troops had performed everything he wished, and that his object had been accomplished—as by sending the troops up by land the rebels took their field artillery from the river, so that it was an easier matter for our fleet to run by, in order to cut off the supplies which the rebels were daily receiving by the way of Red River.

This object, thus stated, affords a key to this dangerous but patriotic enterprise. It was a key however, which even the officers in command were not allowed to have at the time. It seems to have been what is usually called a *feint*, indispensable in war, but of the object, and even of the perils of which at the time the troops knew almost nothing.

It may not have been distinctly stated as it should be to give a full understanding of the facts in the case, that on the 14th of March, 1863, Com. Farragut made an attempt with eight gun-boats and steamers, to pass the rebel batteries at Port Hudson. They started about eleven o'clock at night. The rebels, by some means, discovered the movement, and opened upon our ships. The Mississippi frigate being large, ran aground, and was abandoned and burned; sixty-five of her crew having been killed, drowned, or taken prisoners. The Hartford and Albatross only succeeded in passing the fort, the remaining five having been repulsed.

On the 27th of March, Capt. Howes remarks, that the drilling of four hours each day, after their return to Baton Rouge, together with guard duty, left but a short time for rest, especially as they had no lieutenant on duty. In five days more, viz: on the 1st of April, he is suffering from an attack of fever, and is off duty, of course. On the 3d, we find him in the general hospital, one of the Essex soldiers, Albert F. Burnham being detailed to attend him as nurse. It was not until the 17th, that he was able to rejoin the regiment, which, by that time, had moved down near the hospital and was encamped upon a level, beautiful spot near the center of the city, consequently but a short distance from the Mississippi River.

The lamented F. Gilbert Mears, also rejoined the regiment the same day, having been quite sick at the arsenal hospital. There was an alarm at midnight, between the 17th and 18th (April,) in consequence of an order from Col. O'Brien, requiring Capt. Howes to be prepared to form his company at a moment's notice, as it was announced that seven hundred rebel cavalry, outside of our pickets, were expected to make a raid into the city during the night. The alarm, however, proved groundless, and instead of a fight, the paymaster's arrival on the 23d, filled or might have filled their mouths with laughter, and their tongues with singing, and nobody have thought the worse of them for it.

Lieut. Sanders was detailed with twenty men on the morning of the 24th, for an expedition up the river to capture some cattle, which was in part a failure, as they obtained but four cows with a few horses and mules.

Capt. Howes' journal of the 5th of May, has the following painful entry : " F. Gilbert Mears was taken sick quite suddenly yesterday, and was taken to the hospital. He appears to be failing fast. Visited Mr. Crockett at the arsenal hospital. He is very sick and cannot live long. . . . . . Wilkins James of Company D is quite sick in the hospital.

May 7th. Mr. Crockett died suddenly yesterday, and we have buried him under arms to-day at the cemetery. Sergeant Mears is no worse, and the surgeon thinks he may recover ;" an expectation, which, alas ! was never to be realized, except to be again disappointed. On the 9th of April, we find Wilkins James "not so well," though Mr. Mears seemed somewhat improving. Four others came on the sick list the same day, viz : John Kellcher, Morty Duggan, Aaron Low, and Leonard Burnham. It was also on this same 9th of May, that the mortar boats began bombarding Port Hudson. The reports could be heard distinctly. Capt. Howes' company made choice of John F. Ford of Salem for second lieutenant, in the room of Lieut. Lee, resigned. Lieut. Sanders was at the same time sick, and off duty. Orders were received on the 12th of May, to cook two days' rations and be ready to march at half an hour's notice. On the 13th, one of the partially recovered soldiers, Solomon A. Riggs, came up from the hospital at New Orleans, and joined the company, though unable to do duty. As an offset to this gratifying announcement, however, we learn that on the same day, the 13th of May, Wilkins James died, and was buried the day following.

In obedience to orders received on the 18th inst., Capt. Howes took up the march for Port Hudson at half-past two o'clock, leaving twenty-four of his company behind, however, sick. At dark they halted and encamped on Merritt's plantation, and near Dudley's brigade, which, however, had been there some days. The heat of the day, together with the dusty state of the roads, made the march one of great fatigue. As soon as the muskets could be stacked, the men threw themselves upon the ground and soon knew the blessings of sleep. Marching orders were received next day, (19th May,) at noon. A march of three miles on the Port Hudson road brought them to a plain on which the whole force was brought into line of battle. This was five miles from the Port Hudson entrenchments. Our batteries shelled the woods, says the gallant captain, but we could not tempt the rebels out to a fair stand-up-fight. Three prisoners were brought in on the 20th inst., who reported that there were seven thousand troops inside the entrenchments. Capt. H. was detailed as officer of the picket guard. Early on the morning of the 21st, he received orders to report to the regiment with the picket guard. The troops were then falling in for the march, and at eight o'clock it was commenced. After a march of about four miles, the rebel artillery opened on our advance. Our artillery was now sent to the front and forced the rebels back, though slowly. Our advance was hotly contested. At three o'clock, our regiment was ordered to the front to support a battery then in position. Companies B, D and E, of the right wing, under command of Lieut. Col. O'Brien, were stationed in the woods on the right of the road, and about fifty yards in rear of the battery. The left wing were stationed on the left of the road. Capt. Howes proceeds to say, "the rebels opened a terrific fire on our battery, and we were obliged to lie down to escape the terrible shower of shot and shell that was flying about us. One of our company, Benjamin Crowell of Lynnfield, was killed by a cannon ball. After lying in this position nearly an hour, the rebel infantry charged on the left wing of our regiment, and compelled them to fall back. The right wing sprang to their feet and were in line in a moment. The rebels came up to a fence on the road, and poured a volley of musketry into our ranks. As we were outflanked, the lieutenant-colonel ordered us to fall back and rally on the colors. We fell back about seventy-five yards, formed our line again, (being all the time under their fire,) and opened on them with our musketry. The rest of the brigade came up at this time and charged on them, taking sixty-two prisoners, besides killing and wounding quite a number. The loss of our regiment in this battle was two killed, seven wounded, and eleven prisoners. Company E lost one killed, Crowell, above mentioned, and three prisoners, one of whom was James B. Kimball of Essex."

The battle here described took place, it should be remembered, on the 21st
47

of May, 1863, and was the first that Company E had seen. A mark of honor was put upon this company at the close of the fight, well understood and appreciated by military men, of however doubtful significance it might seem to others, viz: *they were put on picket duty the night following the battle, after having done the same duty the very night before;* thus showing that the company had acquired a reputation for *courage and endurance, not always secured by nine months' men.*

A rebel flag of truce was sent in next morning, 22d inst., asking permission to take away their dead, their prisoners having been sent down to Baton Rouge under guard. On the 23d, our regiment were sent a mile to the rear, where they remained that day. They received orders at ten o'clock in the evening to cook two days' rations, and be ready to march at day-light next morning. The cooks were busy all night, of course; but all was ready at the hour, and at sun-rise they were on the march for Port Hudson. Before starting they heard the welcome rumor that Gen. Banks had crossed the river above Port Hudson with his forces, and would join them the next day. The great heat of the day compelled the troops to cast off all superfluous clothing; and overcoats, blankets, etc., lined the road over which they marched.

While on the march to Port Hudson, and within about two miles of it, a long, loud cheering from the regiments in the rear announced the arrival of Gen. Banks. The glorious Forty-eighth were not slow in giving him three tremendous cheers. When within about one mile of the Port Hudson works, the troops halted, and established picket lines. Gen. Sherman, it was ascertained, had arrived from New Orleans, and had formed his forces on the left; while Gen. Banks encircled the right, leaving ours (says Capt. H.) under Gen. Augur, in the centre, thus making a chain seven miles long around the rear of Port Hudson, the right and left of which rested on the Mississippi. Nothing of moment was done that day; one of our batteries indeed, opened fire on the works of the enemy, and it was responded to. Our troops slept quietly by the side of their stacked arms. Slight firing upon the pickets indeed, occasioned the forming of the men into line a few times, through apprehension of an attack.

May 25th, no fighting except with artillery; on the 26th, Capt. H. was detailed as officer of the picket-guard (about sixty men), thus relieving the old guard, which had been stationed one-fourth of a mile in advance of our forces. He had a reserve of fifteen men, who remained with him a short distance in rear of the line. No firing that night.

On the morning of the 27th, the scene changed, and the quiet of the two preceding days gave way to rapid artillery firing all the forenoon, the discharges averaging, as Capt. H. judged, twenty per minute. Our troops were passing through the picket line to the front all the forenoon. A charge was made on the rebel works, about noon, which was unsuccessful. At noon, the officer of the day ordered Capt. H. to post his reserve on a road leading to the front, and to permit none but wounded men to pass to the rear. Some attempted to pass through, on pretence of being wounded, but as every man was examined, many were ordered back to their regiments. Ambulances were constantly passing to the rear, filled with the wounded and dying. It was ascertained on the next day that the Forty-eighth lost *seven* killed and forty-one wounded in the attack on the 27th. Lieut. Col. O'Brien was killed at the head of the storming party. Five commissioned officers were wounded, and the Acting Brigadier General, Col. Chapin of New York, fought his last fight on that memorable though unsuccessful day.

Capt. H. was, shortly after, detailed to take command of twenty-five men belonging to the Forty-eighth, to go out under a flag of truce to bury the dead, lying near the rebel works. Each of the three other regiments in this brigade also detailed twenty-five men, making one hundred in all, under command of Col. Johnson of the Twenty-first Maine, for the same melancholy duty. We found, says Capt. H., sixty-three bodies, which we took a short distance to the rear, and buried in trenches. Two were found living but badly wounded, who were removed to the hospital at the rear. A fact is here stated by the Captain, going to show that some sparks of humanity still linger in human bosoms, where we should otherwise suppose them to be utterly extinct. "Many of the rebels came out of the fort, and joined us while we were collecting the dead. They brought out beer for us to drink, and joined freely with us in conversation."

On the 31st of May, Capt. H. was detailed as captain of the skirmishers consisting of forty men, and stationed in the edge of the woods, about four hundred yards from the rebel works, and was ordered to hold that portion, if attacked, until reinforced from the rear. He stationed two men in the tops of the trees to watch the movements of the enemy. Seven volleys of musketry were received from the rebels during the day, but no one was injured, and the fire was not returned, for the reason that it was thought unadvisable to betray the strength, or rather the weakness, of the Union force. The captain might well say they found themselves much exhausted when relieved next morning, having been on duty, and without sleep, *fire* of the thirteen nights since leaving Baton Rouge. One alarm only disturbed the rest of the following night.

The duties of the company were more or less active, consisting largely in guarding the ammunition, the commissary stores, teams and forage belonging to the brigade, and the plantations in the rear, as well as keeping the roads well guarded leading into the camp. It was in this position and discharging these duties, that the company was occupied until the final surrender of Port Hudson, which took place on the 8th of July following. Company E were ordered to join their regiment on the next morning, July 9th, and march into that long rebellious Port Hudson, now rebellious, it is believed, no more. The steamers at the landing received them, and at dark started down the river, stopping a few minutes only at Baton Rouge, and proceeding on to Donaldsonville, arriving there at eight o'clock next morning. The 10th of July, was excessively hot, and while lying upon the ground, Capt. H. received a sun-stroke, on account of which the surgeon ordered him to Baton Rouge, as unfit for duty.

The Forty-eighth came up from Donaldsonville on the 2d of August, and on the 8th, they received orders to turn in their muskets and equipments to the Quartermaster, which was done on Sunday the 9th. At four o'clock they embarked on board the steamer Sunny South for Cairo, Ill., where they arrived August 17th, having stopped at Natchez, Vicksburg, Memphis, Helena and Columbus.

From Cairo, they disembarked on the afternoon of the 18th, taking the cars for Boston, via Indianapolis, Cleveland, Buffalo and Albany. They reached Boston on Sabbath morning, August 23d, and arrived at the old homestead in Essex, on the afternoon of the same day.

Capt. H. and his men were mustered out of the United States service September 3d, being eleven and a half months from the time of mustering in. The event gave great joy to all households, except, of course, those which had been made desolate by the death of loved ones away. For those smitten and mourning families, the feelings and the tears of sympathy are not and shall not be wanting.

LAMONT G. BURNHAM.

Lamont G. Burnham was born August 5, 1844, and was the son of Washington and Mary Burnham. He was a volunteer in Capt. Howes' company.

Mr. B's. journal commences on the 8th of June, after arriving in the Mississippi River, and immediately after a raid on Clinton, under date of June 8th, being eighteen days after the fight at Plain Store, Port Hudson. Our company, says Mr. B., is guard over the baggage train. The regiment is encamped at the Plain Store. During the night two regiments came out from the fort and attempted to spike some of the guns in Gen. Sherman's division, but were repulsed, and driven back to the fort. In the morning of the 9th of June, he went one and one-half miles for a canteen of water, and although at that early season, he found blackberries on the way. That night "heavy firing was commenced by our batteries about dark, and continued through the night." This continued through Wednesday, June 10th, and the night following. "Several of our men were wounded. Received the Boston Journal and the Essex Register of May 25th." The firing seems to have been continued through Thursday the 11th. An election of a Lieutenant-Colonel took place on the 12th, to supply the vacancy occasioned by the death of Lieut-Col. O'Brien. Capt. Stanwood of Company B was chosen, and by this election, says Mr. Burnham, "we lost our place on the right wing of the regiment, which was much regretted. Numbers of rebels came from the fort and gave themselves up—two hundred in the whole. Our regiment was moved from Plain Store to the front; and part of the day was employed in clearing a road through the ravine, to carry ammunition to the battery in front, and the remainder of the day in supporting a marine battery of nine inch Dahlgren guns. Back to the store at night, and again to the front, marching in all about twelve miles that day. At twelve o'clock the firing of the large guns ceased, and a flag of truce was sent in, demanding the surren-

der of the fort, which was replied to by Gen. Gardiner, that his duties to the
Southern Confederacy would not permit him to surrender the fort.

"Severe fighting commenced on Sunday morning the 14th, all along the
whole front. At about eight o'clock, our forces under Gen. Grover, charged
and took the outer line of fortifications on the right. Along the whole line
we were within a few hundred yards of the fort, and a continual fire of musketry was kept up through the day. Some of the officers on the left of the
Forty-eighth were wounded."

"There is something grand," remarks this young soldier, "in the flashes
of musketry, and the sheet of flame and the heavy booming of the big guns,
and the line of fire from the shell as it flies through the air, and the explosion, dealing death to those around." Ah! how many like Lamont G. Burnham have seen those flashings of the musket and that sheet of flame; how
many have heard the booming of the big guns and seen the line of fire, and
instead of recording it at the battle's close in poetic style almost like the
above, have been numbered among those to whom the "explosion" was
death! Well may Lamont add, as he does, "I hope I may never again see
such a sight!"

The next day was one of comparative rest. Appearances indicated that
the rebels were in much stronger force than had been supposed. Long trains
of ammunition wagons poured into the enemy at intervals all day (the 15th).
Neither was the fighting really renewed on Tuesday, although our siege batteries and sharp-shooters were not wholly silent. Preparations were, however,
made for another attack. Volunteers to the number of one thousand were
called for as a storming party. "The brave Forty-eighth furnished twenty-
seven." The term for which the nine months' men of Co. A, in the Forty-
eighth, enlisted, expired on the 16th of June. The journal of this youthful
soldier is so instructive that it ought not to be lost. On the 17th of June
(1863), still at Port Hudson, he says "Co. A, which refused duty yesterday
on account of their time being up, were drawn up in line before Col. Paine,
and a company with fixed bayonets and loaded guns behind them, and each
man was asked separately if he would do duty. All but four complied, who
were placed under arrest to be sentenced by court martial."

On the 19th of June, the time for which Company E enlisted, expired,
but nothing appeared like preparations for leaving for home. It was not forgotten of course, but the experience of Company A, the day before, operated
to prevent a man from refusing to do duty. News of the surrender of Vicksburg reached Port Hudson. The journalist makes the affecting entry on the
21st of June, that F. Gilbert Mears died of chronic diarrhœa.

AARON LOW.

Aaron Low, aged 29 years, was born in Essex; he was a farmer, and the
son of Warren and Mary Low. He enlisted September 8, 1862, in Company E, Forty-eighth regiment, Capt. Howes; went into camp at Wenham,
and there remained until December. At this time the regiment was sent to

Readville, where they remained until they were ordered to New York. The passage was made on board the Constellation.

Mr. Low's journal is filled with the result of his observations at almost every stage of the expedition. It is difficult from such a superabundance of matter to make a selection. He arrived at Fortress Monroe, however, on the 8th of January, 1863. "It (the fort,) can be seen," he observes, "opposite the Rip Raps, and further away is Sewall's Point." On the morning of the 9th, when they were expecting a Virginia sun, they encountered a snowstorm. On the 10th, he writes that there had not been much sickness on board, although three of Company E had been in the hospital, and to-day he says there has been a gloom and sadness cast over the men by the sudden death of Mr. Peabody, one of their number, a man not far from fifty years of age. This was the second death that had then occurred in the company. The funeral took place on Sunday, the 11th, at a short distance from Hampton. From the cupola of the hospital they had a splendid view of the ruins of the village of Hampton that had been burnt by the rebels. Mr. Low's habit of observation would not allow him to be idle when there was anything to instruct. The country around the hospital, he observes, is level, and most of it apparently productive, notwithstanding the air of desolation around. The large, smooth fields that were apparently in a high state of cultivation when the rebellion commenced, are now covered over with a rank, coarse vegetation. On the road to Hampton they saw a few scattering apple-trees, and one small orchard of apple and peach-trees, though untrimmed and thriftless, and in sad contrast with the productive orchards of old Massachusetts. "The Hygiene hospital," Mr. Low writes, "where poor O. H. P. Sargent's life went out, in the flush of his manhood, has been taken down, to give better range to the guns of the fort, as after McClellan's defeat before Richmond, an attack on the fort was anticipated." "It was with feelings of sadness," he continues, "that I stood upon the spot, consecrated by the sufferings of so many of those who have left all to serve the country. I took a sprig or two from the shrubbery as mementos of Sargent, whose eyes mayhap have looked on them before they were closed in death."

On Wednesday, January 14th, the ship sailed for New Orleans with a good breeze, and on the 16th, the sea had become very rough, producing seasickness, as a matter of course. On Sabbath, the 18th, it is interesting to observe that the New Testament is read; the men were around on the deck, some reading the Bible, or whatever they could find to while away the time.

Mr. L. complains of the absence of books and papers as one of the most serious of privations, though he admits that "one cannot feel lonesome among so many, as there are so many phases of human nature to study."

We find our Forty-eighth up the Mississippi River shortly after the above, and from Baton Rouge on the 7th of February, Mr. L. records the feeling of transport which pervaded the troops on the arrival of their chaplain, Rev. Dr. Spaulding of Newburyport, with letters from home. On the 9th the unusual appearance of the season is thus described: "Robins and sparrows are quite plenty, and the frogs peeping in the evening, make it seem more like Spring than Winter;" and at 10 o'clock on the night of the 10th of February, after posting his guard, he says, the air is as warm as September or June, and the peeping of frogs and the hum of insects make the illusion complete.   Lieut. Brown of Ipswich inspected them, the 12th of February. After a stroll in the woods in the afternoon of the same day, he says, there are many very large trees of sweet gum and white wood, measuring from four to seven feet through, and fifty to seventy-five feet high, clear of limbs. There are also noble specimens of lime and white oak and magnolia.   There does not appear to have been any care taken of these noble trees for a long time, as many are standing thirty to fifty feet high, branchless and barkless. Within the circle of a few rods, I counted the remains of five enormous trees, seven to eight feet in diameter, and from one hundred to two hundred feet high, which had been cut down years ago, and a small part carried away.

Sickness is mentioned on the 27th of February.   "Have been down to the general hospital where Solomon A. Riggs, Horace Burnham, J. Daniels, and J. Jewett are.   The boys are all getting along well.   The hospital was formerly a deaf and dumb asylum.   Went to see the ruins of the State House, once a splendid building, costing nearly a million and a half of dollars.   At the time it was burnt it was occupied by our troops and by rebel prisoners; it is supposed to have been set on fire.   The charred remains of State documents, pamphlets, marble mantles, and fire-places besides the ruins of costly furniture are all lying in a confused mass in the tanks below.   The building stood a short distance from the river, the banks on this side being much higher than on the other."

IRA FRANCIS BURNHAM.

Ira Francis Burnham was born in Essex, November 21, 1844; his father's name was Ira Burnham, and his mother's Harriet; occupation formerly, farming; since the war, vessel-building.   He enlisted in the Forty-eighth Regiment, in September, 1862; was mustered in at Wenham, and was there from the middle of September to the last of November.   "Our regiment consisted of eight companies, and near the last of November, six companies were ordered to Readville, where we remained till after Christmas.   Near the last of December we were ordered to Groton, Ct., by rail, thence by steamer to New York, where we remained about five days, and thence by sailing vessel, the Constellation, left for Fortress Monroe, and again, in about one week, left in same vessel for New Orleans, where we arrived February 1st.   The grass was then green; oranges upon the trees looked inviting.   Our next place of destination was Baton Rouge.   Some sickness made its appearance about this time.   Solomon A. Riggs and Horace Burnham, also Maurice Callehan had been sick on the voyage from New York.   We left the two former at New Orleans.   Andrews came up about the 1st of May.   Horace B. was discharged for disability, at New Orleans.   Our first fight was at Plain Store, so called, near Port Hudson.   Not being able to do full duty, I was appointed Col. Stone's orderly. Col. Chapin commanded our brigade at the time of our attack on Port Hudson. My duty as orderly, was to report to the adjutant-general of the brigade, the state and condition of our regiment, which statement was prepared by our Adjutant Ogden, showing the number sick or in any way disabled, and the number ready for duty. I was in both assaults on Port Hudson, one in May and the other in June. After the May attack, our regiment was sent back to Plain Store, as a rear guard. We remained there till the evening before the June attack; this attack was on the Sabbath. Neither attack, as is well-known, was successful; the fort did not surrender till July 8th. I received my bounty of $200 after being mustered in, and $13 per month while in the service. In case of our advancing money for our uniforms, it was afterwards refunded. I was in the hospital at Baton Rouge about nine weeks, with fever."

SOLOMON A. RIGGS.

Solomon A. Riggs, the son of Asa and Anna Riggs, was born in Essex, November 7, 1834. He enlisted in the Forty-eighth Massachusetts Volunteers, Company E, at the time of its formation. Mr. Riggs' fortunes as a soldier are almost told when it is stated that he was in Company E, inasmuch as the history of the company has already been so particularly told by the captain and others. He was sick, however, and sent to the hospital at New Orleans; though we find him, when only partially recovered, namely, on the 13th of May, leaving the hospital to join the company, though still unable, says the captain, to do duty. This it will be recollected, was on the same day when Wilkins James died, and was buried.

JOHN F. HART.

John F. Hart enlisted in the Fourteenth Regiment, Company A, afterwards made First Heavy Artillery. His enlistment was in August, 1862, and they reached Camp Cameron at Cambridge the same day. They remained there about one week, when they received their uniforms and equipments, and left for Washington, being ordered to join the said First Heavy Artillery, then numbering about fifteen hundred men. The history of this soldier is so nearly identified with that of Joseph W. Tucker, that perhaps little more need be said, than to refer the reader to the sketch of Mr. Tucker, except where the statements are *strictly personal.*

JOSEPH W. TUCKER.

Joseph W. Tucker was 35 years and six months old when he enlisted, viz., on the 2d of August, 1862. He was born in Boston, March 20, 1827. The Fourteenth Massachusetts, Company A, into which Mr. Tucker enlisted, was subsequently made, as before stated, the First Massachusetts Heavy Artillery. Mr. Tucker left Essex August 13, 1862, and arrived at Camp Cameron in Cambridge the same day. On the 21st of August, he found himself in Washington, and along with other Essex soldiers, attached as above stated, and stationed at the fort five and a half miles from Washington, in Virginia.

In three days more they were ordered to reinforce Gen. Pope, then at Cloud's Mills, and were in what was called Pope's defeat, and in the battle of Fairfax, five miles beyond the court-house, and at the close of the battle, the same day, were ordered to Fort De Kalb, there to do garrison duty. In three weeks, Mr. T. was detailed for hospital duty at Fort Craig. Here he remained seventeen months.

GEORGE F. BURNHAM.

George F. Burnham, 2d, son of Joel and Mary Burnham, was born April 15, 1837. He enlisted in Company E, Capt. Howes, Forty-eighth Massachusetts, Col. Stone, for nine months. His fortunes being identified with those of the company, need not, as indeed in his absence, they cannot be minutely described. He received his discharge with the company, and returned with them.

JAMES HORACE BURNHAM.

James Horace Burnham, son of Michael and Patience Burnham, enlisted at the age of 19 years, being in July, 1862, into the Thirty-ninth Massachusetts, Col. P. S. Davis, Company A, Capt. Nelson. This regiment left the State on the 6th of September, and were ordered to the defenses of Washington, where they remained until July 6, 1863, when they joined the Army of the Potomac. Their first engagement was at Mine Run, Va., on the 29th and 30th of December, 1863, although they had had some skirmishes under Gen. Meade; indeed the army had been under Gen. Meade wholly till this time, when the command was taken by Gen. Grant. In the following Spring they crossed the Rapidan, and attacked the rebel army, May 6th, at the Wilderness, Va. The fighting continued until the 8th, when he was wounded by a rifle ball in the abdomen. This was the fight near Spottsylvania Court House, and that ball he carried till the 14th of March, 1865, when it was extracted at the Summit House hospital in Philadelphia. Up to the time of being wounded Mr. B. had never been away from the regiment, although he had had a typhoid fever, disqualifying him for duty some eight weeks. He never joined the regiment after the ball was extracted, and after the surrender of Lee, was discharged.

ISRAEL F. ANDREWS.

Israel F. Andrews, aged 30 years, shoemaker, was the son of Israel and Kezia Andrews, and born in Essex. He enlisted for nine months, in Company E, Capt. Howes, Forty-eighth Regiment Massachusetts Volunteers, August 28, 1862. He was in the battle at Donaldsonville, and the siege at Port Hudson. His history, except when strictly personal, is so incorporated in the interesting sketch given by Capt. Howes, like many others, that it is thought sufficient to refer the reader to that sketch.

HORACE BURNHAM.

Horace Burnham, son of John and Sarah C. Burnham, was born in Essex, February 20, 1843. He enlisted in August, 1862, into Company E, Capt.

48

Howes, Forty-eighth Massachusetts Volunteers, for nine months. He was taken sick before seeing any service, and continued so until discharged. He was absent from home just nine months.

LEWIS BURNHAM.

Lewis Burnham, aged 18 years, was the son of Noah and Caroline Burnham; ship carpenter, born in Essex. He enlisted September 8, 1862, in Company E, Forty-eighth Regiment Massachusetts Volunteers. His regiment left the State on the 27th of December, to join Gen. Banks' command at New Orleans. He was taken prisoner, July 13, 1863, but released on parole the next day. He came home by the way of Cairo, and thence by land.

ALBERT F. BURNHAM.

Albert F. Burnham, 2d, was born in Essex, November 1, 1840. He was a ship carpenter, and the son of Ebenezer and Susan T. Burnham. He enlisted August 30, 1862, in Capt. Wheatland's Company E, afterwards Capt. Howes', Forty-eighth Massachusetts Volunteers. After encamping first at Wenham, September 19, 1862, and then at Readville, the regiment was ordered to the Mississippi River to join the command of Gen. Banks. Mr. B. states that he was not in any battle, was never wounded, nor in any hospital, nor at any time a prisoner; received bounty and wages as did all others of that regiment and company.

ALPHONSO M. HARDY.

Alphonso M. Hardy, aged 19 years, and a line maker, was born in Essex, and was the son of Daniel and Mary Hardy. He enlisted August 23, 1862, in Capt. Howes' Company E. He was discharged from Camp Lander, at Wenham, for disability, October 1, 1862.

ANDREW JACKSON.

Andrew Jackson, aged 28 years, was the son of Jotham Jackson. He enlisted in Company E, Massachusetts Forty-eighth Regiment, September 19, 1862. His subsequent history is not known.

LUTHER HAYDEN.

Luther Hayden, aged 44 years, was born in Braintree, and was hotel-keeper and stabler, and the son of Barnabas and Rusby Hayden. He enlisted August 25, 1862, in Capt. Howes' Company E, Forty-eighth Massachusetts Regiment. Mr. Hayden's history is part and parcel with that of all the members of this company substantially. He was consequently one of those to whom Capt. Howes' compliment of good soldiership applies, and to which the reader is again referred.

LEONARD BURNHAM.

Leonard Burnham, at the time of enlistment, on the 28th of August, 1862, was 22 years of age, and the son of Michael and Patience Burnham. Mr. B. went into camp at Wenham, September 15th, and was mustered into the service of the United States, in the Forty-eighth Regiment, on the 19th of

September, Company E, Capt. Howes. He was with the regiment and followed its fortunes until the 11th of April, 1863, when he was taken sick and went to the hospital. [See sketch of Capt. Howes, p. 364 and onward.] Mr. B. remained at the hospital two months and three weeks, at the close of which term he joined the regiment before Port Hudson, on the 3d of June, and was with them through the remainder of that siege, also in a skirmish at Donaldsonville. He came home with the regiment, and was mustered out of service on the 3d of September, 1863, at Wenham.

JOHN McEACHEN.

John McEachen, was born in Port Hood, Nova Scotia, July 2, 1837; occupation ship carpenter; son of John and Mary McEachen. He enlisted on the 30th of August, 1862, in Company E, Forty-eighth Massachusetts; mustered in, September 19, 1862, and his history is fully described in that of the other members of the company from Essex, to which reference is to be made. His own statement, however, is brief and may be inserted in a few words, thus: "I was in the first fight at Port Hudson Plain, May 21, 1863, also in the unsuccessful second attack, May 27th. Our place of encampment was in front of Port Hudson. I have not been wounded or ever been made a prisoner of war. For two months, however, I was in a hospital for medical treatment."

ROBERT PREST.

Robert Prest, aged 37 years, is a wheelwright by trade, and has a wife and four children; son of William and Jane Prest. He was born near Plymouth in England; enlisted in Company E, Forty-eighth Massachusetts. He was detailed as ambulance driver at New Orleans, until February 10, 1863, when he was discharged, his time having expired. In October, 1863, he re-enlisted as artificer, in the Twelfth Company Unattached Heavy Artillery, Capt. Richardson. The regiment was stationed at Fort Pickering, Salem Harbor (February, 1864).

MAURICE CALLEHAN.

Maurice Callehan was born in Ireland, and enlisted in the Massachusetts Forty-eighth, Col. Stone, Company E, Capt. Howes. The history of Maurice Callehan as given by him *verbally* (except so far as involved with others of Company E, and therefore unnecessary to be repeated,) informs us that he was taken sick in about two days after going on board the Constellation at New York, bound for the Mississippi. "I was better," says he, "on arriving at Baton Rouge, February 4th. I think I remained there about two months, doing guard duty. I was in the battle at Plain Store, and in both attacks on Port Hudson. I was sick again when on the Baton Rouge road for about three weeks, where we were without shelter of any kind, except the shelter-tent and the trees, together with a rubber blanket. This tent consists of two pieces of cotton cloth, buttoned together. Our physician was Dr. Hurd, but I was sick nearly a week before he was called. In addition to the fever, I was afflicted with chronic diarrhœa. After the surrender of

Port Hudson, we were ordered down the river to Donaldsonville. I was with the company the rest of the time, and returned home with them. I was never wounded, though I was several times unwell, besides the two sick-nesses referred to above."

JOHN KELLEHER.

John Kelleher was born in Ireland. He enlisted in the Forty-eighth, Company E, as a nine months' man, and was at Camp Lander until the re-moval of the troops, first to Readville, and shortly after to New York, and thence, on the 2d of January following, by water to New Orleans. He was at Port Hudson in the memorable attack upon that place, and fired about twenty-five rounds, as he thinks. The station of the Forty-eighth was im-mediately under the guns of the fort.

THOMAS MAHONY.

Thomas Mahony was born in Ireland. . He enlisted in the Forty-eighth Regiment, Company E, and at the same time with other members from Essex. Mr. M. continued with the company all the way to Port Hudson, so that his history, like that of Mr. Kelleher last mentioned, is involved in theirs, and has already to a considerable extent been told, or will be found closely con-nected with that of Marston, Kimball and Lamont G. Burnham.

CHARLES P. CROCKETT.

Charles P. Crockett's personal history is lost, except to his friends at a distance, and beyond our reach. It is known, however, that he enlisted in Company E, Capt. Howes of the Forty-eighth, Col. Stone. The occasional allusions to him in the sketch by Capt. Howes and others, furnish the melan-choly facts of his illness and death on the banks of the Mississippi, while en-gaged in the line of his duty.

JAMES B. KIMBALL.

James B. Kimball was a member of the Massachusetts Forty-eighth, Col. Stone, and of Company E, Capt. Howes. Mr. Kimball was detailed with nine others, for the hospital department, on January 1, 1863, and thereby made *non-combatant*. When not engaged in the duties of this office, the members of this corps have opportunity for making observations upon pass-ing events more extensively and accurately than officers or soldiers can gen-erally do. Mr. K. was wide awake to his advantages in this respect, and not slow to improve them. Officially, the ten men in the hospital service are familiar chiefly with surgical instruments, tourniquets, bandages, lint, stretchers and quinine, and a part of their active duty consists in placing wounded men upon *stretchers* and carrying them to the surgeons in the rear. This implement is believed to be somewhat modern as it is now used, and may be described as consisting of two side-pieces of wood, corresponding to a farmer's hay poles, but connected with a sacking bottom upon which the wounded man is laid. One soldier at each end carries the load with ease. But a preliminary duty is frequently to apply the lint, the bandage, and finally the tourniquet, used to stop blood with. Mr. Kimball early noticed the difference in different men, with regard to the ability to bear heavy surgical operations—some resolutely declining chloroform, though it was always at hand, and declining also to be strapped to the table. He has seen men hold out a right arm to the surgeon and suffer the amputation, not only without wincing, but almost with the fortitude of Covey, the English marine, who, after losing both legs by a chain shot, called out to a comrade, "Shove them along here, and let me have one more kick at the French before I go for 't." Mr. K. was captured by the rebels in May, and was with them *forty-nine* days, when Port Hudson capitulated. Of the style of living among the rebels Mr. K. is fully competent to speak. It has been remarked by others, that had Vicksburg *not fallen*, and had a supply of provisions been obtained, we might have knocked at the door of Port Hudson in vain. Any assault might have been attempted with terrible slaughter. "We were allowed four ears of Indian corn per day only," says he, "and yet we fared as well as the rebels. This corn was frequently musty, and whether eaten raw, or as *cracked corn*, or boiled in lye and made into *samp*, so called, it was far from being wholesome, producing diarrhœa, though perhaps not in a very aggravated form." He lost twenty-two and a half pounds of flesh in forty-nine days.

Our army took possession of Port Hudson on the 8th of July, when Mr. K. was relieved and returned home with the other nine months' men, their time of service having now expired. Mr. Kimball's experience in the hospitals enables him to speak upon matters connected with that department, and his observation in many things has led to the same results at which surgeons themselves have usually arrived. As before stated, he remarked the usual absence of pain in gun-shot wounds. The exceptions usually made by surgeons are in cases of injury to the joints. Surgical operations among the rebels, so far as witnessed by him, were as skillfully performed as in our own army. One of the evils incident to war, is the impossibility of attending to cases in season. Theophilus Ponsley of Salem was taken at the same time Mr. Kimball was. He was wounded by a shell in the leg, taking off all the fleshy part. It was in the afternoon that the injury was inflicted, and his case could not be reached till the next day, when it was too late, his death having taken place in the morning.

Our army, as Mr. K. states, and as agrees with the printed reports, having fought for nine hours at Plain Store, on the 21st of May, made three other distinct charges upon the rebels during the siege. Although our soldiers in the excavation in front of the enbankment entirely escaped the heavy cannonading, they yet suffered fearfully from the small arms. Mr. Luther Hayden became acquainted, after the surrender, with a rebel soldier, who, before the surrender, shot fifteen of our men in the ditch. His guns were loaded for him, sometimes by the wounded. When taking aim at the sixteenth Yankee, the soldier entreated for his life. "Throw away your gun and come here," said the half chivalrous rebel, which the Union man, under those circumstances, was nothing loth to do.

MARK FRANCIS BURNHAM.

Mark Francis Burnham was the son of Mark and Mary C. Burnham. He enlisted December 15, 1863, in the Second Massachusetts Cavalry, Col. Charles Lowell, Capt. MacIntosh. They were first ordered to Long Island in Boston Harbor, where they remained about one month, after which they were sent to join the regiment at Vienna, Va., for drilling, and remained here for some six months. Mr. Burnham represents his *first day's work in the saddle to have been most exhausting.* A part of the regiment, from previous training, were able to sustain the fatigue; but one hundred and eighty-five like himself were in the saddle, as before said, for the *first time.* His first day's service lasted from three o'clock in the morning until two o'clock of the next morning, being twenty-three hours, having had but three short stops for refreshments, and traveling *sixty miles.* Such was his sense of prostration that on dismounting he fell to the ground. Their first fighting was at Ashby's Gap, and it was heavy. They were then between Washington and the main army defending Washington. In March, 1864, they were at Drainsville, Va., and thence crossed the Potomac at Edward's Ferry on the 16th of July, where they joined Sheridan's army. Mr. B. was finally mustered out of the service at Fairfax Court House, July 22, 1865.

By way of recapitulation in part, it may be stated that Mr. B. was present at the grand consummation of the surrender of Lee's army, after having fought at Ashby's Gap, Fort Stevens, Rockville, Poolesville, Summit Point, Halltown, Opequan, Winchester, Waynesboro, Cedar Creek, South Anna, White Oak Road, Berrysville, Charlestown, Dinwiddie Court House, Five Forks, and Appomattox Court House. Four horses were shot under him in these battles, two having been so at Winchester. He relates one escape which he may well consider providential, as follows: In June, 1864, some seven hundred cavalry had been, on one occasion, ordered to Point of Rocks. Six men besides himself were detailed to go up the canal in a boat with rations; while on shore they were surprised by about forty of Mosby's guerrillas. As they advanced, the seven Union soldiers fired their guns, but had no time to reload, and retreated. Four were captured at once. He with two others fell into a ditch somewhat concealed by the tall overhanging grass. *He* was not discovered by the guerrillas, but the two other surrendered themselves. In the result, five of the seven died in the horrors of Libby Prison, and one alone besides himself escaped to tell the story.

ALBERT ANDREWS.

Albert Andrews, son of Ira and Martha Andrews, was drafted, July 10, 1863, being the first draft ordered by the President of three hundred thousand men. He was assigned to the Sixteenth Massachusetts, Lieut Col. Waldo Merriam then commander, and Company A, Capt. Joseph S. Hills. They were first sent to Long Island, in Boston Harbor, where they remained about ten days, and thence were ordered to join the main army at Beverly Ford, on the 31st of August, 1863; and thence to Culpepper Court House.

On the 27th of July, 1864, they were transferred to the Eleventh Battalion of Infantry, commanded by Col. Charles C. Rivers, James F. Mansfield, Captain. He fought in the following battles, viz : Locust Grove, Wilderness, Spottsylvania Court House, Coal Harbor, Hatcher's Run, siege of Peters-burg, which surrendered April 2d, from which time till April 9th, the army followed Lee, when he surrendered. He was discharged, July 14, 1865, at Four Mile Run, having never been wounded. He was, however, taken sick in September, 1864, of chronic diarrhœa, and sent to the hospital in New York, where he remained two months. Mr. Andrews speaks well of the hos-pital treatment, and remarked that a free library of some hundreds of volumes was established for the benefit of the soldiers, and he there read the life and works of his townsman, Hon. Rufus Choate, once teacher of the district school in Essex, where his father Ira Andrews was a pupil.

CHARLES E. MARSTON.

Charles E. Marston, enlisted in the Forty-eighth Regiment of Massachu-setts Volunteers, on the 23d of September, 1862, and was stationed at Camp Lander, Wenham. He left with his regiment for Readville, on the 4th of December following, and on the 27th of the same month, the regiment was under marching orders for New York, where they arrived on Sunday the 28th, at seven and a half A. M.

As the diary of Mr. Marston was carefully kept, extracts will be made somewhat freely. The regiment embarked on board the sailing ship Constel-lation, on Friday, January 2, 1863, at twelve and a half, noon. After speaking the ship Crown Point, for New York, one hundred and forty-five days from Bombay, Mr. Marston shared with others the bane of every voy-age, sea-sickness, but in addition to that had a severe attack of nettle rash, so called, lasting three days. During a gale of some severity on the 5th, the soldiers were all ordered below, and none but sailors were allowed on deck. Cape Henry was made on the 8th, this being the first glance of " Old Virginia's shore." While lying at anchor in the mouth of the Bay on the 8th, J. Peabody was taken sick, and died on the 10th. The New Ironsides arrived there from Philadelphia that day. The ship sailed for New Orleans on the 15th of January, and after the usual varieties of weather, arrived off the mouth of the Mississippi on or about the 29th. Fort Jackson was passed on the 31st.

On the 12th of February the first general inspection took place, by Lieut. Brown of Ipswich, "a very smart officer and aid-de-camp to Gen. Grover. Gen. Banks passed our camp on the 9th of March."

An incident in negro life is recorded by Mr. Marston, on the 1st of April, 1863, at Bayou, Montecino. After having been down to the river and seen the gunboat Seneca, they came to a negro hut. The negroes were outside. There was a corpse in the house on the table, covered with a white cloth ; it was very small and a woman knelt beside it. There were four candles on the table, one at each corner.

While at Camp Williams near the State House, on the 6th of April, "had orders to be in readiness to march at a moment's notice, as an attack was expected in the night. On the 7th, started out one mile to cut down trees. On the 9th, we were detailed to go to the funeral of the Captain of the One Hundred and Tenth New York regiment.

On the 19th of May, went to Port Hudson Plains and returned at night. On the 21st of May, started for Port Hudson, Upper Plains; had a battle; Benjamin Crowell, killed; J. B. Kimball, E. Southwick, and T. Pousley, missing, probably taken prisoners." On the 26th, they went to support the Fourth Battery. On the 27th, "an assault on Port Hudson, Col. O'Brien killed." "July 7th, news arrived that Vicksburg was taken, and Port Hudson surrendered on the 8th of July. The Union troops went in on the 9th. At seven o'clock P. M., same day, left for Donaldsonville on board the Louisiana Belle, and arrived at seven A. M. on the 10th. Capt. Howes and five others left for Baton Rouge, sick. On the 12th, the Forty-ninth Massachusetts and Sixth Massachusetts Battery went out, took ten prisoners and returned at night. On the 13th, left the river, marched three miles, and bivouacked. A battle commenced at ten o'clock, and ended at four P. M.; had to fall back; the Forty-eighth and One Hundred and Sixty-first New York, were the last to leave the field. Missing at roll on the 14th, Lewis Burnham, Solomon A. Riggs, J. L. Ford, P. Caldwell; on the 17th, the two former arrived back." On the 20th, Mr. Marston had an attack of nettle rash and diarrhœa with fever, having got wet for two nights; was much relieved by ice and lemon. His loss by weight in sixteen days was fifteen pounds. On Sabbath 26th, went to church at the hospital; got a book and at night another. On the 28th, he was sick again. An inspection took place on the 9th of August. "Went on board the Sunny South same day and left for Cairo, eight hundred and sixty miles up the river; passed steamers Diana, Autocrat, Baltic and one unknown; passed Port Hudson at six A. M. Commodore Farragut burned this place, because the people killed some of his men while ashore. Saw an alligator on the shore; passed a rebel iron-clad at nine A. M., and two iron-clad rams at twelve o'clock M."

On arriving at Natchez they found six steamers, and left on the 11th. "This city is on a hill." In going up the river they passed the mansion of the rebel Gen. Williams, and arrived at Vicksburg on the 12th. "August 15th, arrived at Memphis; we afterwards went back to Fort Pickering, one mile, and stopped to coal; a very handsome place, buildings mostly of brick. On the 16th, passed Island No. 10, and on the 17th, Columbus, (Ky.) and at ten o'clock, A. M., we arrived at Cairo, (Ill.)"

Mr. Marston was in three battles during his nine months' service. First, at Port Hudson Plain, the fight lasted nine hours, on the 21st of May; already referred to above, when Benjamin Crowell was killed. In this fight, by far the most considerable of the three, the troops were lying down while loading and firing. Mr. Crowell raised his head upon his elbows in order to see the enemy, when it was taken off by a solid shot.

LYMAN B. ANDREWS.

Lyman B. Andrews, son of Capt. Moses and Susan Andrews, born March 20, 1841; enlisted August 2, 1862, in Company E, Capt. Howes, Forty-eighth Regiment, Col. Stone. He was with the regiment throughout the campaign, and discharged at the same time.

GEORGE C. CLAIBORNE.

George C. Claiborne was born at Shapleigh, Me., October 30, 1819. His father was William H. and his mother Abigail Claiborne; came to reside in Essex, in 1845. Mr. C. enlisted in a company of mounted rifle rangers under Gen. B. F. Butler, November 6, 1861, and was sent to Ship Island in the Gulf Division; but was detailed with ten others to take charge of a load of horses, one hundred and fifty-three in all, sent to that island, by the transport Black Prince, of one thousand and sixty tons. The ship encountered a disastrous storm on her passage, during which the horses broke loose, and by the roll of the vessel, were so thrown together that but few reached the island alive. The balance of the company arrived at the island shortly after the Black Prince. This company of rangers, commanded by Capt. James M. McGee, belonged to, or made a part of Gen. Shepley's Brigade. After some three months' service at the island, they were ordered to New Orleans. It was during the service at the island, in the saddle, however, that Mr. Claiborne received an injury in the artery of his left leg, on account of which he was discharged on or about the 11th of June, 1862, and finally left New Orleans, near the last of July following, for home.

NATHANIEL HASKELL.

Nathaniel Haskell, though residing in Gloucester at the commencement of the rebellion, is an Essex boy, and his record is worthy of preservation. He enlisted in Company G, Massachusetts Eighth, and we find him at the Relay House, Washington Junction, in Maryland, as early as the 26th of May, 1861. "Who would have thought," says he, in a letter to his mother, "that I would have slept in the capitol of the United States." Yet so it was. He arrived there but a short time before the lamented Col. Ellsworth was killed at Alexandria, and his mortal remains were carried by the place of encampment on the 25th of May, 1861. Mr. H. received with much gratitude clothing sent him by the ladies of Gloucester, Mass., as one of Company G, in the Massachusetts Eighth. He writes his first letter while lying on the ground, with a little box for his desk; "while in the tent," he says, "some are writing and some are telling stories. But it is Sunday," he writes, "and the bell is now ringing for meeting, and I guess I shall go."

On the 5th of June, we find him rejoicing in having a plenty to eat, and a plenty to wear, and saying he never felt better in his life. "We don't have to work very hard," says he, "but drill six hours a day." On the 5th of June, "there were acres and acres of strawberries close to us, at five cents a quart," and he says that in regard to *both the price and the quantity,* as well as quality, they altogether exceeded anything that Mount Hunger had to show, (the celebrated garden of Abel Burnham in Gloucester, Mass.)

In the immediate neighborhood of Baltimore, on the 10th of July, 1861, Mr. Haskell says in his letter: "Only think! we are on a secession man's ground, and our stars and stripes are waving over it. When we first came here, he tried to drive us off. There are about fifteen thousand troops in Baltimore and around the city, besides six pieces of artillery all loaded and pointing two up each street, while we are marching through it."

No one can be so ill-tempered as to forbid the soldiers having a little pastime when safe occasion offers. The soldier, Haskell, in a letter from Annapolis, dated December 10, 1861, says "to-day, one of our boys had a letter from a lady in New Jersey, although they had never seen each other in the world. I will tell you how it was. As we were coming along, he wrote his name on a piece of paper, with a request that whoever picked it up would write to him. He put the paper into his handkerchief and threw it out of the cars. The letter received in reply to the request was quite a patriotic one." On the 25th of December, he writes in good spirits (Christmas day) and says "folks may say what they have a mind to, but soldiering is a gay life, and if you don't believe it, judge for yourself. I have weighed one hundred and seventy-six pounds to-day, so that my gain in the army has been sixteen pounds." He afterwards re-enlisted for coast defence, and served till the close of the war.

HERVEY ALLEN.

Hervey Allen, son of Joseph and Orpha Allen, enlisted in December, 1864, for one year, for coast defence in forts in the vicinity of Boston.

GILMAN ANDREWS.

Gilman Andrews enlisted in Capt. Babson's Company for coast defence, and like twelve others served to the close of the war.

FRANK E. ANDREWS.

Frank E. Andrews, son of Francis E. Andrews, enlisted like the foregoing for one year for coast defence. Discharged at the close of the war.

ADDISON COGSWELL.

Addison Cogswell, son of John and Elizabeth Cogswell, enlisted in Capt. Babson's Company for coast defence at the same time as the foregoing, having the same service to perform, and was discharged at the same time. Mr. Cogswell's residence was in Gloucester, but he properly passes for an Essex soldier, as he helps to fill our quota.

WILLIAM B. LOW.

William B. Low, aged 17 years, was born in Essex, and was the son of Caleb and Rachel Low. He enlisted the 3d of December, 1861, in Capt. Bartlett's Company I, Twentieth Massachusetts Volunteers, infantry. After being mustered into camp they were ordered to Poolesville, Md. He was in the battle at Yorktown under McClellan, also in the seven days' battle, so called. He received a flesh wound in the leg at Antietam battle, and another in the thigh at Gettysburg. He was also in the Fredericksburg battle under Burnside and Meade. He was appointed corporal in 1862; came home November 16, 1863, and remained twenty-five days, when he returned to his regiment at Stephensburg.

In addition to the above, for which obligations are due to J. C. Choate, town clerk of Essex, for the use of the records made by him, not only in this, but in numerous other cases, the following facts and incidents are derived from Mr. Low the soldier, himself. They are miscellaneous, and do not follow in strictly chronological order. "At the Fredericksburg battle on the 11th or 12th of December, 1862, out of sixty men in our company, we lost thirty-five." He was wounded by a spent ball at Antietam battle on the 17th of September, 1862, and carried off to the hospital. "Gen. Dana commanded our brigade—Sedgwick the division, and Sumner the corps. At Gettysburg, the rebels shelled us two hours on the last day. I was wounded in the thigh the third day. Col. Revere was killed, and Col. Nacy had his left arm shot off. Only three officers of our regiment came out of the battle unhurt, of the whole seventeen that went in. Our captain, Abbot, son of Judge Abbot, has since been made major. Our regiment was near the centre, which is said by the official reports, to have been harder pressed than any other part of the army." In answer to questions put to him, Mr. Low says the music is never played in battle; and as to disposing of the men in open order to prevent slaughter, it is not done. In the battle of Savage's Station, in July, we first drove the rebels, but after dark they drove us. Col. Meagher's (Irish) regiment was alongside of ours; a spirited fellow on a mule carried their flag. Savage's Station is, say ten to twelve miles from Richmond; we could see the steeples at times. Surgical operations are performed in a very short time. I have seen Doctor Hazard with his sleeves rolled up and pants all bloody, while amputating limbs. Chloroform is used freely. At Yorktown, we saw the very spot, as we were told, where Cornwallis surrendered.

DANIEL CALLEHAN.

Daniel Callehan was born in Ireland; enlisted in Company E, Capt. Howes, Forty-eighth Massachusetts Regiment. He survived the campaign and returned with the company. It is not known that he was sick or wounded while in the service. It may, however, be added that he has since died, viz: September 18, 1864, leaving a widow and three children.

WILLIAM E. LOW.

William E. Low, aged 19 years, was born in Essex, by trade a shoemaker, was the son of Rufus and Mary Eliza Low. He enlisted October 9, 1861, in Company I, Capt. Hobbs, Twenty-third Regiment Massachusetts Volunteers, infantry; ordered to join Gen. Burnside. He was in the battles of Roanoke Island, Newbern, Kinston and others. His regiment remained at

Newbern about a year, and was then ordered to Hilton Head, S. C., where they remained two days and returned to Newbern, and from that place to Fortress Monroe. He came home on furlough on the 1st of July, and returned on the 24th, (1863). On returning to the army he was sent to join Gen. Butler's expedition up the James River, during which he fought in two or three engagements. After this he was ordered to join Grant's army, near Richmond, and at Coal Harbor was severely wounded in his face, receiving a ball at the corner of his mouth. This wound occasioned three months' hospital treatment, at the close of which his three years had so nearly expired that he was discharged.

WILLIAM H. ANDREWS.

William H. Andrews, aged 34 years, shoemaker, was born in Essex, and the son of Eleazer and Judith Andrews. He enlisted June 30, 1862, for six months, in the Mechanics' Light Infantry, Capt. Staten ; was sent to Fort Warren, Boston harbor, and was discharged January 1, 1863, his term of enlistment having expired.

ALBURN ANDREWS.

Alburn Andrews, aged 19 years, born in Essex, was the son of Eleazer and Judith Andrews. He enlisted June, 1862, for six months in the Salem Mechanics' Light Infantry, Capt. Staten, and was sent to Fort Warren on garrison duty. He was discharged on January 1st, his time having expired. He re-enlisted in December, 1864, for one year, and was discharged at the close of the war, that is, after a service of about seven months.

JOSEPH GILMAN ALLEN.

Joseph Gilman Allen, aged 32 years, born in Essex, was the son of Joseph and Orpha Allen ; ship-carpenter. He enlisted June, 1862, for six months in the Salem Mechanics' Light Infantry, before mentioned, and was discharged at the expiration of the time of service, viz., January, 1863.

ALFRED M. BURNHAM.

Alfred M. Burnham, aged 19, shoemaker, was born in Essex, and the son of Nathan and Sarah Burnham. He enlisted in June, 1862, for six months, and was ordered to Fort Warren ; being attached to the Salem Mechanics' Light Infantry, Capt. Staten, and was discharged January 1, 1863, the term of service having expired. In something like a year and a half after this discharge, he was drafted and paid three hundred dollars commutation. He subsequently re-enlisted and was sent first to Galloup's Island, thence to Fort Warren, where he remained about one month, and thence to Marblehead, where he remained until within twelve days of the expiration of his time. During the said twelve days he was again at Galloup's Island.

JESSE BURNHAM.

Jesse Burnham, aged 38, is a ship-carpenter and has a wife and two children ; born in Gloucester, son of Jesse and Sarah R. Burnham. He enlisted in the company last above mentioned, and had the same place of destination, but was put upon garrison duty. Discharged at expiration of term of service.

JACOB BARTLETT.

Jacob Bartlett, aged 21, was born in Salisbury; shoemaker; son of Ezekiel W. and Elizabeth Bartlett. He enlisted at the same time with the last above mentioned for the same term; had the same destination and was discharged at the same time.

OTIS BURNHAM.

Otis Burnham, son of Andrew W. and Mary Ann Burnham, was born March 15, 1839. He enlisted in June, 1862, in the Salem Mechanics' Light Infantry with eleven others, mentioned above and below, and was stationed at Fort Warren for six months. On re-enlisting he was stationed a part of the time again at Fort Warren, and the remainder of the time at a fort in Marblehead. Mr. B's. *third* enlistment was as one of the *one hundred days' men*, to serve in the forts for the defense of Washington, where he remained from four to six weeks, and the balance of the time at Fort Delaware, some forty miles from Philadelphia, and at Readfield. Mr. B. regrets that he did not keep a journal of events during his army life, as dates are so easily forgotten.while the events themselves may be long remembered.

JOHN F. GILBERT.

John F..Gilbert, aged 19, blacksmith, was born in Rockport; son of William G. and Elizabeth Gilbert. He enlisted for six months, and into the same company as the above, ordered to the same place, and was discharged at the same time and for the same cause. Re-enlisted in December, 1864, and served in forts for coast defence; discharged at close of the war.

WEBSTER HOWES.

Webster Howes, aged 31 years, ship carpenter, was born in Chatham; son of Collins and Rhoda Howes. He enlisted like the former for six months, viz., from June, 1862, to January 1, 1863, into the same company, and was ordered to Fort Warren for garrison duty and guarding prisoners.

IRA ANDREWS, JR.

Ira Andrews, Jr., was the son of Ira and Martha Andrews; age not obtained. He was one of the Fort Warren soldiers, enlisting and serving and being discharged with them.

EDWARD LOW.

Edward Low was born in Essex, September 20, 1835, and the son of Enoch and Elizabeth McKeen Low. His destination was to Fort Warren. Term of enlistment and discharge, the same as in the other cases of the Fort Warren soldiers.

WILLIAM H. McINTIRE.

William H. McIntire, son of Nathaniel and Hannah McIntire, was born in Essex, and was 30 years and four months of age when he enlisted. Like the preceding, he enlisted (July 1, 1862,) for six months, and was ordered to Fort Warren. The same general duties devolved on all the above, and all were discharged together.

ALBERT E. LUFKIN.

Albert E. Lufkin enlisted August 4, 1863, to serve in a fort at Gloucester, where he remained about two months, when he was ordered to the forts in the vicinity of Washington. Here he remained until the 17th of September, 1865. He is the son of Jonathan and Thirza Lufkin.

GEORGE C. HARDY.

George C. Hardy, aged 29 years, by trade a machinist, was born in Essex, and was the son of Daniel and Mary Hardy; enlisted August, 1861, in Company A, Capt. Brewster, Twenty-third Massachusetts Regiment of infantry. The regiment left Camp Stanton at Lynnfield, October, 1861, for Annapolis, Md., and remained until December, 1861, when they were ordered to Roanoke Island, thence to Newbern, to Kinston, and subsequently to Little Washington. The regiment left the latter place in February, 1863, for Morris Island in Charleston harbor, and was in the assault on Fort Wagner. Mr. H. came home in August, 1863, on thirty days' furlough, which was extended ten days on account of his health. He then returned to Folly Island, Charleston harbor, and was placed in command of a schooner, to carry despatches of the signal corps from Hilton Head to Morris Island.

HARLAN PAGE BURNHAM.

Harlan Page Burnham, aged 20 years, born in Essex, was a sailor and the son of Zaccheus and Susannah Burnham; enlisted November 6, 1861, in Company E, Capt. Hooper, Twenty-fourth Regiment Massachusetts Volunteers, infantry. Left camp at Readville in December, 1861, for Annapolis, Md., and ordered to join Gen. Burnside's command. He was sick three months from April, 1862, and again most of the time in 1863. He was not in the assault on Fort Wagner, as at first understood, being sick, but was ordered to Morris Island and thence to St. Augustine, Fla., where the troops remained some four months, after which they were ordered to Jacksonville, (Fla.) where they arrived the day before the battle of Olustee. Having here done duty as provost guard. they were next ordered to Gloucester Point, opposite Yorktown. Mr. Burnham's statement is full of interesting historical events, but comes too late to be inserted in full. It will be put upon file for future reference.

WILLIAM LUFKIN.

William Lufkin, aged 57 years, was born in West Gloucester, and had a wife and three children. Enlisted in 1861, in Company K, Capt. Cook, Thirtieth Regiment Massachusetts Volunteers, infantry; died of fever in New Orleans or vicinity.

ZENAS BURNHAM.

Zenas Burnham, aged 36 years, widower, with one child, by trade a ship carpenter, was born in Essex, and was the son of Job and Lydia Burnham. He enlisted September 10, 1862, in Company A, Capt. Todd, Nineteenth Regiment Massachusetts Volunteers; was in the battle at Ball's Bluff; discharged on surgeon's certificate of disability, signed by Dr. E. A. Bradley.

MOSES COOK.

Moses Cook was the son of Edward and Ellen Cook. He enlisted in Capt. Babson's Company for the defense of the coast; first two months at Fort Warren, one month at Galloup's Island, and four months at Marblehead. He was enlisted for one year on the one hundred dollar bounty, and was discharged in seven months, at the end of the war.

ANDREW FRANK BURNHAM.

Andrew Frank Burnham was the son of Andrew and Augusta Burnham. He enlisted in Capt. Babson's Company for coast defense for one year, on the one hundred dollar bounty offer. He was a part of the time at Fort Warren, a part of the time at Galloup's Island, and subsequently at Marblehead, but was discharged in about seven months, being the close of the war.

FRANCIS BURNHAM.

Francis Burnham, son of Nathan and Sally Burnham, aged 23, was born in Essex. He enlisted in December, 1864, like the two preceding, for one year, for coast defense. Stationed in forts in Boston harbor and vicinity. Discharged July 15, 1865.

OTIS STORY.

Otis Story was the son of Elisha Story. He enlisted at the same time as the three preceding, into the same company, was in the same service, and discharged at the same time.

JOHN E. LEE.

John E. Lee, aged 23 years, married, shoemaker by trade, was born in Essex, and was the son of Zaccheus and Ann Lee. He enlisted December 1, 1861, in Company C, Capt. Devereux, Nineteenth Regiment Massachusetts Volunteers, for three years, but was discharged from Carver hospital at Washington, after remaining there two months, on surgeon's certificate of disability, signed by Dr. E. A. Bradley, May 29th, 1862. It should be stated that he had a pleurisy fever in the hospital at Poolesville, beginning early in March, 1862. He was subsequently removed to the general hospital at Washington, and from there to Carver's hospital, whence he was discharged as above stated.

HERVEY LUFKIN.

Hervey Lufkin, son of Thomas and Eliza Lufkin, enlisted in December, 1864, for one year, in Capt. Babson's Company, for coast defense; discharged in seven months, being the close of the war.

ROLLINS M. BURNHAM.

Rollins M. Burnham, son of Zaccheus Burnham, deceased, and Susannah Burnham, was born May 31, 1844, enlisted April 16, 1861, in the First Minnesota Regiment, where he was at that time residing. In this regiment he served eighteen months, when he was honorably discharged. He subsequently enlisted in the regular army, Nineteenth Regiment, First Battalion, Company A, of the United States Infantry. He was in the first Bull Run battle in July, 1861, and at Ball's Bluff, and in all Gen. Sherman's battles up to the time of leaving Atlanta.

SAMUEL Q. JONES.

Samuel Q. Jones was born in Essex, May 22d, 1840, son of Abraham and Mary Jones; by trade a ship-joiner, enlisted October 16, 1861, in the Third Massachusetts Cavalry, commonly called Mounted Rifle Rangers. Mr. Jones in his own written account, somewhat abridged, says: "Read's Mounted Rifle Rangers were got up in 1861, and went into camp at Lowell in August. We were encamped at Lowell about one month when orders came to break camp and go to Boston, there to take the steamer Constitution for Ship Island. . . . . On our way there we went into Hampton Roads and anchored below the fort; remained there two weeks, and while there saw the rebel gun-boat Merrimac come down to Sewall's Point and steam back again." It appears from Mr. Jones' statement, that after remaining here to have the ship cleaned, they pursued the voyage. On the coast of North Carolina they found one of our gun-boats in a damaged condition and towed her back to Hampton Roads, and "after forty-two days," says the soldier, "we arrived at the place of destination. There had been twenty-five hundred men on board. There was but one house on Ship Island at that time, though others have been since built. A dreary place for soldiers, though they did not grumble." After a season of drilling at the Island the troops took transports for New Orleans. During the bombardment of Fort Jackson, the transports laid some days below the fort; but proceeded up to the city on the day of the surrender. Mr. Jones says it was a grand sight, during the bombardment, to see the fire-rafts float down in the night. They were intended by the rebels to float against our vessels and burn them, but in this they were defeated. Mr J. says our troops landed in the city on the 1st or 2d of May, 1862. He himself was taken sick soon after with chills and chronic diarrhœa, and did not expect to recover. He was discharged after being ill about six months, although he had been able to be on duty all the time, except about one month. The troops were about this time ordered to proceed about ninety miles up the river to protect the plantations, and he soon began to recover. His weight increased from one hundred and twenty to one hundred and eighty pounds in less than two months. In the Spring of 1863, they went through the Red River campaign which lasted three months, and were once defeated. They were next ordered to join Sheridan in the Valley. This campaign was a "tough one." They fought at Fisher's Hill and Cedar Creek. In this last battle Jason Hatch was killed by a ball through his left breast and heart. " When I found him," says Mr. Jones, " I wrote his name on a slip of paper and pinned it on his pocket. On procuring others to assist in burying him, it was found that somebody had done it, but on examination it was found he had been buried but one foot deep. We dug a new grave and placed a board at the head, with his name, regiment and company." Mr. Jones was promoted corporal in 1862, and sergeant in 1863.

JASON HATCH.

Jason Hatch was born in Charlestown, Mass., son of Jacob and Sarah Hatch. He enlisted as a Rifle Ranger, otherwise called mounted riflemen, in the same company with William D. Coose and Samuel Q. Jones, all of Essex. He was killed in battle at Cedar Creek.

GEORGE S. WENTWORTH.

George S. Wentworth, aged 29 years, married, shoemaker, was born in Stoughton, son of Ellis and Mary A. Wentworth. He enlisted August 12, 1868, in Company E, Capt. Preston, Thirty-fifth Massachusetts Regiment, which joined the Army of the Potomac, and was in the battle of Fredericksburg, under Burnside, also at Antietam and Gettysburg. The regiment was subsequently ordered to the Army of the West, in East Tennessee, and was at Knoxville in February, 1864.

ASA STORY.

Asa Story, son of Michael and Lydia Story, was born in 1829 ; enlisted July 26, 1862, in the Massachusetts Thirty-ninth, Col. Davis, and Company A, Capt. Nelson. He died of typhus fever, November 11, 1862. His remains were brought home and re-interred in about two weeks after his decease. He was never in battle. He left a widow to mourn his death.

WILLIAM D. COOSE.

William D. Coose, son of William and Polly Coose, was born in Rockport ; was 23 years old when he enlisted in the Third Massachusetts Rifle Rangers, October 15, 1861, Capt. S. T. Reads. After remaining at Lowell until January, 1862, they were ordered on board the steamer Constitution for Ship Island, where they finally arrived, February 8th. After remaining there two months they left for New Orleans. They performed escort duty, for Gen. Butler about six months. They next went into camp at Carrolton, and thence about seventy miles up the river. Here they operated as a scouting party under Col. Davis, the force consisting of Read's Rangers and three other companies. " We whipped the enemy three hundred strong," says Mr. Coose, " and burnt five railroad stations." They were in all the Red River campaign. He was in the battles at Winchester, September 17 ; at Fishersville the 22d ; at Cedar Creek, October 19, and all through the campaign under Sheridan in the Valley, up to November 19, when he started for home. Arrived home November 26, 1864.

50

CONSTANTINE BURNHAM.

Constantine Burnham, was born in Essex, September 17, 1844 ; son of Adoniram and Nancy Burnham. He enlisted December 19, 1863, in Company L, Capt. Martin, Second Regiment Massachusetts, Col. John Frankle, heavy artillery. In January 1864, the regiment was ordered to Norfolk, Va. In the summer of 1864, he was in the hospital about five weeks with typhoid fever. Their next encampment was at Portsmouth, Va., where they were drilled four hours daily. He was in the second battle at Kinston, in March, 1865, where the fighting lasted three days. He was not wounded at all. He is understood to have served in the latter part of his time in Company I, Capt. John D. Parker.

WILLIAM A. HASKELL.

William A. Haskell, aged 33 years, enlisted January, 1864, in Company B, Capt. Emory, Fifth Massachusetts Cavalry. He has a wife and three children ; born in Hamilton, Mass., son of Elias and Sally Ann Haskell. Mr. H. was in the same Company with Charles Fields, and he may be said to have substantially the same history.

ALFRED LUFKIN.

Alfred Lufkin, aged 30 years, was the son of Josiah and Mehitable Lufkin. He was born in Essex, shoemaker by trade ; has a wife and one child ; enlisted August 5th, in the Eleventh Unattached Company of Heavy Artillery, stationed at the fort, at Eastern Point, Gloucester.

PRINCE A. ANDREWS.

Prince A. Andrews, was the son of Obed and Ruth Andrews. He enlisted into the Second Massachusetts Volunteers, Col. Gordon, and from the trifling and imperfect information obtained, it can now only be known that he was mustered out on the 28th of May, 1864.

RUFUS ANDREWS.

Rufus Andrews, aged 33 years, shoemaker, was the son of Ira and Martha Andrews, and has a wife and two children. He enlisted August 5, 1863, in the last named Eleventh Unattached Company of Heavy Artillery, stationed in the fort at Eastern Point, Gloucester.

WILLIAM HOWE BURNHAM.

William Howe Burnham, son of Winthrop Burnham, was born in Essex, April 8, 1840. He enlisted November 27, 1861, into Company H, Capt. Devereaux, Nineteenth Massachusetts Volunteers. This company left the State, December 10th, and arrived at Philadelphia, at ten o'clock on the evening of the same day. On the 13th of December, they were ordered up the Chesapeake and Ohio Canal to Muddy Branch Locks, Md., where they joined the regiment, which regiment formed a part of the Corps of observation on the upper Potomac. The following Winter was spent in drilling and doing guard duty until the 11th of March. Marching orders were received at that time, when the regiment to which Mr. Burnham was attached joined the brigade and proceeded up the canal to Harper's Ferry. The march was continued the same day of arriving there, to Charlestown, Va., where they encamped in an oak grove adjoining the field where John Brown was hung. There was much marching and counter-marching until the 24th of March, when they were ordered to take the cars and proceed to Washington. The troops encamped just back of the Capitol until the 28th, when they proceeded to Fortress Monroe, and thence on the march to Hampton, where Gen. McClellan was encamped with one hundred thousand strong. On the 4th of April, they marched up the Peninsula to Big Bethel, and thence to Yorktown the next day. They were under fire for the first time on the 7th of April, losing, however, but one man killed and two wounded. They remained in front of Yorktown until its evacuation by the rebels, on the 3d of May.

Mr. Burnham's statements are full, explicit and interesting, but somewhat more voluminous than the already swollen size of the book will warrant us in inserting. He (Mr. B.) was discharged from the service on the 11th of March, 1863. The following is a synopsis of his service in the army: entered and discharged as above stated: April 7, 1861, in skirmish at Yorktown; April 7th, to 4th May, at the siege of Yorktown; May 7th, in the battle at West Point; June 25th, at Fair Oaks; June 29th, at the battles at Orchard Station and Savage's Station; June 30th, at Glendale; July 1, at Malvern Hills.

JOHN B. BURNHAM.

John B. Burnham, aged 23 years, shoemaker, was born in Essex, and was the son of Nathan and Sarah Burnham. He enlisted in November, 1861, in Capt. Devereaux's Company H, of the Nineteenth Massachusetts infantry. He was in the battle at Fair Oaks, and was taken prisoner during the seven days' battle on the Peninsula, and carried to Richmond where he was held until paroled. An exchange of prisoners was effected about the first of September, and he was ordered to report himself at the camp in Readville.

JAMES FREDERIC HASKELL.

James Frederic Haskell, farmer, was born in Essex; son of Enoch and Nancy Haskell. He enlisted on the 19th of October, 1861, into Company I, Twenty-third Massachusetts Volunteers, infantry. He died on board the Suwannee steamer, on the 3d of February, 1862, and was buried at sea. His disease was measles and inflammation of the lungs. His age was 19 years, 7 months, and 21 days. Young and more ardent and aspiring than was generally supposed, unexpectedly to all, he sought the battle-field. Short was the march of this youthful hero. In one hundred and seven days from the time of his enlistment, of disease contracted in the army, "he slept the sleep that knows no waking."

WILLIAM A. ANDREWS.

William A. Andrews, aged 15 years, was born in Essex, shoemaker, son of William Allen A. and Esther B. Andrews. He enlisted December 2, 1861, in Company H, Capt. Devereaux, Nineteenth Regiment Massachusetts Volunteers, infantry. He was in the battles of the Peninsula, and was wounded on the 30th of June, 1862, in the battle of White Oak Swamp, and has not been heard from up to this time (February, 1864); is supposed to have died of his wound.

HENRY C. MEARS.

Henry C. Mears, aged 15 years, farmer, was the son of Samuel and Sarah Ann Mears; born in Essex. He enlisted in 1861, served thirteen months, and was then discharged on a surgeon's certificate of disability. He however re-enlisted, October 1, 1863, in the Second Regiment Massachusetts Heavy Artillery, Col. Frankle, in Company B, Capt. N. B. Fuller. He was appointed corporal upon his re-enlistment, and the regiment was ordered to Fort Macon, N. C.

GEORGE COGSWELL.

George Cogswell was born in Essex, March 12, 1827; parents, John and Lucretia Cogswell. He enlisted December 9, 1864, for one year, into the Twenty-fifth Massachusetts, unattached. Ordered to Galloup's Island, nine miles down Boston Harbor, and thence to Fort Warren, where they were drilled until the 20th of February following, under Capt. Fitz J. Babson, thence to Fort Miller in Marblehead, and subsequently to Fort Glover under Lieut. Dunn. Mr. C. was taken sick at Fort Miller, and remained so from the 15th of February till the 1st of March. He was mustered out in July, 1865.

ANCILL K. BUTMAN.

Ancill K. Butman, aged 41 years, shoemaker; was born in Essex, son of John and Hepzibah Butman. He enlisted December 2, 1861, in Capt. Devereaux's Company H, Nineteenth Massachusetts Volunteers, infantry. He was discharged on a surgeon's certificate of disability from Chesapeake hospital, Fortress Monroe, on the 3d of November, 1862. His disease was rheumatism.

WILLIAM H. H. BURNHAM.

William H. H. Burnham, aged 22 years, was born in West Gloucester. He enlisted in February, 1862, in Company L, Capt. Andrews, Fourteenth Regiment, Heavy Artillery. He was detailed as major's orderly; discharged January 5, 1864, on a surgeon's certificate of disability. His disease was fever and ague. He was in no battle.

WILLIAM H. HAYDEN.

William H. Hayden, aged 21 years, was born in Stoughton; son of Luther and Sarah Ann Hayden. He enlisted in April, 1861, into Capt. Todd's Company A, Nineteenth Massachusetts Volunteers. He was in the battles of Yorktown, Fair Oaks, and Fredericksburg, also the seven days' fight on the Peninsula under Gen. McClellan. He was detailed as Gen. Stone's orderly, and at length was taken sick and discharged on a surgeon's certificate of disability, March 10, 1863.

AARON HERBERT STORY.

Aaron Herbert Story, aged 17 years, was the son of Aaron and Aurelia Story. He enlisted October 21, 1861, in the Twenty-third Massachusetts Volunteers, Company B, Capt. Martin. On the 21st of November, 1863, we find him stationed at Newport News, Va. He was subsequently made Fife Major in the regiment of Col. Kurtz, where he is understood to have remained until his discharge, October 13, 1864.

DAVID E. CLIFFORD.

David E. Clifford, aged 37 years, was born in Salem, son of Peter and Hannah Clifford. He enlisted on the 26th of June, 1861, for three years, in Company E, Capt. Allen, Twelfth Massachusetts Volunteers, and was ordered to join Gen. Banks at Harper's Ferry. He was in the battle of Cedar Mountain on the 8th of August, 1862, and at Bull Run on the 30th of the same month. He lost a finger in this battle and was sent to the Caspar Hospital, Seventh street, Washington. Here he remained about ten days, and was then sent to the hospital at corner of Bond and Cherry streets, Philadelphia, where he remained until the 15th of December, 1862, when he was discharged on surgeon's certificate of disability.

EDWARD EVERETT McINTIRE.

Edward Everett McIntire, aged 18 years, shoemaker, was born in Essex; son of Nathaniel and Hannah McIntire. He enlisted the 2d of December, 1861, in Company C, Twenty-fourth Massachusetts Volunteers, Capt Pratt. They were ordered to join Gen. Burnside's brigade, and were in the battles at Roanoke Island and Newbern, and also in the assault of Fort Wagner, July 15, 1863. He was in the hospital but once, and that but for a short time. In addition to the battles above specified Mr. McIntire was at Kinston and Goldsboro' in 1862, and went with his regiment to St. Augustine, Florida, early in October, 1863.

Mr. McIntire states verbally, that by far the severest fighting which he saw during his three years in the army, was at Newbern. This battle it will be recollected occurred in 1862. He afterwards re-enlisted and was stationed in different forts for coast defense in the vicinity of Boston.

MONSIEUR M. ANDREWS.

Monsieur M. Andrews, aged 24 years, by trade a shoemaker, was the son of Benjamin and Lydia Andrews; enlisted 31st of December, 1861, into the Thirtieth Regiment, Company K. Mr. Andrews was never wounded, but suffered from sickness severely. He was attacked with typhoid fever on reaching New Orleans, which disqualified him from active service for two months, commencing about the 10th or 12th of May, 1862. His second attack of illness was about the 1st of June, 1863. His ailment was chronic diarrhœa, the bane of the army under a southern sun and lying too often upon a southern soil. This attack lasted four months, and was the cause of his discharge. He was, however, more than a merely passive sufferer by the war. On the 5th of August, 1862, he was in a battle about half a mile in the rear of the State House at Baton Rouge. This occurred shortly after returning from Vicksburg, where they were, about the 1st of August. The battle near the State House, referred to, lasted about eight hours. "We had," says he verbally, "but about two thousand five hundred men; and more than one in ten were sick; in our company nearly half. The spies informed the rebels of the sickness among our soldiers, and this induced them, with five thousand effective men under Gen. J. C. Breckinridge, to attack us. We contended successfully with them for eight hours and drove them. This, however, was owing to the fact that we had artillery in which they were deficient, viz: The Fourth Massachusetts Battery, the Sixth Massachusetts Battery, Nims' Battery, and the First Maine. The fight commenced at three o'clock in the morning We lost about seventy killed and two hundred and fifteen wounded; and the rebels left three hundred dead and seventy wounded on the field. The rebels had expected the co-operation of their river ram, Arkansas, but she had run aground six miles above, and was *hors de combat.* They had, however, some fourteen field pieces, but our batteries did excellent service. Gen. Thomas was killed with a rifle ball through the head. The rebels lost their Brig. Gen. Clarke, and his aid, Col. Lovell, also Capt. A. H. Todd, a brother of Mrs. Lincoln, wife of the President of the United States. We also captured thirty prisoners." Mr. Andrews re-enlisted in December, 1864, for one year, for coast defense, in Capt. Babson's company, but was discharged at the close of the war.

GEORGE ROSS.

George Ross, born in Ipswich, February 18, 1817, was the son of Samuel Ross; enlisted in the Thirtieth Massachusetts Regiment, Company K. This regiment was at first under command of Lieut.-Col. Joseph H. French. Mr. Ross enlisted for three years, and was mustered in at Lowell. They sailed from Boston in the Constellation, and after a voyage of thirty-three days, says the soldier, with some detention at Fortress Monroe, they arrived at Ship Island. After a detention of five or six weeks, they proceeded to the Mississippi River. At the time of their arrival at Ship Island, it may be stated, the United States fleet of gun-boats and mortar-boats was lying there; each of the latter carrying one mortar and two guns, and there were, he says, twenty of them, all moved by sails, being of eighty to one hundred tons burthen. This fleet preceded the troops, there being some eighteen to twenty thousand of the latter, up the Mississippi to the capture of Fort Jackson, which took place after a bombardment of about six days. They were afterwards landed at New Orleans, and quartered in a large sugar store and other large buildings. The place for drilling was an immense building, he thinks an Odd Fellows' Hall, well-carpeted; here they remained some two months, being drilled twice a day. In July they proceeded to Baton Rouge and thence to Vicksburg, soon after which he was taken sick; it proved to be an epidemic among the troops. Of one hundred and one men in this company, only eighteen, he says, were fit for duty. On the authority of the Gloucester (Mass.) newspaper, it may be stated, there were but one hundred and thirty-two in the whole regiment fit for duty. Mr. Ross states that during the progress of his fever, his *hearing*, which had long been imperfect, became for the time entirely lost, so that his discharge was on that account.

GEORGE ROSS, JR.

George Ross, Jr., was the son of the foregoing. Although he enlisted on the Rockport quota, yet as he had lived with his father in Essex, he seems entitled to notice with our soldiers. His *march* was, like far too many others, *a short one*. He was drowned while lying off Fort Jackson. He seems to have stepped upon one side of a small boat which tipped, and as is believed, he went over backwards, and being heavily equipped, sunk to the bottom before his father's eyes; though no one at the time knew who it was. He was 18 years old, and was married a short time before enlisting.

RUFUS E. MEARS.

Rufus E. Mears was the youngest son of Samuel and Lydia Mears, and was 21 years old when he enlisted in the Thirty-ninth Regiment, Company A, under Col. P. S. Davis and Capt. George S. Nelson. He was in the battles of Mine Run, Wilderness, Spottsylvania, North Anna, Tolopotomy, Bethesda Church and Petersburg. He was taken prisoner at the Weldon Railroad, August 18, 1864, and died in a rebel prison at Salisbury, October 26, 1864.

DANIEL BURNHAM.

Daniel Burnham, aged 30 years, shoemaker; son of Nimrod and Susan Burnham; was born in Essex; enlisted, August 15, 1862, for three years, in the Thirty-ninth Regiment, Col. Davis, Company A, Capt. Nelson, and was mustered in at Camp Stanton, at Boxford. Mr. B. left Boxford with the regiment on the 6th of September, 1862, and arrived at Washington city on the 8th; marched to Arlington Heights on the 9th, and three days afterwards moved to camp Chase. The regiment marched for Edward's Ferry, on the 14th of September, where they arrived on the 17th, and here, on the night of the 22d, the troops were called out to stop the rebels from crossing. October 1st, the regiment was sent to Conrad's Ferry, and on the 6th, was again ordered up the river, to prevent another threatened crossing. On the 12th, they were marched to Seneca's Mills, and on the 21st to big Muddy Branch. After remaining awhile at the cross roads, they marched to Poolesville on the 21st of December. Here the regiment remained until the 15th of April, when they again marched to Washington. During

this march the rain fell heavily, and the mud was in full character
with itself in a Virginia soil.   The progress on the 15th was but seventeen
miles.   At Rockville, where the encampment was made, the rain continued
through the night, the clothes of the soldiers being wet through, of course.
On the next day the progress was still less, viz., but fifteen miles.   The
weather continued stormy, and the mud, if possible, deeper than before.   On
the 17th, they made but five miles.   Washington seems not to have been
reached till the 18th of April, when this soldier went on guard, at the army
headquarters, near Gen. Halleck's office.   Four hundred of the regiment
were now detailed at different parts in the city, for provost duty.

The troops, or a portion of them were allowed to see the lions of the Federal city, of course having themselves been " the observed of all observers."
On the 6th of May, says Mr. Burnham, in a letter to the writer, " I had a
pass to go round the city ; went into the Capitol, Patent Office, Smithsonian
Institute and President's house.   Mr. B. kept a journal up to this date, at
least, from which the above extracts have been made.

A short description given by Mr. Burnham, of the morals of the Essex
soldiers in the Thirty-ninth, Company A, in a letter dated 8th of September,
1862, from Rappahannock station, is so honorable to them that it is tran-
scribed entire.   After speaking of Sabbath-breaking and other enormities in
the army, he says : " With great pleasure I can assure you that the Essex
boys respect our meetings, and enjoy the religious privileges which we have,
and none of them take any part in the open profanity which prevails in the
army to such a great extent ; and this for one thing does me good and comforts me in what I always believe the unspeakable blessing of a Sabbath
School education."   On turning to the records of the largest Sabbath School
in Essex, it is perceived that *nine* out of the fourteen soldiers in the Thirty-
ninth, had been members of that Sabbath school.   Mr. Burnham was killed
in the battle of the Wilderness, May 6th, 1864.

WILLIAM GILBERT DODGE.

William Gilbert Dodge, aged 15 years, was born in Essex ; son of Moses
and Sally Dodge, both deceased.   He enlisted August, 1862, in Company
G, Capt. Trull, Thirty-ninth Regiment Massachusetts Volunteers, infantry ;
ordered from Camp Stanton, Lynnfield to Virginia.   This regiment had
been in no battles down to February, 1864, but was generally on the march ;
stationed in camp near Mitchell's Station, Virginia, at the latter date above.

DAVID LEWIS STORY.

David Lewis Story, shoemaker, aged 19 years, was born in Essex, son
of David Story, 2d, and Susan Story ; enlisted August, 1862, in Company
K, Capt. E. L. Giddings, Fortieth Regiment Massachusetts Volunteers, infantry.   They were ordered to join the army of the Potomac and afterwards
sent to Folly Island, Charleston harbor, and from that place to Hilton Head.
The regiment had been in no battles up to February, 1864.

Statements like this last, however, will not apply to the subsequent history of this distinguished regiment. It elevates the sensibilities of any inhabitant of Essex to know that Essex " boys " belonged to it. Unlike many others, this regiment served a part of the time as *mounted infantry* and was detailed to the column intended to operate in Florida. Here, indeed, it served in that capacity, bearing its part in all the conflicts in which the Fortieth was engaged, especially (as Essex men are pleased to know) at Olustee, February 20, 1864, and at Cedar Creek, March 1, 1864 ; our idea being that leaden balls have seldom rained as they rained there. And it is most gratifying to add in the words of Adj. Gen. Schouler's report, made January, 1866, that "too much cannot be said of the *men* composing this regiment. There never was a case of desertion to the enemy, says the report, and though often under the most trying fire, and called into duties deemed almost impossible, yet it can never be said that the Fortieth ever run, or even showed the white feather."

The following extracts of a letter from this soldier at a much earlier stage of the war, to his young brother, are introduced to show that our soldiers, although often but young and inexperienced, were still by no means discontented or unhappy when away, and even amidst the perils of war. He dates at Camp Ethan Allen, September 26th, 1862 : " Dear brother, I have just come in from the woods and thought you would like to hear from me. About four hundred of us have been out into the woods, detailed to cut down trees, and you better believe we have *cut some*. There are so many detailed from every company, and they have been at work now for about three days. They let the trees remain just where they happened to fall. The reason for cutting them is partly because they obstruct our view of the rebels, and partly that the trees may obstruct their march. The woods belong to the rebel Gen. Lee, and his house is right in sight of the woods. They estimate the wood we have cut at *twelve hundred cords*, and it is the very best kind. Our living is good, much better than it was at Boxford. We have been expecting an attack by the rebs every night since we have been here. The place was taken from them about one year ago, and there are graves all round back of the hill. We have picked up lots of balls," etc. Want of room forbids making further extracts.

TIMOTHY ANDREWS, JR.

Timothy Andrews, Jr., was born in Essex, May 7, 1820 ; spar-maker by trade ; son of Timothy and Susan P. Andrews. Enlisted August 18, 1862, in Company A, Capt. Nelson, Thirty-ninth Regiment, Massachusetts Volunteers, infantry. Went first to Camp Cameron, and thence to Boxford at Camp Stanton. The regiment was first ordered to Poolesville, Maryland, thence to Harper's Ferry, and thence to Washington, where the Thirty-ninth were on guard for some time. They were afterwards ordered again to Harper's Ferry and Hagerstown. On the 15th of December Mr. Andrews was detailed on the ammunition train. It was at Poolesville that he slept his first sleep upon the bare ground, and it would not have been very surprising if it had proved his last. A rain came on in the night, so that when they awoke, the water was some three inches deep around them, yet so deep had been their sleep from fatigue, that they knew nothing of it till morning! Mr. A. was appointed by the Colonel to go to Washington for horses, and the character of his army life was now so far changed that his time was chiefly spent at regimental headquarters at first, and afterwards he was made carpenter at brigade headquarters. After marching to Poolesville on the 21st of December, his first duty was the erection of a hospital for the sick. In January following he was ordered for the third time to Washington for another supply of horses and mules. The 19th of August, 1864, was a disastrous day for the Thirty-ninth Massachusetts Volunteers, losing in two days, as they did, two hundred and forty men, killed, wounded and prisoners. After this date, Mr. Andrews' duties were chiefly in the ordnance office as an assistant clerk under Capt. Trembly of the One Hundred and Fourth New York Volunteers.

The compiler of this chapter regrets the small amount of space assigned to the sketch of this soldier. By far the most important and interesting page of his army life has come to hand at so late a day, (dated December 21, 1867,) that to make room for it within these limits, is utterly impossible. It will go upon file with much other unpublished though important matter, and remain for future reference.

GEORGE F. BURNHAM.

George F. Burnham, aged 27 years, shoemaker, born in Essex, son of Silas and Sarah Burnham; enlisted July, 1862, in the Thirty-ninth Regiment Massachusetts Volunteers, Co. A, Col. P. S. Davis; mustered into the United States service August 20th, at Camp Stanton, Lynnfield. They were ordered to Washington and were on guard duty for some time. On the 24th of December, 1863, they were in camp at Mitchell's Station. Mr. B. was in the battles of Mine Run, Wilderness, Spottsylvania, Gravelly Run and Five Forks. He was wounded at Spottsylvania May 8, 1864, and was then sent to Washington where he remained until September. He was discharged in June, 1865.

JOHN C. CHANNEL.

John C. Channel enlisted in the Thirty-ninth Regiment, Col. P. S. Davis, Company A, Capt. Nelson. For a full description of the operations of this regiment, reference may be had to the sketches of Albert A. Haskell, Daniel Burnham, Willbur Burnham, and Asa Story, all of whom died in the service or were killed, also to the sketches of George Washington Burnham, James Horace Burnham and others who survived. Mr. Channel was discharged for disability under his enlistment, and afterwards was drafted, but exempted on account of disability.

GEORGE F. GUPPY.

George F. Guppy was born in Rochester, N. H; son of Samuel and Philenia Guppy; enlisted August 15, 1862, in the Thirty-ninth Massachusetts Volunteers, Col. P. S. Davis, Company A. He was discharged at an early date, on a surgeon's certificate of disability.

ALBERT A. HASKELL.

Albert A. Haskell, was born February 12, 1843; son of Francis and Mary K. Haskell. He enlisted in July or August 1862, in Company A, Capt. Nelson, Thirty-ninth Massachusetts Volunteers, infantry, Col. P. S. Davis. The regiment left camp at Boxford for Washington, September 6th, remained there and at Poolesville during the winter and spring. Left Washington for Harper's Ferry and Hagarstown in May, 1863, and joined the army of the Potomac, and were held in reserve at the attack on Fredericksburg, under Gen. Meade, after which time they were in camp at Mitchell's Station, until the latter part of April, 1864. As the history of this regiment is like others, minutely described by Adjt. Gen. Schouler in his admirable reports, it seems unnecessary here to go much beyond the personal history of the soldier. The circumstances of his capture as a prisoner took place on the 18th of August, 1864. From the letters written by him to his friends, a few incidents may be gathered to relieve the dullness of statistics. On the day of Col. Davis' death, July 11, 1864, Mr. H. writes thus: "I am very sorry to write that Col. Davis was wounded by a shell very badly. I am afraid it will prove fatal. He was wounded through the thigh, tearing one leg terribly. He will be missed very much in the regiment. The boys feel very bad about it."

In a previous letter of June 3, 1864, he says "I have been up to the First Massachusetts, this forenoon. They are on the same line as ourselves, but their time is out to-morrow and I suppose they will leave us. I tell you it makes a fellow feel a little homesick sometimes, to see the men going home, *right to our own homes*, and we can't go ourselves; but our time will come after awhile, and if we live, happier will be the meeting," a hope alas! never to be realized; and as showing that he had a full appreciation of the dangers of army life, he says in the same letter: "Our regiment has fourteen months from to-morrow *and what there is left of us* on that day will be happy boys;" a hope as deceptive as the former; and again he says. "we have advanced the main line, since I last wrote home, about a quarter of a mile, and built new works." The following incident reminds one of a few similar events that occurred in the Revolutionary war, and takes away the idea of *personal hatred*, even among hostile troops. "A week ago to-day, the pickets that were out, made an agreement not to fire upon each other, unless one or the other advanced. After that, they got to *trading* our *hard tack* for their corn bread—coffee for tobacco, &c., but the officers stopped it. Now we hoot at each other a little, but not a gun is fired; while on our right, where we were about ten days ago, they keep up a firing all the time." Mr H. describes the military works erected by them, and inserts a drawing of them made by himself which ought to have a place in this sketch, as showing his native tact in delineating objects presented to the eye.

The dreadful process of starvation in the case of this youthful soldier,

lasted one hundred and sixty-six days, ending only with his life on the 31st
of January, 1865. Some of the details of the horrors of Salisbury prison,
will be found in the sketch of George Washington Burnham, a fellow-
prisoner of Mr. Haskell, but who survived. By a memorandum furnished
by surviving friends, it appears that he was taken prisoner of war, at the
battle of the Weldon Railroad, was thence carried to Libby prison, thence
to Belle Island, and finally to Salisbury prison, where he died at the time
above stated. The Wilderness, Weldon Railroad, and Petersburg, were the
principal battles in which he fought.

OLIVER HAZARD PERRY SARGENT.

Oliver Hazard Perry Sargent, aged 34, was born in Gloucester; ship
carpenter. He enlisted at Essex, in the Twenty-second Massachusetts Volunteers, Company G, in October, 1862, the headquarters of which were at
Camp Wilson, Hall's Hill, Va. Mr. Sargent, like several others from
Essex, was an easy and ready writer, and kept his friends constantly informed
of army movements, both great and small. The following extracts of a letter from him while at Hall's Hill, in Gen. Fitz John Porter's division, will
give an idea of his talent at description, and will also convey an idea of army
life, under date of February 17, 1862.

"My Dear Sir: I have no doubt you have found the exact position of Hall's
Hill, near which we are encamped. Draw upon the map a straight line from
Chain Bridge to Munson's Hill, and from Ball's cross-roads to Miner's Hill.
The lines will cross at Hall's Hill. Col. Cass, with the Ninth Massachusetts, is
immediately in our front, with the Eighty-third Pennsylvania, Fourteenth New
York, Fourth Michigan, the Fourth Rhode Island Battery and Griffin's Battery
(Regulars), composing Morale's Brigade. Near us on Hall's Hill, are the
Second Maine, Eighteenth Massachusetts, Follet's Battery, and Twenty fifth
New York, composing with our regiment, Martindale's or the Second Brigade.
Near us on the other side, is the Seventeenth New York, and in our rear the
Forty-fourth New York, Sixty-third Pennsylvania, and the New Jersey
Stockton Regiment, and on Mount Olivet, a little farther in the rear, the
Fifth Massachusetts Battery, composing Gen. Butterfield's Brigade. In ad-
dition to these are two cavalry regiments just in our rear, one from Pennsylvania, the other (McClellan's Rangers) from Kentucky, altogether composing
Gen. Porter's division. . . . . . It is a grand army. I have seen seventy-
five thousand men on one field since I have been here, and on several
occasions have seen reviews of forty thousand. . . . . . Col. Wilson was out
to see us yesterday, and told us we had only to wait for the traveling. Two
long trains of artillery are in Washington ready to move. One of the trains
has one hundred sixty-eight pound cannon; the other has one hundred
one-hundred pound cannon. In addition to these, there are several batteries
of light artillery and two hundred wagons loaded with ammunition. The
army has been building a road from Georgetown to Alexandria and Lees-
burg turnpike. It is done by laying logs at the bottom and covering them

with poles and dirt. It is rough, but it keeps us out of the mud. Before this road was built our wheels sank to the hubs. It was awful The worst thing I have seen in the army, is the management in the hospital department. Every morning the sick are marched up to the hospital tent, and obliged to wait, *out of doors*, in the open air, whatever the weather may be. It is strange that no more are sick, or that any recover. The sick are well cared for when really in the hospital; and yet I pity any man who is sick here. Another curious matter is the method of punishment adopted It is often ridiculous. Think of a boy carrying a barrel on his shoulders with his head through a hole in the head of the barrel, and 'thief,' perhaps, written on the side. I saw a boy thus at work for three days, from reveille to tattoo, stopping only to get dinner, until he fell from exhaustion. The lieutenant in charge would not let any one pick him up. I took the boy up, and told the lieutenant to make his charges if he pleased. I have heard nothing from it since. The ball and chain is a common mode of punishment. I have seen a great many men at work on the roads and fortifications, with a six pound ball attached to one end of a six foot chain, the other being round the prisoner's leg. Other modes of punishment are, carrying a log, the gag, cutting down the pay, shaving one side of the head and knapsack drill. . . . . . I am in the Quartermaster's department, and have charge of all the teams, twenty-five in number. I ride about the country more than any man in the camp. . . . . . Our Capt., Jesse A. Gove, is a captain in the regulars and has been for ten years. He had command of one thousand men in Utah, and took on eight hundred and fifty of them when he came here. He is a fine officer."

But Mr. Sargent has passed away by the undiscriminating fate of war. As he filled a somewhat larger space in the public eye at home, however, than soldiers often do, it will surprise no one to find one leaf more bestowed upon him here, than there would otherwise have been. He was made an orphan at the age of nine, his father having died in 1832, and his mother in 1836. We find him an apprentice to Mr. Ezra Perkins, senior, of Essex, when ten years old, beginning work at the shoemaking trade. At the district school he was a diligent scholar. Books were among his dearest companions, and yet many avenues to knowledge seemed to open before him, as they always will where the love of it is strong. It is believed there were few lessons recited even by classes to which he did not belong, to which he had not an open ear. Few were the teacher's remarks, especially at a general or miscellaneous exercise, which he did not hear and remember. In looking over his life-long diary of little short of fifteen hundred folio pages, in two large ledger volumes, there is most conclusive evidence of the truth of the above remark. He has been known to remark that his school teacher at Essex once recommended the keeping of a journal, to his scholars, but who could have anticipated such a result as this? The keeping of this journal, it is believed, was never intermitted, and it enables us to account for his self-culture, for his close thinking and mental train-

ing generally. He would seem to have adopted Dr. Franklin's rule for the
farmer :

> " Plough deep, while sluggards sleep,
> And you shall have corn to sell and to keep."

As a member of the village debating club, he distinguished himself at
at once. He saw with ease how error could be assailed and truth defended ;
and his flow of language was ready and happy. Notwithstanding the ob-
scurity of his beginning in Essex, Mr. Sargent was not slow to find his true
level among our young men. He was called to preside at the annual town
meeting when but almost a youth, and shortly after, he was made both town
and parish clerk, and his records had the public approval, as appears from
the fact that he continued to fill both offices, till he laid them down to obey
what he believed to be his country's call. Mr. Sargent represented the
town in general court in 1857, was one of the special county commissioners
till he surrendered his commission on going into the army. He was a justice
of the peace for several years, and held his commission till he died. Various
other offices also, he was called upon from time to time to fill, a fact showing
how well he stood in the estimation of the public.

But the object of this appendix to the town history, compels us to confine
ourselves to the soldiers *as soldiers*, and here we must leave him " alone in
his glory."

SIMEON SWETT.

Simeon Swett enlisted in Company I, Twenty-third Massachusetts, Col. John
Kurtz, and in 1864 was under the command of Col. A. Elwell. The personal
history of this volunteer is not known to the compiler at the present date,
December 30, 1867.

WILLIAM P. HASKELL.

William P. Haskell enlisted June, 1862 in the Fourteenth Massachusetts
Volunteers, Company A, Capt. Shatswell. It is painful to commence a sketch
of the soldiers of the regiment named above, with a record of death ; yet
such is the Divine appointment. William P. Haskell died at Fort Albany on
the 6th of January, 1862, at the early age of 17, of disease contracted in the
army, viz. : erysipelas in his left side. The following letter from Lieut. Smith
contains the sad details :

FORT ALBANY, Va., January 6, 1862.

MRS. HASKELL,—*Dear Madam :* It becomes my painful duty, this morning, to inform you of the sudden and unexpected death of your son William
P. Haskell. He had been sick but four days and none of us thought him so
near his end. Yet 'tis even so. Death has snatched another of our comrades, from our midst, and deeply do we mourn his loss. He was ever willing to perform his duties, was alway kind and obliging and cheerful. Little
did we think he would so soon be called from us. His sickness was erysipelas ; it spread all over his left side and looked badly. The doctor said it
was impossible to send the body home ; that it must be buried here for he
turned so fast ; otherwise we should have sent it home. He was buried this

morning near Fort Albany. He had the company as an escort, and a corporal's guard fired over his grave. A prayer was made by our chaplain, and the funeral procession moved to the grave. Peace to his ashes! He was a kind, brave and good boy, and a true soldier. He had *three dollars* in money in his pocket, which I send you by William Burnham, and the rest of his things we will save for you. Deeply sympathizing with you in the loss of your son, I trust his death may be sanctified to you and yours. I am, dear madam, yours most truly,   J. C. SMITH,

First Lieut. Com'd'g Co. A, Fourteenth Mass. Regiment.

STEPHEN P. ANDREWS.

Stephen P. Andrews, aged 25 years, son of Eleazer and Judith Andrews, enlisted June 8, 1862, in Company A, Capt. Shatswell, Fourteenth Massachusetts Volunteers. His regiment was afterwards made a heavy artillery regiment, designated as the Massachusetts First and was stationed in the forts in the vicinity of Washington up to February, 1864, or later. He was promoted Corporal, October 22, 1862, and came home on a furlough of thirty days November 11, 1863, having re-enlisted for three years. He took part in the following named battles, viz: at Spottsylvania Court House, May 19th; at North Anna River, May 23d; at Salem Church, June 2d; at Cold Harbor, June 4th and 5th; near Petersburg, June 16th. He was wounded in his right shoulder, but returned to duty December 4th. On the 1st of January, 1865, he was promoted Sergeant. In addition to the battles above named, he was also in battle on the 5th of February and 25th of March near Hatcher's Run, and on the 31st of March, at South Side Railroad, and was wounded in his right hand. Discharged at Philadelphia, Pa., June 19, 1865, by reason of a gun-shot wound received in battle, after a term of service of three years, eleven months and fifteen days.

DAVID BRAINARD BURNHAM.

David Brainard Burnham, mason by trade, was born in Essex, and was the son of John S. and Clarissa Burnham. He enlisted August 14, 1862, in Company E, Capt. Sawyer, in the Fourteenth Massachusetts Volunteers, infantry. Ten other Essex men were enlisted about the same time into the same regiment, viz.: William H. Hull, Osgood E. Burnham, Albert F. Burnham, J. J. Parsons, Charles A. Burnham, John S. Jones, J. Frank Hart, Joseph W. Tucker, H. Nelson Andrews and Jeremiah Poland, Jr. They were ordered to Camp Cameron, in Cambridge, to wait for the filling up of the regiment. They finally left for Washington, August 18, 1862, and arrived there on the 20th. On the day of their arrival there, they were marched over the long bridge and stationed in different forts on Arlington Heights. While at Fort Albany, the above named Essex men were so divided and disposed of as to fill the vacancies in different companies. D. B. Burnham, W. H. Hull, A. F. Burnham, O. E. Burnham and J. J. Parsons were attached to Company E, and the remaining six to Company A.

The regiment was immediately put under marching orders, and had barely
time to draw clothing, and none at all to drill, before the march commenced,
viz : on the 23d of August, for Cloud's Mills, eight miles from Washington.
Other troops soon began to arrive, and on the following morning the field as
far as eye could see, was covered with men, tents, artillery, horses, mules, etc.
The Eleventh, Sixteenth, Nineteenth and Twenty-second Massachusetts, were
among them.   These troops had now just arrived from the Peninsula, and
the whole corps were to join the army of Gen. Pope.   On the 26th of August, at nine o'clock P. M., the march commenced of twelve miles, halting
at two o'clock A. M.   After a few hours' sleep, such as could be had upon
the *bare ground*, they commenced a hurried march, as news had arrived that
the rebels were cutting the New York Fourth Heavy Artillery in pieces.
They met the New York troops retreating in a completely demoralized condition, having only two pieces of artillery.   They were in a panic and left
their two pieces of artillery in their flight.   Our troops laid here for twenty-
six hours with their rifles loaded, and no less than eleven times in that twenty-
six hours were called to arms, as the rebels were trying to flank the Union
troops.   At six and one-half o'clock, on the 28th, orders were given to return to the forts ; the order, however, was given to each man *in a whisper*.
The object of this was but too well understood during the night following, as
the rebels shelled the ground, they had just left, heavily.   Our troops on their
return to the Heights were so divided as to garrison eight forts, and here they
remained from the 30th of August, 1862, until the month of May, 1864.
Our troops while here often practiced target-shooting with the large guns, the
corporals acting as gunners.   Each one would naturally try to excel, but it
is gratifying to learn that our lamented townsman, Osgood E. Burnham, discovered quite uncommon skill in this to him, new mode of warfare.   During
the twenty months' stay of our troops at this station, they were visited by
distinguished persons, as the President, the Russian Embassy and others,
who often addressed the troops in patriotic terms.

On the 14th of May, 1864, however, orders were received to march to the
front as *Infantry*, and next day, Sunday, they took transports at Alexandria,
and proceeded down the river to Belle Plains.   At this time only two Essex
men remained in Company E, viz., D. Brainard and Osgood E. Burnham.
It may be proper to say, that Parsons and A. F. Burnham, had been discharged.   W. H. Hull was sick in Washington.   The troops arrived at Belle
Plains 17th of May, at nine o'clock, A. M., and marched thirty-four miles to
Fredericksburg, and from thence to the extreme front.   On the 19th says D.
B. B. the subject of this sketch, at four o'clock P. M., " we became engaged
with Ewell's corps which had attacked a supply train."   We lost five hundred and seventeen killed and wounded, fifty-four being shot dead.   The
fight continued till nine o'clock P. M.   The result was a Union victory.   " It
would be hard," says Mr. B., " to describe my feelings when first going into
battle, but I determined to do my duty let what would come."   A ball struck
his rifle out of his hand and also took off the middle finger of his left hand.

Just then he saw Osgood E. Burnham fall, having received a rifle ball in his left hip. With the aid of another soldier he carried Osgood to the rear. Osgood was too faint with loss of blood to reach the surgeon's tent and was laid for a short time in a barn, but as soon as circumstances would permit, was put into the surgeon's hands, being carried upon a stretcher by four men. That was the last time, says Mr. B., that I ever saw my much loved cousin and brother soldier. He was a *model* soldier in camp, and a very brave one in battle. His first and highest ambition was to *do his duty*. When he fell, indeed, the words "wife" and "mother" were almost the only words that fell from his lips. He at length died of lock-jaw, having taken cold probably. Jeremiah Poland, Jr., also received his death wound in that battle, and H. Nelson Andrews was wounded in his hand.

ALBERT FRANK BURNHAM.

Albert Frank Burnham was born in Gloucester, October 2, 1839, and was the son of Francis Burnham, 2d, and Polly Burnham. He enlisted July 23, 1862, in Company E, Capt. Sargent, Fourteenth Massachusetts Volunteers. The regiment was stationed, as before mentioned, in the forts near Washington. He was ruptured in February, 1863, and sent to the hospital, where he remained ten days, when he returned to the regiment, and remained until July, 1863. On the 23d of October, 1863, he was transferred to the Invalid corps; came home, November 12th, on thirty days' furlough; then returned to the regiment and was with it until February 7, 1864, when he was discharged on surgeon's certificate of disability, by order from the War Department, No. 9, certificate being signed by Surgeon N. R. Mosely. It is painful to add that this soldier died at his father's residence in Essex, August 14, 1866, of consumption. He was an only child.

CHARLES A. BURNHAM.

Charles A. Burnham, painter, aged 25 years, was born in Essex; he is married, and has a wife and three children. He was the son of John Fiske and Joanna Burnham, and enlisted August, 1862. His regiment, the Fourteenth (infantry), after their departure for the seat of war, was changed to a heavy artillery regiment. The Fourteenth Regiment, above named, left Camp Cameron, at Cambridge, August 18, 1862, and arrived in Washington on the 20th. At Fort Albany, they were divided into squads, and Charles A. Burnham, the above-named soldier, became a member of Company A, a large number of the men in that company being from Ipswich. In September, 1862, by order of the War Department, this regiment was organized as before stated, as heavy artillery, and to remain so during their whole term of service, though when ordered to the front in May, 1864, they were to act as *infantry*.

WILLIAM H. HULL.

William H. Hull enlisted in August, 1862, in Company E, Capt. Sawyer, Fourteenth Regiment Massachusetts Volunteers, infantry. They were first

52

ordered to Camp Cameron, in Cambridge, for the purpose of filling vacancies, but shortly left the State for Washington, and arrived there in the same month.   Soon after arriving at Washington and crossing the long bridge across the Potomac, they were stationed in different forts on Arlington Heights.   For additional details the reader is referred to the sketch of D. B. Burnham, p. 407.

GEORGE WASHINGTON BURNHAM.

George Washington Burnham was born February 22, 1830, and was the son of Michael and Thirza Burnham.   He enlisted in the Thirty-ninth.   His history being involved with that of Albert A. Haskell, Rufus E. Mears, Daniel Burnham, and others in the same regiment, and substantially the same, need not be minutely repeated.   His verbal statement is that on the 18th of August, 1864, in company with Albert A. Haskell, (see p. 403,) he was captured with some two thousand others, and kept at Petersburg, Va., and at Ship Island, some four days : thence, first to Libby prison, in Richmond, where they remained but two days, after which they were removed across the James to Belle Isle.   Here they found themselves among seven to eight thousand Union prisoners.   The battle in which these prisoners were captured was at Weldon railroad.   From Belle Isle they were removed to Salisbury prison, N. C., from which receptacle *of living death* they were not discharged until February 22, 1865.   At first and for a time, they were allowed flour bread, but afterwards corn bread made of the corn and cob ground together.   Once in four or five days, and sometimes only once in about *ten* days, they were allowed a "bit of *beef*," if so it might be called, sometimes liver, lights, *tripe uncleaned*, and once in a while a little sorghum. "There were five days," 'not consecutive indeed, says Mr. B., "*when we had no food whatever.*"   The prisoners were confined by a close board fence, with a guard on the outside so elevated that they could see over.   On one occasion our soldiers being driven to desperation by hunger, attempted to break out, but were fired upon by the guard.   Sixteen were killed and about forty wounded.   There was, of course, no other attempt to break.   Mr. B. says there was no sickness, *as such*, in the prison, but the want of *shelter* was as destructive to life as hunger itself.   After a parole was finally ordered, the soldiers were sent first to Greensborough, say fifty miles, the whole distance, except about fifteen miles, being performed on foot.   The effect of prison-life, as might be expected, was different upon different men.   Mr. Burnham's eye-sight was impaired, and continued so a long time, so that when sent to Greensborough, he was unable to do night-marching with any safety, falling into culverts, &c.   He thinks many others were similarly affected.   The *scurvy* was also one of the sequels of prison-life, as jaundice had been one of the earlier ailments of it.   Chronic diarrhœa did not affect him particularly, until paroled and on the way home.   The almost endless fighting at the Wilderness, the battle at Weldon railroad, before mentioned, and that at Petersburg, were the principal, if not the only battles in which

Mr. B. was engaged.   "We had no chaplain or surgeon in the prison except rebels.   The soldiers," says Mr. B, "were not all young men by any means, though generally so.   In our company one was sixty years old, a Mr. Gibbs, and a 'right good soldier he.'   Some others were fifty or over, and yet excellent soldiers."   Mr. Burnham believes that explosive bullets were used by rebs to some extent, though the fact has not been referred to by any other Essex soldier, perhaps because not questioned with regard to it.   A soldier from Danvers on his immediate left, Mr. B. thinks, was shot with one of these dreadful missiles, as an explosion appeared to him to take place when the ball struck, which it did in the head.   The soldier in falling, fell upon Mr. B.

OSGOOD E. BURNHAM.

The sketch of this fallen soldier has already been somewhat fully given by his relative and friend, David Brainard Burnham (see page 407), but a distinct notice is certainly due to so fine a soldier as he.   He was born in Essex, December 23, 1835; his parents, Luke and Mary Burnham, both survive.   He enlisted on the 6th of August, 1862, in Company E, Fourteenth Massachusetts Regiment, the same being afterwards changed to Massachusetts First, Company A.   At the time of enlistment, Col. Green commanded the regiment, and Capt. Sargent the company, but their places were subsequently and permanently supplied by Col. Tannat and Capt. Thomson.   Mr. Burnham was made corporal of Company E, on the 16th of October, 1863, which office he held until his death.   He was wounded in the battle of Spottsylvania, on the 19th of May, 1864; was carried first to Fredericksburg, and afterwards to Washington, D. C., where he died in Campbell Hospital on the 28th of May, being nine days after the wound.

The case of this soldier would afford matter for much useful reflection were we not almost precluded in sketches like these from indulging in it.   It may, however, at least be said that it is probably far from being the first time, when very great native modesty has been found to have been united with an equal amount of valor and intrepidity, such as nothing short of the battle-field can well develop.   The precious life it is true, is a great price to pay, but he undoubtedly perceived himself becoming more and more equal to the occasion, and could have said perhaps, with Adjutant Stearns in a letter to his father from some part of the same great battle-field, "father, I am twice the man I ever was before."

HORATIO NELSON ANDREWS.

Horatio Nelson Andrews, son of Joseph and Hannah Andrews, was born June 17, 1836.   He enlisted August 6, 1862, in Company A, Fourteenth Regiment Massachusetts Volunteers, infantry, Col. William B. Green, Capt. Nathaniel Shatswell, of Ipswich, Mass.   They arrived, says Mr. Andrews, in Virginia just in season to take part in the disastrous campaign of Gen. Pope, in which were fought the memorable battles of Bull Run, Centreville, Chantilly, &c.   They were stationed at Arlington Heights for nearly two years, most of which time was on detached service at Division or Brigade Head-quarters, and during which time, the regiment was changed from the Fourteenth Infantry to the First Massachusetts Heavy Artillery, Col. Thomas R. Tannat of Manchester, Mass. They crossed the Rappahannock at Fredericksburg with the regiment of one thousand seven hundred and fifty men in time to take part in Grant's campaign, at a battle in Spottsylvania, in which the regiment lost between three and four hundred men, killed and wounded, among whom were Jeremiah Poland, Jr., and Osgood Burnham of Essex. Mr. Andrews states that he was mustered out at the close of his term of service ; the regiment, then consisting of two hundred and fifty men, in front of Petersburg, Va., having lost nearly one thousand four hundred men in about two months. He received his final discharge, July 21, 1864. He states that he received a pension from the United States for injuries received at Spottsylvania, which consisted of a slight wound in the hip, and in the hand the loss of a finger.

JOHN J. PARSONS.

John J. Parsons enlisted in August, 1862, in Company E, Capt. Sawyer, Fourteenth Massachusetts Regiment, Col. Green. He continued in the same company (E) after a part of the Essex men who enlisted at the same time, were attached to Company A, in the same regiment. His history may be considered as described in that of others in the same company, except when personal, and the facts relating to this point we are unable to give at this date, (December 31, 1867).

MORTY DUGGAN.

Morty Duggan, born in Ireland, county of Cork in 1822 ; enlisted in the Forty eighth Massachusetts, Col. Stone, Company E, Capt. Howes. So perfectly is the personal history of Mr. Duggan identified with his company, and so fully are the services of it set forth by Capt. Howes, (see p. 364 and onward,) also by Mr. Aaron Low and Mr. Lamont G. Burnham in their several journals herein contained, that it is conceived no separate description will be thought necessary.

JOSEPH PROCTER, JR.

Joseph Procter, Jr., carpenter, son of Joseph and Elizabeth G. Procter, born in Essex December 14, 1834 ; enlisted in the Forty-eighth Massachusetts, Company E, Capt. Howes, as a drummer. The fortunes and the services of this ardent and patriotic soldier may be read out in the long sketch given by Capt. Howes, before referred to, to which, as well as that given by Mr. A. Low, the reader is referred.

CHARLES W. PROCTER.

Charles W. Procter, son of Joseph and Elizabeth G. Procter, was born in Essex, December 12, 1838. He enlisted as a fifer, and was connected with Company E, Forty-eighth Massachusetts throughout the entire service of nine months.

JOHN CRAFTS, JR.

John Crafts, Jr., son of John and Nancy Crafts, born October 23, 1819. His first enlistment was on the 9th of November, 1861, in Capt. Tyler Read's Company A, Second Massachusetts Cavalry, and he was discharged July 14, 1862, for disability. Mr. Craft's second enlistment was the 7th of October, 1862, in Capt. Howes' Company E, Forty-eighth Massachusetts Volunteers, Col. Stone. He was in the battle at Plain Store, and at Donaldsonville, for some account of which, see the sketch of Capt. Howes.

FRANKLIN CRAFTS.

Franklin Crafts enlisted two years before the war in the regular army, and was stationed in Nebraska at the commencement of the rebellion. He came to Cincinnati in the summer of 1861, and was thence ordered into Virginia, and was engaged in the battles of Port Republic and at Fredericksburg. He enlisted the second time in October, 1862, in Capt. Howes' Company E, Forty-eighth Massachusetts, Col. Stone, and was with the same regiment and company until their discharge.

WASHINGTON WILKINS JAMES.

Washington Wilkins James, son of John and Eliza James, was born in Essex, February 13, 1841. He enlisted in the Forty-eighth Massachusetts, Col. Stone, Company D, Capt. Noyes. From the statement of Capt. Howes of Company E, we obtain the only facts relating to this youthful soldier. Under date of May 5, 1863, Capt. Howes says: " Wilkins James is quite sick in the hospital." And by an entry on the 9th, it appears he was not so well. It is painful in the extreme to add, that " he died on the 13th of May, and was buried the following day." He found his grave where so many multitudes of precious lives were laid down for their country's good, on the banks of the rolling Mississippi. Peace to the memory of the soldier wherever his ashes lie.

FRANCIS G. MEARS.

Francis G. Mears, son of William H. and Mary Ann Mears, was born September 1837, at Essex. He enlisted in the Forty-eighth Massachusetts, Col. Stone, Company E, Capt. Howes; died at Baton Rouge, June 21, 1863. The military life and its honorable though painful close in death, is sufficiently narrated in the sketch of the Forty-eighth, by Capt. Howes, page 364 and onward, but may be recapitulated here in part. He had had a sickness at the arsenal hospital previous to that of which he died, but so far recovered as to rejoin the regiment on the 17th of April, 1863. He was, however, taken down again on the 4th of May, following, and was at once removed to the hospital. He grew sick rapidly and as Capt H states, " appeared to be failing fast." He improved somewhat afterwards, it appears, as by the journal of the ever attentive Captain it appears that " on the 4th of the month, Mr. Mears was somewhat improving." It has been often remarked, however, that there is *one foe*, which even the bravest and the best cannot

meet, and before which all alike must fall. And accordingly, on the 21st of
June, 1863, this youthful warrior laid off his mortal armor forever, and like
multitudes of others, many of whom were no doubt equally brave, sleeps
on the banks of the mighty Mississippi at Baton Rouge.

It should have been before stated that Mr. Mears was in the line of promotion when taken sick, having been made a sergeant.

SAMUEL MEARS, JR.

Samuel Mears, Jr., was the son of Samuel and Lydia Mears. He was
38 years of age at the time of his enlistment, which was in July, 1862,
in the Thirty-ninth Massachusetts, Company A, Col. P. S. Davis, and
Capt. George S. Nelson. Mr. Mears was not engaged in any regular battle,
and was discharged for disability, in January, 1864. He was re-enlisted
however, in the same year in the Thirteenth Veteran Reserve, in the month
of July, and was finally discharged in January, 1865.

WILLIAM C. HOWARD.

William C. Howard being by *marriage* and *residence*, in part, an Essex
man, and for that reason inserted here, was born at Fall River; son of
Stephen and Lucy Howard. He enlisted at the age of 27 years, in the
Third Maine Regiment, Company A, Capt. Sawyer. He was sworn into the
United States service, June 5, 1861, at Washington. On the 15th of July,
following, they were marched to Centerville, Va., eight miles from Bull Run.
He was in the first Bull Run fight about five hours, when they fell back
twenty-eight miles to Alexandria, where they encamped until the 5th of
April, 1862, when the army were ordered down to Fortress Monroe and
thence to Yorktown, twenty-four miles, where they remained until the 28th
of May. Mr. Howard was in the battle at Williamsburg, about the last of
May, and also at Fair Oaks, where he was taken with a fever. This was
the last of his service in the Third Maine. The Colonel of this Maine regiment was O. O. Howard; Capt. Sawyer commanded this company.

On the 12th of August, 1862, he enlisted in the Tenth Vermont, where he
served until the 3d of July, 1865, making two years and ten months. While
in this regiment he fought in the first battle of Mine Run, on the 24th of
November, 1864, and next in the Wilderness battle on the 5th of May.
Here he lost two of the fingers of his right hand while on picket. The next
battle was on the 2d of April, 1865, breaking the lines before Petersburg, and there they chased " old Bob. Lee," as the rebs used to call him, several days and captured Lee's rear guard of five thousand men, on the 6th of
April. This, says Mr. Howard, was called Sailor's Run, and was the last
battle of the Army of the Potomac, so he says he had the pleasure of saying
he was in *Bull Run first, and Sailor's Run last.* His Colonel was William
Henry, Lieut-Colonel, J. Hunt, and Company, H. And to recapitulate, Mr.
Howard fought as follows, viz.: in the Third Maine, July 21, 1861, at the
first Bull Run battle; in 1862, at Williamsburg and at Fair Oaks; and in

the Tenth Vermont, as follows :   November 27, 1863, at Mine Run ; May 6, 1864, Wilderness ; April 2, 1865, when he lost his fingers ; April 6, 1865, Sailor's Run, being seven battles in all.

ROBERT WALLACE ALLEN.

Robert Wallace Allen, was enrolled September 6th, 1862, being the day preceding his 14th year, and was shortly mustered into the service at Camp Lander, in Wenham, thence assigned to the Fifth Regiment, Company E, Col. Pierson, Capt. John Kent.   He did not return with the regiment, but went on board the gun boat Arletta, Capt. William Wright, Salem.   He was discharged from the United States Naval Hospital, at Brooklyn, N. Y., and from the service, December 21, 1864.   Not much fighting was done while the Fifth Massachusetts Regiment was stationed in North Carolina.   It had a part, however, in several small expeditions.   At the time of the battle at Fort Fisher, March 25, 1865, this soldier was under hospital treatment.

ALBION BURNHAM.

Albion Burnham, son of Samuel and Sallie Burnham, enlisted October 15, 1863, when at the age of 23 years, as first mate of the ship Carnation, and was stationed for a time off Port Royal.   The Carnation was engaged as a part of the blockading squadron in the capture of Charleston, S. C., in February, 1865.

LYMAN H. CHASE.

Lyman H. Chase, (alias Lyman B. Chase,) enlisted in the Fifth Regiment, Col. Pierson, Company K, Capt. Crafts, for *three* months.   And after the expiration of that time during which term the regiment was under the command of Brig. Gen. Lawrence, M. V. M., it volunteered to return for *nine* months, when the President, in 1862, called for three hundred thousand nine months' men.   It appears by Adjutant Gen. Schouler's Report for 1863, p. 117, that after the re-enlistment for nine months, this regiment left Boston the 22d of October, in transports for Newbern, N. C.   It should be observed that while acting as three months' men, "this regiment acted a brave part in the first disastrous battle of Bull Run."   Mr. Chase was 26 years old at the time of his first enlistment.   By the Adjutant General's Report for 1863, it appears that Mr. Chase was acting as wagoner.

JAMES HOWE BURNHAM.

James Howe Burnham, son of Abel and Esther Burnham, was drafted into the army, July 10, 1863, and was first mustered into the Eighteenth Massachusetts Regiment, but afterwards transferred to the Thirty-second, Company I.   He was in the battle of the Wilderness and in several skirmishes, but never wounded.   His entire term of service was twenty-three months and nineteen days, and he received his discharge on the 20th of June, 1865.

JOHN L. MARTYN.

John L. Martyn, enlisted in December, 1861, into Company H, Massachusetts Twenty-fourth, Col. Stevenson.   He is believed to have been at the siege at Fort Wagner, but the details of his army life are not now available.

JOHN S. JONES.

John S. Jones, ship-carpenter by trade, aged 30 years, was born in Essex, and was the son of Abraham and Mary Jones; has a wife and two children. He enlisted August 2, 1862, into Company A, Capt. Shatswell, Fourteenth Regiment. He was detailed to work as a carpenter. On the 29th of May, 1863, he met with the accident of cutting off his great toe, and was sent to the hospital. Left for home, September 30, 1863, on furlough for fifteen days, with orders to report at the expiration of his furlough at the Mason General Hospital, Pemberton square, Boston. He remained there until the 5th of December, when he was transferred to the invalid corps, stationed at Camp Sumner, Wenham. The carpenter-work for which he was detailed was that of getting out timber for gun-carriages.

JEREMIAH POLAND, JR.

Jeremiah Poland, Jr., aged 34 years, was the son of Jeremiah and Betsey Poland. He enlisted first, December 31, 1862, in Company A, Fourteenth Massachusetts Regiment. Re-enlisted December 31, 1863, at Fort DeKalb, in Company A, First Massachusetts Heavy Artillery, Capt. A. A. Hosmer, for three years, and came home on thirty days' furlough. Mr. Poland, according to the sketch given of David B. Burnham (p. 407), is believed to have received his death wound in the battle of Fredericksburg, May 19, 1864. But he is known to have died May 21, 1864, having been wounded by a shell in his body, also in one of his legs.

EDWIN A. HOWES.

Edwin A. Howes, aged 27 years, ship-joiner by trade, was the son of Collins and Rhoda Howes; and was born in Chatham; a widower with one child. He enlisted May 11, 1861, in the Second Regiment, Massachusetts Volunteers, infantry, and left the State July 8, 1861. He was in Gen. Patterson's command at Martinsburg, under the immediate command of Gen. Banks, from August, 1861, till September, 1862. On the date of his enlistment he was appointed corporal, and on the 20th of June was made fourth sergeant of Company F. On the 1st of October, 1862, he was appointed color sergeant, and on the 8th of December, following, was promoted commissary sergeant of the regiment. He was in the battle of Winchester on the 25th of August, 1861, and in that at Cedar Mountain, August 8, 1862. Mr. Howes was attached to the Twelfth Army Corps at Antietam, and was in the battle of September 17, 1862; also when Burnside was crossing at Fredericksburg, this corps was held in reserve, and was not engaged in the battle. It was, however, in the battle at Chancellorsville and at Beverly Ford, also at Gettysburg. On the 2d of August, 1863, this corps was ordered to New York to quell a riot there on account of the draft, and was absent from the army four weeks. On the 24th of September, 1863, they were ordered to East Tennessee to re-enforce Gen. Rosecrans, and since that time have been a part of the Army of the Cumberland. Mr. Howes had been in all the battles in which the regiment had been engaged up to the time of his promotion to the office of commissary sergeant, except during the six weeks in the Spring of 1862, when he was in the hospital at Frederic City, Md. Mr. H. re-enlisted for three years on the 30th of December, 1863, as commissary sergeant of the Second Massachusetts Volunteers, infantry, and came home on a thirty days' furlough in January, 1864. Mustered out of service, August 1, 1865. Whole term of service, four years, two months, twenty days.

DANIEL DUGGAN.

Daniel Duggan, aged 26 years, laborer, was born in the county of Cork, Ireland, and was the son of Dennis and Honora Duggan. He enlisted May 20, 1861, in Company F, Capt. Mudge, Second Massachusetts Regiment, infantry, and was sent to Camp Cameron, Roxbury, and there remained till August 8th. The regiment was then ordered to Western Virginia. He was in the battle and retreat at Ball's Bluff, and was in the second Bull Run battle, also at the battles of Cedar Mountain, Antietam and Gettysburg, besides many skirmishes. In one of these battles he received a flesh wound in the leg. In September, 1863, his regiment was ordered to East Tennessee, where he remained on guard duty until the 7th of January, 1864, when the regiment was ordered home on furlough, he having previously re-enlisted. He arrived home on January 21st. The furlough was for thirty days. He was mustered out July 26, 1865. His whole term of service was four years, two months, fifteen days.

ROBERT W. BURNHAM, JR.

Robert W. Burnham, Jr., aged 21 years, ship-carpenter by trade, was born in Essex; son of Robert W. and Clara Burnham. He enlisted for three years as band musician in the Second Regiment, Massachusetts Volunteers, Col. Gordon. He left Camp Andrews, Roxbury, for the seat of war July 8, 1861; was discharged by a general order, No. 9, after fifteen months of hard service, during which time the regiment was in two or three battles, besides being almost continually on the march. They arrived home September 8, 1862. The number of the original members of the regiment at this time was six hundred only, out of ten hundred and forty that left Camp Andrews one year and two months before. Mr. Burnham enlisted again in the band of the third brigade, twelfth army corps, and was sworn into the service of the United States April 16, 1863. The brigade arrived at Stafford Court House, headquarters of the brigade, April 20th. They left the Army of the Potomac September 26, to join the Army of the West in Tennessee, and January 7, 1864, they left Tullahoma for home with the Second Massachusetts Regiment, having re-enlisted for three years. Arrived home January 21, 1864. Mr. Burnham kept a journal daily, from which the following facts are chiefly derived. We shall feel precluded by the crowded state of the book from inserting much that would deeply interest the reader, but must find room for the following: " June 8, 1862, crossed the Potomac to Falling Waters; bivouacked for the night; constant rain. On the 11th, marched towards Martinsburg; encamped at Bunker Hill, distance eighteen miles; 12th, to Newton, eighteen miles. On the 15th, Gen. (late Col.) Gordon made his farewell address to the regiment. . . . . July 6th, marched four miles; crossed the Shenandoah; passed through Front Royal and encamped. . . . . On the 28th, grand review; 30th, our band played at a funeral here. August 9th, formed in line of battle nine miles from Culpepper, on the right of Banks' command; heavy firing of artillery till six o'clock; grand charge of infantry from the enemy on the whole line; assisted in carrying off the wounded; narrowly escaped being taken prisoner."

GUSTAVUS S. PERKINS.

Gustavus S. Perkins, aged 28 years, was the son of Abraham and Abigail Perkins. He received his commission September 1, 1861, as Second Assistant Engineer of the Colorado steamer, and was ordered to Mobile, where he served fifteen months. He then received a furlough of two weeks, after which he was ordered on board the Donaldson, stationed on the blockade off Wilmington. He here served as First Assistant or head Engineer until Autumn, when, after another short furlough, he was ordered on board the Gettysburg on the blockade off Wilmington. He remained there till the end of the war, being in the engagement at Fort Fisher. After this engagement he was allowed another furlough of three months, after which he received his discharge, September, 1865.

GEORGE DODGE.

George Dodge enlisted in the Massachusetts Twenty-third Volunteers, infantry, Col. John Kurtz, Company I, Capt. Hobbs, which was ordered to join Gen. Burnside's army. This company was in the battles of Roanoke Island, Newbern, Kinston and others. After remaining at Newbern about a year they were ordered to Hilton Head, S. C., where they remained but two days, when they returned to Newbern and thence to Fortress Monroe, where they remained as late as February, 1864. Col. Raymond, who at one time commanded this regiment, pays a compliment which every soldier in the regiment ought to share. "Their excellent conduct, while I had the honor to command them, their coolness and bravery under fire, their vigilance and fidelity at all times displayed, entitles them to the highest praise . . . . . . I shall account it the greatest honor of my life, that I have been privileged to command them." We regret to say we are unable to obtain other facts relating to Mr. Dodge.

RUFUS BURNHAM.

Rufus Burnham, ship-carpenter, single man, was the son of Humphrey and Eliza Burnham, and was born in Essex, November 17, 1838. He enlisted May 9, 1861, in Company F, Capt. Patterson, Second Regiment, Massachusetts Volunteers, infantry. They were ordered to Martinsburg under Gen. Patterson, and were in the battles of Winchester and Cedar Mountain. Mr. Burnham was discharged February 26, 1863, on a certificate of disability, signed by Surgeon Gen. Dale. This soldier died at his father's in Essex, on the 22d of January, 1867, aged 29 years and 2 months, much lamented.

CHARLES PERRY LUFKIN.

Charles Perry Lufkin, shoemaker by trade, was born February 19, 1843, and was the son of John P. and Elizabeth Lufkin. He enlisted December 2, 1861, in Company C, Capt. Pratt, Twenty-fourth Regiment, Massachusetts Volunteers. They were ordered to join Gen. Burnside's division, and were in the battles of Roanoke Island and Newbern, and were then ordered to Charleston harbor, and were in the assault on Fort Wagner, on the 25th of July, 1863, when Mr. L. was struck in the back by a ball from Fort Sumpter. He was carried to Beaufort hospital where he died on the 1st of August, 1863, from the effects of the wound. The first effect of the ball was to produce paralysis of the legs only, but his whole system shared in it, and he died as above stated. His grave is in the National Cemetery at Beaufort, and affectionate comrades placed a head-stone above the consecrated spot where sleep the remains of Charles P. Lufkin. Besides the battles named above, he was in the secret expedition to Columbia, March 8, 1862; in the battle at Vanter's Creek, June 5, 1862; at Rawle's Mills, November 2; Kinston, December 14; Whitehall, December 16; Goldsboro, December 17,—all the above being in North Carolina; also at James' Island, S. C., July 16, 1863, and at Morris Island, July 18, 1863.

CHARLES F. MORSE.

Charles F. Morse, aged 33 years; enlisted in Company H, Nineteenth Regiment, Massachusetts Volunteers, Capt. Devereaux, which was ordered to join the Army of the Potomac under Gen. McClellan. They were in the seven days' battles on the Peninsula, also, at the battles of Yorktown and Fair Oaks. He was taken sick on the march to Antietam, and sent to the hospital at corner of Fifth and Buttonwood streets, Philadelphia, where he died after a sickness of two months, aged 33 years. He was in the service about eighteen months, and leaves a widow and three children. A member of the same company and an acquaintance of this soldier, states that Mr. Morse, like some others, frequently expressed his fears, that he never should survive the campaign, and for some reasons had no expectation of ever reaching home again.

REUBEN ANDREWS.

Reuben Andrews, aged 25 years, by trade a shoemaker; was the son of Obed and Ruth Andrews, and was born in Essex. He enlisted November 25, 1861, in Company H, Capt. Devereaux, Nineteenth Regiment, Massachusetts Volunteers. The regiment, as before stated, was ordered to join McClellan's army. He was in the battles on the Peninsula and at Yorktown, and died at Harper's Ferry, October 27, 1862, of typhoid fever. He left a widow and one child. For further allusions to Mr. Andrews, see the sketch of John C. Butman.

CHARLES EDWIN ANDREWS.

Charles Edwin Andrews, aged 26 years, shoemaker; was the son of Ira and Martha Andrews, and was born in Essex. He enlisted in Company H,

Capt. Devereaux, Nineteenth Regiment. They were, as before stated, ordered to join the Army of the Potomac. Mr. Andrews was in the battle at
Yorktown, and was killed by a ball through his head, in the seven days'
fight on the Peninsula, at White Oaks. This battle was on the last day of
May and first day of June, 1862, and he sleeps with multitudes of others
on the banks of the Chicahominy River. It is said of him, that from the
time of his enlistment, he had a premonition of the final event, and while
putting on the military dress at Salem, made some remark to a comrade
strongly indicative of the sad result. Reference may also be had to the
sketch of J. C. Butman, page 424.

ERASTUS HOWES.

Erastus Howes, was born in Chatham, Barnstable County, July 4, 1834,
and was the son of Enoch and Azubah Howes. He enlisted on the 17th of
October, 1861, for three years, into the Massachusetts Twenty-fourth, Col.
Thomas G. Stevenson, and Company C, Captain Robert H. Stevenson.
He was sworn in as a Massachusetts volunteer at Readville, and mustered
into the United States service at Annapolis, in December, 1861. Mr.
Howes sailed with the Burnside expedition to Hatteras, N. C. The following is a list of the battles in which he was engaged, from an early period
to the literal close of the war. The first was that at Roanoke Island, N. C.,
on the 8th of February, 1862; secret expedition to Columbia, N. C., March
8, 1862; Newbern, N. C., March 14, 1862; Tranter's Creek, N. C., June
5, 1862; Rawles Mills, N. C., November 2, 1862; on detached service
from December 1, 1862, to June 20, 1863; at Newbern N. C.; joined the
regiment at Folly Island, S. C., July 10, 1863; battle of James Island,
S. C., July 16, 1863; charge on rifle-pits of Fort Wagner, Morris Island,
S. C., August 18, 1863. On the 25th of September, the regiment, being very
much reduced in numbers by hard service and *malaria*, were ordered to St.
Augustine, Florida, to recruit health. Re-enlisted at the latter place, on the
4th of January, 1864, for *three years*. Ordered to the Army of the James;
joined Butler's command. Captured Bermuda Hundred, Va., May 6, 1864,
and the battle of Petersburg Railroad, Va., followed on the 13th. Mr.
Howes was wounded while charging a rebel battery, and sent to the hospital
at Point Lookout, Md.,—thence transferred to Veteran Reserve Corps, April
13, 1865. He was ordered to Washington, D. C., in August and placed on
duty in the Capitol prison, and as an appropriate conclusion to his military
career, was an assistant at the hanging of H. Wirz.

LIEUT. CYRUS ANDREWS.

Lieut. Cyrus Andrews, was born at Essex, and was the son of Israel Jr., and
Keziah Andrews. He enlisted at Gloucester, Mass., October 18, 1861, joined
the Twenty-fourth Regiment at Readville, and was mustered into the service
on the 23d. About the last of October, the same year, he was ordered with
Companies A, B, C and I, to guard prisoners at Fort Warren in Boston

harbor. Joined the regiment again at Readville, on the 2d of December, but on the 9th, left for Annapolis, Md. Arrived there December 12th, and on the 21st were detached for duty on board the steamer Eastern State and remained on board till the battle of Roanoke Island on the 8th of February, 1862. It was the fate of Mr. A. to double stormy Cape Hatteras no less than fourteen times. He was in the battle of Roanoke Island, N. C., on the 8th and 9th of February, 1862, and it was the grateful duty of this regiment (Twenty-fourth,) to receive the surrender of all the rebel prisoners taken on the island, two thousand five hundred in number. Mr. A. was also with his regiment at the battle of Newbern, 14th of March, 1862, and at those of Kinston, 14th of December, Whitehall on the 16th, and Goldsboro, on the 17th of the same month and year (1862.) He left North Carolina for Hilton Head, S. C., in January following, and remained on St. Helena Island, S. C., for three months, and thence was ordered to Brook Island, S. C., where he remained until July. He was at the siege of Morris Island through July and August, and took part in the charge on the rifle-pits on the 26th of August, 1863. When subsequently and next at St. Augustine, Fla., on the 4th of January, 1864, Mr. Andrews re-enlisted, and was mustered in as a veteran volunteer. After a furlough of thirty days, he reported himself at Washington, D. C., and after remaining three months at Arlington Heights, he joined Butler's force at Gloucester Point, Va. On the 2d of May, 1864, embarked on Butler's expedition up the James, landing at Bermuda Hundred. He was engaged in the battles of Green Valley, Chester Station, and Drury's Bluff, all in the same month of May, at the latter of which, he was slightly wounded. In June following he was in the battle of Richmond and Petersburg Railroad, also in that at Weir Bottom Church. The army moved across the James on the 13th of August, and fought in the battle of Deep Bottom on the next day; in that at Deep Run on the 16th of August, and again at Flusser's Mills on the 18th. Mr. A. was in the siege of Petersburg in August and September, 1864, also at New Market Heights on the 29th of September. He saw fight again at Four Mile Run in October, and at Darbytown Road at two different times in the same month. After considerable other service, we find him detailed in July, 1865, to take charge of Castle Thunder Prison, under Capt. W. J. O'Brien, where he remained until the 22d of January, 1866.

Mr. Andrews had been appointed corporal in June, 1864, and sergeant on the 1st of December, the same year, and was finally promoted lieutenant January 1st, 1866.

THOMAS A. MORSE.

Thomas A. Morse, son of Samuel and Anna Morse, was 20 years of age when he enlisted. He enlisted in the Nineteenth Massachusetts Regiment, Col. Hinks, Company H, Capt. Charles Devereaux. This soldier fought, as he states, in fifteen battles. He was wounded in a muscle in the right arm, and was discharged on the 21st of December, 1863.

The published report enumerates the battle at Ball's Bluff, before Richmond, the second Bull Run, Antietam, Fredericksburg, all previous to January 1, 1863. Many of the battles referred to by this soldier may have been, and probably were, of minor importance. That at Gettysburg, in July, however, could not have been called so. The regiment was marched to the front; and finally took their position on the left of Cemetery Hill, being the centre of the line of the army. That position they kept, under heavy artillery fire until five o'clock P. M., on the 2d of July. On the morning of the 3d inst., this regiment was " for one hour and forty minutes under the most terrific cannonading during the war." Second Lieut. S. S. Robinson, was killed by a round shot, besides whom several men were killed or wounded. The regiment to which Mr. Andrews belonged (Nineteenth,) secured a large number of flags, among which were the colors of the Fourteenth, Nineteenth, Fifty-third, and Fifty-seventh Virginia Regiments. Three of them were taken from the hands of the rebel color bearers, and one was picked up beyond the stone wall. Of the other engagements in which this soldier fought, we have not room to speak.

WILBUR BURNHAM.

Wilbur Burnham was born in Essex, May 24, 1842; parents, Nathan Burnham, 3d, and Margaret B.; carpenter. He enlisted in Essex, July 28, 1862, under the call for *three years' men*. With ten other Essex men he joined the Thirty-fifth Regiment at Lynnfield, but that regiment being larger than was allowed by army regulations, the company to which he was attached was transferred, and became Company A, of the Thirty-ninth Massachusetts. Col. P. S. Davis, was commander of the regiment, and Capt. George Nelson of the company to which the soldier belonged. The company was mustered in at Lynnfield on the 18th of August, and he was appointed corporal the same day; he was soon after promoted as sergeant, which position he held at the time of his death. The Thirty-ninth Regiment was removed to Boxford after remaining at Lynnfield a short time, but left the former place for the seat of war on the 6th of September, 1862. They were at once detailed for picket duty up and down the Potomac, and so continued to be during the then ensuing Autumn and Winter, not being engaged in battle at all. On the 31st of December, this Thirty-ninth Regiment was in bivouac near Mitchell's Station, Va., and they remained on picket and provost duty through the Winter on the northern side of the Rapidan. It was in Washington that the death of this young and rising warrior occurred. While on a march to guard rebel prisoners in the lower part of the city, he was suddenly seized with a fainting fit, and was conveyed to the hospital. It was at first supposed that the attack was sun-stroke, but it soon developed itself as varioloid, with typhoid fever of a most malignant type, which terminated his life on the 21st of May, 1863; and it may with confidence be added, that if among the thousands of the patriotic young men of the Union army, there was one who was actuated by a spirit of pure patriotism, Wilbur Burnham was that young man. As one of the *twenty-four* fallen brave of Essex, he is entitled to honorable mention.

JOHN VARNUM.

John Varnum enlisted at the age of 28 years, into the Massachusetts Thirty-ninth, Company A, Col. P. S. Davis, and Capt. George S. Nelson. The battles in which he was engaged were those of the Wilderness, Spottsylvania, Laurel Hill, Hatcher's Run, and White Oak Swamp. He was slightly wounded at the battle of Laurel Hill.

EZRA F. BURNHAM.

Ezra F. Burnham, was the son of Ezra and Mary Ann Burnham. He served in the United States steamer Gettysburg, Lieut. R. H. Lamson, commander. He enlisted at the age of 20 years. While in the service he was in the engagement at Fort Fisher, and received his discharge May 19, 1865.

EDWARD W. LANDER.

Edward W. Lander was born in Salem, Mass., January 9, 1835. His occupation both there and in Essex was that of a barber ; has a wife and three children. He enlisted at Essex, July 19, 1862, in the Fourth Massachusetts Light Battery, Capt. C. H. Manning, (who raised the battery,) although it was afterwards commanded by Capt. George G. Trull. Capt. Trull was not commissioned until October 21, 1862. Mr. Lander was mustered into the service July 21, 1862, at Camp Cameron in Cambridge. He says, " I never was wounded nor in the hospital from sickness," and adds, " I never was really hungry, but have eaten raw salt pork and hard tack. I never was a prisoner." On the 13th of January, this battery, then at Brashear City, was ordered up Bayou Teche with Gen. Weitzel's Corps to Camp Bisland, where it participated in the fight on the next day with the rebel gun-boat J. A. Cotton and the rebel land forces, and on the 16th returned to Brashear City, after which it went to Fort Pike. In the meantime, the men of the two sections of the battery, which had been left at Carrolton, La., had become so much disabled by the miasma arising from the surrounding swamps, that one hundred and ten out of one hundred and fourteen in camp being unfit for duty, they were ordered to Fort Pike to recruit their health. While here, several expeditions were sent out along the lake ; some to Bay St. Louis, where valuable light-house equipments and stores were captured, also to Pass Christian and Pearlington, where starving and destitute families were found and sent to New Orleans. " On the 28th of February our battery was ordered to Baton Rouge, and on the 13th of March it went with the expedition to Port Hudson, whence, after the object of the expedition was accomplished, we returned to the swamps for rest a short time. On the 21st of May we marched for Port Hudson and were actively engaged throughout the siege. . . . . . From the time of the surrender of Port Hudson till the 19th of September, we were passing up and down the great river, between Port Hudson and Donaldsonville, and on the 19th we were ordered to Camp Bisland to join the army engaged in the expedition to Opelousas. On the 11th of October we were engaged with the enemy at Vermillionville. On the 17th of November we arrived at New Iberia, where the battery, having re-enlisted, was mustered into service for three years more. This re-enlistment took place on the 4th of January, 1864. After our furlough had expired, we returned to New Orleans and were stationed for a while in the city. On Monday, September 3d, we were ordered to Morganza Bend, where we spent some time in drill and target-firing." Omitting much which might be related, Mr. Lander states, that on the 13th of October their left section went up Red River on an expedition, and returned in the evening with a few prisoners. On the 10th of November they were ordered on board the Ohio Belle, bound for White River, and landed at Duvall's Bluffs. He calls it a bad place for landing a battery. The mud was up to the hubs of the wheels. On the 25th of November they went on board a steamer for Memphis, Tennessee, on an expedition after the rebel General Hood. Hood retreated after a slight skirmish, but they did not follow him on account of the badness of the roads. Other skirmishing took place subsequent to the above, but not of a very important character. The last order before Mr. Lander's discharge was issued on Thursday the 9th of February, in pursuance of which they took the steamer Corrinthia for Dauphine Island, where his discharge took place, his time having expired.

JOHN C. BUTMAN.

This sketch of John C. Butman may also be considered as applying to the following named soldiers, who enlisted at the same time, except wherein it is strictly personal, viz: William A. Andrews, Charles E. Andrews, Reuben Andrews, Ancill K. Butman, Charles F. Morse, Thomas A. Morse, John B. Burnham and William Howe Burnham. John C. Butman, son of John and Hepzibah Butman, was born December 28, 1819. Occupation, vessel-painting, enlisted at Essex, November 27, 1861, and was mustered and sworn in, December 10th, following. The above named soldiers left Salem on the same day, December 10th for Muddy Bank, say thirty-five miles above Washington city, and remained there until the 11th of March, 1862. On that day, they were ordered to strike their tents and move down the Potomac some sixteen miles to Edward's Ferry; halted there for refreshments the same afternoon, and immediately went on board a canal boat and proceeded up the river till midnight. "On the next morning we were towed to Harper's Ferry. Leaving the boat at that place we crossed the river on a pontoon bridge, and marched in a southerly direction about two miles into Virginia, and thence on to Winchester. At Berrysville, we found the road lined with Union soldiers, shouting victory; being now returning from the battle of Winchester. We learned that all the dwellings between us and Winchester, were filled with the dead and dying. We were now ordered into line and marched by the very field where John Brown was hanged. We were soon after halted and remained two nights in a grove near Gen. Banks' headquarters, and thence proceeded to Bolivar, a small town where most of the houses had been evacuated. Our regiment was divided into squads, large or small, according to the size of the house we were to occupy. The roads were very muddy and the weather very rainy. Some twenty men were detailed to procure a supply of straw for the men to sleep upon. In about one week more we were ordered to the 'Soldier's Retreat' at Washington." [The remainder of Mr. Butman's statement, though interesting, is omitted, having already occupied more than the space assigned to it.]

CHARLES H. FIELDS.

Charles H. Fields enlisted in the first battalion of the Fifth Massachusetts Cavalry, Col. Russel, Company B, Capt. Cyrus Emery, December 25, 1863, for three years. Mr. Fields was born in Byfield Parish, Newbury, June 23, 1823. He had been a seaman for about eleven years at one time, and followed other and laborious occupations previous to enlisting. His wife died while he was absent in the army, leaving several children. The regiment was mustered in at Readville on or about January 4, 1864, and remained there till the 5th of May, following, when they were ordered to proceed to Washington. The three battalions then consisted of about nine hundred men; they arrived there on the 7th of May, and by Gen. Casey's order were dismounted and marched next day to Camp Stoneman, in Maryland; shortly after, they were ordered again to Washington, and thence to Camp Casey, two miles from Long Bridge. On the 13th of May they were ordered to Fortress Monroe and to report themselves to Gen. Butler; they arrived on the 15th, and proceeded the next day to City Point, at the junction of the James and Appomattox, where they remained a month for drill. This regiment was the first on the field at Petersburg, on the 15th of June, having commenced their march for that place an hour and a half sooner than the orders required. There had been a battle some four days before, viz., on the 11th of June; but their first fighting commenced as above stated, on the 15th of June, 1864, and may be said to have lasted eleven days. The whole country between the James and Appomattox, as far westerly at least as Petersburg on the Appomattox and Bermuda Hundred on the James, and so down to the junction, may be said to have been battle ground those eleven days. Our troops drove the rebels in the first of these battles at Petersburg, June 15, 1864, though it was a hotly contested battle. Mr. Fields belonged to the band (twenty-one in number), and they were used as soldiers in battle, though not required, on any occasion, to stand guard. Our troops captured three forts and three breastworks during those eleven days. It should have been stated that Mr. F. was at City Point about a month before the battle at Petersburg on the 15th, for drilling. After the battle above mentioned they were ordered to Bermuda Hundred, on the James River, when another battle was fought, and the troops continued from that time to be used where most wanted, during the remainder of the said *eleven days*. At the expiration of this time, they were ordered from Bermuda Hundred to Point Lookout in Maryland, at the junction of the Potomac and the Chesapeake Bay, for the purpose of drilling, and guarding rebel soldiers, there being fifteen thousand at that place. They remained at Point Lookout from the last of July to the 26th of March, 1865, then left for Deep Bottom, so called, on the James River, five miles from Richmond, and remained there till the 4th of April, and at that time joined in the charge upon Richmond. It ought to be stated that the first colonel, Russell, had been degraded and sent home to Boston. The new colonel (Adams), had informed the regiment Sunday night (the day before the charge), of the plan of Gen. Grant for the attack on Richmond, and counseled them to show a specimen of their valor, as it would be, he said, a case of life and death.

After the surrender of Richmond, this colored battalion was ordered to the Rio Grande, the great river separating Texas from Mexico. They were located at the mouth of the river, and were on duty here, five and one-half months, though sickness began to prevail in the form of chronic diarrhœa at an early day. Mr. Fields was sick during the entire campaign of five and one-half months, and indeed, his system was not free from it for at least fourteen months. They were here attached to the Twenty-fifth Army Corps, colored. There were one thousand four hundred and seventy in the regiment who went to Texas. The whole colored army corps consisted of about sixty thousand. Of the one thousand four hundred and seventy above named who went to Texas, only one thousand one hundred and four came back, three hundred and sixty-six having been left either sick or dead. Maj. Gen. Sheridan was chief in command. The colored-corps' commander was Gen. Weitzel; indeed, it was under him that they had entered Richmond. Their brigadier in Texas was Gen. Cole.

MICHAEL COY.

Michael Coy was born in the county of Galway, Ireland, March 9, 1829; his occupation had been farming. His statement, verbally made, is as follows, viz: "I enlisted June 9, 1862, in Company F, Capt. Garlick, Fortieth Massachusetts, Col. Dalton. Went into camp at Boxford. Our guns were not furnished us till we left the camp. When we left Boxford, we were ordered to Washington. Our first stop was at Philadelphia, but that was short and only for refreshments, and we proceeded immediately to Baltimore and thence to Washington by rail. Our first destination was to Arlington Heights, five miles from Washington, on the Virginia side. We remained at the Heights until March, 1863, when we were ordered down the river to the Peninsula. There we remained on service about a month, during which we were in the battle at Bottom's Bridge, on the 2d of July, 1863, which lasted about half a day. We drove the enemy, although we lost seven hundred and fifty men. Our next battle was at Seven Pines." [The soldier may sometimes be inadvertently incorrect, in regard to the *order* in which events occurred. In this case, I find the battle of Seven Pines was first officially reported in the Tribune of *February 6th*, instead of being *subsequent* to Bottom's Bridge fight]. "While there, we occupied the fortifications of Gen. McClellan early in the war, now nearly in ruins. Our next march was to Alexandria, Va., and thence to Williamsburg, Va., by rail. We were expecting a battle with Lee, but were too late to do any fighting, as a battle had already taken place. We saw the field where it had been fought, and the dead horses upon it. We learned that the Union forces had been victorious and Lee had retreated." [On turning to the published reports of events at Williamsburg in 1863, I find but two recorded, viz: that the Union cavalry fell into ambush there on the 7th of February, and that the Union camp was broken up April 11th. Neither of these facts appear to coincide so fully with the soldier's statements as could be wished]. The soldier (Coy) says he never was wounded in battle, nor sick, nor was he ever a prisoner of war, but was once wounded in his ankle, by running against a bayonet lying on the ground in the night. This injury disabled him about six weeks, during which time he was under hospital treatment. On inquiring of him whether he was ever where the balls flew, he replied, that in all the battles where he fought, men and horses were falling all around him. "At Olustee," says he, " we lost two hundred and fifty in *two hours and forty minutes.* We were driven off the field in that battle. Previously to this fight we had been used as cavalry about six months, but on arriving at Olustee, we dismounted and fought on foot. Every *fourth man* was detailed to hold the horses during the fight. We were finally discharged in June, 1865, the war being over."

By the Adjutant General's Report for 1864, page 859 and onward, it appears that this regiment (Fortieth Massachusetts), "was one of the few Massachusetts regiments that served in the far-off State of Florida. It took part in the brave battle of Olustee." After a full record of the history of this Fortieth Massachusetts, the report concludes by saying : " No better battalion ever left the old Bay State. The banner which was entrusted to the regiment to defend and honor, has never been lost, and it will be placed beside other battle-stained and weather-beaten colors in the Capitol of the State. The battles enumerated by Coy in which he was actively engaged, should have been before stated. They were at Bottom's Bridge, Seven Pines, Charlottestown ; Saint Mary's Creek, and Olustee, Florida ; Cold Harbor, and Ball's Bluff, Va., these two being the heaviest. There were also a few others not now recollected.

SUMMARY OR RECAPITULATION

OF THE NAMES OF THE ESSEX SOLDIERS, AS ARRANGED IN THEIR SEVERAL REGIMENTS OR OTHER ORGANIZATIONS.

The figures refer to the pages where a sketch of each may be found.

MASSACHUSETTS SECOND INFANTRY.

MASSACHUSETTS FIFTH.

MASSACHUSETTS SEVENTH.

Stationed at Fort Warren.

Allen, Joseph Gilman .	. 388	Burnham, Jesse . .	. 388
Andrews, Alburn .	. 388	Burnham, Otis . .	. 389
Andrews, Ira, Jr. .	. 389	Gilbert John F. . .	. 389
Andrews, William H. .	. 388	Howes, Webster .	. 389
Bartlett, Jacob O. .	. 389	Low, Edward . .	. 389
Burnham, Alfred M. .	. 388	McIntire, William Henry .	389

MASSACHUSETTS EIGHTH.

Haskell, Nathaniel 385

MASSACHUSETTS TWELFTH.

Clifford, David E. 397

MASSACHUSETTS SIXTEENTH.

Andrews, Albert 382

MASSACHUSETTS EIGHTEENTH.

Burnham, James Howe 415

MASSACHUSETTS NINETEENTH.

Andrews, Charles Edwin	. 419	Butman, Ancill K. .	. 396
Andrews, Reuben .	. 419	Butman, John C. .	. 424
Andrews, William A. .	. 396	Hayden, William H. .	. 396
Burnham, John B. .	. 395	Lee, John E. .	. 391
Burnham, William Howe	. 394	Morse, Charles F. .	. 419
Burnham, Zenas . .	. 391	Morse, Thomas A. .	. 421

MASSACHUSETTS TWENTIETH.

Low, William B. 386

MASSACHUSETTS TWENTY-SECOND.

Sargent, O. H. P. 404

MASSACHUSETTS TWENTY-THIRD.

Dodge, George . .	. 418	Sargent, George H.	
Hardy, George C. .	. 390	Story, Aaron Herbert	. 397
Haskell, James Frederic	. 395	Swett, Simeon . .	. 406
Low, William E. .	. 387		

MASSACHUSETTS TWENTY-FOURTH.

Andrews, Cyrus (Lieut.)	. 420	Lufkin, Charles P. .	. 419
Burnham, Harlan P. .	. 390	Martyn, John L. .	. 415
Howes, Erastus . .	. 420	McIntire, Edward E. .	. 397

MASSACHUSETTS TWENTY-FIFTH, UNATTACHED.

Cogswell, George 396

MASSACHUSETTS THIRTIETH.

Andrews, Monsieur M.	. 397	Ross, George	. .	. 398
Lufkin, William	. 390	Ross, George, Jr.	.	. 399

MASSACHUSETTS THIRTY-FIFTH.

Wentworth, George S. 393

MASSACHUSETTS THIRTY-NINTH.

Andrews, Timothy, Jr.	. 401	Dodge, William G.	.	. 400
Burnham, Daniel	. 399	Guppy, George F.	.	. 402
Burnham, George Foster	. 402	Haskell, Albert A.	.	. 403
Burnham, G. Washington	. 410	Mears, Rufus E. .	.	. 390
Burnham, James Horace	. 377	Mears, Samuel, Jr.	.	. 414
Burnham, Wilbur	. 422	Story, Asa .	.	. 393
Channel, John C.	. 402	Varnum, John	.	. 423

MASSACHUSETTS FORTIETH.

Coy, Michael . . . 426 | Story, David Lewis . . 400

MASSACHUSETTS FORTY-EIGHTH.

Andrews, Israel F.	. 377	Hayden, Luther .	.	. 378
Andrews, Lyman B.	. 385	Howes, Charles (Capt.)	.	364
Burnham, Albert F., 2d	. 378	Jackson, Andrew	.	. 378
Burnham, George F., 2d	. 377	James, Washington Wilkins		413
Burnham, Horace	. 377	Kelleher, John .	.	. 380
Burnham, Ira F.	. 375	Kimball, James B.	.	. 380
Burnham, Lamont G.	. 372	Low, Aaron	.	. 373
Burnham, Leonard	. 378	Mahoney, Thomas	.	. 380
Burnham, Lewis	. 378	Marston, Charles E.	.	. 383
Callehan, Daniel	. 387	McEachen, John .	.	. 379
Callehan, Maurice	. 379	Mears, Francis G.	.	. 413
Crafts, Franklin	. 413	Prest, Robert	.	. 379
Crafts, John, Jr.	. 413	Procter, Charles W.	.	. 412
Crockett, Charles P.	. 380	Procter, Joseph, Jr.	.	. 412
Duggan, Morty	. 412	Riggs, Solomon A.	.	. 376
Hardy, Alphonso M.	. 378			

FIRST MASSACHUSETTS HEAVY ARTILLERY.

All having first enlisted in the Fourteenth Volunteers, infantry.

Andrews, H. Nelson	. 411	Hart, John F.	. .	. 376
Andrews, Stephen P.	. 407	Haskell, William P.	.	. 406
Burnham, Albert Frank	. 409	Hull, William H.		. 409
Burnham, Charles A.	. 409	Jones, John S.	.	. 416
Burnham, David B.	. 407	Parsons, John J.	.	. 412
Burnham, Osgood E.	. 411	Poland, Jeremiah, Jr.	.	. 416
Burnham, William H. H.	. 396	Tucker, Joseph W.		. 376

SECOND MASSACHUSETTS HEAVY ARTILLERY.

Burnham, Constantine   . 394 | Mears, Henry C.   .   . 396

ELEVENTH MASSACHUSETTS HEAVY ARTILLERY, UNATTACHED.

Andrews, Rufus .   .   . 394 | Lufkin, Alfred .   .   . 394

TWELFTH MASSACHUSETTS HEAVY ARTILLERY, UNATTACHED.

Burnham, Abner.

FOURTH MASSACHUSETTS LIGHT BATTERY.

Lander, Edward W. 423

SECOND MASSACHUSETTS CAVALRY.

Burnham, Mark F. 382

FIFTH MASSACHUSETTS CAVALRY.

Fields, Charles H.   .   . 425 | Haskell, William A. .   . 394

CAVALRY OR MOUNTED RIFLE RANGERS.

Claiborne, George C. .   . 385 | Hatch, Jason   .   . 393
Coose, William D.   .   . 393 | Jones, Samuel Q.   .   . 392

UNITED STATES NAVY.

Burnham, Albion   .   . 415 | Perkins, Gustavus S. .   . 418
Burnham, Ezra F.   .   . 423 |

AT FORT SUMPTER AND OTHER FORTS.

Lufkin, Albert E.   390

MAINE AND MINNESOTA.

Howard, William C. .   . 414 | Burnham, Rollins M. .   . 392

CAPT. BABSON'S COMPANY FOR COAST DEFENSE.

Enlisted for one year from December 4, 1864, but discharged at close of the war.

Allen, Hervey   .   . 386 | Cogswell, Addison   .   . 386
Andrews, Frank F.   . 386 | Cogswell, George   .   . 396
Andrews, Gilman   .   . 386 | Cook, Moses   .   . 391
Burnham, Alfred M. .   . 388 | Haskell, Nathaniel   .   . 385
Burnham, Andrew F. .   . 391 | Lufkin, Hervey .   .   . 391
Burnham, Francis   .   . 391 | Story, Otis .   .   . 391
Burnham, Otis   .   . 389 |

A part of the above are re enlistments.

OBITUARY.

Names of Essex soldiers slain in battle during the War of the Rebellion, or who died subsequently of wounds received, or diseases contracted in the army:

	AGED ABOUT.	
	Years.	Mo's.

CHARLES EDWIN ANDREWS, killed at the battle of White Oak, June 1, 1862, - - - - - - - - - - 27

REUBEN ANDREWS, died of fever at Harper's Ferry, October 27, 1862, - - - - - - - - - - 26

WILLIAM A. ANDREWS, wounded June 30, 1862; not seen afterwards, - - - - - - - - - - 16

DANIEL BURNHAM, killed at the battle of the Wilderness, May 6, 1864.

OSGOOD E. BURNHAM, wounded May 19, 1864; died May 28, 1864, - - - - - - - - - - 29

WILBUR BURNHAM, died at Washington of fever, May 21, 1863, 21

JOHN C. CHANNEL, died after arriving home.

CHARLES P. CROCKETT, died at Baton Rouge, May 6, 1863.

GEORGE DODGE, circumstances and time of death not known.

ALBERT A. HASKELL, died in Salisbury prison, June 30, 1865, 22

JAMES FREDERIC HASKELL, died on board the steamer Suwanee, February 3, 1862, - - - - - - - - 19 7

WILLIAM P. HASKELL, died January 6, 1862, - - - - 17

JASON HATCH, killed in battle at Cedar Creek, October 19, 1864.

WASHINGTON WILKINS JAMES, died May 13, 1863, - - 22

CHARLES P. LUFKIN, died of wounds received at Fort Wagner, July 29, 1863, - - - - - - - - - - 20

WILLIAM LUFKIN, died of fever in the vicinity of New Orleans, 57

JOHN L. MARTYN, unknown.

FRANCIS GILBERT MEARS, died at Baton Rouge, June 21, 1863, - - - - - - - - - - 26

RUFUS E. MEARS, died in Salisbury prison, October 26, 1864, - 24

CHARLES F. MORSE, died at hospital after a sickness of about two months, - - - - - - - - - - 23

JEREMIAH POLAND, Jr., died May 21, 1864, - - - - 34

GEORGE ROSS, Jr., drowned in the Mississippi River, April 29, 1862, - - - - - - - - - - 18 9

OLIVER H. P. SARGENT, wounded at Yorktown, May 4, 1862; died May 30, 1862, - - - - - - - - 41

ASA STORY, died of fever, November 11, 1862, - - - - 33

ADDRESS OF WELCOME.

The following extracts from a "Welcome to the Soldiers," delivered July 4, 1865, at the town celebration in Essex, by the compiler of the foregoing sketches, may form a not unfitting close to the foregoing chapter:

The 4th of July has opened upon us jubilant, and yet with some clouds of sorrow upon its brow;—jubilant, because the defiant Palmetto flag is furled as we believe forever, and America for the third time is free. And yet with much of sorrow to many, because it finds us mourning for the unreturning brave. The tear stands upon many a household hearth to-day. The general joy, however, will preponderate and moderate that grief and assuage it. The living soldier has returned from the war with untarnished laurels, and the slain heroes are reposing, every one in his bed of honor.

WELCOME TO THE SOLDIERS.

To the commanding officer of the day, (Capt. Howes of the Forty-eighth,) late commander on a very different field, and to the brave soldiers all, I would say, you may be familiar with the worthlessness of human praise, and it is not to be denied that it is sometimes empty; but it does please us, and we cannot help it, to *welcome you home from the war this day*. It relieved our hearts somewhat, to break your gentle morning slumbers with the music of the village gun, and the bell and the band, and it will please us as much to lull you to sleep in the same peaceful way to-night.

Till an hour ago, I had supposed it would be the agreeable duty of the orator of the day [B. H. Smith, Esq., of Gloucester,] to pronounce our welcome in his more fitting terms, and I did not intend to make his task the harder by many words of mine. Rather would I have smoothed his part, by informing him that in this phalanx of veteran men, the wounded and the unwounded, he would see the heroes of *three and twenty battle-fields*. Without strict regard to chronological order they have fought at Yorktown, Antietam, Fredericksburg, Roanoke Island, Gettysburg, Newbern, Kinston, Cedar Mountain, Wilderness, Fair Oaks, Seven Pines, South Mountain, Atlanta, Chattanooga, Plain Store, Port Hudson, Winchester, Spottsylvania, Cold Harbor, Olustee, Donaldsonville and in the Red River campaign, besides in numerous skirmishes, many of them not quite taking the name of *battles*. And here are the men, who have met no foe on any of these fields of war, before whom they could not stand, though the brown hair of every one of their heads has whistled to the wind of rebel bullets. We do not for a moment forget our glorious, but unreturning *twenty four*. Peace, peace, to their hallowed memories! On the future monument, of which I love to dream, shall all their names be carved.

Essex has put one hundred and forty-three of her own citizens into the country's service, besides thirty-nine strangers, and thirteen substitutes; making the number of one hundred and ninety-five in all.

Mr. Commander, brave men in arms, ladies, teachers and scholars of the town schools, officers of the town, and citizens generally :—It was the strong declaration of a Fourth of July oration, in 1863, that rather than live under a dishonored flag, and in a broken Union, it would be better that the last man and the last dollar should be followed by the last loved woman and the last dime, and they by the last dear child and the last white cent. This, he admitted, might be called a strong American exaggeration. He could not of course tell how much of life and treasure would be wasted. But you know *now* how small a portion of that treasure has been needed, and how few of those precious lives have been yielded, terrible as the war has been in both respects. With us, save the "sheeted spirits" of our beloved *twenty-four*, nearly all are here or on their way home, AND THE WAR OVER! and the flag not "dishonored," nor the Union "broken." There is "no *unfinished* conflict," no "unrighted wrong;" and there will not long be, I think, any "unsettled question." I admit that some say otherwise. Dr. Loring and Mr. Dana think the war not over, I believe. Should there, by any possibility, be another appeal to arms, *it must be short*, with a million men like you, all ready. The manly energies of these glorious fellows would carry them, at once, if needed, to another Antietam, or South Mountain, or Port Hudson, or Gettysburg, or Fair Oaks, or to cross the Rapidan, as they have done, on a pontoon in the night! Especially, fellow-citizens, hear me, ESPECIALLY should a *delinquent Legislature pass a law, allowing the town to pay the bounty to our first forty-seven enlisted soldiers, which all others have received, which they ought to have had, and which they shall yet have!*

OUR SOLDIERS NOT DEMORALIZED.

Having noticed the noble *military* bearing, as well as the *fine civil* and gentlemanly bearing of our returned soldiers, I have but little sympathy with the oft-uttered sentiment that the *demoralized troops* are prepared as they return to *demoralize the community.* How it may be sometimes, elsewhere, I have no means of knowing, but how truly may it be said of some of the Essex soldiers, *they went out boys*, but have come back men in the best sense of the word! Military life has elevated the character and made the man, in multitudes of cases in the history of wars. Adjutant Stearns wrote home after having been in the army but a few months, " Father, I am twice the man I ever was before." That the temptations are sometimes strong in army life there can be but little doubt; but as respects our own soldiers, I have sometimes put the question, do you know of any Essex soldier who was *perfectly temperate* before the war, who became decidedly and hopelessly intemperate in the army; and as yet I hear of none.

SOLDIERS SHOULD HAVE SUBSTANTIAL PAY.

Let us manifest our regard in some way which they can appreciate. This, I fear, is not always done. I have heard of a so-called philanthropist, who

55

would read a lecture to a soldier on the sin of *playing cards*, when the soldier's *left arm* had been shot off a little above the elbow, and the *right* amputated just below!—and another, who was advised never to lose any more precious time in *dancing*, when he had had both legs taken off by a shell! That is not the philanthropy that I love.

And now let me say to the soldiers, that what we failed to do as a reception on Sunday, the 22d of August, 1863, as well as on other less noticeable days of your return, you will please to understand us as doing NOW.

WELCOME, *a thousand times welcome home, Mr. Commander, and soldiers, all.* You are to eat no "salt hoss," and drink no *swamp water*, on our account to-day. You will be invited to dine at a table spread by the very fairest of fair hands; and I can close in no more fitting words than those of the Rev. John Howe, I think, and say, soldiers, soldiers, "*may your* MOON *become more and more like the* SUN, *and your* MIDDAY SUN *become seven-fold brighter than it is!*"

WAR AID OF THE LADIES.

Turning awhile from the soldiers, for there is *beauty* here as well as *chivalry*, fair *women* as well as *brave men*, I cannot but imagine what brought the faces and the forms of our fair friends here to-day, when they knew well enough, that with the men of war among us, much of our talk to-day would be about the *grim business* of bloody fields! Four years ago to-day, ladies, your needles were employed in making havelocks for the army, and in five days more, (July 9,) you put them upon Capt. Fuller's men, and indulged in the pretty fancy that you had made them soldiers. What inexperience, united with what patriotism! In twelve days more, (July 21), the terrible defeat at Bull Run took place, and away went all of our confidence in havelocks. You could have wept; but *weeping* would not fight battles, and we found it time to prepare better for the war. But to repeat my question, what has brought sweet smiling woman here to-day? It was *not* because the war could not have been *commenced* without her. Alas, it could have been, and it was. But believe me, it could not *have been conducted and concluded* as it was, without *infinitely greater loss of blood*, had she not stood by, to minister to the wounded and the dying; to put on the bandage, to adjust the tourniquet, to aid the surgeon, if not almost to guide the amputating knife;—to wipe away the moisture of the fever;—to beat up and smooth down the pillow, and when nothing more could be done, to reach the cup of water; to point upwards, and to speak of that wondrous One, who has the rod and the staff, and who puts the everlasting arms underneath! and when the last pulse had fluttered in one and all was over, and the soldier's form was forever still, then to proceed to another and another.

I say the war could not have been concluded so bloodlessly as it was, without the presence of woman, any more than the Crimean war could. My fair friends, whose name was it that floated over all other names at Sebastopol at the close of that war? Was it Raglan's, the Gen. Grant of that battle? No. Was it Toddleben's the wonderful engineer? No. Was it

St. Armand's, as great a man, I suppose, as either? No. It was the name of Miss Florence Nightingale—and that's whose it was. And now does any one venture the fool's question, and ask who our American Florence Nightingale is? I shall let George S. Hillard answer,—"the reason we have no one in *particular*, is because we have so many *in general*.

If the presence of Florence N. during a battle and at its close, may have been compared to a star looking down upon a troubled sea, as it has been, our country has certainly had a *galaxy*, a *milky way of them*, hushing the troubled waters all to rest. I shall always honor the memory of Miss Kean the actress, for taking the fainting head of the dying President in her lap, and upon her diamond dress;—but bear in mind, this was at Ford's theatre, and with two thousand people to look on, whereas the army nurses must often, from necessity, be beyond all human observation.

"A WALK ABOUT TOWN."

[THE gifted author of an interesting History of Candia, N. H., (Rev. F. B. Eaton) has, near the close of his work, published at Manchester in that State, in 1852, introduced a large variety of matters, often of a kind more familiar and interesting to the young, than he chose to insert in the body of the book, under the agreeable title of a "Walk about Town." We trust it will be no violation of the rules of authorship-etiquette, if with this explanation and acknowledgment, the same happy thought is followed in a sketch of Essex, and a part of the remaining pages, after the manner of "Charming Fare," be entitled "A WALK ABOUT TOWN."]

THE ANCIENT MEETING-HOUSES.

It is painful to notice how little remains by which to identify localities, once memorable but now forgotten or unknown. A skeleton of a tradition may be floating in the air, but how unsatisfactory! "We ask for the *monuments* of Richard's Christian men," while "they show but the bones of the infidel Saracen." It is to this day uncertain whether the first meeting-house in Chebacco was upon the same side of the county road where the buildings of Capt. Joseph Choate now stand, or upon the opposite side; there being printed authorities in favor of both. So too, the exact locality of the *second* meeting-house is lost, although three years ago, viz., in 1864, the underpinning stones marked the square perfectly. The *bell* of that structure which called the generations of Rev. Mr. Wise's day to go up for worship as often as the smile of the Sabbath appeared, might have been preserved through coming years, while on the contrary, all that is now known of it is the tradition that when struck it always seemed to say "skillet," giving some diminutive idea of the size of it, as well as the fact of its having been a *cracked* bell. This at least, was the construction which the wags of that day would and did put upon it. That bell weighed one hundred and sixty pounds! And it now seems incredible as well as painful that it was not preserved, so much light would the very sight of it have thrown upon the true history of that day!

But sometimes *acts*, and even *words*, as well as *things*, become monuments for perpetuating events, *when well authenticated*, and none other should be allowed to appear on the page of history. Indeed, granite and marble are too cold to hold the record of very much that the living desire to know.

A very short " walk," southerly, from the *second* meeting-house, which stood within some twenty-five feet of the present town pound, brings us to the site of the third house of worship, and which was built in 1752, for Rev. Mr. Cleaveland's society. · A union of this society with that just referred to having been effected in 1774, the united society erected the *present* Orthodox church in 1792. When erected, and until remodeled in 1842, it was crowned with a small dome, and that dome was surmounted by a ball. A deed of valor and daring was performed by one of the young men of that day, which has never been recorded; Thomas Giddings, then of Chebacco, now living at a great age in Maine, unless very recently deceased, went up to the ball, stood upon it with one foot, and swung his hat! This feat was witnessed by many, and was related to the writer a few years since by Mr. John Choate, since deceased, who witnessed it, being then a small boy. The height of that ball from the ground cannot now be precisely determined. It was probably eighty feet. The bell of the present house is a noble one, never says *skillet*, like the former, nor does it sound like one.*

---

* A passage of words once described by Capt. James Perkins, late of Londonderry, N. H., is thought worth preserving, relating, as it does, to the location of the present Orthodox church, built, as above stated, in 1792. The people were not unanimous with regard to the spot where it should stand, as had indeed been the case in Rev. Mr. Wise's day, many years before. Jonathan Cogswell, Jr., Esq., and his friends had selected the old gravel pit, where the three roads met, and Thomas Choate and his friends, chiefly from the south side of the river, had a preference for the spot *where it now stands*, undoubtedly the best in the town. A short specimen of the " logic and the wisdom and the wit," if not of the " loud laugh " itself, lets us into the spirit of the times. Squire Cogswell with a few, but well chosen words, when urging the superior advantages of the gravel pit lot, would be let into by John

BRIDGE CONTEMPLATED IN 1852.

Remains of the horse bridge across the river, referred to in a former part of this work, are still visible upon its banks at the farm of the late Adam Boyd, formerly of Jonathan Cogswell, Esq. As vessel building has increased, good building lots have become scarce. It has been already stated that the demand for *larger vessels* than formerly, made it necessary at length to build wholly *upon the banks of the river*. It was this fact that led a large number of the citizens of Essex in 1852, to petition the Legislature to authorize the County Commissioners to allow a bridge to be constructed at the same place where the horse bridge before referred to, formerly stood. A part of the design of the petitioners was to open a road beginning at or near the mouth of the lane leading by the house, then of Col. John P. Choate, now Mr. E. K. Lee, and continue it upon a straight course by the house of Mr. Boyd, and so on, to and over the river, and to strike the Gloucester road, nearly opposite the house of Mr. Oliver Pierce. This, it will be seen, would have thrown open vessel-building lots all the way from the contemplated bridge to the creek which separates the Boyd farm from that of Messrs. Albert and Jonathan Cogswell. The petition was referred to the Legislative Committee on Roads and Bridges, before whom a long and patient hearing was had, in the Senate-chamber, on the 2d of March, 1852. The case on the part of the petitioners was ably presented by William D. Northend, Esq., of Salem, attorney at law, and that of the town as respondents, by

Emerson, " You're all *self,* Squire, just cause you live close to it." Mr. Cogswell continued to urge his reasons coolly, when Mr. Emerson applied the touch of ridicule, "Squire, Squire," said he, raising his voice, "I guess it will do very well, Squire ; go up on the hill, take a hand-sled, and you can slide right into the window." Squire Cogswell's words grew fewer, as they approached the climax, only adding, " If you'll set it at the gravel pit, I'll level the spot." Ordinarily, this might have settled the question, but Mr. Choate threw in the make-weight, "If you'll go to the hill *I'll* fix the spot." This, along with the recollection of Mr. Emerson's *hand-sled* settled the question, the " Squire " himself surrendering as gracefully as circumstances would admit.

Obed B. Low, Esq., of Boston, attorney at law, and formerly of Essex. The committee reported a bill agreeably to the prayer of the petitioners, but it failed to pass; the grand objection being that of interrupting the navigation of the river, and more especially the passage of vessels built above. An incidental advantage of the proposed road and bridge would have been a considerable shortening of the distance from Ipswich to Gloucester.

INDIAN RELIC.

About the year 1810, a cellar was dug opposite the house of George W. Burnham, trader, for the dwelling-house now owned and occupied by the heirs of John Boyd, deceased, but then being built for Thomas M. Burnham, father of O. H. Perry Burnham, of Boston. One of the workmen, Moses Andrews, senior, deceased, in excavating, struck a stone, which, upon having the earth removed, presented the appearance of a man's head. It was of granite. Such was the interest taken in this head that Mr. B. had it set up upon the corner post of his front yard. A little paint was added, to mark the features, and it remained there for years. On removing to Boston Mr. Burnham carried the stone head, and at length sold it to a gentleman of Boston interested in antiquarian matters, who also sold it to other parties, upon a representation, it is said, of its being the work of *Roman hands*, inasmuch as the features were to some extent imitations of the Roman. It was purchased by two gentlemen from Europe, Danes, and was long exhibited in an antiquarian collection of curiosities at Copenhagen, where it was seen and recognized by an American Captain, formerly of Chebacco. This head was of course the work of the *red man of America*, made with no other tool than a stone hatchet, and may have been, and no doubt was, an object of worship. That any well informed European traveler could have made himself believe it was the work of the Romans, and most of all that it should have been admitted into such a Museum, upon such a representation, is not a little surprising. If imposition was practiced upon a traveler from abroad, it is some satisfaction to know, it was by no Chebacco man. The original finding of the head, indeed, was verified by the finder, Mr. Andrews, who signed and swore to the affidavit setting forth the facts. But no *opinion* of his made any part of his affidavit.* It is now said, that on its being sent back to Boston, damage was demanded for deception. Of this, however, nothing certain is now known.

WITCHCRAFT.

No one, it is presumed, could take a very long *walk about town*, without a frequent disposition to inquire, not only what manner *of stones and buildings* formerly stood here, but also and more especially, what kind of *men and women and children* dwelt here. No reference is made by this inquiry to such men as William White, or John Cogswell, or Goodman Bradstreet, or any others, male or female, whose names were never allowed to die; but to the *mass of men*—to the three hundred of the rank and file of old Chebacco at the close, if you please, of the seventeenth century. The pulpit was doing its work gloriously and had been from the beginning; so the press was throwing off its weekly *seven by nine;* and the common school scholars were studying Dilworth and the Psalter. But all this left a vast amount of unoccupied mind and talent, that must and would train itself. Arrivals from England were occasional, and all loved to hear from *fader-land;* and on a great variety of subjects England pitched the tunes for us to sing. And now, would it not be past belief for example, in a community, settled half a century before the *Salem witchcraft*, if no legendary tales upon that fruitful topic should find ears to fall upon, in old Ipswich and its Chebacco child? Yes, *past belief*, it must have been, that *none* of the gentry who everywhere else could *ride through the air upon a broomstick and pass in*

*and out through the smallest key-hole of your chamber as
easily as through the widest open door*—if none of this
gentry ever ventured over Hatfield's Bridge, the bridge
where the towns of Ipswich and Essex now meet.

The gifted author of the History of Gloucester, p. 321,
remarks that "no account of the part borne by Gloucester
men in the expedition to Louisburg would be complete
without the story of Peg Wesson," the witch. It is true
that not every town is able to point to the proven fact of
the existence of any particular *Peggy*. But inasmuch as
the historic record proves the fact (see Felt's History of
Ipswich), that Chebacco men helped to drag Sir William
Pepperell's cannon across the beach at Louisburg, who will
presume to say that Chebacco men were not as really
brought up in the fear and belief of witchcraft *in general*
and Miss Wesson's claim to her honors as a witch *in particular*, as though they had really lived along side of "the
old building on Back street, in Gloucester," or even in the
"Garrison" itself. We have high authority for gathering
up legendary tales and ancestral recollections. We confess with shame to a remissness in this part of "everybody's duty;" and with a tearful regret that so much is
lost irrecoverably, would claim for the honor of our birth-
right upon *Hog Island*, that the old homestead was honored with a now and then visit from "Peggy Wesson" or
some kind friend of hers. How else are we to account
for the fact that the farm-*horse* was sometimes found
hitched to the corner of the house at an early hour in the
morning, "all of a lather," with his mane tied into un-
questioned witch-knots, when a few minutes inquiry among
the three or four families upon that island satisfied you
that nobody had been out of their house for the night ;
unless the horse had been taken once in a while to ride
upon, instead of the broomstick ?

The propitious horseshoe was not nailed up upon every
dwelling in town for the *exclusive purpose of attaching the
clothes line to it, by any means.*

56

And then, as those days and scenes gradually passed away, other events bordering on the marvellous would come in to the aid of superstitious belief—the *rag-man* was always ready to come down chimney after the boy that could not help playing Sunday. The story of the Babes in the Wood could not long satisfy the demand for exciting incident, and what was wanting in fact would be supplied by fancy. Real advance or retrocession in society can be detected only by weighing and guaging the masses of one epoch, against their descendants of another epoch, in the *same scales ;* that is, determining the status of the public mind at different periods in regard to the same matters. If the superstition and ignorance of a given age melt away before actual intelligence, education and refinement in that which succeeds it, then society has advanced ; the *percentage* is not so easily determined. It is *something,* indeed, almost *everything,* to know that the load of the *night-mare* is removed forever, without being obliged to prove just what that load weighed. It is not pretended that there is no room for further improvement. Superstitious observances and bad signs are yet fellow-boarders and dear friends of the *skeleton,* which we are told is to be found in *every house.* But when even light literature, and more especially that which is substantial, comes *in at the door,* the gentry above named must *go out at the window.*

It is not the most agreeable task in the world, in the abstract, to hold up the past age to the present, but we hold to *progress,* and insist that it is a better world to live in than it was once ; a better world than when Paul fought with wild beasts at Ephesus ; better than when the Hebrew children were cast in a furnace of fire ; or to come down to New England's day, it is a better world to live in than when the *raw heads* and bloody bones of the nursery stood by every member of the family, man and boy, as long as they lived. At the close of the last century, like the close of the preceding, the moral atmosphere, if not full of witchcraft itself, was so impregnated with a *re-siduum* of it, that it wanted another hundred years to settle in. When a boy would rather have his ears boxed than go down cellar alone, or go to bed in the dark, and this fear of the invisible, permeated through every order of society; there was very nearly an end to social and commercial intercourse. Nothing was too absurd not to have votaries. Men would sometimes reason as correctly upon *wrong* principles, and unestablished facts, as they would at other times reason *incorrectly* upon *right* ones. When the imagination was heated, it became a race-horse without a rider. An incident or two may illustrate. For many years at about the close of the last century and the commencement of the present, a Chebacco gentleman of the first respectability was a member of the board of selectmen, and as the meetings of the board were held in the body of the town at Ipswich, and frequently continued into the evening and night, he would often be returning at midnight. The remarkable fact connected with these nocturnal rides, was that in crossing Haffield's bridge, a *light was generally, if not invariably, kindled up upon each of the horse's ears;* coming on quietly, but unmistakably, as he entered at the northern end of the causeway, and as quietly leaving them on his leaving the causeway at its southern terminus. It was never injurious to the venerable traveler; but *what was it,* and *what its business?* The tradition that aids us in the investigation is, that during some of those years when the causeway was low, and consequently often overflowed by the tide, a traveler had been lost there or came to grief or damage, and though this part of the case was not very clearly verified, yet it was surely *believed,* and the town was thus punished in the person of one of its principal officers, until the road, causeway and bridge were properly raised above the tide; for after that was done the selectman was neither troubled nor honored with any more lights upon his horse's ears when passing that bridge.

PERSONAL REMINISCENCES.

Some of our boys and young men may, perhaps, have quite as much fondness for *active* as for *still* life, and will tell us that the *natural scenery* of the town speaks for itself, and they can read out all it has to say; but *of the people of former years who are now, and have been long abroad*, whom they have not seen and are not likely to see, they would like to know something, especially if they have made any mark worth remembering.

In a walk about town not long since, the site of the first Falls school-house brought to mind the long-a-go pupils, or at least some of them. Their history has already been made the subject of a sketch in a former chapter of the present History. Reference is had just now to some of the common name of Burnham, as Westley, Samuel, Zaccheus. A later "walk" along the site of the old North school-house, when standing between the present dwellings of Jonathan Low and David Mears, has called up the green memories of others, and some of whom have spent most of life abroad. Among those who drank of the old North school spring, still living and active, but unknown to most persons under twenty years of age, was Thomas Sewall, [now the Rev. Dr. S. of the Methodist Episcopal church, fifty years old]. His residence in Essex was not perfectly continuous after the age of boyhood, and yet he attended our school as late as about 1832. He was a fine speaker and reader, having enjoyed the instructions of Prof. Russell at Phillips Academy, in Andover.

In the Spring of 1842, our young friend, having graduated at Middletown, Conn., and having entered upon the study of theology, went upon a foreign tour in company with Rev. Dr. Durbin with whom he was then studying, and several other gentlemen. Their travels lay through parts of England and several other countries of Europe, Arabia and the Holy Land. While in England, he visited many spots made dear by the recollection of his child-hood reading and nursery training. "This letter" says he, in writing to an Essex relative, "I have pressed to the tombstones of John Bunyan, Isaac Watts, and the Wesleys, *just for the notion of it.*" But it was an in-stance of his personal, individual prowess and bodily activity that is to be here recited, a case where a Che-bacco school-boy beat an Arabian runner on his own sands. Some twenty in all were upon the camels together, or perhaps some resting in walking and loitering. "I sup-pose," said our Thomas, to one of the Arab guides, "you are a swift runner?" It was said pleasantly and taken so, yet with the addition, "if you will come down, I show you," giving him to understand he felt it to be a chal-lenge. A wager must always be laid in such a case, and Sewall merely threw down a few *pice*, knowing he should lose them. The Arab on the other hand laid down the best things he had—his sword and belt, knowing he should win. The ground was marked off and the judges appointed. Sewall commenced by a *good* but not his *best* run. He perceived almost at once, however, that he was fully up with the Arab. His first thought was that it was but a *make-believe* on the Mahometan's part, till a glance assured him that the man of the desert was doing his best. Our Essex boy, on perceiving that, quickened his pace, and there upon the yielding sands of that sandy country, Thomas Sewall *beat the Arab and took the trophy by unanimous consent.* The interpreter of the company told our countrymen that he could hear the Arab with deep mortification, declare that there was n't a man on the desert that could run so. Before the final separation of that little caravan, such was the deep humiliation of our Arab runner, for the loss of his sword and belt, that Mr. Sewall *made him a present of* the former, and if our recol-lection is correct, paid him something for the belt, which he exhibited to American friends on his return home; thus leaving some salutary impressions of foreign etiquette upon the heathen's mind as well as some belief that even an American knows how *to run*. An instance of this same Chebacco boy's native persistence of character in very early childhood, may as well be mentioned, perhaps. When a number of boys much older and larger than himself, were one day at play in the yard, they suddenly all had occasion to go out of the yard, and because the gate would not easily open, they all climbed over except the boy in question. It excelled his power, but he was "not to be beat," and perceiving an opening under the gate, where one would hardly say a kitten could go, he rubbed his way under about as quick as the rest went over. "Well, master Tom," said a venerable lady looking on, "you'll do something yet in the world." As a comment upon this prognostication, the Rev. Dr. Cook, himself, a distinguished Methodist clergyman, remarked to the writer a few years since, "Sir, we consider the Rev. Mr. Sewall as the Summerfield of America.

GEOLOGY OF ESSEX.

The geological character of Essex is deserving of notice. Sienite is the leading element, though President Hitchcock's map exhibits Alluvium in the northern part of the town. Traces of paint deposits have been discovered in at least two different localities, one in the large pasture commonly called White's Hill, and the other in the woodlands. From an out-cropping in a wood-lot belonging to the heirs of the late Zaccheus Burnham, a quantity was taken near the surface, some years since, which upon being sifted merely, was used for the first painting of Mr. Burnham's house. It lasted well and it is believed that the usual manufacturing processes would show it to be a paint of *good*, it may be, *superior* quality. But this is not the only mineral to be found in Essex. The Massachusetts Society for the promotion of Agriculture, in their published "Transactions" for 1861, New Series, Vol. I. Part III. pp. 309, 310, discourse as follows: "Allusion has before been made to limestone in Newbury, and it may be added that *iron* gives evidence of being present to some extent. There is a deposit of iron, it is believed, of great purity in the town of Essex. No exploration has been yet made, but the effect upon the magnetic needle, is without a precedent, as it is confidently believed; viz.: such as to deflect the needle seventy-two degrees in a distance of four rods. The deposit must therefore be greatly concentrated. It may indeed prove to be a combination of minerals of very little value, as is sometimes found to be the case, and still produce all that effect upon the needle above described. Its power, however, exceeds that which was found by Dr. Hitchcock, at Canaan Mountain, Connecticut, and which he describes in Silliman's Scientific Journal, but which deflected the needle only fifty or fifty-two degrees in a distance of ten rods, but which he nevertheless supposed to be iron ore of sufficient purity to pay well for exploring. This deposit of iron, if it be one, is to be met with in a "Walk" less than half a mile from the dwelling-house formerly owned and occupied by the late Asa Burnham.

DESCRIPTION OF SCENERY BY A VISITOR.

A distinguished clergyman, after preaching here in June, this year (1867), took a Monday morning walk about our town, and as is common, saw so much more than native residents ever do see, that no apology will be made for an extract of his "correspondence of the Traveler," as published in that paper of June 20th:

"Do you desire to see a beautiful town, and people living in peace and primitive simplicity? Why, then, leave your dusty *sanctum*, your scissors and your pigeon-holes, and come down to old Chebacco for a day or two. You will find the venerable descendants of the original Pilgrims,—Cogswell, Burnham, Low, Choate, *et alias*, inhabiting the very grounds which those good men received from England's King—bearing their names, their lineaments; thinking their thoughts, sustaining their principles, and realizing to some extent their expectations.

"It would do your soul and body good to see these hardy men of Essex; to taste their hospitality; to observe their thrift and industry, and to hear the stories which they tell of daring exploits on the deep, or of the olden times. Or if you love the Summer breeze and Summer beauty, if you love to gaze on scenery, varied picturesque, enchanting, ascend with me " White's Hill," above the village, on a rosy morning. Turn your eye around from the towers and trees of distant Ipswich, inland to quiet Rowley, thence over hills of deepest green to the silver shimmering of the beautiful Chebacco, as it winds along the vales beneath you ; see it gleam among the foliage of the village at your feet and now dotted with sail, go sparkling in the early beam of day, to mingle gently with the waters of the ocean.

The spot where the Chebacco first meets your eye, reminds you of " that vale in whose bosom the bright waters meet ;" and at the confluence of this beautiful river, with the ocean just before you, rises the rounded form of Hog Island, birth-place of Rufus Choate. . . . . . But come and see the boats we build. None stauncher, trimmer, fleeter, breast the waves of ocean. Mr. Cooper, in the " Pilot," has honored us in making Capt. Barnstable commander of the never-to-be-forgotten Ariel, hail from " old Chebacco," and Capt. Kane had the good sense to sail to the North Pole in timber put together on the Chebacco river.

" Our natural curiosity par excellence, is " Martin's Rock," a mass of cloven granite blocks piled fantastically, no mortal can divine just how or when. On this grotesque aggregation of rock, which rises some dozen feet upon the summit of a rocky knoll, the late Winthrop Low, Esq., erected a liberty pole, fastening it with iron clamps and spikes into the solid base. . . . . .

" But do not understand me to say that our dear old town, though beautiful, is perfect. We want a railroad, we intend to have one ; we want a town-house and town-clock, a high school, public library, hotel and a bank ; we want more charity, less scandal, and less rum, and more than this, we want and ask and invite you, Mr. Traveler, as I said in the beginning, to leave your dusty *cabinet*, your musty books and papers, and the hubbub of the ' Hub,' a day or so, and come and breathe the invigorating atmosphere and see the beauties of the well turned, quiet rolling ' Hub' of old Cape Ann."

EFFORTS FOR A RAILROAD.

The fact that a railroad is upon the programme of facilities which old Chebacco is still wanting, is not wholly voluntary on the part of the people of the town. And as we cannot *ride in a car*, we continue our *walk*, though we find we cannot go far in any direction without crossing some one of the lines already surveyed and even staked out for a railroad within the last few years.

It it sometimes said *reproachfully*, that Essex, the very namesake of the county, is the only town in the county, still without that grand facility. If there were no absolute necessity for a road, it surely would be no reproach to do without it. No town or other corporation ought to lay out a hundred and fifty or two hundred thousand dollars merely for the sake of being in the fashion. But Essex is environed on nearly every side by high land. You can go to neither Ipswich, Gloucester, Salem, Beverly, or Wenham Depot, without encountering hills, rising in *some parts of their ascent*, as rapidly for short distances as the Simplon over the Alps, or the Holy-head road in North Wales; at least we are told so.

The first effort made for obtaining railroad facilities for Essex, was in the Autumn of 1844, at the time when the Eastern Railroad Company were contemplating a branch to Gloucester. The then president of the road, stated to a committee from Essex, that if the corporation could be satisfied that a road from Gloucester through Essex would pay them a certain per cent , such a road would be built without any doubt. The statistics were collected, and a stronger case was made out than he had contemplated ; so much so, that he caused a scientific survey of the road to be made in June, 1845. Probably a stronger case was made in favor of the present route ; at any rate the road was never built, and that phantom ship went on to the rocks a total loss.

Essex moved again in 1848, by petitioning the Legislature to charter a railroad from a point near the center of Essex, over Foster's bridge to the Eastern Railroad, at or near the twenty-second mile post from Boston, the distance from said bridge, being $3\frac{7.8}{100}$ miles. A hearing of the petitioners was had before a Legislative Committee on the 13th of March, and a charter was obtained, but no patronage ever smiled upon that enterprise, and it was *still-born*.

In 1850 again, a company in Boston explored the great Chebacco, or Essex Pond, with a view to the ice trade, and determined to construct a railroad from that beautiful sheet of water to Wenham depot. Such a road could have been continued from the pond to the center of Essex, by our citizens alone. Some important member of the Boston company, however, seceded, as we were told, and all those prospects melted away before the ice melted that Spring in the pond.

Nothing disheartened, however, the Essex friends of a road rallied once more in the Winter of 1865-6. Having before us the example of Rockport and several towns in the western part of the State, a town meeting was called for the purpose of asking leave of the Legislature to use the town's credit to the amount of $50,000. This sum indeed had been voted by the town *in anticipation of the law*, and with great if not with perfect unanimity. The town's action was somewhat premature, although that alone interposed no serious difficulty. Before a new meeting could be called, however, for the purpose of complying strictly with the terms of the charter, local interests antagonized, and upon that rock, this last ship, like that of 1845, went to pieces, a total loss. Upon such a state of facts, moralists must moralize; we have no heart to. Possibly some future *Nelson* may point out a "cause and cure." Oh, come the day! for many who desire to see it, have already died without the sight.

TOWN BURYING - GROUND.

Notwithstanding most of the *recent interments* have been made in the Spring Street Cemetery, yet family considerations still lead to the occasional occupation of the *old* burying-ground. A recent walk has brought us to the fresh grave of John Dexter, late of Manchester but formerly of this town; and as the following sketch contains much of historical value generally, we offer no apology for inserting it, as published in the Salem Gazette of the 15th of October, 1867:

"John Dexter, the subject of this sketch, was born in Malden, in this State, February 16, 1776. He was the son of William Dexter, a farmer, of German descent. He worked on his father's farm when there were no bridges connecting Boston with Charlestown, and it took two days to get a load of hay from the farm to Boston and back again, with the team, having to go round through Cambridge and over the neck. Having a step-mother who was severe with him, he left his father's house at the age of fifteen years, to learn a cooper's trade of Captain Pitchard, of Medford, with whom he worked till about the age of nineteen years, when he went on a voyage to the West Indies as a cooper. He next went a voyage to France, as mate of a vessel. On his return from this voyage he married Judith W. Sawyer, of Gloucester, and established himself as a small trader in Essex, then a portion of Ipswich, called 'Chebacco Parish.' Mr. Dexter soon identified himself with the people he settled among, by engaging in the boat building and clam business. His first vessel was of that description called 'Chebacco Boats,' of eighteen or twenty tons burthen, with two masts, pink stern,—that is, sharp at both ends, but designed to sail only one way,—a kind of craft much used for fishing in those days, along our coast and the shores of Maine, which gave employment to many men and boys, and rendered Wood Island, Damaris Cove, Frenchman's Bay, and Mount Desert, familiar places. He afterwards built many boats, schooners and brigs, some of which he employed in fishing and commercial trade. He engaged largely in the 'bait business,' giving employment sometimes to a hundred men in digging the clams, shocking, packing and marketing. His sales were made in Gloucester, Marblehead, Boston, Cape Cod and elsewhere. That *Bank* in Essex probably never discounted more freely, than while Mr. Dexter was one of the Directors.

" Mr. Dexter being fully identified with the interests of Essex gave his influence on the side of all enterprises started for the benefit of the place. At this time communication between Essex and Manchester was by the way of the ' Old Road,' as it is now called, a crooked, hilly road, as may be easily conceived by those who have never traveled over it, by the names given to some places on that road, viz: the ' Ram's Horn,' ' Steep Pitch,' &c. Hay from Essex to Manchester in those days was teamed around through Hamilton, Wenham and Beverly. Mr. Dexter, in his frequent journeys to Salem, Marblehead, Boston, and elsewhere, in the course of his business, traveled over this old road, and knowing from his acquaintance with the woods lying between Essex and Manchester, in the pursuit of timber for his vessels, that a better way could be had, he earnestly advocated a new road from Essex to Manchester, at a time when the economical policy of the county was to require the towns in which new roads were located to build them at the expense of such towns, which policy naturally caused the strong opposition of those who would not derive any immediate benefit from such road. Mr. Dexter's party prevailed, however, and he spent many days in looking out the best line for the road, and in carrying the surveyor's chain through ' Cedar Swamp.' The road was built, and now affords one of the most pleasant drives in the county, as many of our summer residents from Boston know and appreciate. Over this road now runs a daily coach from Essex to Manchester, and a large amount of heavy teaming of materials for vessel-building is carried. He was a large stockholder in the Essex Mill Corporation, a company that dammed the ' Chebacco River,' at the causeway in Essex, and erected a saw-mill and grist-mill, and run a carding machine ; for at that time the manufacture of cloth was done in families, and farmers raised their own wool, and having their carding done by machinery was thought to be a great advancement in the arts. One incident of the building of this dam, it may not be out of place to mention here. The owners of marsh, above the dam, fearing that their crop of hay would be greatly diminished or spoiled in consequence of the water being kept back on the marsh, sued the corporation for damage ; but before the case came to trial, they were satisfied that the crop had increased rather than diminished. They therefore withdrew their case from court.

" Mr. Dexter, like many others who have prospered in business, had a desire for farming, and in 1836 he gave over his business in Essex (where he had been thirty-eight years) to a son, and bought a farm in Danvers, where he lived about eight years, only four of which, however, he spent on his farm.

" In politics Mr. Dexter was republican, having in early life been a republican of the " old school," afterwards a whig during the existence of that party, and since a republican of the ' Lincoln school.' He voted for President Lincoln, and was a firm supporter of his administration and policy during the war of the rebellion and since. At the time of Mr. Dexter's decease he was living in Manchester with his fourth wife. As I said before, he married in 1798 Judith W. Sawyer, of Gloucester, who died in 1815. By this wife were born all his children, eight in number, three only of whom survive him, one son and two daughters. In 1816 he married Mrs. Sarah Hooper, of Manchester, who lived but a few months. She died in June, 1816, suddenly. He married for his third wife Miss Eliza Elwell, of Gloucester, in 1818, who died in 1842, while they lived in Danvers. Believing in the declaration of Scripture, that, ' it is not good that the man should be alone ' he in 1844 married Mrs. Mahala L. Byer, of Manchester, a lady much younger than himself, but a person well calculated to render his home pleasant in the decline of life. Having been liberal with his means in assisting his children in business, he deliberately made his will many years since, by which he made specific and liberal provision for his widow, free from the restrictions so frequently imposed in such cases. Having lived a life of temperate habits, *in the true meaning of that term*, he enjoyed good health and lively spirits, and at last died from mere exhaustion of the system, having for thirty-three days taken only cold water, with a little wine or cider a few times. Being nearly free from pain, having the full exercise of his reason, with the power of speech to the last, and being constantly attended by his wife or some of his children, his departure from this life could not be contemplated under more agreeable circumstances. He died with hopes full of immortality, fully resigned to the will of God, on the morning of October 2d, aged 91 years, 7 months and 16 days, and was buried in Essex on the 5th, among the graves of two of his wives and his deceased children.

REV. JOHN WISE.

As you enter this ancient burying ground, the most elevated object that strikes the eye, is a monument of sandstone, supported by four granite pillars, near the center of the cemetery and which covers the grave of Mr. Wise. The life of this great man, minister, patriot and statesman, is fully delineated elsewhere, and by many writers. And yet to walk over the fields of the town and among its monuments, without stopping to wipe the dust from Mr. Wise's stone, would almost be one of those sins that are not to be forgiven.

" The *first man* in America ever known *to oppose* the idea of TAXATION WITHOUT REPRESENTATION *sleeps in the grave of the Rev. John Wise, of Chebacco.* For this he was imprisoned, as all the world know, by Sir Edmund Andros, and with other Ipswich men had $5,000 to pay in money as a part of the penalty.

Of the *public* life and acts of Mr. Wise, however, it is not proposed here to say much. The reading world know what his life was and what his acts were, almost "by heart." But a reference to the heretofore published volume of the present History, gives us a hint at that portion of his life, which would be likely to escape the notice of Allen & Sprague, and other biographers. It is admitted that *drapery*, even *tradition* if the world pleases, are terms sometimes applied to sketches of the obscurer portions of a man's life; but the ivy clings not more closely to the oak, than the description and embellishment in this case, gather about the real and substantial part of the narrative, and indeed throughout this work.*

BISHOP'S GRAVE.

In the fourth range of Chebacco wood-lots, number two hundred and eighty-five, as found upon the Commoners' book, is a spot made memorable by the fact of its containing "Bishop's grave." The lot of land belongs to the heirs of the late Jonathan Story, Esq., and lies not far from half-way between the great pond and the road to Manchester. The history of the man buried there, is obscure, but by no means traditionary as the term is often understood. As stated verbally by the late Col. David Story, to the writer and a few others, while at the grave a few years since, this Mr. Bishop, then residing in the south part of the town, was away from home one evening making a call on a distant neighbor. On leaving the neighbor's house, it being intensely dark, he lost his way. We hardly need to be told that search was made, but unavailingly. The body was found the next Spring, on the spot where the head and foot stone lie, and was buried by order of the Selectmen of the town. Col. Story fixed the time at about the year 1770, although he did not claim to be accurate.

---

* Since it has been decided to publish the two volumes of our History in one, the insertion of a farther sketch of Rev. Mr. Wise, becomes unnecessary.

Appendix.

I.

RECORD OF MARRIAGES

SOLEMNIZED BY REV. JOHN CLEAVELAND, DURING THE LAST TEN YEARS OF HIS LIFE.

1790, Jan. 7. Jonathan Perkins and Dorcas Haskell, both of Ipswich.

May 27. Francis Burnham, 3d, and Anna Goodhue, both of Ipswich.

Nov. 22. Solomon Burnham and Elizabeth Kirby, both of Ipswich.

1791, Feb. 12. William Cogswell, 3d, and Mary Smith, both of Ipswich.

Mar. 3. Mark Burnham, Jr., and Margaret Burnham, both of Ipswich.

Mar. 26. Nathaniel Holmes and Susannah Story, both of Ipswich.

Apr. 21. Thomas Lee and Ruth Allen, both of Manchester.

Apr. 21. Arthur Dennis and Lucy Burnham, both of Ipswich.

July 28. Joseph Cogswell, Jr., and Hannah Burnham, both of Ipswich.

Aug. 25. Ezekiel Allen and Mary Procter, both of Manchester.

Sept. 8. Nathan Story, Jr., and Joanna Foster, both of Ipswich.

Sept. 14. Caleb Burnham and Jemima Pulsifer, both of Ipswich.

Oct. 6. Thomas Baker and Mary Choate, both of Ipswich.

Dec. 25. John Emerton and Ruth Rust, both of Ipswich.

1792, Jan. 8. Josiah Poland and Mehitable Lufkin, both of Ipswich

Mar. 11. At Manchester (there being no settled minister there) the Rev. Thomas Worcester of Salisbury, N. H., and Deborah Lee of Manchester.

Mar. 17. Isaac Allen, and Joanna Burnham, both of Ipswich.

Mar. 20. John Edwards, Jr., and Bethiah Foster, both of Manchester.

Apr. 19. Benjamin Patch, Jr., and Martha Low, both of Ipswich.

June 26. John Andrews, 3d, and Susannah Andrews, both of Ipswich.

Sept. 20. David Lull and Miriam Emerson, both of Ipswich.

Sept. 22. Dr. Nathan Jaques and Anna Patch, both of Ipswich.

Nov. 27. Joshua Burnham and Lucy Andrews, both of Ipswich.

Dec. 7. William Linneken of Cushing, and Mehitable Foster of Ipswich.

Dec. 13. Levi Andrews and Hannah Lufkin, both of Ipswich.

1793, Jan. 3. Robert Burnham and Eunice Emmerton, both of Ipswich.

Jan. 10. Samuel Smith and Hannah Choate, both of Ipswich.

Feb. 21. Samuel Low and Elizabeth Giddings, both of Ipswich.

May 1. Titus Nedson and Esther Story, both of Ipswich.

July 8. Thomas Holmes and Elizabeth Story, both of Ipswich.

July 18. John Osmont Craft of Manchester, and Susanna Low of Ipswich.

Oct. 20. Grover Burnham and Martha Story, both of Ipswich.

Nov. 7. James McKinley, and Joanna Burnham, both of Ipswich.

Nov. 28. Isaac Story, Jr., and Susanna Burnham, both of Ipswich.

Nov. 30. Samuel Giddings and Martha Goodhue, both of Ipswich.

Dec. 12. Winthrop Burnham and Mary Cogswell, both of Ipswich.

1794, Feb. 20. Nathaniel Cogswell and Eunice Low, both of Ipswich.

1794, Mar.	19.	Thomas Burnham (now the 4th) and Ruth Cavies, both of Ipswich.
Apr.	10.	Nathan Choate and Mary Perkins, both of Ipswich.
May	13.	Adoniram Haskell of Gloucester, and Ruth Perkins of Ipswich.
Sept.	7.	Solomon Choate, Jr., and Lucy Choate both of Ipswich.
Oct.	2.	Jonathan Burnham and Sukey Burnham both of Ipswich.
Oct.	2.	William Spiller and Anna Poland, both of Ipswich.
Nov.	21.	Jeremiah Choate of Londonderry, N. H., and Mary Story of Ipswich.
Nov.	30.	Zebulon Foster and Polly Story, both of Ipswich.
1795, Jan.	1.	Abraham Channel and Elizabeth Cleaveland, both of Ipswich.
Feb.	19.	Michael Story and Betsey Goodhue, both of Ipswich.
Mar.	29.	Capt. William Allen and Sally Edwards, both of Manchester.
Sept.	10.	Benjamin Jones and Sarah Hasham, both of Manchester.
Nov.	14.	Ezra Burnham and Anna Burnham, both of Ipswich.
Dec.	31.	Benjamin Procter and Susanna Low, both of Ipswich.
1796, Jan.	4.	David Burnham, 3d, and Rachel Choate, both of Ipswich.
Apr.	28.	Joshua Burnham, and Anna Andrews, both of Ipswich.
May	21.	Nehemiah Dodge and Sarah Low, both of Ipswich.
Oct.	20.	Henry Clemant of Weare, N. H., and Mrs. Mary Trendwell of Ipswich.
Oct.	27.	Eleazar Andrews and Molly Andrews, both of Ipswich.
Nov.	10.	Westley Burnham, 3d, and Hannah Story, both of Ipswich.
1797, Jan.	19.	Henry Witham of Gloucester, and Lois Story of Ipswich.
Mar.	23.	Caleb Andrews and Molly Burnham, both of Ipswich.
Mar.	28.	David Andrews, Jr., and Susanna Burnham, both of Ipswich.
Apr.	23.	Abraham Hobbs, 3d, of Topsfield, and Polly Story, of Ipswich.
June	27.	William Lakeman, 3d, and Susanna Brown, both of Ipswich.
July	30.	Moses Andrews and Sarah Andrews, both of Ipswich.
Nov.	2.	Mark Andrews and Polly Ross, both of Ipswich.
Nov.	7.	Robert Rust and Miriam Lufkin, both of Ipswich.
Nov.	8.	Nathaniel Rust, Jr., and Kate Henderson, both of Ipswich.
Nov.	21.	James Brown of Manchester, and Sarah Story of Ipswich.
Nov.	24.	James Butler and Sarah Smith, both of Ipswich.
Dec.	19.	Enoch Haskell and Mrs. Mary Low, both of Ipswich.
Dec.	26.	Israel Dunnels and Mary Story, both of Ipswich.
1798, Feb.	1.	William Norton and Susanna Perkins, both of Ipswich.
Mar.	29.	Nathan Burnham, Jr., and Susanna Burnham, both of Ipswich.
Aug.	10.	William Burnham, 4th, and Eunice Story, both of Ipswich.
Nov.	24.	Abraham Jones and Patty Smith, both of Ipswich.
Nov.	27.	John Smith, 3d, and Betsey Burnham, both of Ipswich.
Dec.	20.	Nathaniel Dodge of Percy, N. H., resident in Ipswich, and Sarah Poland, of Beverly.
Dec.	31.	William Bowers and Eunice Low, both of Ipswich.
1799, Feb.	7.	Elias Andrews and Martha Lufkin, both of Ipswich.
April	6.	Moses Burnham, Jr., and Eunice Andrews, both of Ipswich.
Apr.	22.	Rev. Mr. Cleaveland died.

MARRIED BY REV. JOSIAH WEBSTER.

1799, Nov.	19.	Jesse Story and Eunice Burnham, both of Ipswich.
Dec.	29.	John Mears and Susannah Story, both of Ipswich.
1800, May	4.	John Dodge, and Susaunah Marshall, both of Ipswich.
June	10.	Nicholas Babcock and Betsey May, both of Manchester.
June	28.	Jabez Ross and Hannah Smith, both of Ipswich.
Aug.	10.	John Carnel and Polly Tuck, both of Manchester.

1800, Nov. 22. Joseph Story and Mary Foster, both of Ipswich.
    Nov. 27. John Osment and Anna Morgan, both of Manchester.
    Nov. 27. John Emerson and Mrs. Abigail Allen, both of Ipswich.
    Dec. 4. Dr. Parker Russ and Elizabeth Cogswell, both of Ipswich.
    Nov. 24. William Low, Jr., and Mary Giddings, both of Ipswich.
1801, Feb. 19. John Perkins and Lydia Choate, both of Ipswich.
    Mar. 24. Jacob Burnham, Jr., and Sally Hidden, both of Ipswich.
    Apr. 19. Solomon Cole of Hamilton, and Ruth Poland of Ipswich.
    May 21. Daniel Andrews and Betsey Burnham, both of Ipswich.
    Sept. 17. Israel Andrews and Anna Burnham, both of Ipswich.
    Oct. 29. William Pollard and Nancy Hall, (negroes), both of Ipswich.
    Dec. 3. Jonathan Andrews and Joanna Andrews, both of Ipswich.
    Dec. 24. Asa Burnham and Polly Burnham, both of Ipswich.
1802, Jan. 14. Abel Low and Polly Cogswell, both of Ipswich.
    Mar. 18. John P. Choate, and Lucretia Cogswell, both of Ipswich.
    Apr. 1. David Story and Sally Andrews, both of Ipswich.
    Apr. 8. Epes Burnham and Abigail Craft, both of Ipswich.
    June 6. Jacob Andrews and Eunice Choate, both of Ipswich.
    July 1. Sargent Burnham and Hannah Craft, both of Ipswich.
    July 8. Jonathan Story, 3d, and Polly Burnham, both of Ipswich.
    July 29. James Crawley and Abigail Andrews, both of Ipswich.
    Sept. 4. Capt. William Andrews, Jr., and Betsey Goodhue, both of Ipswich.
    Oct. 12. Moses Haskell of North Yarmouth, and Elizabeth Haskell of Ipswich.
    Nov. 29. Luke Burnham and Eunice Foster, both of Ipswich.
    Dec. 19. John Wells and Bethiah Day, both of Ipswich.
1803, Jan. John Perkins, Jr., and Rachel Smith, both of Ipswich.
    July 21. Zebulon Burnham and Judith Andrews, both of Ipswich.
    Oct. 27. Manasseh Dodge of Hamilton, and Jemima Low, of Ipswich.
    Dec. 1. Oliver Poland and Susannah Woodbury, both of Hamilton (in the absence of Rev. Dr. Cutler in Congress).
    Dec. 22. Seth Burnham and Rachel Burnham, both of Ipswich.
    Dec. 29. Jacob Procter of Gloucester, and Lois Lufkin of Ipswich.
1804, Jan. 5. Timothy Marshall, Jr., of Beverly, and Mary Poland of Hamilton (in the absence of Dr. Cutler in Congress).
    Jan. 26. John B. Cummings of Topsfield, and Martha Knowlton of Hamilton.
    Mar. 7. John T. Tuttle and Nabby Butler, both of Ipswich.
    Apr. 7. Ebenezer Andrews and Susanna Marshall, both of Ipswich.
    July 14. Phinehas Story and Rosanna Burnham, both of Ipswich.
    Aug. 26. Jonathan Story, 4th, and Mrs. Susanna Craft, both of Ipswich.
    Oct. 23. Abel Currier of Chester, N. H., and Sally Quinby of Ipswich.
    Oct. 25. Amos Lee of Manchester, and Margaret Burnham, of Ipswich.
    Dec. 3. Parker Burnham and Martha Lufkin, both of Ipswich.
    Dec. 4. Abner Burnham and Anna Burnham, both of Ipswich.
1805, Jan. 8. Daniel Norton and Hannah Story, both of Ipswich.
    Jan. 10. Jacob Andrews, 4th, and Mary Burnham, both of Ipswich.
    Jan. 17. William Cogswell of Salem, and Lucy Choate of Ipswich.
    May 2. Henry Burnham and Sally Poland, both of Ipswich.
    July 23. Henry Russ and Patty Mears, both of Ipswich.
    Aug. 10. Thomas Giddings and Betsey Story, both of Ipswich.
    Oct. 31. William Burnham and Sally Burnham, both of Ipswich.
    Nov. 14. Jonathan Eveleth and Mary Smith, both of Ipswich.
    Nov. 21. Ebenezer Burnham, Jr, and Lucy Burnham, both of Ipswich.
    Dec. 8. Matthew Hammont and Joanna Lakeman, both of Ipswich.

1806, Jan. 12. William Mears and Lucy Butler, both of Ipswich.
Mar. 26. Stephen B. Hovey and Margaret Stacy, both of Ipswich.
Apr. 8. Benjamin Andrews, Jr., and Martha Craft, both of Ipswich.
Apr. 29. Benjamin Todd, Jr., of Rowley, and Abigail Story of Ipswich.
May 5. Joseph Smith and Hannah Lord, both of Ipswich.
June 8. Abraham Gloss of Beverly, and Judith Lee (negroes), both of Ipswich.

The Rev. Mr. Webster was dismissed, July 23, 1806, and his successor, Rev. Thomas Holt, was installed at Chebacco, January 25, 1809. Mr. Holt's record commences as follows, viz:

MARRIAGES SOLEMNIZED BY REV. THOMAS HOLT.

1809, Sept. 14. Parker Burnham and Mary Hardy, both of Ipswich.
Dec. 7. Richard Tucker and Ruth Goodhue, both of Ipswich.
Dec. 21. Moses Kinsman and Susanna Cogswell, both of Ipswich.
1810, Feb. 15. John McKenzie and Rebecca Burnham, both of Ipswich.
Feb. 28. Enoch Low and Anna Eveleth, both of Ipswich.
Mar. 7. Michael Story and Lydia Story, both of Ipswich.
Apr. 11. Elijah Gove and Ednah Poland, both of Ipswich.
July 4. Daniel Doe and Rachel Pulsifer, both of Ipswich.
Nov. 12. Francis Marshall and Anna Holmes, both of Ipswich.
Dec. 3. Ebenezer Mayo, Jr., of Hallowell, and Fanny Burnham of Ipswich.
1811, Jan. 1. John Smith of Manchester, and Abigail Giddings of Ipswich.
Apr. 10. Noah Burnham and Hannah Marshall, both of Ipswich.
Nov. 17. Winthrop Andrews of Ipswich, and Rhoda Grover of Boothbay.
Dec. 27. John Lang, Jr., of Portsmouth, N. H., and Judith Butler of Ipswich.
1812, Aug. 6. Samuel Burnham and Lucy Andrews, both of Ipswich.
Sept. 20. Oliver Lakeman and Mary Foster, both of Ipswich.
Oct. 11. William Mears and Elizabeth Butler, both of Ipswich.
Oct. 15. Pelatiah Lewis and Peggy Lemous (negroes), both of Ipswich.
Oct. 25. Abel Burnham and Esther Butler, both of Ipswich.
Nov. 12. Jonathan Andrews, Jr., and Hannah Andrews, both of Ipswich.
1813, Apr. 18. Nathaniel Gorton, Jr., and Martha Andrews, both of Ipswich.

Rev. Mr. Holt was dismissed from Chebacco, April 20, 1813. His successor, Rev. Robert Crowell, was ordained, August 10, 1814, and his record of marriages proceeds as follows, viz:

MARRIAGES BY REV. R. CROWELL.

1814, Dec. 23. Ira Burnham and Polly Marshall, both of Ipswich.
1815, Feb. 26. John Burnham and Abigail Herrick.
Sept. 17. Peter Colado of Manchester, and Ruth Story of Ipswich.
Oct. 10. Charles Choate and Polly Low, both of Ipswich.
Oct. 13. William Marshall and Lucy Butler, both of Ipswich.
Nov. 13. Samuel Burnham and Amelia Choate, both of Ipswich.
Nov. 22. Perkins Story and Rachel Burnham, both of Ipswich.
Nov. 28. David Perkins and Lydia Kimball, both of Wenham (there being no settled minister in that town).
Nov. 30. Jacob Butler and Lucy Giddings, both of Ipswich.
Nov. 30. Francis Burnham and Mina Andrews, both of Ipswich.
Nov. 30. William Masury and Hannah Andrews, both of Ipswich.
Dec. 21. Abner Andrews of Gloucester, and Tabitha Burnham of Ipswich.
1816, Feb. 27. Adam Boyd and Ruth Story, both of Ipswich.
Nov. 3. Cornelius Batchelder of Beverly, and Sally Low of Ipswich.
Nov. 27. Samuel Burnham, Jr., and Sally Burnham both of Ipswich.
Dec. 21. Zebulon Andrews and Nancy Low, both of Ipswich.

58

1817, Mar. 20. William Holmes and Mrs. Mary Burnham, both of Ipswich.
      May 28. Thomas Lang of Deerfield, N. H., and Sarah Butler of Ipswich.
      July 9. Benjamin Burnham and Lucy Hardy, both of Ipswich.
      Sept. 2. Thomas Low and Lucy Story, both of Ipswich.
      Sept. 28. Dudley Choate and Sally Channel, both of Ipswich.
      Oct. 7. John Goodhue and Peggy Burnham, both of Ipswich
      Nov. 12. Richard Burnham and Thankful Burnham, both of Ipswich.
      Nov. 30. Dudley Andrews and Sally Low, both of Ipswich.
      Dec. 26. Michael Whitehouse and Polly Burnham, both of Ipswich.
1818, May 14. James Hoaig of Pittsfield, N. H., and Lucy Burnham of Ipswich.
      May 21. Thomas Masury of Wenham, and Lucy Andrews of Ipswich.
      Dec. 13. Mark Andrews of St. George, and Mary Andrews of Ipswich.
      Dec. 17. Capt. Winthrop Low and Mary Cogswell, both of Ipswich.
1819, Feb. 18. Samuel Morse and Anna Andrews, both of Ipswich.
      Mar. 17. Daniel Mears and Hepzibah Butler, both of Ipswich.
      Mar. 31. Jacob Burnham and Joanna Lull, both of Essex.
      May 3. William S. Foster and Mariah Andrews, both of Essex.
      Sept. 2. William Babcock and Mrs. Lydia Murray, both of Manchester.
      Sept. 5. Daniel Bayier and Mahala Lee, both of Manchester, (there being no
               minister there).
      Sept. 12. Joshua Low and Mary Burnham, both of Essex.
      Oct. 10. Samuel Cheever and Mrs. Nancy Cheever, both of Manchester (no
               settled minister there).
      Oct. 31. Zeno Burnham and Hepzibah Cummings, both of Essex.
      Nov. 25. Benjamin Stickney of Beverly, and Eunice Lee of Manchester.
      Nov. 28. John Crumby and Hannah Hill, both of Manchester.
      Dec. 14. William Choate and Lucretia Burnham, both of Essex.
1820, Jan. 25. John F. Burnham and Sarah Burnham, both of Essex.
      Jan. 31. Thomas Choate and Dorothy Emerson, both of Essex.
      Mar. 8. John Goodhue of Essex, and Mary Stanwood of Gloucester.
      Apr. 8. William Lufkin and Nancy Burnham both of Essex.
      May 11. Jasper Lummus of Hamilton, and Sally Choate of Essex.
      May 16. Isaac Day of Ipswich, and Mary Story of Essex.
      July 20. John West, age 75 years, and Lucy Goldsmith, age 40, both of Man-
               chester.
      Oct. 15. Thomas Allen and Lavinia Baker, both of Manchester.
      Nov. 3. Florence McMann of Ipswich, and Sophia Butler of Essex.
      Nov. 7. Asa Riggs of Gloucester, and Anna Andrews of Essex.
      Nov. 23. Thomas Holmes of Essex, and Sally Ayres of Manchester.
      Dec. 14. Francis Burnham and Mary Procter, both of Essex.
      Dec. 24. Samuel Baker of Ipswich, and Susanna Holmes of Essex.
      Dec. 24. Moses Rust of Gloucester, and Lucy Procter of Essex.
1821, Feb. 1. James Burgess and Anna Richards, both of Manchester.
      Jan. 17. Jonathan Cogswell and Sukey Choate, both of Essex.
      Mar. 5. Joseph Tewksbury of Hopkinton, N. H., and Eliza Butler of Essex.
      Mar. 19. Job Burnham and Lydia Holmes, both of Essex.
      Mar. 25. Epes Story and Eunice Burnham, both of Essex.
      Apr. 11. Samuel Caldwell of Marblehead, and Elizabeth Mears of Essex.
      July 22. Joseph Marshall and Sally Burnham, both of Essex.
      May 17. Daniel Leach and Deborah Hill, both of Manchester.
      Oct. 7. Joseph Goodhue of Salem, and Mahala Lemmons (colored persons),
               of Essex.
      Nov. 21. Thomas Hardy and Esther Burnham, both of Essex.

1821, Nov. 29. James Haskell of Gloucester, and Sarah Procter of Essex.
Dec. 6. Stephen Piper of Ashley, and Lucretia Andrews of Essex.
Dec. 8. Nimrod Burnham and Susan Burnham, both of Essex.
Dec. 30. Thomas Dade of Gloucester, and Mary Burnham, of Essex.
1822, Feb. 14. Daniel Cogswell of Ipswich, and Sally Cogswell of Essex.
Feb. 21. Levi Andrews and Achsah Andrews, both of Essex.
Mar. 27. Henry Mears and Abigail Butler. both of Essex.
Mar. 31. Joshua Burnham and Hannah Andrews, both of Essex.
June 10. Benjamin Brown of Ipswich, and Atarah Andrews of Essex.
Nov. 20. Samuel Hibbert of Haverhill, and Sally S. Holmes of Essex.
Feb. 5. Abel Story and Thankful Burnham, both of Essex.
1823, Mar. 20. Adoniram Andrews and Mary Andrews, both of Essex.
Mar. 29. Samuel Mears and Lydia W. Burnham, both of Essex.
Apr. 3. Alfred Burnham and Ednah Burnham, both of Essex.
Nov. 20. John Boyd and Lucy Burnham, both of Essex.
Dec. 28. At Hamilton, Mr. Farr of Gloucester, and Miss Patch of Hamilton.
1824, Jan. 29. Thomas Lufkin and Eliza Haskell, both of Essex.
Feb. 9. Elisha Story and Lydia Boyd, both of Essex.
Feb. 22. Seth Story and Mary Story, both of Essex.
Mar. 21. Jeremiah Poland and Betsey Andrews, both of Essex.
Apr. 5. Moses Rust and Judith Burnham, both of Essex.
Apr. 10. Joel Boyd and Mary Burnham, both of Essex.
Apr. 18. Warren Foster and Judith Burnham, both of Essex.
May 15. Amos Burnham and Polly Story, both of Essex.
June. 1. At Hamilton—Benjamin Woodbury and Thirza Woodbury, both of Hamilton, (there being no settled minister there.)
June 14. Enoch Low and Betsey Burnham, both of Essex.
July 18. Thomas Stamford of Ipswich, and Judith Burnham of Essex.
Aug. 22. Ezra Haskell of Boston, and Emily Haskell of Essex.
Sept. 9. Dr. Josiah Lamson and Rebecca Sargent, both of Essex.
Oct. 28. Joseph Allen, Jr., and Orpah Andrews, both of Essex.
Nov. 22. Samuel Burnham and Sally Andrews, both of Essex.
Dec. 2. John Burnham and Sarah C. Perkins, both of Essex.
Dec. 11. Eleazer Andrews and Judith Andrews, both of Essex.
Dec. 5. Jeremiah Andrews and Eliza Allen, both of Essex.
1825, Mar. 21. Jonathan Lufkin, Jr., and Thirza Marshall, both of Essex.
Mar. 27. John Andrews and Lucy Low, both of Essex.
Apr. 20. Thomas Knight of Manchester, and Lucretia Burnham of Essex.
June 15. Charles Roberts and Charlotte Andrews, both of Essex.
June 15. Weeden Cole of Gloucester, and Mrs. Mary Holmes of Essex.
July 19. Humphrey C. Cogswell of Hampstead, N. H., and Sally H. Burnham of Essex.
July 21. Isaac Farnham of Salem, and Hannah G. Burnham of Essex.
July 28. Josiah Lufkin, Jr., of Gloucester, and Mehitable Burnham of Essex.
Nov. 24. Uriah G. Spofford and Mary Perkins, both of Essex.
Dec. 14. John F. Bannister of Boston, and Abigail Dexter of Essex.
1826, Feb. 7. Michael Story, Jr., and Susan Burnham, both of Essex.
Feb. 19. John J. Butler and Mary Andrews, both of Essex.
Apr. 16. Luke Burnham, Jr., and Mary Burnham, both of Essex.
Apr. 26. John T. Taylor of Danvers, and Maria Perkins of Essex.
May 31. Levi Brown of Ipswich, and Susan Mears of Essex.
Aug. 20, Daniel Gaffney of Gloucester, and Abigail Story of Essex.
Oct. 3. John S. Burnham and Clarissa Burnham, both of Essex.

1826, Oct. 30. Charles Dexter and Judith Allen, both of Essex.
    Nov. 19. Zaccheus Burnham and Susanna Burnham, both of Essex.
    Nov. 19. David S. Andrews and Mary Poland, both of Essex.
    Nov 23. Isaac Annabal of Hamilton, and Sally Burnham of Essex.
    Nov. 26. Elias Savage and Lucretia Choate, both of Essex.
    Nov. 30. Abraham Jones and Mary Quimby, both of Essex.
    Dec. 4. Asa Burnham, Jr, and Mary S. Andrews, both of Essex.
    Dec. 7. Joseph Kilham and Mary Allen, both of Manchester.
    Dec. 26. Warren Low of Essex, and ——— Babcock of Manchester.
1827, Jan. 8. Timothy Andrews and Susan P. Low, both of Essex.
    Mar. 3. William Thomson and Hannah Low, both of Essex.
    Mar. 14. Daniel Whipple of Hamilton, and Hannah Norton of Essex.
    Apr. 29. George Burnham and Ann G. Perkins, both of Essex.
    May 20. Daniel Norton and Lydia Choate, both of Essex.
    July 15. John Herrick of Gloucester, and Mary Andrews of Essex.
    Sept. 30. Abraham Perkins and Abigail Story, both of Essex.
    Oct. 13. Moses B. Perkins and Lydia Procter, both of Essex.
    Dec. 19. Ebenezer Cogswell of Ipswich, and Elizabeth Burnham of Essex.
    Dec. 22. Samuel Giddings and Eunice Burnham, both of Essex.

RECORD OF DEATHS IN CHEBACCO,

AS RECORDED BY REV. JOHN CLEAVELAND DURING THE LAST TEN YEARS OF HIS LIFE.

1790, Feb. 10. Jonathan Marshall, of consumption, almost 75 years.
    Feb. 19. Dennison Cogswell, son of Col. Jonathan Cogswell, Jr., of vital weakness, in 11th month of his age.
    Feb. 20. Widow Martha Burnham, relict of late Capt. Jonathan Burnham of cancer, in her 90th year.
    May 28. Elder Eleazer Craft, of influenza, just entered his 79th year.
    June 13. Ephraim, son of Jacob Burnham, of spasmodic fever, brought on by labor beyond his strength and getting a sudden cold, in his 14th year.
    June 14. Still-born child of Benjamin Cogswell.
    June 20. Male infant of Capt. Jonathan Story, of sore mouth, aged 15 days.
    July 15. Philemon Smith, dropsy and other disorders, in his 23d year.
    July 17. Nathaniel Burnham, son of Job Burnham, of convulsions and worms, near two years old.
    Aug. 19. Wife of Thomas Giddings, of consumptive disorders, between 70 and 80 years of age.
    Oct. 16. Elizabeth Choate, of consumption, in her 20th year.
    Oct. 20. Child of Grover Burnham, 3 days old.
    Dec. 1. Child of Oliver Emmerton. of canker, about two weeks old.
    Dec. 5. Infant child of Jonathan Perkins, of canker, near three weeks old.
1791, Feb. 6. Samuel Low, of bilious disorders, in his 17th year.
    Apr. 13. A female infant of William Burnham, 3d.
    June 9. Capt. Joshua Burnham, of unknown disease, lately arrived from West Indies, in his 55th year.
    June 25. Polly, daughter of Thomas Burnham 4th, a choleric fever, aged 1 year 9 months.
    June 27. Infant of Jesse Burnham.
    July 7. John Choate, Esq., of consumption attended with excruciating pains and a costive habit arising from scirrhuses in his liver, being opened after his death, in his 54th year.

1791, July 13. Elizabeth, wife of Stephen Story, of consumptive decay, in her 74th year.

Sept 21. Patty, daughter of Timothy Ross, of diarrhœa, worms and fever, aged 22 months.

Aug. 28. Polly, daughter of Elisha Story, of an unknown disorder.

Nov. 5. Adoniram, son of James Andrews, of worms and it was thought mortification, in his 3d year.

Nov. 17. A son of Stephen Boardman, of fits, 9 days old.

Dec. 9. Aaron Low, of a nervous fever after a pleurisy, in his 64th year.

1792, Feb. 9. Widow Elizabeth Holmes, of fever and old age, aged about 81.

May 9. Wife of Enoch Haskell, of an unknown disease of the bowels and mortification, aged 59 years.

June 13. Amariah Andrews, of consumption, in his 34th year.

July 10. Billy, son of Titus Nedson, of fits, in his 3d year.

July 18. Benjamin Procter, by falling from his horse into the creek was drowned, about 79 years of age.

July 20. Mary, wife of Grover Burnham, of mortification, aged about 22 years.

Aug. 1. William Cogswell, Jr., and David Lufkin, by a hurricane at St. Martins.

Aug. 11. An infant twin child of Abraham Channel two days after its birth.

Aug. 23. Widow Mehitabal, relict of Solomon Burnham, suddenly, in her 84th year.

Aug. 28. Widow Jane Burnham, chiefly of the infirmities of old age, in her 89th year.

Oct. 23. Mary Cogswell, of fever and canker, aged 51 years.

Dec. 1. Male child of John Emmerton, at its birth.

Dec. 8. Female child of David Lull, soon after its birth.

1793, Jan. 24. Elias, son of Isaac Andrews, of mortification, uncommon, aged 4 months, 25 days.

Mar. 30. Francis Choate, last son of the late John Choate, Esq , deceased, of consumption, in his 17th year.

Apr. 6. Eunice, wife of Jeremiah Choate, of dropsical consumption. We trust she fell asleep in Jesus.

Apr. 12. Francis Burnham, of fever, in his 80th year; who appeared to fall asleep in Jesus.

Aug. 14. Seward Dow, of sudden mortification, aged about 9 years.

Sept. 6. Jacob Goodhue, of palsy, aged about 70 years.

Sept. 17. Billy Story, son of Jonathan Story, Jr., of malignant quinsy, about 1 year, 8 months.

Sept. 26. Margaret, relict of Francis Burnham, deceased, of many disorders, somewhat uncommon, terminating in consumption, in her 78th year.

Oct. 24. Polly, daughter of John Procter, Jr., of quinsy, aged 2 years and near 7 months; a remarkably large child, weighing between 70 and 80 *weight* above 2 months before her death.

Dec. 13. Widow Mary Marshall, of cancer, just entered her 70th year.

1794, Feb. 27. Widow Abigail Jones, of sudden dropsy, aged 69 to 70 years.

Mar. 3. Isaac Perkins, son of Abraham Perkins, by bleeding occasioned by an ulcer in the throat, in his 16th year.

Mar. 5. A female infant of John Cogswell, at its birth.

Jan. 24. Jacob Low, of small pox, in the West Indies, in his 24th year.

Apr. 3. An infant of William Burnham, 3d, at its birth.

June 21. Abigail, wife of Abraham Channel, of consumption, aged 39 years. She gave good evidence of her good estate.

June 29. An infant of Solomon Andrews, at its birth.

1794, July 4. Ruth, wife of John Emmerton, of consumption, in her 25th year. Died hopefully.

Aug. 5. Hannah Foster, of a sudden convulsion of her nerves, after having been in a . . . . . . state for many months, in her 87th year. A person of real piety and truth for many years.

Sept. 9. Ebenezer Mansfield, accidental, aged 61 years.

Sept. 22. Nabby, daughter of Amos Burnham, of consumption, aged 12 years, (and perhaps) 1 month.

Sept. 23. Polly, daughter of Widow Mary Cogswell, of consumption, aged 15 years, (and perhaps) 1 month.

Oct. 2. Male infant of Lieut. Jeremy Choate, of fits occasioned by dysenteric affection, in 4th day of its age.

Oct. 16. Elizabeth, relict of David Burnham, of fever and old age, in her 92d year.

Oct. 23. Sarah, wife of James Eveleth, of fever, aged 74 years.

Oct. 31. Lucy, daughter of Robert and Mary Choate, of malignant quinsy, in her 4th year.

Dec. 16. Francis Choate, son of Stephen C., fever and convulsive fits, 7 months old.

Dec. 19. Elizabeth Butler, of fever, aged 57 years.

Dec. 21. We have news that Stephen Low, Jr., died at sea of fever, aged perhaps 35 years.

Dec. 25. Thomas, son of George Pierce, in West Indies of yellow fever, aged about 18 years.

Sometime in the summer of this year, (1794,) it is supposed Mr. Caleb Burnham and all the crew perished at sea.

1795, Jan. 9. Samuel Nedson, a colored boy, of a violent seizure in his nerves and of fever; son of Titus N., in his 8th year.

Jan. 27. A child of Mr. Riggs, 2 months old.

Mar. 13. Four persons drowned in Chebacco River—a terrible snow-storm.

    Parker Story, in his 35th year, married.

    Thomas Holmes, aged 29 years, married.

    Aaron Story, in his 28th year.

    Moses Pearse, son of George Pearse, about 16.

James Burnham, of an uncommon disorder, at sea.

Apr. 23. Lucy, wife of Joshua Burnham, of fever, aged 29 years and a few months.

May 11. Mehitable, relict of James Burnham, of Manchester, [leaf torn.]

N. B. Parker Story taken up Lord's day, March 15, and buried March 16.

Moses Pearse, taken up and buried May 7.

Aaron Story taken up and buried May 15.

    A Jury of Inquest sat upon each.

Mar. Mr. William Butler, in France, of small pox, aged near 21 years.

June 4. Female infant of Joshua Burnham, aged 2 months.

July 8. Michael Story, who fell on the edge of a broad axe, which was in his hand, from the ridge-pole of a barn-frame just raised, which cut the whole width of it, through his shoulder-blade and ribs into his vitals about 6 o'clock P. M., and he expired about 10 o'clock the same evening, in the 26th year of his age, and left a young wife with an infant and aged father, all to mourn. Two more on the same ridge-pole when it broke, fell with him, and were disastered but like to recover,—William Burnham, a minor, and Titus, a black belonging to Rev. Mr. Cleaveland.

1795, July 29. Two female infants of Robert and Eunice Burnham.

Aug. 7. Moses Burnham, by the extreme hot weather, aged 51 years.

Aug. 25. Ensign Humphrey Choate, of an uncommon bleeding from his bladder for several days, aged almost 75 years.

Dec. 2. Thomas Emerson, at sea, son of the late Nathaniel Emerson, a young man.

Dec. 29. Thomas, son of Joseph Perkins, Jr., of scarlatina squinosa, in his 13th year.

Dec. 30. Asa Perkins, son of Joseph Perkins, Jr., of the same distemper, aged 4 years.

1796, Jan. 8. Eunice, daughter of Robert Burnham, of throat distemper and scarlet fever, aged 2 years.

Jan. 17. John Holmes, son of William H., of throat distemper, aged 15 months.

Jan. 22. Mrs. Sarah Tripwell, a few days after having had thirty quarts of dropsy water taken from her by tapping, in her 76th year.

Jan. 23. Asa, son of Ebenezer Story, of throat distemper, in his 16th year.

Jan. 25. Lucy, daughter of Nathaniel Burnham, of throat distemper, aged 10 years.

Jan. 25. Aaron, son of Aaron Foster, at evening, of same distemper, in his 4th year.

Jan. 30. Miss Abigail Goodhue, at Ipswich town, aged near 80 years.

Feb. 1. Samuel, son of Mr. Hardy, of throat distemper, near 6 years old.

Feb. 3. Hannah Procter, wife of Mr. John P., [record torn off] attended with a most distressing asthma.

Feb. 4. Daughter of Isaac Story, Jr., [record torn off] in her 4th month.

Mar. 12. The widow Mary Cogswell, who had [remainder torn off].

Mar. 27. Widow Anna Jones, of the ja [torn off.]

Apr. 3. Sarah, wife of Mr. Samuel [rest torn off].

Mar. 7. Mary Jones, at the poor-house, aged 72.

Apr. 13. Jonathan Smith, at the poor-house, aged 91 or 92.

May 10. Lieut. Jacob Story, of various disorders of long standing, aged 82.

May 13. Infant daughter of Solomon Burnham, 9 days old.

May 14. Stephen Story, of various disorders of long standing, aged near 80.

May 16. Jesse, son of Jesse Burnham, drowned at E. Haskell's bridge, in his 7th year.

May 21. Solomon, son of Solomon Burnham, of throat distemper, aged about 4 years.

May 25. Hannah, wife of David Andrews, being reduced by fever, and various disorders, aged 25.

May 26. Untimely infant of the last mentioned Mrs. Andrews.

May 28. Widow Sarah Bennet, of a complication of disorders, aged about 62 years.

Aug. 19. Bennet, son of Enoch Burnham, drowned in Chebacco River, against Col. Cogswell's landing, in his 13th year.

Aug. 26. Joseph Page of Salisbury, a ship carpenter, working for Jacob Story, died at his house of putrid fever and mortification in bowels, in his 24th year.

Sept. 25. Nathan, twin son of Nathan Burnham, of bilious fever, 8 years old.

Oct. 6. Infant child of Daniel Burnham, of cough, suddenly, 8 weeks old.

Oct. 8. Stephen, a child of widow Low, of fever, 3 years old.

Oct. 8. Child of Joshua Burnham, at its birth.

Nov. 25. Child of Moses Marshall, 10 months.

Dec. 15–16. Daughter of Jesse Burnham, of cough and other complaints, 17 months.

1796, Dec. 27. Widow Mary, relict of William Allen, suddenly, supposed to be 80 years old.

1797, Jan. 1. Infant of Stephen Story, at its birth.

    Jan. 24. Nehemiah Choate, of lung fever, in his 67th year.

      * 22. Patience, daughter of James Andrews, of cough and fever, aged 1 year and 9 months.

        †Twins of Oliver Norton, one on the day of its birth, the other its 3d day.

        ‡Story, suddenly by an unknown disorder, just entered his 74th year.

        §Andrews, son of James Andrews, Jr., of putrid fever ending in mortification, in the 11th year of his age.

The names of the remaining five upon this page of Mr. Cleaveland's records are lost by some accident in tearing, the corner of the leaf being lost. The remainder of the record is perfect for the year, and throughout, and is as follows, viz.:

    June 28. Westley Burnham, of a fever with mortification, in his 78th year.

    July 22. Miss Jemima Foster, of dropsy and other disorders, in her 77 year; a member of the church—of unspotted character for piety and religion.

    July 28. Michael, son of Ebenezer Burnham, of fever and other disorders, in his 12th year.

    Sept. 1. Sarah, widow of late Joseph Procter, of malignant fever, [record of age torn off.]

    Sept. 28. Martha, relict of Elder Eleazer Craft, of fever, in her 83d year.

    Dec. The aged widow Pearse, of many and great infirmities.

1798, Jan. 7. Infant son of Joshua Burnham, soon after its birth.

    Feb. 8. Elizabeth, wife of Ebenezer Choate, of various disorders, in her 71st year.

    Feb. 10. Ruhamah, wife of Jesse Story, of various disorders for many months, aged 62 years.

    Mar. 29. Son of Capt. Rufus Low, aged 4 days.

    July 4. Abigail, daughter of late John Choate, Esq.; she died at Ipswich town in her 24th year. She gave evidence of falling asleep in Jesus.

    July 14. At Gloucester, Elizabeth, wife of Jonathan Burnham, of a combination of diseases—a good woman—in her 84th year.

    Aug. 25. An infant of James Andrews, Jr., immediately after birth.

    Sept. 2. Infant child of black Peter and Kate, in its 17th month.

    Sept. 11. John, only son of Capt. John Procter, by sucking in the steam of hot coffee, in its 13th month.

    Oct. 19. Anna, wife of John Cogswell, of a short consumption, aged 36 years. She appeared to fall asleep in Jesus.

    Oct. 24. A female child of Aaron Haskell, 16 days old.

    Nov. 2. Israel, son of John Procter, of quinsy, aged 11 months.

    Dec. 12. Moses Lufkin, of dropsy, aged 58.

    Dec. 10. Richard Pearse, a likely young man, mate of the vessel, was washed overboard, with one of the hands, and both were drowned in a storm.

1799, Feb. 3. Zechariah Story, Jr., of Windsor, Vt., of a violent fever, at Mr. David Low's, in his 21st year.

    Feb. 2. Francis Rust, very suddenly, as he was at table, aged 48.

RECORDED BY ANOTHER HAND.

    Apr. 22. Rev. John Cleaveland, pastor of the Second Church in Ipswich, after a long, faithful and successful ministry. He died on the same day of the month on which he was born, being 77 years old.

---

* Month gone.   † Date gone.   ‡ Date and name torn off.   § Date and Christian name gone.

1799, May 18. Deacon Thomas, (Burnham is believed to have been intended though omitted), aged 72 years.

May 31. Lieut. Jeremiah Choate, aged near 44 years.

April or In a foreign part, Isaac Andrews, 45 or 46,—and Daniel Andrews,
May. aged 19 years.

July 23. Widow Susannah Elwell, of consumption, aged 47.

Aug. 20. Joseph Marshall, aged 76.

Sept. [A death is recorded, not legible.]

Nov. 25. Widow Susanna Marshall, an aged woman.

RECORD OF DEATHS IN THE SECOND PARISH OF IPSWICH.

BY REV. JOSIAH WEBSTER.

1800, April. A child of Aaron Giddings, aged almost 4 years.

July 11. John Herrick, drowned, from Gloucester; lived with D. Choate.

Aug. 8. Francis Burnham, aged about 50 years.

Aug. 29. A child of Abraham Jones.

Sept. Wife of John Emerson.

Sept. 27. Ned Choate, negro, church member, aged about 90; from D. Choate's family.

Oct. 4. Elizabeth Perkins, wife of Joseph Perkins, aged 77; church member.

Dec. 19. Capt. Stephen Low, aged about 65.

Dec. 30. Widow Catherine Low, aged 86.
A child of William Burnham.

1801, Feb. Widow Eunice Burnham.

April. Child of Joseph Story was still-born.

Apr. 22. Capt. Moses Burnham, about 40.

April or May. At sea, Moses Burnham, aged about 21.

Aug. 27. Mary Perkins, aged about 20.

Sept. 25. A child of Moses Burnham, aged 13 months.

Nov. 15. Elizabeth, wife of David Burnham, about 86; a professor of religion.

Nov. 26. An infant of Caleb and Molly Andrews.

Dec. 26. Sarah Choate, 28 or 29; a professor of religion.

1802, Mar. 26. Jonathan Burnham, 86.

Apr. 25-6. John Cavis, about 80.

May. Sarah Burnham.

May 13. An infant of Jonathan and Joanna Andrews.

July 4. Nehemiah Story, a church member; aged 81-2.

July 6-7. A child of Abner and . . . . . Poland, about 7 months.

July 29. Thomas Giddings, aged 94.

Aug. 5. Wife of Joseph Perkins, Jr., aged 50.

Sept. 22. Wife of Jacob Cogswell.

Oct. Enoch Burnham.

Oct. Polly, daughter of Stephen Story, 14 years, of lock-jaw.

Dec. 15. James Eveleth, 87 years.

Dec. 27. David Burnham, 89 years.
George Norton, Jr., abroad, aged 21-2.

1803, Jan. 27, Mr. George Norton.
Aaron Low, at sea, aged 21.

Apr. 17. A child of Mr. John Dexter, 2 years.

June 5. Elizabeth, wife of Dr. Parker Russ, aged 29.

Sept. 4. An infant of John Perkins, Jr.

Oct. 5-7. A child of Ebenezer Haskell.

50

1803, Oct. 21.	Betsy Kimball, from Maine, on a visit, suddenly; she was as well as usual in the morning, and died before nine o'clock at night.
Oct. 24.	Lieut. Abraham Perkins, of a cancer, aged 60; a professor of religion.
Nov. 1.	Eben Story, rose well for aught was known, but before he had put on all his clothes, he fell, never spake nor struggled, aged about 60 years.
Nov.	The wife of William Burnham, a Quaker.
Dec. 17.	Timothy, a sprightly son of Benjamin Burnham, who died at Salem, aged 18.
1804, Jan. 19.	Child of Joshua Burnham, still-born.
Jan. 20.	News arrived of the death of John Low, at sea, aged 24 years.
Feb. 11.	Funeral of Garrett's child, a negro.
Feb. 19.	Funeral of Levi Andrews' child, aged 2 years.
Mar. 3.	Funeral of Benjamin Cogswell's child, 1 year, 4 months.
Mar. 16.	Funeral of Eli Haskell's child, an infant.
Mar. 25.	Funeral of Ruth Foster, aged 20.
May 16.	Funeral of an infant child of Parker Burnham.
May 22.	Funeral of wife of Thomas Giddings, who died of consumption.
May 26.	Funeral of Sarah Perkins, daughter of Joseph P., died of consumption, aged 18.
July 3.	Funeral of a child of John Perkins, about one year old.
July 24.	Funeral of Parker Burnham's wife.
July 27.	A child of Jonathan Lufkin, died.
July 31.	Funeral of widow Hannah Burnham, who died of cancer, 59 years.
Aug. 27.	A child of John Dodge, 3 years old, of scarlet fever.
Sept. 2.	A child of Samuel Quimby, about 6 years.
Sept. 3.	Oliver Emerton, died, aged 45.
Oct. 11.	Funeral of a child of Ebenezer Andrews, in Gloucester.
Oct. 12.	Funeral of widow Smith, aged 74.
Oct. 24.	Funeral of Mr. Harlow's child, 2½ years.
Dec. 26.	Funeral of Moses Marshall's youngest child, 2½ years.
1805, Jan. 21.	Wife of Simeon Burnham, a professor of religion, 76 years.
Jan. 30.	Funeral of Nehemiah Dodge's child, still-born.
Feb. 7.	Funeral of Joseph Lemons' child, a negro.
Feb. 9.	Funeral of Jethro Story's child, a negro.
Feb. 22.	Funeral of George Choate's child, aged 19 months.
Apr. 4.	Capt. Joseph Perkins died, aged 85; a worthy member of the church.
May 15.	Funeral of child of Jonathan Story, 4th.
Sept. 9.	Funeral of infant child of Mr. Hardy.
Oct. 6.	Widow Ross died, aged 86.
Oct. 26.	Sukey Burnham died, aged 26, of consumption.
Nov. 4.	Polly, wife of Abel Low, died very suddenly, aged 27.
Dec. 1.	Jacob Cogswell died, aged 79.
Dec. 19.	Dr. Parker Russ died, aged 36.
1806, Jan. 4.	A negro child of Charles and Kate Hall died.
Feb. 1.	Mr. Joseph Perkins, aged 53.
Feb. 17.	A negro infant of Jethro Story.
Mar. 28.	Funeral of a colored child from the country.
Apr. 11.	Funeral of Dinah, a colored woman.
Apr. 16.	Funeral of Joseph Andrews, aged 77 years.
Apr. 26.	Funeral of William Mears' infant child.
May 10.	Funeral of Daniel Andrews' child, died suddenly of quinsy.

DEATHS RECORDED BY REV. THOMAS HOLT.

1809, Feb. 22. Widow Rachel Andrews, of old age, 78 yrs., 6 mos., 3 wks, 2 days.

June 10. Adam Boyd, of quick consumption, 44 years.

July 14. Job, son of Thomas and Betsy Giddings, 2 years, 10 months, 1 week, 6 days.

Sept. 21. Infant child of Zebulon and Judith Burnham, of canker, 2 months, 2 weeks, 1 day.

Oct. 15. Young child of Benjamin, Jr., and Mary Burnham, 1 year, 2 months, 3 weeks.

Nov. 10. Thomas Foster, of consumption, 47 years, 7 months. 1 day.

Nov. 16. Infant child of Zebulon and Polly Foster, whooping-cough and lung fever, 3 months, 2 weeks, 6 days.

Nov 30. Martha, wife of Stephen Boardman, inflammation of lungs, 38 years, 7 months, 1 day.

Dec. 11. Sally Peabody Friend, nervous putrid fever, 15 years, 1 month, 3 weeks.

Dec. 23. Widow Martha Andrews. old age, 90 years, 11 months, 1 week, 4 days.

1810, Jan. 14. Eunice. wife of William Bowers, dropsy, 33 years, 11 months, 2 weeks, 2 days.

Feb. 8. Miss Sally Bennet. lung fever, 54 years, 3 months, 4 weeks.

Feb. 11. Miss Anna Low, old age. 86 years, 11 months, 2 weeks, 2 days.

Mar. 6. Sophronia, twin daughter of Moses Marshall. of a singular cutaneous disease,1 year, 9 months. 3 weeks, 3 days.

June 17. Widow Mary Haskell, old age, 78 years, 11 months, 4 weeks.

July 7. Widow Mary Smith. consumption, 49 years, 1 mouth, 1 week, 1 day.

Aug. 2. Widow Ann Goodhue, consumption, 79 years, 11 months, 2 weeks, 6 days.

Sept. 7. Clara Perkins, consumption, 14 years, 6 months, 1 week, 5 days.

Nov. 1. Widow Mary Choate, palsy and consumption, 78 years, 7 months, 5 days.

Nov. 2. Peter Lewis, colored, quick consumption, 20 years.

Nov. 15. Infant child of James and Sally Perkins. a scald over pit of stomach, 8 months, 2 weeks, 1 day.

Nov. 17. Elizabeth Burnham, consumption, 24 years, 7 months, 4 weeks.

Nov. 25. Child of Nehemiah and Sarah Dodge, dropsy of the brain, 3 years, 2 months, 2 days.

Dec. 20. Infant child of John and Rebecca McKenzie, canker, 2 weeks, 2 days.

1811, Jan. 4. Widow Sarah Andrews, dropsy and consumption, 84 years.

Jan. 18. Zaccheus Burnham, consumption, 24 years, 3 weeks, 5 days.

Mar. 24. Ruth, wife of Capt. Aaron Foster, fever and old age, 83 years, 9 months. 1 week, 2 days.

Apr. 9. Edward, son of widow Susanna Foster, lung complaint, 1 year, 10 months, 1 day.

Apr. 17. Hannah Burnham, lung fever, 60 years, 3 months, 4 days.

Apr. 26. Infant child of Nathan and Elizabeth Story, 3 months, 2 weeks, 4 days.

June Widow Low.

June 22. Westley Burnham, Jr., inflammation of brain, 36 years, 9 months, 1 week, 1 day.

July 6. Young child of Benjamin, Jr., and Mary Burnham, of fits, 3 months, 2 weeks, 4 days.

July 28. Young child of Parker and Martha Burnham, consumption, 6 months, 3 weeks, 5 days.

Aug. 8. Cæsar Conway, colored, consumption, 70 years.

1811, Sept. 18. Child of John and Hepzibah Butman, of languishment, 10 months, 3 weeks, 3 days.

Oct.   6. Zebulon Foster, Jr., consumption.

Oct. 22. Child of Zebulon and Judith Burnham, whooping-cough, 1 year.

Nov. 24. Susanna, daughter of widow Susan Foster, 17 years, 2 months, 1 week, 2 days.

Dec. 13. Bethuel, wife of William Burnham, Jr., 59 years.

Dec. 26. Capt. Aaron Foster, of mortification from diarrhœa, 87 years, 3 weeks, 4 days.

1812, Jan. 10. Lydia, wife of William Holmes, lung fever, 50 years, 3 months, 4 weeks.

Jan.   9. Taff, colored woman, found dead in the house, 50 years.

Feb. 12. Dea. Jonathan Cogswell, 86 years, 8 months, 3 weeks, 2 days.

Mar. 13. Infant son of Nathaniel and Judith Perkins, 3 days.

Mar. 21. Mary Cogswell, consumption, 51 years, 6 months, 2 weeks, 3 days.

Apr.   8. John, son of Capt. John and Elizabeth Eveleth, 1 year, 2 months, 1 week, 1 day.

Apr. 10. Samuel Sewall, consumption, 21 years.

Apr. 20. Abigail, wife of Caleb Marshall, consumption, 24 years, 8 months, 3 weeks, 4 days.

May 29. Nathan, son of Nathan and Susanna Burnham, inflammation in the knee joint, 2 years. 4 months, 4 days.

Aug. 23. Washington, son of William and Eunice Burnham, dropsy of the brain, 2 years, 7 months, 2 weeks, 1 day.

Aug. 23. Infant child of Amos and Margarett Lee, 2 months, 4 days.

Sept. 16. Cyrus Burnham, consumption, 19 years, 9 months, 3 weeks.

Oct. 10. Rachael, wife of Seth Burnham, fever and consumption, 36 years, 2 weeks, 6 days.

Oct. 20. Moses Foster, consumption, 51 years, 11 months, 2 weeks, 2 days.

Oct. 23. Infant child of Joseph and Peggy Lemous, dropsy of brain, 11 weeks.

Oct. 28. Eunice, wife of Jacob Andrews, 3d, cancer in breast, 49 years, 11 months, 2 weeks, 6 days.

1813, Jan.   3. Lucy, wife of Samuel Burnham, consumption, 24 years, 1 month, 3 weeks, 1 day.

Jan. 15. Widow Sarah Norton, palsy, terminating in lethargy, 71 years, 2 months, 3 weeks, 3 days.

Mar.   1. Infant child of Samuel Burnham, whooping-cough, 3 months, 1 week, 4 days.

Apr.   4. Martha, wife of Henry Russ, nervous disorder, 31 years, 8 months, 2 weeks, 1 day.

Apr.   4. Charles Hall, colored, suddenly, 43 years, 10 months, 3 weeks, 3 days.

Rev. Mr. Holt was dismissed, April 20th, 1813.

1813, June 30. Mary, widow of Dea. Jonathan Cogswell, 84 years, 3 months, 18 days.

July   8. William Gorten, 35 years, 5 months.

Oct. 13. Col. Jonathan Cogswell, Jr., said (erroneously) to have been of lung fever, 29 years.

The last mentioned eight deaths are all that appear upon the records during the year 1813.

DEATHS IN THE SECOND PARISH OF IPSWICH, AS RECORDED BY REV. ROBERT CROWELL.

Rev. Mr. Crowell was ordained August 10, 1814, having previously preached here nearly a year.

1814, Jan.   2. Infant child of Aaron Lee, of edematous affection, aged 4 months.

Mar. 16. Wife of John Burnham, of consumption, 34 years.

1814, Apr.	Widow of Ebenezer Low, aphthoe, 84 years.
May	Sally, daughter of Aaron Burnham, consumption, 19 years.
May	Polly, daughter of Ezra Burnham, consumption, 8 years.
June	Daughter of Jeremiah Low, of measles, 4 years.
July 23.	Son of Enoch Low, inflammation of stomach, 1 year.
July 31.	Daughter of Michael Burnham, measles, 3 years.
July 31.	A male infant of Angeline Marshall, 15 days.
July 31.	Washington, son of Jacob Burnham, measles, &c.
Aug. 16.	Widow Lufkin, old age, 93 years.
Sept.	A child of Luke and Eunice Burnham, measles, &c.
Sept. 15.	Noah, son of Abraham and Martha Jones, 3 years, 6 months.
Dec. 7.	Widow Poland was buried, died of old age.
Oct. 14.	Daniel Quimby was drowned, 18 years, 2 months.
1815, Jan. 12.	An infant of Nathaniel Gorton, Jr.
Jan. 29.	Son of Sargent Burnham, inflammation of brain.
Apr. 9.	Son of Capt. Parker Burnham, 4 years.
Mar.	Abraham, son of William Burnham, died abroad, of small pox, 30 years, 11 months.
May	Joshua, son of Benjamin Andrews, abroad, 22 years.
June 4.	Aaron, son of widow Polly Foster, at Charleston, S. C., of cholera morbus, 17 years, 6 months.
July 4.	Widow Molly Rust.
Aug. 1.	An infant of Henry Burnham, 3 days.
Aug. 10.	Judith, wife of John Dexter, liver complaint, 30 years.
Nov. 10.	Matthew Vincent, apprentice of Thomas Choate, nervous fever, 20 years.
Nov. 14.	Mrs. Miriam Lull, of scrofulous consumption.
Nov. 27.	Abraham Jones, lung fever.
Nov. 29.	An infant of Phinehas Story, inflammation of bowels, 3 months, 17 days.
Dec. 20.	Widow Susanna Story, palsy and fever, 73 years, 3 months, 28 days.
	Oliver Emerton and —— Andrews were supposed to have been lost (at sea) this year.
1816, Jan. 4.	Son of Elias Andrews, measles and quinsy, 1 year, 9 months, 7 days.
Jan. 20.	Joshua Burnham, measles followed by lung fever.
Jan. 30.	An infant of Caleb and Polly Andrews, mortification of bowels, 5 days.
Feb. 16.	Ruhamah, wife of Daniel Story, consumption, 20 years, 5 months, 17 days.
Feb. 19.	Widow Sarah Perkins, old age.
Mar. 3.	Tabitha, daughter of Benjamin Burnham, consumption, 27 years, 7 months, 11 days.
Mar. 22.	A female infant of Daniel Story, of tabes, 3 months, 7 days.
Mar. 25.	An infant of Thomas M. Procter.
Mar. 27.	Widow Smith, of old age, 97 years, 3 months.
Mar. 30.	A male child of Michael Burnham, lung fever, 4 months.
Apr. 2.	Child of Sargent Burnham, lung fever.
Apr. 15.	William Holmes, after two days illness with lock-jaw, 26 years, 4 months.
Apr. 16.	An infant of Adam Boyd, soon after birth.
Apr. 23.	Benjamin Andrews, (was baptized Sept. 2, 1753,) of pleurisy fever, 62 years, 7 months.
Apr. 25.	Child of David Andrews, lung complaint and fits, 1 year, 1 month.
May 4.	Simeon Burnham, (baptized March 23, 1729,) of old age and St. Anthony's fire, 87 years, 1 month.

1816, May 20.   Mary, wife of Zebulon Andrews, consumption, 24 years, 9 months.
May 20.   Stephen Choate, of a cancer upon the cheek, 63 years, 6 months.
June 3.   Wife of John Dexter, of lung fever.
July 6.   Infant child of Henry Burnham, 10 days.
July 7.   John Emerson, (baptized Aug. 4,1734,) of dropsy, 81 years, 11 months.
July 24,   Mary, daughter of Benjamin Burnham, Jr., mortification of bowels, 4 years.
Sept. 27.   Widow Mary Burnham, (baptized April 20, 1729,) lethargy and old age, 87 years, 5 months, 7 days.
Oct. 30.   Martha, daughter of John and Lucy Low, aphthoe, 1 year, 7 months.
1817, Jan. 17.   Anna, wife of Francis Marshall, consumption. 29 years.
Jan. 26.   Mary, wife of Benjamin Burnham, Jr., consumption, 41 years, 3 months ; both members of the church, and both met death with a sweet and heavenly calm.
Feb. 5.   Lucy, wife of John Goodhue, consumption, 41 years, 10 months.
Mar. 14.   Mina Story, daughter of Jacob Story, typhus, 17 years, 2 months.
Apr. 2.   Epes Roberts, consumption, 20 years.
Apr. 11.   Christopher Hodgkins, old age, 87 years.
Apr. 14.   Jonathan, son of Capt. Jonathan Eveleth, lung fever, 3 years.
Apr. 17.   Widow Susanna Choate, lung fever and old age, 83 years.
Child of Benjamin Burnham, Jr., hydrocephalus internus, 2 years, 6 months.
Infant child of Eben and Susanna, epilepsy, 5 days.
Sept. 20.   Aaron, infant child of Capt. Joseph Foster, from a scald, 8 months.
Sept. 24.   Male child of Asa and Polly Burnham, hydrocephalus internus, 1 year, 8 months.
Sept. 25.   Ira Burnham, lung fever, 20 years.
Oct. 11.   Philip, son of John Harlow, nervous fever.
Oct. 21.   Elisha Story, lethargy, 64 years, 10 months.
Nov. 27.   Widow Betsey Andrews, consumption, 42 years.
Dec. 23.   William Burnham, consumption and old age, 79 years, 8 months.
Dec. 25.   Sally Andrews, consumption, 26 years, 7 months.
Mr. Jeremiah Choate and Mr. Jonathan Low are supposed to have been lost at sea this year.
1818, Jan. 6.   Widow Hepzibah Cummins, of inflammation of the brain, 46 years.
Jan. 10.   Infant child of John Burnham.
Feb. 18.   Mrs. Lucy Butler, consumption and jaundice, 31 years.
Mar. 4.   Mrs. Polly Millet, pulmonary consumption, 35 years.
Mar. 5.   Samuel Burnham, pulmonary consumption, 26 years.
Widow Hodgkins, paralytic disorder, 80 years.
Oct. 7.   Joanna Giddings, of cancer in breast, died at Salem very suddenly while under the operation of a drawing plaster, supposed to be made of arsenic ; 21 years.
Oct. 17.   Abner Choate, chronic affection of the liver, 25 years.
Oct. 27.   John Foster, of typhus mitior, or low nervous fever, 18 years, 4 months.
Dec. 11.   At Andover, Mrs. Hannah, wife of Robert Crowell, of consumption, interred here ; 27 years, 8 months, 15 days.
Josiah Poland fell from a ship's mast in New York, and was killed instantly, 24 years.
1819, Feb. 1.   Infant child of Mr. and Mrs. Prindle, 8 days.
Mar. 15.   Abigail, daughter of Benjamin and Abigail Cogswell, dropsy of the head, 11 years.
Apr. 10.   Jonathan Cogswell, Esq., old age and fever, 79 years.

1819, May 10. Betsy Burnham, chronic affection of the brain, 31 years.

May 29. John Burnham, consumption, 41 years.

June 5. Nathan Story, lung complaint, 73 years.

June 7. William Holmes, consumption.

June 18. Elizabeth Pierce, consumption of many years, 78 years.

June 17. Funeral of Mary Allen, dropsy of abdomen.

Aug. 7. Infant of Thomas Low, 5 days.

Aug. 7. Mrs. Thomas Choate, suicide by hanging.

Aug 8. Isaac Burnham, old age, 81 years.

Sept. 7. John Low, apoplexy.

Sept. 21. Infant daughter of Capt. Jonathan Eveleth, lung complaint, 1 month.

1820, Jan. 13. Infant son of William Low.

June 16. Ruhama Varney, dropsy and inflammation of brain, 63 years, 9 months, 10 days.

July 16. Infant of John F. Burnham.

Aug. 10. Jacob Burnham, complication of disorders, 68 years, 7 months, 8 days.

Aug. 15. Wife of Capt. John Procter, consumption.

Oct. 19. Thomas Burnham, mortification, 88 years.

1821, Feb. 7. Infant son of Joseph Allen, lung complaint, 5 months, 14 days.

Feb. 16. Sarah B. Story, daughter of Ephraim Story, 9 years, 7 months, 7 days.

Apr. 7. An infant daughter of John Mears, throat ail, 7 months.

Apr. 12. Infant son of John Harlow, Jr., lung complaint, 1 year, 8 months.

Aug. 9. Twin infants of John Goodhue, 2 months.

Aug. 23. Infant of Daniel Story.

Sept. 9. William Howe Burnham, inflammatory fever, 27 years.

Nov. 2. Infant of Samuel Burnham.

Nov. 24. Widow Westley Burnham, old age, 98 years.

Nov. 30. Wife of Jesse Story, liver complaint, 72 years.

1822, Jan. 22. Almira Hardy, dropsy of the chest, 13 years, 9 months.

Jan. 23. Widow Lydia Lufkin, old age, 93 years.

Feb. 16. Widow Ruth Colado, consumption, 33 years.

Feb. 24. Anna, wife of Lieut. Aaron Low.

Feb. 27. Washington Choate, an engorgement of the lungs, 19 years; (member of Dartmouth College).

Apr. 4. Martha, wife of Abel Story, 30 years.

Apr. 9. John Cogswell, old age, 79 years.

Apr. 12. Amelia, wife of Samuel Burnham, consumption, 33 years.

Apr. 13. Son of Samuel Burnham, dropsy of brain, 4 years.

Apr. 15. Wife of James Andrews, 67 years.

Capt. John Butler, very suddenly.

Colored child of Robert Jarret, debility.

Oct. 2. James Andrews, 76 years.

Oct. 18. Eliza Baten, old age, 72 years.

Oct. 16. Child of Thomas Low, Jr., 17 days.

ACCOUNT OF FUNERALS IN ESSEX SINCE JANUARY 1823.

1823. Mr. Thomas Low, died of old age and asthmatic complaint, 76 years.

Apr. 12. Mr. John Story, died in his sleep without waking his companion, 37 years.

July 10. Widow Ann Andrews, old age, 82 years.

Aug. 13. Widow Anna Andrews, old age and dropsy, 94 years, 10 months.

1823, Aug. 14. Jonathan Burnham, extreme nervous debility, 29 years.
    Oct. 7. Wife of Jacob Andrews, Sen., worn out, 70 years.
    Oct. 10. Wife of Perkins Story, consumption.
            Same afternoon—Son of Thomas M. Procter, nervous fever.
    Oct. 20. Wife of Enoch Low.
    Dec. 19. Capt. Jacob Andrews, of cancer near the eye.
    Dec. 20. Jacob, son of Adam Boyd, lingering disorder and bowel complaint, 6 years.
    Dec. 26. Miss Susan Gorton, consumption, 23 years.
1824, Jan. 20. Mr. Ephraim Burnham, 22 years, 2 months.
    Feb. 11. Mr. Abner Poland, old age, 87 years.
    Apr. 10. Mr. Mears, suddenly, after slight illness.
    Apr. 12. Son of Mr. Epes Story, dropsy of the brain.
    Apr. 14. Mr. Daniel Low, old age, 78 years.
    Apr. 16. Son of Daniel Story, dropsy of the brain, 4 months.
    May 13. Son of Capt. Francis Burnham, lung fever, 5 years.
            Mr. Robert Jarret, colored man, of consumption.
    May 27. Mr. Jesse Story, old age, 94 years.
    June 17. Mr. Samuel Hardy, consumption.
    June 18. Mrs. Molly, widow of Benjamin Andrews, consumption, 78 years.
    Aug. 7. Son of Henry Mears, 6 hours.
    Aug. 19. Widow Lucy Procter, old age, 89 years.
    Aug. 31. Samuel Andrews, dysentery, 16 years.
    Sept. 4. Lois Andrews, sister of Samuel, above, dysentery, 27 years.
    Sept. 8. Charles, son of Ebenezer Burnham, Jr., dropsy of brain, 4 years.
    Sept. 23. Emily Andrews, sister of Samuel and Lois above, dysentery, 11 years.
    Sept. 30. Mrs. Lydia, wife of Elisha Story, dropsy, 24 years.
    Oct. 2. Miss Betsy Burnham, consumption, with other diseases, 23 years, 10 months.
    Oct. 27. Harriet, daughter of John Choate, disease unknown, died in 40 minutes after being taken, 11 years.
    Nov. 19. Susan Varney, burnt from her clothes taking fire, 11 years.
    Nov. 25. Almira Andrews, nervous putrid fever, 18 years.
    Nov. 29. Mr. William Burnham. He was returning with a grist from the mill; leaned upon his wheelbarrow, said he was faint, and died instantly in the street, 48 years.
1825, Mar. Child of Mr. Richard Burnham.
    Apr. Child of Mr. Zaccheus Cogswell, a son.
    May Child of Mr. William S. Foster.
    May 16. Child of Mr. Benjamin Burnham, 9 months.
    June 3. Child of Mr. John Butman, 3 months.
    June 28. Wife of William Lufkin, 73 years.
    July 11. Wife of Daniel Norton.
    July 23. Mr. William Burnham, 79 years.
    Aug. 17. Mr. James Crawley.
    Aug. 25. Wife of Mr. Aaron Eveleth.
    Sept. 1. Child of Mr. Enoch Low.
            Child of Mr. Amos Burnham.
    Oct. Child of Mr. Noah Burnham.
            Miss Fanny Burnham.
            Mr. Stephen Story, drowned.
            Jackson, son of Mr. John Story.
            Miss Lois Putnam.

1825, Nov. 22. Washington Choate, son of Rev. R. Crowell, 3 days.

Dec. Mr. Charles Burnham.

1826, Feb. 1. Mr. Samuel Giddings, at work on Saturday and died Sabbath night following, 62 years.

Feb. 3. Daughter of James Eveleth, fever after measles, 4 years.

Feb. 4. Son of Thomas Holmes, 1 week.

Feb. 8. George Choate, Esq., paralysis, 64 years.

Feb. 12. Child of James Eveleth, fever after measles, 2 years.

Feb. 13. Wife of Seth Burnham.

Feb. 22. Mr. Jacob Andrews, old age, 78.

Feb. 25. Infant son of Jonathan Lufkin, Jr., 2 months.

Mar. 8. Lucinda Story, daughter of Abel Story, disease unknown.

Mar. 28. Mr. William Lufkin, old age.

May 23. Mr. Ezra Burnham, consumption, 53 years.

June 23. Mr. Jacob Burnham, from burning, 51 years.

Aug. 27. Daughter of Samuel Mears, 11 months.

Aug. 28. Miss Susan Shales, consumption, 18 years.

Sept. 4. Mr. Francis Marshall, consumption of liver, 39 years.

Sept. 22. Mrs. Peggy, wife of Joseph Burnham, 84 years.

Oct. 3. Mr. Nathaniel Gorton, old age, 84 years.

Oct. 20. Son of Aaron Burnham, Jr., throat ail, 2 years, 8 months.

Oct. 21. Son of Nathaniel Rowe, throat ail, 1 year.

1827, Jan. 28. Female child of Benjamin Andrews, Jr., 1 year.

Feb. 2. Mr. Jonathan Burnham, consumption.

Feb. 21. Mrs. Kate Hall, disease unknown.

Mar. 4. Mr. Ebenezer Burnham, disease unknown.

Mar. 24. Mr. Elisha Burnham, consumption of liver, 33 years.

July 2. Mr. Mark Burnham, asthma and old age, 74 years.

Aug. 13. Widow of George Choate, Esq.

Aug. Sarah, daughter of Capt. James Perkins.

Son of Mr. Richardson.

Sept. 23. Sally, daughter of Thomas M. Burnham, burnt, 23 years.

Nov. 7. Child of Abel Story, whooping-cough.

Dec. 22. Infant son of Thomas Low.

Dec. 23. Infant son of Henry Mears

1828, Feb. 1. Widow Martha Jones, 57 years.

Feb. 24. Child of Joseph Andrews.

Mar. 17. James Nutter, drowned.

Apr. 5. Ebenezer Burnham, 70 years.

Apr. 9. Abigail, wife of Michael Burnham, consumption, 43 years.

Apr. 12. Sarah Marshall, 76 years.

May 20. Emeline Dexter, 19 years.

July 8. James Burnham.

Aug. 2. Abigail, daughter of Adam Boyd.

Aug. 21. Abigail Eveleth, consumption, 42 years.

Sept. 3. Widow Eunice Low, 84 years.

1829, Jan. 3. Abraham Marshall, consumption, 39 years.

Apr. 24. Capt. William Choate, 38 years.

May 22. Miss Mary Giddings, consumption, 20 years.

July 30. Sarah, wife of John F. Burnham, consumption, 32 years.

Aug. 20. Sarah Amelia, child of Capt. Samuel Burnham, 7 months.

Aug. 27. Widow of Enoch Burnham, 70 years.

Aug. 31. Luther, Child of Abel Story, 10 months.

1829, Sept 7.   Mr. William Cogswell, Jr., internal tumor.
     Sept. 17.   Eliz. A., child of Charles Roberts, 1 year.
        18.   Hannah Choate, child of R. Crowell, dysentery, 1 year.
     Nov. 2.   Mrs. Lucretia Savage, 27 years.
1830,   Tabitha, wife of Abner Andrews, 35 years.
     Mar. 31.   Capt. Francis Burnham, Jr., 38 years.
     Apr. 15.   Mary, wife of Timothy Ross, 60 years.
     Apr. 20.   Wife of Isaac Low, 50 years.
     Apr. 29.   Mary, wife of Westley Burnham, 82 years.
     May 30.   Son of Michael Story, 2½ years.
     May 31.   Male child of D. Preston, 8 months.
     June 3.   Moses Marshall, 70 years.
     June 3.   Male child of Tabitha Burnham, 3 weeks.
     June 8.   Female child of Daniel Mears, 1 year, 4 months.   •
           Wife of John Roberts, consumption, 33 years.
     Sept. 26.   Eunice, wife of Moses Burnham, 50 years.
     Oct. 10.   Polly Gorten, of cancer, 49 years.
     Oct. 20.   Mr. Thomas Choate, 78 years.
     Nov. 8.   Son of Henry Mears, 2 years.
     Dec. 6.   Widow Sarah Low, 79 years.
1831, Jan. 27.   Amos Jones, died in Boston of consumption.
     Feb. 3.   William Cogswell, Sen., of old age, 83 years.
     Mar. 31.   Widow Philippa Burnham, 93 years.
     Apr. 10.   Jeremiah Perkins, 46 years.
           Enos Burnham.
     June 26.   Daughter of Thomas Hardy, drowned, 2 years.
     Sept. 6.   Mrs. Sally Kimball, broken limb and dysentery, 79 years.
     Sept. 7.   Widow Lucy Story, relict of Capt. Jonathan Story, old age, 79 years.
     Sept. 9.   Miss Bethula Burnham, 56 years.
     Sept. 9.   Widow Lois Story, relict of Elisha Story, old age, 76 years.
     Sept. 10.   Mrs. Sally, wife of John F. Burnham, consumption, 26 years.
     Sept. 12.   Mr. Nathan Burnham, worn out, 71 years.
     Oct. 4.   Mrs. Abigail, widow of Ebenezer Burnham, consumption.
     Oct. 28.   Mrs. Martha Procter Low, died in Danvers, of fever, 22 years.
     Nov. 16.   Mrs. Abigail Burnham, wife of Amos Burnham, Sen., 72 years.
     Dec. 29.   Grover Dodge, old age.
           Child of John Cogswell.
1832, Jan. 25.   Infant of Henry Mears, 3 weeks.
     Mar. 22.   Hannah Burnham, 4 years.
     May 30.   Mrs. Lufkin, old age, 93 years.
     June 4.   Nehemiah Marshall, found dead in his bed, 32 years.
     July 3.   Nathan Choate, 63 years.
     Aug. 9.   Aaron Giddings, about 75 years.
     Aug. 25.   Widow Butler, 67 years.
     Sept. 19.   Son of widow Denning, (a child).
     Oct. 30.   Daughter of Enoch Low.
     Oct. 31.   Anna Burnham, consumption.
     Nov. 23.   Widow of Isaac Andrews.
     Dec. 21.   Wife of Nehemiah Dodge, 57 years.
     Dec. 21.   Child of Joseph Allen, 7 months.
     Dec. 31.   Daughter of Elisha Story.

II.

COLLEGE GRADUATES,

FROM THE FIRST SETTLEMENT OF CHEBACCO.

Time of Graduation.		Where Graduated.
1689.	Rev. John Eveleth, ...	Harvard University.
1695.	John Perkins, M. D., ...	Harvard University.
1699.	Rev. Francis Goodhue, ...	Harvard University.
1700.	Rev. Jeremiah Wise, ...	Harvard University.
1703.	Rev. Benjamin Choate, ...	Harvard University.
1717.	Henry Wise, A. M., merchant, ...	Harvard University.
1718.	Francis Cogswell, A. M., ...	Harvard University.
1728.	Joseph Wise, M. D., ...	Harvard University.
1794.	Joseph Perkins, Esq., ...	Harvard University.
1818.	George Choate, M. D., ...	Harvard University.
1819.	Hon. Rufus Choate, LL. D., ...	Dartmouth College.
1823.	John D. Russ, M. D., ...	Yale College.
1832.	Hon. Jonathan C. Perkins, LL. D., ...	Amherst College.
1837.	Rev. Thomas Sewall, D. D., ...	Middletown University.
1843.	Judge George F. Choate, Esq., ...	Bowdoin College.
1853.	Prof. Edward P. Crowell, ...	Amherst College.
1861.	Rev. Edward Norton, ...	Dartmouth College.
1865.	Rev. David O. Mears, ...	Amherst College.
1865.	Coeleb Burnham, M. D., ...	Dartmouth College.
1867.	Michael Burnham, ...	Amherst College.

OTHER PROFESSIONAL MEN.

1761.	Hon. John Choate, ...	Judge of Court of Common Pleas.
1770.	Parker Cleaveland, M. D., . . .	
1783.	Nehemiah Cleaveland, M. D., . .	
1785.	Rev. John Cleaveland, Jr., . . .	
1788.	Parker Russ, M. D., ...	
1817.	Asa Story, M. D., ...	Dartmouth College Medical School.
1837.	Eliphalet K. Webster, M. D., . .	Dartmouth College Medical School.
	Rev. Edwin Burnham, ...	
	Rev. George W. Burnham, . . .	
	Rev. Hezekiah Burnham, . . .	
1846.	Jacob Story, Esq., ...	Cambridge Law School.
1847.	Obed B. Low Esq., ...	
1854.	David Choate, Jr., M. D., ...	Massachusetts Medical College.
1861.	J. Howard Burnham, ...	Teacher; State Normal School, Illinois.
1866.	Edward Smith Eveleth, M. D., . .	Columbia College, Medical Department.

III.

REPRESENTATIVES TO THE LEGISLATURE

SINCE THE ADOPTION OF THE CONSTITUTION OF THE STATE, IN 1780.

1781–83. John Choate, Esq.	1842. John Burnham.
1785–86–88. John Choate, Esq.	1843. Rev. John Prince.
1792–93. Col. Jonathan Cogswell.	1844. Moses Burnham, Jr.
1800–13. Col. Jonathan Cogswell, Sen.,	1845. Ezra Perkins, Jr., Esq.
1814–17. George Choate, Esq.	1851. Gilman P. Allen.
1819. George Choate, Esq.	1852. William Burnham, 2d.
1824. Jacob Story.	1853. Rev. John Prince.
1827–30. Jonathan Story, 3d, Esq.	1855. Rev. John Prince.
1833–34. Jonathan Story, 3d, Esq.	1856. Samuel Story.
1835–36. Charles Dexter.	1857. O. H. P. Sargent, Esq.
1837. Oliver Low.	1858. Charles Howes.
1838. George W. Burnham.	1859. Rev. John Prince.
1839. Hon. David Choate.	1861. Ebenezer Stanwood.
1840. Samuel Hardy.	1863. Nehemiah Burnham.
1840. Aaron L. Burnham, Esq.	1865. Timothy Andrews, Jr.
1841. Grover Dodge.	1867. Leonard McKenzie.

In the years 1820–23 inclusive, 1825 and 1826, 1831 and 1832 it was voted "not to send." In 1846, and in 1849 and 1850 there was "no choice." In 1854 there was no representative chosen ; and there is *no record* of any election of a representative in 1847 or in 1848.

STATE SENATORS.

1781–83. Hon. Stephen Choate,	1858. Hon. John Prince.
1840–41. Hon. David Choate.	

DELEGATES TO CONVENTIONS.

1780. Hon. Stephen Choate, to the State Constitutional Convention.
1780. Col. Jonathan Cogswell, to the State Constitutional Convention.
1788. Col. Jonathan Cogswell, to the U. S. Constitutional Convention of Mass.
1788. John Choate, Esq., to the U. S. Constitutional Convention of Mass.
1820. Jonathan Story, Esq., to the State Constitutional Convention.
1853. William J. A. Bradford, to the State Constitutional Convention.

TOWN OFFICERS.

TOWN CLERKS.	TOWN TREASURERS.
1819–24. Joseph Story.	1819–24. Nathan Choate.
1824–29. Jonathan Story, 3d, Esq.	1825. George Choate, Esq.
1830–36. Col. William Andrews, Jr.	1826–32. Nathan Choate.
1836–39. Hon. David Choate.	1832–38. Hon. David Choate.
1840–42. Jonathan Story, Esq.	1839–48. Ezra Perkins, Jr., Esq.
1843–55. Aaron L. Burnham, Esq.	1849–50. Caleb Cogswell.
1856–61. O. H. P. Sargent, Esq.	1851–67. Grover Dodge.
1862–67. John C. Choate.	

MODERATORS OF THE ANNUAL TOWN MEETING.

1819–22.	George Choate, Esq.	1843.	Uriah G. Spofford.
1823–25.	Jonathan Story, Esq.	1844.	Caleb Cogswell.
1826–27.	Elias Andrews.	1845–47.	Capt. John S. Burnham.
1828–29.	Capt. Francis Burnham.	1848–51.	Uriah G. Spofford.
1830–32.	Jonathan Story, Esq.	1852–53.	Rev. John Prince.
1833–36.	Capt. Francis Burnham.	1854.	O. H. P. Sargent, Esq.
1837.	Col. Joshua Low.	1855.	Uriah G. Spofford.
1838–39.	Capt. Francis Burnham.	1857.	Nehemiah Burnham.
1840.	(No record).	1858.	Uriah G. Spofford.
1841.	Uriah G. Spofford.	1859–61.	Charles Howes.
1842.	Capt. Francis Burnham.	1861–67.	Nehemiah Burnham.

JUSTICES OF THE PEACE, Etc.

JUSTICES OF THE PEACE.—Jonathan Cogswell, (1733); Francis Choate, (1754); Col. Jonathan Cogswell, Sen.; George Choate; Jonathan Story, 3d; David Choate; Aaron Giddings; Aaron L. Burnham; Ezra Perkins, Jr.; Oliver H. P. Sargent; John Prince; Nehemiah Burnham; Ebenezer Stanwood; Daniel W. Bartlett.

JUSTICE OF THE PEACE AND OF THE QUORUM.—David Choate.

TRIAL JUSTICE.—David Choate.

CORONERS.—David Choate; Caleb Cogswell.

---••◦•---

CORRECTIONS.

PAGE 108.—DEA. JOHN BURNHAM was the ancester of *a part* only of *the Burnhams in Essex.* To his son JOHN, Jr., were born *Dea. John,* 2d, (father of John, Samuel, Jeremiah and Nehemiah), *Thomas,* (father of Francis, [whose sons were Francis and Nathan,] and of Dea. Thomas), *Jonathan* and *Robert.* To his *other son,* JOSIAH, were born *Josiah,* 2d, (father of Josiah, 3d, William and Abraham), *Jacob* and *Ebenezer.*

The rest of the Burnhams are descended from *a brother* of Dea. John, 1st, named THOMAS, who settled and lived in Ipswich, and *whose son John* removed to Chebacco. To *this* JOHN were born *John, Thomas,* (father of Thomas, [from whom was Winthrop B.,] Jeremiah, Lieut. Nathan, Caleb and Stephen), *Jacob, Capt. Jonathan,* (father of Jonathan, Jr.; and of Francis, whose sons were Capt. Nathaniel, Ebenezer and Jonathan, 3d), and *David,* (father of David, Jr., Westley, 1st, and William).

According to R. H. Burnham, Esq., author of the *History of the Burnham Family,* about to be published, Dea. John, 1st, and Thomas, 1st, were sons of Robert and Mary Andrews Burnham of Norwich, Norfolk Co., England, and sailed for this country in charge of *their maternal uncle, Capt. Andrews,* commander of the vessel *Angel Gabriel.* [See p. 23 of this History].

PAGE 119.—Dea. Low was the *son* of Thomas, the first settler, (see p. 45), *d.* Sept. 8, 1677, and *grandson* of Capt. John Low, commander of the ship *Ambrose*, and Rear Admiral of a fleet of twelve ships, which sailed from England for Salem in April, 1630. To Dea. Thomas' *son Samuel*, were born Samuel, Asa and *Daniel*, (d. 1824, aged 78).

PAGE 130.—The name *William Burnham* should be omitted.

PAGE 148.—The *date* of Dea. John Choate's *death* should be July 17; and the date of his birth, June 15, 1661.

PAGE 168.—The *year* of Dea. Choate's *death* should be 1733; and the *age* of Dea. Seth Story, 86, (according to Felt's History).

PAGE 179, 180.—For *Col. Bayley,* read Col. *Bagley.*

PAGE 200.—The *date* of Dea. John Andrews' *death* in the Parish records, is November, 1750; in the printed church covenant, March 16, 1750.

PAGE 206.—Israel Andrews, (son of James Andrews, soldier at Bunker's Hill,) is still living and more than 90 years of age.

PAGE 226.—Maj. Caleb Low was a brother of Thomas, (father of Jeremiah, Caleb, David, Thomas, Jonathan, Col. Joshua, Abigail, Josiah and Polly).

PAGE 236.—There is *no record* of the election of *Dea. Seth Story,* 2d, to the office of *Elder.* Yet in a record of deaths of that day is the following: "Dea. Seth Story, *afterwards Elder,* died Aug. 11, 1786, aged 93."

According to Savage's Genealogical Dictionary of the first settlers of New England, (Boston, 1862.) *William Story,* the father of Dea. Seth, 1*st,* was a native of *Norwich, Norfolk Co., England,* and embarked for this country, April 8, 1637, at the age of 23. He was a carpenter. *Jesse,* the son of *Dea. Zechariah* was the father of Jesse, Jr., Parker and Ephraim. The sons of *Dea. Seth,* 2d, were *John* and *Ebenezer,* (father of Jonathan).

Most of the *Storys,* however, are descended from Andrew, (pp. 40 and 41), who was probably *a brother* of *William.* The earliest ancester now known of *one branch,* was JACOB STORY. To *his* son JACOB, 2D, were born *Maj. Andrew, Michael, Jacob,* 3d, (father of Andrew, Michael, Abel, Epes, Enoch and Noah), *Elisha,* (father of Elisha), and *Jonathan,* (father of Dr. Asa, Col. David, Esq., Jonathan and Perkins). To his son STEPHEN were born *Stephen,* (father of John, Seth, Stephen and Daniel), *Esquire David* and *Daniel.* To still a *third branch* belonged *William Story,* whose sons were *Master* Joseph, William and Jonathan.

PAGE 246.—Rev. Mr. Cleaveland received his degree of A. B. from Yale College in 1763, and the same year the honorary degree of A. M. from *the same Institution.* The latter degree was *also* conferred on him by *Dartmouth* College, in 1782.

PAGE 253.—The *date* of Dea. *Jonathan Cogswell's death* should be 1812.

PAGE 270.—The *date* of Dea. *Jonathan Cogswell's marriage* should be 1748.

PAGE 274.—*Samuel Burnham* was elected *deacon* in 1828, *Caleb Cogswell, deacon* in 1862, and *Robert W. Burnham, treasurer,* in 1868.

PAGE 284.—This *William Cogswell,* who *d.* February, 1831, aged 83, was a son of *John,* 3d, and grandson of John, Jr.,—son of the first settler.

PAGE 315.—For *Sept.* 4, 1822, read *Sept.* 24, 1822.

PAGE 325.—For Nathaniel *Macintire,* read *McIntire.*

PAGE 325.—Town Statistics for 1850: Population, 1572; Valuation, $390,553; money raised for schools, $1300; for highways, $700; for other town charges, $1200.

PAGE 347.—*Andrew Story* and *Jacob Burnham,* 2d, should be included in the *second* list of vessel builders.

PAGE 359.—For *William Hayden,* read *William H. Hayden;* and for *William S. Howard,* read *William C. Howard.*

PAGE 360.—For George *S.* Burnham, read George *F.* Burnham, 1*st.*

PAGE 361.—For Edward *L.* Lander, read Edward *W.* Lander.

PAGE 363.—For William Haskell, read William *A.* Haskell.

Index.

61

www.ingramcontent.com/pod-product-compliance
Lightning Source LLC
Chambersburg PA
CBHW032018110726
47901CB00004B/1129